THE CAMBRIDGE FOUCAULT LEXICON

The Cambridge Foucault Lexicon is a reference tool that provides clear and incisive definitions and descriptions of all of Michel Foucault's major terms and influences, including history, knowledge, language, philosophy, and power. It also includes entries on philosophers about whom Foucault wrote and who influenced his thinking, such as Deleuze, Heidegger, Nietzsche, and Canguilhem. The entries are written by scholars of Foucault from a variety of disciplines such as philosophy, gender studies, political science, and history. Together, they shed light on concepts key to Foucault and to ongoing discussions of his work today.

Leonard Lawlor is Sparks Professor of Philosophy at the Pennsylvania State University. He is the author of *This Is Not Sufficient: An Essay on Animality and Human Nature in Derrida* and *Early Twentieth-Century Continental Philosophy* and is co-editor (with Ted Toadvine) of *The Merleau-Ponty Reader*.

John Nale earned his PhD in philosophy from the Pennsylvania State University. He is currently Visiting Assistant Professor of Philosophy at the University of North Florida.

THE CAMBRIDGE
FOUCAULT LEXICON

EDITORS

Leonard Lawlor

Pennsylvania State University

AND

John Nale

University of North Florida

CAMBRIDGE
UNIVERSITY PRESS

CAMBRIDGE
UNIVERSITY PRESS

University Printing House, Cambridge CB2 8BS, United Kingdom

One Liberty Plaza, 20th Floor, New York, NY 10006, USA

477 Williamstown Road, Port Melbourne, VIC 3207, Australia

314-321, 3rd Floor, Plot 3, Splendor Forum, Jasola District Centre, New Delhi - 110025, India

79 Anson Road, #06-04/06, Singapore 079906

Cambridge University Press is part of the University of Cambridge.

It furthers the University's mission by disseminating knowledge in the pursuit of education, learning and research at the highest international levels of excellence.

www.cambridge.org
Information on this title: www.cambridge.org/9781108813044

© Cambridge University Press 2014

First published 2014
First paperback edition 2020

A catalogue record for this publication is available from the British Library

Library of Congress Cataloging in Publication data
Lawlor, Leonard, 1954–
The Cambridge Foucault lexicon / Leonard Lawlor, Pennsylvania State University, John Nale, University of North Florida.
pages   cm
Includes bibliographical references and index.
ISBN 978-0-521-11921-4 (hardback)
1. Foucault, Michel, 1926–1984 – Dictionaries.   1. Title.
B2430.F724L38   2014
194–dc23   2013027344

ISBN 978-0-521-11921-4 Hardback
ISBN 978-1-108-81304-4 Paperback

Contents

List of Abbreviations for Foucault's Texts *page* ix
Introduction xv

⌐ I. TERMS

1. **Abnormal** *Dianna Taylor* 3
2. **Actuality** *Erinn Gilson* 10
3. **Archaeology** *Gary Gutting* 13
4. **Archive** *Richard A. Lynch* 20
5. **Author** *Harry A. Nethery IV* 24
6. **Biohistory** *Eduardo Mendieta* 31
7. **Biopolitics** *Eduardo Mendieta* 37
8. **Biopower** *Eduardo Mendieta* 44
9. **Body** *John Protevi* 51
10. **Care** *Stephanie Jenkins* 57
11. **Christianity** *James Bernauer* 61
12. **Civil Society** *Paul Patton* 64
13. **Conduct** *Corey McCall* 68
14. **Confession** *James Bernauer* 75
15. **Contestation** *Leonard Lawlor* 80
16. **Control** *Jeffrey T. Nealon* 83
17. **Critique** *Christopher Penfield* 87
18. **Death** *Arun Iyer* 94
19. **Desire** *Margaret A. McLaren* 99
20. **Difference** *Paul Patton* 102
21. **Discipline** *Devonya N. Havis* 110

22. **Discourse** *Richard A. Lynch* — 120
23. *Dispositif* **(Apparatus)** *Gilles Deleuze* — 126
24. **The Double** *Ann V. Murphy* — 133
25. **Ethics** *Gary Gutting* — 136
26. **Event** *Erinn Gilson* — 143
27. **Experience** *Kevin Thompson* — 147
28. **Finitude** *Ann V. Murphy* — 153
29. **Freedom** *Jana Sawicki* — 156
30. **Friendship** *Joshua Kurdys* — 162
31. **Genealogy** *Charles E. Scott* — 165
32. **Governmentality** *Todd May* — 175
33. **Hermeneutics** *Pol van de Velde* — 182
34. **History** *Judith Revel* — 187
35. **Historical a Priori** *Jeffrey T. Nealon* — 200
36. **Homosexuality** *Nicolae Morar* — 207
37. **Human Sciences** *Samuel Talcott* — 212
38. **Institution** *Robert Vallier* — 217
39. **The Intellectual** *Philippe Artières* — 224
40. **Knowledge** *Mary Beth Mader* — 226
41. **Language** *Fred Evans* — 236
42. **Law** *Andrew Dilts* — 243
43. **Liberalism** *Jared Hibbard-Swanson* — 251
44. **Life** *Eduardo Mendieta* — 254
45. **Literature** *Hugh J. Silverman* — 263
46. **Love** *Margaret A. McLaren* — 270
47. **Madness** *Paolo Savoia* — 273
48. **Man** *Alan D. Schrift* — 281
49. **Marxism** *Bill Martin* — 288
50. **Medicine** *Samuel Talcott* — 295
51. **Monster** *Nicolae Morar* — 300
52. **Multiplicity** *Erinn Gilson* — 304
53. **Nature** *Luca Paltrinieri* — 308
54. **Normalization** *Ladelle McWhorter* — 315
55. **Outside** *David-Olivier Gougelet* — 322
56. **Painting (and Photography)** *Gary Shapiro* — 327
57. *Parrēsia* *Corey McCall* — 334
58. **Phenomenology** *Leonard Lawlor* — 337
59. **Philosophy** *Miguel de Beistegui* — 345
60. **Plague** *David-Olivier Gougelet* — 356
61. **Pleasure** *Margaret A. McLaren* — 359
62. **Politics** *Amy Allen* — 364

63. **Population** *Ladelle McWhorter*   370
64. **Power** *Judith Revel*   377
65. **Practice** *Brad Stone*   386
66. **Prison** *Philippe Artières*   392
67. **Prison Information Group (GIP)** *Leonard Lawlor*   394
68. **Problematization** *Colin Koopman*   399
69. **Psychiatry** *Chloë Taylor*   404
70. **Psychoanalysis** *Adrian Switzer*   411
71. **Race (and Racism)** *Robert Bernasconi*   419
72. **Reason** *C. G. Prado*   424
73. **Religion** *James Bernauer*   429
74. **Resistance** *Joanna Oksala*   432
75. **Revolution** *Mark Kelly*   438
76. **Self** *Lynne Huffer*   443
77. **Sex** *Olivia Custer*   449
78. **Sovereignty** *Banu Bargu*   456
79. **Space** *Stuart Elden*   466
80. **Spirituality** *Edward McGushin*   472
81. **State** *Mark Kelly*   477
82. **Statement** *Richard A. Lynch*   482
83. **Strategies (and Tactics)** *John Nale*   486
84. **Structuralism** *Patrick Singy*   490
85. **Subjectification** *Todd May*   496
86. **Technology (of Discipline, Governmentality, and Ethics)** *Paul Patton*   503
87. **Transgression** *Allan Stoekl*   509
88. **Truth** *Don T. Deere*   517
89. **Violence** *Joanna Oksala*   528
90. **The Visible** *Luca Paltrinieri*   534
91. **War** *John Protevi*   540

II. PROPER NAMES

92. **Louis Althusser (1918–1990)** *Warren Montag*   549
93. **The Ancients (Stoics and Cynics)** *Frédéric Gros*   555
94. **Georges Bataille (1897–1962)** *Shannon Winnubst*   560
95. **Xavier Bichat (1771–1802)** *Patrick Singy*   563
96. **Ludwig Binswanger (1881–1966)** *Paolo Savoia*   567
97. **Maurice Blanchot (1907–2003)** *Kas Saghafi*   572
98. **Henri de Boulainvilliers (1658–1722)** *Robert Bernasconi*   577

99. **Georges Canguilhem (1904–1995)** *Samuel Talcott*   580

100. **Gilles Deleuze (1925–1995)** *Paul Patton*   588

101. **Jacques Derrida (1930–2004)** *Samir Haddad*   595

102. **René Descartes (1596–1650)** *Edward McGushin*   602

103. **Sigmund Freud (1856–1939)** *Adrian Switzer*   609

104. **Jürgen Habermas (1929–)** *Amy Allen*   616

105. **Georg Wilhelm Friedrich Hegel (1770–1831)** *Kevin Thompson*   624

106. **Martin Heidegger (1889–1976)** *David Webb*   630

107. **Jean Hyppolite (1907–1968)** *Leonard Lawlor*   639

108. **Immanuel Kant (1724–1804)** *Marc Djaballah*   641

109. **Niccolò Machiavelli (1469–1527)** *David-Olivier Gougelet*   652

110. **Maurice Merleau-Ponty (1907–1961)** *Federico Leoni*   655

111. **Friedrich Nietzsche (1844–1901)** *Alan D. Schrift*   662

112. **Plato (428–347 BCE)** *Frédéric Gros*   669

113. **Pierre Rivière (1815–1840)** *Jean-François Bert*   674

114. **Raymond Roussel (1877–1933)** *Timothy O'Leary*   676

115. **Jean-Paul Sartre (1905–1980)** *Thomas R. Flynn*   680

116. **William Shakespeare (1564–1616)** *Andrew Cutrofello*   689

117. **Carl von Clausewitz (1780–1831)** *Mark Kelly*   693

Chronology of Michel Foucault's Life (1926–1984)   695

Secondary Works Cited   699

Authors' Biographical Statements   715

Index   721

List of Abbreviations for Foucault's Texts

TEXTS BY MICHEL FOUCAULT IN ENGLISH TRANSLATION

EAIF   *Michel Foucault: Beyond Structuralism and Hermeneutics*, ed. Paul
              Rabinow and Hubert Dreyfus. Chicago: University of Chicago
              Press, 1983.

EAK   *The Archaeology of Knowledge and the Discourse on Language*, trans.
              A. M. Sheridan Smith. New York: Pantheon Books, 1971.

EAW   "Madness, the Absence of an Œuvre," in *The History of Madness*,
              trans. Jonathan Murphy and Jean Khalfa. London: Routledge, 2006,
              pp. 541–549.

EBC   *The Birth of the Clinic: An Archaeology of Medical Perception*, trans.
              A. M. Sheridan Smith. New York: Vintage Books, 1994.

EBHS   "About the Beginnings of the Hermeneutics of the Self: Two
              Lectures at Dartmouth," *Political Theory* 21, no. 2 (May 1993):
              198–227.

ECF-AB   *Abnormal: Lectures at the Collège de France 1974–1975*, trans. Graham
              Burchell. New York: Picador, 2003.

ECF-BBIO   *The Birth of Biopolitics: Lectures at the Collège de France 1978–1979*,
              trans. Graham Burchell. New York: Palgrave Macmillan, 2010.

ECF-COT   *The Courage of Truth. The Government of Self and Others II: Lectures at
              the Collège de France 1983–1984*, trans. Graham Burchell. New York:
              Palgrave Macmillan, 2011.

ECF-GSO   *The Government of Self and Others: Lectures at the Collège de France 1982–1983*, trans. Graham Burchell. New York: Palgrave Macmillan, 2010.

ECF-HOS   *The Hermeneutics of the Subject: Lectures at the Collège de France 1981–1982*, trans. Graham Burchell. New York: Palgrave Macmillian, 2005.

ECF-PP   *Psychiatric Power: Lectures at the Collège de France 1973–1974*, trans. Graham Burchell. New York: Palgrave Macmillan, 2006.

ECF-SMD   *"Society Must Be Defended": Lectures at the Collège de France 1975–1976*, trans. David Macey. New York: Picador, 2003.

ECF-STP   *Security, Territory, Population: Lectures at the Collège de France 1977–1978*, trans. Graham Burchell. New York: Palgrave Macmillan, 2007.

ECM   "Crisis of Medicine or Crisis of Anti-medicine?" trans. Edgar C. Knowlton, William J. King, and Clare O'Farrell, *Foucault Studies* 1 (2004): 5–19.

EDE   Ludwig Binswanger, *Dream and Existence*, trans. Jacob Needleman, Introduction ("Dream, Imagination, Existence") by Michel Foucault, trans. Forrest Williams. Atlantic Highlands, NJ: Humanities Press, 1985.

EDL   *Death and the Labyrinth: The World of Raymond Roussel*, trans. Charles Ruas. New York: Continuum, 2007.

EDP   *Discipline and Punish*, trans. Alan Sheridan. New York: Vintage, 1995.

EEF   *The Essential Foucault*, ed. Paul Rabinow and Nikolas Rose. New York: The New Press, 2003.

EEW1   *Ethics, Subjectivity, and Truth: Essential Works of Foucault, 1954–1984*, ed. James D. Faubion. New York: The New Press, 1997.

EEW2   *Aesthetics, Method, and Epistemology: Essential Works of Foucault, 1954–1984*, ed. James D. Faubion. New York: The New Press, 1998.

EEW3   *Power: Essential Works of Foucault, 1954–1984*, ed. James D. Faubion. New York: The New Press, 2000.

EFB   Michel Foucault, *Maurice Blanchot: The Thought from Outside*, and Maurice Blanchot, *Michel Foucault as I Imagine Him*, trans. Jeffrey Mehlman and Brian Massumi. New York: Zone Books, 1987.

EFC   A. J. Ayers and Arne Naess; Sir Karl Popper and Sir John Eccles; Noam Chomsky and Michel Foucault; Leszek Kolakowski and

Henri Lefebrve, *Reflexive Water: The Basic Concerns of Mankind*, ed. Fons Elder. London: Souvenir Press, 1974.

EFE   *The Foucault Effect: Studies in Governmentality*, ed. Graham Burchell, Colin Gordon, and Peter Miller. Chicago: University of Chicago Press.

EFL   *Foucault Live: Collected Interviews, 1961–1984*, 2nd ed., ed. Sylvere Lotringer. New York: Semiotext(e), 1996.

EFR   *The Foucault Reader*, ed. Paul Rabinow. New York: Pantheon Books, 1984.

EFS   *Fearless Speech*, ed. Joseph Pearson. Los Angeles: Semiotexte, 2001.

EGS   "The Gay Science," trans. Nicolae Morar and Daniel W. Smith, *Critical Inquiry* 37 (2011): 385–403.

EHM   *The History of Madness*, trans. Jonathan Murphy and Jean Khalfa. London: Routledge, 2006.

EHS1   *The History of Sexuality*, volume 1: *An Introduction*, trans. Robert Hurley. New York: Vintage, 1990.

EHS2   *The History of Sexuality*, volume 2: *The Use of Pleasure*, trans. Robert Hurley. New York: Random House, 1985.

EHS3   *The History of Sexuality*, volume 3: *The Care of the Self*, trans. Robert Hurley. New York: Vintage, 1988.

EIKA   *Introduction to Kant's Anthropology*, trans. Roberto Nigro and Kate Briggs. Los Angeles: Semiotext(e), 2008.

EINP   Georges Canguilhem, *The Normal and the Pathological*, with an introduction by Michel Foucault. New York: Zone Books, 1991, pp. 7–24.

ELCP   *Language, Counter-memory, Practice: Selected Essays and Interviews by Michel Foucault*, ed. Donald F. Bouchard. Ithaca, NY: Cornell University Press, 1977.

EMIP   *Mental Illness and Psychology*, trans. Alan Sheridan. Berkeley: University of California Press, 1976.

EMP   *Manet and the Object of Painting*, trans. Nicolas Bourriaud. London: Tate Publishing, 2009.

ENP   *This Is Not a Pipe*, trans. James Harkness. Berkeley: University of California Press, 1982.

EOT   *The Order of Things: An Archaeology of the Human Sciences*, anon. trans. New York: Vintage, 1994.

EPGP   "Photogenic Painting," trans. Dafydd Roberts, in Michel Foucault, *Revisions 2: Photogenic Painting*, ed. Gilles Deleuze. London: Black Dog Publishing, 1999, pp. 81–104.

EPHM   "Preface to the 1961 Edition," in *The History of Madness*, trans. Jonathan Murphy and Jean Khalfa. London: Routledge, 2006, pp. xxvii–xxxvi.

EPK   *Power/Knowledge: Selected Interviews and Other Writings, 1972–1977*, ed. Colin Gordon. New York: Pantheon Books, 1980.

EPPC   Michel Foucault, *Politics, Philosophy, Culture: Interview and Other Writings, 1977–1984*, ed. Lawrence D. Kritzman. New York: Routledge, 1988.

EPR   *I, Pierre Rivière, Having Slaughtered My Mother, My Sister, and My Brother: A Case of Parricide in the 19th Century*, ed. Michel Foucault, trans. Frank Jellinek. Lincoln: University of Nebraska Press, 1982.

EPT   *The Politics of Truth*, trans. Lysa Hochroth and Catherine Porter. Los Angeles: Semiotext(e), 2007.

ERC   *Religion and Culture: Michel Foucault*, selected and edited by Jeremy R. Carrette. New York: Routledge, 1999.

ERD   "Reply to Derrida," in *The History of Madness*, trans. Jonathan Murphy and Jean Khalfa. London: Routledge, 2006, pp. 575–590.

ETS   *Technologies of the Self: A Seminar with Michel Foucault*, ed. Luther H. Martin, Huck Gutman, and Patrick H. Hutton. Amherst: University of Massachusetts Press, 1988.

EWC   "What Is Critique?" trans. Kevin Paul Geiman, in *What Is Enlightenment? Eighteenth Century Answers and Twentieth Century Questions*, ed. James Schmidt. Berkeley: University of California Press, 1996, pp. 382–398.

TEXTS BY MICHEL FOUCAULT IN FRENCH

FAS   *L'archeologie du savoir*. Paris: NRF Gallimard, 1969.

FCF-ANO   *Les anormaux: Cours au Collège de France, 1974–1975*. Paris: Seuil Gallimard, 1999.

FCF-CV   *Le courage de la vérité, le gouvernement de soi et des autres II: Cours au Collège de France, 1984.* Paris: Seuil Gallimard, 2009.

FCF-FDS   *"Il faut defendre la société": Cours au Collège de France, 1976.* Paris: Seuil Gallimard, 1997.

FCF-GDV   *Du gouvernement des vivants: Cours au Collège de France, 1979–1980.* Paris: Seuil Gallimard, 2012.

FCF-LSV   *Leçons sur la volonté de savoir: Cours au Collège de France, 1970–1971. Suivi de Le savoir d'Œipe.* Paris: Hautes Études Gallimard Seuil, 2011.

FCF-NBIO   *Naissance de la biopolitique: Cours au Collège de France, 1978–1979.* Paris: Seuil Gallimard, 2004.

FDE1   *Dits et écrits, I: 1954–1969.* Paris: NRF Gallimard, 1994.

FDE1a   *Dits et écrits, I: 1954–1975.* Paris: Quarto Gallimard, 2001.

FDE2   *Dits et écrits, II: 1970–1976.* Paris: NRF Gallimard, 1994.

FDE2a   *Dits et écrits, II: 1976–1988.* Paris: Quarto Gallimard, 2001.

FDE3   *Dits et écrits, III: 1976–1979.* Paris: NRF Gallimard, 1994.

FDE4   *Dits et écrits, IV: 1980–1988.* Paris: NRF Gallimard, 1994.

FDF   Michel Foucault and A. Farge, *Le Désordre des familles: Lettres de cachet des archives de la Bastille.* Paris : Gallimard-Julliard, coll. Archives, 1982.

FGS   Michel Foucault, "Le Gai Savoir," in Jean Le Bitoux, *Entretiens sur la Question Gay* (Paris: Editeur H&O, 2005), pp. 45–72. Reprinted as "Gay Science," trans. Nicolae Morar and Daniel W. Smith, *Critical Inquiry* 37 (2011): 385–403.

FHF   *Histoire de la folie à l'âge classique.* Paris: Tel Gallimard, 1972.

FHS1   *Histoire de la sexualité 1: la volonté de savoir.* Paris: Tel Gallimard, 1976.

FHS2   *Histoire de la sexualité 2: l'usage des plaisirs.* Paris: Tel Gallimard, 1984.

FHS3   *Histoire de la sexualité 3: le souci de soi.* Paris: Tel Gallimard, 1984.

FKF   Kant, *Anthropologie du point de vue pragmatique* & Foucault, *Introduction à l'Anthropologie.* Paris: Vrin, 2009.

FMC   *Les mots et les choses.* Paris: Tel Gallimard, 1966.

FMFE   *Michel Foucault, entretiens,* ed. Roger-Pol Droit. Paris: Odile Jacob, 2004.

FMMP   *Maladie mentale et psychologie*. Paris: Presses Universitaires de France, 1962.

FNC   *Naissance de la Clinique*. Paris: Quadrige Presses Universitaires de France, 1963.

FNGH   "Nietzsche, la généalogie, l'histoire," in *Hommage à Jean Hyppolite*. Paris: Presses Universtaire de France, 1971, pp. 145–172.

FOD   *L'ordre du discours*. Paris: NRF Gallimard, 1971.

FQC   M. Foucault, "Qu'est-ce que la critique? (Critique et Aufklärung)," *Bulletin de la Société française de philosophie* 84, no. 2 (1990): 35–63.

FSP   *Surveiller et punir*. Paris: Tel Gallimard, 1975.

Introduction

The Cambridge Foucault Lexicon is intended to be an important research tool for scholars working in Foucault studies and more generally in twentieth-century French and European thought. The volume consists of one hundred seventeen entries, written by the world's leading scholars in Foucault's thought. The entries range from the most central and well-known concepts in Foucault's thinking – such as archaeology, ethics, genealogy, history, knowledge, language, madness, philosophy, power, subjectification, and truth – to more obscure themes and notions such as actuality, Christianity, death, double, hermeneutics, homosexuality, love, medicine, multiplicity, painting, plague, race, and war. The volume also includes entries on key figures in Foucault's thinking or key figures for the development of his thinking, figures as obvious as Georges Canguilhem, Gilles Deleuze, Friedrich Nietzsche, Jürgen Habermas, Martin Heidegger, and Immanuel Kant, and as obscure as Xavier Bichat, Ludwig Binswanger, Henri de Boulainvilliers, Raymond Roussel, and William Shakespeare. Each entry attempts to present the notion, idea, or theme in question in a way that is lucid, coherent, comprehensive, and thoroughly researched. Similarly, the entries on figures attempt to present, with utmost precision, the relation of influence (direct or indirect) or relation of appropriation between the figure and Foucault. Within each entry, the reader will find the definitions, structures, and descriptions documented on the basis of Foucault's works (by means of a list of abbreviations found at the front of this volume). By examining the references, the reader will be able to determine precisely which Foucault text is most relevant for the term under consideration and thereby, if he or she desires, be able to read Foucault's own words themselves. For instance, in the entry on "Power," the reader will see several references to a 1982 work called "Subjects and Power" (found both in EEW3, 326–348, and in EAIF, 208–228), and in "Immanuel Kant" the reader will see several references to Foucault's 1961 *Introduction to Kant's Anthropology* (EIKA) and to his 1984 essay "What Is Enlightenment?" (EEW2, 303–320). Out of the shorter texts, "Subjects and Power" and "What Is Enlightenment?" are essential starting points for understanding Foucault's thinking. Although we do not intend that *The Cambridge Foucault Lexicon* be read from cover to cover (the entries are in alphabetical order, first for the terms, then for the proper names), we have provided two ways of reading across the volume. On the one hand, at the end of each entry, the reader will find a list of terms (under the category of "See Also") that intersect with the term under consideration. On the other hand, at the end of the volume, the reader will find an index (of terms and names) that aims to be comprehensive and even exhaustive. (We would like to take this opportunity to thank Joseph Barker, doctoral student in philosophy at Penn State University, for compiling this excellent index.) We would also like to thank Jennifer Wagner-Lawlor who assisted us in the final proofreading of the entire volume. Through these two systems of cross-reference, the reader will be able to construct something like a comprehensive narrative of Foucault's thinking. Finally, at the end, the reader will find "Secondary Works Cited," whose explicit purpose is obvious but that also functions as a sort of Foucault bibliography. For our readers who are not very familiar with Foucault's life, we have also appended a "Chronology of Foucault's Life."

Overall, we hope you will see this volume as a sort of event in Foucault scholarship, and indeed, as Foucault would have wanted it, an event in thinking in general.

Leonard Lawlor
John Nale

I

TERMS

1

ABNORMAL

THE CONCEPT OF the "abnormal" emerges within (and contributes to the construction of) Foucault's understanding of normalization – a key technique that constitutes and bridges two general forms of modern power: disciplinary power and biopower. The abnormal is the "other" that defines the "normal"; it is the object that gives rise to criminal psychiatry (as an attempt to treat, or at least explain, abnormality), and it also becomes a linchpin of modern racism. This presentation shall work from the general to the specific, starting from an identification of the forms of modern power in which the concept of the abnormal functions, through the particular techniques of normalization, to the details of how the abnormal has functioned within these contexts and its significance.

In marking a distinction between modern disciplinary power and biopower on the one hand and sovereign power on the other, Foucault states that although it does not disappear with the rise of modernity, sovereign power does cease to be the predominant form that power takes. The defining characteristic of sovereign power is the "right to take life and let live" (ECF-SMD, 241). This right is graphically illustrated in the opening pages of *Discipline and Punish* through a description of Robert-François Damiens's execution, in which the king's power is violently and publicly exhibited on Damiens's tortured body. In contradistinction to sovereign power, possessed and wielded over others by an individual, modern power is characterized by relations in which actions affect other actions, and in which all parties have the capacity to act. "[W]hat defines a relationship of power," Foucault states, "is that it is a mode of action which ... acts upon ... actions" (EEW3, 340). Moreover, he contends that within power relations, "'the other ... is recognized and maintained to the very end as a subject who acts'" (ibid.). Disciplinary power operates by way of techniques that train individual bodies to become efficient at a limited range of activities, and is primarily a mechanism of institutions (schools, prisons, workplaces). Biopower operates by way of techniques that manage populations (specifically at the

3

biological level of the human species) in order to maximize their overall health, and is primarily a mechanism of the state.

It is apparent from even this brief sketch that the effects of modern power are much more expansive than those of sovereign power. In *Discipline and Punish*, Foucault illustrates that sovereign power's impact, dramatic though it may be, is experienced directly and therefore most intensely only by the condemned person and those who witness his or her execution. Yet within modern societies as Foucault describes them, everyone (with the exception of persons who have been deprived of their capacity to act and hence suffer under conditions of domination) is directly affected by power because we are all involved in navigating power relations. According to Foucault, a key factor in the circulation and proliferation of modern power is the concept of the norm.

In his 1975 Collège de France course "Abnormal," Foucault asserts, "The norm is not simply and not even a principle of intelligibility; it is an element on the basis of which a certain exercise of power is founded and legitimized" (ECF-AB, 50). Simply put, the norm – the idea of having a standard (or that a standard exists or can be instituted) by which to evaluate and thereby determine "optimal" modes of behavior, levels of productivity, states of health, and the like – establishes what is normal (ECF-STP, 57). Once parameters of normality are set, techniques of "normalization" emerge that function to enforce those parameters. These techniques "make normal" in two ways. First, they intervene within both individual bodies and populations in ways that bring them into conformity with particular social norms. Within a disciplinary context, the norm gets established by, for example, schools developing and implementing standards that are intended to promote what is considered to be effective learning. Pupils' bodies are then trained (in *Discipline and Punish*, Foucault discusses methods of teaching and learning proper penmanship) so that they perform in ways that produce desired outcomes.

Second, techniques of normalization enforce normality by reproducing particular social norms (and thereby reinforcing the idea of normality more generally) to the point that they come to be seen not as produced at all but simply as natural and necessary. When norms become sedimented to the point that they are uncritically accepted in this manner, they can be said to be "normalizing." By presenting a limited range of modes of thought and existence not only as desirable but also as given, normalizing norms curtail persons' ability to act. They therefore reduce the fluidity of power relations and threaten to produce states of domination where modes of thought and existence are merely and simply dictated.

Foucault is describing a kind of circular relationship of mutual reinforcement whereby the norm generates the concept of the normal, which in turn generates techniques that, by way of promoting conformity with, reproducing, and thus presenting as ineluctable particular social norms, reasserts the significance of normality. But he also shows that the norm may function to expand power's scope. The norm,

Foucault asserts, "circulates between" the body and the population (ECF-SMD, 253). By forging a relationship between the two targets of modern power, the norm facilitates the spread of (potentially normalizing) power across "the whole surface" of society (ibid.).

Through rearticulating and legitimating both the concept of the normal and particular social norms, techniques of normalization also demarcate boundaries between what is normal and what is not, between what can be made to be normal and what cannot, thereby giving rise to the concept of the abnormal. Within the context of a normalizing society, abnormality can be understood in the most general sense as that which deviates from the norm. Simply put, abnormality is nonconformity or "non-observance, that which does not measure up to the rule, that departs from it" (EDP, 178). Such departure is devalued but it is not, as we might expect, simply "excluded and rejected" (ECF-AB, 50). Rather, the concept of the abnormal plays a role analogous to that of normality in facilitating the circulation of power and proliferating normalizing power relations. Just as techniques of normalization intervene within bodies and populations in such a way as to produce and enforce particular normals that reassert the concept of the normal, these same techniques by means of the same intervention function to identify, define, categorize, observe, and render visible – in other words, produce and enforce – particular abnormals that reassert the concept of the "abnormal." This conceptualization and rendering visible of abnormality is normalizing. In conveying to us what we do not want to be, and what we must try to avoid becoming, the concept of the abnormal effectively reasserts prevailing notions of normality not only by reinforcing prevailing social norms but also by challenging the limits of those norms and thus calling forth new fields of inquiry and producing new forms of knowledge, new institutions, and new state functions – in other words, by producing new norms. From a Foucauldian perspective, then, the abnormal, like the normal, is implicated in normalizing relations of power.

Although his 1975 Collège course focuses primarily on the articulation and function of the abnormal within the context of disciplinary power, as Foucault's most extensive study of this concept *Abnormal* proves instructive in understanding important aspects of his thinking. The genealogy provided in the course illustrates the link between the concept of the abnormal and normalization. Tracing the origins of the modern abnormal individual through the figures of the human monster of the medieval period to the eighteenth century, the individual to be corrected of the seventeenth and eighteenth centuries, and the masturbating child of the eighteenth and nineteenth centuries, Foucault shows that the historical expansion of the category of the abnormal corresponds to an expansion in the scope of normalizing power. Monsters, which violate laws of both nature and society, are rare; Foucault states that they are "by definition the exception" (ECF-AB, 58). The individual to be corrected, by contrast, is commonplace, an "everyday phenomenon" (ibid.). This figure violates normative relations within the economy of the family – that is, the family as a social institution situated within a web of other such institutions, including "the school, workshop, street, quarter, parish, church, police, and so on" (ibid.). The masturbator, violator of familial norms concerning the nature of intimacy (specifically, of one's intimate relationship to one's own body), "seems to be an almost universal" figure (ibid.).

In the face of each of these violations, new fields of study, new forms of knowledge, new institutions and institutional relations, and therefore new norms and techniques of normalization emerge. The cases of Henriette Cornier and Charles Jouy illustrate that violations by the monster and the individual to be corrected lead to the emergence and advancement of the field of criminal psychiatry. Cornier, lacking any apparent motive, the readily identifiable physiological irregularities of the "natural monster," and madness, decapitated a neighbor's child. Her act thus simultaneously invokes and confounds the two fields of inquiry, law and medicine, that would have been called on to make sense of it, thus giving rise to the new field of criminal psychiatry, which uses classical techniques of disciplinary power such as normalizing judgment, surveillance, and examination. In the absence of overt manifestations of abnormality, authorities investigated Cornier's life, studying how she lived and who she was – they examined her *character*. Doing so, they determined that Henriette Cornier's life had deteriorated into "debauchery," that her character was flawed, and that her action reflected those inherent flaws. In other words, they determined that Cornier's abnormality was implicit rather than overt: Cornier was a "moral monster" (ECF-AB, 124).

Jouy's case advances the field of criminal psychiatry and its techniques of normalization. Jouy, a forty-year-old "agricultural worker" whom Foucault describes as being "more or less the village idiot," was charged in 1867 with raping a young girl by the name of Sophie Adam (ECF-AB, 292). Unlike Cornier, who was deemed to have *developed* an immoral, monstrous character (apparent in the fact that she separated from her husband and subsequently twice became pregnant, giving both children up for adoption), Jouy's abnormality was considered to be *innate*. It did not emerge at a particular point in time, nor was it attributed to Jouy's character; instead, Jouy's abnormality, and hence his crime, was attributed to inborn qualities or traits. Authorities subjected Jouy to physical examination in an effort to identify not the cause of his act but "stigmata" – external manifestations of his aberrant nature (ECF-AB, 298). "[Jouy's] act and its stigmata," according to Foucault, "refer ... to a permanent, constitutive, congenital condition. The deformities of the body are, as it were, the physical and structural outcomes of this condition, and the aberrations of conduct, those precisely that earned Jouy his indictment, are its instinctual and dynamic outcomes" (ibid.).

Foucault's analysis shows that as abnormality becomes increasingly ubiquitous it also becomes increasingly implicit. There are two important effects of power associated with this development. First, abnormality becomes more difficult to detect, thereby giving rise to the need for the kinds of normalizing techniques just described that aim to access and illuminate individuals' inherent natures. Second, abnormality becomes part of who we are, not merely a characteristic of our actions: it's not that Cornier and Jouy committed acts that departed from the norm but rather that they themselves *were* abnormal. For Foucault, the cases of Cornier and Jouy make clear that the idea of an inherent human nature itself, whether that nature is normal or abnormal, "is the element in which are articulated the effects of a certain type of power and the reference to a certain type of knowledge, the machinery by which the power relations give rise to a possible corpus of knowledge, and knowledge extends and reinforces the effects of power" (EDP, 29).

While violations by the moral monster and individual to be corrected facilitate the emergence and advancement of a new field of inquiry, new forms of knowledge, and new techniques of normalization, Foucault shows that violations of familial norms by the masturbating child facilitate a redefinition and social repositioning of the institution of the family that is itself normalizing. The eighteenth century witnessed an explosion of discourse on the topic of childhood masturbation that, Foucault asserts, essentially functioned as an antimasturbation "campaign." Although this campaign drew an association between masturbation and abnormal sexuality, it focused primarily on the "somatic" effects of masturbation, which were said to be abnormal physiological development and physical illness. The campaign also identified "seduction by an adult" as being "the most frequent cause of masturbation," the adults in question being nonparental figures ("[s]ervants, governesses, private tutors, uncles, aunts, and cousins") who were present in the family home (ECF-AB, 243, 244). Preventing masturbation and the risk of abnormality associated with it thus required a change in the structure of the family.

This change, Foucault shows, ultimately led to the more general redefinition of the family as an institution. Given the threat they have come to pose, "[i]ntermediaries," the nonparental adult figures, "disappear" from the household (ECF-AB, 247). Parents now have a direct relationship to their children that is also characterized by close physical proximity, enabling them to watch for potential signs that their children are masturbating, as well as for symptoms of emerging physiological abnormality or illness. Yet while this new "possum-like" closeness, as Foucault puts it, allows parents to identify signs and symptoms, treating illness should it occur requires outside medical intervention (ECF-AB, 249). Parents do not possess expert medical knowledge and, moreover, although there can be no denying that masturbation is ultimately about sexuality, it is precisely sexuality that is being disavowed within the family's understanding of and approach to the "problem" of masturbation: that which is in fact at the heart of the issue, sexuality, "is silent within the family" (ECF-AB, 251). In the face of this disavowal, physicians are required not only to treat patients but also to adopt the role of confessor. "Medicine," Foucault notes, "is able to put sexuality into words and make it speak at the very moment that the family makes it visible because it is watching over it" (ibid.).

Foucault is describing here a fundamental change in what is considered "normal" family structure. Specifically, he details the displacement of the "big relational family" by the nuclear family, and the almost simultaneous medicalization of the family that accompanies it (ECF-AB, 249). This new social norm, according to Foucault, exposes the family and its individual members to scrutiny and intervention by a variety of institutions (medicine, pedagogy) as well as by the state (social services, public health). "Restricting the family in this way, and giving it such a compact and close-knit look," he declares, "effectively opens it up to political and moral criteria; opens it up to a type of power and to a technique of power relayed by medicine and doctors together with families" (ECF-AB, 256). This new medicalized nuclear family "functions as a source of normalization.... [I]t is this family that reveals ... the normal and the abnormal in the sexual domain. The family becomes not only the basis for the determination and distinction of sexuality but also for the rectification of the abnormal" (ECF-AB, 254).

Foucault's genealogy analyzes specific figures that both illustrate abnormality as being a departure from the norm and elucidate its historical evolution into a phenomenon that is widespread, pervasive, and threatening, yet also inherent and therefore difficult to identify and root out. In doing so, it provides an account of the identification, definition, categorization, observation, and general rendering visible – in short, the (re)production and expansion – of the abnormal and the normalizing effects of power associated with it. Foucault concludes his 1975 course by providing some insight into the implications such a conceptualization of abnormality would have in the twentieth century and twenty-first century, and in doing so invokes some themes that figure prominently in later work, especially his work on biopower.

The view of abnormality as inherent, Foucault argues, has particularly profound effects in light of the rise and prominence of the science of heredity. Two of these effects he considered particularly worthy of his attention. The first is that "the theory of heredity allows psychiatry of the abnormal" to become "a technology of the healthy or unhealthy, useful or dangerous, profitable or harmful marriage" (ECF-AB, 315). This concern with marriage as an institution will expand into a general social concern with the process of reproduction. The second important effect is that concerns about abnormality as a heritable trait, as something that can be passed on to offspring, give rise to the theory of "degeneration," which posits that the reproduction and dissemination of abnormality throughout a population threatens its overall health. "The degenerate," according to Foucault, is the abnormal individual whose abnormality is inherited and thus biologically based, as well as scientifically "proven" (ECF-AB, 315).

This scientization of abnormality allows the field of psychiatry to "[dispense] with the need to find a cure" (ECF-AB, 316). If abnormality is written into one's genetic code, so to speak, efforts toward "rectification" are clearly in vain. In a reference to the emergence of biopower, Foucault argues that insofar as this is the case, psychiatry shifts its attention away from curing abnormals and toward the "protection" of society from the biological threat that degenerates pose (ibid.). For him, the extent of the abnormal's implication in normalizing power, the propensity of normalizing power to deteriorate into states of domination, and the destructive character of domination itself are perhaps most apparent in this perceived need by a society to ward off what manifests as a threat at the biological level of the human species. "This notion of degeneration and these analyses of heredity" as articulated specifically within psychiatric discourse, according to Foucault, "give rise to" a new form of racism that in turn informs Nazism (ECF-AB, 316). "The new racism specific to the twentieth century, this neoracism as the internal means of defense of a society against its abnormal individuals, is the child of psychiatry," he contends, "and Nazism did no more than graft this new racism onto the ethnic racism that was endemic in the nineteenth century" (ECF-AB, 317).

Dianna Taylor

SEE ALSO

> *Biopower*
> *Discipline*
> *Madness*
> *Normalization*
> *Psychiatry*
> *Georges Canguilhem*

SUGGESTED READING

Canguilhem, Georges. 1962. "Monstrosity and the Monstrous," *Diogenes* 10:27–42.
   The Normal and the Pathological. 1991. New York: Zone Books.
Taylor, Dianna. 2009. "Normativity and Normalization," *Foucault Studies* 7:45–63.

2

ACTUALITY

THE NOTION OF "actuality" in Foucault's work points toward a particular understanding of and relation to present social reality. Understood simply, actuality may be identified with the concrete sociohistorical conditions that define the contemporary moment. Actuality thus concerns the specificity of the "now" in which we find ourselves, but is not the same as the present or as the sum of reality in general. That is, actuality is not equivalent to the present moment; it is not merely a slice of time, not merely a temporal notion. But neither is it equivalent to all that exists; it is not merely an aggregation of what is. In contrast, actuality is a defining set of events that mark the distinctiveness of the current time. Thus, Foucault describes himself to be a kind of radical journalist "insofar as what interests me is actuality, what happens around us, what we are, what occurs in the world" (quoted in Ewald 1999, 82).

Yet, this sense of actuality involves more than a simple interest in current affairs. Comprehension of actuality entails, furthermore, a certain distance from the "now." The relation to the present that defines actuality can be understood as one in which we break with current conditions. Actuality, therefore, is linked to critique and with the attitude that Foucault describes as that of "modernity." Thus, Foucault's notion of actuality is elaborated in relationship to Kant and the Kantian understanding of the limits and critical use of reason. For Foucault, Kant's meditation on Enlightenment is both an analysis that "situates actuality with respect to the overall movement [of humanity into maturity] and its basic directions" and "a reflection by Kant on the actuality of his own enterprise" (EFR, 38; see also ECF-GSO, 11–21 – the English translation of this course renders "actualité" as "present reality"). What distinguishes the Kantian text on Enlightenment as one that concerns itself with actuality is the way it links historical reflection with critical analysis of the present and situates Kant's own philosophical project at this juncture. Thus, the text represents the inauguration of the ethos of modernity that is defined by "a mode of relating to actuality ...

that at one and the same time marks a relation of belonging and presents itself as a task" (EFR, 39). The attitude that engages with actuality – that makes of the present moment an actuality – is thus one in which we simultaneously inhabit our present and begin to move out of it, in which we effect a kind of distance that is only possible because of our belonging to that from which we distance ourselves.

Accordingly, Deleuze characterizes Foucault's thinking of the "actual" by emphasizing "the difference between the present and the actual" (Deleuze and Guattari 1994, 112). The crux of this difference lies in how "the actual is not what we are but, rather, what we become, what we are in the process of becoming…. The present, on the contrary, is what we are and, thereby, what already we are ceasing to be" (ibid.). Whereas the present embodies the limitations of what we are now, what will be left behind, and what will be transformed, actuality is possessed of a certain kind of mobility; in our actuality, we are in movement. In other words, the actual is "the now of our becoming" (ibid.). It signals not some mysterious temporality but rather the movement out of the present into a future that is different from it. Yet, Foucault emphasizes that if modernity is defined by a sense of "perpetual movement" that accompanies ruptures in tradition, we fail to reckon with our actuality if we simply embrace this movement (EFR, 39). Instead, the modern ethos in relation to actuality "lies in adopting a certain attitude with respect to this movement; and this deliberate, difficult attitude consists in recapturing something eternal that is not beyond the present instant, nor behind it, but within it" (ibid.). We can only understand our own actuality by "recapturing something eternal" in the present moment and "grasping it [this moment] in what it is" (EFR, 41). Effective critique, which is accomplished through distance from the present, must also be premised on such attentiveness to the delimiting conditions of the present.

Actuality, therefore, describes a place and time from which critique and transformative action can occur. As François Ewald notes, Foucault poses "the problem of actuality … because actuality is, in this sense, from the moment that one could identify the present, the position of an act which is capable of disrupting the present" (Ewald 1999, 83). Only through the simultaneous comprehension of the present – "the moment that one could identify the present" – and the aforementioned sense of distance from the present is such disruption and transformation possible. In order to effect this distance and to disrupt the present, a deliberate and critical exercise of one's freedom in relation to one's actuality is required; an "extreme attention to what is real is confronted with the practice of a liberty that simultaneously respects this reality and violates it" (EFR, 41). It is through reference to our actuality that critique of ourselves and our era becomes reflective critique, and disruptive action becomes transformative and responsive rather than merely disruptive. Our own practice of freedom must "put itself to the test of reality, of actuality, both to grasp the points where change is possible and desirable, and to determine the precise form this change should take" (EFR, 46). Thus, it is comprehension of and responsiveness to our actuality that makes practices of freedom ethical – that is, reflective – ones. In this way, the movement beyond limits – beyond the limits of the present – is not merely transgression for transgression's sake or novelty for novelty's sake but is a "patient labor" that responds to actuality.

Erinn Gilson

SEE ALSO

> *Critique*
> *History*
> *Immanuel Kant*

SUGGESTED READING

McGushin, Edward. 2007. *Foucault's Askesis: An Introduction to the Philosophical Life*. Evanston, IL: Northwestern University Press.
Patton, Paul. 2010. "Activism, Philosophy and Actuality in Deleuze and Foucault." *Deleuze Studies* 4 (Supplement). Accessed December 6, 2010. DOI: 10.3366/dls.2010.0207.

3

ARCHAEOLOGY

FOUCAULT'S ARCHAEOLOGY IS archaeology of knowledge, where "archaeology" is a metaphor presenting knowledge as something that lies beneath a surface and needs to be uncovered before it can be understood. Husserl had used this metaphor to express how the knowledge to be uncovered by phenomenological reflection was embedded beneath layers of misleading assumptions and interpretations. For example, the truths of our lived experience of the sensory world are covered over by the abstractions and theoretical interpretations of modern science and emerge only through the penetrating gaze of transcendental consciousness. Foucault, however, transforms the Husserlian metaphor in at least two ways. First, he does not see the truths uncovered by his archaeology as essential and ahistorical but as the "truths" characteristic of specific historical modes of thinking; for example, thinking about madness in the seventeenth century or about sexuality in the nineteenth century. Second, archaeology is not the activity of a transcendental subject, constituting the meaning of the world that it knows, but of an inquirer dealing with contingent historical facts about systems of knowledge in a given period.

The method of Foucault's archaeology is to read vast amounts of the writing produced about a certain domain at a certain time, with a view to determining fundamental rules governing the use of language in that written corpus. These, however, are not the formal rules (of grammar and logic, which are not distinctive of a historical period) but the material rules that delimit the substantive boundaries of what can be said about the domain in question. Such rules express the limits of conceivability with a given historical mode of thought (which Foucault calls an *episteme* or a discursive formation). They explain, for example, why seventeenth-century thought could not have made sense of our modern idea that criminals should be primarily punished by imprisonment intended to rehabilitate them or why, unlike us, Renaissance scholars made no sharp distinction between features empirically observed to belong to an animal and stories told about it.

Foucault's archaeology of knowledge is not a theory of knowledge in the sense of analytic epistemology: it is not a philosophical account of the nature of knowledge in general. Nor is it *épistémologie* in the French sense (associated with Bachelard and Canguilhem), a philosophical account of the nature of scientific knowledge. It is a historical rather than a philosophical project, although its historical approach depends on philosophical assumptions about the priority of language over subjective experience. Archaeology is similar to what Canguilhem called the "history of concepts." His two historical studies that have "archaeology" in their titles, *The Birth of the Clinic: An Archaeology of the Medical Gaze* and *The Order of Things: An Archaeology of the Human Sciences*, both contain strong elements of such a history. But archaeological histories are, we might say, radicalizations of Canguilhem's histories in that they focus not on the standard scientific disciplines in a given period (for example, in the nineteenth century, biology, economics, and philology) but on the deeper cognitive structures that underlie such disciplines. In Foucault's terminology, history of concepts operates only the level of *connaissance*, the concepts and theories of particular sciences, whereas archaeology operates at the level of *savoir*, the cognitive structures that define the shared cognitive field in which these concepts and theories are deployed.

Foucault's archaeology, as its embrace of a history of concepts suggests, is closely tied to his effort to come to terms with Hegel. Foucault eschews the "bad Hegel" of the complete System, absolute knowledge, total synthesis, and final necessity, but he wants to preserve the "good Hegel" for whom experience is given its undeniable place as a historical reality but is nonetheless subordinated to a more fundamental objective structure (which in turn, however, allows for new forms of experience whereby we can break out of the pattern set for us by the past).

Archaeology tries to avoid the "bad Hegel" by committing itself to a description of historical concreta that are irreducible to any philosophical synthesis. Particularly important for Foucault, because of its connection with efforts of human self-understanding, is the history of what he calls "the human sciences." Because he aims to write genuine histories of these sciences, based on his own archival research, his projects have to be judged by criteria of factual accuracy that, in principle at least, guard against the Hegelian temptation of fitting everything too neatly into an independently posited philosophical system. On the other hand, within the discipline of history, his archaeologies are much closer to an "idealist history" that deploys broad interpretative schemes, more illustrated than proven by data, than to an "empiricist history" that fears to venture much beyond the bare catalogue of facts. This sort of high-flying history can readily find itself taking on, for better or worse, Hegelian features. The three histories (of madness, clinical medicine, and the emergence of the modern "sciences of man") that preceded Foucault's detailed formulation of the archaeological methodology in *The Archaeology of Knowledge* show the difficulties he faced in trying to devise a historical methodology that was free of Hegelian entanglements.

Foucault's first major book, *History of Madness in the Age of Reason*, makes considerable use of Hegelian concepts – for example, alienation, recognition, unhappy consciousness, master–slave relation – to describe various aspects of the existence of the mad and of society's perception of them. Although such descriptions need not imply a commitment to Hegel's overall metaphysical view, they raise questions as to whether Foucault's account is based solely on the patient archaeological reconstruction of the language of seventeenth-century delineations of madness. Further, *History of Madness* is framed in terms of what Foucault presents as classical reason's effort to exclude madness as its simple denial, rather than (as, Foucault claims, was done in the Middle Ages and Renaissance) treating madness as the essential complement of reason, in continuing dialogue with it. Moreover, Foucault describes these historical developments as changes in the *experience* of madness. If we ask who or what has this experience, the only answer would seem to be reason itself, which, even if it avoids a progressive teleology, seems to posit something like Hegelian spirit as the subject of the historical experience of madness. Foucault himself seems to recognize this in the self-critique of *The Archaeology of Knowledge* when he says that his *History of Madness* "accorded far too great a place, and a very enigmatic one too, to what I called an 'experience', thus showing to what extent one was still close to admitting an anonymous and general subject of history" (EAK, 16, translation modified).

Nonetheless, there are features of the archaeological approach – particularly as developed in Foucault's next two histories, *The Birth of the Clinic* and, especially, *The Order of Things*, that seem suited to avoiding Hegelian pitfalls. First, the focus on uncovering unconscious structures of thought suggests that even the most striking achievements of conscious thinking are, contrary to Hegel, based on and restricted by factors outside consciousness. Second, Foucault's histories avoided any hint of Hegelian dialectical development by renouncing the attempt to explain changes in *episteme*, since he limited himself to archaeological descriptions of the deep structure of thought in discrete periods. Foucault could demonstrate that Renaissance thought took place within an *episteme* quite different from that of the classical age, and that the *episteme* of the classical age was likewise quite different from that of modernity. But he made no effort to account for the processes whereby one *episteme* was replaced by another, choosing instead to present isolated snapshots of different periods.

But neither of these features was a sure protection against Hegelian totalization. Structures that are unconscious for individual human minds at a given time may still be part of the conscious life of absolute spirit. (Even if we require that absolute consciousness be manifested in human consciousness, Foucault's subsequent discovery of these structures can be taken as precisely this manifestation.)

And, as Foucault realized, full-blooded history requires explanations of why changes in thinking occurred. Unless he was able to find a satisfactory explanatory alternative to Hegelian dialectic, he had no reason to think that he had avoided Hegelian history. Moreover, even the avowedly explanation-free history of *The Order of Things* turns, at its most crucial point, to something very like Hegelian dialectic. This occurs when Foucault is trying to show how the modern *episteme*, centered on the concept of man as simultaneously empirical (an object in the world) and transcendental (constituting the world), is on the verge of collapse. In his section on "The Analytic of Finitude," Foucault deploys a series of philosophical analyses that seem designed to show, in classic Hegelian fashion, how successive attempts at thinking of man as both empirical and transcendental make some progress in reconciling the two aspects but eventually fall into contradiction.

The lesson of Foucault's archaeological histories was therefore the need to develop an effective alternative to the dialectical method of explaining historical change. Only in this way could Foucault carry out his project of confronting philosophical thought with a historical reality which that thought could not reduce to itself. It was this need that motivated Foucault's development, beginning with his history of the prison, *Discipline and Punish*, of a complementary historical approach that, with more than a nod to Nietzsche, he presented as his genealogy.

Foucault's *The Archaeology of Knowledge* provides a detailed methodological reflection on what he was doing – or at least moving toward – in the three preceding histories. The fundamental point is that the method is designed to provide historical accounts that are not centered around the activities of human subjects and, in particular, have no place for a transcendental subject that is the source of historical meaning and purpose. Foucault does not deny the obvious fact that humans have a role in making their history, but this role is specified and limited by the discursive formation – a complex of rules that define the sorts of objects, concepts, forms of cognitive authority ("enunciative modalities"), and theoretical viewpoints ("strategies") that are possible in a given historical context. The discursive formation (roughly what Foucault had previously called an *episteme*) is not constituted by the subject but rather provides a place from which subjects speak and know but under strong constraints from the discursive formation. The history occurring within a discursive formation is not devoid of subjectivity, but it is free of what Foucault calls "transcendental narcissism" (EAK, 203).

Consistent with Foucault's flight from totalization, he presents discursive formations as systems of dispersion, not of unification. A discursive formation is not a worldview, conceptual framework, or theory so much as a set of elements from which a variety of conflicting worldviews, frameworks, and theories can be developed. This allows us to "decenter" the subjective unities (ideas, opinions) of individual subjects, which are the primary focus of standard histories of thought (which Foucault labels "doxology"). The impersonal unity of a language disperses and displaces the proper names that dominate nonarchaeological histories. The unity of thought thus becomes language itself, with discursive formations delimiting the field on which traditional conceptual and theoretical conflicts occur.

The archaeological understanding of language is essentially that of Saussure: "a collection of signs defined by their contrasting characteristics and their rules of use" (EAK, 85). For archaeology, however, the basic linguistic unit is not the syllable or the word but the statement, which (as Foucault admitted in correspondence with John Searle) can be understood as something quite like the speech act of analytic philosophy of language. But the analogy with speech acts is best taken as emphasizing that statements are moves in a language game, deriving their meaning from the ways in which they differ functionally from other possible moves. The similarity does not involve thinking of statements as expressing the intentional states of subjects. As Foucault puts it: "The analysis of statements operates ... without reference to a cogito.... It is situated at the level of the 'it is said'" (EAK, 122). Of course, what "is said" is in fact said by some subject or another, but, from an archaeological standpoint, this subject refers merely to "a position that may be filled in certain conditions by various individuals" in accordance with the rules of a discursive formation (EAK, 115).

Nor should we think of these rules as transcendental principles that somehow "constitute" statements as meaningful expressions. Rather, the rules are merely descriptions of statements that have historically occurred and of the relations among them. "Discourse in this sense is not an ideal timeless form that also possesses a history ... ; it is, from beginning to end, historical" (EAK, 117). Foucault does introduce the (admittedly, he says, "rather barbarous") term "historical a priori," which might suggest a remnant of transcendentalism. But he insists that any condition imposed by such an a priori "is not a condition of validity for judgments but a condition of reality for statements"; that is, a condition that itself derives from the given historical reality "of things actually said" (EAK, 127). Foucault sums up his insistence that archaeology is in no way a transcendental enterprise when he says that if rejecting the transcendental means that "one is a positivist, then I am quite happy to be one" (EAK, 125).

For all its importance as a methodological manifesto, *The Archaeology of Knowledge* remains awkwardly related to Foucault's histories. On the one hand, the book formulates an ideal method that, by his own admission, is not fully carried out in the histories (of madness, the clinic, and the human sciences) that precede it. On the other hand, Foucault did not publish another historical study until 1975 (six years after *The Archaeology of Knowledge*), and the new study, *Discipline and Punish*, proclaimed a new, genealogical method, which operates quite differently from archaeology. It is therefore easy to see why Foucault scholars have paid relatively little attention to *The Archaeology of Knowledge*. Nonetheless, it is valuable as a guide to reflection on the methodology of Foucault's early histories, and the account of language and discursive formations is of considerable interest in its own right.

Most important, it is a mistake to think that Foucault simply abandons archaeology in his later histories. Although *The Archaeology of Knowledge* primarily presents the method as a way of studying language (*discursive* formations), it also emphasizes the use of archaeology for understanding the relation of discourse to nondiscursive practices such as "institutions, political events, economic practices and processes" (EAK, 162). This opens the door to its use even when Foucault is primarily concerned with a genealogy that will tease out the causal role of institutions and so on. This happens, for example, in *Discipline and Punish*, where Foucault analyzes the modern practice of punishing those who break the law in terms of the four archaeological categories of object (the delinquent), concept (the criminal character), enunciative modality (the authority of judges, prison officials, parole boards), and strategies (various uses of isolation and work in the treatment of delinquents). In his work on ancient sexuality, Foucault even makes extensive use of the archaeological analysis of discourse. In *The Use of Pleasure*, for example, he offers readings of medical, economic, and philosophical texts that uncover the structure of ancient Greek discourse about sex.

Foucault directly recognizes the continuing role of archaeology in his work by incorporating it as an essential element in his final understanding of his approach to writing history. In his Introduction to *The Use of Pleasure*, he says that his work has been a contribution to "the history of truth," which comprises analyses of (1) discursive "games of truth," (2) the relation of games of truth to power relations, and (3) the relation of games of truth to the self. Games of truth are the various systems of discourse directed toward producing true statements, and so clearly the objects of archaeological analysis. Power relations are the concern of what Foucault initially called "genealogy," and the self is the concern of his final turn to ethics. But both of these later "turns" of Foucault's histories are studied in relation to the games of truth treated by archaeology, which therefore remains essential at every stage of his historical work.

Gary Gutting

SEE ALSO

> *Genealogy*
> *History*
> *Knowledge*
> *Truth*
> *Georges Canguilhem*
> *Georg Wilhelm Friedrich Hegel*

SUGGESTED READING

Bernauer, James. 1990. *Michel Foucault's Force of Flight*. London: Humanities Press, 1990, esp. chap. 4.

Dreyfus, Hubert L., and Paul Rabinow. 1983. *Michel Foucault: Beyond Structuralism and Hermeneutics*, 2nd ed. Chicago: University of Chicago Press.

Gutting, Gary. 1989. *Michel Foucault's Archaeology of Scientific Reason*. Cambridge: Cambridge University Press.

4

ARCHIVE

OUCAULT USED THE term "archive" most commonly in the years 1967–1969, in a number of interviews before and just after the publication of *The Archaeology of Knowledge* as well as in the book itself. In each of these interviews, he offers a definition of the term – all of which are variations on the definition given in *The Archaeology of Knowledge*. After 1969, however, the notion of the archive virtually disappeared from Foucault's vocabulary, as his interests shifted in the 1970s "genealogical" period to the analysis of nondiscursive as well as discursive practices, and in which power relations emerged as the principal framing lens.

The "archive," as Foucault defined it in a 1969 interview, is

> the set of discourses actually pronounced; and this set of discourses is envisaged not only as a set of events which would have taken place once and for all and which would remain in abeyance, in the limbo or purgatory of history, but also as a set that continues to function, to be transformed through history, and to provide the possibility of appearing in other discourses. (EFL, 57)

As this passage illustrates, the archive functions as the set of all statements that constitute a discourse and as the rules or regularities that govern what can be said within a discourse. It is first of all the set of actual discourses – in other words, the archive encompasses "all that has actually been said." "By the archive, I mean first of all the mass of things spoken in a culture, preserved, valorized, re-used, repeated and transformed. In brief, this whole verbal mass that has been produced by men, invested in their techniques and in their institutions, and woven into their existence and their history" (EFL, 66, translation modified). But these discourses are not permanently fixed, immobile, or static – like an atemporal Platonic form. Rather they are transformable and transformed, sometimes disappearing to be replaced by others, and even their constitutive rules are transformable. Discourses are, in other words, practices, and "[t]he 'archive' appears then as a kind of great practice of discourse, a practice which has its rules, its conditions, its functioning and its effects" (EFL, 66).

Discourses are not just amorphous collections of statements; rather, Foucault argues, these discourses obey certain rules or regularities, and these regularities themselves are determined by the archive. As the set of "all that has been said," the archive functions as the limit or boundary for a discourse, and functions to establish the rules or regularities that govern the discourse's transformations. In this way, the archive establishes the "conditions of existence" (EFL, 40) (or, if you prefer a more Kantian phrase, the conditions of possibility) for what can be said within a discourse and provides rules of transformation for these discourses. The archive thus constitutes what Foucault calls a discourse's "historical *a priori*." And so the "archive," as defined in *The Archaeology of Knowledge* (in much more formal and technical, as well as metaphorical, language), is

> first the law of what can be said, the system that governs the appearance of statements as unique events. But the archive is also that which determines that all these things said do not accumulate endlessly in an amorphous mass … but they are grouped together in distinct figures, composed together in accordance with multiple relations, maintained or blurred in accordance with specific regularities; that which determines that they do not withdraw at the same pace in time, but shine, as it were, like stars, some that seem close to us shining brightly from afar off, while others that are in fact close to us are already growing pale. (EAK, 129)

As the "law of what can be said" (the second aspect of Foucault's definition), the archive establishes the regularities that govern statements and discourses, that give them the particular forms and rules that they actually have (rather than leaving them as amorphous masses). The archive functions at a middle level – the level of practices – between language (the rules of which allow for an infinite number of possible coherent expressions, many of which might never be said) and a passive collection (or "corpus") of everything that has been said. At this level of practice, "it reveals the rules of a practice that enables statements both to survive and to undergo regular modification. It is *the general system of the formation and transformation of statements*" (EAK, 130).

Foucault specifies that the archive serves to define two systems or kinds of regularity within discourse: enunciability and functioning. First, the archive defines a "system of enunciability" (EAK, 129) that regulates statements as *events*. That is, the archive determines what can actually be said or expressed at a given moment in history, by whom, with what authority, and so forth. (This is distinct from the grammatical rules that govern a sentence's coherence. Rather, it addresses whether a statement will "make sense" or be accepted, given everything else that is believed in a particular discourse.) Second, the archive defines a "system of functioning" (ibid.) that distinguishes statements and discourses as *things*: "It is that which differentiates discourses in their multiple existence and specifies them in their own duration" (ibid.). Different discourses will recognize different "truths" and different speakers' authority to speak those truths, and the archive delimits how these combinations are assembled.

The archive thus constitutes what Foucault calls a "*historical a priori*": "an *a priori* that is not a condition of validity for judgments, but a condition of reality for statements ... the *a priori* of a history that is given, since it is that of things actually said" (EAK, 127). Unlike a formal (or Kantian) a priori, the historical a priori "does not constitute, above events, and in an unmoving heaven, an atemporal structure; it is defined as the group of rules that characterize a discursive practice" (ibid.). The archive determines the rules of enunciability and functioning that delimit a discourse and enable certain statements within it, and thus functions a priori to constitute that discourse, but the archive is itself malleable and transformable – indeed, each new statement serves to alter it a little bit – and this is what distinguishes it as a *historical* a priori.

The archive remains, however, distinct from a closely related concept, the *episteme*. The *episteme* is "the totality of relations that can be discovered, for a given period, between the sciences when one analyses them at the level of discursive regularities" (EAK, 191). The *episteme* reflects the relations that exist between sciences or discourses, whereas the archive is the set that encompasses these discourses (as well as the relations between them) and gives them their regularities. As Foucault notes, "[t]he archive cannot be described in its totality; and in its presence it is unavoidable" (EAK, 130). "Archaeology," Foucault's method of investigation, is "the never completed, never wholly achieved uncovering of the archive" (EAK, 131).

In sum, the "archive" is a key concept of Foucault's "archaeological" period – indeed, Foucault chose this term in part because of its etymological similarity with "archaeology." It is one of the core "framing" concepts for Foucault's methodological reflection on his earlier, empirical studies (*History of Madness*, *The Birth of the Clinic*, and *The Order of Things*), and thus illustrates his attempt to systematize his thinking up to this point.

Richard A. Lynch

SEE ALSO

Archaeology
History
Immanuel Kant
Maurice Merleau-Ponty

SUGGESTED READING

Flynn, Thomas. 1994. "Foucault's Mapping of History," in *The Cambridge Companion to Foucault*, ed. Gary Gutting. Cambridge: Cambridge University Press, pp. 28–46.

Gutting, Gary. 1989. *Michel Foucault's Archaeology of Scientific Reason*. Cambridge: Cambridge University Press.

5

AUTHOR

For MICHEL FOUCAULT, the term "author" denotes a function within our modern discourse, by which fiction's "proliferation of meaning" is constrained (EEW2, 222). This, of course, is the reversal of the notion that the "author" is an unlimited source of creativity, through which writing gains its power of expression. Instead, the organization and interpretation of texts according to their "author," in Foucault's account, functions like a kind of limiting principle that ultimately restricts the possible meanings created through fiction. The idea of the "author" as an "author-function" can be understood on two different, but interrelated, registers. First, Foucault's most direct engagement with the idea of the author occurs in his 1969 work "What Is an Author?" in which he argues that the idea that the "death of the author" (a notion found in then contemporary literary criticism) will not properly occur until our modern discourse changes into a new form (EEW2, 222). Second, in *The Archaeology of Knowledge*, Foucault argues that the notion of the author is part of a larger "mass of notions" whose function is to guarantee the continuity of historical progression, primarily in terms of understanding meaning as produced solely in and through the subject (EAK, 21). Here, we shall primarily examine the first of these two registers, Foucault's discussion of the author in "What Is an Author?" However, near the end of this entry, we shall briefly look at the role of the author in Foucault's larger understanding of discourse during his archaeological period.

Foucault presented "What Is an Author?" as a lecture in February 1969 before the Société Française de philosophie. As already mentioned, Foucault directly engages with the idea of the "death of the author." The term "the death of the author" is meant to denote the movement within French literary criticism during the 1960s that sought to overcome the idea that a text is both the product and the container of its creator's hidden and secret intentions. This idea has its most explicit articulation in Roland Barthes's 1977 essay "The Death of the Author." In this essay, Barthes argues that writing is "the destruction of every voice, of every point of origin," in the sense that "it is language which speaks" and not the author (Barthes 1977, 142). As such, to write is to "perform" language rather than to transcribe into a material form one's own intentions. Thus, to call for the death of the author is to call for the realization that writing must not be constrained in meaning by the imposition of an author.

"What Is an Author?" begins with Foucault outlining the "two themes" of modern literary theory to which he is generally sympathetic: (1) that writing, conceptually, has been freed from "the theme of expression" (EEW2, 206) and (2) that writing is no longer conceived of as a kind of immortality for the writer, but rather a "voluntary self-effacement" (EEW2, 206). As regards the first, Foucault adopts the general insight from Saussure that language can be understood as a system without reference to a speaking individual. Foucault writes that "Referring only to itself, but without being restricted to the confines of its interiority, writing is identified with its own unfolded exteriority" (EEW2, 206). Since language does not require a speaking individual for its own internal coherence, writing can no longer be thought of as the "expression" of the intentions of the writing subject. The second theme, the author's self-effacement, is linked to the first. If writing can be understood free of the idea that it is originally tied to the writer's expression, then the act of writing itself must, as Barthes puts it, "reach that point where only language acts" (Barthes 1977, 143). Indeed, Foucault tells us that the writer "must assume the role of the dead person in the game of writing" (EEW2, 207).

However, although Foucault adopts the idea of writing, he argues that it is much too quick to claim, as Barthes does in "The Death of the Author," that the death of the author has been achieved. To this end, Foucault shows how two contemporary ideas about how we are to understand the absence of the author in fact presuppose the very entity that they deny. The first notion that is supposed to make sense of the author's absence is that of the work (*œuvre*). As Foucault understands it, the notion of the work determines the relationships between texts in terms of an overall structure that can be explicated in such a way that, supposedly, does not rely on any notion of the author. Yet, on closer inspection, the structure of a work exists only in reference to an individual that has been labeled as an author. The question is: how does one *actually* delimit the sphere of texts accepted as the work? What constitutes, for instance, Nietzsche's work? By what criteria does one choose to accept or reject a grocery receipt as part of a work? Indeed, Foucault asks, "How can one define a work amid the millions of traces left by someone after his death" (EEW2, 207)? The work can only be defined through some reference to those texts that are produced through some kind of presupposed authorial intent. The second notion that is supposed to account for the absence of the author is Derrida's notion of writing (*écriture*) (EEW2, 208). Using language similar to his critique of phenomenology in *The Order of Things*, Foucault argues that this notion of writing "seems to transpose the empirical characteristics of the author into the transcendental" by keeping alive "those representations that formed a particular image of the author" (EEW2, 208–209). Specifically, the idea of writing as absence "seems to be a simple repetition, in transcendental terms, of both the religious principle of inalterable and yet never fulfilled tradition, and the aesthetic principle of the work's survival, its perpetuation beyond the author's death, and its enigmatic excess in relation to him" (EEW2, 208). In other words, the idea that meaning is given through absence seems to take the empirical guarantor of meaning (the author) and, through effacing it, transforms it into the form of a transcendental absence, which is the new guarantor of meaning. As an absence, the author still haunts writing. For Foucault, both attempts to understand the absence of the author therefore fail.

So, what is an author, for Foucault? Foucault claims that the author should be understood not as an element within a discourse but rather as a role that plays a classificatory function (EEW2, 210). That the notion of the author is a *role* rather than an *element* of discourse can be seen through the various problems that arise if we try to equate the role of the author with the element of the proper name. For instance, a proper name is one of simple reference, in the sense that it designates some individual. However, when used in the role of an author, the relation of reference of the name changes. As an author, the name "Aristotle" does not point simply to some individual. Rather, it is descriptive: the name "Aristotle" indicates "the author of the *Analytics*" or "the founder of ontology" (EEW2, 209). Furthermore, imagine if we were to find out that all of Plato's texts were actually written by Aristotle. The relationship of reference between the proper name "Aristotle" and the individual would not change – but the relationship between Aristotle as an author, his texts, and their interrelationships would change.

As such, the term "author" does not simply designate the reference between a proper name and a group of texts. Rather, it is a kind of role that a name can assume, or more specifically a discursive space that may be occupied by a subject, which serves two functions: (1) to "manifest the appearance of a certain discursive set" and (2) to manifest "the status of this discourse within a society or culture" (EEW2, 211). First, the author's name serves to delimit a number of texts and the internal relationship between them (EEW2, 210). For example, "Aristotle" refers to a group of texts that were written by him and the relationships among them such as their chronological order. Second, for Foucault, the name of the author gives a kind of status to the speech of the particular discourse: "it is a speech that must be received in a certain mode and that, in a given culture, must receive a certain status" (EEW2, 211). Thus, the notion of the author must be understood not as an element but rather as a function – specifically, the author-function.

The author-function, in its role of indicating a discursive set and its privileged speech, has four characteristics. First, the author-function is tied to systems of ownership, and it is through these systems of ownership that the author-function is able to set a limit on writing (EEW2, 211). For Foucault, writing is transgressive because it has become bound up with "rules concerning author's rights, author-publisher relations, [and] rights of reproductions" (EEW2, 212). Second, the author-function will vary within a discourse, and across discourses and times (ibid.). That is, this function is not a universal constant. For instance, the valence between author and text in terms of literary and scientific text changed within the seventeenth and eighteenth centuries (ibid.). Previously, literary texts with anonymous authors were accepted on their own terms, whereas the truth of a scientific text was linked to the name of the author. Then, an inversion or chiasm between author and text occurred in the seventeenth and eighteenth centuries. The truth of scientific texts became tied to the content of the text itself rather than the name of the author, and literary texts only became accepted when assigned a proper name. If an anonymous literary text is found, Foucault writes, "the game becomes one of rediscovering the author" (EEW2, 213). Third, the author-function does not spontaneously develop but is instead the result of a long and complex operation (ibid.). To illustrate this characteristic, Foucault argues that the way in which contemporary literary criticism constructs the author is derived from the authentication of texts within the Christian tradition (EEW2, 214). For instance, Saint Jerome wrote that a number of methods must be used to classify texts in accordance with the saintliness of the author, one of which was that if any text contradicted the main thesis of the group of texts, then it was to be rejected. Similarly, Foucault argues that in literary criticism, at a very basic level, there is still the attempt to resolve contradictions within an author's work (EEW2, 215). Finally, the author-function refers to "positions that can be occupied by different classes of individuals" rather than the simple reference to some real individual (EEW2, 216). This can be seen through the examination of the personal pronouns within a mathematical text. As Foucault points out, the author of the preface indicates the writer of the text who "completed a certain task" (EEW2, 216). However, the demonstrations within the text itself do not refer to this same individual author. The demonstrations push the idea of the author into a kind of anonymity, as it is the demonstrations themselves that guarantee the truth of the text, such that anyone could have written it.

The notion of the author is not limited solely to the author of a literary text. In fact, for Foucault, we can understand the founders of various discourses as endowed with the author-function, but in a way that is fundamentally different from the author-function within a literary text, painting, or piece of music (EEW2, 217). The difference lies in the way that the founder of a discourse has "produced something else: the possibilities and the rules for the formation of other texts" (ibid.). This is not to be understood as the possibility of duplication, such as within the founding of the gothic novel. The gothic novel has a certain set of requirements, and for any novel to be gothic, it must fit these requirements. However, the founding of psychoanalysis is much different. The name "Freud" does not designate a series of conditions for the duplication of his texts. Rather, it indicates a set of possibilities and rules for further texts. In addition, unlike a scientific text, the author of a discourse does not participate within the texts that follow the institution of the discourse. For example, the truth of a text in physics is not related back to the work of Galileo, Newton, or Einstein. In Foucault's account, truth in psychoanalysis is always referred back to the work of Freud, its founder. This foundational relation always necessitates, again in language similar to the chapter "Man and His Doubles" in *The Order of Things*, a "return to the origin" within a discourse, in which the modification of a discourse is always related to the work of its founders. Furthermore, by referring the modification of a discourse back to its origin, the author-function guarantees the continuity of a discourse, as this reference back does not allow for modification outside the relation itself.

We have now seen how the author-function operates, its various characteristics, and that it operates not only within literary texts but within the founding of discourses as such. Yet, we have not adequately examined the way in which the author-function is a principle of constraint or limitation, and thus the reversal of the traditional notion of the author. For Foucault, we traditionally understand the author as a source of creative expression, "the genial creator of a work," or a "perpetual surging of invention" (EEW2, 221). However, if we understand the author instead as a kind of discursive position, the assignment of an author to a group of texts does not designate a source of creative invention but rather functions as a limit on how texts can be arranged and understood. Foucault writes,

> The author is not an indefinite source of significations that fill a work; the author does not precede the works; he is a certain functional principle by which, in our culture, one limits, excludes, and chooses; in short by which one impedes the free circulation, the free manipulation, the free composition, decomposition, and recomposition of fiction. (EEW2, 221)

Although here Foucault is discussing fiction, the idea that the author is a principle of limitation can also be seen within the founding of a discourse, specifically as regards Foucault's notion of the "return to the origin." If the modifications of a discourse must always be referred back to its origin (i.e., its founder), then there is no possibility for the discourse to change completely, and thus meaning is constrained. That is, if psychoanalysis is always referred back to Freud, it can never be anything but Freudian. Thus, any proliferation of meaning within psychoanalysis must always be related back to Freud, and through this relation some meanings are accepted whereas others are rejected.

Since the notion of the author is tied to discourse, the author cannot be said to have died or disappeared until our modern discursive formation changes into a new one. That is, our current discourse cannot simply drop the author-function. Its shape must change completely, and in such a way that it does not institute the author-function. In this regard, Foucault writes,

> I think that, as our society changes, at the very moment when it is in the process of changing, the author function will disappear, and in such a manner that fiction and its polysemous texts will once again function according to another mode, but still with a system of constraint – one that will no longer be the author but will have to be determined, or, perhaps, experienced. (EEW2, 222)

As such, for Foucault, when our discursive formation changes into a new one, it is not that the author will die but that it will *disappear completely*.

The notion of the author can also be understood in terms of Foucault's larger project during the "archaeological period" of his career. In *The Archaeology of Knowledge*, Foucault argues that the analysis of the fields of discourse within history requires that "we must rid ourselves of a whole mass of notions, each of which, in its own way, diversifies the theme of continuity" (EAK, 21). When historians analyze historical events, they make use of a set of presuppositions that allow them to constitute continuity. They presuppose a picture of the subject as the source of all meaning, and historical events then become organized in terms of a historical progression, along the lines of the development of rationality. As such, in order to describe historical events in terms of, for instance, rupture and chance, one must rid oneself of all the notions that are related to this picture of the subject. Although Foucault does not explicitly name the author in this discussion, he discusses a number of notions that relate to the discussion of the author in his work "What Is an Author?" Specifically, in *The Archaeology of Knowledge*, the notions of the book and the *œuvre* (work) must be jettisoned. Furthermore, Foucault argues that we must also rid ourselves of two "linked, but opposite themes": (1) the secret origin and (2) the already-said (EAK, 25). In a discussion reminiscent of the "return to the origin" in "What Is an Author?" Foucault argues that historians treat history as a kind of "quest for and the repetition of an origin that eludes all historical determination," since the origin can never be made present (EAK, 36, 25). Furthermore, this secret origin possesses an "already-said," in the sense that the origin has a meaning itself that can never be made manifest, and it is thus the historian's job to unearth and interpret the already-said of history. Both of these themes serve to guarantee the continuity of discourse by relating the understanding of history back to an immutable origin, which, since we can never have its original present to us, requires constant reinterpretation. The origin has the function of guaranteeing continuity, as does the notion of the author in terms of the founder of a discourse. As such, we can see a repetition of this limiting function within his overall project.

We are now in a position to understand the role of the notion of the author within Foucault's "archaeological" period. The author is best understood as a kind of function, which, through a variety of operations, guarantees the continuity of a discourse and its progression into the figure through the limitation of the proliferation of meaning within a given discourse. That is, the author "allows a limitation of the cancerous and dangerous proliferation of significations within a world where one is thrifty not only with one's resources and riches but also with one's discourses and their significations" (EEW2, 221). The notion of the author in Foucault is one of a mass of notions whose function is to guarantee the continuity of discourse, thus disallowing the rupture or change of a given discourse into a new one.

Harry A. Nethery IV

SEE ALSO

Archaeology
Language
Literature

SUGGESTED READING

Barthes, Roland. 1977. *Image-Music-Text*, trans. Stephen Heath. London: Fontana Press.
Derrida, Jacques. 1978. *Writing and Difference*, trans. Alan Bass. Chicago: University of Chicago Press.

6

BIOHISTORY

FOUCAULT FIRST USED this term in October 1974, in the series of lectures he gave at the Institute of Social Medicine, Biomedical Center, of the State University of Rio de Janeiro, Brazil. These lectures followed his 1973–1974 Collège de France course on Psychiatric Power (ECF-PP), in which Foucault was studying the transformation of medicine through the emergence of the hospital as the locus of deployment of a series of new medical disciplines. In the first lecture in Rio de Janeiro, titled "Crisis of Medicine or Crisis of Anti-Medicine?" Foucault wrote: "A new dimension of medical possibilities arises that I shall call the question of biohistory. From this moment forward, the doctor and the biologist are no longer working at the level of the individual and his descendants, but are beginning to work at the level of life and its fundamental events. This is a very important element in biohistory in which we find ourselves" (FDE3, 48). Later in the same lecture, he refers to the appearance of a political economy of health that interacts with the medicalization of society and "mechanisms of bio-history" (FDE3, 57). In the second lecture, "The Birth of Social Medicine," Foucault provides us with another definition: "[b]iohistory – that is, the effect of medical intervention at the biological level, the imprint left on human history, one may assume, by the strong medical intervention that began the eighteenth century. It is clear that humanity did not remain immune to medicalization" (EEW3, 134). The term is used again in 1976 in a review of Jacques Ruffié's book *De la biologie à la culture* (FDE 3, 95). Foucault identifies three fundamental propositions in Ruffié's book. First, for a biologist, "race" only makes sense as a statistical concept; in other words, as a "population" or living whole. Second, the genetic polymorphism of a population is not a liability or degeneration but is instead useful. Genetic purity is an artificial device that makes adaptation difficult. Third, a population cannot be defined or determined in terms of manifest morphological characteristics; that is, in terms of phenotype (FDE3, 96). Foucault concludes with an encomium to the richness of Ruffié's book: "All of them are important [Ruffié's analyses], since what are so clearly formulated here are the questions of both a 'biohistory' that is no longer the unitary and mythological history of the human species over time, and a 'biopolitics' that is not a matter of divisions, conservations and hierarchies but rather of communication and polymorphism" (FDE3, 97). Here he is suggesting that Ruffié's analyses allow us to conceptualize humanity not as a conglomeration of races but as a statistical spectrum of populations all of which are engaged in genetic exchange. Quoting Mayr approvingly, Foucault wrote: "Humanity is 'a pool of intercommunicating genes'" (ibid.). That same year, he used the term in the last chapter of the Introduction to the *History of Sexuality*, where he wrote: "If one can apply the term *biohistory* to the pressures through which the movements of life and the process of history interfere with one another, one would have to speak of *biopower* to designate what brought life and its mechanisms into the realm of explicit calculations and made knowledge-power an agent of transformation of human life" (EHS1, 143). Biohistory thus names both a new conception of the human, as living being, which is now the target and object of political intervention, and also a new conception of life, of the living as such. Up through the middle of the eighteenth century, humans were conceived along Aristotelian lines, namely as animals that had the additional capacity for political existence. Now, however, "modern man is an animal whose politics places his existence as a living being in question" (ibid.). Modern humanity's placing into question its "living being" has two dimensions: what does it mean for the human being to be a living being, and what is the living, what is life? Biohistory therefore names both the trace, or the history of the deliberate, calculated, concerted intervention of power-knowledge into the very biological makeup of humans, and also the history of the different conceptions of the "living" that have been mobilized, deployed, conceptualized, and conjured up to serve the political technologies that aimed to intervene at the level of biological existence. It becomes immediately evident, then, that in order to understand the novelty of biohistory, we have to turn to Foucault's contributions to the history of natural history, the life sciences, and biology. The novelty of the term "biohistory" can only be appreciated against the background of Foucault's sustained and unceasing thinking about the biological sciences and the "living." Insofar as Foucault's theoretical project can be thought of as a "critical history of thought" (EEW2, 459), we must understand "biohistory" as a critical concept in the critical history of the political technologies that have intervened in the biological structure of the human being.

Although it may be argued that the term "biohistory" remains underdefined and undertheorized, to then seemingly dissolve or disappear in the concept of governmentality and the hermeneutics of the subject, it should be noted that Michel Foucault's entire oeuvre is dominated by the question of what it means to be human, to which biohistory is another chapter. This preoccupation appears already in

Foucault's complementary dissertation, and more specifically in the introduction to his translation into French of Immanuel Kant's *Anthropology from a Pragmatic Standpoint* (EIKA). This text was published in 1964, although the translation and research for the translation had been carried out between 1959 and 1960. This introduction, which anticipates the central theses of *The Order of Things* (FMC), focuses on the relationship between Kant's critical philosophy, more specifically the *Critique of Pure Reason*, and the *Anthropology*, as this relationship is encapsulated in the synthesis of Kant's three questions (What can I know? What should I do? What may I hope?) into one question: What is Man? This relationship, however, is paradoxical, for the *Anthropology* makes no reference to the *Critique*, whereas the latter announces and makes space for the former: "The *Anthropology* rests on the *Critique* but is not rooted in it. It inclines spontaneously toward that which must serve as its foundation: not critical, but transcendental philosophy itself. It is there that we will discover the structure and the function of its empiricity" (EIKA, 87–88). This means that man is what Foucault will call in *The Order of Things* the "empirico-transcendental doublet" (EOT, 318). Man is the type of being "such that knowledge will be attained in him that renders all knowledge possible" (ibid.). Man is the being that is both the condition of possibility of all knowledge and the object of knowledge that renders those conditions evident. Man is both object and subject. It knows only as it knows itself. In *The Birth of the Clinic* (EBC), this empiricity or empirico-transcendental doublet appears as the biologization of the study of humans through their being subjected to the "medical gaze" that operates in tandem with the drawing up of a "medical topography": "If the sciences of man appeared as an extension of the sciences of life, it is because it was *medically*, as well as *biologically*, based: by transference, importation, and, often, metaphor, the sciences of man no doubt used concepts formed by biologists" (EBC, 36, italics in original). This medicalization and biologization of man renders him both subject and object of knowledge, implying an inversion of the way finitude was accounted for through the classical period. Whereas for classical thought finitude (death) had no other function than the negation of the infinite, for modern thought, at least since the eighteenth century, finitude has acquired a positive dimension. Finitude as death now takes on a generative function: "The living night is dissipated in the brightness of death" (EBC, 146). Here is revealed the paradoxical nature of the human sciences: man as living entity at the disposal of social medicine is both the founding origin and limit of knowledge (EBC, 197).

Biohistory cannot be properly understood without a consideration of Foucault's "archaeology of the human science" as it was developed in *The Order of Things*. At the center of this archaeology is an analysis of the shifts and caesuras in the *episteme* from the Renaissance, through the classical age, to the modern age. Some of the epistemic breaks Foucault tracks there are those between natural history, the life sciences, and modern biology. The classical *episteme* allowed the study of living entities in accordance with a grammar of similitude or resemblance. This study took the name of "natural history," which according to Foucault "was nothing more than the nomination of the visible" (EOT, 132). Natural history aimed to name, categorize, and locate living entities within a table of visible characteristics – the "simplicity of a description of the visible" (EOT, 137). Natural history, however, is not the same as biology. In fact, biology was not possible, as the concept of life did not exist. For natural history, "All that existed was living beings, which were viewed through a grid of knowledge constituted by *natural history*" (EOT, 128, italics in original). The naturalist therefore was concerned with the signature of the visible but not with life itself. And, for this reason, natural history could not conceive of the history of nature, for temporality, finitude, remained external to the order of living things. By contrast, biology operates on a different epistemic grid. For Cuvier and the natural scientists of the nineteenth century, nature is the realm of the discontinuous precisely because it is alive, that which is "regional and autonomous" (EOT, 273). This discontinuity is possible because now the living organism is the locus of temporality and finitude, for each individual living organism became the distinct exemplar of a form of life that remained irreducible and unassimilable. For biology, life constitutes a "living historicity," and it is on this new ontological grounds that Charles Darwin's theory of evolution became possible. This new ontology and *episteme* has profound consequences for how humans are conceived. In a key passage, the essential instability of this new *episteme* is revealed:

> … man for the human sciences is not that living being with a very particular form (a somewhat special physiology and an almost unique anatomy): he is that living being who, from within the life to which he entirely belongs and by which he is traversed in this whole being, constitutes representations by means of which he lives, and on the basis of which he possesses that strange capacity of being able to represent to himself precisely that life. (EOT, 352)

This is a remarkable passage that is echoed in a tremendously revealing text – in light of which we have to study anything having to do with biopolitics – that Foucault wrote on one of his teachers, perhaps one of the most important intellectual influences on his work, namely Georges Canguilhem (see also EAK, 235). The text, written for the 1978 translation of Canguilhem's *The Normal and the Pathological*, although a revised French translation was published in 1985, was titled "Life: Experience and Science" (EEW2, 465–478). In this text, Foucault wrote:

> The fact that man lives in a conceptually structured environment does not prove that he has turned away from life, or that a historical drama has separated him from it – just that he lives in a certain way, that he has a relationship with his environment such that he has no set point of view toward it, that he is mobile on

an undefined or a rather broadly defined territory, that he has to move around in order to gather information, that he has to move things relative to one another in order to make them useful. Forming concepts is a way of living and not a way of killing life; it is a way to live in a relative mobility and not to immobilize life; it is to show, among those billions of living beings that inform their environment and inform themselves on the basis of it, an innovation that can be judged as one like, tiny or substantial: a very special type of information. (EEW2, 475)

Here Foucault is glossing Canguilhem's determination of life, a concept that elucidates the way in which a living being takes information from its environment and by means of which it structures its environment. It was for this reason that Foucault's teacher gave such systematic importance to the concepts of the normal, the pathological, which in modern biology takes on the form of error, transposition, and mistake. For Canguilhem, as for Foucault, "... life – and this is its radical feature – is that which is capable of error" (EEW2, 476). This claim prepares the ground for his conclusion:

> Nietzsche said that truth was the greatest lie. Canguilhem, who is far from and near to Nietzsche at the same time, would perhaps say that on the huge calendar of life it is the most recent error; or, more exactly, he would say that the true/false dichotomy and the value accorded to truth constitute the most singular way of living that has been invented by a life that, from the depths of its origin, bore the potential for error within itself. (EEW2, 476–477)

Biohistory must then be understood as a concept that belongs to the history of systems of thought, or what Foucault called in his essay on his teacher the history of rationalities. Biohistory is a concept by means of which a living entity has made sense of its environment and itself, precisely in order to intervene in its biological structure as it structures its environment.

Eduardo Mendieta

SEE ALSO

Biopolitics
Biopower
Death
History
Life
Medicine

Georges Canguilhem
Immanuel Kant

SUGGESTED READING

Canguilhem, Georges. 2008. *Knowledge of Life*. New York: Fordham University Press.
Ruffié, Jacques. 1976. *De la biologie à la culture*. Paris: Flammarion.

7

BIOPOLITICS

THIS TERM REFERS to a new modality of producing, circulating, and enacting power that subjects and governs individuals through a set of disciplines that normalize bodies and pleasures and regulations that target political agents as members of a living species. Biopolitics produces and circulates through *biopower*. Biopolitics is a historical marker that designates the transformation of political techniques and procedures in the West that took place between the eighteenth and early nineteenth centuries. If, to paraphrase Gilles Deleuze, power has neither an essence nor is it an attribute but is purely operational and relational, then biopolitics is the name for a new way of producing political effects through new forms of power-knowledge and corresponding *dispositifs* (apparatuses). Foucault first used the term in his 1974 lectures at the State University of Rio de Janeiro (FDE3, 170, 196, 229) and continued to use it in his lectures at the Collège de France, even naming one such set of lectures "The Birth of Biopolitics." Like many of Foucault's key concepts, biopolitics was used with different emphases, denoting different aspects of the transformation of the political techniques that developed over two centuries. The term therefore is not univocal and has many uses and valences in Foucault's problematizations. We can identify at least five different ways in which Foucault used the term: (1) as designating what resulted from the transformation of medicine with the rise of capitalism, (2) as part and parcel of the history of capitalism, (3) as a new form of sovereignty, (4) as a form of power that is distinctive of neoliberal governmentality, and (5) as the title of a chapter in biohistory.

Foucault first used the term in the context of analysis of the transformation of social medicine as it took place during the eighteenth century. He characterized this process in terms of four processes: the appearance of medical authority, not simply in terms of scientific and technical knowledge but the authority bestowed on doctors to attend to the health of individuals and entire social groups. Doctors were now allowed and expected to wield power over the body politic. Their new preoccupation

37

was "public health." This is what the Germans called *Staatmedizine*. Second, new fields and objects for medical intervention and study were identified that were distinct from disease: air, water, terrain, living spaces, sewers, and so forth. The third process was the transformation of the hospital into an apparatus of medicalization that ceases to perform a philanthropic and pastoral function and begins to become the locus of health, of the monitoring of individual and collective bodies. The fourth process was the introduction of a new set of systems and processes for the administering and administration of medicine: data collection, statistics gathering and comparison, in a word the scienticization and mathematization qua statistification of knowledge about both health and disease (FDE3, 50–51). Comparing what began to emerge in the late eighteenth century with what came before, Foucault juxtaposes the theocracies from Constantine to the early eighteenth century with what he calls a "somatocracy." This new regime is one in which the state uses medicine to intervene in the care of bodies, social health, the relations between natality and mortality, morbidity and normality. In fact, paraphrasing Fichte's coinage of an "open commercial state," Foucault talks about an "open medical state," which regulates through pathology. Now that medicine is a technique of political administration, medicine also begins to have an economic function. Foucault thus speaks of the "political economy of medicine" (FDE3, 53). The medicalization of state power and political economy also marked a transformation of society from one that was governed by a system of codified laws produced, protected, and presided over by jurists on behalf of the sovereign to another that is governed by the ceaseless monitoring of the distinction between the normal and the abnormal, the healthy and the pathological. This society of normalization is presided over, guided, overseen, and monitored by the medical authorities. Biopolitics then is another name for somatocracy, the ruling by and through the flesh. The history of medicine therefore is also the history of the medicalization of state power and the emergence of a political economy of health. Biopolitics identifies this new modality of the medicalization of power-knowledge and the transformation of the hospital into a topos for the generation and transformation of a new type of power, biopower.

The second of these three Rio de Janeiro lectures, titled "The Birth of Social Medicine" (EEW3, 134–156), is where Foucault uses biopolitics explicitly, when he says: "Society's control over individuals was accomplished not only through consciousness or ideology but also in the body and with the body. For capitalist society, it was biopolitics, the biological, the somatic, the corporal that mattered more than anything else. The body is a biopolitical reality; medicine is a biopolitical strategy" (EEW3, 137). Biopolitics here is identified as a particular way in which capitalism is able to use, harness, control, subjugate, and exploit bodies. Capitalism views the proletariat body not simply or uniquely as a laboring body, as a body that produces a certain surplus, the source of living labor, to use Marx's expression. It also and simultaneously views the body as part of a collectivity, a biomass, the body of either a part or an entire population. Capitalism entails the socialization of the body; that is, the transformation of the body into an object of continuous social monitoring and control. As Foucault put it in his 1975 *Discipline and Punish*:

> If the economic take-off of the West began with the techniques that made possible the accumulation of capital, it might perhaps be said that the methods for administering the accumulation of men made possible a political take-off in relation to the traditional, ritual, costly, violent forms of power, which soon fell into disuse and were superseded by a subtle, calculated technology of subjection. In fact, the two processes – the accumulation of men and the accumulation of capital – cannot be separated. (EDP, 220–221)

The rise of capitalism entails this new form of biopolitics that viewed the producing body in two ways: individualized and collectivized. In fact, capitalism required a specific modality of power: "The growth of a capitalist economy gave rise to the specific modality of disciplinary power, whose general formulas, techniques of submitting forces and bodies, in short, 'political anatomy', could be operated in the most diverse political régimes, apparatuses or institutions" (EDP, 221). These formulations have to be compared with those from the pivotal last chapter of *La Volonté de savoir*, volume one of *The History of Sexuality*, where Foucault distinguishes between *anatomo-politics* of the human body and *biopolitics of population* (EHS1, 139). In this chapter, however, Foucault is less interested in capitalism per se than in the emergence of a new form of sovereignty. But, before we turn to this use of biopolitics within a general history of the transformation of sovereignty, it is important to underscore that biopolitics refers to the ways in which capitalism disciplines both individual and collective bodies in order to maximize their subjugation and exploitation with the least cost of expenditure of power. In this way, we can understand biopolitics as a calculus of capitalist extraction of wealth that is inversely proportional to the deployment of force and control. The emergence of a whole set of new social spaces for the disciplining of bodies, such as the barracks, the public school, or the university, is most clearly epitomized in the emergence of the modern hospital. Before the eighteenth century, the hospital was not a medical institution, and medicine was not a hospital discipline (FDE3, 510–511). The incorporation of the hospital into modern medical technology is the kaleidoscope through which we can see the permutations that took place in modern political power: new social topoi for the enactment of disciplines that focus on the body and presuppose the productivity of new power-knowledge regimes. What flashes up brilliantly in the simultaneous medicalization of the hospital and the hospitalization of medicine is precisely the convergence of medically sanctioned intervention into individuated bodies that at the same time tracked them statistically as specimens within a certain living mass. Biopolitics thus meant the medicalization of individual and collectivized bodies for the sake of maximizing their output. Disease, morbidity, and infirmity became pathologies that had to be prevented,

cured, and managed, lest individuals and populations become unproductive, underpro-
ductive, or too much of a drain and liability. Biopolitics then is a more proper name for
the political economy that enables capitalism: the political economy of pathology and
health.

In the last chapter of volume one of *The History of Sexuality*, titled "The Right of
Death and Power over Life," Foucault's analytics of capitalism are absorbed within a
broader study of the transformations of sovereign power since the seventeenth century. Foucault describes this transformation in terms of a shift from sovereign power
that took life and let live to a sovereign power that makes life and lets die: "One
might say that the ancient right to *take* life or *let* live was replaced by a power to *foster*
life or *disallow* it to the point of death" (EHS1, 138, Foucault's italics). This new form
of sovereign power establishes its dominion over life, and death becomes its limit.
The juridical existence of the sovereign, its right and *potestas*, are no longer at stake.
Instead, what is at stake is the "biological existence of a population" (EHS1, 137).
This dominion over life, this *fostering*, this nurturing, tending to the life of the body
politic evolved since the seventeenth century along two axes or poles. One is focused
on the body as a machine. The goal was to discipline, optimize its capabilities, direct
its forces so as to maximize its productivity and docility. The body became a machine
for the maximization of economic productivity. The procedure through which the
body became such an apparatus characterized the disciplines. These processes and
techniques constituted what Foucault called an *anatomo-politics of the human body*.
The other pole focused on the "species body, the body imbued with the mechanics of
life and serving as the basis of the biological processes: propagation, births, mortality, the level of health, life expectancy and longevity, with all the conditions that can
cause these to vary" (EHS1, 139). This "species body" was monitored through what
Foucault called "regulatory controls," which constituted a "biopolitics of the population" (ibid.). Thus, we have that this new sovereign power utilizes an anatomo-politics of human bodies that individuates them so as to discipline them most effectively.
This anatomo-politics also controls populations through regulatory controls. Here,
Foucault seems to be indicating that biopolitics is one technique among anatomo-
politics that allows modern sovereign power to maximize its power with minimal
expenditure of control. Here biopolitics appears as one of two political techniques
of the type of sovereign power that puts in question the existence of modern man
as a living being (EHS1, 143). These formulations must be compared with those
Foucault offered in his Collège de France course from 1975–1976, which was titled
"Society Must Be Defended," where the contrast between individuating disciplinary
control and collectivizing control is sharpened. In this course, Foucault claimed:

> Unlike discipline, which is addressed to bodies, the new non-disciplinary power
> is applied not to man-as-body, but to the living man, to man-as-living-being;
> ultimately, if you like, to man-as-species. To be more specific, I would say that

discipline tries to rule a multiplicity of men to the extent that their multiplicity can and must be dissolved into individual bodies that can be kept under surveillance, trained, used, and, if need be, punished.... So after a first seizure of power over the body in an individualizing mode, we have a second seizure of power that is not individualizing but, if you like, massifying, that is directed not at the man-as-body, but at man-as-species. After the anatomo-politics of the human body established in the course of the eighteenth century, we have, at the end of that century, the emergence of something that is no longer an anatomo-politics of the human body, but what I would call a "biopolitics" of the human race. (ECF-SMD, 243)

Still, it is with the emergence of this new form of sovereign power, with its political techniques of anatomo-politics of bodies and biopolitics of populations, that "sex" becomes a "target of power." Since sex is the pivot, the hinge, the point of intersection between the individual and collective body, the normalizing, disciplining, controlling, and regulation of individuals and populations could be pursued with greatest efficacy. Determine how, with whom, and for what purposes individuals have sex and you can establish segregations, hierarchizations, and corresponding practices and ideologies that control and discipline as if automatically. It is through these two political techniques of anatomo-politics and biopolitics that the body became the prison of the soul, especially when the body is thoroughly sexualized, or became the locus of an analytics of sexuality. The administration of sex, through marriage licenses, the encouragement of natality, the management of morbidity, monitoring of prophylactics, abortions, and so forth became a way in which the populations were regulated. Nazism, perhaps the paroxysm of this new form of sovereign power, epitomizes the convergence of these two techniques of power. On the one hand, as a eugenic society, as a racialized society bent on enhancing the racial stock of its population, it exerted an intensification of its medicalized micropowers, while commanding a corresponding unhinged state control (*étatisation*). Here we began already to see the ways in which the rise of biopolitics signals a transformation of the state via the apparatuses of the state. Biopolitics signals the statisation (*Étatisation*) of the state, or more precisely the governmentalization of the state.

   The Collège de France lecture courses for the years 1977–1978 and 1978–1979, called "Security, Territory, Population" and "The Birth of Biopolitics," respectively, should be studied jointly under the title of "History of Governmentality," as Foucault himself noted in the lecture courses (ECF-STP, 108). It is against this history that we have to understand another sense in which Foucault meant biopolitics. The course "Security, Territory, Population" begins with a very explicit claim: "This year I would like to begin studying something that I have called vaguely biopower" (ECF-STP, 1). In the course "The Birth of Biopolitics," in the first lecture, Foucault claimed: "... only when we know what this governmental regime called liberalism was, will we be able to grasp what biopolitics is" (ECF-BBIO, 22). In fact, in the manuscript for this lecture, there are some pages that were not read that contain the following statement: "Studying liberalism as the general framework of biopolitics" (ECF-BBIO, 22, 383). By *governmentality* Foucault meant, first, the processes, institutions, calculations, and tactics that allow the deployment of a very specific type of power that has "population as its target, political economy as its major form of knowledge, and apparatuses of security as its essential technical instrument." Second, governmentality refers to the historical tendency within the West that has led to the preeminence of the type of power that Foucault calls "government." Third, the term names the process by which the juridical state bent on legal justice becomes an administrative state. This later process is called governmentalization (ECF-STP, 110–111). According to Foucault, we must study governmentality in order to be able to understand how it is that population became a concern of the state (ECF-STP, 116). The rise of neoliberalism is an instance of this process of the governmentalization of the modern state that seeks to govern the best by governing the least. Neoliberalism is a new political rationality that no longer operates on the older model of reason of state but rather in the submission of political power to the truths revealed by the market. The market is now the privileged space for the production of truths to which the performance of power must be tethered. Biopolitics must be understood as the type of politics that leads to the governmentalization of the modern state, by means of which its power is deployed through the administration of what we can properly call the welfare state. Biopolitics and neoliberalism converge precisely in that evisceration and reduction of the political to mere administration: the health of the body politic is now simply another of the administrative functions of the state. Biopolitics is the automatization of sovereign power through the reduction of the politics of health, the politics of the body politic, to an administrative task. Biopolitics dissimulates the political and economic exploitation of individuated and massified bodies behind the benign name of a national health-care policy. Eugenics has become normalized with the neoliberal "statification" (*étatisation*) of society.

Biopolitics, finally, names the process by which biopower can be said to have launched biohistory. Biopolitics is thus part of a conceptual triptych: biopolitics deploys biopower in order to produce events and processes that result in a biohistory. Already in his Rio de Janeiro lectures Foucault had referred to the biohistory question that is raised by the possibilities and effects caused by the rise of social medicine. There he makes reference to Darwin in order to foreground the ways in which historical events intervene in the general laws of life. The political economy of health and the medicalization of the body politic became "mechanisms of biohistory" (FDE3, 57). In the last chapter of volume one of *The History of Sexuality*, the rise of the new form of sovereign power that exerts its dominion over life signals the first time in history when "biological existence" is "reflected in political existence." In fact, as Foucault claimed there: "If one can apply the term *biohistory* to the pressures through which the movements of life and the processes of history interfere with one another, one would have to speak of *biopower* to designate what brought life and its mechanisms into the real of explicit calculations and made knowledge-power an agent of transformation of human life" (EHS1, 143). The same year he published volume one of *The History of Sexuality*, Foucault published a short but extremely enthusiastic review praising Jacques Ruffié's book *De la biologie à la culture*, which is important because there he highlights the way in which Ruffié links the question of biohistory to that of biopolitics (FDE3, 95–97). Biohistory, it may be said, is the trace of biopolitics: what biopolitics makes live, how biopolitics makes individuals or populations live, and how it allows or disallows the death of individuals or population, how biopolitics allows or disallows death. Life and death are now thoroughly conditioned by a form of sovereignty that administers life and death as it attends to the construction of highways, prisons, schools, and hospitals, issues marriage licenses and death certificates, and grants certification to those who can rule on the norm of what is normal and what is pathological. Biopolitics names the intervention of political power into the very processes of life itself.

Eduardo Mendieta

SEE ALSO

> *Biohistory*
> *Biopower*
> *Body*
> *Governmentality*
> *Life*
> *Power*
> *Race (and Racism)*
> *Sex*

SUGGESTED READING

Morton, Stephen, and Stephen Bygrave, eds. 2008. *Foucault in an Age of Terror*. London: Palgrave Macmillan.

8

BIOPOWER

W E HAVE A misleadingly straightforward and concise definition of biopower, offered by Foucault at the beginning of his 1977–1978 Collège de France course "Security, Territory, Population": "By this [biopower] I mean a number of phenomena that seem to me to be quite significant, namely, the set of mechanisms through which basic biological features of the human species became the object of a political strategy, of a genealogy of power, or, in other words, how, starting from the eighteenth century, modern Western societies took on board the fundamental biological fact that human beings are a species" (ECF-STP, 1). Foucault also wrote about an "area of bio-power" (EHS1, 140) in which "life and its mechanisms" have been brought into the "realm of explicit calculation and made knowledge-power an agent of transformation of human life" (EHS1, 143). By making life an explicit object of political-economic calculation, biopolitics made the processes of history "interfere" with the movements of life. Foucault called this interference *biohistory* (EHS1, 143; see also FDE3, 48, 57, 95, 207, 208). This analysis of biopower, however, is set against the analysis of the transformation of sovereign power between the classical and modern ages. This transformation is traced through what Foucault calls there an "analytics of power," which maps the shift from "juridico-discursive" power to "biopower." If the former is negative, repressive, punitive, prohibitive, uniform, and enunciated through the law, the latter is productive, generative, disciplinary, regularizing, normalizing, decentered, capillary, heterogeneous, and polymorphous (EHS1, 82–90). In the 1975–1976 Collège de France course "Society Must Be Defended," Foucault juxtaposed anatomo-politics with this biopolitics, with a biopower that began to be established at the end of the eighteenth century and concerned itself with the "processes of birth rates, mortality rate, longevity" that are measured in "statistical terms" (ECF-SMD, 243). Here, as in volume one of *The History of Sexuality*, Foucault is still mainly concerned with the transformation of sovereign power, but now against the background of the slippage of death from the grip of a power that is now evaluated from the standpoint of its ability to make live. Biopower, which regularizes life, is juxtaposed with sovereignty over death. In fact, there are two different systems of power: sovereign power, which took life and let live, and biopower, which makes live and lets die (ECF-SMD, 247–249). But if death escapes sovereign power, death becomes power's limit, its nadir. Racism is the means by which biopower asserts its control over death. Thus, biopower has two modalities, making live and making die, putting to death, as part and parcel of an economy of life: "[R]acism justifies the death-function in the economy of biopower" (ECF-SMD, 258). In the age of biopolitics, then, we should talk simultaneously about biopower and necropower, or thanatopower. In an important interview with Hubert Dreyfus and Paul Rabinow conducted in 1983, Foucault responded to the question of whether he "should be writing a genealogy of bio-power" in light of his recent preoccupations with the "genealogy of problems, of *problèmatiques*," by saying: "I have no time for that now, but it could be done. In fact, I have to do it" (EEW1, 256). This answer is perhaps coy, as in fact most of his work through the late seventies and early eighties had been a genealogy of modalities of biopower. In this same interview, Foucault identifies three possible domains of genealogy: "First, a historical ontology of ourselves in relation to truth through which we constitute ourselves as subjects of knowledge; second, a historical ontology of ourselves in relation to a field of power through which we constitute ourselves as subjects acting on others; third, a historical ontology in relation to ethics through which we constitute ourselves as moral agents" (EEW1, 262). A genealogy of biopower would be part of a historical ontology of how we have constituted ourselves as objects of medical power-knowledge, how we govern ourselves as living entities, and how we relate to ourselves in terms of an ethics of life, a practice of life that is both a subjection and also resistance. In the Collège de France course from 1978–1979, "The Birth of Biopolitics," Foucault set out to discuss biopolitics in relation to the history of governmentality, albeit without referring to biopower directly, though noting that in order to understand biopolitics we have to understand power: "The term itself, power, does no more than designate a [domain] of relations which are entirely still to be analyzed, and what I have proposed to call governmentality, that is to say, the way in which one conducts the conduct of men, is no more than a proposed analytical grid for these relations of power" (ECF-BBIO, 186). The concept of biopower thus must be studied from within three different moments in Foucault's work: in terms of an "analytics of power," that is to say, in terms of the transformations of sovereign power between the seventeenth and twentieth centuries; in terms of what he called the "history of governmentality"; and in terms of a historical ontology of what he called the era of biopower.

Of all the places where Foucault discusses how his work is not about a theory of power but about the analysis of power relations, perhaps the most incisive and elucidating is "The Subject and Power," which he wrote in the early 1980s. In this work, Foucault states that an analytics of power "demands that a certain number of points be established":

> 1.) *The system of differentiations* that permit one to act upon the actions of others;
> 2.) *The types of objectives* pursued by those who act upon the actions of others;
> 3.) *Instrumental modes*: whether power is exercised by the threat of arms, by the effects of speech, through economic disparities, by more or less complex means of control; 4.) *Forms of institutionalization*: these may mix traditional conditions, legal structures, matters of habit or fashion (such as one sees in the institution of the family); 5.) *Degree of rationalization*: the bringing into play of power relations as action in a field of possibilities may be more or less elaborate in terms of the effectiveness of its instruments. (EEW3, 344–345)

In this differentiation of "points," one can see that Foucault means that in order to analyze power without rendering it an institution, or "something that is acquired, seized, or shared, something that one holds on to or allows to slip away" (EHS1, 94), one must see "why the analysis of power relations within a society cannot be reduced to a series of institutions or even the study of all those institutions that would merit the name 'political.' Power relations are rooted in the whole network of the social" (EEW3, 345). Biopower therefore cannot be reduced to the study of one particular institution, be it the modern medicalized hospital, the *Polizei*, the rise of the welfare state, the modern psychiatric ward, or even the rise of the eugenic state, which became nefariously epitomized in the Nazi state. Nor can it be reduced to the set of differentiations that operate under biopolitics, those that are made under the rule of the norm: healthy versus pathological. Nor still can it be reduced to the analysis of the way in which biopower aims to both normalize and regularize, discipline and control. Biopower also cannot simply be analyzed in terms of the degree of rationalization that may be achieved in terms of modes of mathematization through statistical analysis of regulatory control. Power is produced, circulated, augmented, diffused, and made efficacious, but also resisted, countered, opposed, and refracted, diverted by the field of relations that is established among institutions, disciplines, and rationalities, with their respective subjects of discipline and control, modes of knowing and rendering into objects of knowledge, and calculus of maximization of governmentality with the least expenditure of force. An analytics of biopower, to put it positively, therefore requires that we be attentive to the field of forces that is constituted by the emergence in the late eighteenth century of a series of disciplines, objects of knowledge, modes of analyzing, and set of preoccupations. Biopolitics, which attends to the human being as a member of a species, generates biopower through its *dispositifs*: sexuality, race, productivity, health, mortality, fertility, and so on. If one of the key aspects of biopolitics is the treatment of humans as a population, then biopower is what fashions, monitors, surveys, controls, and secures populations in terms of a calculus of forces: health, hygiene, and vitality, but also infirmity, sickness, old age, vice, and degeneracy. Biopower is generated by the emergence and interaction among the fields of the general vitality of populations, their pathologies, and everything that may affect both either positively or negatively: the environment, whether it be determined by nature or humans (i.e., geography and the urban setting), nutrition, and so on. Biopower thus is also generated by all those institutions that attend to the disciplining of individuals and the control of a population in terms of either normalization or regularization: schools, barracks, prisons, and hospitals, but also the philanthropic, government, and nongovernment agencies that monitor whom we marry, whether we are healthy, whether we have been vaccinated, everything that falls under the general umbrella of "public health." Death, however, as that which is internal to life, the very manifestation of life, is also a concern of biopolitics. It can be said that for Foucault what characterizes the age of biopolitics is that death itself is now an object of an economy of life. The political economy of health, the general politics of life, assumes two extreme forms under the same continuum: life and death. The politics of life, biopolitics, is a politics of death, a thanato-politics. The politics of health has as its Janus face a politics of pathology. This dual aspect of biopower is eerily illustrated at the extreme ends of its excesses: absolute power over life turns into absolute power of death, and vice versa. For Foucault this is illustrated in the absurdity of nuclear weapons: either sovereign power "uses the atom bomb, and therefore cannot be power, biopower, or the power to guarantee life" or "at the opposite extreme, you no longer have a sovereign right that is in excess of biopower, but a biopower that is in excess of sovereign right" (ECF-SMD, 253–255). This excess of biopower appears when humans can generate, modify, and proliferate life, such that human life itself ceases to be human and becomes monstrous and beyond human sovereignty. The threat of nuclear war and the possible abolition of humanity by biotechnology – which is nothing but a manifestation of biopolitics – exhibit brilliantly how biopower is a power over life and death inasmuch as it makes live by killing and kills by making live. Nuclear weapons and biotechnology, whether as positive genetic engineering or negative eugenic modification of the human genotype, are the two extremes within which all life is determined in a new way of generating power. As excesses of biopower, nuclear annihilation and biotechnological chaos are headings in a new chapter in *biohistory*.

In the Collège de France from 1977 through 1979, which Foucault says should have been called a "history of governmentality" (ECF-STP, 108), the analysis of biopower in terms of an analytics of sovereign power turns into an analysis of biopower in terms of the "governmentalization of the state" in particular and of governmentality in general. One of the consequences of biopolitics, as the control of populations through mechanisms of regulation and security, is that it makes the problem of "sovereignty even more acute" (ECF-STP, 107). The transformation of sovereign power between the eighteenth and nineteenth centuries is no longer the replacement of sovereign power by something like biopower. Rather, as Foucault notes, what we have is a "triangle: sovereignty, discipline, and governmental management" (ibid.).

Within this triangle, however, there is the preeminence of a type of power that is called "government." Thus, now biopower has to be seen as a *dispositif* (apparatus) of the governmentalization of the state and the statification (*étatisation*) of society. Biopower is now generated by government, where this is to be understood as government over others and over ourselves that exhibits a particular calculus: to govern best by governing least. Biopower is now generated and circulated by the instruments that are internal to what it aims to direct (*diriger*): the life of a population. Biopower directs that which is both singular and collectivized, individuated and massified. This is power that attends to every individual while never losing sight of the whole: *Omnes et singulatim* (EEW3, 298). Biopower as a modality and operationality of power that is generated and circulated through attention to the life of populations has its genealogy in *pastoral power* as well as in *raison d'État*. The *dispositifs* (apparatuses) of natality, sexuality, race, health, mortality, diet, and so on have descended from the processes by means of which the state has been governmentalized; that is, submitted more and more to the logic internal to that which the state attends to and less by the logic that is internal to the state itself. The governmentalization of the state has meant, simultaneously, the statification of society (ECF-STP, 109). Biopolitics is the acme of this dual process by means of which the development of the lives of the individuals qua members of a living species, a population, entails simultaneously "the strength of the state" (EEW3, 322). This strengthening of the state, this statification of society, which makes the micropowers of the state more capillary and diffused through society, is governmentality. Governmentality is but the synergy of the "encounter between the technologies of domination of others and those of the self" (EEW1, 225). The analysis of biopower in terms of governmentality turns, then, into a study of political rationality and technologies of the self.

Foucault famously claimed toward the end of his life that "it is not power, but the subject, that is the general theme of my research" (EEW3, 327). There is a way in which all of Foucault's work can be read as prodigiously creative exercises in the study of different forms of *subjectification*, of becoming and being made into a subject (i.e., technologies of the self). The general study of these different technologies of the self Foucault called "hermeneutics of the self" (EEW1, 225; ECF-HOS). The eschewal of a theory of power for an analytics of power relations always meant to refer us back to the dual issues of subjection and subjectification, of domination and resistance, of control and revolt. To ask about the "how" of power rather than the "what" or "whence" of power means to direct our critical attention to processes of subject formation; it means to "give oneself as the object of analysis of *power relations* and not power itself" (EEW3, 339). Foucault's works thus should be understood as genealogical analyses of different technologies of the self, of political technologies of subjection and subjectification. When he answered Dreyfus and Rabinow that there are "three possible axes of genealogy" (EEW1, 262) that focus on three historical ontological domains (knowledge, power, and ethics), Foucault was gesturing toward a critical analysis of how we have made ourselves what we have become. Toward the end of his life, Foucault began to conceive of his work as a "critical ontology of ourselves" (EEW1, 319), an "ontology of actuality" (FDE4, 688), and an "ontology of the present" (FDE4, 687). The genealogical study of technologies of the self is nothing but the study of how we have become who we have become, not to affirm the immutability of this identity but to disclose its contingency. A critical ontology of ourselves is a critical project that is genealogical in design and archaeological in method. This genealogically oriented critical ontology "will not deduce from the form of what we are what it is impossible for us to do and to know; but it will separate out, from the contingency that has made us what we are, the possibility of longer being, doing, or thinking what we are, do, or think" (EEW1, 315–316). A genealogy of technologies of the self, as a critical ontology of ourselves, aims to give impetus to the "undefined work of freedom" (EEW1, 316). We can now discern a different meaning of biopower and biopolitics, not one that is negative and proscriptive but positive and prescriptive. If biopower refers to a modality of governmentality, the general art of governing others and oneself, in which there is a superseding of the dichotomy of society and state (the governmentalization of the state is at the same time the statification of society), then a politics of life can also signify a form of living, a mode of life, a certain art of living, which can become the locus of power production itself. Life itself can become the germ of a counterpower, counter-conducts, or counterpractices. "There is no power without potential refusal or revolt" (EEW3, 324). Power relations cannot be separated from "freedom's refusal." "At the very heart of the power relationship, and constantly provoking it, are the recalcitrance of the will and the intransigence of freedom" (EEW3, 342). If biopower is a modality of power that aims to control and regularize the life of the individual as a member of the human species, life itself can be the place whence a counter-biopower can be enacted. If biopolitics then marks the transition between politics and ethics, then biopower and thanatopower are met by an intransigent freedom that fashions new, critical, emancipatory forms of living and dying. Biopower incites a new art, *technē*, of living.

Eduardo Mendieta

SEE ALSO

Biopolitics
Death
Governmentality
Life

Politics
Power
Sovereignty

SUGGESTED READING

Bernasconi, Robert. 2010. "The Policing of Race Mixing: The Place of Bio-power within the History of Racisms," *Bioethical Inquiry* 7:205–216.
Rabinow, Paul, and Nikolas Rose. 2006. "Biopower Today," *BioSocieties* 1, no. 2:195–217.

9

BODY

THE STANDARD SCHEMA for discussing Foucault's work posits three periods: archaeology, genealogy, and ethics. Using this schema, Foucault's concern with the body can be summed up in the following way: the body is an *object of knowledge* in the discursive practices revealed in archaeology; it is the *target of power* in the nondiscursive practices revealed in genealogy; and it is a *matter of concern* for techniques of the self of Greek and Roman ethical subjects.

The body first appears in Foucault's work as an object of knowledge in the discursive practices revealed in archaeology. We cannot hope to enter into the dense web that is *History of Madness*, but we can locate some markers. Among the most interesting observations of *History of Madness* is that the nineteenth century was an age of medical dualism in which a spiritualist or a materialist psychiatry was possible; in the nineteenth century, one could say "either madness is the organic disturbance of a material principle, or it is the spiritual troubling of an immaterial soul" (EHM, 212). But we realize we are on the other side of an epistemological break when we read that such dualism is mere "philosophy" for the medicine of the classical age, which insists on a medical unity of body and soul (EHM, 213): "to speak of madness in the seventeenth and eighteenth century is not, in the strict sense, to speak of 'a sickness of the mind', but of something where both the body and the mind *together* are in question" (EHM, 214; italics in original).

In *The Birth of the Clinic*, the body has center stage as Foucault traces the shifting forms of the historical a priori governing medical perception. Hence the relations of life and death, of living body and corpse, of surface and depth, of lesions and processes, and of anatomy and physiology are the central concerns. In its largest outlines, we can say *The Birth of the Clinic* traces a shift from knowledge oriented toward the visible surface of the body to knowledge oriented toward internal processes and forces; not simply a move from space to time but a different articulation of space and time (the inside is still a spatial category after all). We see a similar move in *The*

Order of Things: the key move in the shift from natural history to biology is from the tabular classification of visible surface properties to internal functions and temporal processes. The move to organic functions as the essence of life is the revealing of a temporal dimension. In a celebrated archaeological tour de force, Foucault shows how Cuvier is the decisive break; by positing organic structure as prior to taxonomy, Cuvier could isolate the functions rather than the properties (size, shape, location, etc.) of organs. With Cuvier, life becomes a functional system and a science of life, modern biology, is possible.

We will see this move from surface display to internal temporality in the genealogical register of *Discipline and Punish* (to which we now turn), a move from the surface of the body on which torturers and executioners display the power of the sovereign to the internal forces of bodies, which disciplinary practices harness and make work together. The titles of two key chapters of *Discipline and Punish* indicate our itinerary: from "the body of the condemned" on the scaffold of the sovereign to "docile bodies" trained in disciplinary institutions.

Discipline and Punish presents itself as a study of different stages in the "political economy" of the body, in which it is always "the body and its forces, their utility and docility, their distribution and their submission" that are at stake (EDP, 25). Foucault's focused treatment of the body in *Discipline and Punish* is to be distinguished from the "history of the body" others have attempted, which considers the relation of politics and the biological reality of human populations (ibid.; this is what will later be treated as "biopolitics" by Foucault in volume one of *The History of Sexuality* and in the lecture course published as *Security, Territory, Population*). Here in *Discipline and Punish*, however, Foucault is interested in how the "body is also directly involved in a political field" (ibid.); that is, how, via a "political technology of the body," the body "becomes a useful force only if it is both a productive body and a subjected [*assujetti*] body" (EDP, 26). To conduct this investigation, we need to thematize "a micro-physics of power, whose field of validity is situated in a sense between these great functionings [social institutions and state apparatuses] and the bodies themselves with their materiality and their forces" (ibid.).

We should note the way in which the political technology of the body inherent in disciplinary practices gives birth to the modern "soul" (*âme*) (EDP, 29). The modern soul is a reality formed via discursive and nondiscursive practices targeting the body in the disciplinary matrix of the human sciences. The modern soul is "psyche, subjectivity, personality, consciousness" (ibid.); in *Discipline and Punish*, the soul is the seat of the criminal behind the crime, and in volume one of *The History of Sexuality* that of the homosexual behind the act. The modern soul is historically constituted; it is the "present correlative of a certain technology of power over the body" (ibid.). The modern soul is no religious fiction; it "has a reality, it is produced permanently around, on, within the body by the functioning of a power that is exercised on those punished – and in a more general way, on those one supervises, trains and corrects" (ibid.). In tracing the political economy of the body, in particular, in focusing on the genealogy of the disciplinary "political technology of the body," we see "the historical reality of this soul … [which] is born … out of methods of punishment, supervision and constraint" (ibid.).

In *Discipline and Punish*, we find three different *dispositifs* (apparatuses) of the political economy of the body as a target of punishment: those in which the predominant form is sovereign power, reform punishment, or discipline. For sovereign power, the body of the criminal tortured on the scaffold is the scene whereby the might of the sovereign can be displayed. For the reformers, the body displayed in the punitive city is the site where the idea of punishment could be linked to the idea of the crime. For discipline, bodies are malleable; they are what is to be rendered docile so that productivity increases while political resistance decreases.

Foucault's treatment of the body as a target of sovereign power produces the gut-wrenching and unforgettable opening passage of *Discipline and Punish*. It both describes the way in which the torture and destruction of the body of the criminal displays the dissymmetry of power that reveals sovereign might and reminds us that the bodies of the spectators were essential to the *dispositif* (apparatus) of sovereign power. Sovereign power is quite literally terroristic (EDP, 49); we can speculate, though Foucault does not thematize this dimension, that the terror of the spectators rests on a bodily sympathy, a sharing of the pain of the victim ("feelings of terror": EDP, 58). But this sympathy was both the basis of terror and the basis for possible revolt against the agents of the crown (EDP, 58–65). This is the danger of the scaffold that the reformers thought was too much to risk (EDP, 63).

The body for the reformers was only a means of producing signs, part of a "semio-technique of punishment" (EDP, 103). (Foucault does discuss the "social body" in this context as a term for society [e.g., EDP, 80, 92, 139] but it is only a figure of speech, notwithstanding an interesting reference to the "homeostasis" of the social body in volume one of *The History of Sexuality* [EHS1, 107].) For the reformers, it was not the body that was of interest; what counted was the juridical subject as constituted in social contract theories. Foucault encapsulates the move from the tortured body subjected to sovereign power to the juridical subject that was the focus of the reformers in a justly famous statement: "[F]rom being an art of unbearable sensations punishment has become an economy of suspended rights" (EDP, 11). For the reformers, the body was only a support for life, so capital punishment was simply the deprivation of the right to life (ibid.). This presents us with the logic of the guillotine, which would take life via minimal contact with the body (EDP, 13).

The reformers failed to take hold; the focus of *Discipline and Punish*, what makes it a classic, is the analysis of discipline. With the disciplines, the classical age "discovered the body as object and target of power" (EDP, 136). The body is a machine, though not simply a mechanism; the disciplined body is not simply a "mechanical body – the body composed of solids and assigned movements" (EDP, 155). The machine-body had two registers, the body as object of knowledge, an "analyzable" and "intelligible" body written in the "anatomico-metaphysical" register begun by Descartes, and a "manipulable" body found in the "technico-political" register of military, educational, and medical institutions. Their point of overlap, which Foucault claims to be able to read in La Mettrie's *L'Homme-machine*, is the docile body, "which joins the analyzable body to the manipulable body. A body is docile that may be subjected, used, transformed and improved" (EDP, 136; see also EHS1, 139, where Foucault talks about the disciplinary body as a "machine" when contrasted with bio-political population management).

Although the "disciplines" that constructed docile bodies were not new, they changed scale, object, and modality to the point where they became "general formulas of domination" (EDP, 137). Disciplines work at the intersection of individual and group, producing, by the team of four great techniques – the drawing up of tables, the prescription of movements, the imposition of exercises, and the arrangement of tactics – an individuality with four characteristics: cellular (distributed bodies); organic (coded activities); genetic (trained aptitudes); and combinatory (composition of forces). The summary formula of discipline is: "the architecture, anatomy, mechanics, economy of the disciplinary body" (EDP, 167).

The first two of the four procedures of discipline – the spatial distribution of bodies and the control of time via the timetable – could work with a "mechanical body," a body of "solids" and "movements." But the full flowering of the disciplines needed a "new object" beyond the mechanical body; it needed a "natural" body, "the bearer of forces and the seat of duration" (EDP, 155; see McWhorter 1999, 153). The natural and organic body is the target of the "organization of geneses" (graduated exercises: EDP, 156–162) as well as the "composition of forces" (practices inculcating teamwork: EDP, 162–167). But this natural and organic body constituted by these practices is still part of a machine: "the soldier whose body has been trained to function part by part for particular operations must in turn form an element in a mechanism at another level.... The body is constituted as a part of a multi-segmentary machine" (EDP, 164).

There are many challenging philosophical issues raised by Foucault's treatment of the body in *Discipline and Punish*: What is a "natural" body that is at once a "new object" and part of a "machine"? How can the natural body be "discovered" at a point in time? How could that discovery of the natural body come after and "supersede" the "mechanical" body? How can the natural body be more amenable to incorporation in a machine than a mechanical body? Whatever we might say about Foucault's treatment of the natural-machinic disciplinary body, we cannot claim it to be resting on a raw "nature" outside of culture, for the "natural" body of the disciplines is constituted by its submission to exercises and teamwork. If there is any biology at work here it must be a biology of plasticity: not pure social constructivism, but not raw extracultural nature either. Unfortunately, fully exploring these issues is beyond the scope of this entry, but we can at least mention the school of thought known as Developmental Systems Theory, with its emphasis on epigenetic and even social factors of development, as a possible resource in further exploring the natural-machinic body (Oyama, Griffiths, and Gray 2001).

As might be expected, the body also plays a central role in Foucault's second great genealogy, volume one of *The History of Sexuality*. The major claim here is that sexuality is at the intersection of the disciplines of body and the biopolitical management of populations (EHS1, 145). We see this intersection in the four "figures" of the deployment of sexuality, each of which is an individual body defined in its relation to the reproductive capacity of the population: the hysterical woman (who may neglect her motherly duties), the masturbating child (whose sexual potential is at risk), the Malthusian couple (which must be guided, via economic and political incentives as well as medical interventions, to play its proper role), and the perverse adult (who must be studied and rehabilitated) (EHS1, 105).

The body also plays a key role in Foucault's deflationary nominalism with regard to both "sexuality" and "sex." Far from being a natural kind, a transhistorical essence whose truth we are only now beginning to glimpse via our scientific treatment of what had previously been shrouded in myth and superstition, sexuality for Foucault is a "historical construct," a "great surface network" linking together a series of separate factors: "the stimulation of bodies, the intensification of pleasures, the incitement to discourse, the formation of special knowledges [*connaissances*], [and] the strengthening of controls and resistances" (EHS1, 105–106). Foucault is similarly nominalist when it comes to the notion of "sex" as an "in itself" separate from its components. Foucault is skeptical of "sex" as the "idea that there exists something other than bodies, organs, somatic localizations, functions, anatomo-physiological systems, sensations, and pleasures; something else and something more, with intrinsic properties and laws of its own: 'sex'" (EHS1, 152–153). In another passage, Foucault seemingly ups the ante on his nominalism, as "body" no longer appears, being itself dissolved into its components. Here, in stressing that "sex" has a function in the *dispositif* (apparatus) of sexuality, and there alone, Foucault moves below even "body": "The notion of 'sex' made it possible to group together, in an artificial unity, anatomical elements, biological functions, conducts, sensations, and pleasures, and it enabled one to make use of this fictitious unity as a causal principle, an omnipresent meaning, a secret to be discovered everywhere: sex was thus able to function as a unique signifier and as a universal signified" (EHS1, 154). But we should not place too much weight on this passage, as soon thereafter "bodies" reappear in their role as a component of the "fictitious unity" of "sex." Foucault writes, "sex is the most speculative, most ideal, and most internal element in a deployment of sexuality organized by power in its grip on bodies and their materiality, their forces, energies, sensations, and pleasures" (EHS1, 155).

Finally, there is the famous and cryptic slogan: "[T]he rallying point for the counterattack against the deployment of sexuality ought not to be sex-desire but bodies and pleasures" (EHS1, 157). Although duly noting the enormous commentary on this phrase, a good bit of it devoted to accusing Foucault of an escape to a pre-cultural "nature," we can point to others who see the body here as not an ahistorical body but as the sort of plastic, biosocial body we encountered in *Discipline and Punish* (on both points, see McWhorter 1999, 157 and 251n14), literally a "body politic." We might say that the key to fighting the deployment of sexuality, which claims scientific knowledge of the natural body, is to design, in connection with others, your own disciplinary practices, your own techniques of the self.

With this last phrase, we can move to a very brief discussion of the body as it appears in the last period of Foucault's work. Briefly put, the body is a matter of concern to the ethical subjects in volumes two and three of *The History of Sexuality*. For the Greeks and Romans Foucault examines, there are three areas of concern: dietetics, economics, and erotics. That is, he is concerned with the body as seen in regimes of diet, exercise, and sleep, as mediated by advice by physicians (EHS2, 95–139; EHS3, 97–144); the relation to others in the household (EHS2, 143–184; EHS3, 147–185); and the relation to the beloved (EHS2, 187–246; EHS3, 189–232). These concerns are not those of escaping, as in certain Platonic schemes, the body as the prison of the soul. Rather, the body is one of the matters of concern the ethical subject will have with regard to himself.

John Protevi

SEE ALSO

> *Biopolitics*
> *Discipline*
> *Medicine*
> *Nature*
> *Pleasure*
> *Sex*
> *Maurice Merleau-Ponty*

SUGGESTED READING

McWhorter, Ladelle. 1999. *Bodies and Pleasures: Foucault and the Politics of Sexual Normalization*. Bloomington: Indiana University Press.

Protevi, John. 2009. *Political Affect: Connecting the Social and the Somatic*. Minneapolis: University of Minnesota.

Sawicki, Jana. 1991. *Disciplining Foucault: Feminism, Power, and the Body*. New York: Routledge.

10

CARE

"CARE," A TRANSLATION of the French *souci*, is most commonly associated with Foucault's notion of *souci de soi*, or care of the self. The term "care" often has positive connotations in English, potentially leading readers to believe that care of the self indicates a way of being kind to oneself. However, the term should also be considered in the sense of concern, as when one cares whether or not a dreaded event occurs. Care as concern can hold negative implications and would indicate an anxious relationship with the self. *Souci*, like "care," is equivocal insofar as this single term holds both positive and negative connotations (Kelly 2009, 100). As "care" is the standard translation, it will stand for *souci* for the purpose of this entry.

Le souci de soi is Foucault's translation of the Greek injunction *epimeleia heautou*. Foucault contends that injunction "is indeed the justificatory framework, ground, and foundation for the imperative 'know yourself'" (ECF-HOS, 8). As such, the obligation to care for oneself was more fundamental than the injunction to know yourself; knowing oneself appeared as one of many techniques for taking care of oneself. Foucault's genealogy of the subject reveals a different mode of ethical subjectivity in antiquity than that of the modern hermeneutics of desire, which seeks to uncover the subject's secret truth. In Ancient Greek, Hellenistic, and Roman philosophy, Foucault locates an aesthetic rather than an epistemological experience of the self. In opposition to a hermeneutics of self-discovery, *epimeleia heautou*, or care of the self, provided the foundation for ethical subjectivity.

Care of the self is not "synonymous" with ethics. Rather, "in antiquity, ethics as the conscious practice of freedom has revolved around this fundamental imperative: 'Take care of yourself'" (EEW1, 285). For Foucault, "ancient philosophy can be comprehended ... as a vast project of inventing, defining, elaborating, and *practicing* a complex 'care of the self'" (McGushin 2007, 3). Care of the self as *askesis* extends from Greek, Hellenistic, and Roman thought through Christian philosophy. It dominated ethical thought in the Greco-Roman world and continued its influence through early Christian ethics, when care of the self became associated with self-ishness, individualism, and egoism. With the Hellenistic model of care for the self found in Stoic and Epicurean philosophy, Foucault finds a mode of subjectification that is "*irreducible* to either Christianity or to Platonism" (Gros 2005, 699). In *The Care of the Self*, Foucault argues that in the first two centuries AD, there is an emphasis on "the attention that should be brought to bear on oneself" (EHS3, 41).

This attention is associated with "the practices of self-fashioning that one takes up in order to give one's existence a particular form" (McGushin 2007, 39). Care of the self is a way of relating to oneself in order to elaborate and intensify one's ethical subjectivity. Although Socrates' question in *Alcibiades I or II* – do you take proper care of yourself? – marks a turning point in the history of ethics, Foucault most explicitly associates the injunction to care for oneself with "*la culture de soi*" found in Hellenistic and Roman philosophy (FHS3, 60). Particularly in Stoic and Epicurean thought, care of the self appears as a practical activity rather than an emotional state or theoretical endeavor.

Care of the self is an intensification and fortification of the self. Opposed to introspection or self-hermeneutics that requires an objectification of the self by itself, it aims for an immanent presence to self. In Frédéric Gros's words, "It is not a matter of provoking in the self an interior redoubling by which I constitute myself as an object of introspective observation, but of concentrating myself and of *accompanying myself*" (Gros 2005, 700).

As a "form of attention" or a state of mind, care permeates one's actions (ECF-HOS, 10). Caring is a way of disclosing a problem in the world; it is an anxiety about "what exists and might exist" (EEW1, 325). As a mode of comportment, it is also a way of responding to such a problem. Care is also a "general standpoint" or way of comporting oneself in the world. It is "an attitude towards the self, others, and the world" (ECF-HOS, 10).

Care is more than an attitude or feeling; it cannot be reduced to an emotional or cognitive state of being. *Epimeleia* "designates a number of actions exercised on the self by the self, actions by which one takes responsibility for oneself and by which one changes, purifies, transforms, and transfigures oneself" (ECF-HOS, 11). According to Foucault, *epimeleia* is related to *melete*, which refers to exercise, training, and meditation. Care is an activity or set of practices that use diverse technologies of self, including meditation, writing, dialogue, memorization, practical tests, and so forth: "The *meletai* are exercises, gymnastic and military exercises, military training. *Epimeleisthai* refers to a form of vigilant, continuous, applied, regular, etcetera, activity much more than to a mental attitude" (ECF-HOS, 84). Care is an exercise that one performs on oneself in order to transform oneself and to achieve a "certain mode of being" (EEW1, 282). *Epimeleia*, Foucault writes, "implies labor" (EHS3, 52). Care of the self is a kind of development, sheltering, cultivation, and fortification. Through care, one engages in activities designed to cultivate a reflexive relationship with oneself.

Although in antiquity care of the self mediated the relationship between subjectivity and truth, care of the self is not equivalent to self-knowledge. Care is a mode of perception or attention distinct from knowledge; its primary function is not epistemological. In his 1981–1982 Collège de France lectures, one of Foucault's main tasks is to demonstrate that the imperative to "know yourself" that predominates modern philosophy was subordinate to the injunction to "take care of yourself" in Greco-Roman culture and thought.

Through an examination of the usage of *epimeleia*, Foucault outlines the attributes of care that constitute it as a cognitive activity distinct from knowledge. First, there is a conversion to or pivoting toward oneself by the self. It is a transformation of the subject's "very being" as a subject (ECF-HOS, 27). This conversion requires that one focuses one's attention on taking care of oneself. Second, care of the self is a withdrawal into the self and a retreating from the world for the purpose of self-restoration. However, it is not a severance of one's ties to the world. In care of the self, a distance is created between oneself and the world in order to create a space for careful, deliberate, and directed action. Moreover, medical, legal, and religious texts describe care as a practice; care is a self-cure, an assertion of one's rights over oneself, and an honoring of the self (ECF-HOS, 85–86). Finally, care of the self aims for self-mastery. This is not merely the capacity of restraint but also an active disciplining of the body. Through practical exercises, one obtains a possession of oneself.

The self, as the object of care, is both instrument and *telos*; it is the raw material toward which work is directed and an aim to be obtained. This means that "the truth of the self, and the self as a subject capable of knowing the truth and living the true life, are attained not first and foremost through self-*discovery* but rather through the *poetics* of the self" (McGushin 2007, xviii). However, care of the self is not a solipsistic, narcissistic activity. Rather, it is a way of being equal to oneself and finding pleasure in oneself.

Such a self-relation implies and intensifies social relations in two ways. First, one practices care of the self in order to properly perform one's social role. Foucault explains, "the care of the self enables one to occupy his rightful position in the city, the community, or interpersonal relationships" (EEW1, 287). Care of the self is always exercised in communal and institutional environments. Moreover, care of the self requires the guidance of others; "one needs a guide, a counselor, a friend, someone who will be truthful with you" (EEW1, 287). In order to keep oneself truthful and to avoid slipping into egoism, care of the self demands a master of existence. Care of the self is a way of caring for others and a response to complex social relations. As Foucault states, "Around the care of the self, there developed an entire activity of speaking and writing in which the work of oneself on oneself and communication with others were linked together. Here we touch on one of the most important aspects of this activity devoted to oneself: it constituted, not an exercise in solitude but a true social practice" (EHS3, 51). For example, ethical *parrēsia*, or the practice of truth-telling, is a way of caring for oneself that presupposes a relation with others.

It should not be assumed that, with care of the self, Foucault is trying to revive an ancient ethic. In actuality, he considered such ancient male ethics to be abhorrent (EHS2, 22). Moreover, he believed philosophers should not seek to recover a lost past or forgotten truths. In offering his problematization of ethical subjectivity, Foucault did not defend any particular model for morality. The significance of his problematization of the care of self lies in its "creative activity" that makes a different future possible (EEW1, 262).

Stephanie Jenkins

SEE ALSO

> *Ethics*
> *Hermeneutics*
> *Parrēsia*
> *Self*
> *Plato*
> *Truth*

SUGGESTED READING

Davidson, Arnold. 1994. "Ethics as Ascetics: Foucault, the History of Ethics, and Ancient Thought," in *The Cambridge Companion to Foucault*, ed. Gary Gutting. Cambridge: Cambridge University Press, pp. 115–140.

Gros, Frédéric. 2005. "Le Souci de Soi chez Michel Foucault," *Philosophy and Social Criticism* 31, nos. 5–6: 697–708.

McGushin, Edward. 2007. *Foucault's Askesis: An Introduction to Philosophical Life*. Evanston, IL: Northwestern University Press.

O'Leary, Timothy. 2002. *Foucault and the Art of Ethics*. New York: Continuum.

11

CHRISTIANITY

FOUCAULT'S APPRECIATION OF the dynamics of Christianity was twofold: although it was a lively, influential power in the contemporary world, it could also and had at times become in modernity a demonic force. Foucault's awareness of Christianity's dynamism was in part a result of his personal experience. Recall that Foucault spent a year (1958–1959) in Poland, where he saw the Catholic Church's strong opposition to the Communist government. Of course, Pope John Paul II later brought that resistance to an extraordinary efficacy, as was shown in the massive outpouring of popular support for him during his trip to Poland in spring 1979. That visit was the catalyst for the Solidarity movement, of which Foucault became a strong public advocate. Another important source for understanding Foucault's sense of the religious dynamic is his visits to Brazil in the 1970s, when the military dictatorship was in control. In terms of his own thinking, his project was a "history of the present." This necessarily engaged him in a religious-spiritual analysis because the forms of knowledge, power, and subjectivity that he saw as animating our culture were often constructed, he claimed, in decisive ways in argument or alliance with religious practices and concerns. In a 1975 lecture, he mentioned the insight that would greatly shape his studies of the next decade: what "took place starting in the sixteenth century, that is to say, in a period that is not characterized by the beginning of de-Christianization, but rather, as a number of historians have shown, by a phase of in-depth Christianization" (ECF-AB, 177). This insight subverted Foucault's original plan for *The History of Sexuality* series of volumes where he was to separate out the modern experience of the body from the Christian fabrication of the flesh. (The original title of volume 2 was to have been *La Chair et le corps, Flesh and Body*.) The modern body was enmeshed within the coils of a rebellious flesh, and within those coils was a "moral physiology of the flesh" and the "culpabilisation of the body by the flesh" (ECF-AB, 180, 188).

Foucault had rejected what he later called the "blackmail of the Enlightenment," that either-or acceptance of it as some new rationality, liberated from the superstitions of a religious past (EFR, 40–43). As a result, his history of the present came to ignore the customary epochal divisions and concluded that, between different historical eras, the "topography of the parting of the waters is hard to pin down" (EEW1, 196). In the case of the early modern period, he refused the topography of a religious era yielding to a secular age: early modernity was not a tale of growing religious disbelief but rather witnessed the emergence of an energy that drove both the global missionary activities of European Christianity and a vast religious colonization of interior life. This colonization is what Foucault referred to in 1975 as an "in-depth Christianization" or a "new Christianization." The effect of this missionary effort was the "vast interiorization" of a Christian experience that possessed a double center: the practice of confession and the struggle of the flesh with the spirit and the body (ECF-AB, 177, 193, 188–189). Foucault studied these pastoral practices in a variety of contexts, but his major concern came to be with how they operated in the political domain, because it was there that Foucault saw the demonic force of certain seemingly benign religious practices. He claims that the Christian pastorate introduced a "strange game whose elements are life, death, truth, obedience, individuals, self-identity" that seems to have nothing to do with the Greek notion of the city. Foucault wrote: "Our societies proved to be really demonic since they happened to combine these two games – the city-citizen game and the shepherd-flock game – in what we call the modern states" (EEW3, 311). It is against this background that obedience becomes a key modern virtue, that sex becomes political, and that the vision of genocidal war emerges (EHS1, 137).

To grasp Foucault's understanding of Christianity entails study of his writings on sexuality and on the early Church thinkers (ERC, 154–197). Although he wrote far more on Cassian than Augustine, Foucault may be compared with the latter thinker in his critical concern about institutional power and his anti-utopian appreciation of the moral imperfections within all human endeavors. Quite unexpectedly, Foucault's work has given rise to a lively discussion with theologians and biblical scholars, as well as to fresh perspectives among historians of Christianity.

James Bernauer

SEE ALSO

Body
Conduct
Confession
Power
Religion

SUGGESTED READING

Bernauer, James, and Jeremy Carrette, eds. 2004. *Michel Foucault and Theology: The Politics of Religious Experience*. Burlington, VT: Ashgate.

Carrette, Jeremy, ed. 1999. *Religion and Culture: Michel Foucault*. London: Routledge.

2000. *Foucault and Religion*. London: Routledge.

McSweeney, John. 2005. "Foucault and Theology," *Foucault Studies* 2:117–144.

12

CIVIL SOCIETY

FOUCAULT PROVIDES A genealogy of the concept of civil society in the final lectures of his 1978–1979 course "The Birth of Biopolitics." By "civil society," he means the sense acquired by this term from the middle of the eighteenth century onward. Prior to this period, its use was equivalent to "political society." So, for example, Chapter 7 of Locke's *Second Treatise on Government* was called "Of Civil or Political Society" (Locke 1960). By the time of Ferguson's 1767 *Essay on the History of Civil Society* (Ferguson 1966), the term had come to encompass individuals not only as subjects of law and government but also as subjects of interest who engaged in a variety of economic and other social activities. Foucault presents the emergence of this new concept of civil society as a solution to a problem for existing conceptions of government thrown up by the emergence of political economy and its correlate, the subject of interest or *homo oeconomicus*.

In the penultimate lecture of this course, he drew attention to the incompatibility of the subject of interest presupposed by political economy and the subject of right presupposed by traditional conceptions of sovereign power. By "subject of interest" he means the subject of individual choice or preferences that emerged with the empiricism of Locke and Hume. These individual choices are irreducible, in the sense that they have no further rationale or justification, and nontransferable in the sense that they are the preferences of the subject concerned: "This principle of irreducible, non-transferable, atomistic individual choice which is unconditionally referred to the subject himself is what is called interest" (ECF-BBIO, 272). The subject endowed with certain inalienable rights and the subject of interest are fundamentally different. They stand in different relations to the social and political fields of other subjects of the same kind: the subject of right is integrated into the field of other such subjects by a dialectic of renunciation or transfer of rights (the social contract), whereas the subject of interest is integrated into the economic domain of other such subjects by a dialectic of spontaneous multiplication and convergence (the hidden hand).

These differences pose a challenge to existing theories of the sovereign and sovereign power, namely how to reconcile the government of the economy with the absolute and all-encompassing power of the sovereign. Political economy, in the form of Adam Smith and others, represents a challenge to the power of the sovereign insofar as it denies the possibility of an economic sovereign. Either the economy must be supposed to set limits to the power of the sovereign, or as the Physiocrats suggested he must govern differently and in accordance with the inherent rules when it comes to economic processes. In fact, Foucault argues, what emerged was an entirely new concept of the object of government that was characteristic of a distinctively liberal art of government:

> ... for the art of governing not to have to split into two branches of an art of governing economically and an art of governing juridically, in short, to preserve the unity and generality of the art of governing over the whole sphere of sovereignty, and to keep the specificity and autonomy of the art of governing with respect to economic science, to answer these three questions, the art of governing must be given a reference, a domain or field of reference, a new reality on which it will be exercised, and I think this new field of reference is civil society. (ECF-BBIO, 295)

Foucault identifies four essential characteristics of civil society according to Ferguson. First, in contrast to the opposition between political society and a state of nature relied on by Locke and other social contract theorists, civil society is a "historical-natural constant" (ECF-BBIO, 298). For Ferguson, human beings are social animals, and the natural state of humanity only appears in society. There is no presocial state from which humanity passed into social existence, no moment of transition from nonsociety to society: "The nature of human nature is to be historical, because the nature of human nature is to be social" (ECF-BBIO, 299).

Second, there is no explicit contract or delegation or renunciation of rights at the origin of civil society but rather a mechanism that "assures the spontaneous synthesis of individuals" analogous to the confluence of interests that operates in the economic sphere (ECF-BBIO, 300). However, what binds individuals together in civil society is not just economic interests but a series of "disinterested interests," including instinct, sentiments, and sympathies, both favorably and unfavorably disposed to others; in short, "a distinct set of non-egoistic interests, a distinct interplay of non-egoistic disinterested interests which is much wider than egoism itself" (ECF-BBIO, 301). Moreover, these disinterested interests imply that civil society is always bounded, whether at the level of the family, village, community, or nation.

Economic interests are played out within such bounded societies, even as they threaten to undermine the bonds established on non-egoistic grounds.

Third, civil society is the matrix and basis of political power in the sense that explicitly political power is built on already existing relations of power. Ferguson argues that there is "a spontaneous formation of power" (ECF-BBIO, 303). Prior to the formalization of political and juridical institutions and the justification of particular powers, there are spontaneous distributions of authority, obedience, and roles in the collective decision-making process: "[P]ower already exists before it is regulated, delegated, or legally established" (ECF-BBIO, 304).

Fourth, civil society is the motor of history in the sense that it contains within itself the conditions that bring about disequilibrium. The equilibrium obtained at a given stage between the spontaneous harmony of interests and power on the one hand and the play of egoistic economic interests on the other is susceptible to breakdown by virtue of the emergence of different forms of self-interest. Ferguson refers to the egoism generated by the exercise of power itself, but more frequently to economic egoism as the "principle of dissolution of the spontaneous equilibrium of civil society" (ECF-BBIO, 306). In this sense, Foucault suggests, Ferguson sees the conditions of civil association as equally conditions of dissociation, leading to the transformation of society through the different historical stages of savagery, barbarism, and civilization: the very mechanisms that lead to the establishment of particular forms of civil society are also those that lead to its historical transformation.

Foucault argues that, with the emergence of this conception of civil society in the writings of Ferguson and others, we see the emergence of a new domain of nonjuridical social relations. These are irreducibly historical and bound up with the exercise of government. As such, civil society offers a conception of the domain and objects of government that differs from the juridical field found in Hobbes, Locke, and the social contract tradition. It is an object or domain that provides a solution to the problem for traditional conceptions of government thrown up by the emergence of political economy and *homo oeconomicus*. In this manner, Foucault presents the concept of civil society as the solution to a problem of governmentality rather than a philosophical idea. It is the "correlate" of a liberal governmentality that respects both juridical rules of right and the economy. In this sense, "*homo œconomicus* and civil society belong to the same ensemble of the technology of liberal governmentality" (ECF-BBIO, 296).

Paul Patton

SEE ALSO

Biopolitics
Governmentality
Power
State

SUGGESTED READING

Barry, Andrew, Thomas Osborne, and Nikolas Rose, eds. 1996. *Foucault and Political Reason: Liberalism, Neo-liberalism, and Rationalities of Government*. Chicago: University of Chicago Press.

13

CONDUCT

ETWEEN 1976 AND 1984, Michel Foucault published no books. The first
volume of *The History of Sexuality*, *Le Volunté de Savoir* (somewhat misleadingly
translated as *The History of Sexuality, Volume 1: An Introduction*), appeared in
1976, and Foucault received the initial reviews of the second and third volumes just
before his death in 1984. This was not an unproductive period, just the opposite.
The publication and translation of his seminars at the Collège de France testify to a
tremendously productive period.

During this period, Foucault began to rethink his conception of power relations,
and the strategic conception of power relations that had oriented his work in texts
such as *Discipline and Punish* underwent a revision. Although he never renounced his
conception of power in terms of the micropolitics of power featured in texts such as
Discipline and Punish and the initial volume of *The History of Sexuality*, as well as his
lecture course "Society Must Be Defended," he began to think about the relationship between power and governmentality during this time. At this time, he began his
investigations into the concept of governmentality, which he concisely defined as the
"encounter between the technologies of dominations of others and those of the self"
(EEW1, 225), and conduct cannot be understood apart from this concept. Although
conduct is part of a set of closely connected concepts that animate Foucault's work
during this late period, it remains vitally important in its own right.

The key problem of government is "the conduct of conduct," a phrase (*"con-
duire des conduits"*) that appears in the original French version of "The Subject and
Power" but was not included in the English translation (although it does appear in
the English version of *The Birth of Biopolitics*). Jeremy Crampton cites the original
French passage in which this phrase occurs as follows (Crampton 2007):

> L'exercice du pouvoir consiste à «conduire des conduites» et à aménager la prob-
> abilité. Le pouvoir, au fond, est moins de l'ordre de l'affrontement entre deux

adversaries, ou de l'engagement de l'un à l'égard de l'autre, que de l'ordre du «gouvernement.» (FDE4, 237)

My English translation: The exercise of power consists in "the conduct of conduct," and in building up probablility. Power, fundamentally, belongs less to the order of confrontation between two adversaries or to the order of engagement of one with the other, than to the order of "government."

While the exact phrase does not appear in the published translation called "The Subject and Power," this essay is a worthwhile place to begin a discussion of this important concept. According to Foucault, power relations circumscribe fields of possible knowledge and action:

[Power] operates on the field of possibilities in which the behavior of active subjects is able to inscribe itself. It is a set of actions on possible actions; it incites, it induces, it seduces, it makes easier or more difficult; it releases or contrives, makes more probable or less; in the extreme, it constrains or forbids absolutely, but it is always a way of acting upon one or more acting subjects by virtue of their acting or being capable of action. A set of actions upon other actions. (EEW3, 341)

He proceeds to elucidate this conception of power as determining the field of the possible in terms of conduct. "To 'conduct' is at the same time to lead others." In other words, understanding the various techniques of conduct means raising the question of government and governmentality, understood as "the way in which the conduct of individuals or groups might be directed" (EEW3, 341). Power and governmentality, essential words in Foucault's conceptual toolkit, are linked together in this passage through this notion of conduct. It is also significant that, like the word "subject," it has both passive and active dimensions. Just as one finds oneself both subject to power relations and thereby defined by them, one can render oneself a subject. Foucault explains his project in terms of this dynamic most concisely in a brief resumé of his career. In this brief text, he outlines different modalities of subjectification, or the various ways that one might be rendered or render oneself a subject (in terms of a subject of knowledge and in terms of an object for oneself) (EEW2, 459–461). Similarly, one can be both conducted and conduct oneself. One can permit oneself to be led and contest the terms by which one is led, so one cannot understand conduct without understanding counterconduct.

Arnold Davidson has argued that the notion of conduct is essential for understanding the work of Foucault's later period. According to Davidson, this concept provides the link between Foucault's work on power relations in *Discipline and Punish* and the 1975–1976 lecture course "Society Must Be Defended" and his later work on the ancient ethics and asceticism, which comes to fruition in the 1981–1982 lecture course "Hermeneutics of the Subject" as well as the 1982–1983 course "The

Government of Self and Others" (Davidson 2008). The key to understanding this concept as well as Davidson's claim for its centrality in Foucault's work during this period can be found in Foucault's treatment of conduct and counterconduct in his 1978–1979 course "Security, Territory, Population." Although the bulk of this article will consist of a treatment of the concept within the context of this course, I shall turn to Foucault's treatment of this concept in other essays that he wrote during this period, in particular his dispatches on the Iranian Revolution penned for the Italian news daily *Corriere della Serra* and the French newspaper *Le Monde*.

Foucault introduced the term "conduct" during his lecture of March 1, 1978, in the context of his discussion of the pastorate and its unique technologies for governing individuals, for inculcating a state of obedience. A genealogy of techniques of governing must account for these novel techniques for governing "one and all," above all obedience as an end in itself. As Foucault writes in "*'Omnes et Singulatim'*: Toward a Critique of Political Reason,"

> In Christianity, the tie with the shepherd is an individual one. It is personal submission to him. His will is done, not because it is consistent with the law, and not just as far as it is consistent with it, but, principally, because it is his *will*. In Cassian's *Cenobilitical Institutions*, there are many edifying anecdotes in which the monk finds salvation by carrying out the absurdest of his superior's orders. Obedience is a virtue. This means that it is not, as for the Greeks, a provisional means to an end, but, rather, an end in itself. (EEW3, 209)

Written at the same time as the lecture course and delivered as the Tanner Lectures in October 1978, this text summarizing this genealogy of governmentality hinges on the concept of obedience. As a result of obedience, the individual empties herself of any of the passions characteristic of the individual will (ECF-STP, 178–179). The pastorate provides a field of general obedience in which even mastery (for example, of the priest or bishop) is a function of obedience (ECF-STP, 179). Furthermore, the point is not salvation but rather "an entire economy and technique of the circulation, transfer, and reversal of merits, and this is its fundamental point" (ECF-STP, 183). The pastorate institutes a form of power that generalizes obedience and actualizes it on each individual within its economy. In other words, "the objective of the pastorate is men's conduct" (ECF-STP, 195).

A genealogy of pastoral power is necessary if we are to make sense of governmentality, which represents the early modern profusion of these techniques of obedience into a heterogeneous variety of different spheres of knowledge and power. In his essay "What Is Critique?" Foucault writes:

> This art of governing, of course, remained for a long time tied to relatively limited practices, tied ultimately, even in medieval society, to monastic existence and

practiced above all in relatively restricted spiritual groups. But I believe that from the fifteenth century and right before the Reformation, one can say that there was a veritable explosion of the art of governing men. (EWC, 383–384)

Foucault goes on to distinguish this explosion in two senses. First is "a laicization" of these techniques into realms not traditionally those of the Church and second a "reduction" to various domains: "how to govern children, how to govern the poor and beggars, how to govern a family, a house, how to govern armies, how to govern different groups, cities, states, how to govern one's own body, how to govern one's own mind" (EWC, 384).

But what of conduct? What is the relationship between conduct and the profusion of these arts of governmentality? First, Foucault notes that conduct and counterconduct are co-constitutive. It is not the case that we begin with concrete forms of power that mandate obedience and then subsequently movements of counterconduct materialize to contest these mandates. Rather, the well-ordered field of conduct is constituted in reaction to various threats of disorder in the early Christian world; Foucault cites in this regard Gnostic attempts to contest the disorderliness of matter, but various threats can be found in both Judaic and Christian antinomian movements. Foucault mentions examples of such movements of counterconduct, with Martin Luther's movement figuring most prominently. Revolts of conduct are distinct from political or economic revolts, yet often closely related to them. What distinguishes revolts of conduct is that their object is conduct itself, and their question always concerns how one wishes to be led. In other words, they are never completely autonomous and they never question whether one ought to be led. Rather, they question why and how one must be led in a particular way (ECF-STP, 197).

There is a historical shift in these movements. Beginning in the tenth and eleventh centuries and extending through the Protestant Reformation, these local constestations occurred within the religious realm. Gradually, these revolts began to contest reigning political orders. Examples provided by Foucault include insubordination in the arena of warfare, the proliferation of secret societies during the eighteenth century, and refusals in the area of medicine ranging from the refusal of particular vaccinations and treatments to the refusal of medical treatment altogether by various religious movements. (Foucault's examples remain salient, as these revolutions in counterconduct can still be found in various attempts to voluntarily refuse child immunizations and in the widespread interest in alternative therapies.)

The sheer variety of these examples raises the issue of the difficulty in defining the terms conduct and counterconduct. Although he uses them repeatedly, words like revolt and revolution are inadequate for at least two reasons. First, the term pertains primarily to a political or an economic contestation of authority, whereas counterconduct is not primarily political (although Foucault's examples demonstrate that it can certainly have political implications). Second, revolution connotes a widespread mass movement, and, although movements of counterconduct can indeed manifest themselves in this way, they need not do so. Foucault next proposes the term "disobediance," but dismisses it as too weak and inaccurate. Disobedience is necessary, but it is insufficient for characterizing movements ranging from medieval mystics to Anabaptists and the Freemasons. Foucault reluctantly cites "dissidence" as a possibility, for its aptness to characterize religious movements that contest pastoral power as well as contemporary Soviet dissidents such as Alexander Solzhenitsyn. His texts and activities contest the totalizing power of the Soviet state, forms of power that certainly manifest in the political realm as well as everyday realms of conduct. However, when one uses the word "dissidence," one thinks immediately if not of the Soviet context then of intellectuals who use various interventions in the public sphere to contest the political status quo. In addition to various Soviet dissidents such as Solzhenitsyn that Foucault discusses, dissidents today would include writers and activists such as the Nobel Laureates Vaclav Havel and Liu Xiaobo, but the point remains the same: dissidence as it's commonly thought of today is too restrictive a notion to encompass all the aspects of counterconduct, for it would not make sense to refer to individuals who refuse to vaccinate their children as dissidents. Revolt, disobedience, and dissidence each pertain to an important feature of counterconduct, but each has its limitations. Despite its awkwardness, Foucault settles on counterconduct as the counterpart to conduct.

Foucault next turns to five activities associated with pastoral counterconducts in particular (asceticism, community, mysticism, Scripture, and eschatology). I briefly focus on asceticism because of its centrality in Foucault's later texts and ethics understood as the care of the self. In the context of counterconduct, Foucault discusses the ascetics of late antiquity, desert anchorites such as Saint Anthony or Saint Sabbas the Sanctified. Foucault acknowledges that it seems odd to think of these ascetics as engaging in counterconduct, for what could be more obedient than asceticism? (Certainly this was Nietzsche's view.) Although he acknowledges this dimension of ascetic practice, he notes an important distinction between the obedience demanded by authorities of the early Church and the ascetic practices of these lone individuals in the desert. Foucault cites three important distinctions. First, this was an exercise of the self on the self, and hence recalled ancient ascetic practices (cf. EHS2). Second, these exercises were structured from easier to more difficult as one progressed, with "the ascetic's own suffering" as the "criterion" gauging this difficulty. Finally, asceticism takes the form of a challenge among various anchorites in which individuals would try to outdo one another in fasting or various other forms of suffering, with the ultimate goal being an end to suffering, *apatheia*. Throughout the history of the Church, there have been various attempts to incorporate ascetic practices, but these practices are foreign to pastoral power because of the focus on self-mastery (ELC-STP, 205–207). If asceticism has an uneasy relationship with pastoral power, so do the four other aspects of medieval counterconduct. These five counterconducts form the borderlands of Christianity (ECF-STP, 215). The history of the medieval

Church can be read as various attempts to incorporate these counterconducts that achieved various levels of success.

These five aspects of counterconduct led to various "insurrections of conduct" during the fifteenth and sixteenth centuries. Foucault understands various modern revolutions under this rubric, including the seventeenth-century English, eighteenth-century French, the twentieth-century Russian, and, despite the fact that they are omitted here, the Iranian Revolution and the revolutionary clubs and Soviet workers' councils are concrete manifestations of these insurrections, which pose the question of how one is to be led and how communities are to be conceived of, from the level of the family to that of the state (ECF-STP, 228). The extent and limits of sovereignty are at stake in these insurrections; counterconduct manifests an urge "not to be governed like that." In the passage from Foucault's 1978 essay "What Is Critique?" cited previously, he outlines the profusion in the various arts of government. He goes on to assert that the sixteenth-century question of government "cannot be dissociated from the question 'How not to be governed? [...] How not to be governed *like that*, by that, in the name of these principles, in view of such objectives and by the means of such methods, not like that, not for that, not by them?'" (EWC, 384, Foucault's italics). Such a refusal "to be governed like that" is part of a localized struggle against a specific modality of government; put otherwise, this refusal is a localized struggle against a specific way of being conducted.

The twin concepts of conduct and counterconduct, and their relationships to governmentality and power, provide a necessary context for understanding Foucault's work during this period. I would like to conclude by briefly discussing Foucault's texts on the Iranian Revolution as a means of illustrating this; specifically, I discuss Foucault's "Is it Useless to Revolt?" published in *Le Monde* in May 1979 in light of this discussion of counterconduct. Foucault begins with the observation that an individual or group's refusal to obey stands outside history in an odd sort of way because no grip on power, no techniques of government, are ever so absolute as to render this impossible (EEW3, 449). As Foucault notes in "The Subject and Power," power structures the field of possibility and thereby institutes the rules whereby games of power are played. But the rules of the game are never absolute: there are various exceptions that can amount to tactical refusal. Despite the absolutism of authority, people revolt. Just as the counterconducts that defined pastoral power were liminal, revolts and insurrections of conduct are in a sense outside history if history is a discourse structured by the field of power relations in the same manner as conduct. Just as counterconduct is at the threshold of history, it is at the threshold of religion and politics as well, and the Iranian Revolution is no exception:

> This is the enigma of revolts. For anyone who did not look for the "underlying reasons" for the movement in Iran but was attentive to the way in which it was experienced, for anyone who tried to understand what was going on in the heads of these men and women when they were risking their lives, one thing was

striking. They inscribed their humiliations, their hatred for the regime, and their resolve to overthrow it at the bounds of heaven and earth, in an envisioned history that was religious just as much as it was political. (EEW3, 450)

One of the things that fascinates Foucault about the events that happened in Iran is that they resonate with the insurrections of conduct that one sees in the Western context. Without reducing it to a revolution in the Western vein, he approaches it with these events in mind. The Iranian Revolution fascinates Foucault precisely because it recalls these Western insurrections of conduct as it simultaneously distinguishes itself from them. Foucault concludes the essay by reflecting on his own role as an observer of the conflict. He characterizes his "theoretical ethic" as

"anti-strategic": to be respectful when a singularity revolts, intransigent as soon as power violates the universal. A simple choice, a difficult job, for one must at the same time look closely, a bit beneath history, at what cleaves it and stirs it, and keep watch, a bit behind politics, over what must unconditionally limit it. After all, that is my work; I am not the first or the only one to do it. But it is what I chose. (EEW3, 453)

Based on these remarks, conduct and counterconduct are essential for comprehending not only Foucault's thought but his conception of the task of thinking today.

Corey McCall

SEE ALSO

Christianity
Critique
Governmentality
Power
Revolution

SUGGESTED READING

Barry, Andrew, Thomas Osborne, and Nikolas Rose, eds. 1996. *Foucault and Political Reason: Liberalism, Neo-liberalism, and Rationalities of Government*. Chicago: University of Chicago Press.
Burchell, Graham, Colin Gordon, and Peter Miller, eds. 1991. *The Foucault Effect: Studies in Governmentality*. Chicago: University of Chicago Press.

14

CONFESSION

Foucault's 1975 course at the Collège investigated how the general domain of abnormality was opened up for a psychiatric understanding. Foucault attributed responsibility for this development to the articulation of sexuality as a dimension within all abnormality and, most importantly, on the necessity of each individual to avow a sexual identity (ECF-AB). His desire to analyze the conditions accounting for the appearance of this obligatory avowal of sexuality prompted him to study the Christian practice of confession. His initial examination concentrated on its practice after the Council of Trent (1545–1563), and the expansion of confession to ever-larger numbers of relationships in the period after the Reformation (EHS, 161). A special concern took shape that oriented his approach. He focused on the problematic of governance that appeared in the sixteenth century and that showed itself in the dissemination of discourses on personal conduct, on the art of directing souls, and on the manner of educating children. This intensified Foucault's exploration of the crisis of the Reformation and Counter-Reformation, which provoked in that period an anxiety over the matter of governance by putting in "question the manner in which one is to be spiritually ruled and led on this earth to achieve eternal salvation" (ECF-STP, 115–134). The exploration of the knowledge-power relations engaged in governance directed him to a treatment of the Christian pastorate, and thus to a confrontation with the formation critical to its way of obtaining knowledge and exercising power. The first major statement of the results of his research in premodern Christian experience came with his course "On the Governance of the Living," which he presented in 1980. He presented a Christian practice that embraced forms of power, knowledge, and relation to self very different from pre-Christian practices. We shall turn first to power.

Christian experience represents the development of a new form of individualizing power, that of the pastorate, which has its roots in the Hebraic image of God and his deputed King as shepherds. This power is productive, not repressive. Exercising authority over a flock of dispersed individuals rather than a land, the shepherd has the duty to guide his charges to salvation by continuously watching over them and by a permanent concern with their well-being as individuals. Christianity intensifies this concern by having pastors assume a responsibility for all the good and evil done by those to whom they are accountable and whose actions reflect on their quality as shepherds (EEW3, 308–309). Paramount in the exercise of this pastoral power is a virtue of obedience in the subject, a virtue that, unfortunately, all too often became an end in itself. The obedience that is intrinsic to the exercise and responsibilities of pastoral power involves specific forms of knowledge and subjectivity.

Now we turn to knowledge. In order to fulfill the responsibility of directing souls to their salvation, the pastor must understand the truth, not just the general truths of faith but the specific truths of each person's soul. For Foucault, Christianity is unique in the major truth obligations that are imposed on its followers. In addition to accepting moral and dogmatic truths, they must also become excavators of their own personal truth. In Foucault's words: "Everyone in Christianity has the duty to explore who he is, what is happening within himself, the faults he may have committed, the temptations to which he is exposed" (EEW1, 178). Perhaps the most dramatic illustration of this obligation to discover and manifest one's truth took place in those liturgical ceremonies in which the early Christians would avow their state as sinners and then take on the status of public penitents. Less dramatic but more enduring was the search for truth served by those practices of examination of conscience and confession that Christianity first developed in monastic life. The Christian campaign for self-knowledge was not developed directly in the interest of controlling sexual conduct but rather for the sake of a deepened awareness of one's interior life. "Cassian is interested in the movements of the body and the mind, images, feelings, memories, faces in dreams, the spontaneous movements of thoughts, the consenting (or refusing) will, waking and sleeping" (EEW1, 191). This endless task of self-scrutiny is accompanied by regular confessions to another, for verbalization of thoughts is another level of sorting out the good thoughts from those that are evil: namely, those that seek to hide from the light of public expression. Through its examination of conscience and confession, Christianity fashioned a technology of the self that enabled people to transform themselves. The principal product of this technology was a unique form of subjectivity (EEW1, 178).

Finally, we take up subjectivity. Christian practices produced an interiorization or subjectivization of the human being as the outcome of two processes. The first is the constitution of the self as a hermeneutical reality – namely, the recognition that there is a truth in the subject, that the soul is the place where this truth resides, and that true discourses can be articulated concerning it (EEW1, 95–106). The Christian self is an obscure text demanding permanent interpretation through ever more sophisticated practices of attentiveness, decipherment, and verbalization. The second process is both paradoxical and yet essential for appreciating the unique mode of Christian subjectivity. The deciphering of one's soul is but one dimension of the subjectivity that relates the self to the self. Although it involves an "indeterminate objectivization of the self by the self-indeterminate in the sense that one must be extending as far as possible the range of one's thoughts, however insignificant and innocent they may appear to be," the point of such objectivization is not to assemble a progressive knowledge of oneself for the sake of achieving the self-mastery that classical pagan thought advanced as an ideal (EEW1, 195).

The purpose of the Christian hermeneutic of the self is to foster renunciation of the self who has been objectified. The individual's relation to the self imitates both the baptismal turning from the old self to a newfound otherness and the ceremony of public penance that was depicted as a form of martyrdom proclaiming the symbolic death of the old self. The continual mortification entailed by a permanent hermeneutic and renunciation of the self makes that symbolic death an everyday event. All truth about the self is tied to the sacrifice of that same self, and the Christian experience of subjectivity declares itself most clearly in the sounds of a rupture with oneself, of an admission that "I am not who I am." This capacity for self-renunciation was built from the ascetic power with regard to oneself that was generated by a practice of obedience, and from the skepticism with respect to one's knowledge of oneself that was created by hermeneutical self-analysis. Unlike William James, who saw the satisfactions confession afforded and was puzzled that so many turned from them, Foucault grasped its dangers, and it is this awareness of danger that is distinctive of his analysis of religion. He claimed that there was a "millennial yoke of confession" and that "Western man has become a confessing animal" (EHS1, 61, 59).

Foucault's examination of confession has given rise to a variety of stimulating studies (for example, C. Taylor 2009). Among the most interesting are the studies that bring Foucault's examination of confessional practice to bear on some of the new documentation emerging from the archives of the former Soviet Union. Central to that use is the distinction that Foucault stresses between two forms of Christian confession and that I have mentioned in passing. The first was *exomologesis*, which was a public confession of oneself as a sinner. This was a status, a "way of life," symbolic and theatrical; it was Christianity's ontological confession, "not telling the truth of sin but showing the true sinful being of the sinner. It was not a way for the sinner to explain his sins but a way to present himself as a sinner" (ETS, 42). The second form is *exagoreusis*, the verbal confession in which the individual explores his interior geography of thoughts and desires in the presence of a director to whom obedience is owed. This is Christianity's epistemological confession, its hermeneutics of the self. Despite their differences, these two forms of confession possess an important trait in common. In Foucault's words: "You cannot disclose without renouncing.... Throughout Christianity there is a correlation between disclosure of the self, dramatic or verbalized, and the renunciation of self." It is the loss of that self-renunciation that characterizes the migration of confessional techniques into a modern hermeneutics of the self and its production of a positive identity (ETS, 42–43, 47–48).

But let us become more historically specific. There was a Soviet hermeneutics of the self in which confession and public penance were defining technologies. But Communist self-interrogation and self-fashioning were mutations of Eastern Christianity's practices, which were quite distinct from those of the West. For example, it has been shown that the Central Control Commissions of the Communist Party, which were so important for preserving its order and orthodoxy, imitated the functions of the ecclesiastical courts in the Russian Orthodox Church. These commissions did not wish to punish but rather come to know the defendant and have the individual reveal his or her wrongdoing so that admonition and encouragement of a change of conduct would take place. If the wrongdoing continued, the court or commission would have the person excommunicated from the Church or expelled from the Party (Kharkhordin 1999, 35–74). As a result of the show trials of the 1930s, the confessions of some of the non-Stalinist Bolsheviks may be among the most vivid of the memories that we still carry of Communism. Communism's project of creating new men, of becoming the best one could be, demanded membership in the Party. As part of the application to enter, it was usual to submit an autobiographical statement, and these had common features inasmuch as they were often guided by official questionnaires. The prospective member renounced the superstitions of a religious consciousness and denounced clerical exploitation of the poor. The most important element of these autobiographies was the conversion experience, the applicant's account of how the old bourgeois self was put aside and how one's Communist soul came to be fashioned and embraced. Among the terms for describing this conversion were "transformation," "transition," "remolding," "spiritual break," and "reversal in worldview" (Halfin 2003, 280–281, 56, 49–50, 91, 51).

After 1936, however, the Soviet hermeneutics of the self had a new political context, with the result that there was a significant change in the form of self-presentation. It was in that year that Stalin promulgated a constitution that declared that the "foundation for classless society has already been laid" and that a new stage in the Soviet State's development had begun. Because one now lived in a socialist state, the point of autobiographical statements was to show that one had always been a communist, a revolutionary from birth. Conversion stories fall away from personal accounts. "Whereas in the past autobiographers had drawn on a range of model selves, now there were two basic types: the good soul and the wicked soul" (Halfin 2003, 33, 262). Stalin's ideology determined which was which. This might be regarded as the ontological phase, to use Foucault's term, in the Communist hermeneutics of the self, and it certainly resembles Christianity's penitential form as distinct from the epistemological form of confession. Indeed, in Eastern Christianity, the experience of religious confession was very much subordinated to the penitential expression where the emphasis is on deeds and not an accounting of one's interior life. The prominence of the penitential emerges from Russian monasticism's strong commitment to constant mutual surveillance of the monks by the monks. Fraternal love is demonstrated by the monk's careful observance of his brothers, and Saint Basil the Great even compared refusals to denounce sinning brothers as equivalent to "fratricides." Eastern Orthodoxy's practice of horizontal surveillance among peers contrasts with the "hierarchical surveillance of subordinates by superiors that characterized the West." It was this horizontal technology of the self that Soviet culture embraced and that gave birth to the special role of *Kollektivs* in that culture. The self-knowing that is privileged as a result of this disciplinary matrix is not the confession of one's desires and movements of soul but rather the clarity of grasping how one is regarded in the eyes of others. The Soviet individual did not take shape through analysis of private desire but rather by "submitting to consideration by the relevant group that reviewed his or her morality." That individual's visibility is an inversion of the Panopticon's goal, for now the individual is seen by all and these may see in every direction. "United together around the victim, single persons disappear; they become part of a physically invisible yet terrifying *kollektiv*.... There's nowhere to look for help, there's nowhere to run" (Kharkhordin 1999, 114). And once the Christian conviction that the sinner can always sincerely seek forgiveness is eliminated from this penitential form, then there is created the practices that defined Stalin's regime, a "technology of no mercy" (Kharkhordin 1999, 121, 355, 356, 75–122).

James Bernauer

SEE ALSO

Abnormal
Christianity
Discipline
Ethics
Knowledge
Power
Subjectification
Truth

SUGGESTED READING

Taylor, Chloë. 2009. *The Culture of Confession from Augustine to Foucault: A Genealogy of the 'Confessing Animal.'* London: Routledge.

15

CONTESTATION

THE IDEA OF contestation appears only in early works by Foucault; in particular, in "Preface to Transgression" (on Bataille) and "The Thought of the Outside" (on Blanchot). In fact, it seems that Foucault takes the idea of contestation from Blanchot's writings; he says in "Preface to Transgression": "This philosophy of non-positive affirmation, in other words the testing of the limit, is, I believe, what Blanchot was defining through his principle of 'contestation'" (EEW2, 74). As we can see in this quotation, the idea of contestation concerns the testing of limits. Moreover, it concerns an affirmation that includes a negation. Thus, as Foucault suggests in "The Thought of the Outside," contestation resembles the linguistic strategies of negative theology (EEW2, 151). Yet negative theology is not contestation insofar as it always negates in order to reach a kind of interiority (God). In contrast, for Foucault, the idea of contestation is the negating of a limit in order to exit to an outside or exteriority that is truly outside. To conceive the outside as such, one must recognize that the outside cannot be a container of any sort since then it would have an interior. Having no interior, the outside can never be reached. As one approaches a specific place that seems to be outside, the place appears as something to get inside of. But then, having an interiority, the place is no longer the outside. The outside must be conceived as a nonplace.

If the outside cannot be reached – thus, speaking like the later Foucault, we can say that there is no final escape from power – then contestation must be conceived as an indefinite movement of negation. Each time the one contesting reaches an inside – that is, each time it reaches a limit – it must negate that particular limit. Such an incessant negation means that "contestation does not imply a generalized negation, but ... a radical break of transitivity" (EEW2, 74–75). This comment means that, when the one contesting reaches a limit, he or she must realize that it is aiming not at something but at *nothing*. As the title of Foucault's essay on Blanchot suggests, contestation must be "the thought of nothing (interior)." It does not aim to negate a general limit, but also it does not aim to negate merely a particular limit; that is, nothing general such as a unity and nothing particular such as a difference. Indeed, if contestation still finds itself to be a thought *of* something (of some sort of object), then it must take that something and make it more extreme so that it breaks free from the "of" of transitivity: "To contest is to go as far as the empty core where being attains its limit and where the limit defines being" (EEW2, 75). For Foucault, being is not a being (it is not any of the things that are), which allows being to be conceived as the void (of beings): "being attains its limit." But also, insofar as being is not any of the things that are, it is always defined as that which is over the limit of any being whatsoever: "where the limit defines being."

Although these formulas recall Heidegger, Foucault does not mention him by name. Instead, he stresses that contestation is not the kind of negation that one finds in the Hegelian dialectic. Negation in the Hegelian dialectic brings what one has negated into the "restless interiority of spirit" (EEW2, 152). Contestation, however, goes in the opposite direction. When he negates his own discourse, Blanchot makes it "lose the grasp" not only on what it just said but also on "its very power to enunciate" (ibid.). When language loses it grasp, the grasp made possible by past meaning, when it loses even its power to enunciate, then language no longer internalizes; it has truly passed to the outside. Going in the opposite direction of internalization, contestation therefore is no longer the internalizing memory we find in Hegel; it becomes forgetfulness (ibid.). As forgetfulness, contestation realizes that language must be left behind since it has always referred to interiority or to the exteriority of interiority (or the exteriority relative to and dependent on interiority). Leaving this language of interiority behind, contestation makes language "hollow itself out"; that is, it frees language of the already-said of language so that it is able to say something other than what it has said before. In this way, contested language is, as Foucault says, "a pure origin since it has itself and the void for its principle" (ibid.). But, it is also, as Foucault notes, "a re-beginning since it is past language which, but by hollowing itself out, has liberated this void" (ibid.). Contested language (which is again not the language of negative theology and not the discourse of Hegelian dialectic) is a beginning and a rebeginning. Later, in *The Archaeology of Knowledge*, Foucault calls this beginning and rebeginning the archive. Here, in his essay on Blanchot, he speaks of "not speech, but barely a murmur, barely a tremor, less than silence." By this he means less than the silence of a truth ultimately illuminating itself, but also we have "the fullness of the void, something we cannot silence, occupying all of space, the uninterrupted, the incessant, a tremor and already a murmur, not a murmur but speech" (ibid.). Thus we see ultimately that what contestation aims at is this murmur. Foucault gives us a hint as to how we might understand it. He refers (strangely going beyond Hegel) to Kant's early 1763 essay on negative magnitudes (Kant 2003, 203–241). In this essay, Kant tries to show that negative magnitudes in mathematics refer to affirmative quantities. Thus the negation of contestation does not really result at a void in the sense of "zero = 0." Through the process of hollowing out and negating the language of internalizing memory, contestation constantly tries to reach down to the infinitely small traits of language (and to the small traits of the visible, such as mirrors). These small traits are not unities of language, like meanings or references or even enunciating subjects, but the events of discourse called statements (EAK, 28).

Leonard Lawlor

SEE ALSO

> *Archive*
> *Outside*
> *Resistance*
> *Georges Bataille*
> *Maurice Blanchot*
> *Immanuel Kant*

SUGGESTED READING

Blanchot, Maurice. 1992. *The Infinite Conversation*, trans. Susan Hanson. Minneapolis: University of Minnesota Press.
　1995. *The One Who Was Standing Apart from Me*, trans. Lydia Davis. Barrytown, NY: Station Hill Press.
Kant, Immanuel. 2003. "Attempt to Introduce the Concept of Negative Magnitudes into Philosophy (1763)," in *The Cambridge Edition of the Works of Immanuel Kant, Theoretical Philosophy 1755–1770*, trans. and ed. David Walford, in collaboration with Ralf Meerbote. Cambridge: Cambridge University Press, pp. 203–241.

16

CONTROL

ALTHOUGH FOUCAULT DISCUSSED various types of "control" throughout his career (for example, the control of subjective actions by disciplinary apparatuses and institutions, or the dual control of individuals and populations under the regimes of biopower), it may be that the word decisively enters the lexicon of Foucault criticism with Gilles Deleuze's 1990 essay "Postscript on Societies of Control." In this short essay, Deleuze reminds us that Foucault's texts on the disciplinary society constitute historical work on the conditions that led up to the present rather than representing an exhaustive analysis of contemporary social conditions. As Deleuze writes,

> Foucault has thoroughly analyzed the ideal behind sites of confinement, clearly seen in the factory: bringing everything together, giving each thing its place, organizing time, setting up in this space-time a force of production greater than the sum of component forces. But Foucault also knew how short-lived this model was: it succeeded sovereign societies with an altogether different aim and operation (taking a cut of production instead of organizing it, condemning to death instead of ordering life); the transition took place gradually, and Napoleon seems to have effected the overall transformation from one kind of society into another. But discipline would in its turn begin to break down as new forces moved slowly into place, then made rapid advances after the Second World War: we were no longer in disciplinary societies, we were leaving them behind. (Deleuze 1995, 177–178)

Foucault's vision of the present and future, Deleuze insists, is not one that foresees more discipline, the increasing enclosure of subjects within stifling institutions. Rather, the present and future are characterized by the birth of new forms of power – more open, flexible methods aimed both at controlling individuals and gaining control over large aggregates such as populations, sexuality, health, and even life itself.

The late Foucault organizes these emergent regimes under the rubric of "bio-power," but "control" is the related name that Deleuze appends to these lighter, more effective, and more diffuse methods of subject production in the present and future: "*Control societies* are taking over from disciplinary societies. 'Control' is the name proposed by [William] Burroughs to characterize the new monster, and Foucault sees it fast approaching" (Deleuze 1995, 178, Deleuze's italics). Although Deleuze here insists that he takes the word "control" from Burroughs, he could just as easily have taken it from *Discipline and Punish*, where Foucault describes the "swarming [*l'essaimage*] of disciplinary mechanisms" that eventually reaches a tipping point in biopower, wherein "the massive, compact disciplines are broken down into flexible methods of control" (EDP, 211). Or perhaps Deleuze was influenced by Foucault's sense of the word in a 1984 interview, when he states: "The control of sexuality takes a form wholly other than the disciplinary form that one finds, for example, in schools" (FDE4, 662).

When power produces control in Foucault's late work, that control is consti-tuted less by a disciplinary mastery over specific individuals or populations than it is characterized by power's infiltrating ever more micrological parts of the *socius*, finally saturating even the subject's relation to herself: the discourse of identity (or self-identity) becomes a means of control under the regime of biopolitics. Of course, discipline had its own investments in subjective identity. But people have long been able to resist or reinscribe the brand of control deployed by disciplinary forms of identity: you can escape being a soldier, a wife, or a factory worker by fleeing from the army, the marriage, or the job. But it's much harder to escape the brand of con-trol deployed within the biopolitical field. Take Foucault's primary example of "sex-uality": whether you want one or not, everybody has a sexuality, which is to say a complex of self-understood sexual investments that are not necessarily tied to (or bound by) our more segmented, disciplinary roles. Not everyone has a shared dis-ciplinary identity (mother, student, cop), but everyone does have something like a sexual identity. And this remains the case even if one attempts to resist the practices and discourses of sexuality altogether: asexuality is still a sexuality. In other words, postdisciplinary power maintains control not primarily through a training grid that is deployed and reinforced in myriad institutions but largely through reorganiza-tion of the field in which any individual's self-understanding takes place. The target of control shifts from training the subject's actions at various institutional sites (the subject's relation to the hospital, the family, the school, the army, the workplace) to working primarily on the subject's relation to himself, which is at stake virtually everywhere, all the time.

Paradoxically, Foucault shows us that the more open and flexible any given regime of biopolitical relations, the more effective the means of control. As Foucault suggests in his lecture series "The Birth of Biopolitics," for example, something like neoliberal market capitalism (the market model by which we increasingly understand ourselves and our world) produces a society of control much more efficiently than a society of sovereignty, or a society of disciplinary surveillance. Neoliberal market capitalism is, in short, a much more effective means of social control than sovereignty or discipline ever was, precisely because of its supposed commitment to "openness" and flexibility. Control, like the power relations out of which it arises, can hold better and saturate a greater area of the *socius* when its grip is not merely negative (repressive) but positive (enabling) as well.

Foucault sums up this form of nondisciplinary control in the last lecture of his "Birth of Biopolitics" series in 1979, saying:

> [Y]ou can see what appears on the horizon of this kind of analysis is not at all the ideal or project of an exhaustively disciplinary society in which the legal network hemming in individuals is taken over and extended internally by, let's say, normative mechanisms. Nor is it a society in which a mechanism of general normalization and the exclusion of those who cannot be normalized is needed. On the horizon of this analysis we see instead the image, idea, or theme-program of a society in which there is an optimization of systems of difference, in which the field is left open to fluctuating processes, in which minority individuals and practices are tolerated, in which action is brought to bear on the rules of the game rather than on the players, and finally in which there is an environmental type of intervention instead of the internal subjugation of individuals. (ECF-BBIO, 259–260)

With changes in the dominant modalities, practices, and targets of power, the forms of social control are likewise transmogrified, made lighter and more intense, and simultaneously more individual and more global. The individual's identity becomes the pivot of power for the late Foucault (just as the site of training in institutions had been the primary pivot and control mechanism for discipline). Our relations to ourselves constitute that place where we are most intensely connected to biopower's modalities of social control. But precisely because of that fact, the ethical relation to the self is also a privileged place where we might effectively learn to resist biopolitical control. Where there is power, there is resistance. This helps us circle back to Deleuze's notion that control is a Foucauldian watchword for our contemporary, postdisciplinary times.

Jeffrey T. Nealon

SEE ALSO

Biopower
Discipline
Power
Gilles Deleuze

SUGGESTED READING

Deleuze, Gilles. 1995. *Negotiations: 1972–1990*, trans. Martin Joughin. New York: Columbia University Press.
Nealon, Jeffrey T. 2007. *Foucault beyond Foucault: Power and Its Intensifications since 1984.* Stanford, CA: Stanford University Press.

17

CRITIQUE

CRITIQUE IS THE philosophical mode of reflection that best characterizes Foucault's thought. To this effect, the *Dictionnaire des philosophes* entry on Foucault, pseudonymously self-authored at the end of his life, begins as follows: "To the extent that Foucault fits into the philosophical tradition, it is the *critical* tradition of Kant" (EEW2, 459, my italics). Since it designates the form of thought proper to Foucault's philosophical project, critique thus provides a lens for viewing the coherence, stakes, and trajectory of his work as a whole.

It is significant that Foucault identifies the critical tradition to which he belongs with Kant, who plays an ambivalent but fundamental role throughout Foucault's corpus. In his opening lecture at the Collège de France in 1983, Foucault marks this ambivalence by identifying Kant as the founder of "the two great traditions which have divided modern philosophy": on the one hand, "the analytic of truth," which follows the project of Kant's three Critiques by interrogating "the conditions of possibility of a true knowledge"; and on the other, "an ontology of ourselves," which, emerging from Kant's more minor texts on the Enlightenment and French Revolution, calls into question the conditions that have constituted "the present field of possible experiences" (ECF-GSO, 20–21). In other words, the opposition is between an epistemological critique that establishes the necessary and universal conditions that make legitimate knowledge possible and a political critique that uncovers the historically contingent and singular conditions that have delimited the range of what we can say, think, and do. According to Foucault, the first tradition yields the positivism of "Anglo-Saxon analytical philosophy" (ECF-GSO, 20), whereas the second issues into the "form of philosophy that, from Hegel, through Nietzsche and Max Weber, to the Frankfurt School, has founded a form of reflection in which I have tried to work" (EPPC, 95).

This is neither the first nor the last time that Foucault will counterpose these two Kantian traditions. Five years earlier, in a conference paper entitled "What

Is Critique?" Foucault locates an analogous distinction in "this kind of slippage between *critique* and *Aufklärung* that Kant wanted to denote" (EWC, 382). Whereas the three Critiques inaugurate "an analytical procedure which could be called an investigation into the legitimacy of historical modes of knowing," the question of the Enlightenment opens "a different procedure" addressed "not to the problem of knowledge, but to that of power" (EWC, 393). In Foucault's view, the first form of critical analysis, which is ultimately conducted in the service of securing true knowledge, gives rise in the nineteenth and twentieth centuries to a "scientific positivism" that will become closely linked to the "science of the State" (EWC, 388). In other words, the analytic of truth will serve as a historical support for the techniques of governmental rationality of the modern period, by means of which a state system developed "which justified itself as the reason and deep rationality of history and which, moreover, selected as its instruments procedures to rationalize the economy and society" (ibid.).

By contrast, the second strand of Kantian thought poses the question of the Enlightenment as a "call for courage" for humanity to lift the "minority condition" in which it has been "maintained in an authoritative way" – a condition that, whether in the domain of religion, law, or knowledge, is defined by humanity's "incapacity to use its own understanding precisely without something which would be someone else's direction" (EWC, 386). According to Foucault, this excessive authority that maintains humanity in its subordinate condition is a form of governmentalization, a complex set of strategies operating through and organizing the social, political, and economic institutions, relations, and practices by which the conduct of a population is managed and "through which individuals are subjugated in the reality of a social practice through mechanisms of power that adhere to a truth" (ibid.). Governmentalization thus designates a "nexus of knowledge-power" (EWC, 394) that functions through procedures of subjection to induce and control the behavior of individuals and groups. By analyzing the Enlightenment as the ongoing process through which humanity exits from this subordinate condition, Kant activates a second critical tradition, which Foucault characterizes here as a "critical attitude" (EWC, 383) that calls into question the governance of human beings with respect to what we are, think, say, and do.

Now, in Foucault's view, governmentalization emerges historically in the fifteenth and sixteenth centuries as a kind of secularization and expansion of the function of pastoral power according to which every individual is bound by a relation of absolute obedience to let themselves be governed in each of their actions for the entirety of their lives, and where this submission is mediated by a form of truth linking the self-knowledge of the individual to a dogmatic authority (EWC, 383). Once only the province of ecclesiastical institutions, this individualizing technique proliferates in every new area where the problem of governing is posed: "how to govern children, how to govern the poor and beggars, how to govern a family, a house, how to govern armies, different groups, cities, States and also how to govern one's own body and mind" (EWC, 384). Governmentalization thus emerges as an individualizing and totalizing regime of power-knowledge that produces individuals as subjects in the double sense of being "subject to someone else by control and dependence, and tied to [one's] own identity by a conscience or self-knowledge" (EEW3, 331).

However, according to Foucault, there develops in agonistic tandem with governmentalization a critical attitude that resists it, a practice or "art of not being governed quite so much" (EWC, 384). The three historical points of anchorage for this critical attitude anticipate the three areas where Kant calls for the courage of humanity to exercise its own understanding: in the religious domain, a biblical critique that contests ecclesiastical rule with respect to the truth of the Scriptures; in the legal domain, a juridical critique that asserts the rights of natural law so as to contest unjust political rule; and in the domain of knowledge, a scientific critique that contests unjustified authoritarian determinations of truth (EWC, 383–384). In each of these cases, critique functions to limit an excessive authority by challenging the production of knowledge through which the latter operates, thereby disrupting the techniques of subjection by which humanity is maintained in a minor condition. As "the movement by which the subject gives himself the right to question truth on its effects of power and question power on its discourses of truth," and thus as "the art of voluntary insubordination" and "reflected intractability," "[c]ritique would essentially insure the desubjectification of the subject in the context of what we could call, in a word, the politics of truth" (EWC, 386).

For Foucault, it is this critical attitude that Kant reactivates when he poses the question of the Enlightenment as both a critical analysis of the present condition of humanity and a summons to no longer let what we say, think, and do be governed by dogmatic forms of authority. The two Kantian traditions are thus not merely distinct from one another but diametrically opposed: on the one hand, a positivist analytic of truth enlisted to support the governmental rationality of a state system, and on the other the critical attitude of a historical ontology of ourselves that would precisely resist this form of governmentalization.

Thus, when Foucault situates his own philosophical project within the critical tradition of Kant, it is on the side of the historico-political critique of power-knowledge and its individualizing techniques of subjection. When he returns four years later to Kant's text on the Enlightenment, in "The Subject and Power," stressing the increasing importance of the task Kant set for philosophy "as a critical analysis of our world," Foucault writes that the most fundamental philosophical problem is "the problem of the present time, and of what we are, in this very moment.... [T]he political, ethical, social, philosophical problem of our days is ... to liberate us both from the state and from the type of individualization linked to the state" (EEW3, 336). In its most expansive role, then, critique will be a form of philosophical reflection that, as an ethicopolitical practice oriented by its critical attitude toward governmentalization, aims to free human beings from the processes of subjection by which we have been maintained in a condition of excessive subordination to authority. Hence we see the significant stakes of that tradition of critical thought to which Foucault belongs: "In its critical aspect – and I mean critical in a broad sense – philosophy is that which calls into question domination at every level and in every form in which it exists, whether political, economic, sexual, institutional, or what have you" (EEW1, 300–301).

Further, in order to grasp the coherent trajectory of Foucault's oeuvre through the window of critique, it is important to see how the basic opposition he draws between the two Kantian traditions is anticipated from the beginning of his work by a fundamental antagonism between the form of thought in which he lodges himself and the positivism of the human sciences. Here again, the figure of Kant plays a foundational and ambivalent role. If, in Foucault's view, the emergence of Kant in the history of thought is decisive for the larger epistemic formation of the modern period, this is because of the critical reversal or Copernican turn whereby the finite conditions of the transcendental subject, rather than the infinitude of God, become constitutive for knowledge. Thus, as Gilles Deleuze (1998, 127) notes in his book on Foucault, the Kantian revolution, by which the thought of "constituent finitude" displaces the idea of "original infinity," marks the archaeological rupture with the God-form of the classical formation.

Kantian critique thereby establishes a new possibility for thought through its conception of constitutive limits. From this epistemic opening, two opposed forms of reflection arise: on the one hand, an analytic of finitude that provides the basis for the positivist sciences of man; and on the other, a limit-experience of finitude that critically contests the status of the subject and the mode of individualization proper to the human sciences.

Foucault locates the emergence of the first, anthropological strain of thought in a moment in "Kant's *Logic*, when to his traditional trilogy of questions he added an ultimate one: the three critical questions (What can I know? What must I do? What am I permitted to hope?) then found themselves referred to a fourth, and inscribed, as it were, 'to its account': *Was ist der Mensch?*" (EOT, 371). Indeed, Foucault's chief interest in Kant's *Anthropology*, which he translated and wrote an introduction to as his secondary doctoral thesis, consists in this slippage from critical to anthropological thought, whereby the three Critiques appear retrospectively to have taken as their "secret guide" "a certain concrete image of man" (EIKA, 19). If the Kantian critical turn displaces God and the idea of the infinite as epistemic foundation, "the *Anthropology* indicates the absence of God, and occupies the void that the infinite leaves in its wake" (EIKA, 120).

This movement in Kant from critical reversal to anthropological positivism thus reflects, as though in germ form, the two moments of the broader transformation at the end of the eighteenth century, when the classical *episteme* grounded in God is supplanted by the modern *episteme* grounded in man. The epistemic formation of the modern period becomes circumscribed by the "anthropological circle" (EHM, 512), wherein man serves as both the starting point in the inquiry for truth and the end point to which this knowledge refers back (EOT, 342). Moreover, the anthropological mode of reflection that Kant helps to inaugurate is one in which man becomes tied to his own identity as an object through a form of self-knowledge of which he is also the subject: anthropology "is the knowledge of man, in a movement which objectifies him," and, "at the same time, it is the knowledge of the knowledge of man, and so can interrogate the subject himself" (EIKA, 117). As such, the anthropological circle and the human sciences it founds constitute precisely the kind of positivist knowledge that Foucault will later link to governmentalization and its individualizing techniques of subjection.

It is thus no surprise that the second form of reflection emerging in the wake of the Kantian revolution, which Foucault himself champions, will be opposed to the anthropological positivism of the analytic of finitude. Anticipating the famous final pages of *The Order of Things*, which gesture toward the erasure of man "like a face drawn in sand at the edge of the sea" (EOT, 422), Foucault concludes his *Introduction to Kant's Anthropology* by calling for "the death of man," which would consummate the death of God first made possible by the Kantian thought of constitutive finitude: "Is it not possible to conceive of a critique of finitude which would be as liberating with regard to man as it would be with regard to the infinite?" (EIKA, 124). This other form of critical thought, which Foucault here attributes to Nietzsche, conceives of constitutive limits not by reference to an anthropological question of man's essence but in terms of a limit-experience that problematizes the very status of man qua subject.

Foucault's early work can thus be understood as developing the second line of critical thought, beginning with his articulation of the tragic experience of unreason in *History of Madness*. Foucault describes this work, inspired by Nietzsche's *Birth of Tragedy*, as a "history of limits," or of the constitutive divisions through which a culture takes form by "reject[ing] something which for it will be the Exterior" (EHM, xxix). Foucault's analysis thus takes as its chief object the "limit-experience" of unreason, the exclusion of which is foundational for the historical development of Western reason and culture (ibid.). Yet this experience of unreason is expressed by a broken lineage of tragic artists, running from Sade, through Hölderlin and Nietzsche, to Artaud, whose works, bearing witness to the arbitrary violence of "the division which gives a culture the face of its positivity" (ibid.), provide a privileged site of contestation against the dominant forms of social reality that organize the modern world (EHM, 352). In this way, the project in *History of Madness* to give expression to a constitutive limit-experience opens a historicopolitical critique of Western culture that doubles as an ontology of ourselves. Foucault thus follows "that form of thought to which Nietzsche dedicated us from the beginning of his works and ... that would be, absolutely and in the same motion, a Critique and an Ontology" (EEW2, 75).

The two forms of reflection made possible by Kantian critique therefore oppose one another in the same manner as the two traditions of Kantian critical philosophy discussed earlier. Like the analytic of truth, the anthropological analytic of finitude gives rise to a form of positivist science that binds the individual to herself as both object and subject of self-knowledge; indeed, historically, it will be the human sciences, such as psychiatry, medicine, political economy, and criminology, that are enlisted in support of the normalizing objectives of a state system to manage the conduct of individuals and groups. By contrast, like the critical attitude proper to an ontology of ourselves, the experience of constitutive limits contests these individualizing techniques of subjection, calling into question the historical conditions and dividing practices that have delimited what we can be, think, say, and do.

Thus, from his initial text on the *Anthropology* to his last reflections on "What Is Enlightenment?" Foucault's critical project can be understood by reference to the two contradistinctive traditions of Kantian critique. Foucault never stops opposing, to those positivist forms of knowledge linked to government rationality, a critical ontology of the historical present. The properly Foucauldian form of critique, then, which aims to open new possibilities for what we can think and become through the desubjectification of the subject, constitutes a mode of resistance against the processes of subjection that maintain human beings in a subordinate condition to an excessive authority.

Returning once more in 1984 to the question of Enlightenment, Foucault gives a final account of his own conception of critique. What was articulated in the 1960s in terms of a limit-experience of the constitutive divisions of Western culture, and then in the 1970s as a critical attitude resisting governmentalization, now becomes formulated as "a *limit-attitude*," which is to say, "a philosophical ethos consisting in a critique of what we are saying, thinking and doing through a historical ontology of ourselves" (EEW1, 315). By contrast to the Kantian analytic of truth, which takes as its object the universal and necessary limits that make knowledge possible, the critical limit-attitude discloses the historically singular and contingent conditions that have delimited the present field of possible experience. In other words, rather than an epistemological critique of the "limits knowledge must renounce exceeding," Foucault proposes a historicopolitical critique that aims to "separate out, from the contingency that has made us what we are, the possibility of no longer being, doing, or thinking what we are, do, or think" (EEW1, 315–316). Insofar as it both reflects on our limits as so many mutable historical conditions and issues a call for courage to cross over these limits, "promot[ing] new forms of subjectivity through the refusal of this kind of individuality that has been imposed on us for several centuries" (EEW3, 336), Foucauldian critique can thus be characterized as a fundamentally transformative mode of thought, one that constitutes an ethicopolitical practice of freedom through a historicocritical ontology of ourselves.

To the extent, then, that Foucault fits into the critical philosophical tradition of Kant, it is the second, more radical form of Kantian critique, the "permanent reactivation" (EEW1, 312) of a philosophical ethos "in which the critique of what we are is at one and the same time the historical analysis of the limits that are imposed on us and an experiment with the possibility of going beyond them" (EEW1, 319).

Christopher Penfield

SEE ALSO

> *Finitude*
> *Genealogy*
> *Governmentality*
> *Human Sciences*
> *Madness*
> *Man*
> *Philosophy*
> *Resistance*
> *Truth*
> *Immanuel Kant*

SUGGESTED READING

Butler, Judith. 2002. "What Is Critique? An Essay on Foucault's Virtue," in *The Political: Readings in Continental Philosophy*, ed. David Ingram. London: Blackwell, pp. 212–226.

Deleuze, Gilles. 1988. *Foucault*, trans. Seán Hand. Minneapolis: University of Minnesota Press.

Han, Béatrice. 2002. *Foucault's Critical Project: Between the Transcendental and the Historical*, trans. Edward Pile. Stanford, CA: Stanford University Press.

Oksala, Johanna. 2005. *Foucault on Freedom*. Cambridge: Cambridge University Press.

Veyne, Paul. 1997. "The Final Foucault and His Ethics," trans. Catherine Porter and Arnold Davidson, in *Foucault and His Interlocutors*, ed. Arnold Davidson. Chicago: University of Chicago Press, pp. 225–233.

18

DEATH

EATH IS NOT one of Foucault's core explanatory concepts along the lines of being-towards-death (*Sein zum Tode*) in Heidegger or the death drive (*Todestrieb*) in Freud. It certainly does not occupy the same position in Foucault's oeuvre as discursive formations, *episteme*, power, power-knowledge, and technologies of the self – to name a few – which play very specific explanatory roles within his theoretical framework. That being said, Foucault never ceased to reflect on the question of death in indirect and oblique ways throughout his intellectual life. In fact, he even introduced *The Birth of the Clinic* as a book "about space, about language, and about death" (EBC, ix). In Foucault's reflections, death turns out to be neither a natural phenomenon, whose essence can be ascertained through empirical observation, nor an entity of the metaphysical or transcendental order. One finds that there is something essentially elusive about death, and Foucault tries to capture its elusive essence from three perspectives: (1) from the standpoint of an archaeology of discourse-knowledge; (2) from the standpoint of a genealogy of power-knowledge; and (3) from the standpoint of the relationship between subjectivity and truth.

Foucault's reflections on death from the standpoint of an archaeology of discourse-knowledge find their most intense and far-reaching manifestation in *The Birth of the Clinic* when he discusses death in the context of a radical transformation of medical discourse at the end of the eighteenth century beginning with the work of Xavier Bichat. It is in Bichat's anatomical treatises that Foucault finds a complete reconfiguration of some of the most basic relationships between life, death, and disease. These discursive objects have gained a new essence.

Foucault shows how death from the Renaissance right up to the end of the eighteenth century was conceived as the negation of life. Neither life nor disease can be investigated after death because with death we have the absolute end of life and disease. Since death is something external to life, which imposes itself on life from the outside and brings an end to it, death is in need of an agent. Disease is one of its primary agents. Although the living organism and disease are in opposition to each other and have no intrinsic relationship with each other, as they belong to different orders of being, they are both a part of nature and follow its laws. Were it not for disease and other agents of death, life would go on and on. One dies because one is in a situation surrounded by disease wherein one simply cannot live forever. It means that finitude, which in the case of living beings is their mortality, is only conceived negatively as the absence of infinity – the fact that one cannot prolong one's life forever and cannot possess eternal life. Furthermore, death abolishes all traces of individuality. It levels all the differences among individuals that one observes in life, reducing everyone equally to dust. These relationships between life, death, and disease are "discursive" to the extent that they constitute the background that enables the medical practitioner to experience, record, and analyze the various symptoms in the patient and abstract the specific characteristics of the patient as extraneous to the nature of the disease. Against this background, the medical practitioner arrives at the "pure nosological essence" of the disease and prescribes the patient a suitable remedy.

From the end of the eighteenth century, death is no longer an interruption of life. Instead of being the external limit that constrains life, it now becomes a part of life to the extent that life is now conceived essentially as a process of dying. To live means to die slowly. This novel idea of life finds its broadest formulation, from Bichat onward, in the concept of tissue degeneration. By the very fact that they function and are exposed to the outside world, tissues are prone to wear and tear, which is now conceived as a form of degeneration. Since life is a constant process of dying, death is no longer a single event but a series of degenerative events dispersed throughout the life of the organism. It is only by virtue of this everyday degeneration that the organism can contract disease, which in turn accelerates this process of degeneration. No longer a nosological being alien to life that can inhabit the living body, disease is now nothing but the dying body functioning in a drastically abnormal way. One now distinguishes between the pathological processes of a diseased body and the process of mortification that occurs throughout the organism's existence.

These new discursive relations between life, death, and disease give autopsy its central position. The pathologist can now trace the spread of the disease in the entrails of the corpse by distinguishing those lesions and alterations in the tissue that were the manifestations of the disease from other alterations that were only the manifestations of the more general process of death. Thus it is only after death and during the autopsy that the ultimate essence of the disease can be brought to light. Whereas before the knowledge of life and disease stopped with death, it is now only death that can shed light on the secrets of life and disease. Furthermore, since the interactions between the general process of mortification and the process of accelerated degeneration brought about by disease vary from person to person and are ultimately unique, death is no longer the uniform leveler of lives lived differently. It is rather what individuates every person from the broad monotony of daily life. Every opened-up corpse gives itself to a unique description heralding a transformation in scientific language. Death frees it from the exclusive Aristotelian concern for the universal. Scientific language can now focus on the particular, which has suddenly become paramount. Influenced by the ideas of Maurice Blanchot, Foucault will continue his reflections on the relationship between language and death in *Death and the Labyrinth* and "Language to Infinity." Moreover, death and finitude are no longer understood negatively as the cessation of life. In the concept of tissue degeneration and the morbid organism, they have gained a positive meaning, which Foucault will again discuss in *The Order of Things*.

In volume one of *The History of Sexuality*, Foucault tackles the question of death from the standpoint of the force relations that shape individuals in society. Up until the seventeenth century, the force relations between the sovereign and his subject are characterized by the former's right to acquisition, the ultimate expression of which was the acquisition of the life of the subject through death. This right to acquisition of life is of course not an absolute right. It can be exercised indirectly in war when the sovereign exposes his subject to the threat of death in order to save his position. It can be expressed directly through the death penalty, which the sovereign may issue on a dissenting subject, threatening her life. Life in this regime of force relations is an irreducible, inaccessible brute fact that is extremely fragile surrounded as it is by the random ruthlessness of death. Monarchic power manifests itself in the form of this randomness of death, turning the political life of the individual into one of two modes of death: to die for the sovereign in war or to be executed by the order of the sovereign. The human being is "a living animal with the additional capacity of political existence" (EHS1, 143): death.

From the seventeenth century onward, we witness a radical transformation in the relations of force. Life ceases to be simply an inaccessible brute fact. Medical and social practices bring life more and more within the ambit of knowledge. Power does not manifest itself just as a demand for death. It is now a demand for a certain kind of life. This demand takes the form of an anatomo-politics of the human body: the techniques of discipline employed on the individual human body to increase its efficiency and integrate it into the socioeconomic system through institutions such as the school, the military, the prison system, and the factory. It also takes the form of a biopolitics of the population: the regulation of the biological processes of "propagation, births, mortality, the level of health, life expectancy and longevity" (EHS1, 139). The power of death has given way to the management of life, a management that intrudes into the daily lives of individual citizens in a manner simply unimaginable in the monarchies of yore. Since force relations are characterized by a control over life and a harnessing of its powers, death now eludes the grasp of this new disciplinary power. Death is no longer the common currency in which the public transactions between the monarch and his subject are conducted. Death has retreated into the private sphere and is the only thing that truly belongs to the individual. This genealogical transformation of force relations into a political management of life correlates with the transformation of discourse into anatomical pathology, in which death becomes the inner secret of the individual to be revealed only after a dissection of her corpse. It is certainly not the case that war and killing simply vanish in this new regime of force relations. War and killing go on, sometimes on a scale far larger than anything in the past, but they are now justified in terms of life itself as a means to ward off the biological threat to the life of the population.

Whereas the archaeology of discourse-knowledge and the genealogy of power-knowledge treated death from the third-person perspective as the death of an organism and death of a political subject, from this third standpoint of the relationship between subjectivity and truth, we focus on how the subject relates to its own death. Foucault understands subjectivity as originating in a reflexive experience. This is an experience that involves knowing and acting – an epistemic-praxiological experience – wherein the actor-knower and the object acted once known are one and the same. Subjectivity is an experience of the subject working on itself in order to come to grips with the truth about itself. In Western culture, however, this experience has never remained the same. It has undergone drastic transformations over the course of history. Every particular reflexive experience configures only a specific mode of subjectivity. There is no single essence of subjectivity for Foucault but only different modes of subjectivity whereby the subject is made and unmade. Hence speculative categories such as soul, body, and original experience cannot constitute the starting point of an inquiry into subjectivity.

The reflexive experience in which a specific mode of subjectivity comes into being is conditioned in part by how the subject relates to its own death. Death here has the specific quality of being one's own death. Foucault gives us a concrete illustration of how subjectivity is constituted in the subject's relation to its own death by discussing the Stoic exercise of death meditation (*melete thanatou*), which has its roots in ancient Greek thought. In this meditation, the subject assumes the stance of someone for whom death is imminent. Death provides the subject with a vantage point from which to view its past and present. On the one hand, by thinking of the present moment as if it were the last, the subject is able to comprehend the truth of the action or thought that it entertains at that moment by being forced to ask: Is this the kind of thought or action I would like to pursue if it were my last or is there something better that I ought to be doing, one truly befitting my last moment? On the other hand, one is forced to recall everything one has done in life: If I were to die this moment, have I lived my life in a way that I ought to have done? The vantage point of death brings to the fore the truth of one's present and past. The past and the present are stripped of all the delusion and denials one normally harbors when one is secure in the knowledge that death is nowhere near. To think of one's death is not to think of the future but is only a means to ascertain the true value of one's present and past life. The mode of subjectivity we are presented here is not the contemporary historical consciousness "when it became possible to think that looking at memory is at the same time looking at the future" (ECF-HOS, 464). That would be a different kind of reflexive experience in which one's own death would be experienced in a very different way.

Eschewing the comforts of mere empirical descriptions of death and transcendental reflections on being-towards-death, Foucault devises his own methods to tackle the question of death from three seemingly mutually exclusive perspectives. In the process, death becomes a complex, irreducibly fragmented and dynamic object that presents us a different face as an object of discourse, an object of force relations, and an object of the reflexive experience of subjectivity. Whether we can bring these three faces of death together into a comprehensive whole by showing how the dynamism of discourse, the fluidity of power, and the self-transformations of the subject interact with one another is a question worth pondering indeed.

Arun Iyer

SEE ALSO

Biopower
Finitude
Life
Medicine
Xavier Bichat
Maurice Blanchot
Sigmund Freud
Martin Heidegger

SUGGESTED READING

Deleuze, Gilles. 1988. *Foucault*, trans. Seán Hand. Minneapolis: University of Minnesota Press.
Heidegger, Martin. 2010. *Being and Time*, trans. Joan Stambaugh, revised with a Foreword by Dennis J. Schmidt. Albany: The SUNY Press.
Lawlor, Leonard. 2003. *Thinking Through French Philosophy: The Being of the Question.* Bloomington: Indiana University Press.

19

DESIRE

DESIRE PLAYS A central role in modern subjectivity according to Foucault. In volume one of *History of Sexuality*, Foucault analyzes the way in which desire came to play a dominant role in the discourse of sexuality and correspondingly in our self-understanding. But Foucault questions how and why we have come to understand ourselves in this way. In his earlier work, desire seems synonymous with interest and plays a minor role if any (EAK, 69, 115). But at the end of volume one of *The History of Sexuality*, Foucault explicitly links desire with sex (sex-desire), clearly calling for a new paradigm, an ethics of pleasure rather than sex (EHS1, 157). By Foucault's own description, his three-volume series *The History of Sexuality* is a genealogy of desire ("Culture of the Self," cassette, Foucault Archives; EHS2, 12). In volumes two and three of *The History of Sexuality*, he pursues the question: "Why do we recognize ourselves as objects of desire and not agents/subjects of pleasure" ("Culture of the Self")? The concept of desire is important for understanding Foucault's notions of subjectivity, power, discourse, confession, and sexuality.

In the introduction to *The Use of Pleasure*, Foucault discusses the deviation from his original plan to have a multivolume series on the history of sexuality that focused on what he calls the four great strategic unities that emerged out of the discourse of sexuality during the eighteenth and nineteenth centuries – the hysterical woman, the masturbating child, the Malthusian couple, and the perverse adult. Rather than pursuing these four figures, he explains that a genealogy of the hermeneutics of desire was in order instead: "In any case it seemed to me that one could not very well analyze the formation and development of the experience of sexuality from the eighteenth century onward, without doing a historical and critical study dealing with desire and the desiring subject. In other words, without undertaking a 'genealogy'" (EHS2, 5). According to Foucault, a genealogy of desire would help to reveal the historical constitution of subjectivity, in the form of the desiring subject. Moreover, desire itself is a "theoretical theme" encompassing both sexuality and the Christian experience of the "flesh" (ibid.).

Foucault's genealogy of desire led him to a study of ancient Greece (EHS2) and early Rome (EHS3). In ancient Greece, there was no discourse of sexuality but instead "acts of love" (*aphrodisia*) that linked acts-pleasures-desires. The priority given to each of them changes depending on the historical period; for the Greeks the emphasis was on acts, for the Chinese the emphasis was on pleasure, and for Christians desire became the focus (EEW1, 268–269). Ancient Greek ethics emphasized not the role of desire but the use of pleasure. Ethical subjects moderated their actions but did not ferret out desire (EHS2, 54). In other words, it was not a matter of what was permitted or forbidden but of moderation or excess in terms of pleasure. From the seventeenth century onward, desire played a major role in subjectivity. Foucault attributes this shift primarily to two things: Christianity and the corresponding focus on knowing and controlling one's own desires; and psychoanalytic discourse, which sees desire as the "truth" about the self.

Foucault rejects both the Lacanian notion of desire as lack and the Freudian notion of desire as repressed. In his essay "Desire and Pleasure," Deleuze recounts Foucault saying, "I cannot bear the word *desire*; even if you use it differently, I cannot keep myself from thinking or living that desire = lack, or that desire is repressed. [W]hereas myself, what I call pleasure is perhaps what you call desire; but in any case I need another word than *desire*" (Deleuze 1997, 189).

For Foucault, desire as repression and desire as constituted through the law both rely on the same juridico-discursive conception of power as negative. We cannot liberate our desire without invoking this conception of power that manifests as limit and repression. Foucault develops his analytics of power as a response to the inadequacy of this juridico-discursive model of power (EHS1, 82–83). His analytics of power demonstrates power's productive potential; it does not simply limit but produces new objects, such as desiring subjects, through practices and discourse such as confession. Desire plays a central role in volume one of *The History of Sexuality*; desire becomes the significant act of transgression that needs to be confessed. Good Christians had to follow the imperative: "Not only will you confess to acts contravening the law, but you will seek to transform your desire, your every desire, into discourse" (EHS1, 21). Discourse becomes the vehicle for speaking the truth about oneself, and the truth about oneself is viewed as one's desires. Confession plays the role of tying one to one's desire because it forces the articulation of the unsaid into the said. And through its scrutiny of desires and the compulsion to make them public, the Church imbued them with significance and heightened their importance. Confession serves to individualize and normalize: "The truthful confession was inscribed at the heart of the procedures of individualization by power" (EHS1, 59). Christianity, through its emphasis on discerning and confessing desires, makes desire the central truth about the subject. Subjectivity in the contemporary West cannot be understood outside normalizing power relationships. Power operates through a variety of discourses – religious, scientific, medical, and psychological – to produce the desiring subject. The deployment of sexuality with its multifarious forms of normalization and control operates through desire. This explains Foucault's warning that we cannot attack sexuality through sex-desire but must look to bodies and pleasures for a new understanding of subjectivity based perhaps on an ethics of pleasure (EHS1, 157, 159).

Margaret A. McLaren

SEE ALSO

> *Body*
> *Christianity*
> *Confession*
> *Pleasure*
> *Sex*
> *Gilles Deleuze*

SUGGESTED READING

Deleuze, Gilles. 1997. "Desire and Pleasure," in *Foucault and His Interlocuters*, ed. Arnold Davidson. Chicago: University of Chicago Press, pp. 183–192. Originally published as "Desir et Plaisir," *Magazine litteraire* no. 325 (October 1994): 57–65.
Rajchman, John. 1991. *Truth and Eros: Foucault, Lacan and the Question of Ethics*. London: Routledge.

20

DIFFERENCE

U
NLIKE MANY OF his contemporaries such as Deleuze, Derrida, Irigaray, or Lyotard, Foucault is not usually considered a philosopher of difference in the sense that the concept of difference plays a central role in his thought. Commentators dispute whether his work can be subsumed under a single description, and in the course of his career he put forward a variety of descriptions of his overall project: the history of the different ways in which human beings have been made subjects, power, experience, and the conditions of possibility of certain kinds of knowledge and certain kinds of thinkers. He sometimes described his work as an attempt to carry out an internal ethnography of modern European culture and rationality, one that focused on its limits or systems of exclusion, rejection, and refusal. He defined his problem as that of exposing the implicit systems that imprison us: "I would like to understand the system of limits and exclusion that we practice without knowing; I would like to expose the cultural unconscious" (FDE2, 189). In this regard, some of his work investigated the forms of identity or sameness of modern European culture, while some of it investigated the limits or divisions that defined this culture, notably the divisions between reason and madness, normal and pathological. In this sense, for example, he described *The History of Madness* as the history of a division or a rupture found in every society. By contrast, *The Order of Things* is a history of the way in which European society organizes the resemblances as well as the differences between things into rational schemas: "*The History of Madness* is the history of difference while *The Order of Things* is the history of resemblance, the same and identity" (FDE1, 498).

Although he always denied that he was a structuralist or that he made use of the techniques of structural analysis, in an interview in 1967 he went as far as aligning himself with a nontechnical, generalized, and philosophical structuralism that would interrogate the present moment in history and culture and discern what was happening (FDE1, 581). The Nietzschean conception of philosophy as a certain kind of diagnosis of the present provided one of the most enduring ways in which Foucault described his work (FDE1, 553, 606). He often suggested that the point of his retrospective analyses was to undertake a critique of "our time" (FDE2, 183). On several occasions toward the end of his life, Foucault sought to spell out his own critical relationship to the present by comparing it with Kant's answer to the question "What is Enlightenment?" Foucault argues that this apparently minor work signals the appearance of a new type of question for philosophy, one directed at the nature of the present in which the philosopher lives and writes: "What is happening today? What is happening now? What is this 'now' in which we all live and which is the site, the point [from which] I am writing" (ECF-GSO, 11)? In his own "What Is Enlightenment?" essay, Foucault describes Kant's approach to the present historical moment as essentially negative, unlike the teleological approach in his other writings on history: "He is not seeking to understand the present on the basis of a totality or of a future achievement. He is looking for a difference: What difference does today introduce with respect to yesterday" (EEW1, 305)?

These comments show that Foucault's own understanding of his work bore traces of the philosophy of difference that flourished in France during the 1960s. Not surprisingly, his work toward the end of that decade shows the strongest signs of his alignment with those engaged in the philosophical revaluation of difference. Derrida's *Of Grammatology*, *Voice and Phenomenon* and *Writing and Difference* were published in 1967, and Deleuze's *Difference and Repetition* appeared in 1968 and *The Logic of Sense* in 1969. Foucault published a brief review of *Difference and Repetition* in 1969 in which he summarized this book as announcing the end of the philosophy of representation and the beginning of the philosophy of difference: "At last it is possible to think the differences of today, to think today as the difference of differences" (FDE1, 770). Foucault wrote a longer article on these two books by Deleuze, "Theatrum Philosophicum," which appeared in 1970.

During this period at the end of the 1960s and beginning of the 1970s, Foucault sought to clarify the kinds of differences analyzed in his major studies in the history of systems of thought and knowledge. These undertook the analysis of conditions of possibility of objects of knowledge in the human sciences, where, unlike in Kant, these were considered to be historical conditions underpinning certain kinds of empirical knowledge and practice. Foucault sometimes described this historical a priori as the "cultural unconscious" of a particular society at a particular time. His concern to identify changes in relation to the forms of understanding and treatment of madness (*The History of Madness*), medical science (*Birth of the Clinic*), and the empirical sciences of language, wealth, and life (*The Order of Things*) gave rise to a perception of his work as focusing on discontinuity rather than continuity in the history of the sciences. He responded directly to this perception in response to questions from the journal *Esprit*, published in May 1968, and in response to questions from the Epistemological Circle at the École Normale Supérieure, published in *Cahiers pour l'analyse* in summer 1968 (FDE1, 673–731). Both of these publications anticipate his sustained effort in *The Archaeology of Knowledge* (1969) to theorize the kinds of discontinuities he had analyzed in his earlier work.

In the Introduction to *The Archaeology of Knowledge*, he contrasts the concern with structures and long-term continuities among social historians with the focus on discontinuities among historians of science, thought, and philosophy, describing the latter as "paying more and more attention to the play of difference" (EAK, 6). This contrast, however, is only a rhetorical introduction to Foucault's claim that there is an epistemological mutation under way in the historical disciplines that has made discontinuity a key concept. Historians now work with many different kinds of discontinuities, such as epistemological ruptures or thresholds in the history of the sciences, points of inflection in the growth rate of a population, or the transition from one set of techniques to another in economic, medical, or scientific practices. He counterposes this discontinuist history with earlier conceptions of history as a domain of continuous and orderly progression. On a more general and polemical level, he aligns the latter with humanist and historicist themes ultimately grounded in "the sovereignty of consciousness" (EAK, 12). Foucault's own alignment with the philosophical revaluation of difference is clear in his diagnosis of the source of the attachment to these themes:

> It is as if it was particularly difficult, in the history in which men retrace their own ideas and their own knowledge, to formulate a general theory of discontinuity, of series, of limits, unities, specific orders and differentiated autonomies and dependences. As if, in that field where we had become used to seeking origins, to pushing back further and further the lines of antecedents, to reconstituting traditions, to following evolutive curves, to projecting teleologies, and to having constant recourse to metaphors of life, we felt a particular repugnance to *conceiving of difference*, to describing separations and dispersions, to dissociating the reassuring form of the identical. (EAK, 12, emphasis added)

However, invocations of difference such as these remain largely external to the structure and content of Foucault's analyses. To see how certain features of the philosophy of difference affect the details of his concepts of discourse, discursive formations, and the "statements" (*énoncés*) of which these are composed, we need to examine more closely the manner in which he defines these as systems of dispersion. Foucault begins with the observation that the unity of the discourses such as classical political economy or seventeenth- and eighteenth-century natural history is that of a "dispersion of elements" (EAK, 72). His hypothesis is that the identity of a particular series of dispersed elements can be captured if he can determine "the specific rules in accordance with which its objects, statements, concepts, and theoretical options have been formed" (ibid.). He therefore sets out to define specific discourses or discursive formations by the rules governing the formation of their objects, enunciative modalities, and concepts, as well as the discursive strategies that they make available. Along each of these axes, he finds not well-defined structures but systems of dispersion. So, for example, as far as the objects of discourse in a given field are concerned, a discursive formation such as nineteenth-century psychiatry is defined by a group of relations between the different authorities that govern the emergence, delimitation, and specification of its "highly dispersed" objects (EAK, 44). Similarly, the enunciative modalities of a given discursive formation are not derived from the unity of a subject of knowledge or reason in the manner of Kant but rather from the dispersion of the subject of the discourse concerned:

> In the proposed analysis, instead of referring back to the synthesis or the unifying function of a subject, the various enunciate modalities manifest his dispersion. To the various statuses, the various sites, the various positions that he can occupy or be given when making a discourse. To the discontinuity of the planes from which he speaks.... Thus conceived, discourse is not the majestically unfolding manifestation of a thinking, knowing, speaking subject, but, on the contrary, a totality, in which the dispersion of the subject and his discontinuity with himself may be determined. (EAK, 54–55)

Foucault poses the question whether, and if so how, these systems of dispersion can constitute a unified body of discourse. His answer is that there are, in a given empirical field at a given time, definite relations of dependency between the rules governing each of the four dimensions of discourse. Insofar as these interrelated sets of rules tell us what must be related for a particular statement to be made, a particular concept to be used, a particular strategic option to be followed, we can speak of a system of formation for a given discourse: "To define a system of formation in its specific individuality is therefore to characterize a discourse or group of statements by the regularity of a practice" (EAK, 74). Conceived in this manner, discursive formations are identifiable objects that undergo constant modification while remaining the same. They are temporal entities in the same way that a culture or a tradition exists over time in and through its constantly modulated or varied instances. Defined by sets of relations between dispersed elements, they are differential entities in the sense in which for Derrida a language is a system of *différance* or for Deleuze a transcendent Idea is an open-ended and evolving system of relations.

This conception of discourse and the peculiar character of discursive formations was carried over into Foucault's programmatic remarks in his Inaugural Lecture delivered at the Collège de France in December 1970, "The Order of Discourse." His primary objective in this lecture was to present the case that in every society there are mechanisms for the control of discourse and to identify the important ones for Western European societies: procedures of exclusion and division such as those between reason and madness, truth and falsehood; procedures internal to the order of discourse such as practices of commentary, the principal of authorship, membership of disciplines, discursive societies, subjection to rituals, doctrines, and the social distribution of access to certain kinds of discourse. The overall aim of these mechanisms, he suggests, is to set limits to the proliferation of discourse and the effects of chance in its production and circulation. The philosophical antipathy toward difference is not mentioned by name, but Foucault does list a number of philosophical themes that sustain and support this system of exclusions and limits: the founding subject, the idea of an originary experience, and the idea of universal mediation. These are all themes derived from the Hegelian and phenomenological traditions opposed in different ways by the philosophers of difference.

Foucault's concern with questioning the will to truth and insistence on the density, complexity, and event-like character of discourse is not the same as Derrida's project of drawing attention to the antifoundational role of the play of difference or Deleuze's interest in restoring the philosophical integrity of a concept of difference in itself. However, he shares the same antagonisms toward the philosophical guarantees of consciousness and continuity. Moreover, the methodological requirements of his proposed archaeology of discourse raise theoretical problems that overlap with those raised by the philosophers of difference. First among these is the question of the nature and status of events, which are not themselves corporeal entities but are undoubtedly produced by and have effects on relations between bodies: they occur "as an effect of, and in, material dispersion" (EAK, 231). Foucault's understanding of events closely resembles that of Deleuze, who in *The Logic of Sense* describes events as incorporeal entities expressed in language but attributed to configurations of bodies in the transition from one state of affairs to another. Foucault's conclusion might be read as a description of Deleuze's approach, namely that "the philosophy of the event should advance in the direction, at first sight paradoxical, of an incorporeal materialism" (EAK, 231).

The second problem is that posed by the attempt to conceptualize discursive formations as at once discontinuous with one another and themselves while at the same time maintaining their identity. This is the problem of the status of this discontinuity that cannot be conceived on the basis of the unity of the subject or the temporal instant. Beyond these and outside existing philosophies of time and the subject, we must develop "a theory of discontinuous systematization" (*une théorie des systématicités discontinues*) (EAK, 231; FOD, 60). Foucault's call is echoed by Deleuze's suggestion that philosophy is the "logic" or theory of multiplicities (Deleuze 1995, 147; Deleuze and Parnet 2007, 148). Deleuze's distinctive contribution to this problem of finding ways to conceive of a form of identity or unity that is not identical to itself lies in his elaboration of specific examples of such multiplicities. Thus, in Chapter 4 of *Difference and Repetition*, he outlines a concept of qualitative or pure multiplicities that he variously describes as Ideas, Problems, or Structures. These are differential structures in the sense that they are composed of purely formal elements defined by their reciprocal relations to one another. Thus, for example, Deleuze takes the Idea of society to be a system of differential relations of property and relations of production established between unspecified "supports" of ownership and labor power. Defined in this manner, intrinsically rather than by external relations, the Idea or social structure constitutes "an internal multiplicity – in other words, a system of multiple, non-localizable connections between differential elements which is incarnated in real relations and actual terms" (Deleuze 1994, 183). Deleuze developed further examples of differential multiplicities in his major collaboration with Felix Guattari, *A Thousand Plateaus* (Deleuze and Guattari 1987). However, neither he nor Foucault ever elaborated the theory of discontinuous systems called for in *The Order of Discourse.*

Foucault's "Theatrum Philosophicum" appeared in November 1970, one month before he delivered his inaugural lecture. Judith Revel argues that this text marks an essential turn in Foucault's thought, on the grounds that, over and above its superficial appearance as an account of Deleuze's books, it represented his first explicit problematization of the notion of difference (Revel 1996, 727). This problematization occurs in the form of Foucault's uncritical endorsement of Deleuze's account of the manner in which throughout the history of philosophy difference has been subordinated to figures of identity and sameness, and his account of what is required to overturn that subordination and to free difference: "Categories dictate the play of affirmations and negations, establish the legitimacy of resemblances within representation, and guarantee the objectivity and operation of concepts. They suppress anarchic difference, divide differences into zones, delimit their rights, and prescribe their task of specification with respect to individual beings. On the one side, they can be understood as the a priori forms of knowledge, but on the other, they appear as an archaic morality, the ancient decalogue that the identical imposed upon difference. Difference can only be liberated through the invention of an a-categorical thought" (EEW2, 359).

Foucault's archaeological studies seemed to chart the forms of this dominant image of thought insofar as they sought to identify the system of categories and concepts that enable the distribution of differences and similarities within a given group of empirical fields: "In each case, it is always a matter of reconstituting the manner in which a space is established so that difference can be recuperated within the identitarian regime of the other, understood as the other *of* the same rather than as other *to* the same" (Revel 1996, 729, my English translation, Revel's italics). However, Revel points out, the references to Sade, Artaud, Klossowski, Bataille, and Blanchot throughout this text remind us of Foucault's long-held interest in other ways of thinking differently and thereby thinking difference independently of any relation to the same. In these literary texts, she suggests, we can observe Foucault's repeated efforts to discern the outlines of a "non-categorial thought" and an understanding of difference that is not subordinated to the same (Revel 1996, 731). His early essays on Bataille (EEW2, 69–87) and Klossowski (EEW2, 123–135) represent preliminary stages in this experiment with other ways of thinking of difference. Bataille's concept of transgression proved to be a timid and dialectical step since it is inescapably bound up with the notion of the limit that is transgressed. Foucault's article on Blanchot (EEW2, 147–169) represented a further attempt to discern a thought that, "in relation to the interiority of our philosophical reflection and the positivity of our knowledge, constitutes what in a phrase we might call "the thought of the outside" (EEW2, 150). Foucault's interest in Port-Royal logic and grammar, along with his later interest in the language of schizophrenics, also bears witness to this enduring interest in an a-grammatical, outside thought. Revel points to later evidence of his interest in non-categorial thought in texts such as those by Pierre Rivière and Herculine Barbin.

"Theatrum Philosophicum" stands out as a text in which Foucault acknowledges, via the work of Deleuze, the requirements and the stakes of the philosophical enterprise of thinking difference in and for itself. However, it is a further step to suggest that he engages directly in this project. There is a difference between an interest in thought that does not conform to existing categories and concepts and an interest in thinking differently the concept of difference itself. The latter project was never central to Foucault's work in the way that former was. His final published works returned to the practice of genealogical enquiry designed to expose discontinuities in the ways in which individuals conceived of themselves as the subjects of sexuality. In his Introduction to *The Use of Pleasure*, he links this inquiry with the ongoing task of thinking differently: "[W]hat is philosophy today – philosophical activity, I mean – if it is not the critical work that thought brings to bear on itself? In what does it consist, if not in the endeavor to know how and to what extent it might be possible to think differently, instead of legitimating what is already known?" (EHS2, 8–9).

Paul Patton

SEE ALSO

> *Multiplicity*
> *Outside*
> *Structuralism*
> *Transgression*
> *Georges Bataille*
> *Maurice Blanchot*
> *Gilles Deleuze*

SUGGESTED READING

Patton, Paul. 2010. *Deleuzian Concepts: Philosophy, Colonization, Politics*. Stanford, CA: Stanford University Press.

Revel, Judith. 1996. "Foucault lecteur de Deleuze: De l'écart à la différence," *Critique* nos. 591–592 (August–September): 723–735.

21

DISCIPLINE

"D ISCIPLINE" IS THE term Foucault uses to designate a particular kind of power that operates directly on individual bodies and that may be used as an anchoring point for other types of power. Contesting the traditional philosophical and political notions of power, Foucault rejects the idea of power as mere physical violence and moves away from the Freudian concept of repression and the Marxist notions of production and revolution to a sense of power that is, in Arnold Davidson's words, "physical and calculated without having to be violent" (ECF-AB, xx). Foucault focuses on what he terms the positive aspects of power, the ways in which individuals are coerced into accepting standards for behavior that they believe constitute *the norm*. In doing so, individuals come to act as if they are always under surveillance. By constantly comparing, observing, and examining individual bodies, disciplinary power conditions individuals by dictating their desires and coercing them into particular ways of acting.

Although Foucault formally introduces the idea of discipline in *Discipline and Punish*, one can trace its emergence in earlier texts such as *History of Madness*, in which he explores the institutionalization and treatment of people society regards as mad. There Foucault focuses on the way these persons are managed and on the mechanisms society uses to make madness intelligible within a framework of reason. In doing so, he draws parallels between the confinement of the mad and the separation and exclusion of lepers. His core concern in *History of Madness* is the way that medical institutions exercise power to manage seemingly dangerous individuals, including criminals, the mad, and those who are not productive. Foucault's analysis of these issues prefigures his formal use of *the norm* and *normalization*. He views medical mechanisms and their processes of confinement as a form of *medical gaze*, an exercise of continuous surveillance and visual coercion that anticipates his later work in *Discipline and Punish* and *History of Sexuality*, volume 1: *The Will to Know*.

In *Discipline and Punish*, his well-known treatise on the birth of the prison, Foucault painstakingly describes the concept of discipline and the methods he later terms "disciplinary technology" (ECF-SMD, 242n1). In the first two parts of the text, Foucault delineates the emergence of a new form of power – discipline – that radically differs from "sovereign power," an older form associated with monarchs. Sovereign power is both visible and external, and the monarch invokes public spectacle to demonstrate his absolute domination. *Discipline and Punish* thus begins with the public execution of Damiens for regicide (murder of the king), the most egregious crime in a monarchy and a direct attack on state authority. To reassert and reinforce the sovereign's absolute authority, Damiens was subjected to extreme torture: his flesh was torn from his breasts; he was burned with lead, oil, wax, and sulfur; he was drawn and quartered by horses; and his ashes were scattered to the winds. Under sovereign power, the sovereign's domination is visibly and publicly exercised against the body of criminals who, like Damiens, violate the sanctity of the sovereign's laws.

Foucault contrasts this public spectacle of power with a more modern form of power, one that operates invisibly while simultaneously making its target, the individual body, more visible. In the exercise of disciplinary power, individual bodies are subjected to a continual process of surveillance, examination, judgment, and correction. Disciplinary power employs the norm to correct behavior and transform individuals into *docile bodies* who are measured and ranked by their relationship to the norm (EDP, 137–138). The *norm* is a means of exercising domination, a "positive" standard that directs and sets the outer limits of acceptable behavior. It is not derived from natural law but comes instead from an attempt to make individual bodies both docile and socially useful. *Normalization* is a process involving the "positive technique of intervention and transformation" (ECF-AB, 50). It seeks to manage bodies and delimit dangerous individuals while simultaneously coercing each body into compliance with the norm and productivity. The mechanisms by which we train schoolchildren to be "good" pupils and "good" citizens illustrate how disciplinary power operates through the norm and the process of normalization. Disciplinary power, unlike sovereign power, relies heavily on rewards to induce correct behavior. And when individuals do not comply with the norm, the remedy is not simply punishment but more training and more discipline.

Although discipline is aimed at managing individual bodies, it is concerned not only with minute levels of physical and anatomical functioning; it also aims to manage attitudes and potentialities and to generate knowledge about the individual bodies on which it acts. Through that process, disciplinary power introduces an apparent paradox: it creates and reinforces a kind of individuality, even as it molds individual bodies into useful components of larger social machines, which range from the military and prisons to schools, hospitals, and factories. The individual body is thereby situated in a modern matrix of power, one that is concerned both with how the body operates and with what the body produces.

To further illustrate the shift from sovereign power to disciplinary power, Foucault contrasts discipline with both monastic life and slavery as alternative forms of domination. Foucault argues, for instance, that slavery relies solely on the physical appropriation of bodies through external punishment, whereas disciplinary power manages to control bodies without direct confrontation. And yet, as Foucault explains, although discipline differs from slavery because it is not based on a relation of appropriation of bodies, "the elegance of discipline" lies in the fact that it can dispense with this "costly and violent relation" while remaining no less effective (EDP, 137). One might suggest that the Atlantic slave trade combined both the appropriation of bodies and the imposition of discipline on black slaves to transform them into docile bodies that accept, rather than resist, the slaveholders' norm. Nonetheless, Foucault's essential point is that disciplinary power operates primarily by facilitating an individual's acceptance of the norm and the state's authority rather than through confrontational force and public spectacle.

In Foucault's view, the shift from sovereign power to disciplinary power came about because sovereign power is inefficient. Under sovereign power, public acceptance of the monarch's authority is signified through outward behavior and language, and spectacle is the vehicle by which the sovereign seeks to obtain the desired behavior. But with disciplinary power, society is no longer satisfied with the signifying elements of behavior and language alone. Instead, it seeks to maintain a constant constraint on the body, an efficient, ongoing, and ever-present coercion with political effects.

The shift from a violent external spectacle of power (as in the torture of Damiens) to the ongoing constraints of discipline might seem to be "humane," but Foucault argues that the seemingly humane nature of disciplinary power is false. Discipline is not grounded in an appeal to humanity. Instead, it is a more intense and insidious form of power, one that produces "subjected and practiced bodies" in ways that are more coercive, even if they do not seem outwardly violent (EDP, 138).

After discussing the emergence of discipline and the differences between sovereign power and disciplinary power, Foucault devotes the remainder of *Discipline and Punish* to a detailed description, with examples, of the attributes and technologies of disciplinary power. His focus is on the ways that disciplinary power manages and affects individual bodies, and the technologies through which that power transforms individual bodies into components of a larger social machine. At the core of discipline is the ability to make a body both docile and useful, to subject it to power and thereby improve it. Disciplinary techniques are employed by institutions such as families, schools, prisons, the military, and the state. Society is concerned not only with the operation of the body's physical anatomy but also with the body's engagement in the larger political landscape, such that the body itself becomes a method by which society transforms the individual into a docile and productive citizen.

For Foucault, the use of disciplinary mechanisms by social institutions and modern states becomes singularly important. This focus is in keeping with his sense that the exercise of power has shifted away from a sovereign, and that power is not held like a commodity. In a monarchy, the exercise of authority is personal, and the locus of power resides in the person of the king. Disciplinary power, on the other hand, is relational rather than personal: power circulates through a hierarchical structure, and it relies on the distribution and ranking of individual bodies within that structure. In the lectures course called "Society Must Be Defended," Foucault explains that disciplinary power is not divided between those who have it and those who do not, or between those who hold it and those who are subject to it. Instead, individuals who exercise disciplinary power are interchangeable. Power thus "circulates" through "networks," and individuals are "relays" for power, which both passes through them and is applied to them (ECF-SMD, 29). As a result, power "is never localized here or there, it is never in the hands of some, and it is never appropriated in the way that wealth or a commodity can be appropriated" (ibid.).

The techniques of disciplinary power operate through meticulous control of the body and its very minute functioning. Foucault contrasts this technology with sovereign and juridical power, which operate according to the law rather than the norm. The model, he suggests, is that of turning an ordinary man into a soldier, or transforming an undisciplined child into a well-behaved pupil. These forms of control are exercised not only in this more public domain: they become central in the way society manages criminals. But even as Foucault examines the birth of the modern prison, his larger point is that disciplinary power is present anywhere there is a norm – including the norm that underlies our educational system. If we have come to see parallels between schools and prisons, it is largely because Foucault so clearly sketched them.

At the core of the disciplinary process are three distinct technologies – hierarchical observation, normalizing judgment, and examination – by which individuals are trained and transformed into docile and useful bodies. The process is grounded on the norm, which functions as a principle of coercion and correct action, a standard characterized by basic aspects of "time, activity, behavior, speech, body, attitude, and sexuality" (EDP, 178). The three technologies are employed to normalize each individual body. The first technology, hierarchical observation, allows a person to view subjects from a position of hypervisibility through spatial designs that highlight the power relationship and enforce a visual coercion. Factory floors, military inspections, and school classrooms are all examples. From the vantage point of hierarchical observation, the examiner engages in surveillance and subjects individual bodies to a normalizing judgment that culminates with an examination. The examination is a ritualized means by which each individual is subjected to a disciplinary gaze, compared against the norm, ranked, classified, and ultimately reformed toward the norm. Those who comply with the norm are rewarded and given a higher status within the hierarchy, whereas those who do not receive further training and discipline. The effective use of hierarchical observation requires the distribution of individual bodies in space through enclosure, partitioning, and other methods (EDP, 141). It also dictates "their separation, their alignment, their serialization, and their surveillance" within a field of visibility (ECF-SMD, 242). By doing so, discipline creates "functional sites," spaces in which individuals are located and supervised rather than being excluded. But the distribution of individuals is not merely spatial – discipline is also "an art of rank" in which bodies do not occupy a fixed position but circulate through a network of relations (EDP, 146). Places and ranks are disciplinarily created spaces that are "simultaneously architectural, functional and hierarchical" and transform "dangerous multitudes into ordered multiplicities" (EDP, 148). By fostering a desire for efficiency and good order, the supervision and distribution of bodies seeks to eliminate spaces in which individuals might form collectives and resist.

The technologies of discipline also require the control of activity and the detailed partitioning of time. The two are intertwined: "In the correct use of the body, which makes possible a correct use of time, nothing must remain idle or useless" (EDP, 152). By analyzing space and rearranging activities, discipline becomes the machinery for adding up and capitalizing time, and time itself becomes an aspect of the norm and normative judgment, a means for measuring the extent to which individuals are dominated by discipline. Through the coordination of movement, gesture, and time, disciplinary power extracts from time "ever more available moments and, from each moment, ever more useful forces" (EDP, 153). In the end, individuals cannot escape time; they can only become more efficient in time, and thereby more efficiently dominated.

An individual subjected to these technologies "assumes responsibility for the constraints of power," inscribes "the power relation" within himself, and thereby "becomes the principle of his own subjection" (EDP, 202–203). In effect, discipline trains individuals to become the front-line agents of their own repression. And, in doing so, discipline creates individuals who are easily managed and have great utility for the state.

Through the process of normalization – the "means of correct training" – disciplinary power shapes our notions of what is natural and correct and thus determines our corresponding behaviors, and it does so even in the most routine circumstances. For example, imagine that a teacher enters a kindergarten classroom and rings a bell. The bell signals to the children that they should take their seats, become silent, and await instruction. The ringing of the bell is a simple examination, and the students have learned that this is a moment in which they are being judged for their behavior. The teacher observes the students hierarchically, and the normalizing judgment is this: Do they comply, and how quickly do they take their seats and stop talking? Do they display the proper attitude? And if they do not, what do they do instead? To the extent that students either do or do not master the norm associated with the ringing of the bell, they are deemed to be "good" pupils who are rewarded and promoted for their correct behavior or "bad" pupils in need of further training and in danger of not moving on. The students have internalized that judgment, and by ringing the bell and observing their behavior, the teacher is coercing their compliance with the norm through her normative gaze. For Foucault, the process is a type of control without punishment ("penality"), because individual pupils are rewarded only after an examination, and those who fail to comply with the norm will be shamed for non-compliance and retrained.

Education is a continuous application of all three disciplinary technologies, and it demonstrates the degree to which we accept disciplinary power as common. Hence, education trains us to become accustomed to the partitioning of space, time, and movement, and the system of ranking and rewards encourages individuals to accept the norm. As Foucault explains, "disciplinary coercion establishes in the body the constricting link between an increased aptitude and an increased domination" (EDP, 138). As individuals are rewarded and promoted for their success at complying with the norm, they become increasingly invested in maintaining the norm and the disciplinary process by which they are judged and ranked. This effect is starkly evident in American law schools, where students become obsessed with both the ranking of particular schools and their individual class ranking, and the best students from the best schools become the next generation of law professors – the individuals charged with the discipline of future students. Individuals are thereby defined (and define themselves) by the place they occupy in a hierarchy: their relationship within the context of the whole and to others within that whole. This is why Foucault asserts that individuality is an effect of power.

Foucault uses a variety of modern institutions to illustrate the technologies of discipline (including the military, schools, hospitals, and factories), but the modern prison is his archetypal model for the exercise of discipline and disciplinary power within modern society. Although Foucault did prisoner reform work in France with Groupe d'information sur les prisons (GIP), he did not visit a prison until 1971, when he came to the United States and toured the Attica Correctional Facility in New York state. Foucault's visit to Attica and his reading of Black Panther literature are thought to have influenced his writings on power and possibly prisons.

The "Panopticon," an adaptation of Bentham's concept for the ideal prison, is Foucault's model for the efficient operation of disciplinary technology. It features a central tower with cells surrounding the tower in a backlit circle, an arrangement that allows a central supervisor located in the tower to observe each and every one of the prisoners in their cells. But the Panopticon is more than simply a model prison: it is a symbolic and "generalizable model of functioning" that illustrates the effect of disciplinary technology in everyday life. In its various forms, the panoptic schema serves "to treat patients, to instruct schoolchildren, to confine the insane, [and] to supervise workers" (EDP, 205). The panoptic mechanism is starkly different from a dungeon, and it highlights the ways in which disciplinary power operates differently from sovereign power. Whereas the dungeon is dark, confined, and hidden away, the Panopticon is well lit and visible. The structure of the central tower makes it impossible for a prisoner to verify, at any given moment, whether he or she is being observed. Ultimately, the prisoners are complicit in their own domination: they behave as if they are constantly under surveillance and consequently conform their behavior to the norm. The result is the "automatic functioning of power" through "permanent surveillance" and without the immediate use of force (EDP, 201). In short, the inmates are "caught up in a power situation in which they themselves are the bearers" (ibid.). For Foucault, the elegance of the panoptic mechanism is that disciplinary power functions on multiple levels without the need to physically manipulate prisoners. In the Panopticon, "visibility is a trap" (EDP, 200) in which the inmates themselves are permanently visible and, in Bentham's words, power itself is both "visible and unverifiable" (EDP, 201). Given these circumstances, the individual prisoners ultimately discipline themselves, and their domination is not dependent on any other person. Anyone can take the supervisor's place in the central tower, whereas sovereign power required a specific individual who served as the monarch and who was not interchangeable. Foucault's discussion of the Panopticon thus allows us to see more clearly how disciplinary power operates without a sovereign or the spectacle of public violence.

In the final section of volume one of *The History of Sexuality* and in lectures that date from soon after the publication of *Discipline and Punish*, Foucault begins to argue that a "new technology of power" – which he calls biopower – emerged in the second half of the nineteenth century (ECF-SMD, 242). In Foucault's view, the move away from sovereign power came about through two distinct shifts. First, beginning in the seventeenth century, disciplinary power emerged as an adaptation to demographic explosion and industrialization. And then, in the nineteenth century, there was a second adjustment, which he calls biopower, a power grounded in "the bio-sociological processes characteristic of human masses" (ECF-SMD, 249–250).

Foucault thus conceives of two technologies of power, which were established at different times and yet superimposed on each other. The earlier technology, discipline, centers on the body and produces individualizing effects by manipulating the body "as a source of forces that have to be rendered both useful and docile" (ECF-SMD, 249). The second technology, biopower, is centered on large populations rather than individual bodies. In Foucault's words, biopower is "addressed to a multitude of men, not to the extent that they are nothing more than their individual bodies, but to the extent that they form … a global mass that is affected by overall processes, characteristic of birth, death, production, illness and so on" (ECF-SMD, 243). Under biopower, the focus is on the entire population and on the traits that are deemed to be characteristic of that population. The relationship between disciplinary power and biopower has become increasingly controversial. Some scholars view biopower as a distinct shift away from disciplinary power, whereas others see a more intimate relationship between the two. Efforts to understand the relationship are complicated by the fact that Foucault constantly reevaluates the various forms of power in his growing corpus of previously unpublished lectures. Foucault's lectures from 1975–1976, "Society Must Be Defended," directly treat the interrelationship between disciplinary power and biopower, but they were not intended to be a formal published text. Notwithstanding these difficulties, the lectures in *Society Must Be Defended* suggest that biopower is superimposed on disciplinary power but does not supplant it. Biopower does not exclude disciplinary technology, "but it does dovetail into it, integrate it, modify it to some extent, and above all, use it by sort of infiltrating it, embedding itself in existing disciplinary techniques" (ECF-SMD, 242). This new form of power "exists at a different level on a different scale, because it has a different bearing area and makes use of very different instruments" (ibid.). Both disciplinary power and biopower rely on the norm as a method of control. "The norm is something that can be applied to both a body one wishes to discipline, and a population which one wishes to regularize" (ECF-SMD, 253). But where discipline operates through institutions in which individuals are situated (such as schools, hospitals, or factories), biopower operates through the state apparatus. One can view Foucault's move to biopower as a way to account for the individual effects of power and the way that power creates individuals, while simultaneously seeking to understand the mass effects of power and develop coalitions through which individuals might collectively resist the effects of power. In his later work, Foucault turns away from descriptions of how power operates. He focuses instead on ethics and politics as a means of understanding what he describes as the "art of governing."

Foucault's critics have offered several distinct objections to his account of disciplinary power. For instance, Foucault has been widely criticized for asserting that power is "ever-present." Readers often understand this to mean that because power is everywhere, it is futile to fight against it, or that Foucault's point of view cannot form the basis for effective collective resistance to political domination. That understanding, however, is grounded in a misreading of Foucault's ideas. Foucault has also been criticized through the lens of several prevailing Western political theories because he refuses to provide either normative standards for the legitimate exercise of state authority (as in social contract theory) or a programmatic prescription for political revolution (as in Marxian theory). But Foucault in turn challenges these theories of power for failing to acknowledge the emergence of new forms of power and the resulting transformation of the mechanisms and technologies through which power is exercised.

According to Foucault, social contract theorists mistakenly conceive of power as a static commodity, as one that can be held by a central authority or transferred between entities. Such thinkers also regard power as unidirectional, as a force that is held by some and exercised against others. In Foucault's view, Marxian and Freudian theorists likewise err by failing to question this conception of power, even as they oppose social contract theory and focus instead on overthrowing and replacing the existing regime. By contrast, Foucault conceives of power as dynamic and relational, a matrix of forces that circulate through the population itself and that interact through relay points such as individual bodies, institutions, and mechanisms. Moreover, power is not simply repressive: it adapts and creates new strategies, tactics, and technologies to ensure its continued existence. Under social contract theory, individuals are seen as conscious entities that freely consent to be governed. But, in Foucault's view, our individuality is neither natural nor organic but rather an effect of power and a political construct, and we are shaped by the technologies of disciplinary power before we accept them. If power is "ever-present," then, it is only because each individual carries the effects of discipline within themselves, even before the possibility of consent exists. More recently, scholars have questioned the extent to which Foucault's ideas about discipline and disciplinary power apply in the age of globalization. They also take him to task for not directly addressing either feminism or the racial issues associated with those who were formerly colonized. But in the spirit of Foucault's inquiry, other scholars have adapted his analysis and framework for use in those areas.

In the end, Foucault does not see himself as a theorist of the forms of power, although many scholars do. In *Security, Territory, Populations*, Foucault emphasizes that his analysis of the technologies of power "is not in any way a general theory of what power is" (ECF-STP, 1). Instead, Foucault seeks to trace the history of power's effects on individuals, societies, and states. In his words, the work is aimed at "investigating where and how, between whom, between what points, according to what processes, and with what effects power is applied" (ECF-STP, 2). By studying discipline and disciplinary power's creative transformations, Foucault attempts to engage with politics and ethics and to create a framework by which we might conceive of forms of power that do not operate through domination and normalization.

Devonya N. Havis

SEE ALSO

> *Biopower*
> *Normalization*
> *Power*
> *Sovereignty*

SUGGESTED READING

Binkley, Sam, and Jorge Capetillo, eds. 2010. *A Foucault for the 21st Century: Governmentality, Biopolitics and Discipline in the New Millennium*, new ed. Newcastle upon Tyne: Cambridge Scholars Publishing.

Dreyfus, Hubert L., and Paul Rabinow. 1983. *Michel Foucault: Beyond Structuralism and Hermeneutics*, 2nd ed. Chicago: University of Chicago Press.

Taylor, Dianna. 2009. "Normativity and Normalization," *Foucault Studies* 7:45–63.

22

DISCOURSE

ISCOURSE WAS A central concept for Foucault's thinking throughout his career, but it was not a static concept. From the 1960s "archaeological" period (inaugurated with studies of madness and medicine, developed through studies of the human sciences, and culminating in a theoretical metareflection and synthesis) through the 1970s "genealogical" period (highlighted by studies of penality and sexuality) and the emerging "ethical" period of the 1980s, Foucault's views on the signification and significance of "discourse" shifted and evolved. Two key texts – *The Archaeology of Knowledge* (1969) and volume one of *The History of Sexuality* (1976), both of which represent a relatively complete development of a particular "period" or line of thought – illustrate the shifting roles that "discourse" has played in Foucault's thought.

Foucault's most important studies in the 1960s were devoted to the historical emergence or transformation of one or more discourses: madness and psychopathology in *History of Madness* (1961), medicine in *The Birth of the Clinic* (1963), and linguistics, biology, and economics in *The Order of Things* (1966). *The Archaeology of Knowledge* attempted to articulate and systematize the methods that underlie these earlier studies, even as it "includes a number of corrections and internal criticisms" (EAK, 16). The central organizing or framing concept for this systematization is "discourse," or, more precisely, "discursive formations." Foucault states, "Whenever one can describe, between a number of statements, such a system of dispersion, whenever, between objects, types of statement, concepts, or thematic choices, one can define a regularity (an order, correlations, positions and functionings, transformations), we will say ... that we are dealing with a *discursive formation*" (EAK, 38). A discourse is a set of statements that are correlated with each other, among which certain regularities (or rules of appearance, formation, transformation, etc.) obtain. Discourse is not language (in the sense of grammatical rules and a lexicon) but is rather a practice; a discourse consists of all the statements that have been made within it. Foucault terms the sum of these statements a discourse's "archive," and this archive determines which new statements are or are not possible and who can or cannot speak them. These discourses are not fixed and invariable, but rather are bound by all the prior statements and altered by every new statement that is made within a given discourse. Discourses can arise, be transformed, and disappear; they are fragmentary and incomplete. Once discourses have been recognized as the organizing fulcrum or framework for sciences and disciplines, then other apparent "continuities" – the book, the oeuvre, the author, etc. – can be displaced, and the rules and regularities actually governing statements' interactions can be discerned.

According to Foucault, "[D]iscourse is constituted by a group of sequences of signs, in so far as they are statements…. [T]he term discourse can be defined as the group of statements that belong to a single system of formation" (EAK, 107). Hence, discourse constitutes a "network of statements" that "forms a complex web" (EAK, 99, 98). It is this network that gives statements their status and coherence. This field within which statements are situated includes (1) "all the other formulations with which the statement appears," (2) "all the formulations to which the statement refers," (3) "all the formulations whose subsequent possibility is determined by the statement," and (4) "all the formulations whose status the statement in question shares" (EAK, 98–99). Discourse does not presuppose a sovereign subject or cogito (and thus allows a critique of the philosophy of the subject and an escape from the "crisis that concerns that transcendental reflexion with which philosophy since Kant has identified itself; … which, above all, concerns the status of the subject" [EAK, 204]). Instead, discursive regularities establish who can speak, in what voice, and with what authority. For example, with the rise of hospitals and clinics, medical discourse will be restricted to clinically trained doctors – only doctors will be able to make medical judgments or pronouncements with authority; other "practitioners," such as midwives, will be marginalized and discounted. Hence, discourses serve ultimately to delimit and define what constitutes knowledge:

> Knowledge is that of which one can speak in a discursive practice, and which is specified by that fact …; knowledge is also the space in which the subject may take up a position and speak of the objects with which he deals in his discourse …; knowledge is also the field of coordination and subordination of statements in which concepts appear, and are defined, applied, and transformed …; lastly, knowledge is defined by the possibilities of use and appropriation offered by discourse…. [T]here is no knowledge without a particular discursive practice. (EAK, 182–183)

In sum, discourses are the complex networks of statements that make knowledge possible; that delimit what can be said, or understood, within a particular discourse; and that determine who can speak (or at least speak with authority or be heard) within that discourse. They are, in this sense, a priori – they establish the conditions of existence for any given statement. But discourses are themselves transient, discontinuous, and situated within a history that makes their alteration and disappearance possible:

> Discourse in this sense is not an ideal, timeless form that also possesses a history; ... it is, from beginning to end, historical – a fragment of history, a unity and discontinuity in history itself, posing the problem of its own limits, its divisions, its transformations, the specific modes of its temporality rather than its sudden irruption in the midst of the complicities of time. (EAK, 117)

The Archaeology of Knowledge represents the acme of Foucault's epistemological work. Because he attempts to use discursive formations as the framework within which historical and philosophical phenomena are to be studied, he has been characterized as a "structuralist" – a label that he very explicitly rejected. Foucault's analysis of discursive formations is, however, analogous to other, "coherentist" epistemological approaches – approaches that claim a belief is justified not because it rests on a foundation but because of its coherence or connection with other beliefs (Kvanvig 2008). American philosopher William James articulated such a theory of truth in his 1907 lectures on *Pragmatism*: "[I]deas (which themselves are but parts of our experience) become true just in so far as they help us to get into satisfactory relation with other parts of our experience" (James 1981, 30). And Otto Neurath (a member of the Vienna Circle) argues that science as a whole is coherentist: "[W]e still know that basically 'everything is fluid', that multiplicity and uncertainty exist in all science, that there is no *tabula rasa* for us that we could use as a safe foundation on which to heap layers upon layers. *The whole of science is basically* always under discussion" (Neurath 1983, 118, Neurath's italics). Foucault's account is largely in agreement with Neurath's account of science – what is "true" is a function of the discursive formation's rules and regularities, what the discourse permits – but archaeological description seeks to work at a metalevel, analyzing the rules behind the transformations in discourses themselves.

We have seen that Foucault wrote *The Archaeology of Knowledge* in part to "correct and criticize" aspects of his earlier work and thought. But this text did not constitute a final word either. Foucault continued to criticize, revise, and correct his own thinking, and hence, in his later "genealogical" and "ethical" periods, "discourse" no longer held a central organizing/framing role for his analyses. A number of the themes on which Foucault would later focus, as well as some of the later revisions and corrections of the *Archaeology*, can already be detected in it. First, several themes are touched on that will become much more important foci in volume one of *The History of Sexuality*. One such theme is "repression," about which Foucault is suspicious in both works. In the *Archaeology*, Foucault explicitly states that statements' "exclusions" are not to be understood as repression: "[W]e do not presuppose that beneath manifest statements something remains hidden and subjacent" (EAK, 119). In *The History of Sexuality*, Foucault will explicitly challenge "the repressive hypothesis" as a misunderstanding of sexual discourse. Sexuality, too (the central topic of the later work), is a theme anticipated in the *Archaeology*. In its closing chapters, Foucault proposes "the archaeological description of 'sexuality'" as a possible direction that he could pursue:

> Such an archaeology would show, if it succeeded in its task, how the prohibitions, exclusions, limitations, values, freedoms, and transgressions of sexuality, all its manifestations, verbal or otherwise, are linked to a particular discursive practice … [a]n analysis that would be carried out not in the direction of the episteme, but in that of what we might call the ethical. (EAK, 193)

But there are also a number of tensions within the *Archaeology* with which Foucault will struggle. One important such tension is the relationship between discourses and "non-discursive reality." The *Archaeology*'s analyses are focused on discourses and say very little about nondiscursive objects; however, a "complete" approach cannot neglect these elements. And Foucault's later works will much more explicitly bring the nondiscursive into his analytic framework. This shift will displace discourse from its central, framing position – a position that will in the coming years be occupied by power relations. Indeed, power relations are already implicit in much of what Foucault says in the *Archaeology*, in his discussion of discursive "strategies," and even in his understanding of discourse itself:

> In this sense, discourse … appears as an asset – finite, limited, desirable, useful – that has its own rules of appearance, but also its own conditions of appropriation and operation; an asset that consequently, from the moment of its existence (and not only in its "practical applications"), poses the question of power; an asset that is by nature, the object of a struggle, a political struggle. (EAK, 120)

Indeed, one of the key concepts that Foucault is able to define on the basis of his analysis of discourse – knowledge (the book is, after all, entitled *The Archaeology of Knowledge*) – will be conjoined in later analyses with power: "power/knowledge."

As Foucault increasingly emphasized analysis of nondiscursive elements, discourse still remained an important concept or analytical tool, but it was no longer *the* central organizing frame for his analyses. Discourse, in Foucault's later works, is better understood as speech, language, whether spoken or written, an important part of but no longer the critical framework for understanding our social milieu. This shift is quite clear in volume one of *The History of Sexuality*. An important component of this text's work is an analysis of discourse, in particular sexual discourse: "Yet when one looks back over these last three centuries with their continual transformations, ... around and apropos of sex, one sees a veritable discursive explosion" (EHS1, 17); "[t]here was a steady proliferation of discourses concerned with sex – specific discourses, different from one another both by their form and by their object: a discursive ferment that gathered momentum from the eighteenth century onward" (EHS1, 18). Nevertheless, discourse is being reframed: "But more important was the multiplication of discourses concerning sex in the field of exercise of power itself" (ibid.). It is now one element within a larger framework defined by the operation of power relations, and discourses are juxtaposed against, on a par with, other institutions in this new framework. (Indeed, Part IV of *The History of Sexuality* is one of Foucault's most sustained, explicit elaborations of his new framing theory of power relations.) And so sexuality "appears rather as an especially dense transfer point for relations of power" (EHS1, 103). The way power relations permeate sexual discourse is illustrated, for example, by repression and resistance to it. It has been argued that we repress our sexuality, and so we can free ourselves from repression by engaging in more open discourses about sexuality. On the contrary, Foucault argues, these attempts at resistance merely serve to reduplicate and multiply the already existing discourses about sexuality – discourses that facilitate control and normalization of sexuality – and so attempts to break out from repression serve merely to play into and reinforce the normalization of sexuality that we were seeking to escape. Thus:

> The doubts I would like to oppose to the repressive hypothesis are aimed less at showing it to be mistaken than at putting it back within a general economy of discourses on sex in modern societies since the seventeenth century.... The object, in short, is to define the regime of power-knowledge-pleasure that sustains the discourse on human sexuality in our part of the world. (EHS1, 11)

Discourses are now sustained by a regime of power/knowledge relations.

The example of "resistance to repression" serving to reinforce, not escape, sexual normalization, as well as Foucault's commitment to self-critique as illustrated by the evolving signification and significance of "discourse," have important implications for Foucault's ethical thinking. Both illustrate a need for tentative, provisional judgments and a willingness to constantly reconsider and revise what we accept as knowledge. As Foucault put this in a 1983 interview, "My point is not that everything is bad, but that everything is dangerous. If everything is dangerous, then we always have something to do" (EEW1, 256).

One of the most salient features of all of Foucault's work is its relentlessly self-critical character. At each stage of his thinking, he reexamines, criticizes, and attempts to revise and correct earlier ideas. The evolution of "discourse" illustrates this character. In *The Archaeology of Knowledge* it becomes the organizing and framing concept that allows Foucault to revise and correct his earlier studies. By volume one of *The History of Sexuality*, it, too, has been revised, corrected, and resituated; "discourse" is no longer the linchpin for a theoretical framework but rather an important set of elements within a different conceptual framework articulated around power/knowledge relations. Indeed, this essential revisability is a key feature *internal to* Foucault's understanding of discourse itself and discursive formations – hence his emphasis on historical discontinuities in *The Archaeology of Knowledge*. And this essential revisability underscores the provisional character not only of Foucault's (and our) claims to knowledge but his (and our) ethical claims, too. The changing role of "discourse" in fact reveals an important constant of Foucault's thought, as well as a tool or lesson for the rest of us.

Richard A. Lynch

SEE ALSO

> *Archaeology*
> *Language*
> *Practice*
> *Statement*
> *Structuralism*

SUGGESTED READING

Dreyfus, Hubert L., and Paul Rabinow. 1983. *Michel Foucault: Beyond Structuralism and Hermeneutics*. Chicago: University of Chicago Press.

23

DISPOSITIF (APPARATUS)

OUCAULT'S PHILOSOPHY IS often presented as an analysis of concrete "*dispositifs*" or apparatuses. But what is an apparatus? First of all, it is a skein, a multilinear whole. It is composed of lines of different natures. The lines in the apparatus do not encircle or surround systems that are each homogeneous in themselves, the object, the subject, language, and so on, but follow directions, trace processes that are always out of balance, that sometimes move closer together and sometimes further away. Each line is broken, subject to *changes in direction*, bifurcating and forked, and subjected to *derivatives*. Visible objects, articulable statements, forces in use, and subjects in position are like vectors or tensors. Thus the three main instances Foucault successively distinguishes – Knowledge, Power, and Subjectivity – by no means have contours that are defined once and for all but are chains of variables that are torn from each other. Foucault always finds a new dimension or a new line in a crisis. Great thinkers are somewhat seismic; they do not evolve but proceed by crises or quakes. Thinking in terms of moving lines was Herman Melville's operation: fishing lines, dividing lines, dangerous, even deadly, lines. There are lines of sedimentation, Foucault says, but also lines of "fissure" and "fracture." Untangling the lines of an apparatus means, in each case, preparing a map, a cartography, a survey of unexplored lands – what he calls "field work." One has to be positioned on the lines themselves, and these lines do not merely compose an apparatus but pass through it and carry it north to south, east to west, or diagonally.

The first two dimensions of an apparatus, or the ones Foucault first extracts, are the curves of visibility and the curves of enunciation. Because apparatuses are like Raymond Roussel's machines, which Foucault also analyzed, they are machines that make one see and talk. Visibility does not refer to a general light that would illuminate preexisting objects but rather is made up of lines of light that form variable figures inseparable from an apparatus. Each apparatus has its regimen of light, the way it falls, softens, and spreads, distributing the visible and the invisible, generating or eliminating an object, which cannot exist without it. This is true not only of painting but of architecture as well: the "prison apparatus" as an optical machine for seeing without being seen. If there is a historicity of apparatuses, it is the historicity of regimes of light but also regimes of statements. Statements in turn refer to lines of enunciation where the differential positions of the elements of a statement are distributed. And the curves themselves are statements because enunciations are curves that distribute variables and a science at a given moment, or a literary genre, state of laws, or social movement is precisely defined by the regimes of statements they engender. They are neither subjects nor objects but regimes that must be defined for the visible and the utterable with their derivations, transformations, and mutations. In each apparatus, the lines cross thresholds that make them either aesthetic, scientific, political, or whatever.

Third, an apparatus contains lines of force. One might say that they move from one single point to another on the previous lines. In a way, they "rectify" the previous curves, draw tangents, surround the paths from one line to another, operate to and fro from seeing to speaking and vice versa, acting like arrows that constantly mix words and things without ceasing to carry out their battles. A line of force is produced "in every relationship between one point and another" and moves through every place in an apparatus. Invisible and unspeakable, this line is closely combined with the other but can be untangled. Foucault pulls this line and finds its trajectory in Roussel, Brisset, and the painters Magritte and Rebeyrolle. It is the "dimension of power" and power is the third dimension of space, interior to the apparatus and variable with the apparatuses. Like power, it is composed with knowledge.

And finally, Foucault discovered lines of subjectification. This new dimension has already given rise to so much misunderstanding that it is hard to specify its conditions. More than any other, this discovery came from a crisis in Foucault's thought, as if he needed to rework the map of apparatuses, find a new orientation for them to prevent them from closing up behind impenetrable lines of force imposing definitive contours. Leibniz expressed in exemplary fashion this state of crisis that restarts thought when it seems that everything is almost resolved: you think you have reached shore but are cast back out to sea. And as for Foucault, he sensed that the apparatuses he analyzed could not be circumscribed by an enveloping line without other vectors passing above or below: "crossing the line," he said, like "going to the other side" (EEW3, 161)? This going beyond the line of force is what happens when it bends back, starts meandering, goes underground or rather when force, instead of entering into a linear relationship with another force, turns back on itself, acts on itself or affects itself. This dimension of the Self is not a preexisting determination that can be found ready-made. Here again, a line of subjectification is a process, a production of subjectivity in an apparatus: it must be made to the extent that the apparatus allows it or makes it possible. It is a line of flight. It escapes the previous lines; it escapes *from them*. The Self is not knowledge or power. It is process of individuation that affects groups or people and eludes both established lines of force and constituted knowledge. It is a kind of surplus value. Not every apparatus necessarily has it.

Foucault designates the apparatus of the Athenian city-state as the first place where a subjectification was created. According to his original definition, the city-state invents a line of forces that moves through the *rivalry between free men*. From this line on which a free man can have command over others, a very different line separates itself according to which the one who commands free men must also be master of himself. These optional rules for self-mastery constitute an autonomous subjectification, even if it is later called on to furnish new knowledge and inspire new powers. One might wonder whether lines of subjectification are the extreme edge of an apparatus and whether they trace the passage from one apparatus to another. In this sense, they would prepare "lines of fracture." And lines of subjectification have no more of a general formula than other lines. Cruelly interrupted, Foucault's research was going to show that processes of subjectification eventually took on modes other than the Greek mode, for example in Christian apparatuses and modern societies. Couldn't we cite apparatuses where subjectification no longer goes through aristocratic life or the aestheticized existence of free men but through the marginalized existence of the "excluded"? The sinologist Tokei explains how freed slaves in a way lost their social status and found themselves relegated to an isolated, plaintive, *elegiac* existence from which they had to draw new forms of power and knowledge (Sárkány, Hann, and Skalník 2005). The study of variations in the processes of subjectification seems to be one of the tasks Foucault left those who came after him. I believe this research will be extremely fruitful, and the current endeavors toward a history of private life only partially overlap it. Sometimes the ones subjectivized are the nobles, the ones who say "we are the good" according to Nietzsche. But under other conditions, the excluded, the bad, the sinners, or the hermits, monastic communities, or heretics, are subjectivized: an entire typology of subjective formations in changing apparatuses. And with these apparatuses we have combinations to be untangled everywhere: productions of subjectivity escaping the powers and knowledge of one apparatus to reinvest themselves in another through other forms to be created.

Apparatuses are therefore composed of lines of visibility, enunciation, lines of force, lines of subjectification, lines of cracking, breaking, and ruptures that all intertwine and mix together and where some augment the others or elicit others through variations and even mutations of the assemblage. Two important consequences ensue for a philosophy of apparatuses. The first is the repudiation of universals. A universal explains nothing; it, on the other hand, must be explained. All of the lines are lines of variation that do not even have constant coordinates. The One, the Whole, the True, the object, and the subject are not universals but singular processes of unification, totalization, verification, objectification, and subjectification immanent to an apparatus. Each apparatus is therefore a multiplicity where certain processes in becoming are operative and are distinct from those operating in another apparatus. This is how Foucault's philosophy is a pragmatism, a functionalism, a positivism, and a pluralism. Reason may cause the greatest problem because processes of rationalization can operate on segments or regions of all the lines discussed so far. Foucault pays homage to Nietzsche for a historicity of reason. And he notes all of the importance of epistemological research on the various forms of rationality in knowledge (Koyré, Bachelard, Canguilhem) and of sociopolitical research into the modes of rationality in power (Max Weber). Maybe he kept the third line for himself, the study of types "reasonable" in potential subjects. But he refused essentially to identify these processes in a reason par excellence. He rejected any restoration of universals of reflection, communication, or consensus. In this sense, one could say that his relationship with the Frankfurt School and the successors to this school consists of a long series of misunderstandings for which he is not responsible. And no more than there are universals of a founding subject or exemplary reason that would allow for judgment of apparatuses, there are not universals of the disaster of reason being alienated or collapsing once and for all. As Foucault told Gérard Rauler, there is not one bifurcation of reason; it constantly bifurcates, there are as many bifurcations and branches as instaurations, as many collapses as constructions following the cuts carried out by the apparatuses and "there is no meaning to the statement that reason is a long story that is over now" (EEW2, 433–458). From this point of view, the objection raised with Foucault regarding knowing how to assess the relative value of an apparatus if no transcendental values can be called on as universal coordinates is a question that could lead us backward and lose its meaning itself. Should one say that all apparatuses are equal (nihilism)? Thinkers like Spinoza and Nietzsche showed long ago that modes of existence had to be weighed according to immanent criteria, according to their content in "possibilities," freedom, and creativity, with no call to transcendental values. Foucault even alluded to "aesthetic" criteria, understood as life criteria, that substitute an immanent evaluation for a transcendental judgment every time. When we read Foucault's last books, we must do our best to understand the program he is offering his readers. An intrinsic aesthetics of modes of existence as the final dimension of apparatuses?

The second result of a philosophy of apparatuses is a change in orientation, turning away from the eternal to apprehend the new. The new is not supposed to designate fashion but on the contrary the variable creativity for the apparatuses: in conformance with the question that began to appear in the twentieth century of how the production of something new in the world is possible. It is true that, within his entire theory of enunciation, Foucault explicitly rejected the "originality" of a statement as criterion that is hardly pertinent, that is hardly interesting. He only wants to consider the "regularity" of statements. But what he meant by regularity was the slope of the curve passing through the singular points or the differential values of the group of statements. (He also defined the relationship of forces as distributions of singularities in a social field.) By rejecting the originality of statements, he meant that the potential contradiction of two statements is not enough to distinguish them or to indicate the newness of one in relation to the other. What counts is the newness of the regime of enunciation itself in that it can include contradictory statements. For example, we could ask what regime of statements appeared with the French Revolution or the Russian Revolution: it is the newness of the regime that counts and not the originality of the statement. Each apparatus is thus defined by its content of newness and creativity, which at the same time indicates its ability to transform itself or even to break for the sake of an apparatus of the future unless, on the contrary, it transforms itself for the sake of an increase of force to the hardest, most rigid or solid lines. Since they escape the dimension of knowledge and power, lines of subjectification seem particularly apt to trace paths of creation, which are constantly aborted but also taken up again and modified until the old apparatus breaks. Foucault's as yet unpublished studies on the various Christian processes will certainly open many directions in this regard. One should not believe, however, that the production of subjectivity is left only to religion; antireligious struggles are also creative, just as the regimes of light, enunciation, and domination move through very diverse domains. Modern subjectifications resemble the Greek subjectifications no more than they resemble the Christian ones; the same is true of light, statements, and powers.

We belong to these apparatuses and act in them. The newness of an apparatus in relation to those preceding it is what we call its actuality, our actuality. The new is the actual. The actual is not what we are but rather what we become, what are in the process of becoming, in other words the Other, our becoming-other. In every apparatus, we have to distinguish between what we are (what we already no longer are) and what we are becoming: *the portion that is history, the portion that is actual*. History is the archive, the design of what we are and cease being, whereas the actual is the sketch of what we are becoming. Thus history or the archive is what still separates us from ourselves, whereas the actual is this Other with which we already coincide. Some have thought that Foucault was painting the portrait of modern societies as disciplinary apparatuses in opposition to the old apparatuses of sovereignty. This is not the case: the disciplines Foucault described are the history of what are slowly ceasing to be and our actuality is taking shape within arrangements of open and constant *control* that are very different from the recent closed disciplines. Foucault agrees with Burroughs, who announced that our future would be more controlled than disciplined. The question is not which is worse, because we also call on productions of subjectivity capable of resisting this new domination and that are very different from the ones used in the past against the disciplines. A new light, new statements, new power, new forms of subjectification? In every apparatus, we must untangle the lines of the recent past from the lines of the near future: the archive from the actual, the portion of history and the portion of becoming, *the portion of analysis and the portion of diagnosis.* If Foucault is a great philosopher, it is because he used history for something else: as Nietzsche said, to act against time and thus to act on time in favor, I hope, of a time to come. What Foucault saw as the actual or the new was what Nietzsche called the untimely, the "non-actual," the becoming that splits away from history, the diagnosis that relays analysis on different paths, not predicting, but being attentive to the unknown knocking at the door. Nothing reveals this better than a fundamental passage from *The Archaeology of Knowledge* that applies to all his work:

> Analysis of the archive therefore includes a privileged area: it is both close to us and different from our actuality. It is the edge of time that surrounds our present, overlooks it and points to our present in its alterity; the archive is what, outside of us, delimits us. The description of the archive unfolds its possibilities (and the mastery of its possibilities) starting with discourses that have just stopped being ours; its threshold of existence begins with the break that separates us from what we can no longer say and what falls outside our discursive practices; it begins with the outside of our own language; its place is the distance from our own discursive practices. In this sense it can serve as our diagnosis. Not because it would allow us to draw a portrait of our distinctive traits and sketch out in advance the aspect we will have in the future. But it releases us from our continuities; it dissipates the temporal identity where we like to look at ourselves to avoid the ruptures of history; it breaks the thread of transcendental teleologies; and while anthropological thought would examine the being of humans or their subjectivity, it exposes the other, the outside. Diagnosis in this sense does not establish the recognition of our identity through the play of distinctions. It establishes that we are difference, that our reason is the difference between discourses, our history the difference between times, our self the difference between masks. (EAK, 130–131)

The different lines of an apparatus are divided into two groups: lines of stratification or sedimentation and lines of actualization or creativity. The final result of this method concerns Foucault's entire work. In most of his books, he determines a specific archive with extremely new historical means, the general hospital in the seventeenth century, the clinic in the eighteenth century, the prison in the nineteenth century, subjectivity in ancient Greece and then in Christianity. But that is only half of his task. Out of a concern for rigor, because of a will not to mix everything together, because he has confidence in his readers, Foucault does not formulate the other half. He only formulates it explicitly in the interviews given alongside the publication of his major works: What are madness, prison, and sexuality today? What new modes of subjectification do we see appearing today that are certainly not Greek or Christian? This last question haunted Foucault until the end (we who are no longer Greek or even Christian). Foucault attached so much importance to his interviews in France and even more so abroad not because he liked interviews but because in them he traced lines of actualization that required a mode of expression other than the assimilable lines in his major books. The interviews are diagnoses. It is as in Nietzsche, whose works are difficult to read without the Nachlass that is contemporary to each. Foucault's complete works, as Defert and Ewald imagine them, cannot separate the books that have left such an impression on us from the interviews that lead us toward a future, toward a becoming: the strata and the actualities.

Gilles Deleuze

SEE ALSO

Actuality
Statement
Subjectification
Friedrich Nietzsche

SUGGESTED READING

Deleuze, Gilles. 1988. *Foucault*, trans. Seán Hand. Minneapolis: University of Minnesota Press.
Sárkány, Mikhály, Chris M. Hann, and Peter Skalník, eds. 2005. *Studying Peoples in the People's Democracies: Socialist Era Anthropology in East-Central Europe*. Münster: Lit Verlag, pp. 98–99.

24

THE DOUBLE

FOUCAULT'S DISCUSSION OF the double in the ninth chapter of *The Order of Things* contains one of the most forceful critiques of phenomenology to appear in his early work. The figure of "the double" is invoked here to illustrate a problem posed to phenomenology by virtue of the fact that (1) phenomenology as a method aims at the elaboration of the transcendental conditions of human experience, and (2) that phenomenology situates this examination of the transcendental in the empirical reality of man. The problem that results is one of circularity: the ground of phenomenological inquiry is constantly shifting, such that the subject is implicated in a kind of shadow dance. The effects of the Foucauldian rendering of the modern subject are multiple; Foucault's analysis of the double bears consequences for the possibility of a modern ethics and ultimately leads him to forecast the "death of man."

To speak of "the double," however, is misleading, since there are three doubles that Foucault addresses in *The Order of Things*, each of which marks a paradox that proves troublesome for phenomenology. The three "doubles of man" are the empirical and the transcendental, the cogito and the unthought, and the retreat and return of the origin. The first of these, the doublet of the empirical and the transcendental, refers to the fact that man is at once an empirically determined being and a transcendental subject. Man is a finite existent in the world, subject to the laws of natural science, even as he is the transcendental grounds of these very laws: "he is a being such that knowledge will be attained in him of what renders all knowledge possible" (EOT, 318). A paradox results. The transcendental status of phenomenological investigation is undermined by the fact that man is not only the transcendental grounds of the empirical sciences but also their proper object. For this reason, the subject's knowledge of that world can never be clear or entire, as it finds itself implicated in the appearance of the world in ways that obscure certain kinds of knowledge even as others emerge. This tension grounds Foucault's exploration of the "analytic of finitude," or those various modes of modern thought that understand man to be irreducibly transcendental *and* empirical.

The second paradox or double that marks the modern understanding of man is the double of the cogito and the unthought. This paradox is the consequence of the phenomenological method, where self-reflection is taken to be the paradigmatic means of philosophical investigation. The doubling of the cogito and the unthought relates to the paradox that whatever is thought by the subject is conditioned by the unthought. Stated differently, self-reflection is the means by which what is thought is illuminated, but the subject itself is constituted by the unthought. In contradistinction to the self-transparency that marked the Cartesian cogito, Foucault claims that the modern cogito lacks this transparency and clarity. Foucault's analysis of this second doublet echoes the paradox of the empirical and the transcendental just outlined; it concerns the fact that the modern cogito is conditioned by the unthought such that all attempts at self-knowledge are necessarily blurred and marked by regions of opacity. In the modern *episteme*, what is thought is conditioned by what is unthought, and so the immediacy and transparency of the Cartesian cogito give way to a modern cogito whose attempts at self-knowledge can only be partial, encumbered by blind spots.

The third and final double relates to the relationship between historicity and subjectivity in the modern *episteme*; this double concerns the return and retreat of the origin. In his discussions of the origin, Foucault references the fact that man is marked and determined by a history that is not transparent to him, even as he is charged with rendering this history intelligible; hence man is the product and origin of history at once. The structure by this point is familiar: man serves as the transcendental grounds for a discourse that in part determines him, and for this reason the phenomenological evidence given in self-reflection is distorted and imperfect. Although phenomenology is not marked by the conceit of self-certainty to the degree that Cartesian philosophy is – indeed, one of the basic tenets of phenomenology is that a "view from nowhere" is untenable, as we find ourselves always already implicated in those very discourses through which we examine ourselves – it remains the case that Foucault takes the paradoxical doubles that mark the modern discourse on man to be an indictment of phenomenology's critical aspirations in no uncertain terms.

Foucault's discussion of the three doubles serves not only as an indictment of phenomenology's ability to proceed as a critical project but also as an indictment of the ability of modern thought to formulate an ethics: "For modern thought, no morality is possible. Thought has already left itself in its own being as early as the nineteenth century; it is no longer theoretical. As soon as it functions it offends or reconciles, attracts or repels, breaks, dissociates, unites or reunites; it cannot help but liberate and enslave" (EOT, 328). The attribution of action to thought and the notion that all thought is always already practical are ideas that have marked contemporary philosophy in ways that are difficult to overstate. The legacy of Foucault's discussion of the double, then, lies not only in its indictment of phenomenology as a critical project but in its recognition that, in the modern *episteme*, thought is violent, "a perilous act," by virtue of the fact that thought does not approach the world with innocence but with deep complicity.

Ann V. Murphy

SEE ALSO

Ethics
Man
Phenomenology
Structuralism

SUGGESTED READING

Dreyfus, Hubert L., and Paul Rabinow. 1983. *Michel Foucault: Beyond Structuralism and Hermeneutics*, 2nd ed. Chicago: University of Chicago Press.
Gutting, Gary. 1989. *Michel Foucault's Archaeology of Scientific Reason*. Cambridge: Cambridge University Press.
Oksala, Johanna. 2005. *Foucault on Freedom*. Cambridge: Cambridge University Press.

25

ETHICS

FOUCAULT'S WORK ALWAYS had an ethical impetus in his outrage over "intolerable" contemporary institutions or practices. His histories were designed to trace the genealogical origins of, for example, the treatment of insanity as "mental illness," the punishment of criminals by imprisonment, and the movement to "liberate" sexual behavior through self-understanding. As members of an enlightened modern society, we see no scientifically or ethically acceptable alternatives to these approaches to madness, crime, and sexuality. But Foucault's histories set out to show how they arose from intellectually and morally dubious conceptions that are by no means inevitable. The idea is to provide historical tools for those opposing an intolerable aspect of modern social life.

In every case, Foucault's ethical objection to modern practices seems to have been broadly existentialist: they make people be something they have not chosen for themselves. But he rejected any comprehensive philosophical account supporting this moral stance and simply began from his intense pre-philosophical conviction that the practices were morally intolerable. The issue of an ethics in any philosophical sense was not a meaningful option as Foucault analyzed the intertwined structures of knowledge and power underlying modern social practices.

This, however, began to change when Foucault's historical study of modern sexuality made explicit the central role of the subject or self in the network of social constraints. It was, in particular, now apparent that constraints on our behavior were not only externally imposed (e.g., by confinement in an asylum or a prison); they were also internalized as our own view of our self-identity (e.g., my "liberating" acceptance of my sexual identity). As a result, in the first volume of *The History of Sexuality* (EHS1) (intended as an introductory overview of four further projected volumes on children, women, "perverts," and couples), Foucault highlighted the role of the individual subject (self) for the understanding of modern sexuality.

Extending his studies to the self led, however, to a corresponding extension of the historical scope of Foucault's studies. Although previously he had been able to restrict himself to the broadly modern period (with brief looks at the Renaissance), he now decided that he could not understand the modern self without relating it to the medieval Christian view of the self. This Foucault undertook in a study of medieval sexuality (*Les aveux de la chair*), but, before it was properly finished, he decided that he could understand the medieval stance only by contrasting it with the ancient Greek and Roman history that had preceded it. This led to two volumes on Greek and Roman sexuality, published in 1984. Since this was the year of Foucault's death, the volume on medieval sexuality, in accord with Foucault's dictate of "no posthumous publications," has not appeared.

Foucault's two books on ancient sexuality appeared as the second and third volumes of *The History of Sexuality* (EHS2 and EHS3), even though they did not carry out any part of the history of modern sexuality projected by the introductory first volume. It is not just that the move to Greece and Rome broadened Foucault's historical scope; it also led to a new conception of his topic. His original project, previewed in volume one, was to tell in detail the story of how individual subjects internalized the normalizing structures of society's power/knowledge nexus. But Foucault found in the ancients the possibility of a meaningful construction of the self, which involved not just internalizing external norms or resisting them through counterpower. Rather, it meant the possibility of forging, within the interstices left by social constraints, an autonomous self-identity, a project that could, even in a traditional sense, be called ethical.

Readers of Foucault's previous histories might well wonder how his picture of individuals formed by the social power/knowledge nexus can allow room for any project of ethical self-formation. The answer lies in his (implicit) move from a focus on *marginalization* to a focus on *problematization* ("Polemics, Politics, and Problematizations" [interview with Paul Rabinow, 1984], EEW1, 111–119). Marginalization occurs when the constraints of the power/knowledge network are so strong as to threaten a group of individuals with total loss of identity, allowing them no meaningful place in the society (e.g., the mad, the criminal, the sexually "perverse"). Here there is a choice only between submitting to normalization (and losing self-identity) and asserting self-identity entirely through opposition to the constraining society. All of Foucault's earlier histories (except for *The Order of Things*, which has at best very indirect social significance) concern marginalized groups.

"Problematization," by contrast, is Foucault's term for a set of fundamental issues and choices confronting "mainline" (nonmarginalized) members of a society. Talk of problematization assumes a preliminary definition of a person in terms of social constraints, but in this case (as opposed to marginalization) the constraints allow room for creative self-development in accord with self-chosen goals and standards. Problematization differs from marginalization because problematized individuals are not, by virtue of objective features over which they have no control, subject to an almost total constriction of their choices as is the case for marginalized groups. As opposed to the marginalized, those whose lives are merely problematized have a "social essence" compatible with a significant range of freedom. In the history of ancient sexuality, problematization implicitly replaces marginalization as the focus of the discussion.

Although Foucault's ethical emphasis is on an individual's construction of a self (an identity), he does recognize the role of ethical codes (rules of behavior), the force of which will vary depending on the manner in which a given individual is "subjected" to it. Although Foucault says little about ethical codes, it is reasonable to suppose that he would see them as general frameworks required for life within a given social structure but not necessarily the central concern of ethical life, which is instead the construction of a self.

This construction involves four elements (which Foucault calls the four "modes of subjectification") that characterize an individual's relations to an ethical code (EHS2, Chapter 3 of the Introduction). The first mode is *ethical substance*: the various aspects of life relevant to ethical behavior (in the case of sexual ethics, these would be desires, pleasures, actions, virtues, etc.). Second is the mode of *subjection* (to be distinguished from subjectification), the sense in which an individual is subject to the ethical code (some possibilities are the rigid following of highly specified rules, inspiration by highly general principles, or dialectical reasoning to reconcile principles in tension with one another). Third, the *forms of elaboration* are specific kinds of activity that lead to an acceptance of the ethical code (for example, rigorous training through negative reinforcement, prolonged meditation on paradigm instances found in sacred texts, or imitation of admired mentors). Finally, the *telos* (end) is the ultimate goal posited as the purpose of morality (e.g., social stability, individual enlightenment, control of the passions, or eternal happiness).

Like moral codes themselves, the modes of subjectification that relate individuals to the codes of their societies are not the free creation of individuals. But, in contrast to the code, a given mode of subjectification allows a significant range of choice for some individuals. A particular mode will typically offer alternatives (celibate vs. married life) for its implementation, and any alternative will be underdetermined as to its specific form (e.g., active vs. contemplative religious orders). This allows for individual choice in self-formation, based, for example, on personal standards of aesthetic value, corresponding to what Foucault calls an *aesthetics of existence* (which will be discussed further).

Based on the schema of the four modes of subjectification, Foucault offers case studies of the ancients' problematizations of sexual ethics. These studies are essentially archaeological, looking at the underlying conceptual structures of the ethical thought of the ancient world – first that of the fourth-century Greeks, then that of the Latin and Greek world around the time of Christ. A constant benchmark is the contrast with Christian ethics, which Foucault sees as emerging in the later ancient period from non-Christian sources. The ethical substance of ancient sexual behavior comprises desires, acts, and pleasures (*ta aphrodisia*) viewed as natural goods, though subject to some dangers and concerns (primarily because of their ties to our lower, animal nature and their exceptional intensity). By contrast, Christians, according to Foucault, see sex as in itself intrinsically evil. As a result, the ancients' mode of subjection to the ethical code regarding sexual behavior is the careful use (*chresis*) of pleasures, in contrast to the Christians' denial (austerity), effected either through complete celibacy or through restriction of sexuality to monogamous marriage, directed to procreation.

As to the forms of elaboration, the ancients emphasized self-mastery (*enkratia*), achieved through training (*askesis*) in self-control. We achieve conformity to the sexual code through exercises designed to make reason the master of our desires and feelings. By contrast, for Christians, this internal battle between reason and passion is replaced by a struggle between the self's desire to maintain ultimate control of itself and the imperative for it to yield to God, in whom alone it can find its true identity and happiness. As a result, the telos radically changes from the ancient to the Christian world. For the ancients, the telos is moderation (*sophrosyne*), achieved through the proper use of pleasures to attain the ideal of human freedom in both its negative and positive forms (freedom from domination by passions, freedom for rational mastery of self and others). For the Christians, the telos is total subjection of self to God – the negative freedom of denial of self for the sake of a positive freedom achieved only by living entirely in and through God.

What is the point of Foucault's excursions into the ancient history of sexual ethics? The point is not, as in his previous histories, a genealogy of our current practices that will show their contingent, dubious origins and provide ammunition for attacks on their privileged position. The ancient world is too far removed from ours for such a history to sustain sufficient connection to contemporary concerns; it cannot be what Foucault called a "history of the present." But Foucault thinks he can find in the ancient world a model for an ethics of self-creation that will be relatively independent of the power/knowledge structures of our society. This is by no means a matter of "going back to the Greeks" and reviving their way of ethical life. Apart from the historical impossibility of doing such a thing, there are many central features of their ethics that we would not want to emulate (e.g., their focus on the value – literally phallocentric – of virility, their disdain for women, their acceptance of slavery) ("On the Genealogy of Ethics: An Overview of Work in Progress" [interview with Hubert Dreyfus and Paul Rabinow], EEW1, 256–257).

But Foucault does think we can profitably adapt the ancients' general notion of an ethics based on an *aesthetics of existence*. An aesthetics of existence is a *technē*, a practical method of ethical formation devoted not (like Christianity) to redeeming the self (saving it from Hell and for Heaven) but to creating a beautiful life on Earth

(EEW1, 260). Such an aesthetics derives from an individual's distinctive taste, so that the ethical formation it guides allows for an existence that avoids the full force of social power structures by finding a location within the interstices of these structures where the individual as such can flourish. As we have noted, such a project of self-formation is not available to the marginalized people on whom society imposes an identity. For them, the only choices are submission or resistance. But for those with sufficient status in a society, there are resources for creative self-formation within the social fabric.

An aesthetics of existence has, as Foucault sees it, a significant advantage because it makes ethics an essentially private enterprise rather than the imposition of public (universally binding) rules for how we should live. He acknowledges that we need a minimal universal ethical code to maintain a stable social context for our lives. But this is little except the core injunctions that humans have endorsed for millennia. The remainder of ethical life is a matter for private choice, with in particular no role for public moralities derived from allegedly scientific sources such as sociobiology or psychoanalysis. This privatization provides an alternative to the normalizing characteristic of modern society, since it replaces universal ("scientifically" underwritten) standards of moral perfection with personalized ideals of a "beautiful life" (EEW1, 254). This allows a separate space in which ethics can be practiced in relative independence of "the great political and social and economic structures" (EEW1, 261). This does not mean, however, that an aesthetics of existence cannot include a concern – lacking in ancient Greece – for the marginalized of one's society. Activism on their behalf can be, as it was for Foucault, an integral part of creating a beautiful life.

Foucault's ethics obviously has little to do with the traditional efforts of philosophers to formulate the norms of ethical codes or with the metanormative concerns of analytic philosophers. Nothing he says rejects these projects, but he finds the ethical center of gravity elsewhere, in the private sphere of aesthetic self-formation. A natural objection is that such a self-centered project should hardly be called ethical. It is, however, ethical in its concern with the fundamental values that guide an individual's life. The worry, presumably, is that, since these values concern *self*-formation, they lack the directedness to others characteristic of ethics. But to this Foucault would have two responses. First, there is a moral code that constrains self-formative behavior that would harm others. Second, given that there is no harm to others, it would seem that perfecting oneself is an essential aspect of a good human life. It might be suggested that the perfection in question is tied only to individual preferences (taste) and so lacks the universal quality of ethical goods. But to this Foucault can plausibly reply that, in his view, it is a universal human good that each individual engage in a project of aesthetic self-creation. This, indeed, is Foucault's ethical reason for supporting the struggles of marginalized people.

Another question is whether Foucault's turn to ethics reverses his earlier rejection of philosophy as a study of the subject. It is true that his histories of ancient sexuality work along not just his previous two axes of knowledge (archaeology) and power (genealogy). They add an axis of the individual ethical subject, which "constitutes" itself in the context of the first two axes. But, of course, merely bringing into the discussion the individuals who are the subjects of knowledge and power hardly requires philosophical assumptions about subjectivity. Nor need Foucault's use of terms such as "freedom" and "reflection" be read as committing him to a transcendentalist philosophy. The terms may readily be understood as referring to everyday features of human life (the metaphysical equivalent to Freud's famous reminder that sometimes a cigar is just a cigar). In their everyday sense, freedom and reflection do not imply Kantian (or Sartrean) autonomy. They may, for example, represent the small spark of subjectivity in a context heavily constrained by the social system of power-knowledge. In his books on ancient sexuality, Foucault of course often uses Platonic vocabulary, which smacks of strong autonomy. Moreover, since the power-knowledge constraints of ancient Greece and Rome are no longer relevant to us, he has little to say about them. He is simply looking for modes of thinking about the self (e.g., in terms of an aesthetics of existence) that might suggest strategies in our struggle with modern disciplinary society. None of this provides grounds for concluding that Foucault has lapsed into transcendentalism.

Foucault's account of ethical subjectification does recall Levinas's account of how the encounter with the Other constitutes the I as a subject. But Foucault's "subject" already exists at the center of a world of objects prior to the encounter with the Other. In contrast to Levinas's subject, Foucault's is not constituted *tout court* by the encounter with ethical demands. It is merely constituted as an ethical subject; that is, it develops (partly by its own decisions) distinctive modes of being "subject to" the ethical code. This is an event that occurs within the world of subjects and objects, not one that constitutes this world. Foucault's ethics does not provide necessary conditions for anything other than ethical life itself.

More generally, Foucault's ethics is not a contribution to philosophy in the sense that has defined the discipline since at least Kant and Hegel: as a body of theoretical knowledge about fundamental human questions. He had no such theoretical conclusions to offer us, just ethical and political commitments to the kind of life he wanted to live. This was a life of continual free self-transformation, unhindered by unnecessary conceptual and social constraints. His intellectual enterprise was the critique of disciplines and practices that restrict our freedom to transform ourselves. He did not object to those who continued to build new theoretical structures, and, in some cases, such as Deleuze, he seemed to endorse their results. But he was not really a philosopher in the modern sense. Of course, Foucault's books, like other classics of intellectual history, exhibit enormous philosophical talent and are often of great interest to philosophers. Moreover, as his final work makes clear, although he did not pursue philosophical truth, he did aspire to lead, in the ancient sense, a philosophical life.

Gary Gutting

SEE ALSO

> *Christianity*
> *Problematization*
> *Self*
> *Sex*
> *Subjectification*
> *The Ancients (Stoics and Cynics)*

SUGGESTED READING

Bernauer, James, and Michael Mahon. 2005. "Foucault's Ethical Imagination," in *The Cambridge Companion to Foucault*, ed. Gary Gutting, 2nd ed. Cambridge: Cambridge University Press, pp. 149–175.

Davidson, Arnold. 2005. "Ethics as Ascetics: Foucault, the History of Ethics, and Ancient Thought," in *The Cambridge Companion to Foucault*, 2nd ed., ed. Gary Gutting. Cambridge: Cambridge University Press, pp. 123–148.

Detel, Wolfgang. 2005. *Foucault and Classical Antiquity: Power, Ethics and Knowledge*, trans. David Wigg-Wolf. Cambridge: Cambridge University Press.

26

EVENT

T HE CONCEPT OF "event" plays a central role in Foucault's thinking concerning history and historical methodology, and thus in his archaeological and genealogical methods. Historical events in Foucault's thought are not merely those happenings that would conventionally be labeled "events" – noteworthy occurrences such as the beginning of a war, an election, a death – but rather are more subtle, pervasive, multiple, and diverse shifts that underlie these incidents. With his reconceptualization of the event, Foucault sets his own theoretical practice in contrast to traditional historical practice: it is a counterpractice, specifically a resistance to the governing presuppositions concerning history's continuous teleological development, the unity of the knowing subject, the objectivity of historical analysis conducted by that subject, and the fixity of stable categories of analysis.

Foucault's 1971 essay "Nietzsche, Genealogy, History" elaborates this oppositional relationship by contrasting "effective history" with traditional history. The paired terms – *Herkunft*, descent, and *Entstehung*, emergence – used by Nietzsche to refer to the genealogical investigation of "origins" summarize the approach that defines effective history and the significance of the event in that approach. An analysis of *Herkunft* enables one to go beneath the noticeable happenings of history, the transparently important concepts throughout the history of ideas, and the supposed unities of author and corpus to discern "the myriad events through which – thanks to which, against which – they were formed" (ELCP, 146). Thus, events are formative of what we perceive to be necessary and obvious. The constitutive operation of events, however, is not necessarily a uniform, predetermined, coordinated, or orderly one. In mapping dispersed events in order to give an account of the descent of those things that have been considered given, the "things that continue to exist and have value for us," one enters into the realm of accidents, errors, chance, and divergence (ibid.).

Relatedly, a consideration of *Entstehung* focuses one's attention on the milieu and the means of emergence of events. Events emerge through relations between forces and, more specifically, through relations of conflict, domination, and subjection. Confrontation between forces of varying strength occasions the emergence of the triumphant forces themselves as events. Emergence in this context should be understood not as the long-awaited arrival of something expected, as the product of logical or planned development, but as the fortuitous appearance of something that could only have arisen given the confluence of particular forces. Hence, for Foucault, doing history via genealogy – that is, via an analysis of events – destabilizes foundations, breaks up unities, and reveals fragmentation and heterogeneity in their place.

Genealogy thus disrupts the presumptions of both unity and objectivity by locating within history that which has been regarded as constant and stable; for example, by recasting presumed givens such as "human nature" as both the product of events and as themselves discursive events. It places the historian within history; it interrogates the place from which the historian speaks, the construction of the objects that shape the historian's pursuit of knowledge, and the emergence of the concepts that structure the historian's speech. Genealogy thus brings to the fore events that would previously have lain undiscovered and shifts our focus from major, perceptible, and momentous occurrences to the minor, subterranean "profusion of entangled events" beneath them (ELCP, 155).

Whereas traditional history posits an inevitable continuity among historical events, "effective" history treats events as singular eruptions; an event is "the reversal of a relationship of forces, the usurpation of power, the appropriation of a vocabulary turned against those who had once used it" (ELCP, 154). The presumption of a logical progression of events is rejected, supplanted by the accidental collision of forces that give rise to events of an unanticipated order. Thus, in line with the Nietzschean inheritance that shapes Foucault's understanding of the event, a focus on events is paired with a disruption of the conventional understanding of causal relations. The event indicates a shift from thinking of causality as a linear relation between cause and effect, as efficient causality, to thinking of causality in terms of a set of more complex relations. The idea that events are the effects of chance encounters between forces, however, does not entail that events arise randomly or that the contingency of their emergence is haphazard. Instead, Foucault maintains, for example, that the events that constitute a discursive formation are the product of "the regularity of a practice" (EAK, 74).

Foucault's understanding of the event is also significantly inspired by Deleuze's theory of the event in *The Logic of Sense*. In his review of that text in "Theatrum Philosophicum," Foucault summarizes three dimensions of the event: "at the limit of dense bodies, an event is incorporeal (a metaphysical surface); on the surface of words and things, an incorporeal event is the sense of a proposition (its logical dimension); in the thread of discourse, an incorporeal sense-event is fastened to the verb (the infinitive point of the present)" (ELCP, 175). These three aspects of the Deleuzian theory of the event mark a revolution in the concept and a departure from the ways other traditions – neopositivism, phenomenology, and the philosophy of history, respectively – have conceived the event. When it is understood as incorporeal, expressive of sense, and expressed by the infinitive verb with its emphasis on the fullness of the present, the event is thought of autonomously rather than bound to and conceived in terms of either the physical world and its occurrences (neopositivism), the self and its subjective consciousness (phenomenology), or God or a linear progression of time in which the past anticipates and determines the future (the philosophy of history) (ELCP, 176). Understood as incorporeal sense, the sense of what is said or what happens, events are both effects insofar as they themselves are generated and constitutive forces or causes insofar as they constitute the givens of our world (what is said and what happens).

This view of the event is found in modified form in the concept of the "statement" developed in *The Archaeology of Knowledge*: "[A] statement is always an event that neither the language (*langue*) nor the meaning can quite exhaust" (EAK, 28). Like the Deleuzian event, the statement-event is tied to materiality or corporeality without being reducible to it; it is an incorporeal singularity. Nevertheless, the statement-event is connected both to other statements and to its own socio-historical conditions – "too bound up with what surrounds it and supports it to be as free as a pure form" – and yet also repeatable and thus not limited to "the spatio-temporal coordinates of its birth" (EAK, 104–105). The statement-event is to be understood as singular but not as isolated. Thus, in articulating the order of events, Foucault seeks not to detach the event from the conditions that gave rise to it and the novel repetitions it occasions but rather "to leave oneself free to describe the interplay of relations within it and outside it" that would otherwise remain obscured (EAK, 29).

Erinn Gilson

SEE ALSO

Language
Phenomenology
Statement
Gilles Deleuze

SUGGESTED READING

Colwell, Chauncey. 1997. "Deleuze and Foucault: Series, Event, Genealogy," *Theory and Event* 1, no. 2. Accessed November 11, 2010. DOI: 10.1353/tae.1997.0004.

Deleuze, Gilles. 1990. *The Logic of Sense*, trans. Mark Lester. New York: Columbia University Press.

Flynn, Thomas. 1994. "Foucault's Mapping of History," in *The Cambridge Companion to Foucault*, ed. Gary Gutting. Cambridge: Cambridge University Press, pp. 29–48.

McWhorter, Ladelle. 1994. "The Event of Truth: Foucault's Response to Structuralism," *Philosophy Today* 38, no. 2:159–166.

Nietzsche, Friedrich. 1990. "The Four Great Errors," in *Twilight of the Idols*, trans. R. J. Hollingdale. New York: Penguin.

27

EXPERIENCE

THE CONCEPT OF experience lies at the very core of Foucault's thought. Such a claim can only seem deeply paradoxical even to Foucault's most casual readers. Foucault's thought appears throughout to be adamantly opposed precisely to those philosophical traditions – phenomenology, philosophy of life, hermeneutics, and existentialism, for example – that take lived experience as their ultimate point of reference. This fact, however, obscures the more profound and diverse roles that experience plays in Foucault's work.

In order to see this, we must begin by recognizing a distinction that the English term experience fails to convey. French distinguishes between *le vécu* and *l'expérience*. *Le vécu* (lived experience) is employed in the French tradition to translate the German *Erlebnis* as it was used principally by Husserl in his *Cartesian Meditations* [originally published, in French translation, in 1931] and *Ideas Pertaining to a Pure Phenomenology and to a Phenomenological Philosophy: First Book* [1913; French trans., 1950]. Here it denoted the complex stream of conscious states, acts, and content that one distinctly lives through or undergoes by virtue of the various capacities of human subjectivity. In this sense, *le vécu* designates the inner life of the subject whose attitudes or position-takings (*Stellungnahmen*) with respect to the states of affairs that it encounters are taken, in the strands of phenomenology that derive principally from these texts, to be what brings these states to appearance; that is to say, to be what determinately discloses or constitutes them.

L'expérience is used in a number of different ways, several of which we shall explore, but, most generally, it can be said to possess two primary senses: (1) the complex set of correlations that encompass and make possible both the subjective dimension of lived experience and the objective domain of the states of affairs that it encounters, and (2) the idea of wisdom or learning gained through exploration, experimentation, or a journey of discovery (the sense of being "experienced" at something). In both, *expérience* is cognate with the German *Erfahrung*, the term of art for the process of cognition generally employed by Kant and German Idealism.

Foucault examines the role of the constitutive sense of experience in his famous treatment of the invention of man in *The Order of Things* (1966). There he demonstrates that man comes to exist only when he is identified as the source of the representational form of knowledge that had governed what was knowable in the classical age. In this sense, the subject whose power produces representation becomes itself an object of knowledge. Modern empirical sciences (biology, economics, and philology) emerge precisely at this historical juncture as ways of studying the finitude of man's various representational capacities (perceiving, valuing, and describing). Man is shown to be a resolutely finite object. But he is also, at the same time, the subject that is held to constitute the empirical world and to do so precisely by virtue of his finitude. Modern philosophy – and Foucault here clearly targets the constitutive phenomenology of Husserl, the existential phenomenology of the early Merleau-Ponty and Sartre, and Heidegger's distinctive hermeneutical phenomenology – is thus defined by its attempt to work out an "analytic of finitude" that shows how man, precisely in and through his limitations, is both the transcendental origin of all objects of knowledge and the empirical object itself being studied, both, as Foucault put it, the founding and the founded. Lived experience is but one of the principal names for man as this "empirico-transcendental doublet," Foucault contends, for *le vécu* is the "space in which all empirical contents are given to experience; it is also the originary form that makes them in general possible and that designates their first roots" (EOT, 321). As such, lived experience is nothing other than the dogmatic slumber, the "anthropological sleep," into which modern thought, according to Foucault, has fallen. This sleep, as we begin to awaken from it, from the encumbrance of man himself, Foucault says, opens a new space in which it might become possible to think other than simply in accordance with humanism. In this sense, Foucault's mode of thought is indeed deeply at odds with any appeal to experience in this constitutive sense.

The concept of *l'expérience*, however, plays an important and distinctly different set of roles throughout Foucault's work. We can distinguish four principal senses. Three are concepts with which he was explicitly concerned, what can be termed thematic concepts. Another is a meaning on which he relied but does not analyze directly, which is thus best called an operative concept.

The first of the thematic concepts of experience is methodological and is marked by Foucault's employment of the phrase "form of experience" and its variants. In this sense, experience denotes the object of archaeological-genealogical investigation. Foucault speaks, for example, of studying the "structure of the experience of madness," the "pure experience of order and its modes of being," and the "experience of sexuality." Each of these he takes to be a historically unique "form of experience" composed of a "correlation between fields of knowledge, types of normativity, and forms of subjectivity in a particular culture" (EHS2, 4). Each form is thus a config-uration forged by the reciprocal, though irreducible, interrelations between specific types of knowledge, power, and processes of subjectivization. This configuration, what Foucault elsewhere calls a historical a priori or game of truth, is a histori-cal multiplicity that serves, in turn, as the grid of intelligibility, practice, and self-relation that sets down the rules for what can count as an experience of the specific sort under examination. The task of the archaeological-genealogical method is thus to unearth this shifting fundamental conditioning stratum and to set out the chance lines of historical concatenation of types of knowledge and practices of power and subjectivization by which it emerged.

The second thematic concept of experience in Foucault's work is his famous appeal to "limit-experience." Whereas lived experience is concerned with account-ing for the mundane, the banal, and the commonplace, limit-experience occurs at points in life that are as close as possible to being unlivable. Foucault initially found the resources to think of this distinctive sort of experience in his studies of a lineage of what he called thinkers of the outside: the Marquis de Sade, Friedrich Hölderlin, Friedrich Nietzsche, Stephane Mallarmé, Antonin Artaud, Georges Bataille, Pierre Klossowski, and Maurice Blanchot (EEW2, 150–151). Each, according to Foucault, located moments in the course of ordinary life at which the boundaries that define its very normality become exposed, paradoxically, in and through their collapse. Following this line, Foucault initially conceived of limit-experience as an encoun-ter with the untamed space of the prediscursive that he believed lay anterior to the grids of intelligibility that defined the confines of reason, knowledge, and the nor-mal. Later, drawing from the work of Georges Canguilhem, he came to think of a limit not as what opens on some domain outside lived experience but as a deviation from the norms that structure the environments that we inhabit, a chance error or mutation that occurs within the immanent flow of life and that, as such, creates the possibility of something new emerging precisely within that flow itself (see EEW2, 476–477; cf. FDE3, 441–442).

Now, whether the response to such an encounter is to act out the transgression (Bataille) or to withdraw into the condition of destitution (Blanchot), as Foucault's early writings proclaim, or it is to embrace the creative role of deviance for life itself (Canguilhem), as he was later to advocate, limit-experience is always a pro-cess of desubjectivization, an experiment or ordeal in which the constituting self is wrenched from out of its supposed position of preeminence, exposed in its frailty, and confronted with the task of fashioning itself anew, a practice of freedom, an aesthetics of the self.

The third and final thematic sense of experience is the testimony of the marginal. Experience here denotes the wide spectrum of embodied knowledge that comes from being in a condition of subjugation or exclusion. Foucault never sought to develop a full theoretical account of such experience, but he did, on several significant occasions, appeal to it. One such example was when early on he considered the possibility of writing a history of madness itself; that is, an account of madness as it had been lived by the mad. Yet, even then, he acknowledged that such experience is necessarily intertwined with the cognitive schemes and normative practices that produce it: "The liberty of madness can only be heard from the heights of the fortress in which it is imprisoned" (EHM, xxxii). Accordingly, his subsequent presentations of such testimony – in the two case studies that he assembled from the nineteenth century, of the murderer Pierre Rivère (*I, Pierre Rivère, Having Slaughtered My Mother, My Sister, and My Brother ...* [1973]) and the hermaphrodite Alexina Barbin (*Herculine Barbin: Being the Recently Discovered Memoirs of a Nineteenth Century French Hermaphrodite* [1978]), as well as the introduction he wrote for an anthology of internment reports that he edited, "Lives of Infamous Men" (1977) – were all constructed so that they show the complex way in which these experiences were caught up in and constituted by specific historical techniques of representation and forms of intervention, what he would come to call processes of subjectivization. In each, he sought to give voice to subjugated experiences as they moved within and through the very practices of normality that excluded them as deviant or abnormal.

The final sense of experience in Foucault is more subtle and difficult to detect, but not for that any less significant. Foucault himself never theorized this sense, but he relied on it, and it enabled him to carry out his work. It thus stood behind the research itself, shadowing it, sometimes closely, sometimes from afar.

This sense refers to the concrete experiences born out of social and political struggle, and it has two sides. The first has to do with the motivation underlying Foucault's work. Foucault was directly involved in or witnessed at close hand efforts to reform psychiatric facilities and hospitals, the uprisings against the conditions of prison life, social movements in support of immigrant rights and against racism, and political revolts and revolutions, and he supported, albeit critically, the burgeoning movement for gay liberation. He sometimes explicitly invoked such experiences as being part of what compelled him to investigate specific institutions and practices (see FSP, 39–40/EDP, 30–31). In this sense, these experiences stood, for him, as a wellspring that motivated his research and served to suggest for him specific lines of analysis on which he subsequently drew in his investigations.

The second side has to do with the efficacy or effects of this research. As each of Foucault's works is rooted in a contemporary sociopolitical situation, it has a stake in the configurations of knowledge, power, and subjectivization that are at work in this context. Each study thus necessarily operates within the truth of the concrete experience out of which it arises, and, as such, Foucault acknowledged, his analyses must meet the standards of conventional academic research. This means that they must strive to make and defend verifiable historical claims through the responsible use of source materials. But these works exceed the purview of the classical academic historian in that they also call their readers to an experience of who and what they are or, better, who and what they have become, an experience of modernity itself that would ultimately begin, Foucault held, a transformation in the reader's relationship to the subjects that they themselves have become and the age that has shaped them as such. In this sense, the effect of archaeological-genealogical research is not simply to offer an account of the past but to do so in such a way that it provokes us to think of new ways of relating to ourselves, to one another, and to the traditions and worlds that we share. Foucault did not speak of the intended effects of his research very often, but he did note in an interview that what for him was ultimately at stake in his work was not just the historical cogency of his analyses, as important as that was, but the creation (Foucault calls it a "fiction") of an experience of transformation, of transposition, of conversion even, wherein the current form of our subjectivity is brought to its dissolution and an opening to something new emerges. As such, he said, each of his works is to be read as, in this precise sense, an "experience book" (EEW3, 246). Experience, in this deeply practical and exploratory sense, can thus properly be said to pervade the whole of Foucault's thought and to shadow it there as a continual call for transformation, a constant challenge to refuse what one has become.

Kevin Thompson

SEE ALSO

The Double
Man
Phenomenology
Subjectification
Georges Canguilhem

SUGGESTED READING

Bruns, Gerald L. 2011. *On Ceasing to Be Human*. Stanford, CA: Stanford University Press, chap. 3.
Djaballah, Marc. 2008. *Kant, Foucault, and Forms of Experience*. London: Routledge.
Flynn, Thomas. 2005. *Sartre, Foucault and Historical Reason*, volume 2: *A Poststructuralist Mapping of History*. Chicago: University of Chicago Press, chap. 9.
Gutting, Gary. 2002. "Foucault's Philosophy of Experience," *Boundary 2*, 29, no. 2:69–85.
Han, Béatrice. 2002. *Foucault's Critical Project: Between the Transcendental and the Historical*. Stanford, CA: Stanford University Press, chap. 5.
Jay, Martin. 2006. *Songs of Experience: Variations on a Universal Theme*. Berkeley: University of California Press, chap. 9.

Lawlor, Leonard. 2006. *The Implications of Immanence: Toward a New Concept of Life*. New York: Fordham University Press, chaps. 4–5.

Macherey, Pierre. 1986. "Aux Sources de 'L'Histoire de la folie': Une rectification et ses limites," *Critique* 42:753–774.

Oksala, Johanna. 2011. "Sexual Experience: Foucault, Phenomenology, and Feminist Theory," *Hypatia* 26, no. 1:207–223.

O'Leary, Timothy. 2008. "Foucault, Experience, Literature," *Foucault Studies* 5:5–25.

Rayner, Timothy. 2009. *Foucault and Fiction: The Experience Book*. London: Continuum.

28

FINITUDE

"MODERN MAN," WRITES Foucault, "is possible only as a figuration of finitude" (EOT, 318). Crucially, this does not mean that Foucault understands finitude as paradigmatically modern. Indeed, varying conceptions of finitude have been elaborated across human history; it is not as though the very notion of finitude emerged in modernity. The idea was already in play in the classical period, but only insofar as it was understood in negative relation to the idea of infinity, as marking, for instance, the difference between the human and the divine. Of greater interest to Foucault is the particular conception of finitude that marks the modern *episteme*. In philosophical modernity, man is limited by various discourses on life, labor, and language of which he is both the object and the origin. Modern man is an "empirico-transcendental doublet" to the extent that he appears as an empirical object within the transcendental field of which he is the source. Foucault renders the transition from the classical to the modern *episteme* as a "profound upheaval," an "archaeological mutation," that gives birth to modern man as an "enslaved sovereign" and "observed spectator" (EOT, 312). Although Renaissance humanism and classical rationalism were able to assign human beings a privileged position in the order of the world, modern thought is the first to be able to conceive of "man" because it is able to articulate the epistemic bind that is presented by his finitude. Man is the transcendental source of a field in which he appears as an empirical object, and this poses certain epistemological problems that Foucault claims are devastating for phenomenology.

The figure of finitude concerns "the modern themes of an individual who lives, speaks, and works in accordance with the laws of an economics, a philology, and a biology, but who also, by a sort of internal torsion or overlapping, has acquired the right, through the interplay of those very laws, to know them and to subject them to total clarification" (EOT, 310). Finitude marks this understanding of man as not only an empirical entity but also as the entity responsible for opening the transcendental field in which empirical objects appear. For Foucault, the problem of finitude can be traced back to Kant, for whom man was both an object in the empirical world and the transcendental source of that world. The result is that, as Foucault puts it, "each of the positive forms in which man can learn that he is finite is given to him against the background of his own finitude" (EOT, 314). This realization gives rise to the "analytic of finitude," or the various modes of thought that grapple with the paradox that man is at once an empirical object within, and the transcendental origin of, the modern discourses of life, labor, and language. The paradox is grounded in the fact that it is none other than the finitude of human beings that is the condition for their knowledge *of* that finitude. "Modern culture can conceive of man because it conceives of the finite on the basis of itself" (EOT, 318). Hence Foucault's analysis is concerned with the "repetition of the positive within the fundamental," such that finitude "rests on nothing but its own existence as fact" (EOT, 315). This understanding of man's finitude is one of the hallmarks of modernity on Foucault's account, and the modern conception of finitude is one where it is conceived in "an interminable cross reference" with itself (EOT, 318). The fact that Foucault is inclined to use images of "cross-referencing," "folding," "overlapping," and "internal torsion" in his discussions of finitude marks his understanding of this figure as inherently reflexive, such that "the contents of experience are already their own conditions" (EOT, 339). Foucault's investigations of the analytic of finitude emphasize several moments of paradox, or doubling, that result from conceiving man as the transcendental grounds of empirical knowledge, and the object of knowledge, at once. The analytic of finitude is generative of the three doubles – the transcendental and the empirical, the cogito and the unthought, and the retreat and return of the origin that Foucault explores in the ninth chapter of *The Order of Things*.

Foucault's analytic of finitude outlines various attempts made in philosophical modernity to respond to the problem of finitude, or the idea that man is irreducibly transcendental and empirical. In other words, the analytic of finitude traces various efforts to respond to the idea that man is both constituting and constituted in relation to exteriority. Attempts are made to reduce the transcendental to the empirical, for instance in the positivist aspiration to account for knowledge strictly in relation to the natural sciences. The inverse attempt has been made in transcendental phenomenology by subordinating empirical science to the transcendental field constituted by the subject. In Foucault's account, however, neither effort can resolve the tension that persists here. In the end, neither is successful, a fact that forecasts the demise of the modern *episteme* as Foucault understood it. Man is always irreducibly transcendental *and* empirical; he cannot be one or the other. The projects of philosophical modernity that take the reduction of one to the other as their aim are unsuccessful. Instead, the unending vacillation between the empirical and the transcendental yields a fundamental opacity at the heart of knowledge, and a distance at the heart of the self. The result is that the human subject proves incapable of giving an account of its own genesis. This is one problem that defines philosophical modernity as Foucault understood it.

Ann V. Murphy

SEE ALSO

Death
The Double
Man
Phenomenology
Martin Heidegger
Immanuel Kant

SUGGESTED READING

Dreyfus, Hubert L., and Paul Rabinow. 1983. *Michel Foucault: Beyond Structuralism and Hermeneutics*, 2nd ed. Chicago: University of Chicago Press.
Gutting, Gary. 1989. *Michel Foucault's Archaeology of Scientific Reason*. Cambridge: Cambridge University Press.

29

FREEDOM

REEDOM IS A central concern of Foucault's writing. In his genealogies of the emergence and intensification of disciplinary power, the apparatus of sexuality, and governmentality, he hoped to create a shared experience with his readers of the contingency of present constraints on human possibilities. He attempted to loosen the threshold of acceptance of established ways of thinking and being, including ways of thinking about both power and freedom. More specifically, he encouraged his readers to question humanist understandings of freedom that appeal to a universal moral (hence rational and impartial) core, or to the end state of a universal history of human progress. He did not believe that a society without power relations was possible (or desirable), but this is not tantamount to a denial of freedom. In fact, he wanted to show people that they are freer than they think – to inspire his readers to practice freedom by opening up new possibilities for thinking and being in order to minimize situations of domination in which people are unable to alter the power relations in which they are enmeshed.

Given the centrality of freedom to his project, it is, perhaps, surprising that a commonly received view of Foucault represents him as denying the possibility of freedom at all, as describing modern subjects who are constituted within productive disciplinary and normalizing power relations in which they are trapped. Thus, he is said to confront a problem of agency. Foucault rejected this reading of his work: "The idea that power is a system of domination that controls everything and leaves no room for freedom cannot be attributed to me" (EEW1, 293). Power is not domination. In a domination relation, asymmetrical power relations are fixed, allowing no real possibilities for change. In contrast, Foucault claimed, power relations are "mobile, reversible, and unstable" (EEW1, 292). Foucault described a form of power, pastoral or governmental, in which one tries to control the conduct of another ("a conduct of conduct") to manage their possibilities (EEW3, 341). This form of power is not a negative force that operates by repression and prohibition (though repression and prohibition do exist); instead, it produces knowledge, techniques, subjects, objects, and rationalities. It is a form of power that "makes individuals subjects," gripping them at the level of their everyday behavior and their desire to be normal, healthy, secure, or free (EEW3, 331). Power does not determine us, but it does structure the field of possibilities in which we make choices and constitute ourselves. Moreover, if power relations are everywhere, as Foucault contended, this is because freedom is everywhere. Power relations only emerge because subjects confront a range of possible actions and do not necessarily do or think what others want. Thus power and freedom are coconstitutive.

Foucault typically responded to critics who believed there was no room for freedom in his writings in two ways: (1) by noting that this response takes for granted humanist understandings of freedom that he regarded as inadequate for understanding our situation in the modern West, and (2) by clarifying his own understanding of freedom.

What is wrong with humanism? Foucault's account of freedom can be understood as the correlative of his analytic of power, as we have seen. Moreover, just as disciplinary and normalizing biopower (later described as "pastoral power" or "governmentality") represent an alternative to the model of sovereign power in which power is understood as repressive, centralized, and possessed (by a monarch, a people, a class, whites, men, etc.), the freedom Foucault appeals to represents an alternative to dominant historical understandings. The problem with the sovereign model of power is that it obscures other power relations (biopower) dispersed throughout the field that serve as its matrix – power relations that operate by attaching us to particular identities and self-understandings. The problem with humanist accounts of freedom is similar; they obscure and channel the freedom that we already have by subjecting us to an abstract model of humanity as something to be realized either through universal ethics and obedience to moral and political law or through self-knowledge and technologies of self-improvement. Here freedom is represented as a possession or a state of being rather than a concrete practice.

For example, consider two dominant understandings of freedom that Foucault thought were insufficient. The first, an older humanism associated with liberal theories of sovereign power, defines freedom as a natural human right, as something residing in the presocial individual that is not only transferable to the state for the purposes of security and peace but also a limit on illegitimate state power and legal authority. Here the role of the state is to preserve and protect our natural freedom. The second understanding of freedom, a more recent form of humanism associated with the liberal art of government and the rise of the human sciences and concomitant political technologies of individualization, describes freedom as the progressive development of techniques for training, regulating, examining, observing, measuring, and reforming individuals as well as attending to the health, education, and welfare of both individuals and populations in order to make them more productive. In this case, governmental power is not opposed to human liberty but is a vehicle for cultivating and domesticating it in the name of social progress and universal human flourishing. Hence, Foucault claimed, "Liberalism ... must produce freedom, but this very act entails the establishment of limitations, controls, forms of coercion and obligations relying on threats, etc." (ECF-BBIO, 64).

Both of these understandings of freedom appeal to the humanist ideal of a true or universal humanity. In the first case, humanity is understood as in need of law and order lest it abuse the natural freedom of others who are also inherently free and equal (liberalism), or as naturally predisposed to live peacefully with others and realize its potential as long as its basic needs are met and it is not alienated from its true humanity by oppression or economic exploitation (Marxism). In the second account, the progress of humanity and its freedom is associated with the modern historical process of learning how to domesticate its antisocial nature by cultivating its capacity for developing rational (and moral) institutions and behaviors in order to be free. Furthermore, even if one is a pragmatist about the nature of humanity, one might be inclined to think that these humanist stories about ourselves are indispensable to preserving or securing human freedom.

Foucault was wary of humanist philosophies because of their universalizing tendencies. Concerning liberationist theories of freedom associated with Marxism, for example, he remarked:

> I have always been somewhat suspicious of the notion of liberation, because if it is not treated ... within certain limits, one runs the risk of falling back on the idea that there exists a human nature or base that ... has been concealed, or alienated or imprisoned in and by mechanisms of repression. According to this hypothesis, all that is required is to break these repressive deadlocks and man will be reconciled with himself, rediscover his nature or regain contact with his origin and reestablish a full and positive relationship with himself. I think this idea should not be accepted without scrutiny. (EEW1, 283)

Kantian humanism is equally problematic for him insofar as it presents "a certain form of ethics as a universal model for any kind of freedom" (ETS, 15).

What does he propose instead? When he spoke of freedom, which was rare, Foucault implicitly appealed to two different capacities: (1) our capacity for critical reflection on who we are in the present, a form of historical reflection that he called the "historical ontology of ourselves," and (2) our capacity to transform relations of power through ethical practices of freedom (EEW1, 315). For example, in his reflections on Kant's historical essay, "What Is Enlightenment?" he situated himself within the very Enlightenment tradition he was criticizing. In this essay, Foucault locates Kant's sensitivity to a "historical consciousness that the Enlightenment has of itself" – one that is in tension with humanism (EEW1, 314). In a dramatic reversal of Kant's understanding of critique, he described the historical ontology of ourselves as follows:

> It will not deduce from the form of what we are what it is impossible for us to do and to know; but it will separate out, from the contingency that has made us what we are, the possibility of no longer being, doing, thinking what we are, do or think. (EEW1, 315–316)

Whereas Kantian critique tries to establish necessary conditions for the possibility of experience, Foucault's genealogical writings pose the question: "In what is given to us as universal, necessary, obligatory, what place is occupied by whatever is singular, contingent, and the product of arbitrary constraints" (EEW1, 315)? Hence, freedom in relation to critical thought is our capacity to "step back" from entrenched ways of acting and reacting, to engage in historical reflection on our concepts and practices, and to question them concerning their significance, their conditions of possibility, and their aims. Critical thought identifies historical, and thus contingent, constraints on our possibilities, not necessary ones. In turn, in revealing the non-necessity of present ways of thinking, doing, and being, this form of critical work "seeks to give new impetus to … the undefined work of freedom" (EEW1, 316).

This phrase "the undefined work of freedom" captures the experimental nature of the practices of freedom Foucault invoked in his late ethical writings – writings that explore historical shifts in our self-relations from antiquity to early Christianity. As we have seen, although he understood the importance of moments in which a people or a group throws off the yoke of domination, he did not regard liberation as sufficient. Freedom is not a matter of lifting constraints: nor do laws or institutions guarantee it. "Liberty is a practice," he remarked, and "the guarantee of freedom is freedom" (EEW3, 355–356). Thus he encouraged the cultivation of practices of freedom that might help define new and acceptable forms of life and new forms of subjectivity that resist the government of individualization and sever the ways it enhances capacities (namely discipline) from their aims – rendering subjects more useful and controllable. In appealing as he did to practices of freedom, Foucault drew on Marx's idea that "man produces man." He stated: "[W]hat ought to be produced is not man as nature supposedly designed him, or as his essence ordains him to be – we need to produce something that doesn't exist yet, without being able to know what it will be" (EEW3, 275).

The work of freedom is indefinable because, constituted as we are within myriad power relations, we are not capable of grasping all of the forces operating on us. After all, Foucault's genealogies are not universal or totalizing. He was skeptical about the possibility of grasping everything about our historical situation. His genealogies are specific histories about only some of the forces that make us who we are. And this set of forces is always in motion. As a result, all we can do is experiment with ourselves, engage in practices of self-transformation that might resist some of the intolerable normalizing trends in which we find ourselves, and test the limits of our present sense of possibility. We cannot create ourselves ex nihilo but must work with the materials made available to us, bend them to a different will, deploy them within different strategies, and keep the field of possibilities within which we are constituted open.

Take, for example, a privileged case for Foucault, the case of sexuality. Foucault acknowledged that a number of liberations vis-à-vis sexuality were clearly necessary – liberation from male domination or from compulsory heterosexuality and its morality. Yet to be free of such forces is not tantamount to being a "happy human being imbued with a sexuality to which the subject could achieve a complete and satisfying relationship" (EEW1, 283). Liberation will be followed by new power relationships, which, he noted, "must be controlled by practices of freedom" (EEW1, 284). Accordingly, sexual freedom is not merely a matter of securing the right to express the truth of our desires but our capacity to invent new pleasures and forms of life, to experiment with our bodies and ourselves as they have been constituted within the current apparatus of sexuality in order to produce new experiences and other forms of life. On one of the rare occasions in which he offered advice, he urged gays not to *be* but to *become* homosexual.

In the end, we cannot know in advance where these experiments will take us, whether they will lead to something better or whether they will end up becoming just as intolerable as those we are resisting. This is why our capacity for critical historical reflection on what we have become, an exercise in transforming our self-understanding, is just as necessary as experiments in living. Both are indispensable elements of Foucault's practice of freedom.

Jana Sawicki

SEE ALSO

Critique
Liberalism
Man
Marxism
Power

SUGGESTED READING

Heyes, Cressida. 2007. *Self-Transformations: Foucault, Ethics, and Normalized Bodies*. New York: Oxford University Press.

Ingram, David. 2005. "Foucault and Habermas," in *The Cambridge Companion to Foucault*, 2nd ed., ed. Gary Gutting. Cambridge: Cambridge University Press.

May, Todd. 2011. "Foucault's Conception of Freedom," in *Michel Foucault: Key Concepts*, ed. Dianna Taylor. Durham: Acumen Publishing, pp. 73–81.

McWhorter, LaDelle. 1999. *Bodies and Pleasures: Foucault and the Politics of Sexual Normalization*. Bloomington: Indiana University Press.

Oksala, Johanna. 2005. *Foucault on Freedom*. Cambridge: Cambridge University Press.

Rajchman, John. 1985. *Michel Foucault: The Freedom of Philosophy*. New York: Columbia University Press.

Thompson, Kevin. 2003. "Forms of Resistance: Foucault on Tactical Reversal and Self-Formation," *Continental Philosophy Review* 36, no. 2:113–138.

30

FRIENDSHIP

N A 1982 interview, Michel Foucault announced a new direction for his research that he would never have the chance to follow, much less complete. He declared that "now, after studying the history of sex, we should try to understand the history of friendship, or friendships" (EEW1, 171). His rationale builds on the themes of biopower and governmentality that he began studying during the middle and late 1970s. Accordingly, he offers the hypothesis "that the disappearance of friendship as a social relation" occurring between the sixteenth and seventeenth centuries "and the declaration of homosexuality as a social/political/medical problem" in the eighteenth century "are the same process" (ibid.). That is, the problematization of friendship as an open-ended relationship through which individuals determine their obligations and value to one another on broadly aesthetic grounds and the problematization of homosexuality as an apparent violation and, much more, exploitation of both social and biological rules and processes belong to the same system of biopower forming normative prescriptive rules for individuals on the basis of ostensibly descriptive claims about the population or species as a whole.

The theme of friendship in Foucault's work helps to bridge the apparent gap between Foucault's work on power in the 1970s and his work on ethics in the 1980s. Scholars writing on Foucault's analysis of friendship note that this topic, because it involves a political relationship among many individuals while being determined on aesthetic rather than universal normative grounds of duty, utility, or virtue, rebuts criticisms of Foucault's apoliticism, ethical aestheticism, and critical nihilism. In the second and third volumes of *The History of Sexuality*, Foucault explores ancient Greek and Roman practices of *askesis*, "the work that one performs on oneself in order to transform oneself or make the self appear which, happily, one never attains" (EEW1, 137), in order to offer an aestheticized counterexample to contemporary ethical frameworks rooted in duty, utility, or virtue, which allows the creative costs of these universalizing approaches to become conspicuous. Significantly, this aesthetic sense of care of the self implicates others in friendship by a creative interaction that pushes ethical and political valuations toward aesthetic considerations beyond oppositions of subjectivity and objectivity, activity and passivity, that curtail contemporary discourses.

In the third volume of *The History of Sexuality*, subtitled *The Care of the Self*, Foucault uses the concept of *parrēsia* as both an interpersonal, ethicopolitical relationship of friendship and an epistemological relation to truth in order to question the contemporary standards regarding the individual's relation to knowledge. In contrast to scientific standards according to which individuals passively submit to objective truth, the parrēsiast's relationship to truth consists of the use he makes of truth based first on a personal relationship to those for and with whom the truth may be told. The basis for the parrēsiast's truth owes in part to what he stands to lose or the danger in which he places himself by telling the truth. In another sense, the parrēsiast's truth depends on the beauty with which the truth is disclosed or conveyed in consideration of the power relations involved. As with the ethicopolitical relationship of friendship, the value of parrēsiastic truth depends on an aesthetic valuation judged in terms of creativity expressed within a given set of personal, political, and epistemological constraints rather than being compromised by such constraints as an obligation to empirical observation, systematic unity, methodological verifiability, or metaphysical doctrine as contemporary measures of truth insist.

Foucault connects the practices of friendship associated with the themes of *askesis* and *parrēsia* to discussions of the creation of culture in general and gay culture or homosexual "askesis" in particular throughout a series of interviews in gay periodicals in both America and France published during the 1980s. In this context, the significance of friendship, especially friendships between men, results from the ways that gay culture in the late 1970s and early 1980s constituted a way of life that exposed and challenged standards of heterosexist orthodoxy rooted in and maintained by the institution of the family, whose filiation by means of blood served as an example of the microphysics of biopower operative at the level of industrial society at large. By attempting to create forms of pleasure and relationships between individuals outside the institution of the family ringed by the twin legacies of law and biology, the creation of gay culture, or simply "friendship" between men, challenged contemporary forms of governmentality organized according to the function of biopower. Against the knowledge of homosexuality as the breach of either human or divine law, or else a biological aberration or a violation of natural drives, Foucault counterposes homosexuality as an example of an ethical, political, and epistemic order organized around aesthetic practices in which individuals "face each other without terms or convenient words, with nothing to assure them about the meaning of the movement that carries them toward each other. They have to invent, from A to Z, a relationship that is still formless, which is friendship: that is to say, the sum of everything throughout which they can give each other pleasure" (EEW1, 136).

Ultimately, the invention of forms of relationships that bring individuals plea-sure does not belong exclusively to homosexuals more than heterosexuals because these two forms of sexuality, among others, are implicated in the production of one another through biopolitical power relations. Moreover, these relations constitute "a legal, social, and institutional world where the only relations possible are extremely few, extremely simplified, and extremely poor. There is, of course, the relation of marriage, and the relations of family, but how many other relations should exist, should be able to find their codes not in institutions but in possible supports, which is not at all the case" (EEW1, 158). Accordingly, the counterexample of ancient prac-tices of care of the self confronts the atomistic individualism of modernity with the question of what individuality can mean as a singular expression produced amid a community of contending forces and games of truth in which the paramount ques-tion "what can be played?" (EEW1, 140) becomes unavoidable.

Joshua Kurdys

SEE ALSO

Ethics
Homosexuality
Parrēsia
Power
Truth

SUGGESTED READING

Garlick, Steve. 2002. "The Beauty of Friendship: Foucault, Masculinity and the Work of Art," *Philosophy and Social Criticism* 28:558–577.
Lynch, Richard A. 1998. "Is Power All There Is? Michel Foucault and the 'Omnipresence' of Power Relations," *Philosophy Today* 42:65–70.
McLaren, Margaret. 2006. "From Practices of the Self to Politics: Foucault and Friendship," *Philosophy Today* 50:195–201.
Webb, David. 2003. "On Friendship: Derrida, Foucault and the Practice of Becoming," *Research in Phenomenology* 33:119–140.

31

GENEALOGY

W E MAY UNDERSTAND the word "genealogy" in the context of Foucault's work to name a way to form a distinct kind of knowledge. This knowledge, Foucault says, requires meticulous and patient work on all manner of documents and institutional and social practices. It is especially attuned to relations of power and to both the subjection and transformation of individuals. One of its leading goals is to show the specific ways in which social institutions, forms of recognition, and ways of life have come to be as they are and how they in some instances oppressively marginalize other people. A second leading goal is to develop interruptive knowledge that can lead to liberating options for those marginalized people and those who unwittingly oppress themselves.

Foucault's genealogical way of thinking has its roots in Nietzsche's *On the Genealogy of Morals*. Although he did not appropriate Nietzsche's ideas about the overman, will to knowledge, eternal return of the same, or will to power, he nonetheless accepted the importance of Nietzsche's insight that formations of knowledge and values are always also formations of power (in Foucault's language, formations of power relations). To understand the meaning of authoritative knowledge and value, a genealogist in the Nietzschean lineage usually follows the lines of relations of power that are historically developed and that establish social identities, basic inclinations in individuals, and hierarchies of rank and influence in given cultures. Further, the genealogist can trace the formation of some definitive capacities in people that are often taken as unchanging aspects of human nature. Morality itself (and not only specific morals), conscience, guilt, the ability to forgive, and the capacity for self-sacrificial love are examples of such aspects in Nietzsche's work. Foucault also accepted in Nietzsche's thought the importance of the reformation (or transvaluation) of current values by the power of a new kind of knowledge that is formed by a genealogical approach to those values. We will return to this claim and its importance in Foucault's work.

In his 1971 essay "Nietzsche, Genealogy, History," Foucault says that genealogical work

> must record the singularity of events outside of any monotonous finality; it must seek them in the most unpromising places, in what we tend to feel is without history – in sentiments, love, conscience, instincts; it must be sensitive to their recurrence, not in order to trace the gradual curve of their evolution, but to isolate the different scenes where they engaged in different roles. (ELCP, 139–140)

These goals mean that genealogical research requires an exceptionally careful knowledge of details that often seem accidental to the momentous events that are usually studied by traditional historians. It also means that genealogical knowledge and thought, as Foucault understood them, do not begin with images of changeless essences or principles, an expectation of reasonable, evolutionary progress, or "the metaphysical deployment of ideal significations and indefinite teleologies" (ELCP, 140). Genealogists look for the specific sites where a direction of development might begin, such as efforts to see what happens inside a diseased body (a major factor in early research hospitals) or clusters of problems that within certain conditions demand resolution. Foucault found, for example, that the struggle with an intolerable cluster of incompatible problems involving concern for health and "normal" practices and values in ancient societies helped to form some of the most distinctive aspects of Western sexuality. Genealogists look for situations where traceable lines of descent began to form various practices, institutions, and accepted truths. They look for specific beginnings and not for definitive, original identities: "What is found at the historical beginning of things is not the inviolable identity of their origin; it is ... disparity" (ELCP, 142). The definitive characteristics of things are "fabricated in a piecemeal fashion from alien forms ... [from] the details and accidents that accompany every beginning" (ELCP, 142, 144). In other words, values and truths, for example, that we frequently take as unchanging and natural are in fact often the product of processes that bear many mutations and transformations of elements that are not at all like those values and truths.

Foucault, like Nietzsche, emphasized systems of subjugation and domination that accompany the formation of what particular groups of people consider routine and normal. Genealogy, Foucault says, intends to show in various lineages "not the anticipatory power of meaning, but the hazardous play of dominations" (ELCP, 148). Such dominations occur by means of rituals, procedures, rights, and obligations all of which are structured by rules: "[H]umanity installs each of its violences in a system of rules and thus proceeds from domination to domination" (ELCP, 152).

Foucault elaborates this Nietzschean thought with an observation that we will find has particular importance for him when he gives accounts of marginalized individuals and effective types of resistance to centers of power: "The nature of these rules allows violence to be inflicted on violence and resurgence of new forces that are sufficiently strong to dominate those in power. Rules are empty in themselves, violent, and unfinalized; they are impersonal and can be bent to any purpose" (ELCP, 151). They can be used, for example, against the people who had control over them. When that happens, individuals can "overcome the rulers through their own rules" (ibid.). This kind of reversal can happen in interpretations as well as in other kinds of political activity. For our purposes, I note in an introductory way that for Foucault genealogical knowledge can be effective in disrupting stable patterns of life that dominate, suppress, and otherwise injure other people. It can function as a "reversal of a relationship of forces," appropriate a vocabulary, and turn it "against those who had once used it" (ELCP, 154). It can create a countermemory – a transformation of history into a totally different form of time than that found in narratives that provide uninterrupted linear accounts of causes and effects. Rather, in the countermemory that Foucault develops, there are no clear lines of efficiently caused development. There are multiple crosscurrents of circumstances and often discontinuous events in which conflicts, impositions, new problems, and networks of practices and values form unstable assemblages of identity and authority. In that countermemory formed in genealogical knowledge, such assemblages and events constitute genealogies – descents of culturally inherited traits in the ways people find meaning and certainty, connect with each other, and organize themselves in all dimensions of their lives. "Countermemory" names the knowledge that genealogical accounts of these descents provide.

To carry out his Nietzsche-inspired genealogical project, Foucault found that he needed to distance himself from professional philosophy as he found it in France (EHM, 575). He pulled away from the kind of philosophizing that proceeded on the basis of interpretation of canonized philosophical texts in order to expand the range of knowledge and understanding of human, social lives. The traditional approach in his judgment constituted a self-totalizing tradition that turns people away from events that happen in the world, turns them from the surfaces of living occurrences and toward abstract historical narratives and various kinds of logics and principles that developed within the canonizing traditions. Foucault found that he needed to turn away from "unceasing commentary" on philosophical texts, away from the authoritative practices, values, and critiques that originated in the Western philosophical canon. He wanted to develop a different approach and discipline, a new kind of knowledge regarding specific people's lives and organizations (insane people and their doctors and hospitals, for example; or prisoners and prisons and their keepers; or those with unquestioned authoritative knowledge and the people who are subject to that knowledge) (EHM, 577). He said, "I don't think that an intellectual can raise real questions concerning the society in which he lives, based on nothing more than his textual, academic scholarly research"

(EEW3, 285). To carry out these intentions, he needed to focus on "the conditions and rules for the formation of knowledge to which philosophical discourse [for example] is subject, in any given period, in the same manner as any other form of discourse with rational pretension" (EHM, 578). "I set out to study and analyze the 'events' that came about in the order of knowledge, and which cannot be reduced either to the general law of some kind of 'progress', or the repetition of an origin.... For me, the most essential part of the work was in the analysis of those events, the bodies of knowledge, and those systematic forms that line discourses, institutions, and practices" (ibid.).

Foucault's intense exposure as a young man to marginalized people whom he found to be repressed and silenced owing to their social identities and prevailing attitudes toward those identities had a major and formative impact on his approach to genealogy. As a young man, he had close contact with colonialized people and those who were recognized as sexually and morally deviant. The two years he spent as a psychology student in Hopital Sainte Anne had an especially strong effect. He reports that "there was no clear professional status for psychologists in a mental hospital. So, as a student in psychology (I studied first philosophy and then psychology), I had a very strange status there" (EEW1, 123). He had virtually no supervision and was not officially on the staff. He had no special identity within the structure of the hospital. That allowed him to talk openly and freely with the patients for hours without representing anyone or anything. He listened to them and thought with them, hearing their experiences and, in a certain sense, hearing their silence within the institution that intended to help them. Although at that time Sainte Anne's was, according to Foucault, one of the best hospitals of its kind in France, he was aware of the disjunction between the hospital's formation – its intentions, procedures, and understanding of mental illness – and the patients' own lives and identities there. He heard *their* voices, *their* lack of influence, *their* constrictions in both the hospital and in the larger society. Their subjugation formed their identity as insane. He formed a lasting interest in the ways such structures, authority, and practices formed as well as in the voices and experiences of marginalized people.

Like Nietzsche, Foucault needed, in order to follow the interests and directions that he found for himself, a revised vocabulary, manner of thinking, and method of research in comparison with those of standard philosophical and historical practice. Because of these shifts, his genealogical work often seems counterintuitive in the contexts of traditional good sense and what is understood as responsible methods of reflection. He also found in the process of carrying out his genealogical projects that he experienced occasions of unexpected pleasure as he learned to see some aspects of the world around him as though for the first time. His sensibility – his feelings, commitments, assumptions, and values – transformed, and he felt energized and motivated to move on toward new experiences of truth, power, and agency.

In 1978, Foucault said:

> In writing *Madness and Civilization* and *The Birth of the Clinic* I meant to do a genealogical history of knowledge. But the real guiding thread was this problem of power.... I had been doing nothing except trying to retrace how a certain number of institutions, beginning to function on behalf of reason and normality, had brought their power to bear on groups of individuals, in terms of behaviors, ways of being, acting, or speaking that were constituted as abnormality, madness, illness, and so on.... It's true that the problems I pose are always concerned with particular and limited questions. Madness and even prisons are cases in point. (EEW3, 283, 285)

For Foucault, orders of knowledge constitute orders of power that find their expression in types of authority, such as in the sciences, medical disciplines, governmental agencies, and systems of education and punishment. Orders of knowledge and power also find expression in the institutions that carry and apply the orders' rules and procedures. They constitute networks or systems of power and knowledge that have the effect of forming individuals who direct themselves according to what is established as normal and right. They also have the effect of establishing hierarchies of importance that range from those who have varying degrees of power to those on the margins who have no constructive part in the networks of power that marginalize and silence them. Marginalized individuals in the Western lineages have included the mad, the poor, the ill, the young, women, homosexuals, the conquered, and others who appear or act in ways that are recognized as inferior or abnormal.

In Foucault's genealogical understanding, then, individuals, institutional formations, systems of established knowledge, what is known as truth, and issues of power can be distinguished but they cannot be separated in their occurrences. Individuals are subject to them in the individuals' social identities and in their own self-relations. By his genealogical studies of specific lineages of established knowledge, truth, and institutional formations, Foucault intends to show how systems of authority and truth have also formed systems of subjection for individuals in various times and situations. Late in his career, for example, he emphasized that the question of power is "not only a theoretical question but a part of our experience" (EEW3, 328). He emphasized the form of power "that applies itself to immediate everyday life and categorizes the individual, marks him by his own individuality, attaches him to his own identity, imposes a law of truth on him that he must recognize and others have to recognize in him. It is forms of power that make individuals subjects" (EEW3, 331). By "subject" he means "[both] subject to someone else by control and dependence and tied to his own identity by a conscience or self-knowledge. Both meanings suggest a relation of power that subjugates and makes subject to" (EEW3, 338).

Although Foucault refined his understanding of subjects and *relations* of power (as distinct from a metaphysical entity called power), during his life he in fact viewed all of his work as experimental, exploratory, and subject to change. We can say that his genealogical project is given focus as well as continuous transformation and refinement by problems he uncovers in the connections among individuals, knowledge, institutions, and relations of power.

In *Discipline and Punish: The Birth of Prisons*, for example, Foucault traces the formation of prisons, the modern identity of "the prisoner," the various types of knowledge that developed during that process, and the systems of observation, control, and punishment that carried out the intentions and applied the truths taught by knowledgeable authorities (EDP). Foucault considered *Madness and Civilization: A History of Insanity in the Age of Reason*, for a second example, an archaeological study of psychiatric knowledge and the silence of the insane in the formation of that knowledge (EHM). But the formation of that knowledge is also one of the sovereign powers that rationality and the institutions it formed gained in the recognition, imprisonment, silencing, and treatment (or the curing apparatus) of the insane. In both cases, the studies trace the formations of powerful institutions and knowledge, as well as the identities of separated and suppressed individuals. This frequent combination of subjection and marginalization of groups of people in lineages of emerging and developing bodies of knowledge, truth, and established forms of authority mean in part that "archaeological" studies and "genealogical" ones are not mutually exclusive in Foucault's view. In their different emphases, they can be mutually supportive as well as interwoven. (Archaeology focuses on the emergence and formation of various mutational, regulatory, and guiding structures, such as those of accepted truths, authoritative discourses, and networks of practice and value. Genealogy focuses on relations of power and their dynamic modes of operation. In both cases, interwoven as they might be in particular studies, individuals and their subjective formations are always crucial issues.) This combination also means that alertness to the processes of formation of individual subjects, the formation of their kinds of subjectivity, which achieves strong and prominent emphasis in his later work, was significantly, if nascently, present in many of his early studies. The formation of institutions, relations of power, and the subjection of individuals are not separable in Foucault's genealogical work.

In the context of this discussion, *genealogical ethos* means a sensibility and disposition that pervade Foucault's genealogical work. When people, for example, are attuned in a particular study to the way he thinks, the operation and definitive attitudes and intentions in it, and the feelings and conceptual structures that compose it, they will probably experience a considerable departure from many familiar and "normal" types of scholarly, thoughtful writing. They will see the importance of all manner of records, documents, diaries, codes of conduct, and instructions that are relevant to the subject at hand, such as hospitalization of patients in the eighteenth century or ancient sexual practices. They will confront the questionability of many assumed values, such as the primary importance of certain types of argument, knowledge, and logic, the value of the "enduring questions" of Western philosophy, or the unquestioned value of many accepted truths. Foucault's intentions were to interrupt particular normal practices of professional thought and scholarship, to put in question his own authority as well, and to encourage options that might occur to the reader rather than provide definitive answers. Indeed he intended to create an atmosphere that allows the emergence of alternatives to normal attitudes and ways of life (including his own). He wanted to pose problems that nag people. He wanted to write works that are a source of disturbance and irritation to comfortable recognitions, categorizations, and assumptions, and to put in question knowledge that contributes to oppression and marginalization of other people (as well as of ourselves).

In his genealogical work, as we have seen, he traced the lineages of the formation of such things as particular truths, normal practices, pervasive attitudes, and institutions that play major roles in a society. These intentions and projects create a sensibility that people can experience as they read him and think with him. It is one that leaves readers free to consider the problems and questions that emerge in the course of the study without authoritative resolution of them. At best, from Foucault's point of view, readers will feel as they read his writings at least a degree of liberation from subjecting formations in themselves and their societies, feel free enough to engage them, question them, and see alternatives to them. The ethos of Foucault's genealogical texts does carry with it values, knowledge, and movements of thought that make claims on the way readers live as well as disturb some of the certainties in what and how the readers know. But these claims happen within an approach that attempts always to describe how various structures, practices, and relations of power operate rather than to state what the essential nature of anything is. As Foucault said, "the problem is how things happen," and not what things are (EPK, 50). He wanted to know, for example, how relations of power are specifically exercised and how individuals and agencies exert power over others (EEW3, 357).

This move to the priority of the "how" and away from essences in his work engenders an expectation of change rather than enduring truths, of the possibility to transform what has seemed inalterably fixed. It can engender energetic political activity with a sense of caution about all solutions and most particularly one's own preferred solutions (EEW1, 256). Within his work, readers "know" that essences are mutable and metastatic. Foucault was not drawn to fatalism. He intended to make evident the way subjection happens and the ways it developed in an atmosphere that accentuates the possibility of its transformation. We are speaking of an ethos that stimulates varieties of active commitments in spite of the absence of metaphysical foundations as well as stimulating in some cases feelings of elation in the emergence of options for life changes.

Although Foucault's emphasis on relations of power, institutions, and forms of recognition might seem to ignore the importance of individuals, he wrote in an essay published in 1982 that the goal of his work since the early 1960s "has not been to analyze the phenomena of power, nor to elaborate the foundations of such an analysis. My objective, instead, has been to create a history of the different modes by which, in our culture, human beings are made subjects.... [I]t is not power, but the subject, that is the general theme of my research" (EEW3, 326–327). He then proceeded in the remainder of the essay to discuss *relations* of power and strategies to resist some of them. The point in the quotation is that he is interested in the ways subjection happens, and he could not carry out that interest if he analyzed phenomena of power. The latter would be no more than a theoretical and generalized undertaking. He wanted to create an account, a genealogical history, of the specific ways people are made into either objective subjects by some types of disciplined knowledge (such as the subject who produces or labors or is merely an example of a larger category like that of biological life) or made into individuals who subject themselves by the way they identify and objectify themselves. He wanted to develop knowledge of specific lineages of *relations* of power in order "to know the historical conditions that motivate our [objectivizing] conceptualization." To develop the knowledge he wanted, he said, "we need a historical awareness of our present circumstance" (EEW3, 327), adding,

> I would like to suggest another way to go further toward a new economy of power relations, a way that is more empirical, more directly related to our present situation, and one that implies more relations between theory and practice. It consists in taking the forms of resistance against different forms of power as a starting point.... [I]t consists in using this resistance as a chemical catalyst so as to bring to light power relations, locate their position, find out their point of application and the methods used.... [I]t consists of analyzing power relations through the antagonism of strategies. (EEW3, 329)

Although in these statements Foucault pointed toward an expanded strategy for exposing certain power relations in order to understand types of individual self-relations, he is also tacitly stating a primary aspect of his own genealogical thought. Early and late, he developed strategies to interrupt and put in question all manner of power relations and the effects of those relations on individuals. His purpose was to expose particular networks of "normal" and largely unnoticed power that subjugate people, teach them to make themselves subject to these subjugations, and establish

regimes of knowledge to support and advance those networks. To carry out his purposes, he created alternative knowledge about many realities in our present circumstances, ranging from the formation of the human sciences to medical knowledge
and practice, economic systems, and sexual identities. Throughout these projects,
he looked toward freeing individuals (including himself) from particular, subjecting
power relations and toward the creation of regions for alternatives to those relations
rather than toward definitive solutions.

The knowledge Foucault generated by his studies, at best, leads to transformative experiences for individuals. "[M]y problem," he said in 1978,

> is to construct myself, and to invite others to share an experience of what we
> are, not only our past but also our present, an experience of our modernity,
> in such a way that we might come out of it transformed. Which means that
> at the end of a book we would establish new relationships with the subject
> at issue: the I who wrote the book [*The History of Madness* in this example]
> and those who have read it would have a different relationship with mad-
> ness, with its contemporary status, and its history in the modern world.
> (EEW3, 242)

The use of pleasure, on the other hand, consists in taking the early steps toward
a genealogy of the subject of ethical actions (or types of individuals, ethical self-
formation in the Western lineage) that includes a genealogy of desire as an ethical problem (EHS2; see also EEW1, 262ff). He raises such questions as: How
have people constituted themselves as ethical subjects? What kinds of subjectification have operated in the process of individuals making themselves into particular
ethical subjects? What kind of self-forming activity might we now engage in to
become ethical subjects who are at least to some degree free of those subjectifications (EEW1, 265)? In the context of the present discussion, we can say that a major
aspect of Foucault's own self-forming activity is found in the genealogical knowledge that he developed and the transforming effects that he reports this work had
on him. We can also say that he hoped that people who read his work would find
the ethical dimension he found in it, that they would be motivated to find out more
about their own ethical subjectivity, the subjections included in it, and alternatives
to the ways they recognize themselves as obligated to certain values and the lineages that operate in them. Foucault's genealogy thus has both political (as we saw
earlier) and ethical dimensions. It is conceived as a type of power relation that can
move both the author and readers to action in the public sphere and in individuals'
relations with themselves.

Charles E. Scott

SEE ALSO

Ethics
History
Power
Subjectification
Truth
Friedrich Nietzsche

SUGGESTED READING

Blanchot, Maurice. 1990. "Michel Foucault as I Imagine Him," in *Foucault/Blanchot*, trans. Jeffrey Mehlman and Brian Massumis. New York: Zone Books, pp. 61–109.

Davidson, Arnold. 1986. "Archaeology, Genealogy, Ethics," in *Foucault: A Critical Reader*, ed. David Couzens Hoy. Oxford: Blackwell, pp. 221–234.

Mahon, Michael. 1992. *Foucault's Nietzschean Genealogy: Truth, Power, and the Subject*. Albany: The SUNY Press.

May, Todd. 1993. *Between Genealogy and Epistemology: Psychology, Politics, and Knowledge in the Thought of Michel Foucault*. University Park: Pennsylvania State University Press.

Scott, Charles E. 1990. *The Question of Ethics*. Bloomington: Indiana University Press.

Visker, Rudi. 1995. *Michel Foucault: Genealogy as Critique*, trans. Chris Turner. London: Verso.

32

GOVERNMENTALITY

T HE TERM "GOVERNMENTALITY" makes its appearance relatively late in
Foucault's career. It does not appear in any of his published work but is instead
central to two series of lectures he gave at the Collège de France from 1977 to
1979. These two lecture series, "Security, Territory, Population" and "The Birth of
Biopolitics," are centered on a historical development of the idea of governmentality
from its predecessors in the Christian pastoral to its contemporary practice of neoliberal governmentality.

Foucault offers a definition of governmentality in his lecture of February 1,
1978. This definition has three elements, each of which needs to be unpacked in
order to understand why he coins this, in his terms, "ugly word" (ECF-STP, 115):
"First, by governmentality I understand the ensemble formed by institutions, procedures, analyses and reflections, calculations, and tactics that allow the exercise
of this very specific, albeit very complex, power that has the population as its target, political economy as its major form of knowledge, and apparatuses of security
as its essential technological instrument" (ECF-STP, 108). This first characteristic
marks the idea that governmentality is not simply a matter of what is usually called
government. Governmentality is not just whatever it is that governments do. In
fact, as Foucault remarks later in this lecture series, "the emergence of the state as
a fundamental political issue can in fact be situated within a more general history
of governmentality.... [T]he state is an episode in governmentality" (ECF-STP,
247–248).

If governmentality is not simply a matter of governing institutions, then what
is it? As Foucault notes, it is an ensemble, a coming together or emergence of a set
of practices that come to occur largely through the institutions of the state. These
practices have as their object populations, which are to be mobilized and understood.
This understanding, and the uses to which it can be put in mobilizing populations,
is had through political economy. (Here, of course, we see a traditional theme of

Foucault's at work: the intertwining of knowledge and power.) Finally, this object and this knowledge are realized largely through the apparatus of security.

Turning to the next element of governmentality, Foucault says,

> Second, by "governmentality" I understand the tendency, line of force, that for a long time, and throughout the West, has constantly led towards the preeminence over all other types of power – sovereignty, discipline, and so on – of the type of power that we can call "government" and which has led to the development of a series of specific governmental apparatuses (*appareils*) on the one hand, [and, on the other] to the development of a series of knowledges (*savoirs*). (ECF-STP, 108)

The particular interest of this passage lies in the first part, where Foucault posits a preeminence of governmentality over sovereignty and discipline. It is not surprising that Foucault privileges governmentality over sovereignty. Over the course of his career, Foucault often challenges the traditional privileging of centralized forms of power in favor of power that arises from below, beneath the level usually analyzed in political theory. Because of this, the privileging of governmentality over discipline might be unexpected. In fact, as Foucault argues later in this lecture series, discipline can best be understood as a historical form of the exercise of governmentality. This form, Foucault argues in *The Birth of Biopolitics*, is partially displaced by the rise of neoliberal governmentality, a point to which we will return.

The third element of governmentality Foucault addresses is its historical emergence: "Finally, by 'governmentality' I think we should understand the process, or rather, the result of the process by which the state of justice of the Middle Ages became the administrative state in the fifteenth and sixteenth centuries and was gradually 'governmentalized'" (ECF-STP, 108–109). This third element returns us to a familiar theme of Foucault's. Governmentality is the result of a historical process, one that is contingent and has diverse origins. Although the story Foucault tells of the emergence of governmentality in this lecture series is more unified than, say, the emergence of discipline recounted in *Discipline and Punish*, Foucault is at pains to emphasize that there are a multiplicity of sources for the appearance of governmentality. It is not a unified entity but instead a way power has come to be practiced in the West that emerges through an intersection of distinct practices.

Over the course of the two lecture series in which Foucault discusses governmentality, there seem to be four stages of governmental reason, or, more accurately, three stages and a prestage. The prestage is that of the Christian pastorate, followed by the rise of governmentality proper, liberal governmentality, and, more recently, neoliberalism. According to Foucault, "The modern state is born, I think, when governmentality became a calculated and reflected practice. The Christian pastorate seems to me to be the background of this process" (ECF-STP, 165). The model for the pastorate is that of the shepherd and his flock. The shepherd tends to his flock, seeking the salvation of each of its members. This tending is, in contrast to the forms of governmentality that arise later, for the sake of the shepherded. But, as with governmentality, it is a matter of directing and looking after those for whom the shepherd has responsibility. Moreover, as Foucault argues in his Tanner Lecture on Human Values, that responsibility involves a form of individualizing attention that will become a dominant political theme in Western history. In contrast to the political structure of, for instance, the ancient Greek city-state, pastoral power is more personal. The shepherd's responsibility extends to each member of the flock; conversely, each of the members owes a personal obedience to the shepherd. And at stake in these relationships is not merely the operation of the polis; it is the souls of both shepherd and flock. We can see in this operation the seeds of later concerns with discipline and the formation of the subject. In describing this prestage of governmentality, Foucault suggests that the elements of subjectification that have appeared in the works preceding these lecture series have their seeds in far earlier arrangements of power than is treated in those works.

Foucault summarizes this particular form of politics by showing its continuity with modern governmentality:

> Christian pastorship has introduced a game that neither the Greeks nor the Hebrews imagined. A strange game whose elements are life, death, truth, obedience, individuals, self-identity – a game which seems to have nothing to do with the game of the city surviving through the sacrifice of its citizens. Our societies proved to be really demonic since they happened to combine those two games – the city-citizen game and the shepherd-flock game – in what we call the modern states. (EEW3, 311)

The question then becomes, how are these themes taken up in the emergence of modern governmentality and the state?

It is in the sixteenth century that the concern with conducting the affairs of men and women outside the authority of the church arises. The foundation of ecclesiastical authority is the underlying assumption that people have a particular nature, given to them by God, and that the role of governing them is that of ensuring that nature conforms to Christian requirements. With the Renaissance, and later the Reformation, the unitary assumption behind this form of operation (which is a continuation of the Christian pastoral) goes into eclipse. Political authority, rather than being rooted in God, must now find its own rationale, and in two senses. It must find its forms of justification, and it must find its methods of operation. These two senses come together with the emergence of and debates around *raison d'État*. It is unsurprising that Machiavelli's writings are at the center of this emergence and debate. It is not that everyone followed his views but rather that they formed the touchstone for the question of how to conceive the role of governing others, and with it the character of the state. Central to this discussion, however, is the idea that a state has to preserve itself and that practices of government are dedicated to that preservation.

Over the course of the next hundred years, the first phase of governmentality emerges, in both practice and theory. Central to this phase is the project of the mobilization of the forces of the polity, the forces that make it up. (These forces will later, with the development of biopolitical techniques, have the name of *population*.) In this mobilization, Foucault traces what he calls "two great assemblages ... a military-diplomatic apparatus, on the one hand, and the apparatus of the police, in the sense the word had at the time, on the other" (ECF-STP, 296). The goal of these assemblages was to harness the powers over the governed in order to maximize the health and growth of the polity while at the same time retaining its unitary character.

The role of the military was to preserve the tenuous equilibrium between states that was emerging alongside the development of the states themselves in Europe. The police, by contrast, had a number of different roles. It was concerned with the size and health of the population as well as the proper development and circulation of goods. Its goal was the proper development and sustenance of the nation's forces. Instead of the police as we know it – the internal force of violence maintaining social order – the rise of the police in the seventeenth and eighteenth centuries had a much larger purview. According to Foucault, "Generally speaking, what the police has to govern, its fundamental object, is all of the forms of, let's say, men's coexistence with each other" (ECF-STP, 326).

Over the course of the eighteenth century, this model of the police and its functions changes. With the rise of early capitalism and of the economic thinking that accompanied it, it was no longer taken for granted that the internal development of a nation's forces should be the focus of police intervention. Instead, the market should be allowed a freer reign to develop the strength of a nation's forces. For instance, free trade rather than state intervention to promote exportation over importation was said to lead to a healthier state of a national economy. This thinking and practice gives rise to what has become known as liberalism. One should emphasize here that liberalism is not simply a matter of the state leaving individuals alone but rather of a change in how policing is to operate. Rather than actively inserting itself into the economic mechanisms of society, the police instead become responsible for the security of the population, especially the protection of the natural operation of the capitalist market.

The liberalism of the later eighteenth and nineteenth centuries is not, for Foucault, simply a matter of laissez-faire. Rather, it involves a different type of governmentality. This governmentality is predicated on two concepts: the naturalness of market mechanisms (derived from Adam Smith and others) and the necessity of particular kinds of freedoms. It is the latter that prompts Foucault to give the name *liberalism* to this type of governmentality. He emphasizes that liberal governmentality is not simply hands-off. The freedom promoted by liberalism is not just any kind of freedom. It is instead a matter of particular types of freedom that must be developed and sustained in order to support the "naturalness" of market mechanisms. "Liberalism, as I understand it, the liberalism we can describe as the art of government formed in the eighteenth century, entails at its heart a productive/destructive relationship [with] freedom.... Liberalism must produce freedom, but this very act entails the establishment of limitations, controls, forms of coercion, and obligations relying on threats, etcetera" (ECF-BBIO, 64).

Liberal governmentality has three aspects, each of which was dedicated to the creation and nourishment of a proper relationship of individuals to one another in the context of a capitalist market. The first is security in the face of danger. Freedom implies danger, and the nineteenth century was filled with various dangers that had to be recognized and, to the extent possible, contained through governmental intervention. Some of these Foucault has addressed elsewhere: degenerative forms of sexuality, the proliferation of disease, and so on. The second aspect of liberal governmentality involves control and coercion. It is discipline, in the particular and famous sense that Foucault has given it. Mechanisms of discipline mold people into the kinds of individuals consonant with a society of the market and capitalist relationships. Of course, these two aspects of governmentality work hand in hand. The constant threat of various dangers can be alleviated, or at least contained, through the development of disciplinary forces. Danger justifies discipline, and conversely, discipline alleviates danger.

Finally, liberal governmentality requires the management of crises that periodically beset a society characterized by freedom and market relationships. Foucault cites several of these, but perhaps the most important is the New Deal, an attempt to sustain freedom through overwhelming governmental intervention and control. It is precisely these forms of management that are seen by neoliberals after World War II to be the source of the ills for which liberalism is supposed to be the cure. In Foucault's words:

> All of those mechanisms which since the years from 1925 to 1930 have tried to offer economic and political formulae to secure states against communism, socialism, National Socialism, and fascism, all these mechanisms and guarantees of freedom which have been implemented in order to produce this additional freedom, have taken the form of economic interventions, that is to say, shackling economic practice, or anyway, of coercive interventions in the domain of economic practice. (ECF-BBIO, 69)

In the wake of World War II, and particularly the experience of Nazism, liberal governmentality will be criticized, first by the German and Austrian ordoliberals, then by American neoliberals, in favor of a governmentality that operates very differently from that of traditional liberalism.

Ordoliberalism, whose most famous representative is probably Friedrich von Hayek, is seen by Foucault against the background of state power exemplified by Nazism. For the ordoliberals, Nazism is not a historical aberration; it is a lesson in the dangers of concentrating power in the state. States seek to accrete power, whether through Nazism, fascism, socialism, or even New Deal liberalism. The end of this accretion will be some form of state dominance over the lives of people, undermining their freedom. In order to forestall this, the state must be prevented from gaining so much power. A free market is the key route to doing so.

The building of a free market, however, is not simply a matter of less government but instead of a different kind of governmentality, one that does not *allow* a free market to develop naturally but instead intervenes politically *for the sake* of a market. There is no assumption of the naturalness of a market, as there was in earlier liberalism (although, as we saw, this naturalness did not preclude governmental intervention). Foucault states: "Government ... has to intervene on society as such, in its fabric and depth. Basically, it has to intervene on society so that competitive mechanisms can play a regulatory role at every moment and every point in society and by intervening in this way its objective will become possible, that is to say, a general regulation of society by the market" (ECF-BBIO, 145). Governmentality, then, is not divorced from a liberal economy; it is instead intimately bound to it.

This bond is not, of course, merely a matter of more government. That would run directly counter to the concerns over state dominance expressed by the ordoliberals. Instead, it is a matter of a different style of governmentality, one that focuses on people not in their roles as citizens or individuals but in their role as participants in a market economy. This role comes to prominence slightly later in the rise of American neoliberalism in the figure of *homo oeconomicus*. For *homo oeconomicus*, the goal of living is that of making the proper investments with the best return. Such investments are not merely economic but concern the whole of one's life. For examples of this, Foucault turns to the thought of Gary Becker, for whom decisions about marriage, children, schooling, and all other aspects of one's life could be understood in terms of various investments made with the hope of maximizing different yields.

In a striking analysis, Foucault discusses Becker's view on punishment in contrast to Foucault's own analysis of discipline in *Discipline and Punish*, published several years before this lecture series. The operation of penal policy, according to Becker, should not be one of intervening on particular individuals in order to create docile bodies. Instead it should be to set up negative externalities to crime that make it a bad investment for criminals. These negative externalities – for example, prisons – however, are themselves expensive. So a society has to balance its investments in the creation of negative externalities with the cost of those externalities in order to come up with the most efficient system for deterrence of crime. This kind of approach is far different from that of discipline, which seeks instead to ensure compliance by means of individual intervention on particular bodies. As Foucault comments,

> [W]hat appears on the horizon of this kind of analysis is not at all the ideal or project of an exhaustively disciplinary society.... [W]e see instead the image, idea, or theme program of a society in which there is an optimization of systems of difference, in which the field is left open to fluctuating processes, in which minority individuals and practices are tolerated, in which action is brought to bear on the rules of the game rather than on the players, and finally in which there is an environmental type of intervention instead of the internal subjugation of individuals. (ECF-BBIO, 259–260)

What is at issue in neoliberal governmentality, then, is not merely the government or the state but instead a type of governmentality, a set of practices that, while associated in many ways with the state, is instead a style of governing rather than simply a set of institutions. By focusing on governmentality, Foucault is able to answer some of the critics of his work that charge him with a failure to address larger macro-political issues without lapsing into the juridical model of power that he criticized in his genealogical writings.

Todd May

SEE ALSO

> *Christianity*
> *Liberalism*
> *Sovereignty*
> *State*
> *Subjectification*

SUGGESTED READING

Barry, Andrew, Thomas Osborne, and Nikolas Rose, eds. 1996. *Foucault and Political Reason: Liberalism, Neo-liberalism, and Rationalities of Government*. Chicago: University of Chicago Press.
Jessop, Bob. 2006. "From Micro-Powers to Governmentality: Foucault's Work on Statehood, State Formation, Statecraft and State Power," *Political Geography* 26, no. 1: 34–40.

33

HERMENEUTICS

T HERE IS AN apparent paradox in Michel Foucault's attitude toward hermeneutics. Although critical of its goal and method, he exemplifies at its best
the qualities of a rigorous interpreter who tries to separate his own descriptive discourse from the object he describes, whether in his powerful descriptions of
some periods of Western culture or in his painstaking interpretation of Hellenistic
philosophy or little known treatises of the seventeenth century. The paradox is further reinforced when Foucault engages in his last years in what he himself calls a
"hermeneutics of the subject." Nevertheless, Foucault's views on hermeneutics can
be organized along three perspectives: (1) in *The Order of Things*, hermeneutics is
presented as a kind of discourse that can be dated in its arising and thereby relativ-
ized in any universal claim it can make; (2) in *Archaeology of Knowledge*, hermeneutics
is mentioned as a method of investigation that archaeology criticizes and claims
to overcome; and (3) in some of his last works hermeneutics is co-opted as a new
approach to the self, for example in *The Hermeneutics of the Subject*. Let us therefore
examine each of these three perspectives.

In *The Order of Things*, Foucault uses the word "hermeneutics" in two different
senses. He characterizes the age of the Renaissance as the age of hermeneutics and
describes the new discipline of hermeneutics in the nineteenth century as a form of
compensation to the treatment of language as an autonomous object. Regarding the
Renaissance, Foucault argues that in the sixteenth century the prominent role played
by similitude in order to make sense of the world was made possible by the combination of hermeneutics and semiology. By hermeneutics Foucault means "the totality
of the learning and skills that enable one to make the signs speak and to discover
their meaning" (EOT, 29). These two aspects of hermeneutics and semiology in fact
represent what will become the discipline of hermeneutics in the nineteenth century.
Without detailed descriptions, for example of its origin in Ast and Schleiermacher
and further development with Dilthey, Foucault only mentions hermeneutics under

the name of "exegesis," as a discipline that arose when people like Raynouard, Bopp, or the Grimm brothers focused on the organic unity of specific natural languages and turned these languages into new "natural" objects of scientific investigations in philology or linguistics. The treatment of language as a mere object of investigation caused what Foucault calls a compensation in the form of a "formalization," which started to find application in the human sciences; of a "literature," which became a particular use of language that resists theory; and of "exegesis." Exegesis or hermeneutics experienced a renewal of interest owing to the fact that languages are not only organic unities but are also embedded in a tradition and have acquired in the course of time layers of social and cultural influences that can be "interpreted."

In the second perspective we mentioned, that of *The Archaeology of Knowledge*, Foucault takes issue with the very method of hermeneutics rather than examining it as a historical discipline as he did earlier. By tracing the genealogy of hermeneutics in a diachronic perspective in *The Order of Things*, Foucault already contextualized the "rigor" and "principles" of the discipline and showed that the so-called discipline of hermeneutics was rather an effect of the disappearance of discourse as it was prominent in the classical age. In *The Archaeology of Knowledge*, Foucault mounts a full-fledged attack on the hermeneutic method in order to present his own archaeology. Hermeneutics attempts to go back to the arising of meaning and to locate it as a psychological moment, even if unconscious, that is manifested by autonomous signs. In contrast, archaeology "refuses to be allegorical" (EAK, 139). Instead of being "an interpretive discipline" that seeks "another, better-hidden discourse" (ibid.), archaeology treats meaning as an event that can be described in its conditions of possibility irrespective of what speakers or agents intended or meant. Since signs are treated in their materiality, archaeology does not have to abide by the boundaries of works or the self-identity of intentions. In its comparison between works of biology and works of philology without following what "authors" may have meant, archaeology renders irrelevant any effort to recover an author's meaning, to understand authors better or differently than they understood themselves, as hermeneutics of Scheiermacher's or Gadamer's provenance typically does. Because archaeology deals with the materiality of sources and is committed to "the intrinsic description of monuments" (EAK, 7), its description is "purged of all anthropologism" (EAK, 16). This also means that signs are bound to their historical conditions and do not exert their semiotic function across centuries.

This focus on the material and historical conditions of knowledge allows the archaeological description to escape the tyranny of both the propositional level of thought and the ontological nature of things. Regarding the propositional level, Foucault argues that what he calls "statement" allows him to reach the level of what is an "event" that "neither the language [*langue*] nor the meaning can quite exhaust" (EAK, 28). The regularities that archaeology describes among statements or between statements and objects lead to "discursive formations" that generate, in the mathematical sense of a matrix, intentions and meanings. Human beings themselves are shaped by these discursive formations and thus not in charge or in possession of such formations. Regarding the ontological nature of things, archaeology brings to the fore a level of sense that escapes the level of things or, in Foucault's terms, that can "dispense" with them (EAK, 47). Despite the apparent stability of things like metallic pins, the analysis of discursive formations can show that a pin manufactured in the classical age by a single worker in eighteen operations (EOT, 224) and the apparently same pin later on manufactured on an industrial scale rely on two different discursive formations. Because they have different material and historical conditions of possibility, they do not belong to the same "order" of things and thus, strictly speaking, are not the "same" thing.

The claim that archaeology reaches a level that is below subjectivity and below things, as well as the hope to escape hermeneutics, runs against the significant limitations of the results archaeology can show. Although Foucault clearly does not want to describe what he calls "the spirit or science of a period," his "positivistic" attitude of description is compromised by the "hermeneutic" decisions he made in choosing his own fields of investigation in *The Order of Things*. He himself wholeheartedly acknowledges that, had he chosen other fields, the results may have been different. He even accepts the objection he himself raises: "Could not pre-Lavoisier chemistry, or Euler's mathematics, or Vico's history have invalidated all the analyses to be found in *The Order of Things*" (EAK, 158)? Foucault grants that his analyses are limited because he wanted to focus on "one region of interpositivity" (EAK, 159); for example, showing that the classification of living entities in eighteenth-century natural history was made according to the same rules of representation as those enunciated by general grammar, so that natural history in fact used a grammar of classification analogous to general grammar. To require that his limited analysis be corroborated by other fields of investigation would be, he argues, to require that he describe a *Weltanschauung*, precisely what he rejects: "The horizon of archaeology, therefore, is not *a* science, *a* rationality, *a* mentality, *a* culture; it is a tangle of interpositivities whose limits and points of intersection cannot be fixed in a single operation" (EAK, 159, Foucault's italics). The goal, Foucault says, is not to offer a unity of the objects of investigation but to celebrate their diversity by identifying several configurations. Therefore, he says that "Archaeological comparison does not have a unifying, but a diversifying, effect" (EAK, 160).

If the results of archaeology are only valid for the fields chosen by the archaeological method and cannot be extended to other fields and thus cannot be submitted to the scrutiny of other disciplines, it seems that archaeology is ill named, for the way the investigation is presented in *The Order of Things*, at the very least, suggests a kind of rigorous historical investigation that can respond to objections and counterexamples even if these come from fields other than those Foucault examined. If now, as Foucault acknowledges in *The Archaeology of Knowledge*, the results are only valid for the fields investigated and no generalizations should be made to other fields, we in fact have to deal more with the genealogy of a discipline, like economy, biology, or linguistics, than with a systematic study of regularities leading to discursive formations. Equally misused is the term "quasi-transcendentals," by which Foucault characterizes "Life, Labour, and Language" and uses as an alternative to "the transcendental field of subjectivity" (EOT, 250).

It may be this drastic limitation of the claims of archaeology that led to a change of focus in Foucault's works toward a genealogy – and with the paradox that genealogy can better and more successfully accommodate the hermeneutic method that the archaeology rejected. Foucault uses the genealogical method on a variety of topics, like the prison system and the techniques to shape and mold the individual, but came to find its unifying theme in what he calls the "care" or "practice of the self" and can be seen retrospectively as being already at work in the previous studies, although in an inverted form. To the outside structures and institutions rendering the self docile, there also corresponds a self that forms itself through these institutions and through the experiences made possible by such institutions. "The care of the self" was the title of the third volume of the *History of Sexuality*, and the term "hermeneutics" was used in the title of one of Foucault's last courses at the Collège de France, "The Hermeneutics of the Subject." So, we come to the third perspective we outlined.

The hermeneutics of the self is not an investigation of the essence of subjectivity or a history of the subject in Western thought. Instead of an epistemological approach that would put Socrates' *gnoti seauton* in continuation with Descartes' *cogito sum*, Foucault's specific and idiosyncratic hermeneutics focuses on the experience of the self: the self sees itself, experiences itself, and forms itself. In such a view of the self as a practice, the world and others are part of an experience within which a self comes to form itself. Foucault's hermeneutics functions below the level of what could be a stable structure of the self, a substance or an essence of selfhood. The goal is not to "interpret" the self but to accompany its disclosure to itself, as it were, by following the experiences through which a self comes to understand itself or manifest itself. This is more a "hermeneutic attitude" than a hermeneutic method, and it allows Foucault to revisit such notions as *askesis* or *parrēsia* in the Stoics in order to show that they are in fact "practices of the self." *Parrēsia*, for example, is an exercise in truth-telling or being true to oneself. This experience of the truth or this relation between subject and truth makes it clear that the self does not lie in anything that is stable or fixed under the level of experience but rather consists in a set of experiences and as such in a practice.

The hermeneutics of the subject provides a method of investigation that deals with "objects" other than in archaeology in the sense that the experience of the self is different from the discursive formation at the basis of what we call "man." Besides disrupting the common views on the self that either the self only arose with modernity or that there is a continuity between Socrates and Descartes, Foucault's hermeneutics also tempers his own pronouncements in *The Order of Things* that "man will return to that serene non-existence in which he was formerly maintained by the imperious unity of discourse" (EOT, 386). The notion of practice of the self thus not only offers an alternative to any traditional metaphysics of the self. It also mitigates Foucault's own views: his apocalyptical breaks between *epistemes* taking place outside the experience of the self (in his archaeological period) as well as his focus on structures of power that subdue the subject outside its experience. In Foucault's later work, hermeneutics recovers its original humility of being an adjuvant to something that shows itself or somebody who attests to his or her own self.

Pol van de Velde

SEE ALSO

> *Archaeology*
> *Man*
> *Phenomenology*
> *Structuralism*
> *Truth*
> *Martin Heidegger*

SUGGESTED READING

Dreyfus, Hubert L., and Paul Rabinow. 1983. *Michel Foucault: Beyond Structuralism and Hermeneutics*, 2nd ed. Chicago: University of Chicago Press.

Gadamer, Hans-Georg. 1990. *Truth and Method*, trans. Joel Weinsheimer and Donald G. Marshall, 2nd rev. ed. New York: Crossroads.

McGushin, Edward F. 2007. *Foucault's Askēsis: An Introduction to the Philosophical Life*. Evanston, IL: Northwestern University Press.

34

HISTORY

THERE ARE THREE ways to approach the problem of the relation of Michel Foucault to history. The first consists paradoxically in placing Foucault back into the context of his own history. Here we have to understand how, after 1945, a whole generation of young philosophers had played a certain number of references, first of which we must count a specific use of Nietzsche, against the dominant Hegelianism, and more generally against phenomenology as it had been read and taken up in France. In the confrontation that had unfolded, the status and the modeling of history had represented a first-order stake. Foucault, among others, had participated in this "generation," which was rejecting at once the absolute privilege of "the philosophies of the subject" and that of "the philosophies of history" understood generally as linear, continuous, and dialectical. The explicit claim by Foucault, at the end of the 1970s, of this "generational partnership" as the key to his own philosophical trajectory must therefore push us to compose "the history of a certain way of thinking about history" in France after World War II. In short, we must seek to apply to Foucault his own method of inquiry.

In contrast, the second approach consists in staking out what, beyond the reference – internal to philosophical thought – to Nietzsche, has worked over in a unique way the construction of history that Foucault made for himself. There are two massive, contaminating foundations that have undoubtedly displaced and reinvested Foucault investigations *insofar as they are philosophical investigations*. The foundations are works that could at times appear to be on the edge of philosophy or at the intersection of philosophy and the human sciences. One corresponds to the works of Georges Canguilhem; that is, it corresponds to this formidable production of thought set up at the problematic crossroads between the philosophy of sciences and the history of sciences. The other corresponds to a certain historiography connected, in particular, to the Annales School; the 1960s and the 1970s, in Foucault's corpus, will make this historiography appear essentially as if it had two faces: first, a serial and economic history, and then, on the other hand, a microhistory or an event-history fundamentally connected to the minute attention given to the archive.

The third way of approaching the problem consists finally in attempting to understand the astonishing relation that the philosophy that emerges in Foucault's work at the end of the 1970s – in particular, in the course at the Collège de France – has to history. In particular, there are two astonishing "sets" of studies that can help us reflect on the relation to the history of philosophical thought that Foucault constructs when he claims at once to make philosophical thought be the object of a historical inquiry and to lay it out in the present. The first "set" is constituted, between 1978 and 1984, by three texts devoted to Kant and to the question of the Enlightenment. The other "set," in 1983–1984, within the frame of an inquiry into the notion of *parrēsia*, dwells for a long time first on the figure of Socrates, then on the thought of the Cynics. In the two cases, the references – Kant in the first case, Socrates and the Cynics in the second – are traversed by a type of questioning that poses in reality the problem of the *actuality* of philosophical practice and of its being anchored in the present. Likewise, the reflection on what Foucault will then call a "critical ontology of ourselves" or a "critical ontology" of the present cannot fail to be concerned primarily, insofar as it is philosophy, with its own position situated in a certain place in the world and in a certain moment of history of thought, and in a type of specific exercise (that of the type of public speech that the offering of a course implies).

In a passionate interview conducted in 1978, Foucault attempted to account for the historical conditions of possibility of his own thought (see EEW3, 239–297). In this self-analysis, the rupture with phenomenology, particularly with French Hegelianism, is perceived as foundational. The rupture is immediately related to the refusal to agree with a certain model of the history of philosophy, and to the observation that what is then perceived as the dominant university philosophy is obviously unable to match up to the drama of its own times. There, Foucault says that

> Nietzsche, Blanchot, and Bataille were the authors who enabled me to free myself from the dominant influences in my university training in the early 1950s – Hegel and phenomenology. Doing philosophy in those days, and today as well in fact, mainly amounted to doing the history of philosophy – and the history of philosophy delimited, on the one hand, by Hegel's theory of systems and, on the other, by the philosophy of the subject, went on in the form of phenomenology and existentialism. Essentially, it was Hegel who was the prevailing influence. For France, this had been in a sense a recent discovery, following the work of Jean Wahl and the teaching of Jean Hyppolite. It was a Hegelianism permeated with phenomenology and existentialism, centered on the theme of the unhappy consciousness. And it was really the best thing the French university could offer as the broadest possible mode of understanding

the contemporary world, which had barely emerged from the tragedy of World War II and the great upheavals that had preceded it – the Russian revolution, Nazism, and so on. (EEW3, 246)

It is at the intersection of these two imperatives – not becoming a historian of philosophy and yet being at the height of his own epoch – that the concern emerges to break with the representation of a rational, teleologically oriented, continuous, linear history, which is at once the history on which the idea of philosophical thought is grounded and the history, more generally, of human history. The necessity to insert in this *continuum* the violent discontinuity of war is foundational. It implies therefore the investigation of another representation of history that would be susceptible of accounting for the fault line that henceforth traverses the present, and, by a sort of ricochet, redefines as well the way in which we related to the history of philosophy. The name of Nietzsche then returns for good.

What is still more largely at issue is to take up the critique of the suprahistorical viewpoint that history adopts when it claims to be the reassuring and closed unity in which the infinite proliferation of the world is enclosed. The use of Nietzsche serves to deconstruct a history having for its function "to gather up the finally reduced diversity of time into a totality fully closed upon itself" (EEW2, 379) and having in reality always sought to cancel the multiple figures of the disparate and the divergent, of the leap and of change – in a word, it wants to cancel becoming understood as broken linearity. Returning to the singular chance of the event is, in contrast, as Nietzsche recalls for us in *Daybreak*, "to shake the dice-box of chance" (Nietzsche 1982, 130) against the mystification of the unity with which "antiquarian history" is full. It is this "dice-box" that fascinates Foucault.

Foucault therefore "carves out" his own reading on the basis of an object that is at once partial (from the viewpoint of Nietzsche's work) and fundamental (for his own reflection), which is the critique of a certain type of representation of history. And it is on the basis of this object that he is going to be able to summon in the same way two other "mountain ranges" of influence without which it is impossible to account for his work in the 1960s, from *The History of Madness* to *The Archaeology of Knowledge*. The first influence, decisive in many regards, is that of Georges Canguilhem. Two texts, separated by ten years, allow us to take stock of the influence. The first, written in 1968, responds to a certain number of questions posed by the "Epistemology Circle" (see "On the Archaeology of the Sciences" in EEW2, 297–334). The second is an introduction written in 1978 for the American edition of Canguilhem's *The Normal and the Pathological* (see "Life: Experience and Science" in EEW2, 465–478). In "The Archaeology of the Sciences," Foucault says:

> Beneath the great continuities of thought, beneath the massive and homogeneous manifestations of the mind, and beneath the stubborn development of a science

struggling from its beginnings to exist and complete itself, attempts have been made to detect the occurrence of interruptions. Gaston Bachelard has charted out the epistemological thresholds that interrupt the indefinite accumulation of knowledges; Martial Geroult has described the enclosed systems, the closed conceptual architectures that partition the space of philosophical discourse; Georges Canguilhem has analyzed the mutations, displacements, and transformations in the field of validity and the rules for the use of concepts. (EEW2, 299)

And then, ten years later, Foucault says:

First, [Georges Canguilhem] took up the theme of "discontinuity." An old theme that emerged early on, to the point of being contemporaneous, or nearly so, with the birth of a history of the sciences.... Taking up this same theme, developed by Koyré and Bachelard, Canguilhem stresses the fact that for him identifying discontinuities does not have to do with postulates or results; it is more a "way of proceeding," a procedure that is integral with the history of the sciences because it is called for by the very object that the latter must deal with. (EEW2, 471)

Since it is neither a postulate nor a result but a "way of proceeding," we are therefore dealing with a genuine choice of method.

However, in Foucault, these references to the philosophy of the sciences, when he makes them, play a precise role. As he will explain at length in the 1978 Canguilhem text, what is at issue is the construction of an opposition between the "philosophies of subject" and the "philosophies of the concept," between "Sartre and Merleau-Ponty" on the one hand and "Cavaillès, Bachelard, and Canguilhem" on the other. This is an opposition that allows Foucault to reread the history of French thought as "two strains that remained, for a time at least, rather deeply heterogeneous" (EEW2, 466). Obviously, this rereading reinforces his own attempt to undermine a figure of the subject generally understood as autoreferential, solipsistic, ahistorical, and psychologized. Foucault says quite often that this subject, from Descartes to Sartre, has traversed philosophy while rendering it sterile. However, an opposition, from the side of the "philosophies of the concept," allows us, above all, to pose the problem of the relation between the history of sciences and epistemology; that is, at once the problem of the relation to time and of the relation to the historicity of forms of "truth-telling." This is what Foucault says:

The history of science, Canguilhem says, citing Suzanne Bachelard, cannot construct its object anywhere but in "an ideal space-time." And this space-time is given to it neither by the 'realist' time accumulated by historians' erudition nor by the space of ideality which partitions science today in an authoritative way, but by the viewpoint of epistemology. The latter is not the general theory of every science and of every possible scientific statement; it is the search for the normativity internal to the different scientific activities, as they have actually been carried out. So, it involves an indispensable theoretical reflection that enables the history of the sciences to be constituted in a different mode from history in general; and, conversely, the history of the sciences opens up a domain of analysis that is indispensable if epistemology is to be anything else but the simple reproduction of the internal schemas of a science at a given time. In the method employed by Canguilhem, the formulation of "discontinuistic" analyses and the elucidation of the relation between the history of the sciences and epistemology go hand in hand. (EEW2, 473)

What Foucault takes up from Canguilhem's "method," "a philosophy of error, of the concept of the living" (EEW2, 477), corresponds in reality to a stake that is twofold. It is necessary to distinguish the time of the history of the sciences at once from the abstract time of the sciences themselves, on the one hand, and, on the other, from the erudite history of the historians, because both – in different ways, of course – in fact assert the necessity of an absolute continuum. They cannot consider history in any way other than as a linear, ruptureless process. Whether what is at issue is an "idealized" temporal space that is completely freed from the material conditions of its unfolding or a "realist" time reduced to the infinite and continuous accumulation of its different moments, the discourse really does not change. In both cases (the "idealized" space and the "realist" time), one presupposes a linearity without a fault line – and the impossibility that the historian's gaze would be able to distance himself from it, would somehow be able to write the history of this linear history, to set up the epistemology of the continuous form of time itself. Going in the opposite direction, the epistemological viewpoint therefore is going to represent for the history of the sciences the possibility of an approach to time that allows us to question this continuist presupposition. But in another sense, the risk run by epistemology is that of a reproduction of the scientific schemas described within the description itself; that is, the risk of not being able to historicize the scientific discourse and the epistemological grids mobilized by its own analysis. This is why the history of the sciences grants to epistemology itself the status of being something other than a metadiscourse.

The proximity of this twofold stake of Canguilhem's "discontinuist" analyses to Foucault's work from the 1960s is clear. Is *The Order of Things* anything else than the attempt to produce the history of the way in which scientific discourse has constituted, in a given moment, its own fields, its own objects, its own methods, the very form of its knowledge (*savoir*) – and, of course, the form of its history? But we must also ask this question: However we must also ask this question: Isn't *The Order of Things* nothing but the attempt to reintroduce internal schemas into the science within a more general history, which would be that of the different – and successive – forms of "saying-the-truth"? It is within this double historicization that a critique of the "philosophies of the subject" – the other side of Foucault's positive critique – is truly possible. The reason for this is that if, as Foucault correctly recalls, Cartesian philosophy has represented this great rupture of the modernity that has posed for the first time the problem of the relations between truth and the subject, the philosophy of the sciences demands that we totally reformulate the question. This is the case not only because the Cartesian subject has no history in the strict sense – rather it grounds the possibility of history, and of course this lack of history is at the heart of the contemporary critiques of the Cartesian subject – but also because one has to define the conditions for the possibility of a history of truth that does not take the form of a metaphysics of truth. On the contrary, the conditions amount to an archaeology of the way in which the true and the false, truth and error, enter into a relation and mutually define one another on the basis of norms and limits that are constantly being redefined, rearticulated, and readjusted. These norms, moreover, are thinkable only on the basis of the historicization of the *episteme* to which they belong.

The other great contaminating foundation during the same period of Foucault's thinking – and this time it is one outside of philosophy – is a certain French historiography that poses, in particular, the problems of historical causality and linearity, of the selection that the choice of a periodization implies, and it raises the question of the relation to the materiality of the traces that one examines. This allows us to understand at once the way in which Foucault has constructed his own concepts of archaeology and archive, the relations that he has woven with historians – and the collaborations to which the latter have at times produced. This also allows us to understand how Foucault has rejected, thanks to what he borrows from historiography, the generally philosophical ways in which history has been modeled.

In 1967, Foucault granted Raymond Bellour an interview that is entitled "On the Ways of Writing History" (EEW2, 279–296). In fact, Foucault had already agreed to respond at an earlier time to questions from Bellour, just when *The Order of Things* had come out (FDE1, 498–504). At this time, the nearly complete absence of the theme of history was truly astonishing. The problem in fact seemed moreover that of understanding the relation between the analyses in *The History of Madness* and those of *The Order of Things*, or the problem was to explain by way of recourse to the notion of archaeology the way in which one had been able to constitute a sort of homogeneous domain of inquiry. This homogeneous domain is that of an epoch's *episteme*, which traverses all the disciplinary borders in order to constitute the very density of the space in which the different kinds of knowledge are distributed. However, the *episteme* looked to be identical to a historical selection, which was defining the limits of the *episteme*. Foucault seems not to want to open this very problem of periodization. We recall of course the end of *The Order of Things*. There we find the hypothesis of erasure "like a face drawn in the sand at the edge of the sea" (EOT, 387) of the epistemic configuration that appeared at the end of the eighteenth century, whose archaeology Foucault was composing. But in 1966, nothing or nearly nothing that was said indicated the, so to speak, "upstream" of this configuration; that is, moment of its emergence. Therefore, if the themes of transition and transformation, of shifting and discontinuity in history, were considered "in advance" and projected as a possible future hypothesis, they seemed to be evaded as soon as what was at issue was to think what was "behind"; that is, their value as a starting point.

Is it necessary to think, moreover, that these are the organizing moves, the moves of hierarchizations and of distribution on the basis of homogeneity (*episteme*) that have, at this time, interested Foucault? The problem, however, was obvious: either the chosen periodization assured in advance the epistemic homogeneity of the chosen moment or on the contrary it is the staking out of a certain number of isomorphisms that ground the possibility of periodization. In either case, Foucault is commanded to respond to the question that he seems to want to avoid, that of the legitimacy of historical selection for which the *episteme* is – according to the possible ways of reading it – the foundation or the product. And we recall Sartre's very severe critique of Foucault when *The Order of Things* was published: "Of course, his [that is, Foucault's] perspective remains historical. He distinguishes epochs, a before and an after. But, he replaces cinema with a slide show, movement with a succession of immobile structures" (Sartre 1966, 87).

Now we come to the second interview with Bellour, one year after the publication of *The Order of Things*. Here the tone is absolutely different. The problem of Foucault's relation to history and historians is posed there immediately, in particular because, as Bellour recalls in his first question, the reserved welcome the book received has been at once "enthusiastic and reticent." Foucault's answers are extremely precise. On the one hand, the "professional historians" have recognized the book as a book of history. On the other, a very profound mutation of historical knowledge has been at work for the last twenty years; a new generation of historians (Foucault mentioned the names of Fernand Braudel, François Furet, Denis Richet, Emmanuel Le Roy Ladurie, and also the Cambridge school of history and the Soviet school) have undertaken "a new adventure." Now, history has for a long time been the last refuge of the dialectical order, the sacred place in which the relations between individuals and totality have played out. History has often been reduced to the universal relation of causality. Consequently, against this totalizing and untouchable history, what is at issue now is to formulate "the very difficult problem of periodization" and at the same time a genuine "logic of mutation." Therefore, in order to turn history into a philosophy, we have to be interested, above all else, in transformation. Thereby we have returned to the old problem of discontinuity.

It is in this context that we must understand Foucault's archaeology. The term appears three times in the titles of his works: *The Birth of the Clinic: An Archaeology of Medical Perception* (1963); *The Order of Things: An Archaeology of the Human Sciences* (1966); and *The Archaeology of Knowledge* (1969). Up until the beginning of the 1970s, the term characterizes his research method. Archaeology is not a "history" in the strict sense as if what we are trying to do is reconstitute a historical field. Foucault in fact brings into play different dimensions (philosophical, economic, scientific, political, etc.) in order to obtain the conditions of emergence of discourses of knowledge in general in a given epoch. Instead of studying the history of ideas in its evolution, archaeology consequently concentrates on precise historical selections – in particular, the classical age and the beginning of the nineteenth century, whose a priori legitimacy we have seen is difficult to establish.

Now, if we discover in "archaeology" the idea of the *arché* (that is, the problem of the beginning, of the principle, of the emergence of objects of knowledge), we also find the idea of the *archive*, the recording of objects. Foucault specifies the idea in this way:

> I shall call an *archive*, not the totality of texts that have been preserved by a civilization or the set of traces that could be salvaged from its downfall, but the series of rules which determine in a culture the appearance and disappearance of statements, their mode of remaining [*rémanence*] and their erasure, their paradoxical existence as *events* and *things*. To analyze the facts of discourse in the general element of the archive is to consider them, not at all as *documents* (of a concealed signification or a rule of construction), but as *monuments*; it is – leaving aside every geological metaphor, without assigning of origin, without the least gesture toward the beginnings of an *arché* – to do what the rules of the etymological game allow us to call something like an *archaeology*. (EEW2, 309–310)

From *The History of Madness* to *The Archaeology of Knowledge*, the archive represents therefore the set of discourses actually pronounced in a given epoch and that continue to exist across history. To do an archaeology of this documentary mass is to seek to understand its rules, practices, conditions, and the way it functions. That implies above all else a work of recollection of the *general archive* of the chosen epoch. Foucault then treats the archive as constituting series whose distribution and organization, in a given epoch, he analyzes. The proximity to the structural analysis of discourse, which, at this moment, interested Foucault enormously, is obvious. Foucault's archaeology in the 1960s is halfway between serial history and general grammar. Certainly set up on the support of history, it is done on the basis of a historical periodization that grounds its consistency but resembles more a cartography or a diagram than a minute inquiry concerning a past time.

However, at the beginning of the 1970s, the archive changes its status. Thanks to working directly with historians (see *Pierre Rivière* in 1973 [EPR]; *L'impossible prison* in 1978, under the direction of Michelle Perrot [Perrot 1980]; or *Le Désordre des familles* in 1982, with Arlette Farge [FDF]), Foucault starts to assert at once the subjective dimension of his work and starts to take into account a density of the traces with which he is concerned that is nearly existential. It is as if in fact the archive presented past lives. As he notes in a famous text on "infamous men," "This is not a book of history. The selection found here was guided by nothing more substantial than my taste, my pleasure, an emotion" (EEW3, 157). The reading of these fragments, which is often very literary and which he sometimes calls "strange poems," is then in marked contrast to the serial and cartographic approach of the preceding decade. The paradox of a nonhistorian (literary, poetical, philosophical) utilization of historical sources is that Foucault is likewise criticized for this usage. Only gradually will Foucault's interest move toward an analytic of power that is indissociable from a history of subjectivities in the confrontation with this same power. However, a history of subjectivities, a history of anonymous and everyday existences, a history of events, are all at this time at the heart of the renewal of historiography. Event-history, new history, and microhistory are nearby areas from which Foucault has drawn and to which he has contributed (see Jacques Revel 1992) – since what was at issue was to record the methodological tensions, mutations, and moves of the historians' work. But, despite everything, this record is made from within a philosophical reflection.

At the end of the 1970s, these philosophical consequences emerge in all their clarity. Foucault abandons neither archaeology nor the relation to the archive. But he reinvests what was at the beginning something simply borrowed from Nietzsche: the concept of genealogy. Foucault gives Nietzsche's genealogy a new potency. The nerve of this displacement consists in a strategic reversal of the notion of discontinuity.

To start, genealogy is essentially, for Foucault, what allows us to put into play, in history, a principle of dissipation (of the claimed unity of our identity, of our origin), of dispersion and of singularization (of events), and of differentiation (of different historical segments brought to light by a work of periodization). Beyond the dissemination of identities and the critique of the *Ursprung*, the excavation of discontinuities in history nevertheless, in Foucault, takes on accents that are more those of historiography than those of philosophy. Whatever critique may have been formulated concerning the real consistency of the periodizations constructed by Foucault in his works, the selection of distinct *epistemes* or different "moments" nevertheless serves as the essential support for the analysis. Discontinuity is not only a concept but a historiographic practice that allows us to insert difference into the continuum of time by asserting something that is halfway between a sort of staking out of "enduring" averages as Braudel does and the selection of fields of inquiry. And, in fact, this difference plays out essentially "in the background" between what is no longer (and about which it would be necessary to make an archaeology) and what we are. It is in this sense that, if archaeology works on historical materials, at the same time and by ricochet it works toward our present – because if genealogy is in reality the perception that we are, it is always given on the basis of a background of difference. This difference fractures the history on which we think we are grounded. We are plunged into history, traversed by its determinations, but we can know that only through the differentiation from what we have stopped being, saying, or thinking.

In 1978, for the first time in a penetrating way, Foucault commented on Kant's small text "What Is Enlightenment?" In order to try to determine what the "critical attitude" is, he still puts into play the structure discontinuity/periodization/differentiation, as he had in the preceding decade. For him, the "critical attitude" in fact characterizes the beginning of the modern epoch and is opposed to the demands of the preceding epoch's pastoral governmentality, which in contrast had claimed to direct the conduct of individuals by the truth. Periodization allows us to differentiate between the "moments" (here modernity, there the Christian pastoral). But differentiation, in turn, requires that we question ourselves about the way we belong to some such "moment" of thought. Do we not participate in the modernity inaugurated by the emergence of the critical attitude, or are we separated from it by a "difference" that we must recognize and name?

However, five years later, Foucault twice returns to Kant's text. The first time is in his course at the Collège de France called "The Government of Self and Others" (the session on January 5, 1983 [ECF-GSO, 1–40; I shall be quoting an extract of the January 5, 1983, course, published in *Magazine littéraire*, number 207, May 1984, reprinted in FED4, 679–688]); the second time, one year later, is in a text published in the United States ("What Is Enlightenment?" [original publication in EFR, 32–50, reprinted in EEW1, 303–320; reprinted in French in FDE4, 562–578, FDE2a, 1381–1396]). In both cases, Foucault's approach has fundamentally changed. Periodization is reduced to a secondary level because the heart of Foucault's analysis has now become the present as such:

> With this text on the *Aufklärung*, we see philosophy – and it is forcing things to say that this is the first time – problematize its own discursive actuality, an actuality it interrogates as an event, as an event whose sense, value, philosophical singularity it has to say, and in which philosophy must discover at once its own *raison d'être* and the foundation of what it says. (FDE4, 680)

The attention given to the present is no longer only an induced effect of historical inquiry (induced by differentiation). In itself it becomes the subject matter of philosophical reflection. Does that then mean that Foucault, strangely returning to philosophy, has abandoned history? Or does it mean that, in his final years, he starts to concentrate solely on certain episodes of the history of philosophy to the detriment of this proximity with the historians who had, however, provided so strongly the model for his own work?

In fact, the "excavation of difference" in history is still going to intervene in another way. What is at issue is to make it now pass not only between what has been and what is but between what is our present and what could be tomorrow. Discontinuity is not so much what we have to recognize once it has happened but what we can contribute to construct within our own present. This reversal then gives rise in Foucault to two types of analyses. On the one hand, we have the analysis of the theme of revolution as the power to institute discontinuity within our actuality or present (insofar as revolution is "an event whose very content is unimportant, but whose existence testifies to a permanent and unforgettable virtuality" [FDE4, 686]), and, on the other hand, we have the insistence on the necessity of practice, within the historical determinations that make us be what we are, "the present [*actuel*] field of possible experience" (FDE4, 687). As Foucault says, merging the two types of analyses, "to transform the critique conducted in the form of necessary limitation into a practical critique that takes the form of a possible crossing-over" (EEW1, 315). This "historico-practical test of the limits that we may cross over" (EEW1, 316) is immediately analyzed by Foucault as an *attitude*, as an *ethos* that characterizes philosophy understood less as a body of doctrines than as a practice. It is not possible to have a philosophical practice without being contextualized in a specific epoch. But it also is not possible to have philosophy if one does not risk the attempt at the critique of who we are as "at one and the same time the historical analysis of the limits imposed on us and an experiment with the possibility of crossing over them" (EEW1, 319). And Foucault concludes, "this critique will be genealogical in the sense that it will not deduce from the form of what we are what it is impossible for us to do and to know; but it will separate out, from the contingency that has made us what we are, the possibility of no longer being, doing, or thinking what we are, do, or think" (EEW1, 315–316). From precisely within history, this critique constitutes the indefinite (or undefined) work of freedom for humans.

The way in which Foucault positions himself in relation to philosophy bears the trace of this reorientation. We recall how meticulous Foucault is, from his first works, in his concern with historicizing his objects of inquiry. In other words, he places them back in a general economy of a system of thought connected to a precise periodization. In the two texts that we have just quoted, he seems, however, to be engaged in a procedure that goes in the opposite direction. Not only do the opening sessions of the course on January 5, 1983, concerning the *Aufklärung* really set up, through a chronological leap that is dizzying and to say the least surprising, an entire year devoted to ancient thought, but also the treatment of the Enlightenment seems radically different. Foucault writes,

> After all, it seems to me indeed that the *Aufklärung*, at once as a singular event that inaugurates European modernity and as a permanent process that manifests itself in the history of reason … is not simply for us *an episode in the history of ideas*…. What we're doing is not preserving whatever remains of the *Aufklärung*. What is in question is its event and its meaning (the question of the historicity of the universal). This is what we have to keep present and keep in mind as *what must be thought*. (FDE4, 686–687)

Some months later, Foucault makes this more specific:

> I know that modernity is often spoken of as an epoch, or at least as a set of features characteristic of an epoch; situated on a calendar, it would be preceded by a more or less naïve or archaic pre-modernity, and followed by an enigmatic and troubling "postmodernity." … Thinking back on Kant's text, I wonder whether we may not envisage modernity as an attitude rather than as a period of history. (EEW1, 509)

We can see now that Foucault's discourse tends to replace historical periodization with the problematization of actuality – even if the mode of relation to actuality that we establish is itself historically determined.

The last two years of Foucault's courses at the Collège de France resonate with this tension. Just as the Kant commentary opened the 1983 course, which was, however, devoted to the study of "truth-telling" in the texts of Polybius, Euripides, and Plato, Foucault chose in 1984 to make history again leap beyond itself. In the fifth lecture (February 29, 1984), although the whole analysis had so far been devoted to *parrēsia* (and he had just introduced the example of the Cynics), he makes in effect a digression: "Coming closer to our own time, it would also be interesting to analyze another support of the Cynic mode of being, of Cynicism understood as form of life in the scandal of truth" (ECF-COT, 183). And then he presents what he calls a "history of the Cynical mode," which takes the form of a genealogy of militant forms of life – the asceticism of the Franciscans in secret sociality, participation in an avant-garde artist organization in the nineteenth and twentieth centuries. The historical "unhooking" (*déchrochage*) is obvious. In the following session, on March 7, 1984, more classically, Foucault returns to the analysis of the Cynics. Far from being something incoherent, what Foucault calls "a stroll, an excursus, an errancy" provokes the irruption of the question of the "scandal of truth" – this is the Cynical element par excellence – in *other histories*: those of the Christian Middle Ages, modernity, and undoubtedly our own present. It would be a mistake to consider this irruption as an anachronism. If the way in which the Cynics call forth the scandal of truth is historically determined – and as such not susceptible to being exported beyond its own time – the question is to determine whether the way in which the demand of truth-telling can explode in the public space and affect the world's order such as it has been established at a given moment is in itself a lot more general. If the Cynical response to the problem cannot be ours today, the problem that the Cynics pose merits being posed, even in our own actuality. How is it possible to insert discontinuity without our own present? How is it possible to think of "'today' as difference in history" (EEW1, 309) and tomorrow as difference from today?

In response to this question, Foucault never tires of saying that one cannot shortchange history. Instead, paradoxically, we have to think of freedom within its determinations. Why? Because it does not exist "outside" of history, because we are the products of history. But we can and we must, from the inside of what has made us be, seek to invent different horizons and modes of life. Here we have therefore that in which the scandal of thought and its risk consist: to desire, here and now, *in history*, a different life; that is, also and immediately, *another history*. And Foucault concludes, in the last lines of the manuscript for the last session in 1984, which he did not have the time to read but of which we still have the written trace: "There is no establishment of the truth without an essential position of otherness; the truth is never the same; there can be truth only in the form of the other world and the life that is other" (ECF-COT, 356). Metaphysics has made us used to projecting "the life that is other" in a transcendence that is opposed to history. In contrast, Foucault turns history into the density within which the investigation of difference and the disquietude of the present play out.

Judith Revel

SEE ALSO

> *Actuality*
> *Archaeology*
> *Phenomenology*
> *Truth*
> *Georges Canguilhem*
> *Friedrich Nietzsche*

SUGGESTED READING

Dreyfus, Hubert L., and Paul Rabinow. 1983. *Michel Foucault: Beyond Structuralism and Hermeneutics*. Chicago: University of Chicago Press.

Flynn, Thomas R. 1997. *Sartre, Foucault, and Historical Reason: Toward an Existentialist Theory of History*. Chicago: University of Chicago Press.

2005. *Sartre, Foucault, and Historical Reason*, volume 2: *A Poststructuralist Mapping of History*. Chicago: University of Chicago Press.

Revel, Judith. 2010. *Foucault, une pensée du discontinu*. Paris: Fayard.

Veyne, Paul. 1984. *Writing History: Essay on Epistemology*, trans. Mina Moore-Rinvolucri. Manchester: Manchester University Press.

2010. *Foucault: His Thought, His Character*, trans. Janet Lloyd. Cambridge: Polity Press.

35

HISTORICAL A PRIORI

"HISTORICAL A PRIORI" is a Foucaultian *énoncé* that, like the strange list from Borges that opens *The Order of Things*, seems explicitly designed to provoke mischievous laughter. As Foucault himself observes, "juxtaposed these two words produce a rather startling effect" (EAK, 127): exactly how, one is led to wonder, can an "a priori" (that which is both prior to and independent of all experience) be "historical"? Conversely, how can the shifting materiality of the historical constitute any kind of transcendental condition of possibility? One can only assume that the difficulty of the statement "historical a priori," and the adjacent necessity for some kind of stammering translation between the opposed realms that it names, is central to the practice or concept itself. However, rather than following the road of critique (trying to resolve this empirical-transcendental antinomy at a higher theoretical level), perhaps we should follow Foucault's archaeological practice and simply trace the statement "historical a priori" in its discursive emergence and transformation in his work.

The phrase makes its first, halting attempts at emergence in the guise of the sibling phrase "concrete a priori," which is used in the *History of Madness* (see EHM, 130, 376, for example) and in Foucault's 1963 book *The Birth of the Clinic: An Archaeology of Medical Perception*. In the introduction to the *Clinic*, Foucault writes that, "Medicine made its appearance as a clinical science in conditions which define, together with its historical possibility, the domain of its existence and the structure of its rationality. They form its concrete a priori [*l'a priori concret*], which it is now possible to uncover, perhaps because a new experience of disease is coming into being that will make possible a historical and critical understanding of the old experience" (EBC, xv). As Foucault sums up the *Clinic* book, he uses the actual phrase "historical a priori" for the first time, in tandem with the concrete a priori: "Since 1816, the doctor's eye has been able to confront a sick organism. The historical and concrete a priori

[*L'a priori historique et concret*] of the modern medical gaze was finally constituted"
(EBC, 192).

In the *Clinic* book, this "historical and concrete a priori" seems to name those
discursive and institutional conditions of emergence that have to be in place for the
aesthetic and political practice of the gaze to mutate into the central practice of the
human sciences, and specifically as the linchpin practice of medicine. Importantly,
this early formulation of the "historical and concrete a priori" also suggests the dual
importance of both the empirical and diachronic dimensions involved in Foucault's
thinking about the conditions for a discourse's emergence and transformation. One
cannot, Foucault suggests, easily describe or transform one's own concrete historical
conditions (one cannot, perhaps, diagnose one's own clinic), but one *can* perform a
halting archaeology of how we've arrived at the clinical practices that dominate our
present. In short, only when a new conception of a given phenomenon (a new dominant regime of treatment) has emerged can one hope to name the concrete contours
of the former historical a priori.

In Foucault's archaeological work, then, the historical a priori serves as a
mechanism by which certain specific, bounded, and concrete practices (like the
gaze, which organizes aesthetics) are able to saturate and reorganize domains
seemingly far removed from them (domains like medicine). And, in the process,
these "historical" discourses sculpt new "a priori" objects for their disciplines: they
construct (in the guise of "discovering") new objects and new protocols that enable
different engagements and new methods of investigation. The medical gaze, for
example, allows clinical medicine to invent new enabling possibilities and dangers lurking within the body – a prioris that medicine can then go on to study,
combat, and hopefully outflank. Specifically, new practices and understandings of
health, disease, and death are reconstituted by the emergent historical a priori of
the medical gaze – in the way that Foucault will later show how something like
an "author-function" is historically reconstructed in and through various ways of
handling texts. Like the discovery of abnormality through the medical gaze of
diagnosis, the author is discursively and historically constructed precisely as a kind
of a priori, a grounding mechanism supposedly outside and prior to the object
being examined.

Archaeology, then, is a discourse that emphasizes the emergence of the new
(the historical invention of new a prioris, and thereby new practices) rather than a
discourse dedicated to the rediscovery of the a priori conditions of possibility for
any discursive formation: a discourse of historical emergence rather than philosophical origin. Archaeology is a science of what Foucault calls "positivity" rather than
an investigation of the inevitable lacks, gaps, or slippages that haunt any discourse
from its origin. As Foucault writes, "this form of positivity … defines a field in which
formal identities, thematic continuities, translations of concepts, and polemical

interchanges may be deployed. Thus positivity plays the role of what might be called a historical a priori" (EAK, 127).

The historical a priori is native to Foucault's self-described "archaeological" work. As we've seen, the phrase emerges in *The Birth of the Clinic*, but it is first deployed consistently throughout 1966's *The Order of Things: An Archaeology of the Human Sciences*. In the introduction to *The Order of Things*, Foucault states outright that the book's function is to examine the historical a priori of the human sciences:

> Quite obviously, such an analysis does not belong to the history of ideas or of science: it is rather an inquiry whose aim is to rediscover on what basis knowledge and theory become possible; within what space of order knowledge was constituted; on the basis of what historical a priori ... ideas could appear, sciences be established, experience reflected in philosophies, rationalities be formed – only, perhaps, to dissolve and vanish soon afterwards. (EOT, xxi–xxii)

In constructing and mobilizing such a historical a priori for the emergence and transformation of the human sciences in Europe, Foucault goes on to demonstrate in *The Order of Things* that the nineteenth-century triumvirate of life, labor, and language –the discourses of biology, Marxism, and linguistics – all emerge in the context of the same historical a priori: the search for new practices of analysis in the wake of the epistemic breakdown of representation in the early modern period. As linguistics turns away from Adamic understandings of language (the sense that things are represented and their meaning guaranteed by their original names), so, too, does economics gradually turn away from discussions of ground rent (as natural, representational value) to discussions of money and credit, while biology abandons the plant (fully representable from root to flower) as the primary marker of life and slowly adopts the unrepresentable vitalism of animality to model this emergent object called "life" (see EOT, 287–304).

Although the *énoncé* historical a priori is deployed at strategic points throughout Foucault's work of the period, it receives its most thorough theoretical articulation in *The Archaeology of Knowledge* – most specifically in the chapter, "The Historical A Priori and the Archive" (EAK, 126–131). In a fashion characteristic of that book on the whole, Foucault spends much of his time separating out his practice and conceptual apparatus from more recognizable methodological presuppositions in play in philosophy, the history of ideas, history of science, or sociology. The first traditional concept that Foucault rejects is the formal a priori of mathematics and transcendental philosophy: "[T]here ... would be nothing more pleasant, or more inexact, than to conceive of this historical a priori as a formal a priori" (EAK, 128). He continues in the *Archaeology*, "this a priori does not elude historicity: it does not constitute, above events, and in an unmoving heaven, an atemporal structure: it is defined by the group of rules that characterize a discursive practice: but the rules are not imposed from the outside" (EAK, 127).

Following the *Archaeology*'s characteristic discursive move, then, Foucault's historical a priori is defined almost exclusively negatively, in terms of what it *isn't*:

> not a condition of validity for judgments, but a condition of reality for statements. It is not a question of rediscovering what might legitimize an assertion, but of freeing the conditions of emergence of statements, the law of coexistence with their others ... [a]n a priori not of truths that might never be said, or really given to experience; but the a priori of a history that is given since it is that of things actually said. (EAK, 127)

So the historical a priori is far from constituting an interruption or absence at the *arché* of any discourse (a secret silently said or repressed at the origin); rather, it functions as the positive condition (the operating system, so to speak) of the "archive" – a "complex volume" of "different types of positivity" (EAK, 128): "first the law of what can be said, the system that governs the appearance of statements as unique events" (EAK, 129) and that which afterward "differentiates discourses in their multiple existence and specifies them in their own duration" (ibid.).

Following along from Foucault's own practice of negative definition, it may help to think about ways that the historical a priori differs from its two closest analogues in French thought of the 1960s: the Marxist discourse of ideology critique and the phenomenological emphasis on philosophical conditions of possibility. First, Foucault wishes to distinguish the historical a priori from the Marxist concept of ideology – understood as the falsely naturalizing and hegemonic "common sense" that serves to ensure the reproduction of dominant ideology by covering over the true kernel of class antagonism. Recall that for Louis Althusser ideology consists of a subject's imaginary relation to her real conditions of existence, and ideology as such functions as a theoretical a priori that is made concrete in institutions. For the Althusserian Marxism dominant in Foucault's archaeological period, ideology names that hidden but normalizing force of unacknowledged consensus – "what you think before you think" – which the science of ideology critique would consistently unmask as a limiting brake on new, emergent, or revolutionary thinking. As such, Althusser's notion of ideology can seem on the surface to be very similar to Foucault's discourse of the historical a priori.

Elsewhere, however, Foucault outlines three specific objections to the Marxist notion of ideology critique:

> The first is that, like it or not, it always stands in virtual opposition to something else that is supposed to count as truth.... The second drawback is that the concept of ideology refers, I think necessarily, to something of the order

of a subject. Thirdly, ideology stands in a secondary position relative to something that functions as its infrastructure, as its material, economic determinant. (EEW3, 307)

For Foucault, the historical a priori is – unlike ideology – not primarily a set of ideas or limiting constructs, and thereby the historical a priori cannot be characterized as either true or false. In other words, Foucault's historical a priori is not primarily a set of ruling-elite interests that, before the fact, limits or censors what can be said or thought (which is precisely the function of hegemonic ideology). Rather, the historical a priori functions a bit like the phrase that Foucault later borrows from his teacher, Georges Canguilhem. Any given period's historical a priori is neither true nor false, but certain statements can be shown to reside "in the true" or "in the false." In other words, in order to be heard as either "true" or "false" at a given historical juncture, a statement first has to be judged "within the true," able to be evaluated as bearing in some functional way on a given discourse (see "The Discourse on Language," EAK, 224).

The historical a priori is not, as ideology would have it, akin to the blinders that an author has to wear in order to engage in normative discourse, but rather the historical a priori functions as the baseline of enabling discursive practices and thematics that all participants – whether they are speaking for or against a supposed normative discourse – have to follow in order to be relevant to a given truth procedure in the first place. As he continues in the *Archaeology*, Foucault argues that the historical a priori functions as

> a more extensive space than the play of influences that have operated from one author to another, or than the domain of explicit polemics. Different oeuvres, dispersed books, that whole mass of texts that belong to a single discursive formation – and so many authors who do or do not know one another, criticize one another, invalidate one another, pillage one another, meet without knowing it and obstinately intersect their unique discourses in a web of which they are not the masters, of which they cannot see the whole, and of whose breadth they have a very inadequate idea. (EAK, 126)

At that level, the historical a priori allows discursive participants to distinguish between what Nietzsche calls "timely" and "untimely" discourses – discourse that actors are able to use or understand and those pronouncements that are, by definition, not assimilable into existing discursive paradigms. More than that, perhaps, the historical a priori functions as a selection mechanism that decides which statements survive and become housed in the archive and which ones pass unheard, unconsidered, forgotten as soon as they are uttered. But Foucault stresses that such forgetting or ignoring is not primarily a "repressive" operation, as it might be understood for the critic of ideology (i.e., only those statements in sync with the dominant modes of power are allowed to pass into the archive). Just as for Foucault "there are no machines of freedom, by definition," there are no inherently repressive ideological mechanisms at the level of the historical a priori.

However, understanding the historical a priori as the conditions for any discursive event to be seen as relevant within a given domain – as being "in the true" – flirts not so much with the Althusserian science of ideology critique but with the other great enemy of Foucault's *Archaeology of Knowledge*: Derrida's deconstructive focus on the linguistic "conditions of possibility" for the emergence and functioning of a discourse. On that register, barely a page of the *Archaeology* goes by without some kind of stinging critique of any and all discourses of hidden depth or absent origin – a theoretical a priori of any kind, even one of absence, gap, lack, or trace. As Foucault clearly writes, what he seeks in concepts like the historical a priori is "not a condition of possibility but a law of coexistence": the historical a priori and the statement constitute "something more than a series of traces" (EAK, 107). The statements that comprise and transform the archive of the historical a priori are "not defined by their truth – that is, not gauged by the presence of a secret content" (EAK, 120). In other words, the domain of the historical a priori is characterized neither by the masked (historical) content of ideology nor by a species of hidden originary (a priori) gap or lack that haunts all language usage.

In his most pointed criticism of Derrida in the *Archaeology*, Foucault points out that the hazardous historical a priori of discourse "can be purified in the problematic of trace, which, prior to all speech, is the opening of inscription, the gap of deferred time [*écart du temps différeré*]: it is always the historico-transcendental theme that is reinvested" (EAK, 121). And just as ideology for Foucault entails a certain privileged understanding of subjectivity, so, too, does the whole phenomenological legacy of *Dasein*, that "subjectivity that always lags behind manifest history, and which finds, beneath events, another, more serious, more sober, more secret, more fundamental history, closer to the origin, more firmly linked to its ultimate horizon (and consequently more in control of all its determinations)" (ibid.). In short, Foucault's archaeological apparatus insists that the historical archive of discontinuously constructed statements, and not the quasi-transcendental conditions of discourse's general possibility, governs the reception and impact of the statement: why certain statements are received as relevant and influential and others – the vast majority of all statements – are not. The historical a priori does its work at the material level of discursive emergence – with positivities, things that are actually said – rather than ventriloquizing the quasi-transcendental murmur that exists in the originary ether before things are said (which remains, in Foucault's reading, the domain of deconstruction, phenomenology, and ideology critique).

In closing, and as a passing and final example of the work of the historical a priori, one could conjecture that Foucault's own reception in the English-speaking world was configured by the historical a priori operating within linguistic-turn structuralism and poststructuralism in England, Australia, and North America. For "French theory" to have resided "within the true" in the 1970s and 1980s, it had to be based on – and somehow speak positively to – the historical a priori of the linguistic turn, and so Foucault's archaeological work on discursive formation was received as a type of linguistically based structuralism or poststructuralism. In short, Foucault's archaeological work was understood as akin to the work of Barthes or Derrida rather than constituting a wholesale critique of linguistic-turn thought and its obsessions with language's inevitable lacks, gaps, and absences. Outside that "postmodern" legacy, one can perhaps more easily read these early Foucauldian formulations of the statement, the archive, and the historical a priori as archaeological predecessors to his midcareer thinking about mobile *dispositifs* of power, and the late works' emphasis on "modes of veridiction" – similar notions to be sure, but ones stripped of the historical a priori's apparent emphasis on language and discourse.

Jeffrey T. Nealon

SEE ALSO

Archaeology
History
Language
Jacques Derrida
Immanuel Kant

SUGGESTED READING

Djaballah, Marc. 2008. *Kant, Foucault, and Forms of Experience*. London: Routledge.
Han, Béatrice. 2002. *Foucault's Critical Project: Between the Transcendental and the Historical*, trans. Edward Pile. Stanford, CA: Stanford University Press.
Webb, David. 2013. *Foucault's Archaeology: Science and Transformation*. Edinburgh: Edinburgh University Press.

36

HOMOSEXUALITY

THE CONCEPT OF "homosexuality" designates for Foucault a problem that stems out of the larger issue concerning the emergence of sexuality during the nineteenth century (FDE2a, 1112). This claim does not simply reiterate Foucault's understanding of this notion, namely that "homosexuality is a notion that dates from the nineteenth century, and thus, ... it is a recent category" (EGS, 386). More significantly, it points out that a specific sexual practice that was not an important problem during the eighteenth century (FDE2a, 1351) and even during ancient times (FDE2a, 1105–1106; Veyne 1985, 29) became one only when the definition of one's individuality was vested in one's sexual behavior. And so, individuals who previously had sexual relations with another person of the same sex experienced them as *libertinage* or as an active or passive role within a relationship (FDE2a, 1136). Their sexual experience was definitely not a homosexual experience or a region of sexual experience isolated from all other sexual practices and forms of pleasure (EFS, 387; EAK, 190).

For Foucault, homosexuality is not a transhistorical notion ("une catégorie sexuelle ou anthropologique constant" [FDE2a, 1111; Halperin 1995, 45]). It is not a notion equally applicable to all cultures and periods as "an obligatory grid of intelligibility for certain concrete [sexual] practices" (ECF-BBIO, 3). Nor is it a name that refers to a natural kind (EHS1, 105; Halperin 1995, 45). It is rather a term that has a certain historical emergence, and, in order to understand this notion, it is important to grasp its conditions of possibility. As a reminder, however, to claim that the notion of homosexuality emerges in a specific historical context does not fully commit Foucault to the claim that homosexuality is socially constructed. And though Foucault's history of sexuality is written from the standpoint of a history of discourses, he does not openly endorse this kind of explanation (Halperin 1995, 4). For example, when Foucault is asked whether the predisposition for homosexuality is innate or socially conditioned, he simply replies "I have strictly nothing to say on this matter. *No comment*" (FDE2a, 1140). How did homosexual behavior become vested in individual identity to such an extent that it marked the inner essence of the person?

Foucault points out two significant modifications caused by the discursive explosion of the nineteenth century. First, this quantitative phenomenon, this proliferation of discourses speaking about sex, produced "a centrifugal movement with respect to heterosexual monogamy" (EHS1, 38). The sexuality of the legitimate couple not only began to function as a norm but also cast light onto the "peripheral sexuality" of children, mad men and women, criminals, and "the sensuality of those who did not like the opposite sex" (ibid.). Even though this series of discourses about homosexuality "made possible a strong advance of social control into this area of 'perversity'," such a form of sexuality continued to be tolerated nonetheless, and this is how "homosexuality began to speak on its behalf, to demand that its legitimacy or 'naturality' be acknowledged" (EHS1, 101). Yet, as Foucault points out, as long as this act of fighting against being imprisoned within this notion of homosexuality was only a pure reactivity, or a "reverse discourse," this strategy failed "to shift homosexuality from the position of an object of power/knowledge to a position of legitimate subjective agency" (Halperin 1995, 57).

For Foucault, a world of perversion emerges in the nineteenth century, "an entire sub-race race was born, different ... from the libertines of the past" (EHS1, 40), which could not be explained in repressive terms since "the severity of the codes relating to sexual offenses diminished considerably in the nineteenth century and that law itself often deferred to medicine" (EHS1, 40–41). The novelty consists in the emergence of perversion as a medical object (FDE2a, 322). We see here the creation of an entire system of knowledge that does not simply classify those "incomplete" sexual practices (i.e., homosexuality) within an organic, functional, mental pathological framework but does so in order to manage them. This new form of power, which was supposed to control and survey perversions instead of enforcing a repressive system based on prohibition, brings "an additional ruse of severity" (EHS1, 41) by incorporating those perversions and producing *a new specification of individuals* (EHS1, 42–43). This is how "the nineteenth-century homosexual became a personage" (EHS1, 43). The homosexual was more than a type of life or anatomical/physiological shape, he was a medical object to be explained by appealing to either his past or his childhood. "Nothing that went into his total composition was unaffected by his sexuality" (ibid.), and so he became a "case study" (FSP, 225–227). This is the moment when the psychological, psychiatric, medical category of homosexuality is constituted, and as soon as it is constituted it becomes a form of sexuality different from sodomy (a legal category defined by a type of sexual relation). Homosexuality is understood as a "quality of sexual sensibility," a "contrary sexual sensation," a "kind of interior androgyny," "a hermaphrodism of the soul." Hence, "the homosexual was now a species" (EHS1, 43).

This new modality of power coupled with a medical and psychiatric system of knowledge did more than render visible these "aberrant sexualities." It implanted in the perverts' bodies a permanent reality as a new *raison d'être*. The entire sexual domain was "placed under the rule of the normal and the pathological," so there had to be something "in the depths of the organism" (EHS1, 44), like a dysfunction or a symptom, of the sexual instinct. Once the sexual instinct is couched in functional terms, perversions, including homosexuality, "become a natural class of diseases" (Davidson 2001, 14).

Starting in the nineteenth century, homosexuality became not merely a sexual perversion but a specific psychiatric object, a dysfunction of the sexual instinct that requires, like all other psychic diseases (i.e., madness), therapy, intervention, and ultimately control: "The homosexual is a medical patient of psychiatry" (Davidson 2001, 22). This is the subtle way in which the medical and psychiatric system of knowledge incorporates sexual "instinctual disturbances" not merely to label them or to classify them but in order to set up a "network of pleasures and powers" that defines true ways of being oneself, a truthful sexuality, and thus it defines our most inner truth (FDE2a, 937).

Certainly, people like Gide, Oscar Wilde, Hirschfeld, and others fought against the "historico-poltical takeover" (FGS, 47) of this notion of homosexuality that was imposing more than a form of experience or pleasure but a certain identity, a certain relation to oneself. Hence, in earlier struggles, it was important to fight for certain rights for sexuality, rights for pleasure (EGS, 388). However, for Foucault, the battle for gay rights, as important as it is, should be only an "episode" and not "the final stage" of this struggle (FDE2a, 1127). The reason is that it is very "hard to carry on the struggle using the terms of sexuality [or homosexuality] without … getting trapped by notions such as sexual disease, sexual pathology, normal sexuality" (EGS, 388).

Homosexuality should not be a notion for an already existing desire, but "something to be desired" (FDE2a, 982), a way of life to be invented, "a becoming gay" (FDE2a, 1555), which "makes ourselves infinitely more susceptible to pleasures" (FDE2a, 984). This is why for Foucault homosexuality has little to do with sexual liberation. Resistance is not a negation but a creative process (FDE2a, 1560), so to be gay is to define and develop a certain way of life (FDE2a, 984). How does one define a homosexual way of life?

Foucault does not propose a generalizable definition for a homosexual way of life since such a discourse could be easily idealized, and imposed back as a norm on other homosexuals. In this sense, he understands his role more as a facilitator than as a leader of the gay movement (FDE2a, 1153). For him, although it is important to be creative and experiment with new relations and forms of pleasure, it is equally important to be aware of the dangers built into this notion. So, homosexuality is a strategic position (a historic opportunity [FDE2a, 985]) from which one has to constantly create new ways to relate to oneself and to others (an aesthetics of existence [EHS2, 10–11]).

In the reevaluation of the notion of homosexuality ("this rejuvenation ... of the instruments, objectives and axes of the struggle" [EGS, 389]), Foucault puts forward "the theme of pleasure." In order to escape the medico-psychological presuppositions embedded in the notion of desire, Foucault proposes the word *pleasure*, "which in the end means nothing, which is still ... rather empty of content and unsullied by possible uses." He contends, "there is no 'abnormal' pleasure; there is no 'pathology' of pleasure," and thus a mode of life where the self transforms itself into a source of pleasure would avoid "the medical armature that was built into the notion of desire" (EGS, 388). As long as the apparatus of sexuality cannot normalize pleasures, it would not be able to redefine the inner essence of the subject, so the previous dictum "tell me what your desire is, and I'll tell you what you are as a subject" (EGS, 389) would not function anymore.

And since for Foucault "pleasure has no passport, no identification papers" (Foucault in Halperin 1995, 95), a way of life that would focus on the intensification, modulation, and multiplication of sexual pleasures would not only function as a way of "decentering the subject and fragmenting personal identity" (Halperin 1995, 94; FDE2a, 940) but would desexualize the body (FDE2a, 1557; FDE2a, 321) and also free those pleasures from organ specificity (degenitalization of pleasure). It is a way to invent oneself, to transform one's body into "a place for the production of extraordinary polymorphous pleasures, detached from the valorization of sex" (EGS, 396–397). As an effect of such a strategy for creating pleasures, new forms of relationships, new forms of gay sexual practices are produced (FDE2a, 1556). And Foucault can only feel sorry for "those unhappy heterosexuals" (EGS, 400) who do not have places (e.g., baths, love-hotels [FDE2a, 779]) where they can cease to be a subject and experience all sorts of possible encounters and pleasures. But how can one define through certain sexual practices a relational system, a homosexual style of life?

This is possible if homosexuality is understood as an ascetic mode of life, as a kind of spiritual exercise, as a practice of self-mastery in relation to oneself and to others. This "homosexual *askésis*" instead of being a synonym for less pleasure, calls for more intensified, multiplied, novel forms of pleasure. And all those pleasures are not attainable unless there is mutual friendship, love, trust, fidelity, and companionship among the gay individuals (FDE2a, 983). A homosexual mode of life is ultimately "an art of living," a care for the self and for the others, where sexual choices have an effect on one's entire life (FDE2a, 1144; FDE2a, 1114).

In some ways, Foucault's work does not provide an 'improved' definition of homosexuality "but, on the contrary, [an] attempt to empty homosexuality of its positive content, of its material and psychic determinations, in order to make it available to us as a site for the continuing construction and renewal of continually changing identities" (Halperin 1995, 122).

Nicolae Morar

SEE ALSO

Ethics
Life
Love
Sex

SUGGESTED READING

Cohen, Edward. 1988. "Foucauldian Necrologies: 'Gay' 'Politics'? Politically Gay?" *Textual Practice* 2, no. 1:87–101.

Dean, Tim, and Christopher Lane, eds. 2001. *Homosexuality and Psychoanalysis*. Chicago: University of Chicago Press.

Eribon, Didier. 2001. "Michel Foucault's Histories of Sexuality," *GLQ: A Journal of Lesbian and Gay Studies* 7, no. 1:31–86.

Halperin, David. 1996. "Homosexuality," in *The Oxford Classical Dictionary*, ed. Simon Hornblower and Antony Spawforth. Oxford: Oxford University Press, pp. 720–723.

1998. "Forgetting Foucault: Acts, Identities, and the History of Sexuality," *Representations* 63 (Summer): 93–120.

2002a. "The First Homosexuality?" in *The Sleep of Reason: Erotic Experience and Sexual Ethics in Ancient Greece and Rome*, ed. Martha Nussbaum and Julia Sihlova. Chicago: University of Chicago Press, pp. 229–268.

2002b. *How to Do the History of Homosexuality*. Chicago: University of Chicago Press.

McWhorter, Ladelle. 1999. *Bodies and Pleasures: Foucault and the Politics of Sexual Normalization*. Bloomington: Indiana University Press.

2009. *Racism and Sexual Oppression in Anglo-America*. Bloomington: Indiana University Press.

Veyne, Paul. 1985. "Homosexuality in Ancient Rome," in *Western Sexuality: Practices and Precept in Past and Present Times*, ed. Philippe Ariès and André Béjin. Oxford: Oxford University Press, pp. 26–35.

37

HUMAN SCIENCES

COMPRISING ANTHROPOLOGY, PSYCHOLOGY, sociology, and certain forms of history, the human sciences both produce knowledge about man and function to guarantee the ordering of modern societies. Yet although anthropology is one of the human sciences, it is also the cultural and philosophical condition for their appearance. Kantian anthropology is the first philosophical marker of the shift that leads to the appearance of the human sciences, for here the move is made from a philosophical perspective that grounds knowledge of the finite on the basis of the infinite to a critical perspective that produces knowledge of the finite on the basis of the finite itself, as it is found in man, that finite being who seeks knowledge (EOT, 312–318). The human sciences therefore depend on a profound cultural shift to a philosophical anthropology that conditions knowledge practices. Although particular human sciences have taken shape at different times, none of them could appear before the transformation in which the finite human being becomes the sole power invoked in the production of knowledge.

Foucault finds that certain debates have been continuously repeated since the appearance of the human sciences: (1) the human sciences claim to be the foundation of all science, even as the extension of their methods to other sciences provokes fears of psychologism and sociologism; and (2) they lay claim to the space traditionally occupied by philosophy, but philosophers object to the naive manner in which they justify themselves (EOT, 346). The repetition of these debates within a definite time period suggests that they respond not to timeless questions but particular conditions that Foucault fleshes out by describing the modern epistemological trihedron and the event in knowledge it provokes, the appearance of man as an object of knowledge (EOT, 347). This trihedron is composed of three planes, formed in the intersection of three dimensions; in the opening formed by these three planes, man appears as the object of discursive practices oriented by the search for truth. The first dimension is that of formal thought, as found in mathematics and physics; the second dimension refers to the empirical sciences, biology, economics, and philology in particular; and the third dimension concerns philosophical thought. In formal thought, order is established via deductively linked propositions, whereas the empirical sciences relate different causal and structural elements via analogies, and philosophy endeavors to develop a thought of the Same. This trihedron is not defined by any single one of the dimensions but by the planes formed between dimensions in working from one to another; for instance, by formalizing the empirical and seeking mathematical regularities within it, or conversely by applying mathematical formulas to the empirical sciences. So, too, the dimension of the empirical sciences and that of philosophy form a common plane, which gives rise to philosophies of life, of alienated man, and symbolic forms by importing concepts of empirical origin into the dimension of philosophy. Conversely, beginning from philosophy, one finds the emergence of radical ontologies that seek to discover the being of the diverse objects of the empirical sciences. Finally, there is a plane defined between the purely formal and the philosophical dimensions, which concerns the formalization of thought. Man appears in the interpositivity of the different dimensions and planes of the trihedron and the pursuit of knowledge and thought rendered possible therein (EAK, 173). The human sciences are therefore both excluded from and included within the trihedron. They are excluded since none of the dimensions or planes that constitute the trihedron determines them completely. Distinct from the objects pursued across the surface of two dimensions, these sciences have rather their own specific object defined by the open interior shape of the trihedron. Yet they are also included in a way because they draw on every aspect of the epistemological trihedron in seeking knowledge of man. They can, for example, attempt to formalize knowledge of human behavior via probabilities; they can draw on philology in order to better grasp man in his specificity; and they borrow the philosopher's inquiry into man's finitude in order to expose it completely in the empirical (EOT, 347). Thus, his being does not determine their character, but rather a complex epistemological configuration brings about man and with this the possibility and necessity of human sciences.

This approach is epistemological rather than ontological because the human sciences are founded not on the being of man but a particular configuration stemming from a transformation in the power of language. Whereas language in the classical age existed as the discourse within which the being of things appears, in the modern age this power is dispersed, preventing such access to being. In the face of this dispersion, the subjects and objects of knowledge can be said to turn back on themselves, revealing a hitherto unknown depth that becomes the reserve of discoverable truth. Thus natural history transforms from a study of formal differences based on a principle of continuity into the study of the life that animates living being, the study of wealth opens onto the depth of the productive forces that generate value, and discourse itself becomes the study of the history of languages. Through its fragmentation, synonymous with the opening of the epistemological trihedron, the figure of man appears as the living, laboring, and speaking subject but also as the object of a knowledge that seeks to know man in all his activities. This requires that the human sciences operate a formal duplication of the empirical sciences in studying man.

Thanks to this duplication, each of the human sciences can be tied back to one empirical science that it doubles, even though it can also draw on the others. As psychology duplicates biology, sociology duplicates economics, and the analysis of literature and myth duplicates philology. In these duplications, each of the human sciences has its own basic set of concepts derived from its model empirical science. Psychology derives the conceptual categories of norm and function from biology, sociology draws conflict and rule from economics, and the study of literature gains signification and a system from philology (EOT, 357). So, although each set is peculiar to its own area, they are applicable throughout the domain of the human sciences, often making it difficult to distinguish between them. Thus, "all the human sciences interlock and can always be used to interpret one another: their frontiers become blurred, intermediary and composite disciplines multiply endlessly, and in the end their proper object may even disappear altogether" (EOT, 358). Indeed, experience has already shown that the human sciences lead not to the apotheosis of man but to his disappearance (EEW2, 265). Yet this is not a defect in the human sciences that could be corrected so much as an instance of what makes them productive; a defect appears only when the interrelation of the distinct models has not been established in advance. And it is through the broad categories provided by the models that "man is able to present himself to a possible knowledge" (EOT, 362). A human science, therefore, not being defined by its object, is not a science at all. For Foucault, there is instead a "human science" whenever norms, rules, and signifying totalities are deployed in the domain of the unconscious in order to analyze the conditions of consciousness, both in its forms and contents (EOT, 364). The unconscious plays the role of a transcendental for the human sciences, which look to it in order to pose and explain man such as he appears to himself. The human sciences thus exist and function because man is epistemologically constituted as an empirico-transcendental doublet (EOT, 318) that "must be a positive domain of *knowledge* and cannot be an object of *science*" (EOT, 367). Man, as an empirical being, is made to stand in for his own transcendental conditions by these "sciences" – thus his empirical being as living, laboring, and speaking is studied as if it were the transcendental condition of all human behavior and activity, including practices of knowing. In this, the human sciences are soporifics that support the thought of man's finitude.

Foucault's accounts in the 1970s, by contrast, emphasize nondiscursive events in seeking the conditions of the human sciences' emergence and maintenance. Rather than unfolding man as an empirico-transcendental doublet, they function "to twin, to couple this juridical individuality and disciplinary individual, to make us believe that the real, natural, and concrete content of the juridical individual is the disciplinary individual cut out and constituted by political technology" (ECF-PP, 57–58). Knowledge of man therefore creates an impasse insofar as appeals to overthrow repressive institutions in the name of the individual's human rights are mistaken about the meaning of those very rights. Although these rights may seem natural or universal, they are inherent within man, a being constituted by normalizing procedures, and so their affirmation is also an affirmation of disciplinary society itself. Moreover, Foucault argues that, "what gave birth to the sciences of man was precisely the irruption, the presence, or the insistence of these tactical problems posed by the need to distribute the forces of work in terms of the needs of the economy that was then developing" (ECF-PP, 73). Various disciplinary tactics were elaborated in response to these questions about how to accumulate men and rationally distribute the bodily singularities of this labor force so as to accumulate capital. Because of the growing importance of discipline, the knowledge of "plants, animals, objects, values, and languages" could no longer remain classificatory, which had sufficed when naming was itself power. The human sciences arise from a transformation in the role of knowledge and contribute to a descending individualization in which discipline aims to produce docile bodies that have been adapted to the goal of accumulating wealth via industrial production. By drawing on the disciplinary context as a primary resource for knowledge of man in general, the human sciences contribute to the shaping of political subjects as docile bodies.

A later inflection of this account is found in Foucault's discussions of biopower, in which the human sciences play an important role since populations and environments can only be grasped and studied through knowledge of man. Emerging around the new realities established in the interplay of techniques of power and their objects, the human sciences would carve out new objects for these techniques, making these "the privileged correlate of modern mechanisms of power" (ECF-STP, 79). By establishing regularities within different segments of the population, the human sciences discover different normalities that then become objects of power insofar as one sort is to be favored over another (ECF-STP, 63). As Guillaume LeBlanc writes, the human sciences "oscillate permanently between the normal to be recorded and the normal to be instituted" (LeBlanc 2005, 168). The human sciences therefore contribute to normalization by producing new kinds of beings within the population – the hysterical woman, sexual pervert, masturbating child, and Malthusian couple (EHS1, 105) – so many kinds whose diagnosis and administration help to regulate and foster the social whole. They also function to grasp the diverse regularities of populations in relation to their environment; thus, for example, questions of hygiene were of vital importance for the security of towns and allowed knowledge of man to develop according to a medical model (ECF-STP, 63–64). Foucault writes, "if the question of man was raised … the reason for this is to be sought in the new mode of relation between history and life: in this dual position of life that placed it at the same time outside history, in its biological environment, and inside human historicity penetrated by the latter's techniques of knowledge and power" (EHS1, 143). Anthropology, understood as the condition from which the human sciences emerged, appeared when human life was discovered to be a historical phenomenon and the conditions within which it occurred could be modified in order to achieve certain effects. In this, man becomes an orienting problem and the human sciences arise as responses offering a therapeutic kind of knowledge that seeks to control or ward off internal and external threats.

Samuel Talcott

SEE ALSO

Archaeology
Biopower
Finitude
Knowledge
Man
Immanuel Kant

SUGGESTED READING

Burchell, Graham, Colin Gordon, and Peter Miller, eds. 1991. *The Foucault Effect: Studies in Governmentality*. Chicago: University of Chicago.
Canguilhem, George. 1968. "Qu'est-ce que la psychologie?" in *Etudes d'histoire et de philosophie des sciences*. Paris: Vrin, pp. 365–381.
LeBlanc, Guillaume. 2005. *L'Esprit des sciences humaines*. Paris: Vrin.

38

INSTITUTION

THE WORD "INSTITUTION" appears throughout Foucault's work in what seems to be an almost banal, nominal sense, most frequently in the plural, and often modified by an adjective ("political institutions" or "psychiatric institutions") or a genitive ("institutions of power"); use of the singular, when it functions as an active verbal noun ("the institution of the Sovereign" or "the institution of sexuality"), is comparatively sparse and frequently occurs in close proximity to similar but not quite synonymous terms that have a special importance to Foucault, such as birth, emergence, and establishment. Compound forms, such as institutionalization, which can have an ambiguous meaning, are rarer still. And sometimes the appearance of the word in the original French can be obscured by translation – the French verb *instituer* is frequently translated as "to establish" and the adjective *institué* as "established." All of this serves to underscore that the word appears to be used in an ordinary, familiar, almost unreflected manner, and as such it might seem absurd to claim that there is a technical sense, or even concept, of institution in Foucault's work. And yet, if we question the familiar and look beyond appearances, we soon find that not only is there a philosophical concept of institution but also and more broadly a thinking about institution that pervades Foucault's intellectual project in an insistent and consistent manner, such that his project might be characterized, at least in part, as the thought of institution, which would have a double sense. On the one hand is the nominal sense of a concretion or crystallization of power relations operating in the social body to subjugate humans and make them subjects and on the other hand the verbal sense, closely associated with both the problem of accounting for change in historical rationalities (as described in the Preface to the English translation of *The Order of Things*) and the later "method" of genealogy that, in part, address that problem. Indeed, it becomes clear that the thought of institution is a point of entry that gives access to most of Foucault's major concepts. In order to examine the double sense of the thought of institution in Foucault's work, it is worthwhile to consider why and how this thought enters into his work. Although the sources and resources for this consideration could be multiplied indefinitely, here the concern will be with just three tightly intertwined approaches: his relation to both structuralism and phenomenology; his rejection of traditional history and appropriation of Nietzschean genealogy as an alternative; and the exigencies of his intellectual project.

First, Foucault's complex and critical relations to both structuralism and phenomenology have been well documented. On structuralism in particular, one can see his own account in "Structuralism and Post-Structuralism," as well as his famously derisive remarks in the Preface to the English translation of *The Order of Things*. Although he does appreciate that structuralism is better suited than phenomenology to account for the effects of meaning in history, his primary objection is that it seeks universal methodological structures that can explain every situation. Foucault instead advocates a historical and genealogical approach that traces how structures emerge from relations of power and games of truth. For him, there is no meaning in history "except in accordance with the intelligibility of struggles, strategies, and tactics" (EEF, 304), and structuralism is not equipped to think of these. His view of phenomenology is even direr, because it posits reason as the founding act of a non- or transhistorical constituting subject that cannot elaborate a history of rationality independently of itself and its constituting function (EEF, 84). Now, when he speaks of "phenomenology," he paints with very broad strokes; he is, however, much more nuanced when he speaks of a particular phenomenologist, Merleau-Ponty, who, in courses no doubt attended by Foucault at École Normale (and later repeated in augmented form during his first two years at the Collège de France), introduced French students to the then unknown work of Saussure and prepared the way for the rise of structuralism in the human sciences. Indeed, Merleau-Ponty's critical encounter with language is an important turning point for Foucault (EEF, 83), as it not only undermines the phenomenological subject but also lays out the first rules of discourse that Foucault will deploy in his earliest works and then considerably develop and formalize in *The Archaeology of Knowledge*, which could be characterized as the rules for a logic of institution of discourse. And it is telling that Merleau-Ponty concludes his 1953–1954 course on "The Problem of Speech" with the announcement that these analyses of language and meaning should allow him "to clarify the nature of institution," a task that he takes up in the next academic year (Merleau-Ponty 1970, 26). The course on institution from 1954–1955 (when Foucault, then an instructor at the École, was immersed in a reading of Nietzsche, and of which he was no doubt aware) offers a definition of institution that parallels the understanding that Foucault will later have. Merleau-Ponty says,

> Therefore by institution, we were intending here those events in an experience which endow the experience with durable dimensions, in relation to which a

whole series of other experiences will make sense [*aura sens*], will form a think-able sequel or a history – or again the events which deposit a sense [*sens*] in me, not just as something surviving or as a residue, but as the call to follow [*un appel à une suite*], the demand of a future.... There occurs a simultaneous decenter-ing and recentering of the elements of our own life, a movement by us toward the past and of the present reanimated toward us. And this working of the past against the present ... results in a picture [*tableau*] of diverse, complex prob-abilities, which are always connected to local circumstances, burdened with a coefficient of facticity, and such that we can never say of one that it is more true than another, although we can say that one is more false, more artificial, and has less openness to a future which is less rich. (Merleau-Ponty 1970, 77–79)

Like Foucault after him, Merleau-Ponty is quite clearly talking about how our historical present is not a necessary outcome of an inexorable linear development governed by necessity, that it is instead the result of diverse and complex probabil-ities that have elective affinities for one another, thus producing a configuration on the basis of local circumstances, and that it contains within it the possibilities for restructuring the field of possibilities in which a subject is inscribed. But, unlike Foucault, what Merleau-Ponty was not yet able to grasp fully in his thinking on institution is the relations of power and the genealogical method necessary to ana-lyze them (see ECF-PP, 14–15). Merleau-Ponty had recognized that the limitations of phenomenology needed to be overcome and a new nondialectical philosophy of history needed be developed. He therefore proposed to develop this new philos-ophy of history on the basis of the logic of institution but died before he was able to develop all the resources necessary to bring this project to fruition. To a certain extent, then, Foucault's project – understood as a genealogy of institution – can be viewed as both a fulfillment of Merleau-Ponty's project and a transcendence of it, insofar as he goes far beyond his predecessor's scope and intent with the genea-logical analysis of the relations of power – but Foucault could not have developed his own thinking on institution without his critical engagement with both struc-turalism and phenomenology, the space for which was sketched preliminarily by Merleau-Ponty.

Second, as Foucault recounts in "Truth and Power," traditional history, for which the concept of the event is central, and its methodological historical anal-yses depend on "the great biological image of progressive maturation" or the logic of unbroken continuity characteristic of evolution or other linear cause-and-consequence models (EEF, 302). Structuralist approaches to history emptied out the notion of the event, dismissing it as trivial, in favor of relations of meaning, which at least had the advantage of not depending on the intervention of a transhistorical or constituting subject to confer meaning in history (EEF, 304). But, for Foucault, neither a traditional nor a structuralist (nor, for that matter, a phenomenological or Marxist) approach to history is able to break from the linear, causal, continuist model that inevitably and inexorably results in the present as a necessary and self-evident outcome – and all of them, to a greater or lesser extent, also depend on a monogenetic origin and a final telos. And yet, as Foucault discovers in his earliest works, these models cannot take account of what actually happens (in medicine, psychiatry, linguistics, etc.) over a relatively short period of time – namely, the sudden transformations in discourse that break with previous veridical and juridical models, thus instituting a whole new regime of knowledge. Foucault's concern is for how to take account of these sudden deviations, accelerations, evolutions, and transformations that do not correspond to the continuist image (EEF, 302), and, moreover, how those that occur in one discourse infect the body of another, combining with what is specific to that other body, mutating accordingly, and spreading throughout the entire social body to make us what we are and trap us in our historical present. Another model of history must therefore be developed, and Foucault does so, first, through an encounter with the new historians, which allows him to resuscitate the concept of event, and second, through his reading of Nietzsche, which allows him to develop his method of genealogy. The new historians realize that the event is not merely an unthinkable and ungraspable irruption but instead distinguish different types of events "differing in amplitude, chronological breadth, and capacity to produce effects," which must be maintained in their dispersion and are in fact thinkable in terms of the relations of power and in terms of their effects. On this basis, and in order to avoid substantializing the event as an irruption that leads inexorably and causally to the present as a self-evident outcome, Foucault undertakes to think of "eventalization," the complex polymorphic processes and the dispersed and diverse "connections, encounters, supports, blockages, plays of forces, strategies, and so on that at a given moment establish what subsequently counts as being self-evident, universal, and necessary," thus multiplying causes that structure the present field of possibilities in which individuals act and are made subjects (EEF, 249). Since no other model of historical analysis can take account of the "plethora of intelligibilities and deficit of necessities" (EEF, 250) at work in the dispersed polymorphic process, Foucault has to invent what, following Nietzsche, he calls "genealogy." As is clear in "Nietzsche, Genealogy, History," a genealogy does not seek origins but instead must "discover the myriad events" that give rise to an institution, and to maintain these diverse "events in their proper dispersion … and to identify accidents, minute deviations, complete reversals, errors, faulty calculations that give birth to things that continue to exist" (EEF, 355). In this regard, genealogy unravels the complex processes of "institutionalization" – that is, the diverse strategies and "a profusion of entangled events" (EEF, 361) that overlap, cohere, intersect, and interfere with one another, eventually crystallizing in an institution – and thus also reveals how the social body is comprised of interrelated institutions that structure the field of possibilities and govern what we are.

Third, frequently – most often in interviews, and notably in "The Subject and Power" – when Foucault recounts the trajectory of his work, he begins by specifying that his objective had "not been to analyze the phenomenon of power" but rather to create an "alternative" history of the "different modes by which … human beings are made into certain kinds of subjects" or subjugated by what seem to be necessity or the determinism of scientific "knowledge" (EEF, 126). Such an alternative history would refer to "more remote processes" that act directly on the body and on behavior, which in turn led him to study complex power relations (EEF, 128). But, he soon discovered that there were no adequate analytic tools available to study them, so these had to be invented. Indeed, the available but inadequate tools were based on legal and institutional models (EEF, 127) – presupposing that institutions already exist as necessary, closed unities that simply deploy power or govern power relations; but this, in his view, is a false conception that merely begs the question. His question is how certain forms of historical rationality – strategies and practices – have allowed those institutions (e.g., the state, the prison, the asylum, but also a concept, a trait, an *episteme*, and our historical present) to arise and acquire the air of necessity, authority, and inevitability. Analyzing power relations on the basis of institutions as already "given" mistakenly locates power "in" the institution, reduces power relations to a function of the institution, and reveals only the mechanisms of power designed to preserve the institution (EEF, 139–140). If the remote processes (or different types of events) and power relations that have "trapped us" in our historical present are to be understood on the basis of their own specific regularity and logic, regimes and practices – if, in other words, we are to understand how power relations shape and structure a field of possibilities for the subject – then the order of analysis must be inverted. Institutions must instead be understood on the basis of power relations; that is, even though power relations may be "fundamentally anchored or crystallized in" an institution, institutions are themselves, and therefore the specific nature of power relations is itself to be "found outside" of and "prior" to the institution as diverse and dispersed practices and strategies that make the institution possible as such (EEF, 140). Hence, Foucault studies not the institution of the prison but rather the practice of imprisonment, not the institution of the asylum but the strategies of internment and medicalization. Viewed in this light, institutions are interrelated and coordinated networks of power relations (overlapping with systems of communications and objective capacities) that have concretized or crystallized as "blocks" or semiregulated systems that are organized and adjusted as a strategic response to a problem (EEF, 136). As can be seen in the discussion of the educational and military institutions in *Discipline and Punish*, these blocks arrange space, manage time, and regulate the internal life and activities of persons, thus making them subjects. In this regard, institutions overlap with "disciplines," integrally contribute to the disciplining of society, and are thus inscribed in the whole network of the social.

So there is indeed not only a concept of the institution but also a thinking of institutionalization at work throughout Foucault's oeuvre. An institution – understood narrowly as a concept or trait, more broadly as the asylum, the prison, or the clinic, or more broadly still as a historical rationality, an *episteme*, or our historical present – must be thought of on the basis of the diverse and complex power relations, events, and strategies or practices that exist outside of and prior to it but come to be crystallized and embodied in it, and they are susceptible to analysis only through a genealogy. Institutions arise in diverse forms, places, and circumstances in response to a problem (e.g., criminality, madness), constitute a regulated and concerted, constantly adjusting system that works to structure the field of possibilities, act directly on the behavior of individuals, ordering space and time, coordinating the body, and thus subjugating the individual as a particular kind of subject, and in this regard are related to both "discipline" and "governmentality." But why be concerned with institutions and institutionalization? Because, as Foucault observes, there is no society, no social existence without power relations – and power relations exist only where and when there is the possibility of freedom. Our historical present has produced us as subjects, limited our possibilities, and seemingly trapped us in our historical present. But the genealogical analysis of institutions reveals that our historical present is not a necessary and self-evident outcome. It did not and need not be this way, and if we are to resist power, if we are to be otherwise and maintain an open future of freedom, then "the task of analyzing power relations" and the institutions in which they are embodied "in their historical formation, their mechanisms of adjustment, appropriation, and reproduction [is] all the more pressing – it is *the* political task inherent in all social existence" (EEF, 141, Foucault's italics).

Robert Vallier

SEE ALSO

> *Discipline*
> *Genealogy*
> *Governmentality*
> *Phenomenology*
> *Power*
> *Structuralism*
> *Maurice Merleau-Ponty*
> *Friedrich Nietzsche*

SUGGESTED READING

Allen, Amy. 2008. *The Politics of Our Selves: Power, Autonomy, and Gender in Contemporary Critical Theory*. New York: Columbia University Press.

Vallier, Robert. 2005. "Institution: The Significance of Merleau-Ponty's 1954 Course at the Collège de France," *Chiasmi International 7: Life and Individuation*: 263–280.

Veyne, Paul. 2010. *Foucault: His Thought, His Character*, trans. Janet Lloyd. Cambridge: Polity Press.

39

THE INTELLECTUAL

OUCAULT PARTICIPATED IN only one struggle, the struggle that, to his eyes, arises from the work of the intellectual. This is the struggle for information. Foucault made use of the position of power that his status as a scholar conferred on him in order to make the mumbling of the world be heard. After 1968, Foucault, with the organization Groupe d'Information sur les prisons (GIP: Prison Information Group), launched his first inquiry on prisons (see Macey 1993, 257–289). He intended to throw some light into this dark affair of society. Thanks to the testimony of families and the inmates, GIP succeeded therefore in making the prison enter actuality, not in the form of a moral problem, or in the form of a problem of general management, but as a place that takes place without history, the everyday, life, events of the same order as those of a strike in a factory or a job action in a neighborhood, etc. As Gilles Deleuze emphasized in 1972, with GIP, a new theory-practice relation is proposed. For the intellectual, the question is no longer to guide struggles by means of his actions or his words. The question is not even to encourage struggles. What is at issue for the intellectual is to turn himself into the relay of local struggles: here women, there inhabitants of a housing project, elsewhere homosexuals (see Miller 1993, 245–284; Allen 2008, 45–72).

That definition of the intellectual does not stop Foucault from getting up in arms each time political power is exercised in a way that is too arbitrary – as in Spain. In 1975, Foucault went to Madrid in order to physically protest the execution of Basque militants. He also supported the dissidents of the East and a number of opponents of Latin American dictators. Invited by the editor-in-chief of the Italian daily newspaper *Il Corriere della Sera*, Foucault twice went to Iran in 1978 (see Eribon 1991, 281–295). There, he encountered certain personalities of the opposition to the regime and was present at several protests. Returning to Paris, he wrote up a long series of "reports." In them, Foucault gave an account of what he saw and heard during this time when the Iranian people revolted against the Shah, trying out in these "reports" what he called a "radical journalism." He was following a dangerous and unique path that outlined, over twenty years, a new relation between the intellectual and actuality: an *antistrategic* morality: "One has to watch out for, a little below history, what breaks history apart and stirs it up, and, at the same time, one has to look, a bit behind the politics, for what must unconditionally limit that politics." In Iran, Foucault witnessed the emergence of a new force. In 1961, he had pursued this open quest for the plentitude of history that is possible only in "the space – at once empty and populated – of all these words without language that make a dull sound be heard for those who are listening." It is this same conviction that encouraged Foucault to support, with Pierre Bourdieu, the Solidarity movement in Poland (see Eribon 1991, 296–308). He went there just after martial law was established at Varsovie in December 1981. It is likewise this same conviction that made Foucault lash out at the position of the recently elected French socialist government of Francois Mitterand, who had refused to take a position in regard to the establishment of martial law. By his criticism, Foucault put in boldface his refusal to become the official intellectual of the new government.

Philippe Artières

SEE ALSO

Actuality
Philosophy
Politics

SUGGESTED READING

Allen, Amy. 2008. *The Politics of Our Selves: Power, Autonomy, and Gender in Contemporary Critical Theory*. New York: Columbia University Press.

Eribon, Didier. 1991. *Michel Foucault*, trans. Betsy Wing. Cambridge, MA: Harvard University Press.

Macey, David. 1993. *The Lives of Michel Foucault*. New York: Vintage.

Miller, James. 1993. *The Passion of Michel Foucault*. New York: Simon and Schuster.

40

KNOWLEDGE

THE OUTSIZED IMPACT of Foucault's thought on all humanistic and social science research fields is notorious. For many scholars in these fields, his philosophical proposals contain productive implications for the deepest questions of methodological approaches and aims. Indeed, his work was in part received as an innovation of a generally *epistemological* kind. Yet, the exact nature of his specifically epistemological contributions is still under dispute among specialists. This entry does not treat these debates but principally addresses some main points of general agreement about Foucault's contributions to philosophical reflection on the topic of knowledge. A suggestion is also advanced that the singularity of Foucault's philosophy of knowledge can be attributed in part to his prioritization of the ontology of epistemology.

Foucault's principal epistemological position can be characterized in a general fashion as historicist and constructivist. Its distinctive character is most often understood to have resulted from Foucault's insistence on the importance of the explanatory triad of the philosophical concepts of knowledge, power, and subject. It may also be characterized by its treatment of a whole host of additional crucial notions: discourse, *episteme*, law, regularity, archive, archaeology, event, statement, actuality, anonymity, positivity, possibility, objectification, subjectification, apparatus, and, of course, history itself. Some of the philosophical figures whose epistemology most influenced Foucault also can be identified: Kant, Nietzsche, and Canguilhem are of chief importance, with Heidegger and Hegel in the background. In what follows, Foucault's thought on knowledge will be sketched in terms of several of these notions and figures.

Note first two well-known distinctions that characterize Foucault's thought with respect to knowledge. The first is a periodizing and methodological distinction applied to Foucault's own corpus. It divides his work by epistemological and methodological approaches into an earlier "archaeological" period succeeded by a later "genealogical" one, commonly held to have begun in the early 1970s. Indeed, *Birth of the Clinic: An Archaeology of the Medical Gaze* (1963), *The Order of Things: An Archaeology of the Human Sciences* (1966), and *Archaeology of Knowledge* (1969) all underscore the centrality of something called "archaeology" in their titles. The genealogical period is commonly dated to the 1971 essay "Nietzsche, Genealogy, History," with Foucault's theoretical presentation of the distinctive importance of a Nietzschean-inspired method of exposing the historical contingencies of the relations between knowledge on the one hand and forms of power and exercises of will and desire on the other.

The second distinction is one that Foucault draws between two French terms pertaining to knowledge: *savoir* and *connaissance*. In ordinary usage, both words may be rendered in English as "knowledge." Since Foucault employs them with differing technical senses, they are often left untranslated. In a 1978 interview, he explains these senses. By *savoir* he designates

> a process by which the subject undergoes a modification through the very things that one knows [*connaît*] or, rather, in the course of the work that one does in order to know. It is what enables one both to modify the subject and to construct the object. *Connaissance* is the work that makes it possible to multiply the knowable objects, to manifest their intelligibility, to understand their rationality, while maintaining the fixity of the inquiring subject. (EEW3, 256)

Foucault supplies several examples from his work to clarify this distinction. He describes his 1961 book *The History of Madness in the Classical Age* as an effort to show that the constitution of a *savoir* about madness is *at once* the production of the object called madness *and* the production of a subject who knows the mad. He holds the same view about the dual production of certain historically contingent knowing subjects and their epistemological objects in the cases of the social and life sciences.

This bilateral, constitutive epistemology of subject and object has implications for projects of knowing in the modern period. One implication is that such knowledge projects take experiences that mark out the very borders of the traits that canonical Western philosophy considers typical of the human being – rationality, living animality, and sociality or lawfulness – and make these experiences into objects of knowledge. Thus, in modernity there arise organized inquiries into the experiences of madness, death, and crime. The organized bodies of knowledge that are psychiatry, the life sciences, and criminology are constructed around these objects of madness, death, and crime. But in each body of knowledge, to develop knowledge of these objects is equally to constitute certain specific types of subjects: the rational subject, the living subject, and the lawful subject. So, the particular knowledge of various objects that is produced is an instance of *connaissance*. But the very process of simultaneously constituting the particular type of subject that is created in producing a particular *connaissance* is an instance of *savoir*. As Foucault specifies: "there is always this involvement of oneself within one's own *savoir*" (EEW3, 257). This is stipulative; by definition, a kind of knowing is not *savoir* unless it is a form of epistemological co-constitution of subject and object.

A point of great importance about Foucault's thought on epistemology is that it seeks consistently to be an ontology of knowledge. This point is plain when we consider Foucault's thought on knowledge in the light of Kantian epistemology. Kant's transcendental philosophy challenged traditional metaphysics with an epistemology that rigorously limited the legitimate reach of human knowledge. It did so by making fundamental the question of what conditions the very possibility of various forms of knowledge. For Foucault, this question of conditions means that an essential move in Kantian philosophy is the establishment of a fundamentally modal basis for human knowledge; it implies that philosophical inquiry into knowledge concerns the conditions for the possibility of knowledge and not the conditions for the existence of knowledge. It also means that a distinction is drawn between conditions for possibility and conditions for existence, and thus that even if conditions for possibility were to be understood to be conditions for possible *existence*, the latter is not synonymous with conditions for *actual* existence.

Foucault's insistence on the theoretical goal of an ontology of actual, not possible, statements is essential to his philosophy of knowledge. In this insistence on the importance of creating an ontology of actual statements, Foucault is particularly focused on the special kinds of statements that are the province of scientific practice, following the thought of Georges Canguilhem. That is, his concern is with statements whose intrinsic aim is to claim to be true. From Heidegger, Foucault retains an attention to language as a multiform phenomenon and the view that propositional language is a secondary or deficient mode of language whose primary mode is expressive, meditative, and lyrical. He argues that the division between true and false "emerged between Hesiod and Plato" and demoted nonpropositional forms of discourse or saying in relation to propositional forms, which sought knowledge precisely *as* the division between true and false on the propositional level (EAK, 218). Thus, ritual, performative, poetic, or dramatic kinds of speech were no longer the sorts of speech identified with knowledge. This historical emergence of the division between true and false in propositional language developed continually in Western culture thereafter, although it still characterizes modern forms of knowing (ibid.).

But the set of all actually uttered statements that make truth claims is plainly not unlimited, does not exist of necessity, and does not have the specific content it has of necessity; it is limited, it need not have occurred, and it need not have occurred with the specific content it has. To analyze this limitation and indeed rarity, Foucault employs the notions of rule and regularity. But if the limited set of what is actually said is neither limited according to traditional conceptions of possibility nor determined to be necessary, in what sense and by what means is it limited or governed by rules? The answer to this question reveals Foucault's positivism, in a traditional sense of the term; that is, as a philosophical position that prioritizes the lawlike character of reality. Positivism in this sense elevates the nomological character of reality, ranking it epistemologically above other customary contenders such as the purely empirical, intelligible, rational, or transcendental. In the present case, this implies that statements occur as elements in systems of statements and that these systems are rightly described in terms of rules. It is thus the historical occurrence of systems of statements that conforms to rules for those occurrences. Note that it is not a matter of statements conforming to rules for their being true but for their being and for their being claimants to truth. The task of the thinker interested in "the historicity of knowledge," then, is to identify and expose the real, but obscured, nomological order that subtends and epistemologically governs the production of systems of actual statements.

Foucault describes this nomological epistemic principle as "the historical *a priori*." Derived initially from Husserl, the expression "historical *a priori*" means

> an *a priori* that is not a condition of validity for judgments, but a condition of reality for statements. It is not a question of rediscovering what might legitimize an assertion, but of freeing the conditions of emergence of statements, the law of their coexistence with others, the specific form of their mode of being, the principles according to which they survive, become transformed, and disappear. An *a priori* not of truths that might never be said, or really given to experience; but the *a priori* of a history that is given, since it is that of things actually said. (EAK, 127)

However, the sort of regularity of this nomological order is not that of the recurrence of identical items, whether they be statements or discourses. Rather, Foucault seeks to describe the fundamental epistemological matrix, or "*episteme*," of an epoch, which makes possible its specific "system of dispersion" of discourses (EAK, 37, 47). He defines this technical term: "By *episteme* we mean, in fact, the total set of relations that unite, at a given period, the discursive practices that give rise to epistemological figures, sciences and possibly formalized systems…. [I]t is the totality of relations that can be discovered, for a given period, between the sciences when one analyzes them at the level of discursive regularities" (EAK, 191). The historiographical method of archaeology aims to expose the simultaneous and successive differences between the discourses of an era, not an underlying common identity that would unite such discourses. As Foucault puts it:

> Where previously the history was told of traditions and invention, of the old and the new, of the dead and the living, of the closed and the open, of the static and the dynamic, I would set out to tell the history of perpetual differences;

more precisely to tell the history of ideas as a set of specified and descriptive forms of non-identity. (EFE, 62)

This search for a system of dispersion implies that there can be a form of regularity that governs the divergences, rather than the resemblances, between discourses of a single epoch.

In an interview with Jean Hyppolite, Foucault supplied a laconic formulation of a thesis about contemporary philosophical anthropology that is central to *The Order of Things*. The modern era, he offered, is a thoroughly anthropological period in which the anthropology that prevails "is a transcendental that seeks to be true at the level of nature" (FDE1, 480). This remark expresses the common Foucauldian position that modern thought is marked by the repetition of the empirical in the transcendental (EOT, 316). Joining a Kantian idiom with a Nietzschean critique of modernity, Foucault argued that a massive reorientation of knowledge took place between the classical and the modern ages. The sort of transcendental in force in modern thought is determined by the absence or death of God in the Nietzschean sense (EIKA, 117, 124). This is so because the death of God produces a problem for the question of knowledge; absolute knowledge, or divine or totalizing knowledge, is no longer possible, and this has crucial implications for human self-knowledge. Foucault essentially identifies a difference in the sorts of finitude, infinity, and knowledge possible with the absence of a divine epistemological position. The finitude of the classical age, and specifically human finitude, was conceived through a negative relation to the divine infinite. Moreover, human finitude in the classical age explains both ontologically and epistemologically; it explains that man exists with a specifically limited empirical nature – his living, laboring, and thinking is inferior to God's existence, works, and thought – and that this epistemically limited man cannot have absolute knowledge of these specific contents of his finitude.

Modernity, by contrast, must have a fundamentally different notion of finitude, and of human finitude. On the shift to this modern conception of finitude, Foucault writes: "The experience taking form at the beginning of the nineteenth century situates the discovery of finitude not within the *thought of the infinite*, but at the very heart of those contents that are given, by a finite act of knowing, as the concrete forms of *finite existence*" (EOT, 316, my italics). The concrete forms are those that human beings confront in physical need and death, labor, and speech. Each will become the occasion for the emergence of an empirical science in modernity. Foucault sees modern thought itself as directed to the question of whether empirical knowledge of finitude is possible. The Cartesian answer to the question had relied, still, on God's guarantee of the epistemological reliability of human cognition, given the correct rules for the direction of the mind, in an "ontology of the infinite" (EIKA, 117). Hence, it did not confront the truly modern question of what can be known and how it can be known in the absence of infinite or absolute knowing. By contrast, in Foucault's view, Kant eschews an ontology of the infinite but still must ground empirical knowledge in something other than itself (EIKA, 118). Foucault's thesis is that it is the figure of "man" himself who begins in this period to occupy the double and collapsed role of an epistemic knot in which finitude is paradoxically grounded. This "strange empirico-transcendental doublet" that is man "is a being such that knowledge will be attained in him of what renders all knowledge possible" (EOT, 318). A chief thesis is that the historical emergence of modern man is contemporaneous with and required for the advent of the empiricities of the life and human sciences. Specifically, in modernity, the sciences of biology, economics, and linguistics succeed the domains of natural history, the study of wealth, and philology that flourished during the classical age. The only "transcendental" level found in modern thought is that of the "quasi-transcendentals" of life, labor, and language that operate to structure respectively the new empirical inquiries of biology, economics, and linguistics. In the epistemology of modernity, "it is a question of revealing the conditions of knowledge on the basis of the empirical contents given in it" (EOT, 319), for neither life, nor labor, nor language is itself an empirical object of study, yet each governs the investigations of a new empirical science. Finitude, as Foucault puts it, "never ceased to refer back to itself" (EOT, 317). The evacuation of the divine infinite leaves God's theological partner, man, to play out the relation between grounding principle and grounded claims in a solitary epistemic ouroboros.

From Nietzsche, Foucault derives a dynamic, historical epistemology; that is, one that employs the notion of force or power at its heart. This orientation toward providing an explanation in terms of forces grounds the historiography that Nietzsche terms "genealogical" and Foucault explicitly redeploys. Nietzsche holds that the most "important proposition" for "historiography of any kind" is the principle that separates the origin from the purposes of a given historical phenomenon to be understood. As Nietzsche puts it: "[T]he cause of the origin of a thing and its eventual utility, its actual employment and place in a system of purposes, lie worlds apart" (Nietzsche 1967b, 77). All events, for Nietzsche, are recurrently lent new purposes through fresh interpretations. These successive interpretations are always the products of an imposition; that is, the supplanting by force of one interpretation by another. The force at issue is a will to power that manages to compel something, which is therefore weaker, to assume a specified function. In his classic example, the history of punishment is the history of the changing relations between the persisting practices of punishing, on the one hand, and the ever-varying ends or functions attributed to those practices. Genealogical historiography refuses a commonly held teleological presupposition that the present purpose of a practice accurately indicates and historically carries the causal explanation for its origin. Punishment as a practice with a corrective end was historically grafted onto punishment as pure venting of anger at a wrong. The difference between these two forms of punishment is so great – the second requiring the introduction of notions of guilt, conscience, measurable wrong, and equivalence of wrongs and penances – that the nature of the successive form cannot be explained by its sharing a common cause, aim, function, or effect with the preceding form. Genealogical historiography requires, then, that the account of the development of the phenomenon under investigation trace independently varying linkages of practices with their imposed meanings, including those linkages that occur on the basis of discontinuity of cause, aim, function, or effect. Further, it must do so by taking as fundamental what Nietzsche terms a "will to knowledge," a "will to truth." Active, imposing forces of will and desire are the sources of all knowledge seeking; curiosity is never indifferent. Thus, for Nietzsche, knowledge creation is, like interpretation, a forceful imposition, a phenomenon that must be described in terms of power.

We find a version of this position in Foucault's critique of our common contemporary understanding of the scientific discourse as free from the realm of distorting, partial desires. Here, he identifies a self-blindness intrinsic to the conventional conception of scientific discourse: "True discourse, liberated by the nature of its form from desire and power, is incapable of recognizing the will to truth which pervades it; and the will to truth, having imposed itself upon us for so long, is such that the truth it seeks to reveal cannot fail to mask it" (EAK, 219). Scientific pursuits of truth as customarily conceived will produce only truths that protect that version of truth as yielded by an indifferent, nonwilling knower. Both Nietzsche and Foucault reject this conception of knowledge produced by indifferent, unwilling knowers whose conclusions are thus allegedly compelled purely by the facts of the matter. For both thinkers, knowledge must be understood in terms of power.

Indeed, there is scarcely a more important element in Foucault's philosophy of knowledge than his conception of "*pouvoir-savoir*," or "power-knowledge" (FDE1a, 1565). Foucault details many versions of power-knowledge, but we can take the variant of disciplinary power-knowledge as a prime example. In Foucault's analysis of the prison in *Discipline and Punish*, the aforementioned bilateral epistemology of subject and object is developed more fully in conjunction with the notion of power; in particular, with the notion of disciplinary power. For Foucault, this was historically the first to emerge of two variants of biopower. Part of *Discipline and Punish* is devoted to the argument that this new form of power, which Foucault calls the power of the Norm, emerges in the regime of discipline in the classical age, at the start of the seventeenth century. The hospital and the school are models of disciplinary power, this essentially new form of social control. They are sites of the advent of a new kind of training that is characterized by hierarchical observation, normalizing judgment, and the examination, a technique at the heart of a growing practice of surveillance. Hierarchical observation coerces precisely by means of observation, which itself is made possible by architectural design, new forms of documentation and a new form of penality that takes the statistical norm, rather than the law, as its principle of operation. The creation of visible individuals is a chief aspect of the novelty of this system of discipline. But it is the invention of a "homogeneous, continuous, functional power" that concerns Foucault. It is the power of the Norm that is important here, and Foucault distinguishes this power from several others that precede it and that often continue to operate parallel to it after its emergence: the powers of the Law, Word, Text, and Tradition.

Discipline, with its new disciplinary technology of description, is a specific, novel conjunction of power and knowledge. Importantly, discipline is not simply hierarchical organization, normalizing judgment, and the examination, and the new hierarchizing, constant, and functional form of surveillance they permit; the critical points here are that discipline is simultaneously the creation of knowledge and that this knowledge *is a form of power*. Here, Foucault intends to expose a form of objectification that rigorously is tied to practices that simultaneously produce both an object of knowledge that is a peculiar kind of subject or, better, a particular kind of subjected being. Through discipline, the individual "is constituted as effect and object of power, as effect and object of knowledge" (EDP, 192). What is to be considered distinctive about disciplinary power is its dual, simultaneous "subjection of those who are perceived as objects" and "objectification of those who are subjected" (EDP, 185). The term "object" here designates the object of a gaze, control, and increasingly formalized scientific and administrative knowledge. *Discipline and Punish* is replete with references to, and criticisms of, the history of science contemporary to Foucault. He charges it with failing to analyze the gradual constitution of the epistemological object of scientific and administrative inquiry that is *equally* the subjection of human beings to those forms of practiced knowledge as social control, to the disciplinary form of power-knowledge.

Philosopher and physician Georges Canguilhem was one of the principal architects of twentieth-century "*épistémologie*," or the current in French philosophy of science that is known in Anglophone terms as "French historical epistemology." The term "epistemology" in this case differs from customary contemporary Anglophone usage and refers more narrowly to philosophical inquiry into questions of knowledge limited to the sciences. Although Foucault adapts and extends Canguilhem's thought on knowledge for his own purposes, Foucault shares a number of critical epistemological orientations with his teacher. First, they analyze scientific knowledge in terms of discourse, and they consider discourse as inevitably historical. This means that they understand science to be an inescapably cultural practice and product. However, both rigorously refuse the position that science can be understood as the pure issue of economic, political, or ideological forces. To do so would be to miss radically the distinctive nature of scientific discourses, which cannot count as such unless they seek to demonstrate what is to count as real. In other words, they are discourses singularly designed to put forth statements purporting to be true. Canguilhem offers two important points about this distinctive aim of science. One is that a statement must first achieve the status of being intelligible as expressing a scientific proposition in order subsequently to be judged to be true or false. The history of scientific debate shows that achieving this status of intelligible eligibility for veridical expression is a condition that is satisfied neither easily nor constantly. A second point is critical for understanding the nature of Foucault's constructivism. This constructivism turns on the characterization of the object of scientific discourse. If there is an object of science, what sort of item can it be? Canguilhem's epistemology of the sciences distinguishes between three sorts of objects: a natural object, a scientific object, and an object of the history of the sciences (Canguilhem 2005, 202–203). A crystal of itself is a given, natural object. Once that natural object is the object of a scientific discourse on its causes, development, and features, Canguilhem argues, there then exists a scientific object that is a cultural artifact distinct from the natural object. Further, the object that historians of the science of crystallography study is neither of these but the process of the historical constitution of scientific objects.

Foucault extends and greatly enriches these positions by articulating elaborate conceptual-practical histories of the processes of scientifization and depicting the substantial variation in epistemic criteria for scientific formalization. He explicitly aims to expose the changing procedures for the "objectification of objectivities" or for "the 'objectification' of those elements which historians consider as objectively given" (EFE, 86), for he does not take the fact that scientific discourse necessarily includes claims to truth about its objects to imply that the historian of science treats the question of the truth of these discourses. Foucault insists that his prime *epistemological* question is not the question of the legitimacy of scientific knowledge nor of what makes such knowledge possible. He explains:

> [T]he analysis of the episteme is not a way of returning to the critical question ("given the existence of something like a science, what is its legitimacy?"); it is a questioning that accepts the fact of science only in order to ask the question what it is for that science to be a science. In the enigma of scientific discourse, what the analysis of the episteme questions is not its right to be a science, but the fact that it exists. (EAK, 192)

The remark makes clear that Foucault's philosophy of knowledge may be understood to resist a trenchant separation of epistemology from ontology and to ontologize historical epistemology, for, as we have seen, one of his principal arguments about the modern character of knowing asserts that there has been a radical shift from classical knowledge understood only and necessarily in relation to an infinite other's absolute *thought*, on the one hand, to modern knowledge understood only and necessarily through the newborn figure of *existing* man on the other. Knowledge thus mutates from ancient nonpropositional forms of lyrical, interrogative, ritual, and poetic utterance to Socratically narrowed propositional and declarative truth, to knowledge of man as God's negative declination, to modern, allegedly post-theological knowledge constituted in the life and human sciences, with the notion of man as existing subject and object of his knowledge. Man's finite *being* continues the epistemic grounding of knowledge that was handed down from a dying *thinking* God. Thus, Foucault's own ontologization of epistemology amounts to a profound acceptance of the historically singular nature of modern knowing – as knowing what is and is actual – that his very account of modernity provides.

Mary Beth Mader

SEE ALSO

Archaeology
Genealogy
Historical a Priori
Power
Truth
Georges Canguilhem
Immanuel Kant
Friedrich Nietzsche

SUGGESTED READING

Gutting, Gary. 1989. *Michel Foucault's Archaeology of Scientific Reason*. Cambridge: Cambridge University Press.
Han, Béatrice. 2002. *Foucault's Critical Project: Between the Transcendental and the Historical*, trans. Edward Pile. Stanford, CA: Stanford University Press.
Han-Pile, Béatrice. 2003. " Foucault and Heidegger on Kant and Finitude," in *Foucault and Heidegger: Critical Encounters*, ed. Alan Milchman and Alan Rosenberg. Minneapolis: University of Minnesota Press, pp. 127–162.
    2005. "Is Early Foucault a Historian? History, history and the Analytic of Finitude," *Philosophy and Social Criticism* 31(September): 585–608.
Koopman, Colin. 2010. "Historical Critique or Transcendental Critique in Foucault: Two Kantian Lineages," *Foucault Studies* 8:100–121.
Lawlor, Leonard. 2003. *Thinking through French Philosophy: The Being of the Question*. Bloomington: Indiana University Press.

41

LANGUAGE

Throughout Foucault's corpus, a general theme is repeated: the very forces that constitute subjects and their surroundings harbor an "outside" or internal "transgression" that undoes their previous work and makes room for the creation of new possibilities. Thus, in one of his earliest pieces, an introduction to Ludwig Binswanger's book on the existential analysis of dreams and existence, Foucault argues that the imagination "traps" us in the images it produces. But this same imagination, in its "authentic" expression or "*ars poetica*," "destroys and consumes" these images and "refers [us] back to the origin of the constituted world" (EDE, 71–74). This self-reflexive schema is still in play two decades later when Foucault describes power relationships as requiring "points of resistance" for their very existence (EHS1, 95) – points that can "reverse" these relationships (EEW3, 346). This schema is not Hegelian: the transformations involved are not the fulfillment of a preset pattern of development or any other source that transcends them. They are only new possibilities opened up by the endogenous undermining of previously determining forces – a self-transgression that is continually repeated.

Foucault's treatment of language conforms to this self-reflexive schema. More specifically, the schema links two seemingly disparate ways in which Foucault talks about language, especially during the "archaeological" phase of his work: "discourse" and "literary language." These two ways of speaking of language are tied together because Foucault presents literary language as transgressing the "limits" of the enclosed structures of institutionalized discourse that language has also created. We might follow one of Foucault's own metaphors and refer to this process as the creative work of anonymous voices. Thus he says he would have liked "to lodge" himself "in a nameless voice" that had "long preceded" him and what he might say (EAK, 215, 237). Elsewhere he speaks of language or discourse starting in "the anonymity of a murmur" (EEW2, 222, 91, 94, 97, 101, 150, 153, 154) or multitude of voices (EAK, 100). Foucault sees his "inclination" to surrender willingly to these voices as a means of avoiding direct confrontation with the "anxiety" we have over their fecundity and errant nature, the "dangerousness" of the "materiality" of their discourse (EAK, 215–216, 228, 231). But he is more critical of a second response to this materiality: the constant "institutionalization" of language by rules that control the proliferation and direction of discourse. In particular, he sees a "will to truth" at the heart of this rule mongering or "logophilia." He therefore lauds Nietzsche, Artaud, Bataille, and all others who attempt "to remold" this will and turn it on that version of itself which tries to "justify the taboo" against seeing truth as involving "power and desire" and hence as intrinsically heterogeneous and part of the endless production of discourse. Indeed, Foucault says that the thinkers he names and their subversion of linguistic institutionalization "stand as signposts for our future work" (EAK, 219–220), part of which includes his well-known genealogies of truth.

To understand Foucault's idea of language further, we must first clarify its institutional mode and then see in detail how literary language cuts against the latter's grain. In his archaeology of the human sciences, Foucault reveals a "positive unconscious of knowledge ... that eludes the awareness of the scientist and yet is part of scientific discourse" (EOT, xi). His task is to uncover the "rules of formation" that constitute this unconscious and produce the "discursive formations" or "*epistemes*" through which persons perceive and think about themselves and the world. In the "classical age," for example, the scientific *episteme* for what we would now call biology, economics, and linguistics is constituted by representing things through neutral and transparent signs incorporated into tables and charts. This approach leads to seeing language as designating mental "representations" and converting ("analyzing") their simultaneous presentation into verbal orders of succession; for instance, our perception of a green tree as "The tree is green" (EOT, 79–80, 82). The role of classical age linguistics ("General Grammar") is therefore "to define the system of identities and differences" that these verbal designations presuppose and employ in particular languages (EOT, 91). In his consideration of this and other discursive formations, Foucault makes his own discovery: the principal elements of discursive formations are neither the "sentences" of linguists nor the "propositions" of logicians; rather, they are "statements" (EAK, 86–87). Unlike sentences and propositions, statements are repeatable only within the types of formations in which they in fact occur; for example, a judge's "Guilty as charged!" uttered as part of judicial discourse. In repartee or any other use outside official legal employment, such a statement would follow different rules of formation and thus be a different statement despite its use of the same words and syntax (EAK, 100, 104–105).

When the *episteme* of the classical age is replaced by the completely different rules of formation for knowledge in the modern age, the three sciences Foucault considers become the products of hidden or transcendental sources of constitutive power (EOT, 244–245, 314–315, 364–365, 385–386). A language, for example, becomes, among other changes, the manifestation of a people's "will" (EOT,

290) and the internal generation of new evolutionary forms of itself (EOT, 236, 287, 294, 338). It also loses the centrality it had enjoyed in the classical age as the "initial, inevitable way of representing [the] representations" of the other fields of knowledge. Although language is now just "one object of knowledge among others," it is still important as our means of expression. This leads to supplementing the reigning "philology" of Bopp with formalism and hermeneutic interpretation as approaches for understanding language (EOT, 296, 298–299). But when the *episteme* of the modern age begins to break apart and the idea of "man" is "erased, like a face drawn in sand at the edge of the sea," language becomes the central key to all knowledge once again (EOT, 338–339, 342, 387). Indeed, linguistics as a "pure theory of language," along with psychoanalysis and ethnology as formal sign systems, becomes a "counter-science" to the prevailing human sciences based on the notion of man (EOT, 379–382, 385). This formal treatment of language is paralleled by the view of literary language as autonomous or "with nothing to say but itself" (EOT, 300, 383). Gary Gutting states this twofold development succinctly: "What literature develops as an experience of 'the end of man', linguistics would develop as a structural analysis that undermines man's central place in language" (Gutting 1989, 217). Thus once again language doubles back on or transgresses itself, freeing itself (momentarily) from the limits of the institutions to which it and our anxiety continually give rise.

Foucault's development of language as self-reflexive is further clarified in a series of papers he wrote during his archaeological period. In three of these, "Preface to Transgression" (EEW2, 69–87), "The Thought of the Outside" (EEW2, 137–146), and "Language to Infinity" (EEW2, 89–102), he characterizes the "being of language" (EEW2, 149) as a "transgression" or an "outside" that creates a "void" allowing language to multiply itself to "infinity." In "Preface to Transgression," for example, Foucault proclaims that "the death of God restores us ... to a world exposed by the experience of its limits, made and unmade by that excess which transgresses it" (EEW2, 72). These limits and this transgression are reciprocally related. To exist, a limit must be crossable; and for transgression to mean anything it must cross something real. But the limit is real as a limit only because, brought up "to the limit of its being ... and made to face the fact of its imminent disappearance," it "imprisons" its transgressive excess and once more brings the latter right up to "the horizon of the uncrossable" – thereby inciting another crossing (EEW2, 73). Foucault adds that transgression is not "negative" – it affirms the "limited being" that is also "the limitlessness into which [transgression] leaps as it opens this zone to existence for the first time." But it also contains nothing "positive": "no content can bind it, since, by definition, no limit can possibly restrict it" (EEW2, 74). Transgression is, in other words, a "nonpositive affirmation," a "yes" to proceeding "until one reaches the empty core where being achieves its limit and where the limit defines being" (EEW2, 75).

Having characterized the idea of transgression as a limit that incessantly crosses itself, a line that closes up behind itself after each traversing of itself, Foucault goes on in the same article to connect it explicitly to language. He counsels that we not seek a "discursive language" or "language of dialectic" to speak of our experience of transgression; rather, we should make this experience speak "from where its language fails" (EEW2, 77). Following Georges Bataille, he clarifies the site of this "failure" by claiming that "communication" is an "opening" or "limit" where "its being "surges forth ... completely overflowing itself, emptied of itself to the point where it becomes an absolute void" (EEW2, 80). Language creates this void through dispersing the subject who would speak it, "multiplying [the subject] within the space created by its absence" (EEW2, 79, 83, 85) and thus also momentarily unraveling institutionalized discourse. Foucault notes that Bataille marks this limit of language, the point where language "challenges itself," with the image of the "eyes rolled back in ecstasy" (EEW2, 83), suggesting "the most open and the most impenetrable eye." As in the line that closes up behind each of its self-traversals, these rolled-back eyes cross "the limit of day and night" but only "to find [that limit] again on the same line from the other side" (EEW2, 82, 83). Foucault adds that this image of the eye "delineates the zone shared by language and death, the place where language discovers its being in the crossing of limits," the void or death that is also the location of language's constant rebirth (EEW2, 84). But the hollowing out of this void does not mean that we stop talking: "the experience of the limit, and the manner in which philosophy must now understand it, is realized in language and in the movement where it says what cannot be said" (EEW2, 86).

In "Language to Infinity," Foucault provides the most specific ways in which language "says what cannot be said." Before proceeding to that article, however, we should first note the special features of Foucault's "The Thought of the Outside." In this article, Foucault makes use of Maurice Blanchot's trope the "outside" to reinforce and vary what he has already said about the relation between transgression and language. Similar to the treatment of this latter relation, he says that "the experience of the outside" involves effacing the subject, negating our current discourse, and consequently regaining for language the void in which it unfolds (EEW2, 149–150) or "toward which, and outside of which, it speaks" (EEW2, 153). It therefore allows us to understand the commonplace "I speak" as more profoundly "an absolute opening through which language endlessly spreads forth, while the subject – the 'I' who speaks – fragments, disperses, scatters, disappearing in that naked space" (EEW2, 148). In this article, Foucault emphasizes more than in the others that this "spreading" of language consists of new beginnings that are also "rebeginnings": new beginnings because each is a "pure origin" in the sense that its "principles" are itself and the void, and rebeginnings because it is "the language of the *past* in the act of hollowing itself out" that frees up the void to begin with (EEW2, 152, my italics). He is also emphatic in declaring that the void is not a silent abyss: "the continuous streaming of language" is what "precedes all speech, what underlies all silence" (EEW2, 166). Although this streaming always concerns contents that already exist, language, "in its own being," is a "waiting" that "no object could gratify" – hence a "forgetting" that always falls "outside of itself" and yet is equally a "wakefulness" or "acute attention" to both what is "radically new" (the "wait drawn outside of itself") and what is "profoundly old" (a wait that "has never stopped waiting") (EEW2, 167). Foucault dramatizes this language that is forever and patiently outside itself by saying that it "brings to light" the meaning of origin and death. The "pure outside" of the origin (that is, the "transparent endlessness" of the streaming of language) never "solidifies into a penetrable and immobile positivity," and the "perpetually rebegun outside of death" (the incessant new beginning and hence "death" that the void allows and that constitute the streaming) "never sets the limits at which truth would finally begin to take shape" and end language's proliferation of itself. Thus language is "that softest of voices ... bath[ing] the belated effort of the origin and the dawn-like erosion of death in the same neutral light, at once day and night" (EEW2,168).

In "Language to Infinity," Foucault goes further than in the two other articles in specifying the language that speaks in the void. Literary language is taken here in the narrower sense of modern literature. Both it and the preceding literature, such as the *Iliad* and the *Odyssey*, are attempts to escape death, this time in the literal sense of the word. The approach of death, our fear of it, is a limit that creates a void "toward and from which we must speak." From within this "infinite space," our storytelling suspends our most fateful decisions, momentarily fending off our demise, but also allowing us to hear within our speaking another language that precedes us, continues endlessly, and will therefore persist after we are gone, a language that, like an image in a limitless play of mirrors, duplicates or "pursues itself to infinity" (EEW2, 89–90). In traditional epics, this infinity of language was placed outside itself – the promise of immortality or "a real and majestic infinity in which [the epic] became a virtual and circular mirror, completed in a beautifully closed form" (EEW2, 94). But since the end of the eighteenth century, literature has allowed the gods to disappear and the infinity of language to become its reliance on its own self-duplication for fending off death. If earlier literature, and also "Rhetoric," always repeat "the figure of the Infinite that would never come to an end" (EEW2, 100), modern literature, like Jorge Luis Borges's "library of Babel," is a "simple, monotonous line of language left to its own devices, a language fated to be infinite because it can no longer support itself upon the speech of infinity" (EEW2, 100). It finds within itself, rather than from without, the power to divide or duplicate itself: "[a] language that repeats no other speech, no other Promise, but postpones death indefinitely by ceaselessly opening a space where it is always the analogue of itself" (EEW2, 100).

In his portrayal of modern literature in this article, Foucault focuses on the ways in which language speaks of itself. For example, he looks for "faults" or signs in literature that indicate the doubling back of language, its self-representation. Thus Borges's condemned writer in "The Secret Miracle" is permitted by God a year of suspended time before his execution to complete a drama that no one will ever read and that endlessly repeats its beginning. In Denis Diderot's *The Nun*, Suzanne explains the history of a letter to a correspondent that is the actual letter she is writing, an oversight of which Diderot was apparently unaware. And Scheherazade's account of why she is forced to tell stories for a thousand and one nights is itself an episode of *A Thousand and One Nights* that, in effect, reduplicates the whole tale (EEW2, 91–93). But if these sorts of "faults" indicate the superposition of a language on itself – its "secret verticality" – the works of the Marquis de Sade and "tales of terror" are languages that multiply or "double" themselves excessively and make themselves utterly transparent or "thin" through their single-minded effort to "produce effects," such as ecstasy or terror (EEW2, 95, 99). Because this conceit is their aim, they "could and should … continue without interruption, in a murmuring that has no other ontological status" than that of "confiscating [the space of its language] in a gesture of repetitive appropriation" (EEW2, 96–97). In effect, the extreme openendedness and "pastiche" of this form of literature, its mercurial "seeking the limits of the possible," "designates the project of subjecting every possible language, every future language, to the actual sovereignty of this unique Discourse" of self-multiplication (EEW2, 95–96). Foucault thinks that his description of these different ways in which literary language speaks of itself may constitute the beginnings of an "ontology of literature" (EEW2, 92).

Up to this point, we see that Foucault portrays language as a self-reflexive schema, as a transgression or something outside that crosses and recrosses itself to infinity, continually unraveling the institutionalized discourses it and anxiety create along its serpentine way. It remains to address the relation between language or saying and the visible or seeing – between words and things. A poem is a calligram or "tautological" when its lines of words are constructed so as to form literally a visual representation of their topic. Foucault praises the painter René Magritte for "unraveling" the calligram by setting up an "instable dependency" between the written caption and the visual figure that he has drawn on a surface (ENP, 21–22, 26). This instability gives rise to a number of contesting "voices" or articulations of the meaning of the text in relation to the figure. Thus the words "Ceci n'est pas une pipe" ("This is not a pipe") written under the drawing of a pipe can signify that the latter is not the word "pipe," that the line of words themselves are not the drawn pipe, or that the "drawn" text (for the words are "drawn images" in the picture) + the "written" pipe (for the pipe can be viewed as an extension of the text) are not the "mixed" pipe of the traditional calligram (ENP, 26–28).

In a second version of *This is not a pipe*, Magritte draws the pipe and the line of words within a framed support mounted on a tripod, also part of the picture. The pipe and the words taken together now look like either a painting or writing on a blackboard. Magritte adds to this picture the image of a larger pipe hovering over the tripod and what it is holding up to the viewer (ENP, 29). We might say that the added "model" pipe makes clear that the first pipe is not a pipe and that this is what

242 / FRED EVANS

the text is saying. However, "Ceci n'est pas une pipe" can now legitimately mean that even the model pipe in the picture is also not a pipe. Indeed, we cannot even say that any one of the pipes through which we blow smoke is the model for any of the drawn pipes. How would we justify choosing one of the "real" pipes over the others to have this privileged status? Moreover, the drawn ones do not present themselves in the artworks as mere imitations: we say spontaneously that they *are* pipes even though we know we can't use them like the "real" pipes (ENP, 20). Foucault concludes from this that we must replace the idea of instances "resembling" a real model with the idea of "simulacra" or "a network of similitudes," of elements in a series that repeat each other without the guidance of a Platonic form or other type of model (ENP, 47, 49, 52). Magritte's unraveled calligram therefore illustrates that there is an unstable dependency among words and things in all their possible venues. For Foucault, this fecund instability implies the murmur of many anonymous voices, each articulating a different version of what the relation between the sayable and the perceivable means in the Magritte painting or in any other setting, each voice contesting with the others for greater audibility (ENP, 37, 48–49; cf. Deleuze 1988, 7, 50, 55). Thus the anonymous voices or murmurings to which Foucault continually refers are the basis of language but also the visible, moving "to infinity" in innumerable new beginnings that are also rebeginnings.

Fred Evans

SEE ALSO

> *Contestation*
> *Discourse*
> *Knowledge*
> *Literature*
> *Structuralism*
> *Georges Bataille*
> *Maurice Blanchot*
> *Raymond Roussel*

SUGGESTED READING

Deleuze, Gilles. 1988. *Foucault*, trans. Seán Hand. Minneapolis: University of Minnesota Press.
Gutting, Gary. 1989. *Michel Foucault's Archaeology of Scientific Reason*. Cambridge: Cambridge University Press.

42

LAW

"Law" (*loi*), AND its related concept of "right" (*droit*), occupies an ambivalent location within Foucault's thought. On the one hand, Foucault never self-consciously prioritized law as an object of analysis in and of itself or offered an account of the law on the same level he approached other concepts. Moreover, throughout the mid- to late 1970s, in his published books, seminar courses, public lectures, and interviews, Foucault offered a concept of power explicitly distinguished from the law. Linked with sovereign and juridical power, the law would have to be displaced as the dominant framework for understanding modern force relations. On the other hand, Foucault's oeuvre is replete with references and engagements with the law (*loi*),and with various laws and rights (*droits*). Law is always in the foreground of his historical accounts of madness, punishment, and sexuality. In interviews, he spoke at length on the legal reforms of prisons and sexual practices (EPPC, 178–210, 271–285; EFL, 279–292). His interest in Kant, especially in his attention to the concepts of critique and enlightenment, gravitated around notions of autonomy and the possibility of self-legislation within the context of obedience (EPT, 41–82, 97–120). His early literary dialogue with Maurice Blanchot playfully depicts the law as inescapably mutable, elusive, and as "the shadow toward which every gesture necessarily advances" (EFB, 35).

Most importantly, the law is integral for understanding the various modalities of the operation of power, the fabrication (and self-fabrication) of subjects, and the terrain of ethical comportment in ancient, modern, and contemporary society. Foucault's own methodological claims notwithstanding, the law can be said to occupy a central place in his thought in both explicit and implicit ways. Readers of Foucault must always approach the concepts of law and right (as with nearly any other important concept in Foucault's lexicon) as always related to and possibly constitutive with other techniques of power/knowledge. In a 1981 interview, Foucault put his relationship with the question of law and rights this way:

> I have always been interested in the law, as a "layman"; I am not a specialist in rights, I am not a lawyer or jurist. But just as with madness, crime and prisons, I encountered the problem of rights, the law, and the question that I always asked was how the technology or technologies of government, how these relations of power understood in the sense we discussed before, how all this could take shape within a society that pretends to function according to law and which, partly at least, functions by the law. (EPT, 142)

Foucault's most direct and explicit engagement with the concept of law itself can be found in the first volume of *The History of Sexuality*, where he takes up the question of power directly (EHS1, 81–102; FHS1, 107–135). Through the classical age and into the modern period, the law came to represent sovereign power in a primarily juridical and monarchical form. Insofar as a juridical notion of power was figured primarily as repression and prohibition, all deployments of power have been "reduced simply to the procedure of the law of interdiction" (EHS1, 86; FHS1, 113). Historically, this association of the law with sovereignty emerged during the Middle Ages, leaving the law overly determined by monarchical or sovereign power. Such an account of law, however, fails to adequately "describe the manner in which power was and is exercised" during even that period. Yet it nevertheless "is the code according to which power presents itself and prescribes that we conceive of it" (EHS1, 87–88; FHS1, 116).

We remain too focused, Foucault argues, on this representation of power, its mode of legalistic analysis, and its narrow objects and instruments:

> One remains attached to a certain image of power-law, of power-sovereignty, which was traced out by the theoreticians of right and the monarchic institution. It is this image that we must break free of, that is, of the theoretical privilege of law and sovereignty, if we wish to analyze power within the concrete and historical framework of its operation. We must construct an analytics of power that no longer takes law as a model and a code. (EHS1, 90; FHS1, 118–119)

Such an "analytics of power" (rather than a "theory" of power) therefore requires that "it free itself completely" from the "juridico-discursive" representation of power that looks to the law as an expression of power's prohibitive, repressive, or negative force (EHS1, 82; FHS1, 109). To give a proper history of sexuality (in particular) and an account of the analytics of power (more generally), it is therefore necessary to "rid ourselves of a juridical and negative representation of power, and cease to conceive of it in terms of law, prohibition, liberty, and sovereignty" (EHS1, 90; FHS1, 119).

To "escape from the system of Law-and-Sovereign" (EHS1, 97; FHS1, 128) and in turn to "replace" the privilege of the law with a "strategical model" focused on "a multiple and mobile field of force relations" (EHS1, 102; FHS1, 135) is necessary because this displacement is "in fact … one of the essential traits of Western societies that the force relationships which for a long time had found expression in war … gradually became invested in the order of political power" (EHS1, 102; FHS1, 135). This, most famously, is why we may finally "cut off the head of the king" in our political thought and analysis (EHS1, 88–89; FHS1, 117). Although a monarchical/juridical/sovereign theory of power has been "characteristic of our societies … it has gradually been penetrated by quite new mechanisms of power that are probably irreducible to the representation of law" (EHS1, 89; FHS1, 117). Foucault insists there has been an important shift in how power operates such that the law, as an account of power itself, stands in the way of our analysis, masks our understanding, and ultimately blocks potential paths of resistance when power appears in seemingly nonlegal, nonjuridical, or nonprohibitive forms such as discipline and normalization.

Objects of analysis should therefore be taken up from the point of view of power, which requires that one "must not assume that the sovereignty of the state, the form of the law, or the over-all unity of a domination are given at the outset; rather, these are only the terminal forms power takes" (EHS1, 92; FHS1, 121). The law itself (if such a thing can be said to exist) is therefore an instance of power/knowledge, and specific codified laws can be read as a "crystalized form" of power (EHS1, 92–93; FHS1, 122). In this sense, the law and right are to be studied as important "mechanisms" in the "grid of intelligibility of the social order" but never as some "primary," "central," or "unique source" from which power "emanates" (EHS1, 93; FHS1, 122).

This language of displacement has led some readers of Foucault with interests in jurisprudence and the sociology of law to insist that Foucault "expelled law" from both his own analysis of power and ultimately from modernity itself: "It is apparent that the most distinctive features of Foucault's account of the historical emergence of modernity led him to present a view which can be aptly summarized as the expulsion of law from modernity" (Hunt and Wickham 1994, 56). In the place of law, we find discipline, the concept of the norm, and the emergence of biopower: "Foucault identifies law and sovereignty with a pre-modern form of negative, repressive power which is progressively overtaken by a new mode of operation, or technology, of power, namely disciplinary power.… Enter power (in various guises); exit law" (Golder and Fitzpatrick 2009, 13). In this reading, the law is said to be fundamentally incompatible with the modern disciplinary power.

This view appears to be supported in particular by the first two lectures of *Society Must be Defended* (ECF-SMD, 1–41; FCF-FDS, 3–36), published separately as "Two Lectures" in *Power/Knowledge* (EPK, 78–108). Proponents of the "expulsion thesis" routinely point to these lectures, and to Foucault's claims that sovereignty and discipline are "so heterogeneous that they cannot possibly be reduced to each other" (EPK, 106) and that "[t]he discourse of discipline is alien to that of the law," replacing a "code of law" with "a code of normalization" (ECF-SMD, 38; FCF-FDS, 34). Although the "expulsion thesis" has become a dominant interpretation of Foucault's account of law, it has been challenged substantially in recent years on multiple fronts. These critiques have noted that Foucault's account of law is always offered in conjunction with other concepts, most importantly discipline and governmentality. Moreover, other readers have rightly noted that Foucault maintained an important distinction between the "juridical" and the "legal" that the expulsion thesis fails to account for.

Moreover, there are also moments within both *The History of Sexuality* and the 1976 lectures that push directly against the expulsion thesis. Although Foucault expresses the need to "escape" from the law, he argues for the "replacement" of the privilege of power-law with an analytics of power in hopes of "ridding" ourselves of that privilege. Foucault never claims that law disappears. He writes, "I do not mean to say that the law fades into the background or that the institutions of justice tend to disappear, but rather that the law operates more and more as a norm, and that the judicial institution is increasingly incorporated into a continuum of apparatuses ... whose functions are for the most part regulatory" (EHS1, 144; FHS1, 190). In this sense, the methodological "displacement" of law is necessary in order to understand how law is a part of the "relations of subjugation" and how those relations "manufacture subjects" (ECF-SMD, 265; FCF-FDS, 239). Modern disciplinary power, in particular, is exercised at the point of contact between discipline and sovereignty (ECF-SMD, 37–38; FCF-FDS, 33–34). If modalities of power are "invading" and "increasingly colonizing the procedures of law," they are also "increasingly in conflict with the juridical system of sovereignty" (ECF-SMD, 38–39; FCF-FDS, 34–35). It is through conflict and colonization, at the limits of two heterogeneous systems that cannot be reduced to each other, that we find a "perpetual exchange or confrontation" between discipline and the law as a principle of right. Taken together, "[s]overeign and discipline, legislation, the right of sovereignty and disciplinary mechanisms are in fact the two things that constitute ... the general mechanisms of power in our society" (ECF-SMD, 39; FCF-FDS, 35). In general, the role of law in Foucault's thought is subordinated to the task of constructing an analytics of power, in no small part as a corrective to an impoverished yet persistent conception of power that is identified with the law at the expense of other modalities or emerging forms of power in a given time and place.

This is not to say that the law is not vitally important to Foucault's study of "the how of power" (ECF-SMD, 24; EPK, 92; FCF-FDS, 21). Rather, Foucault was not primarily interested in the law for its own sake and was deeply suspicious of the effects of taking the law or theories of right for granted. According to Foucault:

> So, these are connections, relationships of cause and effect, conflicts, too, and oppositions, irreducibilities between this functioning of the law and this technology of power, that is what I would like to study. It seems to me that it can be of interest to investigate juridical institutions, the discourse and practice of law from these technologies of power – not at all in the sense that this would totally shake up history and the theory of law, but rather that this could illuminate some rather important aspects of judicial practices and theories. (EPT, 142)

In particular, Foucault's interest in juridical institutions, legal discourse, and the practice of law was vitally important in illuminating the fabrication of subjects. Three select moments in Foucault's work are illustrative of both the law's productive tension with other discourses and the law's fundamental mutability in relation to the emergence or redeployment of political subjectivities.

First, in *Abnormal*, Foucault focused his attention on the relationships between legal, medical, biological, and psychiatric discourses to show how there occurred in the nineteenth century "the insidious invasion within judicial and medical institutions, exactly at the frontier between them, of a mechanism that is precisely neither medical [n]or judicial" (ECF-AB, 41; FCF-ANO, 38). This "invasion" took the form of an increasing reliance on "expert knowledge" into judicial proceedings (ECF-AB, 18; FCF-ANO, 18). Although various sorts of "abnormal individuals" came into existence as legal categories, they did so only through the reconfiguration of legal knowledge with respect to other modes of knowing. Abnormality itself, Foucault explains, can be defined through the interplay between legal and medical knowledges, each themselves discourses of power/knowledge, in which a figure like the "human monster" is simultaneously a legalistic notion as well as a contradiction of the law. By sitting at the limit of possibility as a breach of the laws of society and nature, the monster in fact becomes the very "principle of intelligibility" through psychiatric and biological knowledge, speaking the "truth" of an anthropological subject that is categorically dangerous (ECF-AB, 56–57; FCF-ANO, 52). The introduction of Article 64 in the French penal code, establishing that no crime could be said to have occurred when the individual accused was in a state of dementia, opened the door to a juridicomedical basis for criminology, the transformation of penal law in the coming century, and the figuration of individuals accused of crimes as dangerous in their being (ECF-AB, 18; FCF-ANO, 18).

Second, the figure of the delinquent in *Discipline and Punish* illustrates the productive force of the law at its border with disciplinary power (EDP, 264–268; FSP, 269–274). Perhaps here more than anywhere else in Foucault's work we can see how law and power (in this case disciplinary power) are always related in various (and possibly oppositional) manners. Disciplinary power, Foucault notes, contains within it punitive and prohibitive force, a "small penal mechanism" (EDP, 177; FSP, 180). Discipline, in fact, relies on the failure of some persons to be properly normalized, "recalcitrant" subjects, who necessarily fail to adhere to the norm (Golder and Fitzpatrick 2009, 69). Thus, discipline is not contrary to law but is deeply dependent on it, if not co-constitutive with it. Discipline, Foucault notes, constitutes an "infra-law," a "counter-law," and it operates "on the underside of law" to generate both obedient subjects and hopelessly delinquent ones (EDP, 222–223; FSP, 224–225). And it does so precisely through its tension and relation with discipline. Law does not simply recede in modernity, but rather it "is inverted and passes outside itself," allowing for a generalization of the power to punish not through "the universal consciousness of the law in each subject" but through the broad sweep of disciplinary surveillance (EDP, 224; FSP, 225). We are, as docile bodies, as citizens, and as delinquents, fabricated as subjects by virtue of the law's ability to mold and adapt itself to the emergence of disciplinary power.

Third, *The Birth of Biopolitics* describes the production and transformation of the liberal subject by the law in relation to the economic discourse of the past three centuries. Twentieth-century neoliberal economic theorists would call for a return of the law and a revaluation of the juridical under strictly economic terms. Central to this revaluation was the redeployment of the classical figure of *homo œconomicus*. At the heart of the nineteenth-century paradox of criminal subjectivity was an "ambiguity between the crime and the criminal" (ECF-BBIO, 250; FCF-NBIO, 255). Under a juridical system that was necessarily focused on responsibilities for *acts*, individuals themselves would have to be disciplined as dangerous and irrational failures of self-government. The "solution" was found in fabricating a distinct category of *homo criminalis*, the productive failure of the law's ability to contain a classical utilitarian and economic calculus (ECF-BBIO, 250–251; FCF-NBIO, 255–256). The neoliberal approach would be to reintroduce the law, not as a framework within which to pursue economistic outcomes but rather as the "rules of the game" according to which *homo œconomicus* must play; that is, it tends to subject the law to economic principles rather than incorporate economic principles into the law. Paradoxically, we should therefore expect the growth of judicial discourse under neoliberalism, "because in fact this idea of law in the form of a rule of the game imposed on players by the public authorities, but which is only imposed on players who remain free in the game, implies ... a revaluation of the juridical" (ECF-BBIO, 174–175; FCF-NBIO, 180). Such a revaluation, Foucault notes, comes only through the critical redeployment of neoliberal subjectivity, of *homo œconomicus*, effectively rejecting the entire notion of delinquency, *homo criminalis*, and throwing out the bulk of criminological power/knowledge. The law is revalued on economic terms, not as a sovereign source of authority or as the infra-law of discipline (with its pathological production of monsters and delinquents) but instead as the ground rules for "free" entrepreneurial subjects responding to penal practices as market prices. The law, in Foucault's careful account, always continues to adapt and shift in relation to new modalities of power, *dispositifs*, and subjectivities. It is far from a fixed or universal form in Foucault's thought but instead represents one aspect, technique, or manifestation of historically contingent modalities of power.

In the closing pages of *Discipline and Punish*, Foucault states that the carceral technique, now generalized throughout society, represents as a system a "new form of 'law': a mixture of legality and nature, prescription and constitution, the norm" (EDP, 304; FSP, 310). The resurgence of the juridical in the twentieth century, subordinated to economic rationality, likewise could be seen as a "new" form of law, one that Foucault seemed presciently aware of before many of his contemporaries. And in a telling line from *Society Must Be Defended*, Foucault claimed that, "If we are to struggle against disciplines, or rather against disciplinary power, in our search for a nondisciplinary power, we should not be turning to the old right of sovereignty; we should be looking for a new right that is both antidisciplinary and emancipated from the principle of sovereignty" (ECF-SMD, 39–40; FCF-FDS, 35). The ability of law to be new, and to call for a "new" law as well as a new "law," reflects its ability to change in relation to the contingencies of history. The discomfort that many legal theorists express about Foucault's thought reflects, perhaps above all, a discomfort with Foucault's refusal to attribute an ahistorical universality to law. It is a contingent – however particularly powerful – instance and practice of power/knowledge among many others. Foucault would never give a "theory" of law, nor would he elevate it to a point of priority in the study of power or the self, but it is consistently present throughout his work, and like so many of his most powerful insights, handled with flexibility and care.

Andrew Dilts

SEE ALSO

> *Freedom*
> *Governmentality*
> *Liberalism*
> *Power*
> *Subjectification*
> *Maurice Blanchot*

SUGGESTED READING

Baxter, Hugh. 1996. "Bringing Foucault into Law and Law into Foucault," *Stanford Law Review* 48, no. 2:449–479.

Ewald, Francis. 1990. "Norms, Discipline, and the Law," trans. Marjorie Beale, *Representations* 30:138–161.

Golder, Ben, and Peter Fitzpatrick. 2009. *Foucault's Law*. London: Routledge.
    eds. 2010. *Foucault and Law*. Surrey: Ashgate.

Hunt, Alan, and Gary Wickham. 1994. *Foucault and Law: Towards a Sociology of Law as Governance*. London: Pluto Press.

Rose, Nikolas, and Mariana Valverde. 1998. "Governed by Law?" *Social and Legal Studies* 7:541–551.

Strauser, Joëlle. 2004. "Loi(s)," in *Abécédaire de Michel Foucault*. Paris: Les Editions Sils Maria, Les Editions Vrin.

Tadros, Victor. 1998. "Between Governance and Discipline: The Law and Michel Foucault," *Oxford Journal of Legal Studies* 18 no. 1:75–103.

Wickham, Gary. 2006. "Foucault, Law, and Power: A Reassessment," *Journal of Law and Society* 33, no. 4:596–614.

43

LIBERALISM

LIBERALISM, IN FOUCAULT'S account, is best understood as a historically specific form of political reason that organizes, directs, and imposes limits on the apparatus of governmentality (ECF-BBIO, 20). As a rational discourse that developed internal to governmental practice itself, eighteenth-century liberalism tied together a new empirical knowledge of the dynamics of the economy and the population with the burgeoning policy apparatus of the administrative state, formulating a precise agenda for the most effective application of governmental power in support of the "natural" growth of the market and society. As a critical doctrine wielded by individuals and groups subject to governmental control, however, liberalism has also constantly confronted governments with the question of whether they have not crossed the line to govern too much, destroying the capacity for self-maintenance and self-transformation supposedly built into the very fabric of civil society and the economy (EEW1, 75).

Both the critical and the governmental deployments of liberalism are grounded on a fundamental principle of "*laisser faire, passer, et aller*," which, as Foucault interprets it, "means acting so that reality develops, goes its way, and follows its own course according to the laws, principles, and mechanisms of reality itself" (ECF-STP, 48). Because this central principle refers simultaneously to the preeminence of a "free" or "natural" path of development and the need for governmental action in support of such development, liberalism is perpetually plagued by the problem of determining whether socioeconomic development requires increased governmental intervention, perhaps to remove irrational or unnatural obstacles to growth, or whether it necessitates only greater governmental restraint. Liberal reason attempts to resolve this difficulty by deciphering the "true" needs of the population, the economy, and civil society in the very nature of the objects themselves. Through this scientific determination of the "truth" of society, liberal reason continues to shape, limit, and extend governmental practice today, and it is in this respect that Foucault dubs liberalism a "regime of veridiction" (ECF-BBIO, 36).

Foucault's description of liberalism as a "regime of veridiction" or a form of "political reason" immediately distinguishes his approach from at least two other prominent interpretations. Most importantly, Foucault's analysis sets him at odds with the dominant Anglo-American philosophical conversation insofar as he denies the theoretical centrality of the normative problem of liberal justice. Foucault argues that the liberal discourse of justice, which asserts the preeminence of the juridical rights of the sovereign individual subject over the power of the state, possesses only a strategic, contingent link to actual liberal governance (ECF-BBIO, 42–43). The juridical framework emerged in the seventeenth and early eighteenth centuries as a tactic for turning the apparatus of the law against the absolute authority of the monarch, grounding the legitimacy of political power in the individual subject's consent to a contractual transfer of rights instead of in the divine right of the king (ECF-BBIO, 7–9). Liberal governance, by contrast, justifies its authority by way of its scientific knowledge of the "real" needs of society and of the natural process of circulation in the market; it is not the sovereign subject of rights that thus serves as the essential unit of liberal political reason but *homo economicus* – the generalized man of exchange, production, and competition. If these two heterogeneous forms of thought – the juridical and the governmental – have forged an alliance over the past three centuries, Foucault contends, it is only because the legal mechanisms of individual rights have proven an effective bulwark for securing the unhindered, naturally beneficial intercourse of individuals in the market (EEW1, 76–77). Liberal governments of course frequently deploy the vocabulary of juridical rationality – rights, justice, and legitimacy – but Foucault argues that it is the flourishing of the market, and not the consent of the juridical subject, that in the final analysis verifies or falsifies the excellence of governmental practice (ECF-BBIO, 43). "Consequently," he writes, "the market determines that good government is no longer simply government that functions according to justice" (ECF-BBIO, 32).

Foucault understands the political philosophy of liberal justice to be but a minor strategic partner to liberal governmental thought, but we must nevertheless be careful to distinguish this *strategic* analysis of liberal thought from the more dismissive interpretation of Marxist ideology critique. Liberal freedoms are not merely a fictive ideological superstructure produced out of the "real" economic exigencies of the capitalist class; they are the refined product of multiple technologies of power that construct subjects as agents of exchange, production, and competition according to the truths spoken by political reason. These freedoms are produced along multiple and frequently contradictory vectors: juridical norms protect the entrepreneurial activities of the individual subject; tariffs, monopolies, subsidies, and their abolition are variously deployed to promote the free flow of labor and capital; disciplinary modes of surveillance guarantee the profitability and productivity of individual behavior; and new forms of social insurance and social security are developed to shelter individuals from the costs of some particular economic liberties (ECF-BBIO, 63–68). Liberal governmentality "consumes freedom," Foucault writes, "which means that it must produce it … it must organize it" (ECF-BBIO, 63). The rubric for this production of free liberal subjects, furthermore, stems directly from scientific conceptions of the true and natural health of the economy, the market, society, or individuals. Theoretical debates concerning the rights of the subject or the truth of the market are not just smoke and mirrors; these debates in fact continue to shape the deployment of new apparatuses of power and are thus central to the constitution of our political present. Recognition of the influential role played by liberal reason is thus essential for understanding, mapping, and contesting the experience of governmentality, discipline, and biopolitics now and into the future (ECF-BBIO, 22; EEW1, 79).

Jared Hibbard-Swanson

SEE ALSO

Freedom
Governmentality
Law
Marxism

SUGGESTED READING

Hindess, Barry. 1996. "Liberal Government and Techniques of the Self," in *Foucault and Political Reason*, ed. Andrew Barry, Thomas Osborne, and Nikolas Rose. Chicago: University of Chicago Press, pp. 19–36.
Read, Jason. 2009. "A Genealogy of Homo-Economicus: Neoliberalism and the Production of Subjectivity," *Foucault Studies* 6:25–36.
Rose, Nikolas. 1999. *Powers of Freedom*. Cambridge: Cambridge University Press.

44

LIFE

THERE IS NO other way to analyze Foucault's engagement with the concept of "life" than through reference to his relationship to his teacher, mentor, and advocate Georges Canguilhem. Foucault biographies chronicle the different ways in which Canguilhem was central in Foucault's own intellectual and professional itinerary. Yet the former's deep influence on the latter has yet to be properly studied (the essays by Paul Rabinow and Pierre Machinery are indispensable points of departure). Foucault himself acknowledged on several occasions his debt and gratitude to his teacher and, above all, the author of both *Knowledge of Life* (Canguilhem 2008 [1952]) and *The Normal and the Pathological* (Canguilhem 1991 [1943, 1966]). In a letter to Canguilhem from June 1965, Foucault wrote:

> When I began to work, ten years ago, I did not know you – not your books. But the things I have done since I certainly would not have done had I not read you. You have had a great impact on [my work]. I cannot describe to you precisely how, nor precisely where, nor what my "method" owes to you; but you should be aware that even, and especially, my counter-positions – for example, on vitalism – are possible only on the basis of what you have done, on this layer of analysis introduced by you, on this epistemological eidetics that you invented. Actually *The Birth of the Clinic* and what follows it derive from this and, perhaps, are completely contained within it. Some day I shall have to come to grips with exactly what this relationship is. (quoted in Eribon 1991, 103)

This is surely a telling admission, especially when one considers that Canguilhem's works are not listed in the bibliography of *The Birth of the Clinic*, though there is one indirect citation to him in chapter eight, endnote 48, when Foucault cites his *Knowledge of Life* as a warrant for the affirmation of Bichat's "vitalism" (EBC, 144).

In his inaugural lecture at the Collège de France on December 2, 1970, Foucault publicly acknowledged his gratitude to his teacher in the following way:

> If I have wished to apply a similar method to discourse quite other than legendary or mythical narratives, it is because before me lay the works of the historians of science, above all, that of Monsieur Canguilhem. I owe it to him that I understood that the history of science did not necessarily involve, either an account of discoveries, or descriptions of the ideas and opinions bordering science either from the side of its doubtful beginnings, or from the side of its fall-out; but that one could – that one should – treat the history of science as an ensemble, at once coherent, and transformable into theoretical models and conceptual instruments. (EAK, 235)

In the introduction for the English translation of Canguilhem's *The Normal and the Pathological*, written in 1977, Foucault offers a synoptic and synthetic analysis of his teacher's work while also evaluating his place within twentieth-century French thought. In fact, he wrote,

> [T]ake away Canguilhem, and you will no longer understand very much about a whole series of discussions that took place among French Marxists; nor will you grasp what is specific about sociologists such as Pierre Bourdieu, Robert Castel, Jean-Claude Passeron, what makes them so distinctive in the field of sociology; you will miss a whole aspect of the theoretical work done by psychoanalysis and, in particular, by the Lacanians. Furthermore, in the whole debate of ideas that preceded or followed the movement of 1968, it is easy to find the place of those who were shaped in one way or another by Canguilhem. (EEW2, 466)

This introductory essay, later edited and published in French with the title "Life: Experience and Science" furthermore maps the history of French thought in terms of a "dividing line" that crosses all the other dividing lines that have configured the physiognomy of that thought. That dividing line is "one that separates a philosophy of experience, of meaning, of the subject, and a philosophy of knowledge, of rationality, and of the concept" (EEW2, 466). On one side of the line, Foucault places Sartre and Merleau-Ponty; on the other he places Cavaillès, Bachelard, and Canguilhem. It is evident that Foucault is placing himself on this side of the dividing line. In this text, Foucault foregrounds four key ways in which Canguilhem reshaped the fields of the philosophy and history of science. First, Canguilhem took up the theme of the discontinuities in the history of the sciences. These discontinuities are not simply a result of battles against "resistances," "preconceptions," or "obstacles" in such a way that a narrative could weave them into a seamless story of triumph over error, prejudice, and ignorance: "The history of the sciences is not the history of the true, of its slow epiphany" (EEW2, 471). Science and the history of science cannot naively assume that truth as such is what it delivers, but at the same time it cannot adjure what it takes to be true, or affirms to be true. Canguilhem, following Cavaillès, shifts the ground from truth to "truthful discourses" and "truth-telling." In this way, the history of science becomes the history of the different practices of "truth-telling," of how the true is both discovered and fashioned. Second, Canguilhem triangulated among the scientist, the historian of science, and the epistemologist in such a way that the history of "truthful discourses" is not arbitrarily and extraneously discontinuous but internally and systematically punctuated by breaks brought about by methodological self-reflexivity that challenges the epistemic transparency of scientific concepts. Third, Canguilhem brought the history of science from the heights of abstraction (mathematics, astronomy, mechanics, physics) to the "regions where knowledge is much less deductive" (EEW2, 470), namely the life sciences, where he was able to decipher and make evident the uniqueness of those concepts operating in medicine, biology, anatomy, and other areas. Canguilhem showed us how it was not possible to have a science of the living "without taking into account, as something essential to its object, the possibility of disease, death, monstrosity, anomaly, and error" (EEW2, 474). Using Canguilhem's language, we could say that his fundamental insight was to demonstrate that life is concerned not with the normal, or normality, but normativity, namely the generation of new norms. Life is not simply that which resists death and keeps it in abeyance by the muted healthy functioning of the organism. In Canguilhem's words: "Life is the formation of forms" (Canguilhem 2008, xix). Fourth, inasmuch as Canguilhem's work was about the history of the life sciences, he raised the question of knowledge as such, of what constitutes knowledge and how that knowledge comes to intervene in the object of that knowledge itself. According to Foucault: "Through an elucidation of knowledge about life and the concepts that articulate that knowledge, Canguilhem wishes to determine the situation of the *concept in life*. That is, of the concept insofar as it is of the modes of that information which every living being takes from its environment and by which conversely it structures its environment" (EEW2, 475, Foucault's italics). Foucault summarized his assessment of Canguilhem's work in this way:

> Enlarging on the point, we could say that the constant problem in Canguilhem's work, from the *Essai sur le normal et le pathologique* of 1943 to *Idéologie et rationalité dans l'histoire des sciences de la vie (Ideology and Rationality in the History of the Life Sciences)* of 1977, has been the relation between science of life and vitalism: a problem which he tackled both in showing the irreducibility of the problem of disease as a problem essential to every science of life, and in studying what has constituted the speculative climate, the theoretical context of the life sciences. (EINP, 18–19)

This sentence is not included in the edited version translated in EEW2. This is an important sentence because it also applies to Foucault's own work with respect to the concept of life and the problem of vitalism, which in his 1965 letter to Canguilhem he identified as something to which he offered a counterposition.

In addition to the texts we have cited, there are four other important places in Foucault's work where he directly addresses the concept of life. In Chapter 8 of *The Birth of the Clinic*, provocatively titled "Open Up a Few Corpses," Foucault discusses the revolutionary effect of Xavier Bichat's work in the history of medicine. Bichat's discovery of anatomical pathology allowed a radical rethinking of death. Whereas in the classical period death was an absolute external to life, the nadir of a horizon ever receding into forgetfulness and nonknowledge, after Bichat death was made multiple, internal to life, integral to the living. In Foucault's words:

> Bichat relativized the concept of death, bringing it down from the absolute in which it appeared as an invisible, decisive, irrecoverable event: he volatilized it, distributed it throughout life in the form of separate, partial, progressive deaths, deaths that are so slow in occurring that they extend even beyond death itself. But from this fact he formed an essential structure of medical thought and perception: that to which life is *opposed* and to which it is *exposed*; that in relation to which it is living *opposition*, and therefore *life*, that in relation to which it is analytically *exposed*, and therefore *true*. (EBC, 144–145, Foucault's italics)

After Bichat, life is no longer thinkable merely as either the name for the functioning of a mechanism or the catalysis of chemical reactions. Life is now to be thought of on its own grounds, grounds traced by the confrontation with disease and death. Death, in fact, has become the great "analyst of life," for it is death that reveals "the space of the organism" and the "time of the disease" (EBC, 144). Death that calls to account life, before which life must give an account of itself, has become the retinal image of the "eye that unties the knot of life" (ibid.). It is for this reason that "[v]italism appears against the background of this 'mortalism'" (EBC, 144–145). Death has acquired a positivity and truth that it had never possessed before, but, by the same token, so has life. If "[t]he living night is dissipated in the brightness of death" (EBC, 146), then it is also true that the night of death is illuminated by teeming, vibrant, exuberant life. Both of these, nonetheless, are caught in the gaze of a medicalized eye.

In the conclusion to *The Birth of the Clinic*, Foucault notes that when death became a basic presupposition of medical knowledge, it ceased to be an abstract, general, ethereal, and desingularizing eventuality. Instead, death became *embodied* and discrete in individuals. Death could now be individualizing. In this way, medicine participated in the formation of a "science of the individual" (EBC, 197). In modern thought, then, the question of individuality is intricately tied to the question of death; that is, the question of human temporality. If figures like Bichat, Freud, and many others who approached the question of human finitude in terms of human mortality are central to European culture, it is not simply because they were philosophers who happened also to be doctors but because "medical thought is fully engaged in the philosophical status of man" (EBC, 198). In other words, it is because medical knowledge allows us to think of finitude in terms of teeming, plural, volatized death that we can now tell a truth about the human condition: we are living beings who are both subject and object of their medical gaze, a gaze that looks at us as beings individualized by the exposure and threat of imminent and immanent death.

The second point of reference for Foucault's discussion of life is *The Order of Things*. In fact, Chapter 8 in Part II is titled "Labor, Life, Language." Section three of this chapter is simply named "Cuvier." In fact, Cuvier is to *The Order of Things* what Bichat was to *The Birth of the Clinic*; namely, the personification is a major shift in the way Europeans thought about life. Cuvier, in fact, marks the discovery of life itself, the living proper. Foucault puts it this way:

> From Cuvier onward, it is life in its non-perceptible, purely functional aspect that provides the basis for the exterior possibility of a classification. The classification of living beings is no longer to be found in the great expanse of order; the possibility of classification now arises from the depths of life, from those elements most hidden from view. Before, the living being was a locality of natural classification; now, the fact of being classifiable is a property of the living being. (EOT, 268)

During the classical age there could be a history of nature because nature itself was conceived in terms of a great chain of being, or the cosmic *scala naturae*, whose order and intelligibility were granted by divine providence or the logic of a mechanism held together by mathematical and dynamic lawfulness. In the eighteenth century, nature becomes discontinuous and heterogeneous because it is alive, and life is always singular, concrete, diverse, incipient, and vital; that is, unexpected and incalculable. Foucault continues:

> From Cuvier onward, the living wraps itself in its own existence, breaks off its taxonomic links of adjacency, tears itself free from the vast, tyrannical plan of continuities, and constitutes itself as a new space: a double space, in fact – since it is both the interior one of anatomical coherences and physiological compatibilities, and the exterior one of the elements in which it resides and of which it forms its own body. But both these spaces are subject to a common control: it is no longer that of the possibilities of being, it is that of the conditions of life. (EOT, 274)

Life, in other words, is that which is alive by virtue of certain internal coherence and compatibilities that enable its living, but also that which is self-sustaining and self-enhancing in a given milieu or environment. Life is self-relation through relating to an environment. Life is thus doubly singular and doubly individualizing, for to live is to generate norms for its health but to do so within a given horizon of constraints, or scarcity or abundance. With Cuvier, another break became possible, from natural history to a history of nature; that is, from the ahistoricality of nature to the temporality of the biological. In Foucault's words: "It is true that the Classical space ... did not exclude the possibility of development, but that development did no more than provide a means of transversing the discreetly preordained table of possible variations. The breaking up of that space made it possible to reveal a historicity proper to life itself: that of its maintenance in its conditions of existence" (EOT, 275). The name for this historicity that is proper to life itself is what we call evolution, which has had profound consequences for European thought. One of those consequences was a turn toward "animality" as the privileged locus for the manifestation of life's historicity. It is in the animal that life makes evident its distinct historicity in terms of its plurality, its wildness, its disorder, and its unforeseeable discontinuities. It is in the animal that life's originality and vitality are made most evident, but it is in a unique animal, the human animal, that life's own generativity is most provocatively embodied. In the last chapter of *The Order of Things*, Foucault carries forward the link between the human, the animal, and the human sciences, which aim to give an account of human beings, as both subject and object of their knowledge:

> [M]an for the human sciences is not that living being with a very particular form (a somewhat special physiology and an almost unique anatomy); he is the living being who, from within the life to which he entirely belongs and by which he is traversed in his whole being, constitutes representations by means of which he lives, and on the basis of which he possesses the strange capacity of being able to represent to himself precisely that life. (EOT, 352)

The human being is the living being whose life is itself sustained or exposed by the concepts it generates in order to make sense of its own life. Human knowledge, as what is proper to the human animal, is part of his living, of his being alive, of his persevering in his life. Here, we should recall what Foucault was to write a decade later in his introduction to Canguilhem's *The Normal and the Pathological*: "Forming concepts is a way of living and not a way of killing life; it is a way to live in a relative mobility and not a way to immobilize life; it is to show, among those billions of living beings that inform their environment and inform themselves on the basis of it, an innovation that can be judged as one likes, tiny or substantial: a very special type of information" (EEW2, 475). If "[a]s the archaeology of our thought easily shows, man is an invention of recent date ... [a]nd one perhaps nearing its end" (EOT, 387), should we not also ask whether the human animal may intervene in his own living organism under the direction of his own representations, accelerating not only the disappearance of the idea of the human that has guided us but perhaps also his own very biological being?

This last question brings us to the third point of reference for Foucault's discussion of life, which we find in the last chapter of *The Will to Knowledge*, known in English as *The History of Sexuality*. There we can read this powerful passage: "For millennia, man remained what he was for Aristotle: a living animal with the additional capacity for political existence; modern man is an animal whose politics places his existence as a living being in question" (EHS1, 143). This putting into question the living of the human by politics is what Foucault calls biopolitics. The recognition of "life's" entry into history, however, is not something that is new in Foucault's late work. As we have seen, he had already been thinking about the relationship between a new conception of life, in medicine and modern biology, and the way in which humans could now be individualized under the gaze of the doctor who gazed at their living body through the lens of teeming death. In his later work, the accent is on the "political" uses of this medical knowledge. With a new concept of life and death, especially from the perspective of how it affects our self-understanding as human animals, the political itself is reconfigured. In fact, a new form of sovereignty emerges that manifests itself not by killing but making live. From the eighteenth century forward, death, life, and disease have configured a conceptual trinity that also forces us to reconfigure the field of the political. Inasmuch as death becomes immanent to life, and disease its auguring, annunciation, and threat, politics is now called to account before the tribunal of life, of the living. Politics becomes the securing, preserving, nurturing of life. Politics must become a means to intervene in the life of the human life, not simply by the force of the conceptions and representations it circulates but also by the institutions it constructs and empowers to frame the milieu of human existence. In the modern age, the new concept of life gives way by means of a new conception of politics to a technology of life. This technology of life, or biopolitics, is pivoted on the axis formed by two intersecting vectors of power: one aiming to discipline bodies, the other aiming to regulate populations.

In his last course at the Collège de France during the academic year of 1983–1984, Foucault returned to the question of life, but now from the perspective of what he called an "aesthetics of existence" (ECF-COT, 162). The course, published with the title *The Courage of Truth*, is a close analysis of *parrēsia*, courageous, fearless, truthful discourse. The analysis, however, is carried out against the background of a rethinking of Kant's question "What is Enlightenment?" which Foucault had undertaken the year before, in the course from 1982–1983, "The Government of Self and Others." For Foucault, Kant's question was about giving an account of oneself in relationship to one's age in terms of a "truth-telling," or game of veridiction. The study of *parrēsia* in this last set of courses became a lens through which to analyze how "modes of veridiction, the study of the techniques of governmentality, and the identification of forms of practice of self interweave" (ECF-COT, 8). It is this interweaving that Foucault also aimed to make evident in his rethinking of the question of the Enlightenment, which he already had initiated in his 1977 essay on Canguilhem. In this last course, the entwinement between life and knowledge is articulated in terms of what Foucault calls "true life" (*alêthês bios*). As he put it: "What I wanted to try to recover was something of the relation between the art of existence and true discourse, between the beautiful existence and the true life, life in the truth, life for the truth" (ECF-COT, 163). "Truth-telling" is the name for a practice through which the true life is pursued, through which certain practices of the self are formed that establish forms of government of self and others. *Parrēsia*, as a practice of telling the truth about others and oneself, as a distinct form of ethical practice, has as its essential object a mode of life, an aesthetics of existence, an *askesis* of the self. In other words, the analysis of fearless speech leads us to rethink both the subject and its relation to both knowledge and truth. Here we are again on the common ground between Foucault and Canguilhem. As Foucault wrote in his introduction to Canguilhem's *The Normal and the Pathological*:

> This historian of rationalities, himself so "rationalistic," is a philosopher of error – I mean that error provides him with the basis for posing philosophical problems; or, let us say more exactly, the problem of truth and life. Here we touch on one of the fundamental events, no doubt, in the history of modern philosophy: if the great Cartesian break raised the question of the relation between truth and subjectivity, the eighteenth century introduced a series of questions concerning truth and life, *The Critique of Judgment* and the *Phenomenology of Spirit* being the first great formulations of these. And since that time this has been one of the great issues of philosophical discussion. Should life be considered as nothing more than one of the areas that raised the general question of truth, the subject, and knowledge? Or does it oblige us to pose the question in a different way? Should not the whole theory of the subject be reformulated, seeing that knowledge, rather than opening onto the truth of the world, is deeply rooted in the "errors" of life? (EEW2, 477)

The nuclear age has become the biotech century. The age of the atom bomb has given way to the age of the gene. Whether as the threat of planetary annihilation, a global thanatology, or as the promethean promise of new life through genetic manipulations of vegetable and animal genotypes, a globalized biopolitics, at the heart of our age is the concept of life that enabled new sciences, new technologies, new forms of political power. The question of life has become the more urgent precisely because the very grammar, code, and language of life are claimed to have been deciphered, promising to enable us to call forth into existence new forms of life.

Against the background of a teeming mortalism, one that calls life to give account of itself in terms of a death that is produced by direct manipulation of life, we may have to oppose what has been called vitalism but which Leonard Lawlor has called a "life-ism" (Lawlor 2006). At the center of this vitalism or "life-ism" is a regard for the novelty of life. Or as Canguilhem put it: "Intelligence can apply itself to life only if it recognizes the originality of life. The thought of the living must take from the living the idea of the living" (Canguilhem 2008, xx). This intelligence that applies itself to life is nothing other than what Foucault called the "true life" and an "aesthetics of existence." A concept of life can itself intervene in the art of living. Life is a concept that can spell death or life.

Eduardo Mendieta

SEE ALSO

Biohistory
Biopolitics
Biopower
Death
Finitude
Medicine
Parrēsia

SUGGESTED READING

Canguilhem, Georges. 1991. *The Normal and the Pathological*, with an introduction by Michel Foucault. New York: Zone Books.
———. 2008. *Knowledge of Life*. New York: Fordham University Press.
Lawlor, Leonard. 2006. *The Implication of Immanence: Towards a New Concept of Life*. New York: Fordham University Press.

45

LITERATURE

I N 1966, FOUCAULT published his provocative "archaeology of the human sciences" that would have been entitled "Words and Things" had there not been a book of that title in English. Hence *The Order of Things* became its substitute title (EOT). Although much attention to this study was concerned with Foucault's radically revised view of the "history of ideas," hidden in the interstices between each of the *epistemes* that designate the dominant but latent mode of thinking and conceptualizing of each epoch ("resemblance" for the Renaissance, "representation" for the seventeenth- and eighteenth-century neoclassical era, "man" for the nineteenth through the mid-twentieth century, and something like "structure" for the postmodern mode of thinking that was appearing on the scene in 1966) was the key role of literary texts. The critical status of literary texts came in the form of what Foucault called "threshold texts," writings that demonstrated the limits of a particular *episteme* and also indicated features of the new *episteme* that would replace it. In this sense, literature for Foucault was not some trivial source of entertainment but it was also not the product of a celebrated creative activity. Rather, literary texts would participate in a discursive practice that would prevail in a particular era. As with other important French figures of his time (Sartre, Derrida, Cixous, and Kristeva, for example), literature would be brought into conjunction with philosophy, political theory, psychology, sociology, and historical studies.

Between the Renaissance and the neoclassical age, between the *episteme* of "resemblance" and that of "representation," Foucault in *The Order of Things* offers a reading of the Golden Age Spanish writer Miguel de Cervantes's celebrated picaresque novel *Don Quixote*. Foucault shows that the "hero" of *Don Quixote* (in the first of the two books that comprise the novel) appears as a great "knight errant" (reminiscent of those associated with medieval gallantry) who roams the countryside offering his services in multiple acts of good will. He singlehandedly (with the help of his aide Sancho Panza) attacks a giant threatening the people, confronts a foreign army approaching the town, and saves Dulcinea, a damsel in distress. With ironic flourish, the reader is amused to learn that the giant is actually a windmill, the army is a herd of sheep, and Dulcinea is a washwoman conducting her daily chores. Foucault shows that Don Quixote himself in fact "resembles" ("acts like" or "is analogous to") an anachronistic medieval knight, the windmill resembles a giant, the herd of sheep an oncoming army, and Ducinea a damsel in distress. Each of these instances in this literary text are indications of a Renaissance mentality and mode of thinking that resonates with scientific studies offered by Galileo (when what he sees in his telescope resembles the planets in the sky), by Machiavelli (when he advises that an effective prince will need to resemble both the lion and the fox), and by Cervantes's contemporary Shakespeare (when, in *Romeo and Juliet*, one finds a description of the main characters as "star-crossed lovers" – resembling stars that are out of their orbit).

The important role of the literary text becomes evident when in the second book of Don Quixote the "hero" of the story hears from townspeople of a "great knight errant" who has been performing wonderful feats of gallantry. Don Quixote recognizes that he himself is "represented" (presented again) in these stories. Hence there is a shift from an age of "resemblance" to that of "representation." Similarly, between the age dominated by "representation" and its replacement, the "anthropological age of man," the Marquis de Sade's writings mark the shift that is taking place. Between the "representation of desire" and the function of the "empirico-transcendental doublet" (the combination of objectivity and subjectivity) that constitutes "man" in the Kantian era, the Marquis de Sade's *Justine* (whose virtuous main character is treated as the neoclassical representation of the scene of the libertine's excessive practices) is juxtaposed with the alternate and subsequent role of a modern "object" subjugated by the sadistic desiring "subject." De Sade's various late eighteenth-century novels, such as *Juliette* and *Philosophy in the Bedroom*, demonstrate even more intensely that no longer is desire "represented" on the scene (as clear and distinct ideas are represented to Descartes, as grammar is represented by Arnaud and the seventeenth-century Port Royal logician-grammarians, and as Madame de Lafayette's illicit lovers – the Princesse de Clèves and the Duc de Nemours – seek to represent to themselves the moral course of action given the intensity of their love affair).

The postmodern turn in the human sciences that was taking place around the time of *The Order of Things* in 1966 was also signaled (according to Foucault) by the writings of Nietzsche and the nineteenth-century French symbolist poet Stephane Mallarmé that were produced decades in advance. Long before the postmodern *episteme* began to take shape in the latter half of the twentieth century, Nietzsche and Mallarmé – through the literary quality of their texts – were offering a new way of thinking. Their work came to mark the thinking of the human sciences in terms of structure, sign system, figuration, discourse, interface, difference as operative between subject/object, transcendental/empirical, and knower/known in lieu of being constituted by them. Although Nietzsche was more of a philosopher than a literary figure, in many contexts his aphoristic style (see *Beyond Good and Evil*) and his narratological philosophizing (as in *Thus Spoke Zarathustra*, written in the 1880s) mark a radical shift in thinking from the comprehensive and all-encompassing critical and philosophical enterprises of Kant and Hegel. Similarly, Mallarmé's emphasis on "correspondences" and symbolic formations (rather than references to realities in the empirical world) provides a "threshold" to the postmodern thinking that would take more than half a century to realize.

Each of these "threshold texts" – literary expressions of a new way of thinking – marks a difference between the dominant *episteme* and that appearing on the scene at the margins of the contemporary. Literature, then, takes on something like a prophetic role, one that provides a hinge with attitudes, ways of articulating the relation between words and things of a subsequent era – before its time. Hence literature is not just the description of how things are at any one epoch but the foreshadowing of perspectives to come. Jean-Paul Sartre, in *What Is Literature?* (1947–1948), had proposed that writing ("*écrire*") has as its dominant task that of the "free" writer (subject) addressing the "free" reader (also a subject) demonstrating the reader's "freedom" through the novel or theatrical piece. Maurice Merleau-Ponty, another of Foucault's predecessors, in his unfinished *Prose of the World* (composed in 1951–1952), proposed that literature should be an instance of "expression" more than an act of "communication" and "engagement" of the writer (as Sartre had proposed). As in Sartre, literature would be a manifestation of an active subjective consciousness – "embodied" in Merleau-Ponty's philosophy, "engaged" in Sartre. The bridge to Foucault comes as Merleau-Ponty offers his notion of the "speaking subject" and the "spoken subject." Merleau-Ponty's embodied, expressive, gesturing subject opens a space for prose and the importance of the writer. But, for Foucault, the subject–object relation as a description of the human is still inscribed within the prior "modern" *episteme*, that of the "anthropological," "empirico-transcendental doublet" known as "man," or what Sartre (drawing on Henri Corbin's translation of Heidegger's *Dasein*) called "human reality." Hence Roland Barthes's *Writing Degree Zero* and his essays on the New French novelist Alain Robbe-Grillet, all from the early 1950s (during Foucault's later twenties) already signaled a different way of thinking about literature. For Barthes, literature is best described as "writing," and writing is situated at the intersection of "style" and a moment in time. Writing is at "zero degree" because it does not invoke either the activity or subjectivity of the writer nor is it constituted as an object of investigation as the product of a writer's subjectivity. Writing can be characterized as "bourgeois" writing, "revolutionary" writing, and so on. Writing at that time had already taken on the character of what Foucault a decade later would call a "discursive practice."

For Foucault, literature has an entirely different function from what Sartre and Merleau-Ponty offered; it is thereby more like that of the cultural critic and semiologist Roland Barthes. For Foucault, literature means "literary texts," and "literary texts" participate in a discursive practice of a particular era. Or, to be more precise, literary texts mark the edge of a discursive practice that is in the process of becoming marginalized in favor of a new *episteme*. With respect to the *episteme* of the human sciences, what we have called the "postmodern" *episteme*, Foucault identifies in particular the structuralist formulations in the areas of ethnology (Claude Levi-Strauss's structural anthropology), psychoanalysis (Jacques Lacan's structural psychoanalysis), and political theory (Louis Althusser's structural Marxism). In many ways, Barthes was the most eloquent theoretician of this new structuralist and even poststructuralist attention to the hinge or "text" between a conscious subjectivity and an empiricist objectivity. And Barthes's cultural criticism, much of which was focused on literary practices (from Greek theatre, to Racine's seventeenth-century plays, to Robbe-Grillet's "new" novels) demonstrated the unique and special status of the kind of sign systems that constitute Foucault's notion of the "*epistemé*." Literature, then, is "epistemic," an effect of the human sciences, a site of "*jouissance*," a place of pleasure in the text that is neither in the subject nor in the object but rather in the semiological spaces between them.

Three years before publishing *The Order of Things* (1966), Foucault wrote a monograph on the French writer Raymond Roussel (1877–1933) entitled *Death and the Labyrinth* (1963). Like many of the figures identified in *The Order of Things*, Foucault was fascinated with this writer, poet, and novelist because of his marginal status in the grand literary canon. Just as Barthes "discovered" Robbe-Grillet, Foucault discovered Roussel. And like Robbe-Grillet's novels, such as *Le Voyeur* (1955), *Jealousy* (1957), and *In the Labyrinth* (1959), the neutral space of writing – something like what Barthes called the "middle voice" (from the Greek grammatical form) – elaborated through repetitions and, in the case of Roussel, reiterated parentheses – became the focus of literary and theoretical elaboration.

Already in 1961, when Foucault produced his mammoth *History of Madness in the Age of Reason*, in order to demonstrate how mad people were treated in Europe in the Middle Ages, he cited the 1494 literary text by Sebastian Brandt entitled *The Ship of Fools* (*Narrenschiff*). The *Narrenschiff* narrates how mad people would be put on a ship that circulates throughout the rivers of Europe. The ship would occasionally stop in a city or town situated along the river. The passengers would attempt to enter the town, but in short order they would be sent off to the next city or town since they would be treated as undesirables with respect to any of these locations. Here, for Foucault, the content of the literary text is offered as a demonstration of the way people wrote about or thought about things and the world at that time.

Three years after publishing *The Order of Things*, Foucault produced another major work: *The Archaeology of Knowledge* (1969). Much of Foucault's extended study of the methodology behind *The Order of Things* and his rethinking of the "history of ideas" was in fact an attempt to respond to the criticisms lodged against what historians regarded as a significant broadside to their whole enterprise. After all, why would a historian want to emphasize "discontinuity" rather than "continuity" in history, or focus on marginal figures (such as Cuvier, Bopp, and the Brothers Grimm), or to think about the interstices between historical "periods" rather than attend to the major outlines and conditions of the epoch itself? And even literary historians at the time would be worried about designating noncanonical writers as worthy of celebration. In *The Archaeology of Knowledge*, Foucault gave less attention to literature and more to the relations between ideas, norms, and practices at a given time. In *The Archaeology of Knowledge*, Foucault addressed the structures of his own "theoretical practice" (as Althusser would have called them) rather than narrating the development of thought, language, and social and political theory (as he had done in *The Order of Things*).

However, in 1968 (the year before the publication of *The Archaeology of Knowledge*), Foucault wrote a piece entitled "What Is an Author?" Both of these texts came in the wake of the events of May and June 1968, which resulted in Foucault being given carte blanche to create the most exciting new philosophy department in France at the newly established University of Paris-VIII – Vincennes, which was later moved to Saint-Denis in the north of Paris. This new department (UER, as they were called) included Deleuze, Jean-Francois Lyotard, and later Jacques Rancière and Alain Badiou. But once Foucault was elected to the newly created Chair of the History of Systems of Thought at the Collège de France in 1970, he had to leave the University of Paris-VIII to those he had hired to develop its fame and reputation. In the 1968 Éditions du Seuil *Tel Quel* volume entitled *Théorie d'ensemble* (which includes groundbreaking essays on the contemporary status of literary study by Roland Barthes concerning the "death of the author," Jacques Derrida with his famous "*Différance*" essay, Julia Kristeva on the theory of the text and semiology, and others), Foucault contributed his famous "What Is an Author?" essay. Foucault's account of the "author-function" rather than the positional, ego-centered "author" marked a whole new way of thinking about literary practice. Along with Barthes (whom Foucault eventually was able to support for the Chair of Semiology to join him at the Collège de France), Foucault participated in this group theory of literature in order to show that it was time to displace the authorial hegemony in favor of the structures of literary practice. The assignment of an author to a text was in order to create a rational entity associated with a particular text, not to celebrate a specific individual's creative powers. Literature, then, for Foucault is linked to texts, discourses, and archives rather than to authorial presences or sources of creativity.

The publication of *The Archaeology of Knowledge* was followed on December 2, 1970 by Foucault's inaugural lecture at the Collège de France, entitled "L'Ordre du discours" ("The Discourse on Language"). This presentation set the stage for the next thirteen years of lectures held at this celebrated institution on topics concerning systems of repression and disciplining (e.g., prisons), political theory, government and self-government (care for the self), sexuality and confession, the courage to say the truth, and others. The role of literature became subjugated to the concern with discourse, language, and the statement or enunciation (*énoncé*). Can "fiction" say the truth? Can language be a site of truth or falsity? Can literary texts as well as political treatises and philosophical narratives provide a locus for saying the truth? When invited to lecture as visiting professor at the University of California at Berkeley in fall 1983 (later published as *Fearless Speech* [EFS]), Foucault decided to focus on "Discourse and Truth," in particular as a study of the ancient Greek notion of "*parrēsia*," a term meaning variously "free speech," "frankness," "saying everything," or "full disclosure." For these lectures, he gave full attention to the tragedies of Euripides (fifth century BCE), though the term continued to be used well into the patristic period of the fifth century CE. Foucault continued to follow this mode of thinking from Socrates to the Roman Cynics and Stoics during his final year of lectures (1983–1984) at the Collège de France, entitled "The Courage to Truth."

Parrēsia entails that the speaking subject – the subject of the enunciation – also serve as the subject of the "enunciandum" (what is at issue, namely the speaker). This rhetorical device means that the speaker seeks to persuade by demonstrating the "courage to say the truth." And *parrēsia* played a key role in the conception of the Athenian democracy as offering a government in which one could speak openly and frankly. Importantly, in Euripides' tragedies, especially the *Ion* and the *Orestes*, Foucault focuses on the question of who has the "right" and "courage" to speak the truth. Furthermore, he devotes special attention to four other Euripides plays: *The Phoenician Women*, (411–409 BCE), *Hippolytus*, (428 BCE), *The Bacchae*, (407–406 BCE), and *Electra* (415 BCE). For instance, in *The Phoenician Women*, Euripides explores the conflict between the two sons of Oedipus (Eteocles and Polynices) when Eteocles refused to follow the agreement to let his brother rule Thebes after the first year, hence preventing the "democratic" "free speech" of his brother and the people of Thebes. The sovereign not giving up power is linked to "madness" as well as the prevention of "free speech" (*parrēsia*). In *The Bacchae*, a herdsman brings a message that could have consequences for the messenger himself. So he asks Pentheus the king if he can "speak freely" (*parrēsia*) and without punishment if the king does not like the content. Pentheus grants the herdsman his request, placing the sovereign in a situation in which he gives power to the slave to say what he needs to say without adverse consequences. Similarly, in *Electra*, the daughter, Electra, and her mother, Clytemnestra, confront one another. Electra asks her mother not to punish her for speaking freely, but in the process her mother asks Electra to use her *parrēsia* to prove that Clytemnestra was wrong in killing Electra's father, Agamemnon. The result of this call for speaking frankly had adverse results for Clytemnestra, as she was then killed by Electra's brother Orestes after demonstrating that she had indeed killed her husband without sufficient justification. What is important here is that Foucault continued, right up to the end of his career, to draw on literary texts in order to demonstrate how discursive practices are crucial to the articulation of ways of thinking and knowing at a particular time.

Reading his later texts and lectures, many of which included instances drawn from literary writings, Foucault was able to activate his understanding of political, social, and intellectual accounts of truth, madness, courage, power, governmentality, biopolitics, sexuality, and the many other themes that preoccupied him over the years leading to his untimely death in late spring 1984. Literature would no longer be the product of a creative, originating author but rather one of many instances of articulating ways of thinking and producing knowledge in different periods and places. Literature would neither be privileged nor denigrated over the course of Foucault's career. He gave literature new vitality and significance both in signaling new ways of thinking and as demonstrative of the multiple discursive practices of an era.

Hugh J. Silverman

SEE ALSO

Author
Language
Parrēsia
Friedrich Nietzsche
Raymond Roussel
Jean-Paul Sartre
William Shakespeare

SUGGESTED READING

Barthes, Roland. 1967. *Writing Degree Zero*, trans. Annette Lavers and Colin Smith. New York: Hill and Wang.

Merleau-Ponty, Maurice. 1973. *Prose of the World*, trans. John O'Neill. Evanston, IL: Northwestern University Press.

Sartre, Jean-Paul. 1988. *What Is Literature?* trans. Bernard Frechtman et al., intro. Steven Ungar. Cambridge, MA: Harvard University Press.

Silverman, Hugh J. 1997. "Sartre/Barthes: Writing Differences," in *Inscriptions: After Phenomenology and Structuralism*, 2nd ed. Evanston, IL: Northwestern University Press, pp. 236–253.

46

LOVE

OVE, LIKE DESIRE and pleasure, has undergone significant historical transformations. Foucault noted this shift as early as his *Histoire de la folie a l' âge
classique*, claiming that in Platonic culture love related either to "a blind corporeal madness or to a magnificent intoxication of the soul," whereas after the Age of
Reason, love was seen either as within reason or unreasonable (FHF, 103). Since the
Age of Reason, the family became the norm of social relations, and love outside of
this social relation was considered unreasonable (FHF, 104). Much of Foucault's discussion of love analyzes ancient Greek and early Roman texts in which one can see
how love came to be viewed so narrowly as to apply only to the family and to marital
relationships. Foucault discusses love in his later writings, notably *The Use of Pleasure*
and *The Care of the Self*, as well as his later lectures, such as "The Hermeneutics
of the Subject." Three themes emerge in Foucault's discussions of love: love as an
erotic relationship between two people, love of the truth, and love as a form of
self-transformation. In *The Hermeneutics of the Subject*, he states, "Love (*eros*) is a
form/modality through which the subject transforms himself to become capable of
truth" (ECF-HOS, 16). Love and *askesis*, practices or work on the self that aim at
the transformation of self, are capable of moving one toward the truth (ibid.). Much
of Foucault's discussion of love in volume two of *The History of Sexuality* focuses on
an analysis of what Plato says about it, examining the relationships between men
and boys in ancient Greece. In volume three of that work, he turns to early Roman
texts, primarily Plutarch's *Dialogue on Love* and Pseudo-Lucian's *Affairs of the Heart*,
observing how these discussions center love firmly within the conjugal relationship.

Foucault undertakes an analysis of love in part to trace the shift from "an economy of bodies and pleasures" to the desiring subject. In ancient Greece it was not
whom one loved but how one loved that was important. However, Foucault claims
that the focus on specific relationships reveals an anxiety about them; ancient Greek
texts focus on the pederastic relationship between men and boys. "[T]his inquiry

concerning relationships with boys took the form of a reflection on love" (EHS2, 201). This relationship as articulated in writings by Plato, Aristotle, Aristophanes, Xenophon, Pliny, and others acknowledges that the role of men differs from that of boys. Men are the active partner (the lover rather than the beloved), men have a different status – they are older than the beloved boy and have more wealth, more knowledge, and more experience (EHS2, 194–195; EHS3, 197). This inequality between lovers was problematic, in part because the relationship changes when the boy becomes a man. In its purest form, love for boys should transition from love of their beauty to friendship (*philia*) based on love of their virtue. The erotic or love relationship between men and boys appears in the relationship between a master and his student. Both seek the truth, and for Plato love (*eros*) is a relation to truth (EHS 2, 239). Significantly, the love between men and boys should focus on the beauty of the soul of the boy and not include sexual relations. This sublimation of *eros* to a "pure" relationship based on virtue and friendship is, according to Foucault, one source of the shift from an ethics of pleasure to an ethics of desire (EHS2, 244–245).

For the Greeks, discussions focused on proper and improper ways to love, centering on the relationships between men and boys. In the Roman and Stoic texts, the question shifted from how to love to whom to love, but divergent arguments were put forth about whether it was "natural" for men to love boys or women.

Foucault claims, "The debate between the love of women and the love of boys … is the confrontation of two forms of life, of two ways of stylizing one's pleasure, and of the two philosophical discourses that accompany these choices" (EHS3, 218). Love accompanies discussions of pleasure (*aphrodisia*) in early Greek and Roman texts, and in part it is the relationship between the two that reveals the character of love. In texts such as Lucian's *Affairs of the Heart*, a paradox is revealed in men's love for boys. If the purest form of love – linked to philosophy, virtue, and the pursuit of truth – excludes the pleasures (*aphrodisia*), then it is incomplete. But if it includes the pleasures, then it is base rather than virtuous.

This paradox is not present in relationships between men and women, as Roman texts assert that marriage must include both Eros (love) and Aphrodite (pleasure). Plutarch argues that conjugal love between a man and a woman is the most perfect form of love; this leads to a new erotics. This new erotics privileges the marital relationship as the site of reciprocity, virginity, and complete union. If we think of the second and third volumes of Foucault's *History of Sexuality* as a genealogy of love (as well as a genealogy of desire), we can see the shift from a conception of love that centers on relationships between men and boys to the conception of love that privileges the marriage relationship and the family. However, the restriction of love to marriage in ancient Roman texts does not presage a Christian ethics of prohibition, because the ethical substance is different. For the ancient Greeks, "the ethical substance was acts linked to pleasure and desires in their unity," whereas for Christianity it is sexuality (EEW1, 263).

In later essays and interviews, Foucault turns from a historical exploration of love to a discussion of love in contemporary homosexual relations. In "Friendship as a Way of Life," he argues that people are disturbed not by sex between men but by love. Love goes against law, rule, and habit because of its "multiple intensities, variable colors, imperceptible movements and changing forms" (EEW1, 137). Foucault views love between men as opening up new possibilities for relating and for friendship. In this sense, love can be transformative (like pleasure) in a way that desire is not.

Margaret A. McLaren

SEE ALSO

Desire
Friendship
Homosexuality
Philosophy
Pleasure
Plato
Truth

SUGGESTED READING

Deleuze, Gilles. 1997. "Desire and Pleasure," in *Foucault and His Interlocuters*, ed. Arnold Davidson. Chicago: University of Chicago Press, pp. 183–192. Originally published as "Desir et Plaisir" in *Magazine litteraire* no. 325 (October 1994): 57–65.
Eribon, Didier. 2001. "Michel Foucault's Histories of Sexuality," *GLQ: A Journal of Lesbian and Gay Studies* 7, no. 1:31–86.

47

MADNESS

N THE JAPANESE version of his famous reply to Jacques Derrida's criticism of *History of Madness* (Derrida 1978, 31–63), Foucault wrote that

> Derrida thinks it is possible to recast the meaning of my "project" in the three pages dedicated to the analysis of a text recognized by the philosophical tradition [that is, Descartes'] ... [m]aking it useless to discuss 650 pages of a book, useless to analyze the historical material that is brought to light there ... if we can denounce a shortcoming in its fundamental relationship to philosophy. (ERD, 578)

Besides the specific content of this polemic, this passage is a good introduction to Foucault's approach to madness: here he is claiming to treat madness not as a philosophical object placed outside of time but as a result of complex historical processes. By studying madness, Foucault makes use of a set of disparate materials, from medical treatises to juridical documents, from literature to canonical philosophical texts, from paintings to asylum architecture, and he discusses in great detail many small facts and events. Madness is historical, but its history is a very special one. In the first Preface of *History of Madness*, in 1961, he said that to write

> the history of madness will therefore mean making a structural study of the historical ensemble – notions, institutions, judicial and police measures, scientific concepts – which hold captive a madness whose wild state can never be reconstituted; but in the absence of that inaccessible primitive purity, the structural study must go back to that decision that both bound and separated reason and madness; it must tend to discover the perpetual exchange, the obscure common root, the originary confrontation that gives meaning to the unity and the opposition of sense and senselessness. (EHM, xxxiii)

Writing the history of madness means writing the history of the separation between reason and the various forms taken by its opposite, unreason. And, at the beginning of this inquiry, a fundamental ambiguity is evident: madness is something more than a merely historical product, as its structure escapes, at least in part, the historical process of modern civilization and constitutes its tragic and negative side. Another source of interest can be found in Foucault's biography. During the 1950s, he had access to an internal point of observation on madness, since he studied and taught psychology and psychopathology, published several papers and a short introductory book on mental illness (FMMP), and worked in a laboratory of experimental psychology. For all of these reasons, madness plays a very important role in Foucault's thought. For him, it is one important field of reflection on the relations between philosophical and historical work, a field of reflection about the practical origins of objects of knowledge, and it is a constant source of reinterpretation and new elaborations of his own research. Both an object constituted within history and the focal point for a tragic and Nietzschean philosophy of history, madness will become in the 1970s one of the main places for the emergence of the concept of the power/knowledge apparatus.

There is a familiar description of the events that bring psychiatry into being as a positive science and as a legitimate therapeutic practice at the end of the eighteenth century. According to this account, at that time madness was finally recognized as mental illness, a scientific discourse was constituted in order to know it, and a set of therapeutic practices gained the status of the application of a solid theory. Also, medical science is said to have brought with it a new philanthropic and humanistic attitude toward the mad, as symbolized by Pinel's gesture – immortalized by Muller's and Fleury's nineteenth-century paintings – liberating the mad from chains at the Bicêtre hospital in 1793. With Pinel in France, Tuke in England, and Wagnitz and Reil in Germany, a style of positivistic thinking finally captured madness, described it as mental illness, and started to cure it. This is the standard account Foucault wants to destroy in his *History of Madness*, and for two main reasons. First, it presupposes that madness is a transhistorical object, whose identity would have finally been recognized by physicians as mental illness at the end of the eighteenth century. Mental illness is not the same thing as madness, or unreason, and we need to study what these things were in the centuries that preceded the constitution of a positive science of the mind. They were complex and global experiences rather than individuated and fixed objects. Second, the standard account of the history of psychiatry implies that a "liberation" of the mad occurred, thanks to a more precise knowledge of madness. But for Foucault we are "able to demonstrate the backdrop of social sensibility against which the medical consciousness of madness had begun to take shape" (EHM, 78–79). Madness is not immediately an object of knowledge and scientific observation but the result of a historical, social, ethical, and political experience of the separation between reason and unreason. In

Foucault's words: "Our scientific and medical knowledge of madness rests implicitly on the prior constitution of an ethical experience of Unreason" (EHM, 91). As Canguilhem brilliantly summarized, the "look [*regard*] of reason – cold, impartial, objective, or so it believes – is thus in fact secretly oriented by a distancing reaction.... In the history of civilization, fear has traced out the object of observation" (Canguilhem 1997, 24–25). Foucault wants to describe the historical experience of the separation between reason and unreason, which conditions the possibility of the constitution of scientific knowledge. This experience, both collective and individual, places unreason at a distance and only then individuates a family of well-shaped and recognizable illnesses. In order to do so, Foucault concentrates on the classical age, but he also discusses the immediately previous and the immediately following periods. It is a history of structural changes and differences in social sensibilities and perceptions.

Although during the Renaissance all European hospitals had places for madmen, this remained a small-scale phenomenon. In the Renaissance, madness was visible and possessed a language to express itself. In the paintings of Bosch and Bruegel, in the words of Brandt and Erasmus, in theatre and literature, and finally in the masterpieces of Shakespeare and Cervantes, madness was a daily experience, and a very important one. Madness was a cosmological force, linked to the dark powers of the world, and the madman was the speaker of this negative world of unreason. Even in philosophical and literary works, the mad demonstrates the madness of every man and leads readers and spectators to the discovery of the impossibility of a human knowledge of the world.

In the middle of the seventeenth century, a sudden change takes place in Europe. Epitomized by Louis XIV's royal decree of 1657, this is what Foucault calls the Great Confinement. The changing of the structure of social, political, and ethical experience of the mad led to a massive internment of fools in particular buildings, which were half prisons and half houses of correction. These buildings grouped these people together with other nonworking people. The world of confinement was now populated by madmen, victims of the infamous *lettres de cachet*, "the venereal, the debauched, the dissolute, blasphemers, homosexuals, alchemists and libertines" (EHM, 101). The separation of the mad from the society of reason had nothing to do with medicine, which during the classical age dealt only with abstract classifications, trying to mold itself according to the taxonomies of natural history. The models of the German *Zuchthäuser*, the English Workhouse, and the French *Hôpital Général*, institutions that aimed not at healing the insane but at excluding them, spread everywhere in Europe. But this exclusion also had some positive effects: it created a new social space of perception where the mad are reduced to silence, deprived of their own language; the mad of the classical age end up in a synthesis between an individual excluded and imprisoned by the law and a socially guilty human being. Secret kinships between the mad and all kinds of social, moral, political, and sexual deviants percolated, and these will become the object of the positive style of thinking about madness of the nineteenth century.

By the mid-eighteenth century, the uniform experience of unreason starts to lose its unity and self-evidence. A new structural transformation takes place owing to changes in the political and economical practices of government and assistance to the poor, political denunciations of the system's arbitrary nature, and the lamentations of the other inmates, who started to complain that they had to be confined with the fools. The great enlightened reformers of the Revolution will find only the mad in the confinement houses, which are the product of 150 years of separation and internment. At this point, the hospital becomes the asylum, a place of healing in itself, a huge therapeutic device, but once again medical knowledge has nothing to do with this space. It is the structural transformation of the experience of madness and of the internment that results in the asylum being a place of healing and scientific observation, not the other way around. The "liberation" of the mad from physical constraints coincides with a new regime of moralization guided by the family order and religion (Tuke at Bethlem), as well as the building of a detailed system of judgments, punishments, and moral gratifications within the asylum (Pinel at Bicêtre and the Salpêtrière). Moreover, a renewal of the meaning of older means of treatment, a separation between "the physical" and "the moral," begins to emerge. For example, whereas in the classical age cold showers were thought to treat at the same time the body and the soul, and their relations, now they are explicitly used to punish, to obtain confessions and recognition of one's own fault – in other words, they are addressed to "the moral." In a highly controversial passage of his historical account (for the most detailed critique, see Gauchet and Swain 1980), the famous "moral treatment" is presented by Foucault as nothing more than a means for a more subtle control of the behavior of the mentally ill, and is in no way a therapeutic practice that could be deduced from a coherent system of knowledge. In Foucault's words, "The asylum of the positivist age, which Pinel is credited with having founded, is not a free domain of observation, diagnosis and therapeutics: it is a judicial space where people are accused, judged, and sentenced, from which they can only be freed by a translation of this judicial process into the depths of psychology, i.e. through repentance" (EHM, 503).

The structure of the experience of the asylum is shaped by the contrast between the madman's silence and the physician's gaze, the acts of recognition of their own madness that mad people necessarily had to perform, and the formation of the patient/ physician couple as the main character of the asylum. In this way, madness becomes the object of an emerging anthropology. Moreover, whereas in the classical age madness affected both the mind and the body in their unity, a new space now became open: that of the separation between the psychological and the organic, the spiritual and the biological, that characterizes mental medicine up to our day. Nineteenth-century psychiatry is built on this anthropological turn that transformed madness into mental illness and slowly organized itself around the notions of the ill will and the instincts and less and less around that of an intellectual error, as Locke and the *idéologues* of the eighteenth century would have it (ECF-AB, 156–160). In the 1970s, Foucault will be more precise about the disciplinary constitution of human subjectivity and of the psyche itself through disciplinary techniques, but in order to do that he had to question some of the ideas he used to write *The History of Madness*.

Between the details and the intricacies of Foucault's refined historical narrative, a tragic philosophy of madness is present in *The History of Madness*. As is clear from the 1961 preface, madness is for Foucault a sort of Kantian *noumenon*: we cannot know it in its "primitive purity," but nonetheless its presence silently guides the history we are writing. At the same time, madness has a kind of permanent Nietszchean and tragic structure. There is a tension between a tragic and cosmic conscience of madness on the one hand and a critical, discursive, and anthropological one on the other. The separation between reason and unreason takes place in history, but at the same time it is a point of origin of our history. Only after the separation between reason and madness took place did we become able to recognize and manage that difference. Before that separation, reason and unreason, tragedy and critique, were bound together. Moreover, even if his book is the story of the triumph of reason, this silent background of unreason possesses a strange continuity and places itself in a "vertical dimension" (EHM, 67) with respect to history. It runs underneath history, ready to reemerge where positive science seems to triumph. In our world of science, unreason finds its way in the words and images of Nietzsche, Artaud, Roussel, Van Gogh, and Goya. Even if reduced to silence by scientific discourse, madness can find its own language, unintelligible to the language of reason. The opposition between madness and mental illness is to be understood as the opposition between a discourse grounded in the long historical process of internment and the essential language of unreason. Foucault states: "What is called 'mental illness' is simply *alienated madness*, alienated in the psychology it has itself made possible" (EMIP, 76). The ambiguity of Freud's role in Foucault's writings of the 1960s is to be placed here: Freud carried on the discourse that reason utters *on* madness and, at the same time, found a place for its original language. This is also one of the main reasons why Foucault was very interested in literature during the 1960s, because he found a singular affinity between literature and madness in what he used to call the "absence of work," where "work" must be understood as the work of reason, history, and the positive consciousness of our civilization. In his words, "Madness neither manifests nor narrates the birth of a work … ; it outlines an empty form from where this work comes … ; this is the blind spot of the possibility of each to become the other…. [I]t is also the place from where the language of literature comes" (EAW, 548). Foucault himself wanted to find a new language in order to capture that silence and to write the history of the experience of madness, not of psychiatry, medicine, or other discourses *about* it. As he wrote in the 1961 preface, he wanted to write "the archaeology of that silence" (EHM, xxviii), but "once Foucault's idea of archaeology had matured, it appears that an archaeology can only be of what is said" (Hacking 2006, xii).

The editorial story of the reeditions of *History of Madness* is eloquent. In the 1972 edition, the first preface was eliminated and the word "Unreason" – capitalized, which is unusual for French books – canceled from the title (from the 1961 *Folie et Déraison. Histoire de la folie à l'âge classique* to the simple *Histoire de la folie à l'âge classique*). Starting from the end of the 1960s, Foucault began to explicitly criticize some of the conceptual tools he made use of in *History of Madness*. In 1969, he wrote that the concept of experience he used was too vague, and for that reason he left room for a subject, even if collective, of history, a subject that he wants now to completely dissolve: "Generally speaking, *Madness and Civilization* [that is, *History of Madness*] accorded far too great a place, and a very enigmatic one too, to what I would call an 'experience,' thus showing to what extent one was still close to admitting an anonymous and general subject of history" (EAK, 16, translation modified). Concepts like "repression," "alienation," and "essence" – all unproblematically employed in *History of Madness* – were also eventually criticized and abandoned. Even more radically, Foucault strongly argued against any kind of exteriority, and a passage such as the following seems implicitly meant to contrast the tragic tendency of *History of Madness*:

> It is an illusion to believe that madness … speaks to us on the basis of an absolute exteriority. Nothing is more interior to our society, nothing is more interior to the effects of its power than the unhappiness of a madman…. We place the "mad" in the outside that is creativity or monstrosity. And yet, they are taken into the network; they are formed and function in the apparatuses of power. (FDE2a, 77)

Parallel to this demystification of the madman, who is neither a hero nor a mere victim but a simple vector in the mechanism of power/knowledge, Foucault will lose interest in writing about literature after the 1960s. Thanks to the notion of a power/knowledge apparatus, Foucault became able to recognize that every human phenomenon is radically historical and that outside of a specific apparatus there are only other specific apparatuses. The fundamental gap between medical knowledge and the practical treatment of madness that *History of Madness* identified as a central feature of the classical age and interpreted within the global framework of the internment of unreason will be filled, in the 1970s, by specific analysis of power relations and power/knowledge apparatuses. If treatment is separated from scientific knowledge, this is because the madman is primarily a target of power relations and not because he is the repressed voice of an essential and tragic force called unreason.

The first lecture of Foucault's 1973–1974 course on psychiatric power is more explicit, and here he individuates four points of distance from his previous work on madness: (1) Madness is not to be approached from the point of view of a history of representations or perceptions but from the point of view of the history of a power apparatus, considered "as a productive instance of discursive practices." (2) It is wrong to say that madness has been the object of violence, because violence is never a wild force but always inserted in strategic and regulated mechanisms of power/knowledge. (3) The notion of an institution is to be abandoned in favor of that of power relations and asymmetries. Whereas the former implies a crystallized equilibrium of power between already constituted subjects – the patient and the physician – the latter terms provide access to the concrete scenes of struggle that take place between doctors and patients and shape their roles and identities. (4) The notion of family is completely useless to make a historical analysis of madness, so far as it appears only with psychoanalysis, as nothing more than a late product of a complicated and long history (ECF-PP, 12–16).

The figure of Freud is again emblematic of this reformulation. Whereas in *History of Madness* Freud is said to have taken up again the dialogue between reason and unreason that positivism reduced to a monologue of reason, in the 1970s Freud and psychoanalysis are seen from the viewpoint of power/knowledge apparatuses, be it as an apparatus that captures the discourse of hysterics after it resisted Charcot's neurology (ECF-PP, 321–323) or an apparatus of sexuality that works within the normalization of society (EHS1, 130). This shift in Foucault's thought about madness does not invalidate his previous historical analyses of *History of Madness*, but it places them in a different frame. The historicity of madness eventually took over, at the expense of the tragic and Nietzschean interpretation of it. In the 1970s, madness and mental illness will lose their unity in Foucault's discourse, which now focuses on very specific figures of abnormality: the "dangerous individual," the hysterical woman, the pervert, the monomaniac, certain forms of the delinquent. Madness is no longer an "overall structure" (EMIP, 76) of human experience but a fragmented object of knowledge and power, to be placed within the historical analysis of the process of government of human beings.

Paolo Savoia

SEE ALSO

Abnormal
Human Sciences
Language

Literature
Psychiatry
Sigmund Freud
Friedrich Nietzsche
William Shakespeare

SUGGESTED READING

Artières, Philippe, Jean-François Bert, and Luca Paltrinieri, eds. 2011. *Histoire de la folie de Michel Foucault, Regards critiques – 50 ans*. Caen: PUC-IMEC.
Roudinesco, Elizabeth, ed. 1992. *Penser la folie: Essais sur Michel Foucault*. Paris: Galilée.
Still, Arthur, and Irving Velody, eds. 1992. *Rewriting the History of Madness: Studies in Foucault's Histoire de la folie*. London: Routledge.

48

MAN

ALONG WITH THE submission of his Doctorat d'État, *Folie et déraison. Histoire de la folie à l'âge classique* to Georges Canguilhem and the Sorbonne in 1961, Foucault also submitted his complimentary thesis, a French translation of *Kant's Anthropologie in pragmatischer Hinsicht* (1833) accompanied by a hundred-page "Introduction à l'Anthropologie de Kant." Although much of this Introduction recounts the history of the construction of Kant's text, a clear thesis on the importance of this text emerges, namely that Kant's *Anthropologie* situates "man" – der Mensch – at the center of philosophical reflection. And insofar as Foucault, like many others, sees Kant's Copernican Revolution effectively setting the new ground rules for all subsequent philosophical discourse (see, e.g., EIKA, 106) – which is to say that Foucault agrees that all philosophy after Kant is, in the strong sense, post-Kantian – it is not at all surprising to find that "man" appears as the central figure in the work that announces Foucault as a major philosophical voice: *The Order of Things*. Subtitled *An Archaeology of the Human Sciences*, Man – which from here on I will capitalize insofar as a part of my thesis is that "Man" functions as a proper name for Foucault – emerges as the central protagonist within the *episteme* of modernity, an *episteme* whose conditions of emergence form the basis of Foucault's analysis in *The Order of Things*.

"Man is only a recent invention, a figure not yet two centuries old," Foucault announces near the end of the Preface (EOT, xxiii; see also 308, 386–387). To all but the most careless of readers – of which, unfortunately, Foucault has had far too many – what should be clear is that Man is not simply a name for human beings, members of the species *Homo sapiens*. Instead, Man is a conceptual figure that emerges at the beginning of the nineteenth century as the central figure in the epistemic shift from the classical to the modern age. Although *The Order of Things* charts this epistemic shift in minute detail, the basic outline of this shift is relatively easy to characterize. The classical age (roughly the seventeenth and eighteenth centuries) was the age of representation: what *is* can be represented in thought, and knowledge is simply the representation of reality in the form of ideas. The relationship between reality and its representation in thought – or in language – is simple and straightforward. When one proceeds carefully and avoids error (think of Descartes' understanding of error in terms of the will getting in the way of the proper functioning of reason), reality will dictate itself to the attentive mind and will allow itself to be represented as it is in itself. Its order will be self-evident, and the task of the scientist or the philosopher is simply to lay out the appropriate grid or table (think of Linnaeus) that will accurately represent relations of identity and difference.

This model of the classical age – the age of rationalism and empiricism, the age of the rise of modern science – is not unfamiliar. But Foucault adds something to the model by noting a certain absence:

> In Classical thought, the personage for whom the representation exists, and who represents himself within it, recognizing himself therein as an image or reflection, he who ties together all the interlacing threads of the "representation in the form of a picture or table" – he is never to be found in that table himself. Before the end of the eighteenth century, *man* did not exist. (EOT, 308, Foucault's italics)

Man does not appear until the classical *episteme* begins to break down, which is to say Man appears with the emergence of a new *episteme* that arises after representation has become problematic. This, according to Foucault, was what Kant recognized in his *Logic* when he referred the "traditional trilogy of questions"– "What can I know?" "What must I do?" "What am I permitted to hope?" – to a fourth "ultimate one": "*Was ist der Mensch?*" ("What is Man?") (EOT, 341). Man, in other words, has now entered the table of knowledge; Man is a part of the grid insofar as "the identities of representation have ceased to express the order of beings completely and openly" (EOT, 303) but express, instead, how those beings are presented to Man's *experience* (cf. EOT, 341). This, for Foucault, is the inevitable consequence of Kant's Copernican Revolution. When Kant outlined the transcendental conditions of experience, he showed that Man inevitably intervened between reality and the representation of that reality as knowledge. Man thus puts a halt to the increasingly disorganized representations of the classical *episteme* and in so doing heralded the birth of the modern *episteme*, in which "anthropology as an analytic of man ... became necessary at the moment when representation lost the power to determine, on its own and in a single movement, the interplay of its syntheses and analyses" (EOT, 340).

Just what is this figure Man, whose analysis stands at the foundation of the modern *episteme*? Foucault provides his answer in terms of "four constituent segments" (EOT, 337), each of which situates Man between two conflicting poles that form the basis of *The Order of Things*' ninth chapter, "Man and His Doubles": the analytic of finitude, the transcendental and the empirical, the cogito and the unthought, and the retreat and return of the origin:

    i. Man's finitude is, paradoxically, endless. It is infinite in the sense that it characterizes every aspect of his analysis: his body, which is limited; his language, which exceeds his ability to master; his labor, which is never sufficient. According to Foucault, "At the foundation of all the empirical positivities, of everything that can indicate itself as a concrete limitation of man's existence, we discover a finitude – which ... is expressed not as a determination imposed upon man from outside ..., but as a fundamental finitude which rests on nothing but its own existence as fact" (EOT, 315). This is not to say that finitude did not exist in the classical *episteme*; of course it did. But there, finitude was understood in terms of its other, the infinite. At the beginning of the nineteenth century, on the other hand, finitude is discovered at the foundation of the empirical contents given to thought, rendering finite all acts of knowing and every concrete form of Man's existence. Man, Foucault concludes, "is possible only as a figuration of finitude" (EOT, 318).

    ii. Within the analytic of finitude, Man appears situated between the empirical and the transcendental, "a strange empirico-transcendental doublet" (EOT, 318). What this means is that with the beginning of the nineteenth century, all inquiry came to be understood as inquiry into the empirical contents given to experience, with the further understanding that what is given to experience is itself a function of the transcendental conditions that make experience possible. And what this means, of course, as Kant understood so well, is that all inquiry within the modern *episteme* would, at bottom, be inquiry into the question "What is Man?"

    iii. From this follows directly the double of the cogito and the unthought: if Man "is that paradoxical figure in which the empirical contents of knowledge necessarily release, of themselves, the conditions that have made them possible, then man cannot posit himself in the immediate and sovereign transparency of the *cogito*" (EOT, 322). The modern cogito is not Descartes' cogito, because the modern "I think" cannot think the conditions that make its thought possible. At the archaeological level, the unthought is not something that befalls Man; it is Man's "Other," his twin, born not *of* him or *in* him but *alongside* him (EOT, 325).

    iv. The final constituent segment of Man is his relation to the origin. Whereas in the classical age the possibility of representation was predicated on the availability of the origin as a site to which one could return, the modern *episteme* can no longer conceive of such an origin. Instead, the origin has been historicized, which is to say that, in every approach to the origin, what Man discovers is that this origin has always already begun. In this sense, Man finds that in his attempt to return to the origin, that origin is always retreating further into the past.

Having displayed the four constituent segments out of which Man has emerged, we can now see how Foucault answers Kant's question "What is Man?" Man is that figure who "resides in the 'and' of retreat *and* return, of thought *and* unthought, of the empirical *and* the transcendental, of what belongs to the order of positivity *and* what belongs to the order of foundations" (EOT, 340). This figure did not exist before the beginning of the nineteenth century; rather, Man emerged at the birth of modernity, his being simply "that historical *a priori* which, since the nineteenth century, has served as an almost self-evident ground for our thought" (EOT, 344). Foucault's "archaeology of the human sciences" reveals that "anthropology as an analytic of man has certainly played a constituent role in modern thought" (EOT, 340).

But of course Foucault's story in *The Order of Things* does not end here, for he suggests we are perhaps witnessing the birth of a new *episteme*, one whose earliest indications he locates in Nietzsche:

> Perhaps we should see the first attempt at this uprooting of Anthropology – to which, no doubt, contemporary thought is dedicated – in the Nietzschean experience: by means of a philological critique, by means of a certain form of biologism, Nietzsche rediscovered the point at which man and God belong to one another, at which the death of the second is synonymous with the disappearance of the first, and at which the promise of the superman signifies first and foremost the imminence of the death of man. (EOT, 342)

Although Man has been privileged in the discourse of the human sciences since the earliest years of the nineteenth century, Foucault locates the beginning of this end of Man in Nietzsche's doctrines of the *Übermensch* and eternal return, as we see clearly in Foucault's final reference to Nietzsche in *The Order of Things*, where he couples Nietzsche's death of God with the death of man:

> Rather than the death of God – or, rather, in the wake of that death and in profound correlation with it – what Nietzsche's thought heralds is the end of his murderer; it is the explosion of man's face in laughter, and the return of masks; it is the scattering of the profound stream of time by which he felt himself carried along and whose pressure he suspected in the very being of things; it is the identity of the Return of the Same with the absolute dispersion of man. (EOT, 385)

Nietzsche's waking us from Kant's anthropological slumber, which recalls the conclusion of Foucault's introduction to Kant's *Anthropologie*, is tied to his broader view of Nietzsche in *The Order of Things* as the precursor of the *episteme* of the twentieth century, the *episteme* that erupted with the question of language as "an enigmatic multiplicity that must be mastered" (EOT, 305).

It is important to recognize that Foucault's desire to deflate Man as epistemically and discursively privileged was never conjoined with an attempt to eliminate the subject entirely. Instead, Foucault seeks to analyze the subject as a variable and complex function of discourse and power, which, he writes, means not to ask, as an existential phenomenologist might, "How can a free subject penetrate the substance of things and give it meaning?" but to ask instead: "How, under what conditions and in what forms can something like a subject appear in the order of discourse? What place can it occupy in each type of discourse, what functions can it assume, and by obeying what rules?" (EEW2, 221). What this means, and what has been largely misunderstood by many of Foucault's critics, is that his "anti-humanism" was not a rejection of the human per se; it was instead an assault on the philosophically modern idea that sought to place Man in a position of epistemic, metaphysical, and moral privilege that earlier thought had set aside for God. It was also an assault on the phenomenological transhistorical subject who was thought to have escaped the epistemic constraints of the world through acts of phenomenologically reduced reflection. What must be kept in mind whenever one reads Foucault, and especially when he is discussing Man or the subject, is that it is a fundamental axiom in Foucault's work that there is a "history of the subject" to be told (EEW2, 438), and Man is simply one moment in that history. Foucault's work is therefore less an antihumanism than an attempt to think of the human subject after the end of (modern) Man.

It is typical to restrict the discussion of Man to Foucault's earlier works, those associated with his archaeological period. Nevertheless, it is important to note that Foucault recalls this account of Man often in his works of the 1970s, and especially in his lectures at the Collège de France. For example, in the 1973–1974 lectures on "Psychiatric Power," he concludes the lecture of November 21, 1973, where he first introduces the notion of "disciplinary power," by linking disciplinary power with the construction of the "individual" and the emergence of the human sciences. There he defines discipline as "that technique of power by which the subject-function is exactly superimposed and fastened on the somatic singularity" (ECF-PP, 55). And it is "the function of the discourse of the human sciences" to conjoin this disciplinary individual with the juridical individual of the philosophers and legal theorists who is an "abstract individual, defined by individual rights" (ECF-PP, 57). Foucault concludes by noting that "the illusion and the reality of" "What I call Man, in the nineteenth and twentieth centuries, is nothing other than the kind of after-image of this oscillation between the juridical individual … and the disciplinary individual" (ECF-PP, 58).

Linking his reflections on discipline and the birth of the prison to his earlier reflections on Man and the birth of the human sciences is not restricted to the lectures, however. In fact, although it is common to periodize Foucault's work by situating *Discipline and Punish* as the central text in the genealogical period, thereby distinguishing it from his earlier archaeological works, Foucault takes pains in the opening chapter of *Discipline and Punish* to link it to his earlier reflections on Man and the emergence of the human sciences. His goal in *Discipline and Punish* is to move beyond a mere history of punishment by leading us to understand "in what way a specific mode of subjection [*assujettissement*] was able to give birth to man as an object of knowledge for a discourse with a 'scientific' status" (EDP, 24). This specific mode of subjection, tied to relations of disciplinary power and born out of methods of punishment, supervision, and constraint, will disclose the genealogy of the modern soul as "the element in which are articulated the effects of a certain type of power and the reference of a certain type of knowledge, the machinery by which the power relations give rise to a possible corpus of knowledge, and knowledge extends and reinforces the effects of this power" (EDP, 29). Whether understood as the psyche, personality, subjectivity, or consciousness, this "soul is the prison of the body," an "effect and instrument of a political anatomy" that inhabits the object that the human sciences seek to know – Man (EDP, 30). And Foucault returns to this point in the closing pages, after introducing the carceral system as the extension of the penitentiary technique "from the penal institution to the entire social body" (EDP, 298), noting that the panoptic functioning of this new power has given rise to the extension of the examination from specialized institutions (the school, the hospital) to the whole of society. By means of constant and omnipresent examination, the disciplinary power of the carceral system

> required the involvement of definite relations of knowledge in relations of power; it called for a technique of overlapping subjection [*assujettissement*] and objectification; it brought with it new procedures of individualization. The carceral network constituted one of the armatures of this power-knowledge that has made the human sciences historically possible. Knowable man (soul, individuality, consciousness, conduct, whatever it is called) is the object-effect of this analytical investment, of this domination-observation. (EDP, 305)

To mention one final example of Foucault's return to Man in the late 1970s, in his 1978–1979 lecture course "Society, Territory, Population," he relates the concept of "population" to his earlier work, noting that the epistemic rupture that is charted in *The Order of Things* also marks the introduction of the concept of "population" as the new object of the art of government. Population emerges "as the correlate of power and the object of knowledge" and, moreover, "man, as he is thought and defined by the so-called human sciences of the nineteenth century, and as he is reflected in nineteenth century humanism, is nothing other than a figure of population" (ECF-STP, 79).

Alan D. Schrift

SEE ALSO

Archaeology
Finitude
Human Sciences
Language
Nature
Phenomenology
Immanuel Kant
Friedrich Nietzsche

SUGGESTED READING

Canguilhem, Georges. 2005. "The Death of Man, or the Exhaustion of the Cogito?" trans. Catherine Porter, in *The Cambridge Companion to Foucault*, 2nd ed., ed. Gary Gutting. Cambridge: Cambridge University Press, pp. 74–94. Essay originally published in 1967.
Han, Béatrice. 2002. *Foucault's Critical Project: Between the Transcendental and the Historical*, trans. Edward Pile. Stanford, CA: Stanford University Press.

49

MARXISM

"MARXISM" NOW MEANS so many things that perhaps it only makes sense to speak of "Marxism *proper*" as that set of theories that develops and extends the understanding of modes of production, especially the capitalist mode of production, that Marx expounds in *Capital*. Foucault obviously does not fit under this heading, but we must say that he contributes to the idea of historical materialism understood in a broad sense. Indeed, if we define Marxism in this very proper sense, we must say that not only does Foucault not fit the Marxist label, neither does Sartre – and, surprisingly, and despite having coauthored a text called *Reading Capital*, it is at least arguable that Althusser does not fit under this heading either. Comparison with these figures lands Foucault more on the side of Marx. Despite Althusser's innovative reading of the mode of production in structural-synchronic terms, and despite Sartre's understanding of reification as seriality, both figures carry out their work on the terrain of philosophy. Meanwhile, if Foucault was not grounded or interested in political economy in quite the way that Marx was, both still preferred something closer to the social sciences than philosophy – or at least this is true of Foucault up to a point, and both could be described (again, up to a point) by Foucault's term "happy positivism."

This term became attached to Foucault because of a characterization Foucault gave to his own methodology in *The Archaeology of Knowledge*: "If, by substituting the analysis of rarity for the search for totalities, the description of relations of exteriority for the theme of transcendental foundation, the analysis of accumulations for the quest of origin, one is a positivist, then I am quite happy to be one" (EAK, 124). Although Foucault's positivism is unconventional, the core issue is opposition to an analysis of social phenomena that is filled out by subject-centered and/or teleological conceptions, anything tending toward theodicy. As Foucault understood things in the mid- and late 1950s, this opposition was a matter of rejecting the Marxism of the Communist Party of France (PCF) on the one side and Jean-Paul Sartre on the other. (In order to assess Foucault's relation to Marxism, we shall rely on the interview called "Interview with Michel Foucault" [EEW3, 239–297], in which Foucault at least tangentially discusses Marxism.) Sartre, it can be argued, was politically radical and philosophically innovative in his engagement with Marx and Marxism. For the most part, the PCF was neither radical nor innovative; despite the tremendous prestige earned by the Party through its role in the Resistance to the German occupation, from the end of World War II onward the PCF was fundamentally a conservative, "establishment" force. Foucault had joined the PCF for a couple of years in the period 1950–1952; this was the sort of thing done by young people simply "as a matter of course." The more important point, however, is that even as a member of the PCF, Foucault did not consider himself to be a Marxist. Instead, even then, Foucault was avowedly "a Nietzschean communist [which] was really untenable and even absurd" (EEW3, 249).

To encounter something more of Marx and Marxism in the postwar period in France, one had to get around the establishment version, which claimed to be "humanistic" but also not in the least radical. There was also a certain exhaustion of Marxism that any intellectual (if not necessarily all activists) would encounter in the vicinity of the PCF, associated in essence with Stalin. Foucault left the PCF specifically in the wake of the "doctor's plot" to assassinate Stalin – or, it could be said, in the wake of yet another attempt to screw his head around what was clearly "opposed to what one could believe" (EEW3, 249). Out of this kind of experience, some people set about projects of Marxist reconception and regrouping, whereas others pursued a radical current more Nietzschean in cast. Among the former group were not only Sartre but also Althusser – Foucault's teacher but also cothinker, who also interrogated humanism and the organizing role of the concept of the subject.

Whereas Althusser went back into Marx's masterpiece, *Capital*, Foucault drew inspiration from thinkers outside of the academy: Pierre Klossowski, Georges Bataille, and Maurice Blanchot (EEW3, 249). Significantly, Foucault's specific methodologies and investigations, in rejecting humanistic and teleological formulations of Marxism, had more in common with Althusser's reworking of "scientific Marxism" than with Sartre's more ethically motivated attempts to come to grips with the Stalin period and what is opposed to what one could believe. This is also to say that Foucault aimed to be a materialist, which meant rejecting what he saw as the Cartesian thread running through so much of French philosophy, and certainly through Sartre's work. As with Althusser, Foucault was impressed by the "epistemological break" proposed by Canguilhem, but Foucault arguably took this break further than Althusser did. Asked about the role played by "the problematic which revolved around the history of science" in his intellectual formation, Foucault responds by saying that

> Paradoxically, more or less the same as Nietzsche, Blanchot, and Bataille. One
> part was asking how far the history of a science can pose a challenge to its

rationality, indicate its limits, or show its linkage with external factors. What are the contingent effects that go into a science, given that it has a history and develops in a historically determined society? Other questions followed. Can there be a rational history of science? Can a principle of intelligibility be found that explains the different vicissitudes and also, in some cases, the irrational elements that creep into the history of the sciences? Broadly stated, these were the problems raised both in Marxism and in phenomenology. For me, though, the questions were raised in a slightly different way. It was here that reading Nietzsche was very important to me. It's not enough to do a history of rationality; one needs to do the history of truth itself.... Truth itself forms part of the history of discourse and is like an effect internal to a discourse or a practice. (EEW3, 253)

With his application of this methodology in *The History of Madness*, Foucault thought he would gain the attention of "those with highly developed political concerns," or at least "it would appeal to Marxists. And there was total silence" (EEW3, 259).

We might consider two reasons for this lack of interest in *The History of Madness*, at least from Marxists. These reasons have to be considered (again) against the background of not only the conservative orthodoxy of the PCF, and almost all of the Marxism-inspired Left, for that matter, but also against pervasive "economism." Economism is the reduction of the struggle for the transformation of the world to the most narrow forms of economic struggle, most often to trade-union demands that are fully within the terms of the wage contract. On the one hand, then, Marxists (of whatever sort) might wonder what Foucault has to do with the mode of production and the economic sphere; on the other hand, radicals (Marxist or otherwise) wondered what Foucault was doing that might be called liberatory – how was he contributing to an emancipatory politics? The common assumption that Foucault did not relate to economic categories is not borne out by either Foucault's actual investigations or by his own self-understanding. Speaking of *The History of Madness*, Foucault says that

I tried to see how a discourse claiming to be scientific, psychiatry, was formed out of historical situations. I had tried to do a history of psychiatry on the basis of the transformations in the modes of production which affected the population in such a way that problems of pauperization became prominent, but also differences between the various categories of the poor, the sick, and the mad. (EEW3, 259)

Keep in mind that Foucault's investigations were performed in a set of contexts (French, European, Western, global) in which the meaning of the terms "working class" and "proletariat" was being reexamined, and where others, such as Marcuse, were speaking of the "new social movements." Orthodox Marxists did not understand how Foucault's work related to class and class struggle as they understood it, even while many of these Marxists were themselves unable to see beyond the increasingly obvious limitations of their categories.

For those still thinking in Marxist terms, even while attempting to reformulate basic categories such as class, class struggle, division of labor, and the mode, forces, and relations of production, there remained the question of whether Foucault's expansion of the range of inquiry at the same time demonstrated much more deeply what any liberatory project was up against. Foucault cannot be faulted for his realism: showing what people are really up against is not the same thing as pessimism. There is, however, something about the way Foucault understood power, as all-encompassing and all-enveloping, as inseparable from any concept of truth or knowledge, as always co-implicated in any epistemological or scientific project, that seemed to encourage the pessimistic conclusion that people are simply "stuck," too stitched into the webs of power to find freedom as it is understood in the Enlightenment sense – a sense that, to all appearances, Marx inherits and extends. Consider the following seemingly dramatic conclusion that Foucault comes to concerning what many Marxists still consider a pivotal moment:

> Who would disagree now that May 68 involved a rebellion against a whole series of forms of power that were exerted with a special intensity on certain age groups in certain social milieus? For all these experiences, mine included, there emerged one word, similar to those written with invisible ink, ready to appear on the paper when the right reagent is applied – the word "power." (EEW3, 283–284)

Though not everyone will agree with this perspective, let us take it as a given that the "Events of May 1968" and their aftermath remain a crucial reference in any contemporary accounting of Marxism and (what Badiou calls) the "communist hypothesis"; how does Foucault's seemingly singular focus on power help with the further projects of an emancipatory politics?

It is very much worth noting that Foucault's discussion of May 1968 participates in the *Tiers Mondialism* that had spread in France largely as a result of the struggles against French colonialism in Vietnam and Algeria. Foucault compares the experiences of students in Paris and Tunis. Quite possibly the most remarkable passages in "Interview with Michel Foucault," and the ones that say the most about the actual meaning of Marx and Marxism for Foucault's work, are to be found in the pages on "May '68 in France," in which, again with a swerve away from Marxism as it existed in a French and Eurocentric frame, Foucault was most interested in talking about the students in Tunisia:

I remember those cold academic discussions on Marxism in which I had participated in France at the beginning of the sixties. In Tunisia, by contrast, everyone appealed to Marxism with a radical vehemence and intensity and with an impressive enthusiasm. For those young people, Marxism didn't just represent a better way of analyzing reality; at the same time, it was a kind of moral energy, a kind of existential act that was quite remarkable. I felt a wave of bitterness and disappointment when I thought of the gap that existed between the Tunisian students' way of being Marxist and what I knew about the way Marxism functioned in Europe (France, Poland, or the Soviet Union). That's what Tunisia was for me: I was compelled to join the political debate. It wasn't May '68 in France but March '68, in a country of the third world. (EEW3, 280)

Foucault was not in France during summer 1968, so his view of things was likely influenced by his not having seen the actual uprising at its most intense. However, he does press the comparison with Tunisia further and makes it into a point about the various attempts to revive Marxism in the aftermath of 1968:

When I returned to France in November or December 1968, I was surprised, astonished, and even disappointed.... There's no comparison between the barricades of the Latin Quarter and the real risk of getting, as in Tunisia, fifteen years of prison. People in France spoke of hyper-Marxism, of a proliferation of theories, of a splintering into small groups. It was exactly the opposite, the reverse, the contrary of what had intrigued me in Tunisia. (EEW3, 281)

Foucault goes on to speak of "the formation of small groups, ... the pulverization of Marxism into little bodies of doctrine that anathematized each other" (EEW3, 282) in the French scene, while in the other case he asks,

I wonder about the meaning of that enthusiasm for radical rebellion demonstrated by the students of Tunis. What was it that was everywhere being called into question? The way in which power was exercised – not just state power but the power exercised by other institutions and forms of constraint, a sort of abiding oppression in everyday life. What was hard to bear and was always put in question, what produced that type of malaise, and what had not been spoken of for twelve years, was power. And not only the power of the state but the power that's exercised throughout the social body, through extremely different channels, forms, and institutions. People no longer accepted being governed in the broad sense of government. (EEW3, 283)

Despite Foucault's explicit disappointment with the Latin Quarter barricades, and despite what Foucault said later about the "groupuscules" (the little sectarian groups in France), he continued to be politically engaged, as we see in his work for GIP (Prison Information Group). We see this again in his famous discussion with Gilles Deleuze on "Intellectuals and Power" and the idea of theoretical work providing a "tool kit for revolutionaries" (in ELCP, 205–217). Moreover, Foucault helped Sartre distribute the banned Maoist newspaper *La cause du people* in the streets, risking arrest. In North America, the book that brought Foucault to the attention of a wider audience was a collection of interviews and short essays published under the title *Power/Knowledge*, which leads off with "On Popular Justice: A Discussion with Maoists" (EPK, 1–36). It could of course be argued that these engagements had more to do with third worldism, an interest in marginal subjects, and Foucault's more specific intellectual agenda than with topics of concern within orthodox Marxism. Once again, however, we must see Foucault trying to forge an alternative to this orthodoxy, and that he found himself in a milieu with others inspired by the events of May, events and developments in the third world, and the rise of new social movements and new liberatory actors (in the fields of sexuality or in prisons). There was an exceedingly complex negotiation to be accomplished here involving the avoidance of simply falling back into a new "Marxist" orthodoxy on the one side and on the other side the betrayals of the "New Philosophers" (in the 1970s, Bernard-Henri Lévy and Alain Finkelkraut, for example). Whether Foucault was able to avoid these dialectically linked pitfalls really hinges on how helpful his intellectual project is for emancipatory politics – regardless of how we understand this project in relation to some conception of Marxism. In the quotation "People no longer accepted being governed in the broad sense of government," we saw an opening to the questions that would preoccupy Foucault in the last years of his life, which coalesce under the term "governmentality." It is perhaps within the idea of governmentality that we find an answer to the question of emancipatory politics in Foucault. Here Foucault addresses large macropolitical issues.

Bill Martin

SEE ALSO

> *Governmentality*
> *Philosophy*
> *Politics*
> *Power*
> *Louis Althusser*
> *Jean-Paul Sartre*

SUGGESTED READING

Afary, Janet, and Kevin B. Anderson. 2005. *Foucault and the Iranian Revolution: Gender and the Seductions of Islamism*. Chicago: University of Chicago Press.

Badiou, Alain. 2009. *Pocket Pantheon*, trans. David Macey. London: Verso.

Burchell, Graham, Colin Gordon, and Peter Miller, eds. 1991. *The Foucault Effect: Studies in Governmentality*. Chicago: University of Chicago Press.

Jameson, Fredric. 2009. *Valences of the Dialectic*. London: Verso.

May, Todd. 1994. *The Political Theory of Poststructuralist Anarchism*. University Park: Pennsylvania State University Press.

Nealon, Jeffrey T. 2007. *Foucault beyond Foucault: Power and Its Intensifications since 1984*. Stanford, CA: Stanford University Press.

Poster, Mark. 1984. *Foucault, Marxism, and History: Mode of Production versus Mode of Information*. Cambridge: Polity Press.

Smart, Barry. 1983. *Foucault, Marxism, and Critique*. London: Routledge.

50

MEDICINE

MEDICINE PLAYED A central role in Foucault's work from early essays on the history of psychology to his works on the history of sexuality. In an important essay here, "Crisis of Medicine or Crisis of Anti-medicine?" Foucault finds that medicine "is not a pure science, but part of an economic system and of a system of power" (ECM, 19). While highlighting its role in technologies of power and its place in a political economy, Foucault does not neglect its scientific aspect. Rather, this aspect of medicine has made it central to the development of modern society since its truths are the realities on which modern economic and power systems work, enabling the exportation of medical practices to other domains, known as medicalization. Medical practice has determined the ontology of the human being and made knowledge itself into a most dangerous enterprise insofar as it now operates at the species level in an effective yet unpredictable manner. Moreover, it is medical practice that grasps man in his historicity. Modernity, therefore, is tied up with medical practice, making it central to Foucault's project of a historical ontology and the correlative discussions of the modifications that can be pursued on its basis.

Foucault identifies two contemporary myths about medicine: one a naive rationalism, the other a naive antirationalism. The former finds that modern European medicine is thoroughly clinical; that is, defined by the agreement between doctor and patient to listen attentively and speak the truth. According to Sournia, out of this intimate clinical union arises a universal medical science, a rationality that knows no national borders (Sournia 1961). Yet this approach, which looks to a founding contract, is based on an acephalic phenomenology because it treats experience as something unstructured by concepts, as a brute reality accessible to an attentive clinical gaze (EBC, xv). Moreover, Sournia's approach normalizes medical practice by erecting a universal standard against which all particular forms of medicine are implicitly measured and judged. Against this myth, Foucault argues that modern medicine is a social medicine that deploys a scientific leveling of the distinction between normal and pathological in order to treat individual illnesses. Illich's critique of modern medicine in the name of a return to premodern conceptions and practices (Illich 1976) exemplifies the other contemporary myth (ECM, 8), since this antimedicine has already been shaped by modern medical activity. This critique gets caught in the labyrinth of modern medicine because it does not realize that its own dream of collective health and hygiene is historically conditioned by it. For Foucault, the dream of a return to a space of spontaneous, collective health outside medicine is the dream of a medicalized consciousness. Although it might give voice to a collective disturbance about the social role of medicine today, such an antimedicine does little to help reflect on possible actions.

Against these two myths, Foucault recognizes the pervasiveness of medicine in modern society and, instead of encouraging a revolt, responds with a historical examination in order to better grasp what might be done now. In this, he draws on the work of Georges Canguilhem, who reveals processes of normalization in social life brought about by a medicine with scientific pretensions. Positivist medicine brings a methodological presupposition to bear on any illness – namely, that illness is merely a pathological modification of normal functions, of norms that medical science can identify in the healthy being and deploy as standards for diagnosis and therapy in practice (Canguilhem 1991). For Canguilhem, the supposed norms of health are actually the fruits of scientific intervention and thus are norms established by a social practice of experimentation (Canguilhem 2008, 3–22). From the standpoint of the sick individual, by contrast, sickness itself is a normal state of being, since sickness is the state from which health is sought. Scientific medicine therefore normalizes, since it subjects individuals to foreign social norms and judges them according to these norms, not the vital norms and normativity of the living individual.

Foucault investigates medicine not by following Canguilhem's theory of the normativity of the individual but by elaborating his account of normalization by investigating the historical rationality of scientific medicine as this has been embedded in the normalizing projects of medicalization. Medicine has furthered such projects in two ways: (1) through authoritarian imposition on individuals and populations, and (2) by turning attention away from disease as a medical object to health as a social concern (ECM, 13). Combined, these have allowed for authoritarian medical treatment of the abnormal as pathological in an effort to keep society healthy. Modern medicine therefore has supported an open-ended process of medicalization; that is, the production of novel forms of life on the basis of the distinction between the normal and the abnormal. *Abnormal* explains how medical concepts are brought to bear in the fashioning of new juridical categories of abnormality as substitutes for the old category of the criminal. In this, the medical concepts of normality and abnormality allow a transformation in the courts such that the state is now able to seek to correct the behavior of individuals who, though not criminals, are socially abnormal (ECF-AB, 309). This last example is helpful, since it makes clear that this is not the result of a purely medical enterprise but a contested enterprise that takes its sense and meaning from the struggle in which it is engaged. It would therefore be a mistake to think that Foucault simply rejects medicine as merely normalizing or ignores it as irrelevant when founded on scientific truths. Rather, medical activity and processes of medicalization continue to define modern man and the conditions of action.

Advances made in contemporary research led Foucault to proclaim the importance of molecular biology and the coming genetic medicine for medical risk, awareness of which "dates from the moment when the positive effects of medicine were accompanied by various negative and harmful consequences" (ECM, 10). Although the eighteenth century saw the coming of a medicine that socialized disease, thereby transforming it, medical risk remained essentially confined to a very limited group until the twentieth century. But with the advent of molecular biology appear radically novel possibilities for intervention, since genetic modification affects all descendants of an individual. Life, in all its elements and facets, is opened to medical intervention, leaving us anxious about our ability to modify the very future and history of life itself (ECM, 11). Charles Darwin's work inserted history into life, which could no longer be understood apart from it, yet life and the living remained essentially external to questions of the human being. The new genetics, however, shows that human history now has an impact on life itself, and this makes medical sciences and practices dangerous in a way not before known. And among those who know, this provokes serious anxiety about the status of knowledge, since medical science might now produce effects that modify how life comes about. The new possibilities for medicine have direct effects on biohistory, defined as "the pressures through which the movements of life and the processes of history interfere with one another" (EHS1, 143). Unlike Weber, Foucault thinks that capitalism and modernity appear with the realization that species-life, human or otherwise, has entered the domain of knowledge and power (EHS1, 141–142). And scientific medicine is an integral part of a history in which Western societies have had to learn the meaning of this new status and the power over life implied therein.

Foucault's attention to the history of medicine should be read in connection with this, since it is modern medicine that inaugurates biohistorical understanding and reveals best who we are today and the questions that face us. In the medieval period, according to Foucault, medicine was properly clinical; that is, medical activity was undertaken in response to the demands of the individual, yet this period never saw any great advances in medical powers to heal the individual or produce knowledge of the illness experienced. Between 1720 and 1750, however, a series of changes in medical activity removed obstacles to effective practice and scientific knowledge. Four processes transformed the conditions within which medical therapy and knowledge were pursued: (1) the appearance of medical authorities; (2) the appearance of medical fields of intervention distinct from disease, such as hygiene and environment; (3) the introduction of the hospital as the site of collective medicalization; and (4) the introduction of mechanisms of medical administration, such as recordkeeping (ECM, 13). In the late eighteenth-century birth of the clinic, therefore, medicine moves from a properly clinical to a social model within the context of the nation, abandoning its focus on the individual, who constituted an obstacle to its very development as a science (EBC, 64–85). By looking at ill populations, as gathered together in the hospital, and examining the anatomy of those who died within a changed epistemological context, it became possible for medicine to increase its powers (EBC, 105). Thus hospitals became healing machines, to a certain extent, and ceased to be only places where one would go to die. All of this involved a medicalization that inserted the human body into the economy and made health an object of national concern, casting scientific medicine as an element in the life of the nation. As populations blossomed, medicine worked not only to heal the injured but to propose standards of hygiene in order to sustain and shape the laboring population through criteria of normality and abnormality. Since then, medicalization has continued unfettered, such that every domain of human life is amenable to medical techniques, making medicine diabolical since it cannot be escaped (ECM, 14).

The initial insertion of the living body into a social medicine was doubled in the twentieth century with a reinvestment of the body in normalizing systems of health as a commodity. Foucault writes, "Health becomes a consumer object, which can be produced by pharmaceutical laboratories, doctors, etc., and consumed by both potential and actual patients. As such, it has acquired economic and market value" (ECM, 16). An increase in health consumption, however, has led to neither an increase in health standards nor an equalization in the social consumption of medicine. What was envisioned as a plan to redistribute and equalize health care has not succeeded, even though based on an appeal to rights, since the equal right to health is caught in a mechanism that preserves inequality. Foucault links the pharmaceutical industry to this mechanism, arguing that it "is supported by the collective financing of health and illness through social security payments from funds paid by people required to insure their health" (ECM, 18). Doctors, by contrast, are in the awkward position of seeing their profession converted into a mechanism for pharmaceutical distribution from which knowledgeable patients choose. Such enlightened consumerism, even if supported by social financing, has prohibited an equalization of health care, since wealthier members of society alone seek the benefits of socially financed medicine, the poorer consigning themselves to working to support it. And even though the political economy of medicine is to blame for the failure to equalize health consumption or increase health, this is not a state of crisis but rather a state of affairs that has subsisted since the late eighteenth century. If the discourse of rights is incapable of overcoming the biopolitical problems of medicalization, contemporary medicine and antimedicine are also incapable of helping, because of their normalizing or normalized approach. Rather, thinks Foucault, "an examination of the history of medicine has a certain utility. It is a matter of acquiring a better knowledge … of the model for the historical development of medicine since the eighteenth century with a view to seeing how it is possible to change it" (ECM, 19). Knowledge of medicine's history will foster a critical approach to the sciences, practices, and technologies defining our actuality that begins to modify them through this very historical knowledge. Moreover, these histories are important for developing nations insofar as they may be able to avoid the problems the European nations experienced when becoming modern.

Samuel Talcott

SEE ALSO

Abnormal
Biohistory
Knowledge
Life
Man
Georges Canguilhem

SUGGESTED READING

Artières, Philippe, and Emmanuel da Silva, eds. 2001. *Michel Foucault et la médecine: Lectures et usages*. Paris: Éditions Kimé.
Canguilhem, Georges. 1991. *The Normal and the Pathological*. New York: Zone Books.
    1994. *A Vital Rationalist*. New York: Zone Books.
    2008. *Knowledge of Life*. New York: Fordham University Press.
Illich, Ivan. 1976. *Medical Nemesis: The Expropriation of Health*. New York: Pantheon.
Mol, Annemarie. 2008. *The Logic of Care*. New York: Routledge.
Sournia, Jean-Charles. 1961. *Logique et morale du diagnostic*. Paris: Gallimard.

51

MONSTER

FOUCAULT'S HYPOTHESIS CONCERNING the emergence of abnormality is certainly indebted to the views of his mentor, Georges Canguilhem, who once said, quoting Gabriel Tarde, "the normal type is the degree zero of the monstrosity" (Canguilhem 2008, 126). Foucault's analysis reflects Canguilhem's assertion that during the nineteenth century a whole system of knowledge (a sort of normative project [ECF-AB, 50]) structured around the polemical/political concept of norm (ibid.; Canguilhem 1991, 146) made possible the incorporation of deviant individuals. But more importantly, Foucault claims that the constitution of such a domain of analysis made possible a specific apparatus of intervention and transformation of abnormal individuals that was driven by a new form of power, "the power of normalization" (ECF-AB, 26, 42).

Three figures – the human monster, the individual to be corrected, and the onanist – "come together in the nineteenth century to give rise to the domain of abnormality" (ECF-AB, 55). Among those three figures, the monster is the most problematic one, "the fundamental figure around which bodies of power and domains of knowledge are disturbed and reorganized" (ECF-AB, 63). What are the bodies of knowledge that constitute this notion?

The monster is a legal notion that appears in the "juridico-biological domain" (ECF-AB, 56). It represents a double violation, "a breach of the law" both at the level of nature and at the level of society. First, the monster does not merely represent a deformity or a dysfunction of some living organism. Each period, says Foucault, from the Middle Ages to the eighteenth century, has privileged a form of monster. Although for the Middle Ages the monster was a mixture of two species (the bestial man), for the Renaissance it was a mixture of two individuals in one body (Siamese twins), and for the classical age a mixture of two sexes (hermaphrodites). Although the monster was seen as a transgression of natural limits (FDE1a, 659), it nonetheless carried within itself the ambiguity of a "natural form of the unnatural" (ECF-AB, 63,

56). Ultimately, as Foucault points out, "there is monstrosity only when confusion [in nature] comes up against … canon or religious law" (ECF-AB, 63). How is this possible?

Since the monster is a blurring of the limits, it cannot be classified. The confusion in nature introduces a second confusion into the canonical law. For example, should a monster be baptized? Canonical law cannot solve this problem, and thus the monster is a juridical enigma. The monster stands outside of the legal framework; it represents a moment of contradiction of the law, a failure of legal classification, and so it leaves the law with nothing to say (ECF-AB, 56). The monster symbolizes the undecidability of the law (ECF-AB, 64). For these reasons, "the monster is the limit, both the point at which law is overturned and the exception that is found only in extreme cases" (ECF-AB, 56). Thus, the human monster is a double transgression since it combines the impossible and the forbidden.

The nineteenth century, however, brings a new understanding of the monster, and for Foucault this fundamental shift can be observed in the treatment of two figures: the cannibal and the incestuous. They were previously the sign of a mixture of species (ECF-AB, 97) or sexes, and as such they were subject to the criminal law. However, these forms of monstrosity as mixture, these "forbidden consumptions" (ECF-AB, 98) or "alimentary and sexual prohibitions" (ECF-AB, 102), either slowly disappear (hermaphrodites: ECF-AB, 72) or crystallize into a new problem in criminal psychology (criminal monstrosity: ECF-AB, 111). This change resulted from a double shift. First, there was a shift in the type of explanation from pathological anatomy to penal psychiatry (outward vs. inward). Second was a shift in the economy of power to punish (ECF-AB, 75) from an immeasurable system of punishment intended to restore the sovereignty of power to a new measurable punitive structure where a crime was to be punished "at the level of interest that underpinned it" (ECF-AB, 114).

Instead of being condemned for the anatomical structure of their body, for their somatic abnormality, hermaphrodites would be charged for their "perverse sexual tastes" (e.g., the case of Herculine Barbin: FDE2a, 935). Thus emerges "the attribution of a monstrosity that is not juridico-natural but juridico-moral; a monstrosity of conduct rather than a monstrosity of nature" (ECF-AB, 73; Davidson 1991, 57–58). Monstrosity shifts from the domain of nature itself to the domain of conduct while continuing to be seen as a breach of the legal system, so it penetrates every small deviation (ECF-AB, 55) and renders them criminal. In this sense, the monster plays the role of a "magnifying model" since it becomes the very principle of intelligibility, the form of every small deviation or irregularity (ECF-AB, 56).

On the other hand, cases of criminal monstrosity (e.g., the case of Henriette Cornier: ECF-AB, 112) brought to light the fact that motiveless crimes created a blockage in the penal system. Since the penal system operated on a system of motives (*raisons*), in such cases the system could no longer judge and thus was obliged "to come to a halt and put questions to psychiatry" (ECF-AB, 117). The application of the law required two superposable systems of reasons. Not only should the motives for committing the criminal action be established (intelligibility of the act) but also the subject's rational motivation, since according to Article 64, if the criminal was in a state of dementia, no punishment could be applied (ECF-AB, 115).

As a consequence of two simultaneous codifications, psychiatry was institution-alized as a form of "hygiene of the social body" (ECF-AB, 118). First, madness was codified as illness, and as an effect of this codification, all sorts of disorders, errors, and small failures of conduct were captured within a system of the normal and the pathological. From this, public hygiene emerges as a specific form of medical knowl-edge. Second, madness, along with all sorts of deviations, was perceived as danger-ous. For that reason, psychiatry became not simply a system of knowledge of mental illness but more importantly "an absolutely necessary form of social precaution" against a certain number of dangers related to psychiatric disorders. So, the monster, the one present in the smallest deviations of conduct, comes to permeate the social body. At the same time, it is detected and codified as a social danger that has to be normalized (ECF-AB, 119–120).

Certainly, if "monstrosity is systematically suspected to be behind all criminal-ity," a new economy of power (procedures, analyses) is required. Its task is to "enable the effects of power to be increased, the cost of its exercise to be reduced, and its exercise integrated into the mechanism of production" (ECF-AB, 87). As a condi-tion for this power of normalization "to be exercised without gaps and penetrate the social body in its totality," an entire medical process inscribes the slightest irregular-ity into a system of correction and control of crimes.

For Foucault, the modern monster would take two main forms. The first is the political monster, the criminal who breaks the social contract, who "prefers his own interest to the laws governing the society" (ECF-AB, 92) and reverts to a state of nature. The second is the juridical monster, who abuses his own power; for example, a despot, a king, or a prince. These two figures are the two forms of the monster: "the monster from below" and "the monster from above" (ECF-AB, 101). On the one hand, the small thief, the brigand, represents a return to nature, to a state of nature where one's interest prevails over the common good. On the other hand, the despot represents the abuse of power. Foucault states: "In their very twinship, these two figures will haunt the problematic of abnormal individuality" (ibid.).

In short, the category of monster plays a key role in Foucault's genealogy of normality and abnormality. Foucault does not simply show how this category has evolved from a juridico-natural to a juridico-moral concept, but more significantly how this notion, along with the application of a certain norm of conduct, has perme-ated all behavior to such an extent that all individuals, in some degree, are deviants. We are all monsters; hence, *des anormaux*.

Nicolae Morar

SEE ALSO

Abnormal
Life
Madness
Nature

SUGGESTED READING

Canguilhem, Georges. 2008. *Knowledge of Life*, trans. Stefanos Geroulanos and Daniela Ginsburg. New York: Fordham University Press.
Davidson, Arnold. 1991. "The Horror of Monsters," in *The Boundaries of Humanity*, ed. James Sheehan and Morton Sosna. Berkeley: University of California Press, pp. 36–68.
Elden, Stuart. 2001. "The Constitution of the Normal: Monsters and Masturbation at the Collège de France," *Boundary 2*, 28, no. 1:91–105.
Foucault, Michel, et al. 1976. *Généalogie des équipements de normalisation*. Fontenay sous-Bois: CERFI.
Rai, Amit S. 2004. "Of Monsters – Biopower, Terrorism, and Excess in Genealogies of Monstrosity," *Cultural Studies* 18, no. 4:538–570.
Sharpe, Andrew. 2007. "Foucault's Monsters, the Abnormal Individual and the Challenge of English Law," *Journal of Historical Sociology* 20, no. 3:384–403.
    2010. *Foucault's Monsters and the Challenge of Law*. New York: Routledge.

52

MULTIPLICITY

THE NOTION OF multiplicity functions in several distinct ways in Foucault's corpus. Multiplicity is a central theoretical tool in Foucault's analyses of both power and knowledge and their concretization in practices and discourses. Conceptually opposed to unity, it indicates his intent to describe and investigate difference, divergence, and discontinuity and thus contest presuppositions of identity, unity, and continuity. More generally, it is a category of analysis that makes the constitutive operation of relations central to understanding how a given phenomenon or event arises in the manner in which it does. In a more specific and limited way, Foucault also places a certain value on multiplicity as a phenomenon of difference, finding the cultivation of multiplicity preferable to, and a mode of resistance to, the instantiation of unity, centralization, and totalization.

A multiplicity can be understood as a web of relations between elements. Singular points or events are linked in a complex system to compose a multiplicity. Thus, multiplicity not only signifies the undoing of the unity and the identity of a human subject, an object of knowledge, a discourse, a practice, and so on, but also, and more importantly, entails the discovery of the heterogeneous relations that condition, constitute, and give rise to these seemingly unified forms. Via multiplicity, difference and diversity are thought apart from opposition, negation, and dialectical synthesis and in terms of conjunction, intersection, and interaction. Rather than stemming from a framework for meaning that is externally imposed (in the form of unities of theme, style of enunciation, concept, or object), the coherence of a multiplicity derives from the ways in which the elements work together and thus is immanent to their operation: "[W]hen one speaks of a system of formation, one does not only mean the juxtaposition, coexistence, or interaction of heterogeneous elements …, but also the relation that is established between them … by discursive practice" (EAK, 72). Thus, in accord with thinking in terms of multiplicity, Foucault's archaeological method describes "systems of dispersion" and specifies the singular points that define them, "the regularities of a practice," in order to investigate the kinds of formative relations that exist between elements (EAK, 37).

Throughout his work, Foucault describes two general types of multiplicity, which enter into relation with one another: discursive and nondiscursive multiplicities are composed, respectively, of articulable elements (words) and visible elements (things), which together constitute "a multiplicity of relations between forces" (Deleuze 1988, 83). Words and things converge in relations of power and knowledge. Thus, multiplicity is integral to Foucault's conception of power, which functions only through multiplicities. Indeed, power is simply "the multiplicity of force relations immanent in the sphere in which they operate" (EHS1, 92). Because power operates throughout "that whole lower region" – is diffused throughout the social body – Foucault's attention focuses both on multiplicity as diversity and on the domestication of multiplicities, the harnessing of their forces, and the various "mechanisms that analyze distributions, gaps, series, combinations, and which use instruments that render visible, record, differentiate and compare: a physics of relational and multiple power" (EDP, 208). An emphasis on multiplicity enables such an account of relational power. Disciplinary power in particular takes multiplicity as its object. For example, the organizing principle of "the table has the function of treating multiplicity itself, distributing it and deriving from it as many effects as possible" (EDP, 149).

Foucault, however, makes a distinction between this kind of ordered multiplicity and "a nomadic and dispersed multiplicity" that remains untamed, not subject to the hierarchizing structure of disciplinary power (ELCP, 185). The disciplines therefore are "techniques for assuring the ordering of human multiplicities" and creating docile bodies and normalized subjects through such ordering (EDP, 218). Through diverse tactics and to serve particular ends, new ordered and calculated multiplicities are composed out of "the moving, confused, useless multitudes of bodies and forces" (EDP, 170). To function effectively in and through multiplicities, disciplinary power must operate with the least expenditure (of money, energy, etc.) possible, must seek to extend its power as much as possible, and achieve an increase in both utility and docility. To tame the forces and elements that compose an unordered multiplicity – those of a population, for instance – and thus accomplish these aims, disciplinary procedures must order a multiplicity through relations that render it useful and efficient, reduce the forces that make a multiplicity unmanageable or set it at odds with the desired outcome, and master the new forces and capacities that arise in the organized multiplicity, thwarting resistance in advance (EDP, 219). The multiplicity is organized, managed, and enhanced so that it, as a whole, has greater utility than its component parts even as the utility and efficiency of each component is maximized by being individualized.

Thus, because power operates in and through multiplicities, it is no longer a question of where power is but rather of how it functions. Since it is known "with reasonable certainty who exploits others, where the profit goes, between whose hands it passes and where it is reinvested," we must seek to analyze and exhibit how "power is exercised, and by which relays and through which often insignificant instances of hierarchy, control, surveillance, prohibition, and constraint" (FDE1a, 1181). Not unlike how disciplinary power operates directly on multiplicities, arranging them anew in order to maximize utility, multiplicity is a defining feature of neoliberal society. Given the generalization of the "enterprise" form, the individual is located "within the framework of a multiplicity of diverse enterprises connected up to and entangled with each other" and defines herself by her engagement with these enterprises (ECF-BBIO, 241). The individual is not merely situated within a larger multiplicity as a cog in a machine – like the soldier within the unit – but is individualized to an even greater extent as the agent-subject of a multiplicity of enterprises; the individual creates himself as a node within these multiplicities (ibid.). Neoliberal power relations are defined by "a multiplicity of points of view" and by "the non-totalizable multiplicity of economic subjects of interest" who conceive of themselves as operating within a network of power relations (ECF-BBIO, 282).

Yet, Foucault appears to find unique value in the untamed, "nomadic and dispersed" multiplicity. Insofar as it implies an affirmation of difference, and thus the possibility for creativity and resistance, the idea of multiplicity is more than just a compelling category for analysis of the intricacies of power relations. In particular, multiplicity is understood as a countermovement in relation to totalization and centralization. Although resistance is possible from within organized multiplicities – which are simultaneously totalizing and individualizing, hierarchical yet decentralized, differentiating yet homogenizing – nomadic multiplicity, which is composed of unformed forces, presents a greater resource. Whereas organized multiplicities operate with an orientation to a particular end (efficiency, utility, docility, etc.), are constructed in order to achieve this end, and thus can only enter into specified kinds of relations, nomadic multiplicities remain open to a diversity of relations and constituting myriad undetermined assemblages. Their potential for alteration is unrestrained by predetermined ends, patterns of relation, and organization.

Erinn Gilson

SEE ALSO

Difference
Event
Power
Gilles Deleuze

SUGGESTED READING

Deleuze, Gilles, and Félix Guattari. 1987. *A Thousand Plateaus: Capitalism and Schizophrenia*, trans. Brian Massumi. Minneapolis: University of Minnesota Press.

53

NATURE

IN A SOMEWHAT banal way, one can say that nature consists of what is produced independently of human action, what existed prior to humanity, and what will exist after humanity is gone. It would be what is independent from culture in which the object, the ideas, and the institutions created by humans participate. Nevertheless, these distinctions are in no way obvious, since a large part of the objects populating our environment are seminatural and semicultural, insofar as they are products of the ways humans transform nature. Moreover, ethnologists have shown that in non-European cultures the nature-culture distinction does not have the same sense and often does not exist as such. The distinction is entirely cultural. Nature can therefore appear as a universal only within our culture.

By defining itself as an "ethnology of our culture," Foucault's archaeology inspired Lévi-Strauss's idea of regrounding anthropology on the universal codes of human cultures (Lévi-Strauss 1963, 33–34). Thus archaeology wants to bring to light the grammatical structure of a symbolic system that exceeds the activity of a subject, a subjectless transcendental or an "objective a priori" (Canguilhem 1975, 362). Nevertheless, Foucault precisely contests the anthropological pretension of knowing *human nature* objectively. The idea of a human nature restored by the sciences is for Foucault nothing but a "pious wish" (EOT, 379). In its philosophical or scientific version, the anthropological project only reveals the weak point in the nature-culture distinction: the place of man, which is conceived at once as a natural being and as a product of culture.

From this point, two important consequences follow. First, Foucault considers the key to the nature-culture opposition to be the concept of *human nature*, and consequently that archaeology will have to detect all the different historical meanings of this concept, in particular, in the *human sciences*. Then, this attempt to open up the nature-culture opposition to a discussion will take on less the form of an ethnology of distant cultures than that of an archaeological history aiming at our system of beliefs, our conceptual configurations. It is obvious that the problem with which this archaeological history is concerned lies less in discovering whether a human nature exists than in understanding the meaning of the constant reference to this nature within the framework of philosophy, the human sciences, and in ethical and political practices (Judith Revel 2008, 95–97). In order to do this, we must precisely avoid presupposing the invariant of a "human nature," which would identify immediately with an origin or a "universal" (FDE2, 103).

Foucault's three books of the 1960s bear witness to this antinaturalism, which is at the same time an antimetaphysics. In *History of Madness*, Foucault shows how the concept of "human nature" has been mobilized within the framework of the birth of modern psychiatry. Reason has been progressively identified with the nature that is properly human, and in this way man is distinguished from animals. This identification is made by excluding the experience of an unreason that in the classical age was identified with animality. If this animality represented then a sort of counternature, an absolute danger of indifferentiation between man and animal "from the moment when philosophy became anthropology, and men decided to find their place the plentitude of the natural order, the animal world lost that power of negativity, and assumed the positive form of an evolution between the determinism of nature and the reason of man" (EHM, 151). Madness "is the unperceived side of order," but this order is at once Nature and reason. This is why the figure of the mad opens onto the question at once of the division of the reasonable and the unreasonable (or the "nature of reason") and the division of the rational and the irrational in nature (or the "reason of nature"). Medical knowledge of the nineteenth century then constitutes madness as a nature that is not human. Instead, it reveals to man his relation with animals and his seminatural and semicultural condition. Madness "is no longer an absolute perversion within counter-nature, but the invasion by a neighboring nature" (EHM, 435), with the mad being unable to recognize his nature, that of being a rational animal. This is why the cure, before converting the mad into a reasonable being, is organized around myths of the "three Natures": Nature as health, which can disappear; Nature as reason, which is latent; and Nature as truth, which presents itself by means of the correct use of reason. It is by the discovery that he is alienated from his truth that the madman will be able to restore Nature as reason and reestablish his Nature as health (EHM, 473).

In *The Birth of the Clinic*, illness takes over the ambiguous place of madness. In the eighteenth century, illness is discovered between "counter-nature" and "nature." Thanks to Bichat, illness is placed between life and death and thereby loses its characteristic of being counternature (EBC, 153–155). By means of the archaeology of the human sciences, what is at issue then is to show the paradox of a reason that affirms the freedom of man as a fact of nature while turning man into the target for an objectifying knowledge that subjugates man to the necessary laws of the cosmos. This paradox discovers its classical formulation in *The Order of Things*. In this book,

Foucault shows not only the historicity of human nature but also the specificity of the relation that this historicity maintains with physical and biological nature in modernity. In the classical *episteme*, nature is present as a collection of things that one can read by means of the play of analogies and correspondences. Words and things (the French title of *The Order of Things* is *Les mots et les choses*, meaning *Words and Things*) are interwoven, and nature itself is given to knowledge by means of naming, which explains the importance in the classical *episteme* of the "well-made language." However, the person speaking this language is absent from knowledge. Representation has no subject; it represents itself by means of the doubling reflection of the picture. The concept of human nature exists, but only insofar as it assures the connection between imagination and resemblances in the order of representation (EOT, 71). Human nature is nothing but a "fold of representation over itself"; it is somehow entangled with the nature of things. In the modern *episteme* in contrast, man is detached from the great continuum of nature by assuming a specific location: he is a being whose nature "would be to know nature and himself consequently as a natural being" (EOT, 310). Modern man no longer belongs to the same regime as the other natural beings since he is supposed to know an objective nature that is over and against him. The development of modern European science first produced the distinction between humanity as subjects of knowledge and agents of the transformation of things and animals and vegetables, which are objects of a knowledge that must reveal the system of the necessary causes of their interrelation. All of modern science will try to explicate the laws of this "objective" nature (Hadot 2004). But this schema is complicated by the Kantian redefinition of nature as a system of laws based on the categories of human understanding and by the appearance of anthropology, the specific knowledge of humanity, which appears as the subject and object of knowledge, this "strange empirico-transcendental doublet" (EOT, 318). Thus, modern philosophy will look for the key to all knowledge in an empirical knowledge of human nature, although this nature is itself only a particular configuration of modern knowledge. It is this confusion that Foucault denounces through the phrase "the anthropological slumber": "What Kant had ambiguously designated as 'natural' in that emergence [of the transcendental] had been forgotten as a fundamental form of the relationship to the object and resurrected as the 'nature' in human nature" (EIKA, 122).

In the works from the 1970s, Foucault pursues and radicalizes his historicization of the notion of "human nature." When he presented Foucault's candidacy for the Collège de France, Jules Vuillemin spoke of a history of systems of thought "without any human nature" (Eribon 1991, 218). In "Nietzsche, Genealogy, History," Foucault describes a model of history that "will leave nothing below the self": historical configurations replace the nature, the life and the body, for whom modern science describes the immutable biological and physiological laws. Genealogy "must expose a body totally imprinted by history and the process of history's destruction of the body" (EEW2, 376). In an analogous way, the genetics of populations shows that we must not look for "raw and definitive biological facts which, from the bottom of 'nature,' would impose themselves on history"; rather we must think of the "interference" between the movements of life and the process of history (FDE3, 97). The principle that Foucault reappropriated in his historical analysis of modern biopolitics is reasserted in the final pages of volume one of *The History of Sexuality*: "[W]hat is needed is to make [the body] visible through an analysis in which the biological and the historical are not consecutive to one another ..., but are bound together in an increasingly complex fashion in accordance with the development of the modern technologies of power that take life as their objective" (EHS1, 152).

Thus the question of human nature is henceforth problematized within the framework of a historical analysis of practical configurations in which it is presented at the same time as penetrable by a technology of power and as a support for and external limit of human action over its own life (since humans are living beings). In its dual version of being disciplinary and regulatory, biopower manifests this ambiguity of the discourse of human nature. The *norm*, introduced at once by the human sciences and the disciplinary apparatus, is a "mixture of legality and nature, prescription and constitution" (EDP, 304). In effect, the norm defines the way one belongs to a society by means of conformity to a *nature*: "The discourse of disciplines is about a rule: not a juridical rule derived from sovereignty, but a discourse about a natural rule, or in other words a norm" (ECF-SMD, 38). Nevertheless, the norm ascertains and prescribes a "natural" state of things: "[T]he norm is not at all defined as a natural law, but rather by the exacting and coercive role it can play in the domains in which it is applied. The norm, consequently, lays claim to power" (ECF-AB, 50). Therefore, the "natural" norm must be understood as a cultural construction that acquires its meaning only within a political technology, a technology directed at human "life" by establishing regularities of conduct imposed by disciplines as the truth of nature. The "human monster," "the natural form of counter-nature," incarnates the negative exception of this paradoxical political order for which human nature is both the model and the target. Excluded from the "authentic nature" of the man who enters into the social contract and is social, the human monster can be the object of a medical pathology (ECF-AB, 54–55). This intertwining of the juridical and the biological is the basis for the pathologization of criminal conduct. The juridico-penal knowledge of the infraction of the law is penetrated by a pathology of criminal conduct referring guilt to illness and illness to the disorder of the individual conduct. The "nature" of the dangerous individual (that is, a virtuality of criminal acts) becomes the true support of the crime and what allows one to decide the punishment for the act (EEW3, 187). The body of the "counter-nature" individual threatens society by provoking the degeneration of the entire species.

The construction of the concept of "human nature" is also analyzed within the framework of the birth of liberalism, understood as the technology of government that is directed at a population. From this viewpoint, liberalism itself is a certain kind of naturalism, for it must respect the "nature" of the objects being governed while intervening continually in them. If for the theoreticians of natural law nature designates immutable characteristics that the governors must absolutely respect, "nature" then becomes "something that runs under, through, and in the exercise of governmentality.... It is the other face of something whose face is visible, visible for the governors, in their own action" (ECF-BBIO, 16). To act politically means, for the first liberals, to recognize the intimate correlation of the "physical order" and the "moral order" in order to adapt human action to natural reality (ECF-STP, 47). A population, as a set of individuals living in a territory, is the image of this "penetrable naturalness" that must be managed, while respecting its laws and mechanisms, by concerted interventions on the milieu, the architecture, the food, the mores, and so forth. The "nature" of the population is "such that the sovereign must deploy reflected procedures of government within this nature, with the help of it, and with regard to it" (ECF-STP, 75). But here "nature" is not a sort of primitive, biological domain or a simple ideological product. It is constructed in the constant transition between the actions of the governors and those of the governed. Foucault shows finally that this "human nature" is less a "substrate," less an order that precedes human actions, than a form of relation between humans. It is the permanent correlate of an action through which they construct their political reality.

In the last two volumes of *The History of Sexuality*, Foucault underscores several times the importance of the concepts of "nature" and "counter-nature" in the definition of a moral code concerning the rules of sexual conduct and, more generally, the rules of a dietetics in Greek and Roman antiquity. Between the "moral code" and the development of a nonuniversalist ethics of individual conduct, the concept of "nature" plays a particular role for the philosopher, who, according to different schools, must either make his behavior conform to nature or must know nature in order to modify his behavior (EHS3, 35). Let us emphasize, however, that here the concepts of "nature," "counter-nature," and "human nature" do not have the same meaning as in modernity. More than evoking a biological necessity, the object of a "knowledge," they express the system of the permitted and the forbidden, the distinction between moderation and immoderation, or still the difference between man and woman (EHS2, 44, 159). Thus, "the opposition between the knowledge of things and knowledge of oneself can in no way be interpreted, in the Epicureans as well as in the Cynics, as the opposition between the knowledge of nature and the knowledge of the human being" (ECF-HOS, 243, translation modified). Knowledge does not concern the "self" insofar as it is the object of a true discourse. The knowledge of things as "truths of nature" must be coordinated with an "art of living" that allows the being of the subject to be modified. In the Epicureans, the knowledge of *physis* lets humans liberate themselves from worries and fears that paralyze their free existence. For the Stoics, the "vision that plunges into" the things of nature is first a spiritual exercise by which the philosopher relativizes the importance of wealth, pleasures, and glory, and thereby he grasps his place in a universe ruled by rational laws (ECF-HOS, 271–279). In contrast, the Cynics completely overturn the theme of natural existence by transforming it into the scandal of a life that is lived entirely in public: "[N]o human prescription may be accepted in the Cynic life if it does not conform exactly to what is found in nature and in nature alone" (ECF-COT, 263). The exaltation of the naturalness of "right life" results in the positive evaluation of animality. Animality is no longer the point of absolute differentiation in relation to the human. It becomes a model of behavior, a challenge to face perpetually, an exercise that must lead to the manifestation of the truth directly in one's own existence.

Does this reevaluation of the animality and of the "naturalness" of existence coincide with the reevaluation of a "nature-body"? Does it assure the overcoming of a dualism between a "hedonist vitalism" that, still in volume one of *The History of Sexuality*, is based on bodies and pleasures, and a "historicist constructivism" within which sexuality "would be entirely *constituted*" (Haber 2006)? In fact, Foucault does not seek to overcome the opposition between nature and history by adopting one term over and against the other. Rather, he tries to deconstruct the opposition historically by showing that it depends on cultural codes that have been historically formed. In Foucault, therefore, there is no "historicist" phase, then a "naturalist" phase. There is a permanent work of historicization showing the strategic functions of the concept of "nature" within several cultures.

It is in this sense that we can understand the 1971 debate that pits Noam Chomsky against Foucault (EFC, 133–198). According to Chomsky, the concept of "human nature" designates innate organizing principles in each human being, principles that determine his social and individual behavior. This "nature" can be redirected by an inventiveness and creativity that function by the same rules. The most important philosophical task then consists in reconstituting the connection between a concept of human nature that acknowledges the freedom and creativity of humanity and a humanitarian social theory. For Chomsky, the establishment of a solid concept of human nature could be the basis of a political action following a "true" notion of justice. In contrast, according to Foucault, "human nature" is not a scientific concept but an "epistemological indicator," an organizing concept that designates the space in which the discourses on man are lodged. Thus, Foucault does not think that the principle of regularities detected by the human sciences defines the mind or human nature. The notions of human nature, of the realization of the human essence, and of justice are created within our civilization, by our system of power/knowledge. It is impossible to ground a revolutionary political action on those notions, for they are formed in a politico-scientific complex and what is precisely at issue is to overcome that complex. The task for political struggle is not to turn humanity into an object of knowledge so that it becomes the subject of its own freedom (FDE1, 663). The struggle responds solely to the will to take power.

It is really in this political perspective that the notion of "human nature" must be entirely historicized and led back to the work of a culture. By taking into account the body, life, and death, Foucault sought precisely to discuss and destabilize the nature-culture and the nature-history oppositions established in our civilization.

Luca Paltrinieri

SEE ALSO

Abnormal
Human Sciences
Madness
Man
Structuralism
The Ancients (Stoics and Cynics)
Xavier Bichat
Immanuel Kant

SUGGESTED READING

Daston, Lorraine, and Francisco Vidal, eds. 2004. *The Moral Authority of Nature*. Chicago: University of Chicago Press.

54

NORMALIZATION

OUCAULT INTRODUCES AND develops the concept of normalization in a number of lectures at the Collège de France and elsewhere through the middle of the 1970s, but his most extensive published account of it occurs in Part III of *Surveiller et punir*, which appeared in 1975 and then in English translation as *Discipline and Punish: The Birth of the Prison* two years later. There he describes normalizing power as it emerged through the coalescence and refinement of myriad disciplinary practices that aimed to control and cultivate the capacities of individual human bodies.

One of Foucault's many provocative claims in that text is that normalizing power simply did not exist prior to the late eighteenth century. Once it did exist, however, it rapidly pervaded Western industrialized societies and enabled, among other things, the formation of the modern welfare state. By the time of his writing, normalizing power was ubiquitous and thus seemingly unremarkable in its operations, although it was largely ignored in political philosophy. Part of Foucault's task in *Discipline and Punish*, therefore, is to defamiliarize the practices and arrangements that make up normalizing power in order to bring it forward as an object for philosophical, social, and political analysis. He does this primarily by contrasting normalizing power with sovereign power (the more usual object of critique in most political theory), an approach he replicates to some extent in Part V of volume one of *The History of Sexuality* in 1976.

Discipline and Punish opens with a famous description of the execution of Damiens, who had attempted to assassinate the king of France in 1757 and was duly condemned to death. Damiens was not dispatched quickly, by firing squad or guillotine as later capital criminals would be; instead, his complex, hours-long execution was a major spectacle full of pageantry and symbolism, a grand display of the king's power in confrontation with a self-declared enemy. Immediately following this provocative account of public torture, Foucault gives us a timetable, Léon Faucher's list of rules for "the House of young prisoners in Paris" (EDP, 6), drafted in the 1830s. Foucault directs his readers' attention to the contrast in these two "penal styles" (EDP, 7). Whereas Damiens was vanquished, vastly and definitively overpowered by the sovereign he had attacked, Faucher's young prisoners were caught up and inserted into a system of tight control. Unlike Damiens, they were not eradicated; rather, their time, bodies, and conduct were carefully scheduled and regulated, and they were kept under constant surveillance so that the slightest deviation in protocol could be noticed and immediately corrected. This effort to "correct" involved the exercise of a power quite different from the prohibitions and extractions typical of a sovereign regime. It was less centralized, more pervasive, largely detached from any single authority figure, and intimately connected to a new experience of what Foucault calls "evolutive" time (EDP, 160), the temporality of living development.

Damiens came into direct conflict with a king. Faucher's young prisoners were absorbed into a disciplinary system that sought not only to oppose and neutralize them as threats but also to transform them into something that system deemed useful. The point of Damiens's elaborate execution was to make a stunning and awe-inspiring display of sovereign excess. Nothing could be further from the point a century later; punishment was to be efficient (only as expensive as necessary for effectiveness), and, where possible, it was to be productive (it was to add to the regime's capacity in some way so as to offset any necessary expenditure). By the end of the nineteenth century, Foucault tells us, the techniques of disciplinary efficiency had triumphed in penal practice and elsewhere, displacing the deductive techniques of sovereign power. And in the process – in the gradual coalescence of techniques and tactics into extensive strategies – disciplinary power had become normalizing power.

Just as it is important to distinguish disciplinary power from sovereign power, it is important to distinguish disciplinary power per se from normalizing disciplinary power. Disciplines are collections of techniques for acting on bodies not just to extract some "product" such as labor or gestures of fealty (as sovereign power seeks to do) but to change those bodies, to train them to do something they otherwise would not have done as efficiently or at all. Foucault's classic example (EDP, 163) is the training of soldiers to use rifles, which, unlike the muskets that preceded them, had to be loaded, rightly aimed, fired, and reloaded in the heat of the battle very quickly (because the enemy was also able to reload and fire very quickly). Hence, military discipline sought to instill a new capacity in soldiers. In this and similar capacity-cultivating endeavors, disciplines require repetitive exercise or drills, which, in order to bring about improvement in speed, aim, or any other skills an officer, teacher, or factory supervisor might want to develop in a soldier, pupil, or laborer, must be graduated, not simply repetitive, so that the body is challenged and moved to improve. The effect of graduated disciplinary exercises is to slowly change the "natural" behavior of bodies subjected to them, to create new habits or a "second nature." Such techniques had been used in monasteries and convents for hundreds of years before they found their way into secular institutions. But in the eighteenth century, with the invention of new weaponry and wealth-production technologies, new divisions of labor in industry, and the pressure of rapidly rising populations in schools, hospitals, and elsewhere, religious disciplinary techniques were adapted to solve secular management problems and to use resources more efficiently.

Normalization emerged when the refinement and spread of secular disciplinary technologies began to occasion development of new technologies of recordkeeping, techniques both for tracking disciplinary practices and for assessing their effectiveness. A century earlier, the science of statistics had made data analysis possible in unprecedented ways. Eighteenth-century institutional authorities and management theorists adopted statistical analysis, finding it to be a very useful tool for measuring the progress of their charges and comparing them to one another. In time, out of these various management practices and the kinds of knowledge they enabled and incorporated, analysts produced norms – that is, average or typical temporal trajectories for the acquisition of various skills or capacities in various populations of individuals. In other words, statistical analysis of disciplinary records made it possible to project a normal developmental course for virtually any given type of acquisition, to measure an individual's progress against this "norm," and, finally, to categorize some individuals as off course or deviant in relation to their cohort.

Normalizing disciplinary techniques are therefore disciplinary techniques that operate in accordance with such norms, measuring individuals and classifying them with regard to standards of normality. In some cases, normalizing disciplines also generate and deploy techniques for disciplining deviation to bend individuals' developmental trajectories back to a normal developmental path. But they need not do so. In fact, Foucault argues that normalizing regimes of power require the continued existence of a certain amount of abnormality or deviance both to give definite sense to norms in the first place and to justify continued imposition of discipline (that is, to support their maintenance and expansion).

In several important senses, moreover, normalizing disciplines actually create deviation. For example, in *Discipline and Punish*, Foucault argues that normalizing disciplines create the figure of the criminal or delinquent (as opposed to the lawbreaker) (EDP, 101). In his lecture courses of 1973–1974 (psychiatric power) and 1974–1975 (abnormal), he examines the ways in which normalizing regimes of power/knowledge continually produce a "residual" or "residue" (ECF-PP, 53–54), a set of individuals who cannot be assimilated into a given disciplinary system and thus for whom a new set of disciplinary mechanisms must be devised. Thus, for example, modern pedagogical techniques identified children who did not and seemingly could not learn in response to current teaching practices and within existing institutional frameworks. These became the "idiots" or the "retarded," pupils for whom new pedagogical techniques, new disciplinary structures and mechanisms, had to be invented (ECF-PP, 203–214). In this way, pedagogical normalization created the conditions for its own expansion.

In comparison with sovereign power and its technologies of deduction, normalizing disciplinary techniques are demonstratively efficacious in projects of organizing and managing people and of cultivating new resources for exploitation. As a result, they have proliferated. Such techniques, along with the normalizing conceptual frameworks and kinds of knowledge they produce, take hold not only in areas of society where earlier regimes of power had not penetrated but also in what were once strongholds of the older sovereign power such as the courts and penal system. In the process, what Foucault calls "the Psy function" (ECF-PP, 85), meaning the techniques and assumptions characteristic of psychiatry and related fields, increases tremendously in social authority and political and economic clout. But developmental thinking is not confined to psychology; it pervades all of the human or social sciences as well as biology, medicine, and even politics. People begin to think in terms of development, to understand themselves in terms of developmental categories and deviant identities, to understand the world in general as a series of temporally structured, normable occurrences. As a consequence, we see the emergence of a normalized society where everyone and almost everything (from economic trends to crop production) is understood as normal or deviant from some norm in some measurable degree.

Crucial to the spread of normalizing disciplines are close and constant surveillance techniques, for without careful observation of individuals, norms cannot be generated and deviations cannot be noted, classified, or corrected. Surveillance is costly in terms of time as well as material resources, however, so every effort must be made to generate techniques that are minimal in material cost without any compromise of epistemic productivity. In this connection, Foucault points to Jeremy Bentham's architectural design for a model prison, the Panopticon, as the embodiment of the general principle of normalizing (as opposed to sovereign) power (EDP, 208). The Panopticon was to consist of a central tower surrounded by a multistory circle of prison cells. Each cell was barred rather than walled on both its interior and exterior sides, although completely walled off from adjacent cells. This design allowed for natural illumination of cell occupants through the course of the day, so that a supervisor in the tower could monitor all prisoners' behavior at all times. The tower itself was to be afforded no such natural illumination. On the contrary, its windows were narrow, and the interior contained angled partitions to prevent backlighting of the tower's occupant. Thus the prisoners were rendered completely visible, whereas the supervisor was rendered completely invisible. In this architectural arrangement, prisoners might be watched constantly with but the smallest imaginable staff of prison officials. In fact, since prisoners could never be sure when they were or were not being watched, it was possible not to staff the tower at all at times without losing any punitive effect or social order; because prisoners would tend always to behave *as if* they were being watched, they would police themselves with no expenditure on the part of the regime. The Panopticon thus functioned as something like a surveillance machine, operating to influence the conduct of prisoners whether or not it actually had a human operator at any given moment. Bentham suggested that this model could be adapted for use in a variety of other settings, including schools, factories, and hospitals. Indeed, although Bentham's Panopticon itself was never actually built, similar designs have been used in the construction of some such institutions since Bentham's time.

As already noted, normalizing disciplinary practices involve techniques for identifying deviations from normal developmental trajectories. Sometimes specific deviations repeatedly identified within a given population lead to the invention of a deviant identity category – such as the delinquent, the idiot, or the homosexual. These new "species" of abnormal individual are reified both in the kinds of knowledge and practices within which they first become identifiable and, frequently, in the minds and experiences of those to whom new category terms are applied. As individuals assume abnormal identities and understand themselves and their place in the world through those identities, they may join together and challenge the prevailing wisdom about their condition. Homosexuals, for example, may embrace their "abnormal" identity but challenge its pathologization by asserting it as a variant kind of developmental norm. The twentieth century saw several political movements founded on just such a reversal of a pathologized identity. Although such political reversals may alleviate much suffering and thus may have much to recommend them, they are not challenges to normalization per se but only to specific knowledge claims within a given normalizing conceptual framework.

An important means of producing information about deviant individuals and for incorporating deviant identities into the lives of those who bear them is secular confession. Foucault therefore has a great deal to say about the genealogy and epistemological valence of confessional practices in volume one of *The History of Sexuality*, where he traces the formation of sexual identities. Practiced initially in the domain of the psychiatrist but eventually in all sorts of modern venues, confession allegedly externalizes what disciplinarians cannot observe directly, the psychic symptoms of pathology that manifest themselves in dreams, fantasies, and desires. But a major effect of confession is to attach an identity firmly to an individual in his or her own experience, to internalize an identity so to speak. Confession and related disciplinary practices can give corporeal reality not only to abnormal identities but also to normal ones – that is, they can help establish any normalized subjectivity, be it normal or deviant. It is for this reason that Foucault can call his work in *Discipline and Punish* and elsewhere "a history of the modern soul" (EDP, 23) and can view normalizing disciplinary techniques that transform people's experiences of themselves by shaping their conduct as evidence that "[t]he soul is the effect and instrument of a political anatomy; the soul is the prison of the body" (EDP, 30). Our experience of ourselves as normable interiorities constrains the life of our bodies.

Once normalizing power effected widespread interiorization of sexual conduct and the formation of sexual identities on that basis, sexuality came to be seen as the foundation for who and what we are both as individuals and as a species. Efforts to control sexuality as the center of selfhood then became bound up, politically and intellectually, with efforts to control and direct the means for reproduction (and purification and enhancement) of species life. A thoroughly normalized and normalizing phenomenon, sexuality serves as one of the anchor points for and mechanisms within the deployment of "biopower" (see EHS1, 140), the vast network of power/knowledge regimes that emerged in the confluence of disciplinary normalization and population management (EHS1, 145).

As Foucault refined his analysis of biopower through the late 1970s, he revised his concept of normalization considerably. This is most evident in the third lecture of his 1978 course at the Collège de France, "Security, Territory, Population," where he distinguishes disciplinary normalization from what he by this time sees as normalization more properly understood. Normalizing discipline classifies in accord with definite objectives. It then creates optimal sequences for transformation and fixes those processes in its techniques. In its application of these techniques, it divides the normal from the abnormal. It thus starts with a model, a norm, and operates in ways that reinforce that norm (ECF-STP, 57). But in this lecture series Foucault is interested in techniques for managing and transforming not individual bodies but populations, and especially techniques for enhancing populations by altering their norms. Suppose, for example, that a given population, say the residents of a certain city, can be broken down into four subpopulations occupying different quadrants of their territory. Suppose further that it is discovered that residents of one quadrant succumb at a far higher rate to a given disease than do residents of the other quadrants. Efforts can then be made to discover differences in the different quadrants, elements within them that might be altered to effect a reduction in the rate at which residents of quadrant one succumb. And this effort, if successful, will have the effect of reducing the population's overall death rate from that disease. These population-enhancement techniques do not discipline individual bodies to fixed norms; rather, by changing the conditions of life of a population, they cause changes in the norms themselves.

This latter type of technique – techniques used to alter the norms of a population – is what Foucault by 1978 wants to call "normalization." The target of these techniques is a population, not an individual body (even when they entail contact with or manipulation of individual bodies). Like disciplinary normalization, they produce norms through observation, but the operations that characterize population management produce norms only in order to surpass them. Having identified this other set of governmental techniques, the means of population management that he now calls "normalization," Foucault invents a new term to describe the work of modern bodily disciplines: "normation" (ECF-ETP, 57). In retrospect, then, *Surveiller et punir* is a book about technologies of "normation," not normalization. However, most scholars and commentators continue to use the word "normalization" when discussing that work or drawing on it.

Ladelle McWhorter

SEE ALSO

Abnormal
Discipline
Homosexuality
Power
The Visible

SUGGESTED READING

Canguilhem, Georges. 1991. *The Normal and the Pathological*, with an introduction by Michel Foucault. New York: Zone Books.

Heyes, Cressida. 2007. *Self-Transformations: Foucault, Ethics, and Normalized Bodies*. New York: Oxford University Press.

McWhorter, Ladelle. 1999. *Bodies and Pleasures: Foucault and the Politics of Sexual Normalization*. Bloomington: Indiana University Press.

55

OUTSIDE

THE CONCEPT OF the outside is, in Foucault's work of the early and mid-1960s, intimately connected to a number of other concepts that figure prominently in his work of that era, concepts such as language, thinking, transgression, the limit, death, and finitude. Indeed, at stake in much of Foucault's work of that period is the question of thinking and of the possibility of opening up a space from which new forms of thinking might emerge. For Foucault, it is language, particularly in the form of modern literature, that opens up this space in which the subject is made to undergo the experience of thinking of its own unthinkable finitude. In this experience of what he refers to in "The Thought from Outside" and *The Order of Things* as the being of language, the subject is put into contact with a space in which the thought of the Same, which regulates contemporary forms of thinking and knowing, is undone by virtue of its confrontation with what Foucault will at various times call the Other, the problematic, heterotopia, or the impossible. It is this space that Foucault calls "the outside."

In his 1963 homage to Georges Bataille, "Preface to Transgression," Foucault had already discussed the manner in which language, through modern literature, had made possible an experience in which the subject is made to think of its own finitude; that is, its own limit. It is language that, through the "pure violence" of transgression, opens up the space in which the subject is made to undergo an experience that is, for Foucault, "essential to our culture since Kant and Sade – an experience of finitude and being, of the limit and of transgression" (ELCP, 40). And it is the new form of thought made possible by this "impossible" space, in which the subject is made to think the unthinkable of its own finitude, that he will later call the thought from, and of, the outside.

In 1966, Foucault would revisit the connection between the outside, language, and thought in *The Order of Things*. In the preface to that work, he describes the experience of the outside as an undergoing of the problematic, the paradoxical, or what he calls, in reference to Borges, a heterotopia. For Foucault, the experience of the unthinkable is one in which an established order of things is undone, and it is precisely the experience of the problematic, in the form of the heterotopia, that brings about such an undoing. The experience described in the preface to *The Order of Things* is one of difference and alterity: the subject and the epistemic order in which it is placed in a given epoch are put into question through their contact with what lies outside them.

It is significant that Foucault would begin what he himself describes as a "history of the Same," a "history of the order of things," with a discussion of the very alterity that undermines such an order (EOT, xxiv). If *The Order of Things* is, ultimately, a work concerned with thinking, then the preface, in conjunction with the closing moments of the book, can be read as a sort of manual that both indicates the direction for and announces the possible advent of new forms of thinking. This is apparent from the beginning, in Foucault's discussion of Borges. Borges writes of a Chinese encyclopedia, The Celestial Emporium of Benevolent Knowledge, in which it is written that the animals are divided into various classes, the most incongruous and significant of which is the class "included in this classification."

Thus, the project of *The Order of Things* finds its roots in a paradox. The Chinese encyclopedia coerces us into encountering the limit of our own thought, thereby giving birth to the series of questions that lie at the heart of Foucault's project: What is it possible or impossible to think? Under what conditions is it possible to think certain things and impossible to think others? From the start, *The Order of Things* concerns thinking and the conditions for the possibility of new forms of thought (EOT, xv). Borges puts us into contact with a thought entirely unlike our own, and it is precisely in the violence of that encounter that the possibility for new ways of thinking opens up. Foucault proposes to call these instances of disorder heterotopias, and they are inextricably tied to a thought of the outside.

One of the implicit theses of *The Order of Things* is that words and things (that is, language and being) are always placed into relation with one another in a specific manner and according to a specific law. Order itself is a constant, even if the manner in which discourses and their objects are empirically ordered changes along with the historical *episteme*. As such, there always exists within a given historical epoch a knot between words and things, a common space where language and being meet and are most at home with one another and with the mode of thinking of that epoch. This common space is a utopia, and it represents, in a sense, the very limit of our thought, precisely because utopias deploy themselves in "marvelous" and "smooth" spaces that "open up cities with vast avenues, well planted gardens, facile lands" (EOT, xviii). Utopias are not spaces of possibility for thinking because they are already spaces, or rather nonspaces, in which certain forms of thinking have been made impossible by the dominant play of order. They offer comfort because they can only place us into contact with what we already know; that is, with the Same.

For Foucault, the possibility for new forms of thinking requires that violence be done to thought. In heterotopias, the familiar connection between language and being is "untied." Whereas utopias are spaces in which words and things are ordered in such a way as to comfort us, and therefore close off any possibility for new forms of thought, heterotopias "disquiet" us precisely because they forcibly place thought into contact with disorder, with an ordering of discourses and their objects with which thought is unfamiliar and is therefore impossible for it to think (EOT, xviii). In this sense, the heterotopia is a space of impossibility in which lies the very possibility for thinking. Heterotopias open up an "unthinkable space" and "transgress all imagination, all possible thought" (EOT, xvi). They are unthinkable, and this undergoing of the impossibility of the heterotopia is a violent one for thought. This is why Foucault writes of the experience of "disquiet," of "unease" in having thought "shaken" from its "familiarities." But in that violence, in the unthinkability of the outside, lies the very possibility for thinking.

Heterotopias undo the taut and familiar connection between words and things, in the process ruining all of the identities, the very order, to which thought is accustomed. Heterotopias ruin classification, taxonomy, and, ultimately, the manifest ordering of words and things. And this is precisely why they open up the possibility for new ways of thinking. This opening up begins with an experience of profound unease, as thought encounters the unthinkable. But, for Foucault, thinking can only arise out of an encounter with that which cannot be thought: the undergoing of its own finitude, in the form of the problematic or paradoxical, on the part of thought is the necessary condition for the possibility of thinking.

Therein lies the importance of the modern epoch's nascent fascination with the being of language and that of its attempts to arrive once more at a certain unity of discourse, a unity whose dispersion had made the birth of the form of thinking called "man" possible. As the unity of classical representation became undone, man, Foucault explains, "composed his own figure in the interstices of [a] fragmented language" (EOT, 386). And if it is now possible to think of even the mere possibility of the disappearance of man, understood as a concept produced by and producer of the very discourses that purport to take "man" as their object, as a concept therefore manifesting a certain order, it is because the "return of language" in its unity serves to fill the spaces within language where "man" has dwelled since the advent of the modern epoch.

These final moments, in which Foucault wonders for the first time whether it might not be possible to see, in the return of language, the imminent death of man, are intimately tied to his earlier discussion of heterotopias and their relation to thought and order. It is linguistics and literature that pose the question of the being of language in such a way that a space for the disappearance of "man" might finally open up. Literature, in its posing of the question of language to itself, manifests "the fundamental forms of finitude" in their "empirical vivacity." For Foucault, what is announced in literature's posing of the question of language is that "man is 'finite'" (EOT, 383).

Thus, far from bringing "man," as a modern figure of thought, back to his own identity, the experience of literature instead pushes man to the "edge of what limits it," to the outside. In undergoing the experience inherent in literature, man is brought into contact with the unthinkable regions of his own finitude, in the forms of death and madness. It is in this sense that the thought of the being of language is a thought from and of the outside: literature confronts man with the space of his own end, "where death prowls, where thought is extinguished, where the promise of the origin interminably recedes" (EOT, 383). In this sense, the bare experience of language is the very perversion of the analytic of finitude to which the figure of man is so inextricably tied and that Foucault famously analyzes in Chapter 9 of *The Order of Things*.

This bare experience of language opens up a space in which man "undergoes" the "forms of finitude in language," which is another way of saying that the figure of man, the subject, is put into question at its very foundation. In the language of literature, the "figure of finitude" manifests itself, this time not in the positivity of knowledge but in terms of the unthinkable negativity of death: the figure of man finds itself for the first time determined from without, and finitude takes the form of an unthinkable limit. The outside, for Foucault, is precisely the form of thought in which this undoing of the subject takes place. The undergoing of the forms of finitude manifested in the space of literature is one in which the particular ordering of words and things that is man is put into question and in which the possibility for new manifestations of order opens up. The experience of the outside, then, is an experience of "death," of "unthinkable thought," of "repetition," of "finitude" (EOT, 384); it is the undergoing of alterity, and in it the fragile play of identity on which the figure of man was erected is undone as the subject is coerced into contact with a region it must, but cannot, think of: its own limit.

Accordingly, as Foucault reiterates in "The Thought from Outside," his homage to Maurice Blanchot, it is language, in the form of literature, that leads us to "the outside where the speaking subject disappears." In other words, the "naked experience of language," by coercing the subject into an encounter with its own finitude, opens up a space in which the "I am" is undone; therein lies its "danger" to established thought and subjective identity (EFB, 13). In the modern epoch, the opening up of this experience from which the subject is excluded and in which its identity is shattered is to be found in a form of thought that is able to think of the peculiar relation that exists between language and the subject: "the being of language only appears for itself in the disappearance of the subject" (EFB, 15). Or, alternately, the bare experience of language is one in which the unity of the subject is shattered. This is a form of thought that "stands outside of any subjectivity" in order to make apparent "its limits" from without, in order to announce "its end" and "its dispersion"; it is a form of thought that "with respect to the interiority of our philosophical reflection and with respect to the positivity of our knowledge, constitutes what one could call the thought from the outside" (EFB, 15–16). As in "Preface to Transgression" and *The Order of Things*, this thought is the thought of the impossible, of the unthinkable; it demands to be referred not to the unity of the cogito but rather to the fractured I, to the undone and dispersed subject. Thinking, in the sense of creation, occurs only in the shattering of thought, as a result of the violent encounter with the unthinkable. The works of Borges, Sade, Artaud, Roussel, Nietzsche, Mallarmé, Klossowski, Bataille, and Blanchot are all forms of a thought from and of the outside, in the sense that they coerce thought into an experience of language in which it encounters what is for it unthinkable, and in so doing opens up the possibility for a new ordering of the relation between language and being. Only through the undergoing of what is most foreign to it can thought, for Foucault, engage in actual thinking.

David-Olivier Gougelet

SEE ALSO

Contestation
Death
Finitude
Language
Literature
Space
Georges Bataille
Maurice Blanchot

SUGGESTED READING

Blanchot, Maurice. 1992. "Atheism and Writing, Humanism and the Cry," in *The Infinite Conversation*, trans. Susan Hanson. Minneapolis: University of Minnesota Press, pp. 246–263.

Borgés, Jorge Luis. 2000. "John Wilkins' Analytical Language," in *Borgés: Selected Non-Fictions*, trans. Eliot Weinberger. New York: Penguin, pp. 229–232.

Deleuze, Gilles. 1988. "Strategies or the Non-stratified: The Thought of the Outside (Power)," in *Foucault*, trans. Seán Hand. Minneapolis: University of Minnesota Press, pp. 47–69.

56

PAINTING (AND PHOTOGRAPHY)

TWO OF FOUCAULT'S signature essays on painting are especially well known: the analysis of Velazquez's *Las Meninas*, and an essay on René Magritte that includes a striking account of how abstraction displaced representation in Western art. In addition, many of Foucault's texts are studded with acute descriptions of major painters from Breughel to Warhol; he gave lecture courses on quattrocento painting and Manet and published essays on several contemporary artists (Rebeyrolle, Fromanger, Michals). Since one of Foucault's major themes was the relation between visibility and discursivity, it is not surprising to find that painting is a favored site for exploring variations in this conjuncture. Throughout his work, painting and the visual arts serve as emblems of the *epistemes* that characterize distinct epochs of thought. At the same time, Foucault's engagement with contemporary art reveals his sense of its political significance and force. These themes coincide in Foucault's continuing interest in how art forms can break with acquired archives, apparatuses, and practices. In (mostly implicit) contrast with romantic concepts of genius (as in Kant, or more generally in the time of "man and his doubles"), Foucault attempted to analyze and articulate the processes of rupture and transformation that mark specific changes in what is called style. Dominant trends in art history either sought to trace relatively continuous developments (following a Hegelian lineage) or operated with sets of categories derived from *Geistesgeschichte* such as Heinrich Wölfflin's linear and painterly modes. Philosophical aesthetics (as Derrida observes) has systematically (from Plato to Heidegger) given premier status to the linguistic arts of poetry and literature. Both of those ways of understanding visual art are put into question by Foucault's engagement with painting and photography.

In *The History of Madness*, Foucault articulates a distinction between visibility and discursivity in sixteenth-century constructions of madness. He contrasted writers like Erasmus and Sebastian Brant, who treated madness as an occasion for instruction and moral satire, with painters like Breughel, Bosch, and Grünewald, who displayed madness as much more dangerous, eruptive, and invasive than the literary parallels they occasionally followed. This contrast leads to a reflection on a "cleavage" (*partage*) that emerged then between literary and visual art. If texts and images had once been mutually illustrative, now "painting was beginning the long process of experimentation that would take it ever further from language, regardless of the superficial identity of a theme. Language and figure are beginning to take two different directions" (EHM, 16). Whereas Foucault's emphasis in *The History of Madness* involves the presentation of madness, he soon expanded his observation in a review of books by the art historian Erwin Panofsky. He praises Panofsky for mapping the complexity of the figurative and discursive: "chiasm, isomorphism, transformation, translation, in a word, all of the festoon [*feston*] of the visible and sayable that characterize a culture in a moment of its history" (FDE1, 621). In the case of painters like Bosch, the *partage* of discourse and figure meant that the power of the image was "no longer to teach but to fascinate," a power that brings it close to the dream. Earlier, Foucault had developed a highly visual account of dreaming, taking issue with Freud's more linguistic analysis (EDE). He describes sixteenth-century painting as "opening the way for a symbolism more often associated with the world of dreams"; that is, creating a public or collective dream (EHM, 17).

Just as *The Order of Things* is a definitive break with phenomenology, which is trapped in the oscillations of "man and his doubles," so its opening essay on *Las Meninas* can be read as a critical alternative to the concept of painting in phenomenologists like Merleau-Ponty (whose philosophy of ambiguity is seen as a typical product of the analytic of finitude). Merleau-Ponty had taken modern painting, especially as it took shape in Cézanne, to be a form of phenomenological inquiry: it suspends the natural attitude in order to explore forms of intentionality through which the visible world takes shape for consciousness. Foucault reads *Las Meninas* archaeologically rather than phenomenologically. Eschewing anything like the psychological account Merleau-Ponty offers of Cézanne's continuous effort to discover the roots of perception, Foucault articulates the principles by which "classical" painting constructs its representations. As he suggests in *The Archaeology of Knowledge*, he takes it to be possible to delineate the rules, sequences, and transformations that a certain form of painting assumes, embodies, and occasionally disrupts or transforms (EAK, 193–194). He therefore describes *Las Meninas* in terms of its deploying multiple strategies of representation typical of the classical age, including linear perspective and the simulation of "natural" light within the image. Moreover, this remarkable painting pushes the limits of representation by explicitly thematizing the roles of artist, model, and spectator involved in the classical model. Foucault takes note of the painting's apparent attempt to inventory all elements and aspects of representation (the core of the classical *episteme*). In viewing the painting, we must successively imagine the place in front of the picture as occupied by the royal models, the artist, or the spectator (ourselves). No one of these representative functions can claim priority, so the position outside the painting, which seems to promise us a definitive understanding, is instead the scene of an endless oscillation among these constituents of representation. Foucault finally reads this indeterminate oscillation as the sign of an absence marking our modern distance from classical painting and indeed from the entire practice of classical representation. The three oscillating figures could be regarded as analogues of the three *epistemes* analyzed in *The Order of Things*: the sovereign models would personify that of resemblance, the painter that of classical representation, and the spectator that of man, the finite being tasked with comprehending his own finitude (Tanke 2010, 33–40). Foucault's reading of the painting reveals "an essential void: the necessary disappearance of that which is its foundation – of the person it resembles and the person in whose eyes it is only a resemblance" (EOT, 16). The absent figure is "man," who will be delineated more fully as an "empirical-transcendental doublet," a being whose task is to discover the conditions of his own finitude; Foucault will argue that this is an impossible and endless task, one that could be abandoned if, as seems to be happening, the figure of man is erased "like a face drawn in sand at the edge of the sea" (EOT, 386–387).

Foucault's essay is both an instance of *ekphrasis*, the verbal description of a visual work of art, and a reflection on that genre. Given his insistence on the distinction between visibility and discursivity, as well as their multiple forms of conjunction, it should not be surprising that Foucault is sensitive to the question of how his verbal analysis is related to the painting as a visual image. At the same time that the text of the essay is disclosing an absence in the painting, that of man, the writing marks its own distance from the image. The essay itself is divided into two numbered parts. The first proceeds by rigorously excluding any discussion of the historical identities of the figures in the painting or of art-historical context. This has the effect of defamiliarizing the work and forcing us to concentrate on its play of representation, a focus intensified by Foucault enlisting us within a "we," a community of observers under the guidance of a connoisseur. The second section of the essay takes a new turn by asking whether it is now time to name the persons in the image (Velazquez, the royal figures, and their entourage). Warning that this could lead to a reductive approach, Foucault insists that "the relation of language to painting is an infinite relation. It is not that words are imperfect, or that, when confronted by the visible, they prove insuperably inadequate. Neither can be reduced to the other's terms: it is in vain that we say what we see; what we see never resides in what we say." This relation, Foucault maintains, should be kept open, so as to "treat their incompatibility as a starting-point for speech instead of an obstacle to be avoided" (EOT, 9). At the same time, there is no explicit reflection on the feigned community of "we" who follow the path of Foucault's *ekphrasis*. Yet such reflection becomes unavoidable much later in the text, as Foucault introduces the analysis of "Man and His Doubles" by reiterating the absence implied by the painting. It is as if man, "enslaved sovereign, observed spectator," appears "in that vacant space towards which Velazquez's whole painting was directed" (EOT, 312). We readers realize that in order to discover the absence of man in the painting, we ourselves have to assume the initially unnamed position of "enslaved sovereign, observed spectator." Yet once such a position has been named, it becomes possible to take our distance from it and ask, as Foucault does, whether this position is inevitable or rather one that arose in a specific context and is subject to disappearance.

Foucault saw Manet as a painter who rethought the position of the viewer. Soon after publishing *The Order of Things*, Foucault took up temporary residence in Tunisia, where he lectured on quattrocento painting and Manet. His projected book on Manet (*Le noir et les couleurs*) was apparently never completed; however, a transcript of one lecture, along with some passages in "Fantasia of the Library," indicate how Foucault understood a body of work that overturned the conventions of representational painting (EMP). Just as Flaubert produced a self-conscious literature of the library and the archive in a novel like *The Temptation of Saint Anthony* (itself inspired by a painting, as Foucault notes), Manet took the museum and its conditions of display as a frame to be altered and manipulated. Manet, in this analysis, rejected certain fictions of the art of his predecessors. These involved the idea that the canvas was a virtual window on a three-dimensional segment of an actual or possible world, a supposition enabled by the picture's use of linear perspective and the simulation of lighting internal to the painting. Drawing on Foucault's later, more explicit development of the concepts of apparatus and diagram (as in *Discipline and Punish*), we can articulate the lines of Manet's innovations. Bentham's Panopticon realized a diagram of visibility: each individual cell of the prison was observable from a central observation tower, thus encouraging prisoners to assume that they could be the subjects of surveillance at any moment and so discipline themselves to meet the behavioral expectations of the prison system. The museum, which rose and flourished in the nineteenth century, produced another viewing apparatus in which each canvas presented itself to the observer as a window opening onto an imagined scene. Manet effectively transformed this arrangement by creating paintings that insisted on their two-dimensionality and did not simulate an internal source of lighting. One no longer had the experience of looking through a window but of engaging with a flat canvas on the wall. By emphasizing rectangular elements and deliberately distorting perspectival expectations (as in *The Bar at the Folies Bergère*), Manet established a new diagram of viewing. Even the looks of the figures within the painting contribute to unsettling the experience of viewing, either by seeming to stare directly at the viewer (as in the scandalous *Olympia*), looking at the invisible (*The Gare Saint-Lazare*), or forming a set of disconnected gazes (*The Balcony*, with its disturbing trio).

"Force of Flight," an essay on the painter Paul Rebeyrolle, extends the analysis of visual framing explored in the lecture on Manet, making more explicit the possibilities of resistance and rebellion latent in the account of the museum and its diagrams of vision. The subject of Foucault's essay is a series of paintings entitled *Dogs*, each depicting a dog in captivity, in various stages of confinement, struggle, suffering, or escape. Constructed as collages with wire lattices and wooden frames, the works reinforce the materiality of the situations represented. Foucault notes that the conditions of display also emphasize the sense of constriction: "Here you are held fast by ten pictures, that circle a room in which all the windows have been carefully closed. In prison, in your turn, like the dogs that you see standing on their hind legs and butting up against the grillwork?" Who are we who create, gaze at, or turn our eyes away from prisons? Foucault was involved at this time in political activity focused on French prison conditions; he takes Rebeyrolle's series as concerned with "the prison ... a place where forces arise and show themelves, a place where history takes shape, and whence time arises" (FDE2, 401). The featureless windows forming the background of the *Dogs* series are only illusory exits. Leaving through the window would leave the apparatus of confinement intact. Rather, "in human struggles, nothing great ever passes by way of the windows, but everything, always, by the triumphant crumbling [*l'effrondrement*] of the walls" (FDE2, 403). Here, as in his account of Manet, Foucault shows how the apparatus of painting can deploy conventions of representation against themselves, but now the political potential of this reflexive move and its questioning of the viewer has become more evident.

In *This Is not a Pipe*, Foucault traces another route painting has taken in the wake of Manet's undoing of representation. Foucault claims that the movement of twentieth-century abstraction challenged two constitutive principles of Western painting that ruled since the fifteenth century: (1) rigorous separation of linguistic and visual signs, and (2) the assumption that resemblance implies affirmation, or that painting refers to a world external to itself (ENP, 32). Klee is credited with breaking down the first of these protocols by introducing words, letters, and signs (e.g., arrows) as compositional elements into paintings that retain a representational aspect (elsewhere Foucault suggests that Klee has an emblematic relation to his time analogous to that Velazquez had to his [FDE1, 544]). Kandinsky broke with the second protocol by first introducing nonrepresentative "things" into his paintings that were "neither more nor less objects than the church, the bridge, or the knight with his bow," and then producing paintings consisting solely of shapes, colors, and their relations (ENP, 34–35).

Foucault sees Magritte as intensifying the assault on representation begun by Klee and Kandinsky. Foucault does this by challenging both principles: separation and affirmation. Yet Magritte accomplishes this not through abstraction but by pushing the techniques of representation to their limits. Impossible objects and proportions, perspectival distortions, or incoherent but "realistic" scenes are produced with exaggerated representational clarity. Words, sentences, inscriptions, and titles play constitutive roles in Magritte's canvases. So far, Foucault suggests, a painting like *Les deux mystéres* (*Ceci n'est pas une pipe*) can be compared to a calligram, a diagrammatic representation formed by written words and letters. Yet to speak more carefully, he continues, we must describe the work as an "unraveled calligram" in which neither the visual nor discursive order becomes dominant; the painting sets up an unlimited interplay of the two modes.

While Foucault highlights Magritte's rejection of the affirmative sense of the image (the implicit claim to resemble something external to itself), he sees another affirmation emerging in his work. Magritte's paintings affirm the simulacrum or phantasm, the image without an original, and therefore proliferating without limit. Freed from the constraints of resemblance, the image floats free, like the "pipe" in the famous painting. Here Foucault draws on Deleuze's transvaluation of the simulacrum (as in *The Logic of Sense*) that Plato had attempted to marginalize. Other partners in this conversation are Klossowski, whose rethinking of the simulacrum Foucault explored in "The Prose of Actaeon," and Nietzsche, the thinker of eternal recurrence. "Seven Seals of Affirmation," the title of the concluding section of *This Is not a Pipe*, paraphrases that of "The Seven Seals," a song that Nietzsche's Zarathustra sings to celebrate the thought of recurrence. That thought can be understood as a radical intensification of multiplicity, where each moment has an infinite depth. That Nietzsche calls these moments *Augenblicke*, "twinklings of the eye" or "momentary glances," enables Foucault to play on the idea of a multiplicity of the visual image, a theme to which he alludes in his essay on Flaubert (ELCP, 101). Foucault also detected the infinitely multiple or "eternal phantasm" in Pop Art, which he invokes in the last line of *This Is not a Pipe* ("Campbell, Campbell, Campbell, Campbell") and in his brief *ekphrasis* of Andy Warhol's images of repetition in "Theatrum Philosophicum." Arising from those images "that refer to each other to eternity" he discovers that "the striped form of the event tears through the darkness, and the eternal phantasm informs that soup can, that singular and depthless face" (ELCP, 189).

Other possibilities of repetition and fantasy are enabled by photography; these are in turn repositionings of the viewing subject. Foucault followed transformations in the apparatus of the visual arts by investigating several such adaptations and mutations. He provides a brief genealogy in "Photogenic Painting," where he recalls the freedom of experimentation in early photography's many ways of altering and recording the image, before the emergence of a canonical form of photographic art in the early twentieth century. Foucault's focus in this essay is the art of Gérard Fromanger, who produces images by painting over projected photographic images of street scenes and public life. For Foucault, this technique mobilizes the image: "Fromanger's paintings do not capture images: they do not fix them, they pass them on" (EPGP, 95). Here painting abandons any aspiration to fixity and solidity, embodying in its form the nomadic transitivity of contemporary life: "this is the autonomous transhumance of the image ... it agrees to become a thoroughfare, an infinite transition, a busy and crowded painting" (EPGP, 102). Here Foucault introduces the theme of territoriality into his account of art.

In "Thought and Emotion" (1982), Foucault discussed the work of the American photographer Duane Michals (FDE4, 243–250). Emphasizing the dream-like quality of Michals's images and photographic narratives, Foucault returns, in a sense, to themes from his early exploration of the visual, the 1954 essay "Dream and Existence." Michals experiments with photography in a different direction than Fromanger. Whereas Fromanger took painting into the street through photography, Michals captures and provokes fragile moments of "thought-emotion." Foucault endorses Michals's observation that photography has an advantage in provoking thoughts about the unseen, spectral, and dreamlike because it is initially taken to be a more realistic medium than painting. The text is contemporary with Foucault's later writings and lectures on the aesthetics of existence and the process of subjectivization. In *The Care of the Self*, Foucault notes that the physicians and writers on love testify to the power of visual images (*phantasiai*) whether remembered, dreamed, or seen (EHS3, 136–139). Michals, as a gay man whose work alters the possibilities of photography while exploring varieties of sexuality, gender, and fantasy, becomes an exemplar of the self-experimenting artist and the practitioner of an aesthetics of existence.

Gary Shapiro

SEE ALSO

Literature
Madness
The Visible
Maurice Merleau-Ponty

SUGGESTED READING

Deleuze, Gilles. 1988. *Foucault*, trans. Seán Hand. Minneapolis: University of Minnesota Press.
Shapiro, Gary. 2003. *Archaeologies of Vision: Foucault and Nietzsche on Seeing and Saying*. Chicago: University of Chicago Press.
Tanke, Joseph. 2010. *Foucault's Philosophy of Art: A Genealogy of Modernity*. New York: Continuum.

57

PARRĒSIA

ICHEL FOUCAULT EXAMINES the significance of this concept beginning late in his career, as part of his explorations of the care of self in the final two volumes of the *History of Sexuality* (*The Uses of Pleasure* and *The Care of the Self*). *Parrēsia* is also the primary theme of Foucault's final lecture courses at the Collège de France. Most significant in this context are the lecture courses from 1981–1982, *The Hermeneutics of the Subject* and in particular *The Government of Self and Others* given the following year. Additionally, *Fearless Speech*, a transcript of a series of lectures Foucault gave at the University of California–Berkeley in 1983, provides a useful précis of the fuller treatment now provided in these two lecture courses. *Parrēsia* is a central concept for Foucault's work on ethics.

Put simply, *parrēsia* means frank or fearless speech. What interests Foucault about this kind of speech act are the particular conditions under which such speech acts becomes possible. Early in *The Governement of Self and Others*, Foucault contrasts *parrēsia* with other modes. He cites ordinary language philosopher J. L. Austin's theory of speech acts in order to highlight the distinctiveness of *parrēsia* as a mode of telling the truth. Performative utterances are those speech acts that clearly codify the effects that follow from them. When the groom in a wedding ceremony utters the words "I do," those words are sufficient to render him married. This happens because the wedding ceremony takes place in a carefully orchestrated institutional context. It is presided over by either a government official or ecclesiastical authority who declares the wedding to have taken place and the couple therefore married. Everyone knows what is supposed to happen in such situations, for everyone has their own particular role to play, from the audience representing the groom's family, those representing the bride's, and the various members of the wedding party to the presiding official. There are typically no surprises at a wedding or at other similar ceremonial occasions.

The difference between the predictability of the situation that authorizes per-formative speech acts contrasts markedly with that of *parrēsia*. The key for the speech act of *parrēsia* is that it cannot be uttered without risk to the speaker. Parrēsiasts call their own existence into question through the act of speaking freely. Foucault cites several examples during the course of his lectures, beginning with an interpretation of Kant's "What Is Enlightenment?" as a way into an analysis of the ancient Greek and Roman philosophical and literary sources, including such theoretical texts as Plato's *Laws* and Galen's *On the Passions and Errors of the Soul* and literary texts such as Euripides' *Ion* and Sophocles' *Oedipus Rex*.

At stake in the discourse of *parrēsia* are the various challenges by the weak made against the injustices of the strong. These discourses challenge injustices or per-ceived injustices committed by the strong on behalf of those who are not powerful enough to contest the ruler by force. The challenges are not limited to words, how-ever. Foucault cites the practices of hunger strikes in India and certain forms of ritual suicide in Japan as examples of actions functioning as part of this discourse (ECF-GSO, 133). Although he does not mention them, presumably one could expand this list to include civil disobedience as practiced by members of various civil rights movements in the United States, South Africa, and India in the latter half of the twentieth century.

As a result of the confrontation between the just but powerless subject and the unjust but powerful ruler, some accommodation must be made so that the ruler's discourse can be both just and powerful. The reason Euripides' play *Ion* serves as a prototype for parrēsiastic discourse, despite (as Foucault notes) failing to employ the term *parrēsia*, is because it enacts this accommodation in paradigmatic fashion. It is revealed at the end of the play that Ion is the true son of Apollo, thus making it pos-sible for him to legitimately ascend the Athenian throne and avoid the illegitimacy of his apparent father, the tyrant Xuthus. Although the term *parrēsia* itself comes into widespread use only later, during the Hellenistic period, important precursors to this discourse of *parrēsia* can be found in Euripides and Plato.

Ion is important for another reason, for the play enacts the basic relationship between democracy and *parrēsia*. *Parrēsia* and democracy codetermine one another. *Ion* is a story of founding that tells the story of one of the founders of the four tribes of Athens. Thus his act of frank speech will provide the origin of Athens as a democracy. Furthermore, without *parrēsia*, democracy becomes impossible. "Ion needs *parrēsia* so that he can return to Athens and found democracy. Consequently, *parrēsia*, in the person of Ion, will be the very foundation of democracy.... In order for there to be democracy, there must be *parrēsia*. But conversely, as you know ... *parrēsia* is one of the characteristic features of democracy" (ECF-GSO, 155). *Parrēsia* is not the formal, constitutional dimension of democracy, however. Rather, it desig-nates the experience of democratic dissent, in which those who can speak exercise the power to do so (Foucault, citing Claude Lefort, distinguishes between the formal dimension as that of the political and the latter, which includes *parrēsia*, as politics).

Although Foucault was able to do little more than outline the project that would link the ancient conception of *parrēsia* to the modern conception of critique, it is clear that this was his intent. Indeed, he indicates at the outset of *The Government of Self and Others* that his investigation of *parrēsia*, understood as "true discourse in the political realm," would be an essential aspect of his investigations of governmentality around the figure of the prince (ECF-GSO, 6). Finally, this genealogy of true political discourse links up with the critical attitude, the conditions under which one begins to question the various political games of truth under the particular experiences of power relations that constitute individuals as the subjects that they are in relation to others. It is at this point that Foucault commences his reading of Kant's "What Is Enlightenment?" understood simultaneously as a text that examines this question of the conditions under which an enlightened public becomes possible and harkens back to the ancient question of *parrēsia*.

Corey McCall

SEE ALSO

> *Care*
> *Ethics*
> *Governmentality*
> *Truth*
> *Plato*

SUGGESTED READING

Bernauer, James. 2004. "Michel Foucault's Philosophy of Religion: An Introduction to the Non-Fascist Life," in *Michel Foucault and Theology: The Politics of Religious Experience*, ed. James Bernauer and Jeremy Carette. New York: Ashgate, pp. 77–97.
Flynn, Thomas. 1988. "Michel Foucault as *Parrhesiast*: His Last Course at the Collège de France," in *The Final Foucault*, ed. James Bernauer and David Rasmussen. Cambridge, MA: The MIT Press, pp. 102–117.
McGushin, Edward. 2007. *Foucault's Askesis: An Introduction to the Philosophical Life*. Evanston, IL: Northwestern University Press.

58

PHENOMENOLOGY

L IKE OTHER MEMBERS of his generation (for example, Derrida, Deleuze, and Lyotard), Foucault grew up in the 1950s studying phenomenology, but as he got older he distanced himself from it more and more. By the time of *The Archaeology of Knowledge* in 1969, there can be no question that phenomenology was a primary target of Foucault's criticisms (EEW3, 241). The "phenomenology" that Foucault targets is phenomenology as Cartesianism. This is the "phenomenology" found in Husserl's classical texts such as *Ideas I* (1913) and *Cartesian Meditations* (1929) but also in his late *The Crisis of European Sciences and Transcendental Phenomenology* (1936). Phenomenology in its Cartesian (or idealist) version revolves around the concept of internal, subjective experience, "Erlebnis" in Husserl's German, a term usually rendered in English as "lived-experience" and in French as "vécu." For Foucault, phenomenology is the investigation of lived-experience. Thus what is at issue in all of Foucault's criticisms of phenomenology is the concept of experience.

Lived-experience plays such an important role in phenomenology because the phenomenological project consists in reducing all knowledge and existence down to their phenomena or appearance. The appearance of something is a lived-experience. We must notice four things about the phenomenological investigation of lived-experience.

First, for Husserl, phenomenology is opposed to all speculations; all presuppositions must be criticized. As Husserl famously says, phenomenology returns "to the things themselves." The phenomenological slogan of returning to the things themselves means that all claims must be grounded and verified in the evidence of an intuition. Intuitionism forms one pole of the phenomenological concept of lived-experience.

Second, no matter what their intuitive content, lived-experiences have one form: the form of intentionality. Intentionality means that in any experience (be it thinking, seeing, wishing, wanting, imagining, etc.) there is a directedness from me of an intention that endows the object intended with a sense. Intentionality can be explained in the way (based on Husserl's *Logical Investigations* [1901]) I think about (think in the direction of) there being a person over there in the garden. I look out the window and see the person; the intuition of the person verifies my intention; and now I can say with certainty that what I see over there has the meaning of a person. But we can also explain intentionality (based on *Ideas I*) using sense data, which Husserl calls "hyletic data." Among phenomenologists, this explanation is sometimes disputed since it presents the subject as entirely active and creative (while the very concept of hyletic data implies that the subject includes a fundamental level of passivity). In any case, here is how the explanation works: I see an indeterminate shape-color over there. I think it is a person (I think about it being a person). I look more carefully and thereby endow the indeterminate shape-color with the meaning of person; it is a person. In the "hyletic data" explanation of intentionality, the subject is a constituting subject. Given these explanations, intentionality implies that lived-experience is a directedness toward an end. In other words, intentionality implies that all lived-experience is not only intuitionistic but also teleological.

Third, Husserlian phenomenology transforms Cartesianism. Phenomenology being a philosophy of the cogito, a subjectivism, means that the subject is the source of meaning, that it is a constituting subjectivity. Husserl, however, recognizes that, since Descartes conceives the thinking thing as a substance, he conceives it on the model of something found in the world; it is, as Husserl says, "a little tag-end [or a little piece] of the world" (Husserl 1977, 24). Insofar as the cogito then is relative to the world, it cannot be absolute. What Descartes calls the cogito is only the psychological, empirical, or anthropological subject; it is the "me" who exists in the world. Therefore, a transcendental conversion of Cartesianism is required. The conversion happens by reducing the cogito itself to an appearance. Insofar as the cogito (the psychological, empirical, or anthropological subject) appears as an object of an intuition, it receives its sense from some other agency. For phenomenology, what constitutes the sense of the cogito is another subjectivity, called "transcendental subjectivity." With the conversion of Cartesianism, Husserl is *not* positing a separate and second subjectivity (a kind of God) behind the psychological, empirical, or anthropological subject. Although this is paradoxical, Husserl is claiming that, if the psychological subject is me, the sense of the psychological subject is constituted by the transcendental subject; but the transcendental subject is still me. In reference to this relation, Husserl speaks of a "parallelism" and a kind of "doubling" of the psychological with the transcendental (Husserl 1997, 244).

Fourth, we must notice that we have now reached a kind of absolute constituting subjectivity. Yet, just as with the psychological subjectivity, if the absolute subjectivity has a sense, it, too, must be constituted. Absolute subjectivity comes to be endowed with sense, according to Husserl, by means of the fact that it is temporal. For Husserl, all lived-experience is temporalizing. As we saw in the earlier description, there is a temporal expanse to intentionality. It moves from an antici-pating intention to a future verification. The implications of the claim that all lived-experience is temporal are far-ranging. The claim results in Heidegger's statement in *Being and Time* that time is the horizon within which being must be understood. Still within Heidegger, it results in existence (*Dasein*) being defined as transcendence (a futural going beyond), a term that both Sartre and Merleau-Ponty will take up respectively in *Being and Nothingness* and in *Phenomenology of Perception*. Most impor-tantly, however, the claim that all experience is temporal leads Husserl to reconceive phenomenology, in the last phase of his thinking, as historical. It results in Husserl's last great work, *The Crisis of European Sciences and Transcendental Phenomenology*. What *The Crisis* shows is that transcendental subjectivity is conditioned by history but, still being oriented by the idea of intentionality, Husserl argues that history is teleologi-cal. The very purpose of *The Crisis* is to "strike through the crust of the externalized 'historical facts' of philosophical history, interrogating, exhibiting, and testing their inner meaning and hidden *teleology*" (Husserl 1970, 18, my emphasis).

If there is one phenomenological claim that Foucault always contests, it is the claim that history is teleological. As Foucault says in *The Archaeology of Knowledge*, "The essential task is to free the history of thought from its subjection to transcen-dence.... My aim is to analyze this history in the discontinuity that no teleology would reduce in advance.... [My] aim is to free history from the grip of phenome-nology" (EAK, 203). Undoubtedly, on the basis of his early study of Hegel (Eribon 1991, 17–18), Foucault recognized that teleological thinking (and therefore phe-nomenology) is a form of circular thinking. We have seen the circular structure in the concept of intentionality: one intends a meaning that one possesses in advance while not having the intuition that verifies it. Then one intuits the object. The verifi-cation is achieved when the intuition is synthesized with or becomes the same as the intention. Teleological thinking therefore turns history into a continuous progres-sion from an originating intention to a final purpose. In other words, teleological thinking eliminates the event character of history. However, if history is conceived without events, then history is no longer, as Foucault would say, "actual" or "effective" (EEW2, 379–382). In order to free the history of thought from teleology in order to liberate its actual existence, Foucault eliminates not events but terminal truths. In *History of Madness*, for example, it is not the case, according to Foucault, that the truth of madness is hidden, latent, throughout the Middle Ages, the Renaissance, and the classical age. It is not the case that we make progress across the classical age toward the truth of madness, a truth fully disclosed in the nineteenth century (EHM, 425). Instead, the knowledge of madness and the practices in regard to the mad are different in the Renaissance, different in the classical age, and then differ-ent once again in the nineteenth century. The suspension of the belief in terminal truths allows history to appear in dispersion (a dispersion best understood through the concept of multiplicity, as we shall see at the end) (EHM, 164–165). Foucault's historical analyses do not lead us back to an original intention and they do not lead forward to an endpoint. They do not lay out a "dialectical enterprise" (EOT, 248) in which history starts from the same and ends with the same. Indeed, as Deleuze has pointed out, Foucault's thinking aims at making us be other, at thinking otherwise (Deleuze 1988, 119). Thus, we see that what is really at stake in Foucault's criticism of phenomenology's conception of history is the fundamental role that intentionality plays, as if history were one large lived-experience: an intention always seeking *its own* verification. For Foucault, what is at issue in phenomenology is "transcendental narcissism" (EAK, 203).

Foucault's criticism of the phenomenological concept of lived-experience appears in the ninth chapter of *The Order of Things*, "Man and His Doubles" (EOT, 303–343). Somewhat like Husserl's *Crisis*, Foucault's *The Order of Things* locates phenomenology in the movement of the history of Western thought and science. Whereas Husserl sees phenomenology as the culmination of Western philosophy, Foucault locates it at the precise moment of the nineteenth century when Western thinking reaches "the limits of representation" (this phrase is the title of his seventh chapter). According to Foucault, classical thinking (in the seventeenth and eighteenth centuries, in Descartes, for example) was a dualism; it constructed a "table" in which words, without any mediation, represented things. The classical mode of "representing" reaches its limit, however, when the classical modes of "speaking" (logic), "classifying" (natural history), and "exchanging" (wealth) are no longer direct relations of representation. At the beginning of the nineteenth century, these modes of classical thinking transform themselves into the positive sciences of philology, biology, and economy. With the development of these positive sciences, "labor, life, and language appear as so many 'transcendentals'"; that is, they appear as conditions for the possibility of discourse and grammar, exchange and profit, and the living being (EOT, 244). But, labor, life, and language are conditions of possibility in a peculiar sense. The sciences are supposed to be the grounds for knowledge of all possible discourse, exchange, and life. However, within their domain, one finds the one who knows: man. Man then becomes the third term (the mediation) for what in the classical age had been a dualism: he is at once a conditioned item of knowledge and a condition of knowledge. The chapter is called "Man and His Doubles" because of this "at once," because of this "doubling" of man as condition and conditioned. For Foucault, phenomenology appears on the scene when Western thinking (that is, modern thinking) becomes anthropological.

For Foucault, the figure of man that appears at the beginning of the nineteenth century is a figure of finitude. In one sense, man is governed by labor, life, and language; his position in these sciences tells him that he is finite like any other object of nature. Yet, man's finitude has another sense. The positive content of these sciences will not arise unless man has a finite body through which he learns of spatiality, unless he suffers desire through which he learns the value of all things, and unless he communicates in a language through which he learns all other discourses (EOT,

314). In this second sense, man's finitude is not something that comes on him from the exterior (because he has a nature or a history); through the body, desire, and language, human finitude is fundamental (EOT, 315). The very opening to knowledge through which he learns that he is *not* infinite is finite. The dual sense of finitude is grounded in death (and here Foucault seems to base his understanding of phenomenology more on Heidegger than on Husserl; the title of one of the sections of Chapter 9 is "The Analytic of Finitude," which echoes the "Dasein analytic" of *Being and Time*) (EOT, 315). Man's finitude is not only the fact that one is going to die like any other animal but also the fact that man is aware that he is going to die, an awareness that separates humans from "the happy opening of animal life" (EOT, 314). From one end of the experience of finitude to the other, death answers itself. On the basis of the description of the dialectical sameness of the analytic of finitude ("the interminable play of a doubled reference: if man's knowledge is finite it is because he is gripped, without the possibility of liberation, within the positive contents of language, labor, and life; and inversely, if life, labor, and language may be posited in their positivity, it is because knowledge has finite forms" [EOT, 316]), Foucault then outlines a series of doubles: "the empirico-transcendental doublet," "the 'cogito' and the unthought," and "the retreat and return of the origin." As we know already from our description of the phenomenological conversion of Cartesianism and from the transformation of the positive sciences of philology, economy, and biology, the empirical subject and the transcendental subject double one another. "The 'cogito' and the unthought" make a double because the cogito finds itself conditioned by life, labor, and language, which always darkens its transparency; thus the darkness of the cogito makes sure that there will always be more to think, an "unthought" that must be brought into light. "The return and retreat of the origin" is a double because, as the cogito finds itself subject to darkness, its origin always seems to lie in the past. Every attempt to recover the origin seems, however, only to uncover more darkness, so that the origin continues to retreat. But then the very project of thinking seems to be the indefinite recovery of and return to that origin – in the future. In each double, we start from the subject and return to the subject; we start from the cogito and we return to the cogito; we start from the origin and we return to the origin. What Foucault describes each time is a dialectic of the same.

We must not pause over the "empirico-transcendental doublet" since it is here that Foucault discusses "lived-experience" ("vécu," which the English translation calls "actual experience") (EOT, 321). Foucault approaches the discussion of lived-experience by stressing that, because the conditions of knowledge must be revealed on the basis of the empirical contents given within knowledge, two kinds of analyses come into being. On the one hand, there must be an analysis that provides the *nature* of human knowledge (this would analyze the sensory modes of acquiring knowledge); on the other, there must be a *history* of human knowledge (this would analyze the economic and social conditions of knowledge) (EOT, 319). In other words, there would be a truth of basic perception in the body and a truth of the movement of history. Yet, as Foucault argues, this true discourse is ambiguous. It can be a true discourse that refers to the empirical side (whether this be nature or history), or it can refer to a truth that is anticipated by nature and history; it can refer to positivist truth or to an eschatological truth (EOT, 320). It is this ambiguity between positivity and eschatology (reduction and promise) that Foucault sees in the phenomenological concept of lived-experience. Foucault sees this ambiguity in the phenomenological concept of lived experience because, as we described earlier, lived-experience in Husserl seems to consist in two inseparable poles. On the one hand, lived-experience is an intuitionism. Indeed, because Husserl wants phenomenology to accept nothing that is not given in an intuition, he calls phenomenology a "true positivism" (Husserl 1965, 145). On the other hand, lived-experience is teleological, and we have seen how this teleology orients Husserl's *Crisis*. The movement of intentionality (transcendence) is futural. The two inseparable poles make lived-experience be, as Foucault calls it, "a discourse with a mixed nature" (EOT, 321). Lived-experience is at once the reduction of all objects down to their positive givenness, and lived-experience is the promise of the fulfillment of the intention.

According to Foucault, as this mixture, phenomenology (despite Husserl's explicit claims) does not really contest positivism and eschatology; phenomenology confirms them by giving them roots. They have their source in the ambiguity of lived-experience. Because phenomenology only confirms positivism and eschatology, it really does not break free of terminal truths; it remains enclosed in the circle of origin and end. Therefore, Foucault's criticisms of phenomenology amount to the attempt to escape from the enclosure. Such an escape is the very meaning of contestation. In "Man and His Doubles," Foucault therefore asks this question: "The true contestation of positivism and eschatology does not lie, therefore, in a return to lived-experience.... If such a contestation could be made, it would be from the starting-point of a question which may well seem aberrant...: does man truly exist" (EOT, 322, translation modified)? This question created a lot of controversy in Foucault's lifetime since it seemed to suggest that he wanted the actual species of man, humanity, to be destroyed. The question, however, suggests something else. It suggests a kind of thinking or experiencing. With this "aberrant question," Foucault is asking us to think what the world would look like if we did not think in terms of ourselves being at once the condition of knowledge and the conditioned of knowledge. Then we could think about things other than all the things we condition and all the things that are conditioned as we are. What happens if instead we focus on the fact that the doubles never make an identity, that between them there is "a minuscule but invincible hiatus" (EOT, 340)? If we place ourselves at this distance, then we no longer think about the same as ourselves but about something other than ourselves. The experience toward which Foucault is pointing us would not be a subjective experience but an experience that "wrenches the subject from itself"; it would not be an experience lived in the sense of the future returning us to the same life we had at the beginning but an experience of "the unliveable" (EEW3, 241). If the beginning and the end are not the same truth of man, then we move from a kind of finite thinking to a kind of infinite thinking. Or, we move from a finite experience to an infinite experience. No longer do we experience the closedness of a circle. Posing the question of man's nonexistence, we experience what Foucault calls "the outside." To speak of the outside in this way is certainly mysterious (and in fact Foucault refers to mystical thinking when he describes the outside [EEW2, 150]). We can, however, make the outside slightly less mysterious if we realize that it is not the monism of the modern thought of man and it is not the dualism of the classical thought of representation. Although Foucault is never clear about this, the thought of the outside is the thought beyond monism and dualism; the thought of the outside is the thought of multiplicity. In fact, unlike phenomenology, Foucault's thought attempts to make subjectivity multiple. We see this attempt in Foucault's late course called "The Hermeneutics of the Subject" when he discusses the ancient Greek and Latin practice of meditating on death. For the Greeks and Latins, according to Foucault, meditating on death is not thinking that you are going to die; it is not a game the subject plays with his own thoughts, on the object or possible objects of his thought (ECF-HOS, 357). It does not consist in determining the essence of one's thought or the objects of thought, as phenomenology does when it determines the structure of lived-experience as intentionality. Here, Foucault stresses, "a completely different kind of game is involved: not a game the subject plays with his own thought or thoughts but a game that thought performs on the subject himself. It is becoming, through thought, the person who is dying or whose death is imminent" (ECF-HOS, 357–358). Thus, the exercise of meditation on death, instead of confirming that one is human, makes one realize that one is becoming other.

Leonard Lawlor

SEE ALSO

> *Archaeology*
> *Contestation*
> *The Double*
> *Experience*
> *Historical a Priori*
> *Outside*
> *Martin Heidegger*
> *Maurice Merleau-Ponty*

SUGGESTED READING

Deleuze, Gilles. 1994. *Difference and Repetition*, trans. Paul Patton. New York: Columbia University Press, chap. 3.

Derrida, Jacques. 2011. *Voice and Phenomenon*, trans. Leonard Lawlor. Evanston, IL: Northwestern University Press.

Husserl, Edmund. 1965. *Phenomenology and the Crisis of Philosophy*, trans. Quentin Lauer. New York: Harper Torchbooks.

1970. *The Crisis of European Sciences and Transcendental Phenomenology*, trans. David Carr. Evanston, IL: Northwestern University Press.

1977. *Cartesian Meditation*, trans. Dorian Cairns. The Hague: Martinus Nijhoff.

Webb, David. 2013. *Foucault's Archaeology: Science and Transformation*. Edinburgh: Edinburgh University Press.

59

PHILOSOPHY

F ROM THE START, and throughout, Foucault's relationship to the body of
texts, problems, traditions, and methods known as "philosophy" remained
ambiguous. Although trained as a philosopher at the prestigious École Normale
Supérieure, fully immersed in the classical authors, and initially influenced by the
dominant philosophical trends of the time (especially by the effort, in the 1940s and
1950s, to unite Marxism and phenomenological existentialism, which culminated in
the publication of Sartre's *Critique of Dialectical Reason*), he began to look for a way
out of the institution and the philosophical climate of his time very early on. (For
traces of such an influence on Foucault's early work, see EMIP. See also the long 1954
introduction to his own translation of Binswanger's *Traum und Existenz* [EDE].) In
an interview from 1967 (FDE1, 667), he explains how, in the context of the political
struggles of the time (against colonialism in particular) and a growing disaffection
with the USSR after the crushing of the Budapest uprising in 1956, his generation
rejected the existentialist and Marxist inheritance. The ideals of "humanism," "progress," and "historical rationality," on which much of that philosophical edifice had
been built, were collapsing before the eyes of that generation. In addition, a different
kind of revolution, which caught Foucault's attention, was taking place at the time in
the so-called human or social sciences, such as linguistics, religious studies, anthropology, history, and psychoanalysis. They showed philosophy how, by applying the
methods and concepts of structuralism to their own field, they were able not only
to renew themselves and establish connections between domains hitherto kept separate but also think in a way that was less naive, more scientific, and more effective
than phenomenological existentialism and dialectical materialism combined. This is
how the efforts to unite phenomenology and Marxism were replaced by efforts to
combine Marxism with structuralism and psychoanalysis. But Foucault himself was
seeking a way out of phenomenology *and* Marxism – a way out, that is, of the philosophy of experience, the transcendental subject, and the metaphysics of "man" – in

order to arrive at a genuinely *critical* stance with respect to the social and scientific order of his time.

A quick glance at the titles of his works could suggest that he found his way out of this philosophical predicament by abandoning philosophy altogether and turning to history instead. From the very start until the very end, from *History of Madness*, his first book, to *History of Sexuality*, his last book, history seems to be the focus of his thought. Instead of focusing on the traditional problems or areas of philosophy, or on the thought of previous philosophers, his work consisted of *historical* investigations, limited, for the most part, to the classical and modern ages, concerning a wide range of topics, such as madness, crime, or desire and pleasure, the birth of institutions such as clinical medicine or the modern prison, the emergence of disciplines such as psychiatry, the *scientia sexualis*, political economy, biology, or linguistics. (Two significant and historically antithetical exceptions to this general rule can be found in Foucault's work from the late 1970s and early 1980s. *The Birth of Biopolitics* from 1978–1979 [ECF-BBIO] is devoted to a series of analyses of the birth of neo-liberalism in the twentieth century and discusses at length the Chicago School of Economics, whose views and theories have shaped our lives and influenced policies in the last thirty years. At the other end of the historical spectrum, we need to note Foucault's sustained engagement with, and readings of, philosophers of Greek and Roman antiquity concerned with the care of the self and the aesthetics of existence [ECF-COT, ECF-GSO, and ECF-HOS].) Telling, in that respect, are the conditions surrounding the publication of Foucault's main PhD thesis. Initially called *Madness and Unreason (Folie et déraison)*, its publication was rejected by the philosopher Brice Parain, then a series editor at Gallimard, but accepted by the historian Philippe Ariès for his series "Civilisations and Mentalities" with Plon and published in May 1961 under the exact title of *Folie et déraison. Histoire de la folie à l'âge classique*. The subtitle emphasized the historical dimension and credentials of the book. And although we must not forget that Foucault devoted his "secondary thesis," normally devoted to a figure of the philosophical canon, to translating and presenting Kant's *Anthropology from a Pragmatic Point of View*, we need also to recall that he eventually published the translation, but without its long introduction.

For further evidence of Foucault's ambiguous, if not distant, relation to philosophy, one could point to the fact that his first positions as an assistant professor and then as a full professor at the University of Clermont-Ferrand, while in a department of philosophy, were in fact in psychology, and the only Chairs in Philosophy he ever held in a career that spanned twenty-four years were between 1966 and 1969, first at the University of Tunis and then, in 1969, at the newly created University of Vincennes. His Chair at the Collège de France, which he occupied between 1970 and the year of his death (1984), bore the intriguing title of "History of the Systems of Thought" and replaced that of Jean Hyppolite, his teacher, in the "History of Philosophical Thought." Finally, Foucault himself was perfectly content to admit that he only worked with the help of a handful of philosophers, thus suggesting that the vast majority were, for his own purposes, of little or no use at all.

But the truth is that if Foucault breaks with a certain way of doing philosophy, of constructing problems, and with a certain conception regarding the task and goal of philosophy, it is to invent a new way of philosophizing. My aim here is to show that Foucault's work is rigorously philosophical, and that the problem with which he is concerned – namely, the manner in which what he calls *savoirs* (kinds of knowledge) are intimately related to certain apparatuses (*dispositifs*) of power, which in turn generate specific modes of subjectivity – is underpinned by the question of truth, or, more specifically, by the system of exclusion and normativity that truth presupposes, and the historical conditions under which such a system is constituted.

There is no doubt, as I have already suggested, that Foucault was impressed by the way in which structuralism transformed the social sciences, and that his work from the 1960s, most notably *The Order of Things* and *The Archaeology of Knowledge*, bear the mark of that method and approach. However, even before turning to structuralism as a way out of the dominant philosophical and intellectual climate of the 1940s and 1950s, and its commitment to various forms of humanism, Foucault was drawn to a different kind of philosophy, oriented toward the analysis of scientific concepts and procedures. From the time of his doctoral thesis (1961) and at least until the lecture courses at the Collège de France from the late 1970s, his work unfolded not under the banner of "a philosophy of experience, of meaning, of the subject" (EEW2, 465), as he described it famously, and with which much of French philosophy came to be identified after World War II, but under the more discrete, seemingly modest, and more narrow auspices of a philosophy concerned with the conditions of emergence of the sciences and the formation of scientific concepts, and exemplified by figures such as Koyré, Canguilhem, and Bachelard. Foucault saw the latter two in particular as enacting a powerful self-critique of reason itself and its concepts, and emphasizing the ruptures, discontinuities, and contingencies behind the apparent "progress" of science. It is their approach and aspects of their method that he eventually applied to the "human sciences." He sought to identify the points that make possible the shift from one discursive "regime" or "formation" to the next and to show how, in the end, there is more in common between, say, natural history, general grammar, and the analysis of wealth in the classical age than between natural history and modern biology, general grammar and philology, or the analysis of wealth and economics. Such an emphasis on the historical conditions underlying epistemic shifts distinguished Foucault's approach from that of the historian of ideas or the philosopher of science. In *The Archaeology of Knowledge*, for example, Foucault makes it very clear that he is concerned not with the sciences themselves, or their logical propositions, but with what he calls "discourses" and "statements" (*énoncés*) (EAK, 126–131). Whereas the first approach aims to reveal the actual, positive content of the sciences, and thus their "truth" dimension and their "meaning," the second approach ("archaeology") analyzes those sciences from the point of view of their "historical a priori" or "archive"; that is, from the point of view of what makes them "possible and necessary" (EOT, 168).

At the same time, and notwithstanding the obvious Kantian tone of Foucault's approach, the shift from a critical investigation in the Kantian sense (that is, in the sense of the conditions of knowledge and experience as rooted in the faculties of the transcendental subject) to history as the very terrain for the constitution of such conditions is distinctly non-Kantian, and, one could even argue, deprives transcendental philosophy itself of its own grounds and justification. Archaeology, then, is a seemingly transcendental category or method, concerned with the conditions of possibility of knowledge, or, better said, with the real conditions of emergence of knowledge (EAK, 127), except that the conditions in question are not those of knowledge *in general* but of historically and geographically specific "*epistemes*" that do not refer back to, or presuppose, the faculties of the human subject as their point of origin. If anything, archaeology reveals the extent to which there is no ahistorical subject, and thus no being that we can designate as human from the start: subjects aren't constituted a priori but constructed as effects of the *savoir* in question and the practices, discourses, and institutions it makes possible. Foucault also describes his work as the search for the "unconscious" of knowledge; that is, for the autonomous domain, with its rules and structures, that lies beneath or behind what knowledge knows of itself, and the actual knowledge-content (*connaissance*) it pursues (see FDE1, 681–683).

But, one might ask, what is this entire effort, this new method, set of concepts, and series of detailed analyses ultimately with a view to? This is the point, perhaps, at which we begin to put our finger on the distinctly philosophical aspect of Foucault's work, for he does not see archaeology – and, one could argue, even genealogy – as an end in itself. He sees history, and specifically archaeology, as primarily oriented toward, and as a way of engaging critically with, our own present: with the concepts we use, the rationality we operate under, the objects we construct, and the type of subjects we have become. He sees archaeology, and even genealogy, as a tool, rather than an end in itself. To an interviewer who asked him the extent to which his work could be seen as philosophical, Foucault replied the following: "It's quite possible that what I'm doing is somewhat related to philosophy, especially given the fact that, since Nietzsche, the aim of philosophy is no longer to utter a universal and transhistorical truth, but to diagnose" (FDE1, 606). In another interview from the same year (1967), he said the following: "The role of philosophy is to diagnose. The philosopher has ceased to try and say what is eternally. The far more arduous and fleeting task he is now faced with is to say what is happening" (FDE1, 581). Here we have an image of philosophy that in the interview from which the passage is extracted Foucault traces back to Nietzsche. Elsewhere, however, and perhaps surprisingly, he traces it back to Kant – not the Kant of the critical project, who seeks to identify the conditions and limits of human experience and knowledge, but the Kant of the historical essays, and of "An Answer to the Question: What Is Enlightenment?" in particular. In his lecture course at the Collège de France from 1982–1983, Foucault says that Kant's text has always represented for him something like an "emblem" or a "fetish" (ECF-GSO, 7). In his essay, Kant raises the question of *who* we are and what it means to philosophize *today*. He raises the question of philosophy against the backdrop of an event, the Enlightenment, which he defines as "the courage to make use of one's own understanding" and the "*public* use of one's reason." Courage is the subject matter of Foucault's final course at the Collège de France (FCF-CV), to which I shall return. Philosophy, then, insofar as it is bound up with such a project, is identified with an "attitude" and an "*ethos*," best described as the diagnosis and "permanent critique of our historical era" (EEW1, 312). The task of philosophy is thus relatively modest: it does not claim to speak in the name of universal truths and eternal essences, the absolute, or even human nature; it aims simply to understand the present. Such a seemingly modest activity, however, requires a certain "courage" and involves a different conception of truth, to which we shall return. At the same time, the activity of diagnosis, and thus of philosophy, is no longer restricted to those who claim to be philosophers, who address the classical problems of philosophy, or who engage with its history. The critical and diagnostic activity of thought, with which Foucault identifies genuine philosophy, can be found in a number of discourses and disciplines (history, linguistics, psychoanalysis, anthropology, religion, etc.), united by a common suspicion regarding the universal notions of truth, freedom, or subjectivity, and so on.

But how can philosophy reconcile the demand to respond to what is happening, and its task as a diagnostician, with the "archive" and the archaeological point of view? How can the analysis and description of the historical a priori, of the emergence of discourses of truth and knowledge between the seventeenth and the nineteenth centuries, help us understand who we are *today*? What is the relation between today and yesterday, present and past, and to what extent *can* archaeology and philosophy (as diagnosis) work together? Or is there a dimension of philosophy – the dimension concerned with the present – that falls outside the realm of archaeology, and this in such a way that Foucault will eventually need not so much to abandon the archaeological point of view as supplement it with a different kind of approach? As the next section of this essay will make clear, the sense of critique that is required in order to carry out the task of diagnosing our historical era is not that of Kant but that of Nietzsche. It is critique as *genealogy*.

In *The Archaeology of Knowledge*, Foucault makes it clear that the archive and archaeological point of view presuppose a certain distance with respect to their object, and that they can interrogate only the past. It is, Foucault claims, impossible for us to describe our own archive (EAK, 130), for the simple reason that it is from within its rules that we speak and think. In its actual state, the archive is thus uncircumventable. In order to grasp our own archive, we would need the sort of distance that, by definition, we do not have. And yet, the archive does not bear on the remotest of pasts, a past that would be so distant that it would no longer concern us. Rather, its role is to interrogate the threshold of our own present, to reach the point where we understand what we are no longer, without quite understanding what we are. This is the extent to which archaeology itself is a diagnostic tool. The historical perspective is necessary to not take our own situation and present for granted, to question it, and see where it has introduced discontinuities, paradigmatic shifts, and ruptures. It is necessary to see the extent to which we tend to draw general if not universal conclusions, on the basis of our own present experience – an experience that, far from proceeding from a universal truth, human nature, or the essence of things, was shaped as a result of historical contingencies. Those contingencies are the *real* (and not merely possible) conditions of experience. They *are* the (historical) a priori.

But is it enough, Foucault began to wonder in the 1970s, to analyze and describe the discourses of the human sciences and extract their historical a priori? Are the diagnostic and critical aims of Foucault's project sufficiently well served by the purely epistemological level on which archaeology operates? Should we not also ask about the deep *motivations* underlying the type of *epistemes* analyzed hitherto, or, to use a Nietzschean expression, about the "will" that corresponds to the very statements of truth those *epistemes* imply? It is precisely after the publication of *The Archaeology of Knowledge* (1969), which marks the culminating point of Foucault's archaeological period, and before the publication of *Discipline and Punish* (1975), devoted to the birth of disciplinary power and exemplifying his genealogical approach, that, in a short period that includes his first lecture course at the Collège de France, Foucault writes and lectures extensively on Nietzsche, and on the problem of genealogy in particular. (At Vincennes, in February 1969, Foucault taught a course on "Nietzsche and Genealogy." In 1971, as a tribute to Jean Hyppolite, he published "Nietzsche, la généalogie, l'histoire" [FGNH; collected in FDE2, 136–156; in English, in EEW2, 369–392]. In April 1971, he gave a lecture at McGill University on "How to Think the History of Truth with Nietzsche without Presupposing Truth" [included in FCF-LSV, 195–213]. Finally, *La volonté de savoir* [FCF-LSV] sets up a radical opposition between the Aristotelian and the Nietzschean "morphologies of knowing [*savoir*].") Behind the break with the history of philosophy, and even with the history of *philosophical thought*, which his Chair at the Collège de France seems to announce, it is precisely to that history that Foucault devotes his first lecture course, and it is that very legacy that allows his own thought to gain the critical power it was lacking.

At the very beginning of his first lecture course at the Collège de France (1970–1971), precisely entitled "Lectures on the Will to Know," Foucault wondered whether "it is possible to establish a theory of the will to know that could be used as a foundation for the historical analyses" (FCF-LSV, 3). How are we to understand "foundation" in this context? Far from wanting to ground his own historical investigations on more scientific and secure foundations, Foucault opens up a line of questioning that will reveal a multiple, shifting, and ultimately disturbing origin, bound up with interpretation and even "fiction" (FDE2a, 236). Behind what Aristotle, and the entire tradition that followed, saw as the supposedly *natural* desire of human beings to know (*le désir de connaître*), their inborn curiosity, and their inclination to distinguish the truth from the false, built into the very notion of philosophy, there is something quite different: a will to know (*volonté de savoir*) and to truth. Inspired by Nietzsche, Foucault understands this will or desire not as oriented toward, or essentially concerned with, knowledge and truth – that is, not as this essentially epistemic and disinterested drive, emanating from a cognitive subject – but as oriented toward, or intimately bound up with, the will to subjugate and dominate. Truth, in other words, is not just, and not even primarily, a matter of knowledge (*connaissance*). It is also, and primarily, a matter of *power*: whereas knowledge refers to "the system that allows one to give a prior unity, a reciprocal belonging and a co-naturality between desire and knowledge," knowing (*savoir*) is "what needs to be wrested from the interiority of knowledge so as to find in it the object of a will [*vouloir*], the goal of a desire, the instrument of a domination, the workings of a struggle [*l'enjeu d'une lutte*]" (FCF-LSV, 18). The will to truth, and the "veridiction" it generates, are indissociable from a "will to power," a will to dominate and subjugate – indissociable, that is, from what Foucault recognizes as systems or *dispositifs* of power, and institutions such as the asylum, the Panopticon, the school, the market, or the family, which shape, mold, and correct minds and bodies alike. Unlike Nietzsche, though, Foucault does not attribute this will to a form or type of life or an instinct. Through a translation of Nietzsche's *Macht* as *pouvoir* (power, as in political power) rather than *puissance* (potentiality, as in sexual potency), Foucault ultimately displaces the terrain of Nietzsche's analysis and avoids his own naturalism. But he does retain the idea that to every discourse of "truth" concerning the human, such as psychiatry or criminology, belongs a specific distribution and organization of power, a process of subjection (*assujettissement*) as well as subjectification: "The birth of the human sciences goes hand in hand with the installation of new mechanisms of power" (EPPC, 106).

This is how, to use the example of the discourses on sexuality that begin to proliferate in the nineteenth century, Foucault claims that he wants "to deal not only with those discourses, but also with the will that sustains them" (EHS1, 16). In other words, he's not concerned to know whether certain discourses manage to formulate the truth about human sexuality, or on the contrary only generate lies that conceal the truth. Nor is he interested in denouncing the many errors, illusions, naivetes, or moralisms concerning "sex." Rather, he wishes to identify the "will to know" that operates as their support and instrument (EHS1, 20). Specifically, the question is one of knowing how, at a specific time and over a certain period, human sexuality – or, to be more precise, the object that came to be known as "sex" – began to fall under the authority of a discourse and a will oriented no longer toward sensations and pleasure, the law and the forbidden, but toward *truth*; that is, toward the system of opposition and exclusion between truth and falsity, usefulness and danger, or the normal and the pathological. The problem, in other words, is one of knowing how "sex" emerged as an object precisely through its constitution within a scientific discourse, the *scientia sexualis*, and as a result of the need to control, discipline, or "normalize" the sexual body through a number of techniques or "technologies," including that of "telling the truth" about one's actions and desires.

In "The Subject and Power" (1982), Foucault claims that "the main objective today is not to discover, but to *refuse* what we are" (EEW3, 336, my emphasis). And with that goal in mind, philosophy is more necessary than ever, over and beyond its ability to diagnose: "We need to promote new forms of subjectivity by *refusing* the type of subjectivity that has been imposed on us for several centuries" (ibid.). Genealogy, Foucault says in *Society Must Be Defended*, is not just a method; it is also a "tactic," which aims to "set free" or "desubjugate" (ECF-SMD, 10). Such a liberation would signal not the end of power relations (slavery alone, or total domination, for Foucault signals the absence of power) but "a new economy of power relations" (EEW3, 329). The problem, in other words, is no longer just one of diagnosis and even critique. It has also become a problem of creation and invention.

Although Foucault never explicitly says, or never had the time to say, what such technologies could consist of for us *today*, he did engage in a series of readings of such technologies in the ancient world, and of that of the "care of the self" (*epimeleia heauto, cura sui*) in particular, which the Cartesian tradition abandoned in favor of the sole technique of self-knowledge, also inherited from the Greeks. Far from excluding the notion of truth, those later texts all try to bring back into the domain of philosophy questions and practices traditionally associated with spirituality, for if by "philosophy" one means this form of thought that asks about the true and the false, about how to distinguish the true from the false, and how the subject might have access to the true, then we will need to recognize as "spirituality" the set of practices, experiences, and exercises (such as purification, renunciation, and conversion, but also a range of erotic practices) recognized as necessary *in order to* arrive at the truth and through which the subject is constituted as a subject of truth. Foucault claims that those two types of questioning and experiences were never separated in the various schools of philosophy of antiquity, with one notable exception, that of Aristotle, who was subsequently described as *the* philosopher. If the "Cartesian moment" is in that respect exemplary, it is not the founding moment. By turning the question of the access to truth into a question of knowledge, philosophy, especially in its modern phase, cuts itself off from the tradition of the care of the self, which Foucault is concerned with reawakening in his later work.

Let me return to the example of "sexuality." Foucault contrasts such a science of sexuality with the *ars erotica* of ancient Rome, China, Japan, India, and Arabic societies. It is not as if one could not associate the category of truth with such an art. In fact, all those techniques or technologies of the body and its pleasures involve a certain discourse of truth, but it is one that is extracted from the pleasure itself, understood as a practice and recorded as an experience. And pleasure is not considered from the point of view of the law, of what is permitted and what is forbidden, or that of utility, but from the point of view of its intensity, its specific quality, its duration, and other angles. This distinction is crucial because it means that there is room for a discourse of truth that is not that of science – whether sexual, political, economical, or whatever. It is precisely to this *other* truth and this *other* will that Foucault will turn in the 1980s – in relation to the use of pleasures (see EHS2, Chapter 5) but also in relation to ethics and politics, as his final lecture course, "The Courage of Truth," makes amply clear. The question then becomes the following: In relation to ourselves as well as others, can we will something other than domination? Can we approach the problem of government – of ourselves and others – in ways that are not disciplinary and subjugating? Can we invent modalities of power outside the technologies of discipline of the nineteenth century and the more recent, biopolitical technologies of the self? This is what is at stake in Foucault's final phase of thought and in his writings and lectures from the 1980s, which focus on the ways in which, in antiquity, an entire discourse and a large body of literature was devoted to the care of the self, the way to govern oneself and relate to others not as members of a "society," "individuals," or a "population" but as subjects who construct themselves through a series of practical, spiritual, and aesthetic practices aimed at articulating a new assemblage of "truth" and "subjectivity."

In that respect, Foucault is interested in emphasizing the fundamental contrast between the technology of confession, based on the need, if not the command, to speak the truth about oneself as a condition of one's salvation, and the Greek, essentially Stoic and Cynic, practice of *parrēsia*, understood as openness and frankness of speech, as the courage to speak the truth even in the most delicate and dangerous circumstances – a form of discourse, and an attitude, that was contrasted with flattery, rhetoric, and sophistry and involved the subject as a whole. The philosophical life of the Cynic is not one of knowledge and contemplation. It is a life of combat, a "militant" life, Foucault says, fully aware of this anachronistic characterization. The Cynic is aggressive. Like a dog (*kuon*), from which his own name is derived, he bites, barks, and shocks. He attacks his enemies – not the actual people but their vices, illusions, vanity, desires, and passions, as well as their fears and weaknesses, and of course his own, not only with words, sometimes especially not with words, but with blows, with sticks. That is the extent to which he is useful, politically useful. The struggle is also against conventions, laws, and habits, against an entire social and political order. The Cynic is an *agent provocateur*, a *guerrillero*: "Why not practice incest?" he asks; "Why not cannibalism?"; "Why clothes?"; "Why the distinction between public and private, why the private at all, domesticity, marriage, and why marriage between *two* people?" The Cynic works and struggles toward a constant *dépouillement* (a stripping, denuding, shedding) and a *décapage* (a cleaning or cleansing) of existence, his own as well as that of others, to take it to the limit, to strip it to its absolute minimum, to leave no aspect of it unquestioned. We have the image of the dog again, chewing on his bone, cleaning it, exposing it; the dog that guards, attacks, exposes, threatens, cleans, and scours, but in all innocence and sovereignty, out of love for others.

Foucault's relation to philosophy – to the discipline of philosophy, its history and the way in which throughout that history it has tended to construct itself as a particular science, the science of truth itself, and therefore as the science of all sciences – was, and remained, ambiguous and ambivalent. If he turns toward history, it is to question the ontological and transcendental claims that philosophy tends to make. But, in turning to history, he does not turn away from philosophy. Rather, he raises philosophical questions that history itself cannot raise, and he is thus able to bring to the surface the unconscious or a priori of the human and social sciences, the system of truth and power they presuppose, and the modes of subjectivity they generate. That he does with a view to asking who we are *today*, and with the further view of asking whether, and how, we might resist them, how we might create new technologies of the self, new ways of governing oneself as well as others. Let us leave the final word to Foucault himself, who once said: "If someone wanted to be a philosopher but didn't ask himself the question, 'what is knowledge?', or 'what is truth?', in what sense could one say he was a philosopher? And as much as I may say that I'm not a philosopher, if it's truth that I'm concerned with, then I am still a philosopher" (FDE2a, 30–31).

Miguel de Beistegui

SEE ALSO

> *Archaeology*
> *Critique*
> *Genealogy*
> *History*
> *Marxism*
> *Phenomenology*
> *Truth*
> *The Ancients (Stoics and Cynics)*
> *Immanuel Kant*
> *Friedrich Nietzsche*

SUGGESTED READING

Gutting, Gary. 1989. *Michel Foucault's Archaeology of Scientific Reason*. Cambridge: Cambridge University Press.

Han, Béatrice. 2002. *Foucault's Critical Project: Between the Transcendental and the Historical*, trans. Edward Pile. Stanford, CA: Stanford University Press.

60

PLAGUE

I N THE SECOND lecture of his 1975 course on "Abnormal" at the Collège de
France, Foucault drew a distinction between sovereign and disciplinary mechanisms of power by examining the two apparatuses that were put in place to deal
with, on the one hand, leprosy and, on the other, the plague.

In the case of leprosy, the "model of control" used during the Middle Ages was
that of exclusion, which entailed the "rigorous division" of certain individuals from
the others, the constitution of two masses foreign to one another, and the subsequent juridical and political "disqualification" of one of those masses with respect to
the other (ECF-AB, 43–44). Foucault contrasts the model of exclusion with that of
the quarantine, a model used more and more often during the eighteenth century to
combat the plague.

First and foremost, the quarantine, as a model for the control of individuals, is
a mechanism of inclusion: it concerns itself with the "spatial partitioning and control" of plague-infested towns. Certainly, there existed an element of exclusion in the
model of the quarantine, but whereas those suffering from leprosy were cast away
into a "vague territory" and left to fend for themselves, the quarantined territory
immediately became the object of a "fine and detailed analysis, of a meticulous spatial partitioning" (ECF-AB, 44–45). As Foucault had explained during a talk given
in Brazil in 1974, the quarantine model, which involved the partitioning of a space
into districts and the constant surveillance of that space by sentries and appointed
inspectors who recorded everything they saw and in turn answered to a higher medical authority, relied on a medical power that sought

> to position individuals in relation to one another, to isolate them, to individu-
> ate them, to monitor them one by one, to control their state of health, to verify
> whether they were still alive or whether they were dead and in this way to main-
> tain society in a space that was compartmentalized, constantly under surveillance,

and controlled by a register, as complete as possible, of all of the events that had occurred. (EEW3, 146, translation modified)

Throughout these analyses, Foucault associates the model of exclusion with a sovereign, negative mechanism of rejection. On the other hand, the eighteenth-century practice of quarantine, as a model of "political control," corresponds to a different historical process, which Foucault describes as "the invention of positive technologies of power" (ECF-AB, 48). In other words, the model of the quarantine is a properly disciplinary model of control: it effects the spatial repartitioning of a territory and controls the circulation of bodies within that territory through the establishment of a clear medical hierarchy and the creation of a finely regulated network of surveillance and recordkeeping. Thus, as a technique of power, the quarantine functions not through sovereign exclusion but through the mechanisms, proper to discipline, of the "close and analytical inclusion of elements" and the distribution of individual bodies as "differential individualities," mechanisms that "secure the formation, investment, accumulation, and growth of knowledge" (ibid.).

Thus, the significance of the quarantine, as Foucault would later explain in *Discipline and Punish*, lies in the fact that its myriad mechanisms constitute "a compact model of the disciplinary apparatus" (EDP, 197, translation modified). And it is precisely these mechanisms that Jeremy Bentham's Panopticon would later reinscribe in architectural form. Accordingly, if the quarantine represents a model for the disciplinary apparatus put in place in exceptional situations and circumstances, such as an epidemic of plague, then the Panopticon is the "diagram of a mechanism of power brought to its ideal form," its "architectural figure," through which the mechanisms of discipline encountered in the quarantine can be generalized in such a way as to define "power relations in terms of the everyday life of men" (EDP, 205).

David-Olivier Gougelet

SEE ALSO

> *Abnormal*
> *Control*
> *Madness*
> *Medicine*
> *Normalization*
> *Power*
> *Space*

SUGGESTED READING

Crampton, Jeremy, and Stuart Elden, eds. 2007. *Space, Knowledge and Power: Foucault and Geography*. Aldershot: Ashgate.
Dillon, Michael, and Andrew Neal, eds. 2008. *Foucault on Politics, Security, and War*. London: Palgrave.

61

PLEASURE

PLEASURE SEEMS TO be used in at least three different ways in Foucault's work: as an alternative to a discourse of sexuality based on desire; as a feature of the Greek understanding of *aphrodisiac*; and as a practice of the self, or *askesis*.

Foucault contrasts pleasure with desire in a number of his writings and interviews, but it is in volume one of *The History of Sexuality* that he first introduces pleasure as an alternative to desire because he argues that desire is trapped within the logic of juridico-discursive power. Even when power is viewed as productive and constitutive of desire, desire only becomes important within a discourse of sexuality that judges one based on one's desires and seeks to extort the truth from individuals about their desires through confession. Whereas desire is bound up with processes of individualization, normalization, and control, pleasure is not.

In two often-quoted passages from the first volume of *The History of Sexuality*, Foucault points to the possibility of thinking about sex and sexuality differently, by moving away from sex-desire toward bodies and pleasures:

> It is the agency of sex that we must break away from, if we aim – through a tactical reversal of the various mechanisms of sexuality – to counter the grips of power with the claims of bodies, pleasures and knowledges, in their multiplicity and their possibility of resistance. The rallying point for the counterattack against the deployment of sexuality ought not to be sex-desire, but bodies and pleasures. (EHS1, 157)

> Moreover, we need to consider the possibility that one day, perhaps in a different economy of bodies and pleasures, people will no longer quite understand the ruses of sexuality, and the power that sustains its organization, were able to subject us to that austere monarchy of sex, so that we become dedicated to the

endless tasks of reinforcing its secret, of exacting the truest confessions from a shadow. (EHS1, 159)

Some scholars wonder whether Foucault is invoking a prediscursive, natural notion of bodies and pleasures here. Foucault clearly posits pleasure as a point of resistance to the discourse of sexuality. In his subsequent work on the history of sexuality in ancient Greece and early Rome, he explores pleasure in more depth; in these historical periods, it is connected to the techniques of living, rather than repression and negation (EEW1, 89). Insofar as it stands outside the normalizing scientific and religious discourses that since the seventeenth century have constituted the discourse of sexuality, pleasure provides an alternative way of thinking about bodily practices that is not reducible to sex or desire.

Pleasure, however, is not simply an alternative to sex-desire but is also an element of it. It is not the having of pleasures but the classifying of them that is problematic; confession played a role in the "great archive of the pleasures of sex" along with the discourses of science and medicine (EHS1, 63). Power and pleasure reinforce one another, forming a "perpetual spiral" (EHS1, 45). According to Foucault, "Pleasure and power do not cancel or turn back against one another; they seek out, overlap and reinforce one another" (EHS1, 48). Within the discourse of sexuality, pleasure is produced, at least in part, through the classification of perversions. In this way, *scientia sexualis* intensifies pleasures produced within the discourse of sexuality through power and knowledge. According to Foucault, sexuality is a historical construct, "a great surface network in which the stimulation of bodies, the intensification of pleasures, the incitement to discourse, the formation of special knowledges, the strengthening of controls and resistances, are linked to one another, in accordance with a few major strategies of knowledge and power" (EHS1, 105–106). In volume one of *The History of Sexuality*, Foucault shows how pleasure, power, and desire work together to produce sex, which is assumed to be the object of the discourse of sexuality but is instead its product. Pleasure here (pleasures of sex), as linked to power and produced through classification, is part of the apparatus of sexuality based on sex-desire, whereas pleasure as *askesis* opens up new possibilities outside the discourse of sexuality. For instance, when Foucault discusses sadomasochism as an innovative practice, he claims that pleasure is "desexualized" because sadomasochism broadens the notion of pleasure to bodily pleasure rather than simply sexual pleasure (EEW1, 165).

Pleasure plays a primary role in volume two of *The History of Sexuality*, subtitled *The Use of Pleasure*. Given Foucault's rallying cry near the end of the first volume, this is not surprising. *Aphrodisia* (acts of love), a central concept for ancient Greeks, includes acts, pleasures, and desires. These three elements were linked together in a dynamic relationship, and for the Greeks the object of moral concern was not any single element of this ensemble but the relationship among them. In *The Use of Pleasure* Foucault raises the question: "How could one, how must one 'make use' (*chresthai*) of this dynamics of pleasures, desires and acts" (EHS2, 52)?

In a discussion he had with Rabinow and Dreyfus in April 1983, Foucault lays out the different relationship of the three elements of sexual behavior: (1) acts; (2) pleasure; and (3) desire. He claims that these three elements have different emphases at different times in different places. For the Greeks, the act was prioritized, and then pleasure and desire played minor roles. For the Chinese, pleasure was prioritized and then desire, with acts following. For Christians, desire becomes the focus, then the act, with pleasure trailing behind. And for we "moderns," desire has become all important and then the acts, whereas pleasure has nearly disappeared. The following table provides an illustration.

Greeks	<u>acte</u> – plaisir – [désir]
Chinese	<u>plaisir</u> – désir – [acte]
Christian	[<u>désir</u>] – acte – [plaisir]
Modern	<u>désir</u> – acte – ([plaisir?])

The triangular relationship among acts, pleasures, and desires shifts over time, but it is within this triangle that Foucault thinks we can trace the genealogy of the subject.

For the ancient Greeks, the pleasures of the body included the pleasures of food and drink as well as sex. The pleasures were seen as natural, and the main issue was not what was permitted and what was prohibited but how to avoid excess. Sex is not privileged, and its pleasures are viewed as natural along with other bodily pleasures. In fact, Foucault notes that the Greeks were much more concerned with food than with sex. Pleasure is not viewed as bad or evil as it is in the Christian tradition (EHS2, 16). In fact, the important question for the ancient Greeks is not *what* pleasures one has (i.e., the objects of one's pleasure and desire) but *how* one has one's pleasures. The measure of pleasure is quantity; excessive pleasure is self-indulgent. But the moderation of pleasures comes from the person experiencing the pleasures, not from the surveillance or judgment of others. Mastery of the pleasures is synonymous with mastery of the self. Unlike in the eighteenth and nineteenth centuries, when Christianity, medicine, and science categorized one in terms of one's desires, in ancient Greece the emphasis was on how one used one's pleasure, not what gave one pleasure. Thus, as Foucault says, "moral discrimination was more dynamic than morphological" (EHS2, 50). In other words, it did not matter if one's object of affection was a man or a woman. What mattered was how one conducted oneself, whether or not one acted, and if one's actions were in moderation. In his genealogy of the "desiring subject," the move from pleasures experienced through acts (in ancient Greece) to pleasure bound up with desires and identity is the shift from doing to being. This shift from acts to desires corresponds with the creation of categories of sexual identity: "This new persecution of the peripheral sexualities entailed an *incorporation of perversions* and a new *specification of individuals....* The sodomite had been a temporary aberration; the homosexual was now a species" (EHS1, 42–43). Foucault was suspicious of fixed categories of identity, especially sexual identity, because these categories serve to regulate behavior and classify individuals according to their sexual desires. The discourse of sexuality marks desires as important and uses them to categorize individuals. Because it is based on sex-desire rather than pleasure, the ethic of sexuality is tied to the logic of repression and prohibition.

In *The Use of Pleasure*, one can see that the "mode of subjection" implied by the moral problematization of sexual conduct is markedly different for the ancient Greeks than it was after the early seventeenth century. The use of pleasures involved moderation and good judgment in the way that the individual managed his or her sexual activity. As Foucault put it, "It was not a question of what was permitted or forbidden among the desires that one felt or the acts that one committed, but of prudence, reflection, and calculation in the way one distributed and controlled his acts" (EHS2, 54).

In *Care of the Self*, Foucault continues his genealogy of the desiring subject, tracing the shift from an ethics of pleasure to an ethics of sexuality. During the first two centuries CE, Foucault notes an increasing mistrust of the pleasures and the limiting of sexual pleasure to marriage. Nonetheless, the focus on the pleasures at this time did not result in moral codes or prescriptions but in an intensification of the relationship to oneself (EHS3, 39, 41). In antiquity, pleasure was emphasized over desire, and the moderation of one's pleasures was seen as part and parcel of a beautiful life. Thus, choosing to act on one's desires was an aesthetic choice rather than a moral choice.

The use of pleasure in relation to sex comprises one aspect of an overall concern for the self, which includes diet, household relations, and erotic relations between men and boys. Out of this concern or care for the self, Foucault develops his ideas of *askesis* and a stylization of freedom: "The moral reflection of the Greeks on sexual behavior did not seek to justify interdictions, but to stylize a freedom – that freedom which the 'free' man exercised in his activity" (EHS2, 97).

In a number of interviews in the early 1980s, Foucault discussed the possibility of pleasure as *askesis*, as a practice of the self. He noted that contemporary pleasures are intense and innovative. Foucault discussed sadomasochism, drugs, and near-death experiences as having the potential for new forms of pleasure. Pleasure can be found as well in friendships and homosexual relationships. In responding to a question about what young homosexuals need to work on, Foucault said "not so much to liberate our desires but to make ourselves infinitely more susceptible to pleasure" (EEW1, 137). Foucault characterizes pleasure as intense, deep, and overwhelming (EEW1, 129). He advocates an ethics of sexual behavior based on pleasure and its intensification (EEW1, 131). Pleasure also plays a role in forging new models of relationships, particularly friendships between homosexual men. Foucault describes friendship as "the sum of all those things through which [people] can reciprocally give each other pleasure" (EEW1, 135). As relationships move into uncharted territory, possibilities for innovation and creativity open up for a multiplicity of new forms of life not based on discovering the truth about one's desires.

Pleasure provides an alternative to desire and to the discourse of sexuality that shapes us into desiring subjects. Although Foucault is not interested in returning to the ancient Greek notion of ethical practices (nor does he think it is possible), he posits that it provides us with a model where desire and pleasure had a strong connection and, significantly, ethical questions were not linked to scientific knowledge. The choices one made about ethical conduct were aesthetic choices and related to choosing a beautiful life, not to normalization. This escape from normalization and scientific categorization is also implied in Foucault's discussions of contemporary *askesis* of pleasure as these practices of pleasure go beyond our current experiences and may open up new possibilities for relating to others and to ourselves.

Margaret A. McLaren

SEE ALSO

Desire
Ethics
Friendship
Homosexuality
Love
Sex

SUGGESTED READING

McWhorter, Ladelle. 1999. *Bodies and Pleasures: Foucault and the Politics of Sexual Normalization.* Bloomington: Indiana University Press.
Sawicki, Jana. 2010. "Foucault, Queer Theory, and the Discourse of Desire: Why Embrace an Ethics of Pleasure?" in *Foucault and Philosophy*, ed. Timothy O'Leary and Christopher Falzon. London: Blackwell, pp. 185–203.

62

POLITICS

I N A LATE interview, Foucault made the following rather astonishing remark: "in fact what interests me is much more morals than politics or, in any case, politics as an ethics" (EFR, 375). This remark is astonishing not only because the term "politics" runs like a red thread through much of Foucault's work from the early 1970s onward – from his discussions of the politics of health in the eighteenth century to his accounts of the politics of truth and the politics of our selves, not to mention his analyses of biopolitics and political rationality – but also because his work has proved so inspirational for so much contemporary thinking about politics in the disciplines of philosophy and political theory. So what could Foucault have meant by saying that he is more interested in morals than in politics? He goes on to explain that his work is not "determined by a pre-established political outlook" and that it does not have as its aim "the realization of some definite political project" (ibid.). Indeed, as Foucault noted in another late interview, his readers have tried in vain to discern his politics; he has been read variously as a Marxist, an anarchist, a neoconservative, and a new liberal. As he puts it, "I think I have in fact been situated in most of the squares on the political checkerboard, one after another and sometimes simultaneously.... None of these descriptions is important by itself; taken together, on the other hand, they mean something. And I must admit that I rather like what they mean" (EEW1, 113). The inability to place Foucault's work on a spectrum of political ideologies is largely a function of his approach to political questions, which is through the lens of problematization: "I have never tried to analyze anything whatsoever from the point of view of politics, but always to ask politics what it had to say about the problems with which it was confronted" (EEW1, 115). (In this light, Foucault's early defense of his archaeological method as connected to genuinely progressive politics is quite interesting. See "Politics and the Study of Discourse," EFE, 53–72.)

But how, then, does Foucault understand politics? What, if anything, ties together his various uses of the term "politics"? Perhaps the best way to approach this question is to distinguish two different uses of the term "politics" in Foucault's work, a narrower and a wider use. The narrower use, operative in the preceding discussion and in much of Foucault's late work, defines "politics" as a specific domain or field of human activity, distinct from economics, morality/ethics, and religion, concerned with relations of governance. The wider use, by contrast, defines politics simply as the struggle for power, where relations of power are understood to be coextensive with the social body. The transition in Foucault's work in the late 1970s from the genealogy of disciplinary power and biopower to the analysis of governmentality could be understood as a transition from the wider to the narrower conception of politics, as Foucault moved away from the Nietzsche-inspired model of power as war that he formulated in the mid-1970s and toward an analysis of the government of self and others (see Lemke 1997). However, the wide conception never completely disappears from Foucault's work.

Moreover, Foucault never explicitly distinguishes these two uses of the term "politics" in his writings, and the two uses are often intricately intertwined, such that it is not always possible to disentangle them completely. But an implicit acknowledgment of such a distinction can be found in his 1973 lectures, "Truth and Juridical Forms," where he distinguishes his emerging conception of power as capillary and microscopic – which he calls here "infrapower" – from what is "traditionally called 'political power'" (EEW3, 86). The latter refers to the "state apparatus, or to the class in power," whereas the former refers to "the whole set of little powers, of little institutions situated at the lowest level" (EEW3, 85–86); that is, to what Foucault will later call the "micro-physics of power" (EDP, 26).

Foucault's wide conception of politics is exemplified in his discussion of "the politics of truth" in "Truth and Juridical Forms." There, Foucault draws on his reading of Nietzsche to trace the relationship between forms of knowledge and power relations conceived as relations of struggle. "One can understand what knowledge consists of," he writes, "only by examining these relations of struggle and power, the manner in which things and men hate one another, fight one another, and try to dominate one another, to exercise power relations over one another" (EEW3, 12). The result of such an examination would be a "political history of knowledge" or a historical analysis of "the politics of truth" (EEW3, 13). Nietzsche opened the door for such an analysis by demolishing the myth of knowledge purified of power relations, and showing that all knowledge production is woven together with struggles for power (EEW3, 32; see also EPK, 131–133).

Foucault articulates the idea of politics as a struggle for power in its strongest form in his 1975–1976 lecture course "Society Must Be Defended," when he discusses whether it makes sense to invert Clausewitz's dictum and claim that "politics is the continuation of war by other means" (ECF-SMD, 15). This would mean that "the role of political power is perpetually to use a sort of silent war to re-inscribe that relationship of force, and to re-inscribe it in institutions, economic inequalities, language, and even the bodies of individuals" (ECF-SMD, 15–16). The lectures pose the question of whether the model of politics as war is the best way to analyze political power (see ECF-SMD, 23), and Foucault's answer to this question seems to have evolved throughout the mid-1970s. Just prior to the start of 1975–1976 lectures, in a short interview published in 1975, Foucault seems to endorse the idea that politics is the continuation of war by other means (FDE2, 704; cited in Davidson 2003, xiii), but in 1977 he was more sanguine or at least more noncommittal on this point (see EPK, 164). Perhaps his most considered answer to this question is given in the crucial chapter on Method in volume 1 of the *History of Sexuality*:

> Should we turn the expression around, then, and say that politics is war pursued by other means? If we still wish to maintain a separation between war and politics, perhaps we should postulate rather that this multiplicity of force relations can be coded – in part but never totally – either in the form of "war," or in the form of "politics"; this would imply two different strategies (but the one always liable to switch into the other) for integrating these unbalanced, heterogeneous, unstable, and tense force relations. (EHS1, 93)

In other words, politics and war are distinct but nonetheless related strategies for integrating and coordinating the multiplicity of force relations in a particular society. If politics is not in itself war, it and war at least share some central defining characteristics: force and struggle.

In the next two sets of lecture courses, "Security, Territory, Population" (1977–1978) and "The Birth of Biopolitics" (1978–1979), the wide model of politics as a warlike struggle for power recedes and the narrower conception of politics as a distinctive domain linked to governmentality and the problematic of the state gains prominence. And yet, characteristically, Foucault gives this account of politics his own distinctive twist. Rather than starting from a theory of the state, Foucault aims to decenter the state from our understanding of politics and to focus instead on the broader techniques of governmentality and political rationality that undergird and give rise to modern state forms. This is connected to his attempt to displace the problematic of sovereignty from our understandings of politics, for "to pose the problem in terms of the State means to continue posing it in terms of the sovereign and sovereignty, that is to say in terms of law" (EPK, 122). Hence, cutting off the head of the kind means not only constructing a genealogy of disciplinary power, as Foucault did in *Discipline and Punish* and related texts, but also constructing a genealogy of the modern state. Such a genealogy would show "how the emergence of the state as a fundamental political issue can in fact be situated within a more general history of governmentality, or, if you like, in the field of practices of power" (ECF-STP, 247).

In connection with this general aim, in the 1977–1978 lectures, Foucault traces the roots of the mode of governmentality that emerges in the modern state in the late sixteenth and early seventeenth centuries back to its roots in Christian pastoral power (see ECF-STP, lecture 7). He also charts the emergence in the seventeenth century of a conception of the political domain as distinct from the economic, moral, or religious domains, governed by its own distinctive form of rationality, *raison d'État* (see ECF-STP, lectures 10 and 11). Similarly, in the 1978–1979 course, Foucault analyzes the emergence of a liberal mode of governmentality that receives extreme expression in the economic neoliberalism in mid-twentieth-century German and American economic thinking. This mode is distinct from previous modes of governmentality, which had been centered on notions of first sovereignty and later *raison d'État*. These modes can be contrasted by considering the types of questions posed by each art of government:

> At one time these amounted to the question: Am I governing in proper conformity to moral, natural, or divine laws? Then, in the sixteenth and seventeenth centuries, with *raison d'État*, it was: Am I governing with sufficient intensity, depth, and attention to detail so as to bring the state to the point fixed by what it should be, to bring it to its maximum strength? And now the problem will be: Am I governing at the border between the too much and too little, between the maximum and minimum fixed for me by the nature of things – I mean, by the necessities intrinsic to the operations of government? (ECF-BBIO, 19)

For the liberal and neoliberal forms of governmentality, the limits of governmental rationality will be set by political economy. At the conclusion of his lectures on liberal and neoliberal governmentality, Foucault asks: "What is politics, in the end, if not both the interplay of these different arts of government with their different reference points and the debate to which these different arts of government give rise? It seems to me that it is here that politics is born" (ECF-BBIO, 313). Here, politics is tied to the question of governance but is not equated with the state in any straightforward manner; rather, it is connected to processes of what Foucault calls "statification" (ECF-BBIO, 77).

To be sure, what I am calling the narrower and wider conceptions of politics in Foucault's work intersect and overlap in important ways. These two conceptions of politics arguably intersect in Foucault's discussions of governmentality. Here, Foucault doesn't exactly abandon his earlier notion of politics as a struggle for power – even if he moves away from the strong formulation of politics as war that he flirted with in the mid-1970s – but he does seek to connect that notion with politics in the sense of the emergence of specific governance structures and state forms. The result is a genealogical analysis – an analysis that is defined methodologically by its commitment to the irreducibly political nature of truth – of the role that micropowers play in the emergence of the modern state and the development of its distinctive art of government and political rationality.

These two conceptions of politics are also connected through the idea of politicization. In an interview conducted in 1977, Foucault was asked to clarify his understanding of the term "political." "The domain of the political," he responded, is constituted by "the set of relations of force in a given society," and "politics is a more-or-less global strategy for co-ordinating and directing those relations" (EPK, 189). In this context, "the problem is not so much that of defining a political 'position' (which is to choose from a pre-existing set of possibilities) but to imagine and to bring into being new schemas of politicization" (EPK, 190). Here, politicization means thematizing a set of previously unthematized power relations – which are already political in the wide sense of the term – and inventing new schemas for analysis and criticism that show the relevance of these power relations for our understanding of politics in the narrower sense. (See also, in this vein, a 1973 interview in which Foucault claimed that one of the distinctive characteristics of the political movements of that time was the politicization of practices, institutions, and domains of life previously thought of as nonpolitical [FDE2, 428].)

What, then, of Foucault's claim, mentioned at the beginning of this entry, that insofar as he is interested in politics at all, his interest is in politics as an ethics? Here the notion of governmentality is once again central. For Foucault, ethics concerns one's relation to self. When Foucault says that he's interested in politics as an ethics, I take this to mean that he is interested in the interaction between technologies of domination and technologies of the self (on this point, see EEW1, 177). Governmentality, he tells us, is the point of intersection of these two types of technologies, the point where the government of the self connects with the government of and by others. There are interesting examples of the idea of politics as an ethics in some of Foucault's late interviews about gay politics. For example, when asked questions about gay political struggles for increased civil rights, Foucault typically responded by talking about the need for gay men to create new "cultural forms" and "ways of life" (EEW1, 157–158). Gay culture, he says, has the chance to invent "ways of relating, types of existence, types of values, types of exchanges between individuals which are really new and neither the same as, nor superimposed on, existing cultural forms" (EEW1, 159–160; see also EEW1, 137 and 163–164). Such cultural transformations are instances of political engagement inasmuch as they challenge and subvert existing structures of power relations, but their challenge takes the form of a reinvention of ethical forms of relation to self and others: politics as an ethics.

Amy Allen

SEE ALSO

> *Ethics*
> *Governmentality*
> *Homosexuality*
> *Institution*
> *Power*
> *Sovereignty*
> *State*
> *War*
> *Jürgen Habermas*
> *Carl von Clausewitz*

SUGGESTED READING

Allen, Amy. 2008. *The Politics of Our Selves: Power, Autonomy and Gender in Contemporary Critical Theory*. New York: Columbia University Press.

Barry, Andrew, Thomas Osborne, and Nikolas Rose, eds. 1996. *Foucault and Political Reason: Liberalism, Neo-liberalism, and Rationalities of Government*. Chicago: University of Chicago Press.

Biebricher, Thomas. 2005. *Selbstkritik der Moderne: Foucault und Habermas im Vergleich*. Frankfurt am Main: Campus Verlag.

Halperin, David. 1995. *Saint Foucault: Towards a Gay Hagiography*. Oxford: Oxford University Press.

Heyes, Cressida. 2007. *Self-Transformations: Foucault, Ethics, and Normalized Bodies*. New York: Oxford University Press.

Huffer, Lynne. 2010. *Mad for Foucault: Rethinking the Foundations of Queer Theory*. New York: Columbia University Press.

Kelly, Mark G. E. 2009. *The Political Philosophy of Michel Foucault*. New York: Routledge.

Lemke, Thomas. 1997. *Eine Kritik der politischen Vernunft – Foucaults Analyse der modernen Gouvernementalität*. Berlin: Argument.

McWhorter, Ladelle. 1999. *Bodies and Pleasures: Foucault and the Politics of Sexual Normalization*. Bloomington: Indiana University Press.

Moss, Jeremy, ed. 1998. *The Later Foucault: Politics and Philosophy*. London: Sage.

Saar, Martin. 2007. *Genealogie als Kritik: Geschichte und Theorie des Subjekts nach Nietzsche und Foucault*. Frankfurt am Main: Campus Verlag.

Sawicki, Jana. 1991. *Disciplining Foucault: Feminism, Power, and the Body*. New York: Routledge.

Simons, Jon. 1995. *Foucault and the Political*. New York: Routledge.

63

POPULATION

OUCAULT MAKES IMPORTANT claims about population both in Part Five of volume one of *The History of Sexuality*, which appeared in late 1976, and in "Society Must Be Defended," the series of lectures he gave at the Collège de France that same year. However, his most extended and detailed discussion of population occurs in his 1978 lecture series at the Collège de France, "Security, Territory, Population." Population is a central issue throughout the series, but it takes center stage in Chapters 2 and 3, the lectures of January 18 and 25, respectively, where Foucault offers a genealogical treatment of the concept. These two lectures are the key to understanding Foucault's concept of population and the work it does in his critique of liberalism.

Although Foucault acknowledges that political writers before the eighteenth century often raised concerns about population, he argues that the word carried a different meaning then than it would acquire later on. Before the eighteenth century, "population" meant simply the opposite of "depopulation." A state's strength and wealth were measured in part by the number of its inhabitants. Therefore, when wars, famine, or epidemics killed many people or precipitated mass emigration, sovereigns and their advisers worried that their states would weaken. Depopulation had to be offset by population; that is, by a resurgence in the number of inhabitants of a state's territory (ECF-STP, 67).

By the seventeenth century, some political thinkers – in particular, the mercantilists – believed that the number of inhabitants was more than just one element of a state's strength (as their predecessors had thought). In their view, population was fundamental, a necessary condition for all other aspects of that strength. If the number of inhabitants decreased, military might and productivity in agriculture and manufacturing would inevitably suffer (ECF-STP, 68). Mercantilists also believed that a large number of inhabitants created more competition for jobs and thus ensured low wages, which kept prices low and thus increased exports, adding even more to the state's wealth. In the second half of the seventeenth century, English (and then Dutch) mathematicians began compiling mortality tables. (For an overview of this development, see Kreager 1993.) Eventually this statistical data was used to inform official strategies to encourage "population," understood as repopulation or population growth. But this notion of population was still far from the concept that prevailed in the nineteenth century or prevails in demographic discourses today.

We begin to see faint outlines of something like the modern concept of population in seventeenth-century treatises on *raison d'État*, particularly in discussions of the need to control public opinion and squelch sedition. In lecture 11 of "Security, Territory, Population," Foucault states:

> When one speaks of obedience, and the fundamental element of obedience in government is the people who may engage in sedition, you can see that the notion of "population" is virtually present. When one speaks of the public on whose opinion one must act in such a way as to modify its behavior, one is already very close to the population. (ECF-STP, 277)

But the focus is still on strengthening and safeguarding the wealth of the state, not on managing populations per se. Similarly, of the work of Francis Bacon on "poverty and discontent," Foucault writes, "we are very close to population, but Bacon never envisages the population as constituted by economic subjects who are capable of autonomous behavior. One will speak of wealth, the circulation of wealth, and the balance of trade, but one will not speak of population as an economic subject" (ECF-STP, 277–278).

Population as we know it first emerges in the analyses of the physiocrats, Foucault asserts, where a clear distinction is made between individual bodies or subjects and something else, something that is not simply a collection of individuals but rather an autonomous entity with its own behaviors and course of life. The mercantilists had been concerned about food scarcity in great part because it resulted in political unrest and sometimes in revolt. In times of food shortages, individuals were hungry and angry; hungry and angry in aggregate, they might turn violent and destructive. Scarcity of grain was therefore a massive catastrophe, a scourge to be avoided if at all possible. But the physiocrats saw things differently. Whereas the mercantilists focused on keeping prices low so that food would be affordable for everyone, the physiocrats advocated policies that might make prices high, both in times of poor harvests and even in times of abundance. The physiocrats believed higher prices would ensure continued production and the possibility of imports, which would reduce or eliminate the scourge of scarcity, if not for all individuals then at least for the general population. True, after poor harvests, if prices rose significantly, some individuals might be unable to afford sufficient grain and might suffer and starve. But the problem of scarcity and its negative effects would still have been solved, for enough grain in proportion to the population would be in circulation at all times. According to Foucault, "There will no longer be any scarcity as a scourge, there will no longer be this phenomenon of scarcity, of massive, individual and collective hunger that advances absolutely in step and without discontinuity, as it were, in individuals and in the population in general. Now, there will be no more food shortage at the level of the population" (ECF-STP, 41). It is the population that matters in the physiocrats' analysis, not the individual who may or may not starve to death. Foucault continues: "The individual is no longer pertinent.... The population is pertinent as the objective and individuals, the series of individuals, are no longer pertinent as the objective, but simply as the instrument, relay, or condition for obtaining something at the level of the population" (ECF-STP, 42).

And what is population? What is this new level of analysis? "The population as a political subject, as a new collective subject absolutely foreign to the juridical and political thought of earlier centuries is appearing here in its complexity" (ECF-STP, 42). It does not present itself "as a collection of subjects of right, as a collective of subject wills who must obey the sovereign's will through the intermediary regulation, laws, edicts, and so on. It will be considered as a set of processes to be managed at the level and on the basis of what is natural in those processes" (ECF-STP, 70). Just as living beings became manifestations of measurable physiological processes in the late eighteenth century, population became a temporally unfolding epistemic object whose rhythms and fluctuations were amenable to statistical analysis. Like organisms, populations were seen to have their own kind of natural life.

This "naturalness," Foucault says, appears in three ways. First, any given population is dependent for its existence and for the specificity of its character on a set of variables including climate, physical environment, intensity of commerce, laws, customs, religious values, means of subsistence, and so forth (ECF-STP, 70–71). Obviously, then, although this new entity must be directed, it cannot be acted on as a free will; it cannot simply be commanded and expected to obey. Foucault explains, "The population appears therefore as a kind of thick natural phenomenon in relation to the sovereign's legalistic voluntarism" (ECF-STP, 71). Second, despite the fact that any population is made up of individuals who are all very different from one another, eighteenth-century theorists held that "there is at least one invariant that means that the population taken as a whole has one and only one mainspring of action. This is desire" (ECF-STP, 72). If the sovereign gives those desires free play, eventually they will spontaneously produce something like a public or general interest that cannot be attributed to individual people but must instead be attributed to the population itself. This is the population's own natural inclination, disposition, or tendency. Finally, year after year, populations manifest fairly consistent birth rates, mortality rates, and even suicide rates. In other words, they evince a series of natural regularities that cannot be attributed to the wills of the individuals who compose them. In essence, they have a life of their own apart from or at least beyond the lives of the individuals they comprise. Foucault states:

> The population is not, then, a collection of juridical subjects in an individual or collective relationship with a sovereign will. It is a set of elements in which we can note constants and regularities even in accidents, in which we can identify the universal of desire regularly producing the benefit of all, and with regard to which we can identify a number of modifiable variables on which it depends. (ECF-STP, 74)

Taking population thus conceived as the target of administrative and managerial efforts and allowing it to displace the individual subject as the object of governmental activity marks, according to Foucault, "the entry of a 'nature' into the field of techniques of power" (ECF-STP, 75). He sees this as a momentous event across a range of disciplines and institutions. While Quesnay was promoting the idea that real economic government was the government of populations (ECF-STP, 77), Darwin was discovering that population was the key to understanding the relationship between organism and environment and the process of evolutionary change, and the discipline of general grammar was giving way to the discipline of philology as relationships between populations and language were identified and delineated. Population was "the operator that upset all these systems of knowledge [the analysis of wealth, natural history, and general grammar], and directed knowledge to the sciences of life, of labor and production, and of language" (ECF-STP, 78). But population itself is in some important respects a product of the changes it operated to effect: "A constant interplay between techniques of power and their object gradually carves out in reality, as a field of reality, population and its specific phenomena" (ECF-STP, 79).

Most important for Foucault's analysis in the lecture series of 1978, population both participates in and enables the eighteenth-century shift away from sovereign deduction as the primary technology of power and toward technologies of security. Seventeenth-century thinkers were more or less trapped within traditional discourses of sovereignty. Either they conceived of the exercise of power exclusively as juridical or, taking the well-governed household as the model of political relationships, they slipped into paternalism, which led them back again to traditional sovereign power. Both paths of thinking precluded the possibility of anything like political economy. The problem, as Foucault sees it, was that their notion of economic administration was caught up in a particular conception of the family as the object of economic governance. In other words, "the art of government could only be conceived on the basis of the model of the family, in terms of economy understood as management of the family" (ECF-STP, 105). Population provided a way out of this conceptual trap.

> When, however, the population appears as absolutely irreducible to the family, the result is that the latter falls to a lower level than the population; it appears as an element within the population. It is therefore no longer a model; it is a segment whose privilege is simply that when one wants to obtain something from the population concerning sexual behavior, demography, the birth rate, or consumption, then one has to utilize the family. (ibid.)

It is at this point that Foucault introduces the term "governmentality" (ECF-STP, 108). With the advent of population as the object of political science, governmental management of economic processes broadly understood takes precedence over juridical processes of legislation and enforcement. We enter an era in which the administrative state is gradually "governmentalized" (ECF-STP, 109).

So far, this essay has focused on Foucault's genealogical analysis of population in "Security, Territory, Population" in 1978. But, as mentioned earlier, population first appeared as a significant element in his analysis of biopower two years earlier in both his published text *The History of Sexuality*, volume 1: *An Introduction* and the lecture series of 1976, later published in English under the title *Society Must Be Defended*. In Part Five of volume one of *The History of Sexuality*, Foucault writes that biopower – which he characterizes as the power to make live or let die in contrast to the sovereign power to make die or let live – comes into existence where two disparate sets of technologies coalesce. One is normalizing disciplinary power centered on the bodies of individuals, which he refers to as the "anatomo-politics of the body" (and which he had analyzed in some detail in his 1975 volume *Discipline and Punish*). The other is a kind of regulatory power involving what he calls techniques of security, "the bio-politics of the population" (EHS1, 139). These two types of technologies of power merge at crucial points to form the vast network that Foucault calls "biopower" (EHS1, 140), so named because "this was nothing less than the entry of life into history, that is, the entry of phenomena peculiar to the life of the human species into the order of knowledge and power, into the sphere of political techniques" (EHS1, 141–142). From this point forward, political power will claim legitimacy on the basis of its aim to safeguard and at times enhance life. The bloodiest of wars will be fought in the name of preserving life, and the most invasive of interventions will be used to enhance the biological quality of the human species.

Volume one of *The History of Sexuality* is about the central role that sexuality's development played in these historico-political events. There Foucault cites the eugenics movements of the early twentieth century as the epitome of biopolitical population management (EHS1, 148), where the supposed good of the human race, the maximization of its living potential, was put forth as justification and motive for drastic intervention in the reproductive lives of millions of people (in the form of lifelong institutionalization and involuntary sterilization, for example) and, eventually, for the complete elimination of those deemed biological threats to the species's health and evolutionary progress in the "euthanasia" program of the Nazi regime. Genocidal racism is inevitable, Foucault tells us, if sovereign power is to be exercised through the mechanisms of biopolitics, an idea he develops in more detail in the 1976 lecture series. The only way to exercise the right to impose death in a biopolitical world is to fracture the field of species life (ECF-SMD, 255) by establishing subspecies or races of human beings who can be eliminated from the population in the name of biological purification, health, and evolutionary advance.

A slight tension appears to exist between Foucault's account of biopower as a consequence of the conjoining of normalizing discipline and population management in *The History of Sexuality* on the one hand and, on the other, his account of biopolitics as technologies of security as opposed to technologies of discipline in the final lecture of "Society Must Be Defended" and in the lecture series of 1978 discussed earlier. In *The History of Sexuality*, Foucault says biopower exists at the point where disciplinary normalization conjoins with technologies of population management (EHS1, 140); thus it includes disciplinary techniques that target individual bodies. In the two lecture series, however, Foucault seems to reserve the term "biopower" for technologies of security focused on populations in sharp contrast with individualizing disciplinary technologies. (In fact, in the 1978 series, he denies that disciplinary technologies are normalizing in an important way and reserves the concept of normalization for technologies of security. See ECF-STP, 56–57.) We might interpret this difference as a product of the evolution of Foucault's thought from 1976 to 1978 or simply to the need to emphasize different aspects of biopolitical phenomena in different analytic contexts. Even while contrasting disciplinary technologies with technologies of security, Foucault insists that they do not displace one another and that they operate together in important ways:

> Mechanisms of security do not replace disciplinary mechanisms, which would have replaced juridico-legal mechanisms. In reality you have a series of complex edifices in which, of course, the techniques themselves change and are perfected, or anyway become more complicated, but in which what above all changes is the dominant characteristic, or more exactly, the system of correlation between juridico-legal mechanisms, disciplinary mechanisms, and mechanisms of security. (ECF-STP, 8)

It is this complexity that Foucault takes up in his lecture series of 1979, "The Birth of Biopolitics," where he undertakes to study the rise of liberalism in the eighteenth century and neoliberalism in the twentieth. The image of liberty that animates liberalism and its politico-theoretical progeny is that of constant circulation of goods, bodies, and information; liberty is the managerial correlate, therefore, of techniques of security. In Foucault's view, liberalism thus understood is a form of governmentality, and what it seeks to govern is not people (citizens or subjects) but populations.

Ladelle McWhorter

SEE ALSO

> *Biopolitics*
> *Biopower*
> *Liberalism*
> *Medicine*
> *Normalization*
> *Race (and Racism)*

SUGGESTED READING

Bernasconi, Robert. 2010. "The Policing of Race Mixing: The Place of Bio-power within the History of Racisms," *Bioethical Inquiry* 7:205–216.
Morton, Stephen, and Stephen Bygrave, eds. 2008. *Foucault in an Age of Terror*. London: Palgrave Macmillan.

64

POWER

OUCAULT NEVER TREATS power as a stable, unitary, and coherent entity. Rather, he treats it as "relations of power," which assume complex, historical conditions of emergence and imply multiple effects, including effects that lie outside what previous philosophical analysis identified, and in a traditional way, as the field of power. Although Foucault seems at times to have raised some doubts about the importance of the theme of power in his work ("Thus it is not power, but the subject, that is the general theme of my research" [EEW3, 327]), his analyses in fact bring about two noticeable displacements.

On the one hand, if it is true that power appears only when some exercise it on others – the "some" and the "others" never being locked into one sole role but rather, in contrast, each taking on, in turns and indeed simultaneously, each pole of the relation – then a genealogy of power is indissociable from a history of subjectivity. That is, a genealogy of power is indissociable from an investigation of the way in which the being of the subject is at once the result of apparatuses of objectivation undergone and active practices of subjectification. The relations of power fashion and traverse our lives, making us be what we are at the intersection of the multiple determinations that the relations imply. That does not mean that we then have to present a binary reading of power (subjected to power versus holders of power) but that what is really at issue lies in describing the complex "mesh" of power, the interpenetration or the superposition of forms of power, and the variability of its expressions. A relation of power is, by definition, a relation. It is the very form of this relation that Foucault urges us to interrogate.

On the other hand, if power exists only in its actions and if it is precisely a relation, then we return to the question of the "how" of this power to analyze its modalities of exercise. That is, we return to the historical emergence of its modes of application as well as the instruments with which it provides itself, the fields into which it intervenes, the network that it designs, and the effects it implies in a given epoch. More generally, we return to the question of the historicity of its rationality, or what is at issue is to formulate its modes of government.

In any case, what is consequently at issue is not to describe a primary and fundamental principle of power but instead to privilege the historical description of an assemblage in which at once practices, kinds of knowledge, and institutions intersect, and in which the type of objective pursued not only is not reduced to mere domination but rather belongs to no one in the strict sense and varies according to the epochs considered.

As soon as it is given as an analytic of *powers* (in the plural), the analysis of power demands consequently that at once we give an account of the historical diversity of the modes of government (and in a procedure that is classically archaeological) but also of the extreme finesse and variety of *powers* – again in the plural – in our lives. This double dimension – on the one hand the historical investigation and on the other the minute cartography of what Foucault will identify as a plurality of relations and their modes – allows us therefore to redefine, in large measure, the work of the investigation that we are to produce. This investigation will be organized, in particular, around four massive foundations.

First, and above all else, what is at issue is to interrogate the system of differentiations and hierarchizations that allows some people, at a given moment, to act on the actions of others. This system is at once the condition of emergence of a power relation (it is what allows the relation to appear) and its most direct effect (that by which the power relation is translated). Foucault mentions certain systems of differentiation that are grounded in different ways: based on a juridical difference of status and privilege, based on a difference of place (and function) within a productive process, based on a linguistic or cultural difference, and based on a difference of know-how or competence, and so forth. Later, of course, Foucault will be criticized for not having included in the set of "systems of differentiation" the differences of color and gender. (Even though the reference to Foucault has been central in many cases of this kind of criticism, it is in particular the recurrent criticism of Foucault made in postcolonial and subaltern studies and in "Women Studies." More generally, it is close to the very early critique of Foucault that he seems to have taken into consideration only a historical and geographical space limited to the West, and that he has hardly ever questioned this limitation. See, for example, the 1976 "Questions à Michel Foucault sur la géographie" [FDE2a, 28–39]. On page 31 of this interview, the interviewer states: "The spaces to which you refer are indistinctly Christianity, the Western world, Northern Europe, and France, although you do not truly justify or specify these reference spaces.")

Second, since "action upon the actions of others" is the definition that Foucault gives to power (EEW3, 341), the objective of this *action upon the actions of others* must be identified. Nothing indicates that the purpose that some such "government" proposes for itself obeys the same imperatives and is equipped with the same stakes.

Thus it will be necessary to describe, in light of the cases and the periods considered, a rationality that aims at maintaining privileges, the accumulation of profits, the exercise of a function, and so on. It is this variation of governmental rationalities, as well as the historicity of the modes of government that they imply immediately, that is therefore at the center of the analytic of powers.

Moreover, the instrumental modalities of power – the procedures and the apparatuses, the elements, and the institutions that display the application of the procedures and apparatuses and can be, according to the case, armies, discourses, kinds of knowledge, economic disparities, mechanisms of control, systems of surveillance, juridical (the rule) and normative (the norm) instruments, and so on – must in turn be described in their historical variability since they are defined on the basis of a specific context. Looking at only one example – the emergence of the norm at the moment of the birth of liberalism, whose forms Foucault studied in the second half of the 1970s – we see two things. On the one hand, we see that the concept of rule (as it appears in the political grammar of modernity; that is, understood as the juridical expression of sovereignty) is no longer as efficacious as it was able to be. On the other hand, the changes that affected production have redefined political rationality on the basis of a new political economy. In other words, the necessity to govern the workforce implies in fact not only a "disciplinarization" of individual bodies in order to obtain productive benefits from them but also the control of entire populations that the old juridical tool of the "rule" could not effectively manage. In contrast, the new political tool of the "norm" allows us precisely to govern with less cost. In the passage from the "rule" to the "norm," we are able to read the "turning" of a political economy that redefines in large part the stakes, the purposes, and the instruments of a certain rationality of power.

Third, to each of these historical configurations corresponds, of course, different forms of the institutionalization of power, forms that Foucault's analytic cannot pass over in silence. What has to happen is the minute cartography of multiple juridical structures, phenomena of habituation – we know the importance of customary law. What has to be mapped is the very large variety of specific places that possess their own rule and hierarchy, the complex system (like that of the state) that relays and translates a given rationality of government. This has to be done in order to understand how this set functions and produces effects of reality that are often those of an immediate spatialization of power.

Fourth and finally, each configuration of power – or rather each complex economy of power relations – provides itself with a specific rationalization that corresponds to indicators or to criteria such as the effectiveness of instruments, the certainty of the result, the political and economic costs of the apparatuses that are put in place, and so on. The analytic of powers therefore presents itself as a history of different rationalities of government, and it seeks to understand in what way a paradigm gives way, in a given moment, to another. Here let us cite two examples.

On the one hand, we have the displacement of the conception of power such as it was able to appear in the Machiavellian literature of the sixteenth century, a conception Foucault analyzes as being entirely constructed around the problem of the prince's conservation of power. The displacement goes in the direction of another way of thinking that, in contrast, defines power as an art of governing and questions less the constancy of power than its managerial and administrative effectiveness. Foucault reads this displacement obviously as a historical shift that affects the type of rationalization to which one is referred. Likewise, the passage from punishment to surveillance marks in its own way, nearly two centuries later, another "turning" of this political rationality on the basis of which power is defined and that qualifies at the same time power's modes and purposes.

Basically, by characterizing the relations of power as complex modes of action on the actions of others, Foucault displaces in fact, and in a clear way, the analysis of power such as tended to be done by modern philosophical discourse. In modern philosophical discourse, what had really been at issue was simply to consider power outside all history, and the question of power's unity, the homogeneity of its forms, was rarely asked. In contrast, Foucault finds it necessary to put into play at once historical difference and the variety of modes.

The dehistoricization and the crystallization of the question of power around the sole figure of the state are, from this viewpoint, at the center of criticisms that Foucault formulates in regard to the approaches to power that have preceded him. As he insists, "Therefore there would be a schematism that we have to avoid … which consists in localizing power in the machinery of the State, and in turning the machinery of the State into the privileged, central, major, and nearly unique instrument of the power of one class over another class" (FDE2a, 35). Of course, this transition to a "microphysics of power" – understood as an analytic capable of describing the most precise canals through which the relations of power pass, of forgetting neither the discourse nor the practices, nor the institutions, capable of giving an account of the evolution and the shifts that affect the history of the way in which power in the Western world has been conceived and exercised – has given rise to enormous kinds of resistance. In particular, the resistance has come from those for whom, occupying a rigid Marxist reading, the superposition between power and the state was often obvious. The disjunction of the power/state couple is a theme that circulated in an important way in French thought after 1968, in particular under the influence of innovative anthropological works such as those of Pierre Clastres (see Clastres 1989). Although Clastres is cited in a decisive way by Deleuze and Guattari in *A Thousand Plateaus* (Deleuze and Guattari 1987), Foucault never cites him. Nevertheless, the disjunction of the power/state couple is very present in Foucault. The presence of that disjunction does not mean that the theme of the state is not put into confrontation with one of the possible incarnations of power. It means instead that the state cannot claim to represent the unique face of power.

In a similar way, the multiplication of what we have tended to consider as "power" in an infinity of *power relations*, and, within these power relations, the reversibility of positions that each person at once exercises and undergoes – since all of us are, in turn and simultaneously, objects and subjects of power overflows any reading enacted exclusively on the basis of what we have qualified as "class identities." Likewise, for Foucault, the kind of conflict to which some such relation of power can give birth, and the confrontation that can result from it, would not be able to be reduced to this unique variable that class warfare represents. The kind of conflict born of power relations cannot be reduced to class warfare, not only because this class struggle implies that one determines *positions* whereas an analysis of power relations privileges a model that is less binary and more dynamic but also because the idea of class struggle tends to reduce the variety of power relations to one sole relation – that exists and is, of course, central but would not be able to exhaust the complexity of the phenomena of subjectification and strategies of government.

Therefore, the divorce from the classically Marxist analyses of the epoch is clear. These classically Marxist analyses simplify their object and excessively schematize its consistency. That divorce is particularly true in the analyses Foucault produces, in the wake of *Discipline and Punish*, in the courses at the Collège de France in the second half of the 1970s; that is, when he seeks to analyze the ways in which industrialization and the birth of economic liberalism have implied a new grammar of the political, a new rationality, which have taken on the face of a never before seen political liberalism. And, just as the juridical model of sovereignty, such as it existed up to that moment, does not allow us to account for the emergence of this new political economy, the political criticism of the state does not allow us to bring to light the way in which power circulates in the entire social body, power circulating there in order to extract from the social body productive benefits. In short, we lose the variability and the novelty of the phenomena of subjectification that accompany the birth of liberalism, the birth of what Foucault will call, as we know, a "birth of biopolitics." In a similar way, the analysis of "subjects" and "objects" of power would not simply be able to be translated by staging an antagonism with a univocal face thought about on the basis of vis-à-vis or through an inverted symmetry. Rather, it is through the staking out of multiple articulations of power relations (of course, here "class analysis" plays an important part, but it does not represent its ultimate truth) and of the different strategies in play in the relations – and a fortiori, from the moment that power has invested lives in their materiality and has extended the field of its applications to what was traditionally considered as *external to power* – that the minute cartography of the analytic of power projected by Foucault can be constructed.

Beyond the enlargement of the field of inquiry – and beyond the multiple displacements that we have just recalled briefly – there is, moreover, a fundamental element around which Foucault's work in his final years comes to be recentered to a large degree. Indeed, it becomes in many ways the paradoxical keyword of the analyses of power relations with which Foucault is concerned. This is the theme of freedom.

Insofar as power is "an action on the actions of humans," it is exercised only on subjects – either individual or collective – on whom power can really inflict conduct, capture or orient behaviors, administer modes of life, and erect and organize productive potentialities. The key idea is that if humans were not at least in part free, an action on the action of humans would not be thinkable insofar as power would not find the freedom onto which it applies itself. And, consequently, power would not be able to continue to assert itself as power. In short, the relations of power, for Foucault, are exercised only on individuals "who are faced with a field of possibilities in which several kinds of conduct, several ways of reacting and modes of behavior are available. Where the determining factors are exhaustive, there is no relation of power" (EEW3, 342).

Foucault's analysis thereby destroys the idea of a frontal relation between power and freedom. Freedom is paradoxically transformed into a condition of the possibility of power. This implication is in turn reversible. If freedom is necessary so that power can be applied, this logical priority does not, however, turn freedom into an absolute first term; it is not an originary reality, a state of pure freedom, to which we should want to return. We are always traversed by multiple relations of power, in which we act or in which we undergo. We live immersed in a complex web of power relations. Therefore, this indissociability of power and freedom involves at least three consequences.

The first consequence consists in saying that the struggle against power would not be able to be limited to a struggle for liberation, if by liberation we mean the dream of a total elimination of power relations. As Foucault notes, "I have always been somewhat suspicious of the notion of liberation, because if it is not treated with precautions and within certain limits, one runs the risk of falling back on the idea that there exists a human nature or base that, as a consequence of certain historical, economic, and social processes, has been concealed, alienated, or imprisoned in and by mechanisms of repression. According to this hypothesis, all that is required is to break these repressive deadlocks and man will be reconciled with himself, rediscover his nature or regain contact with his origin, and reestablish a full and positive relation with himself" (EEW1, 282). Obviously, we really have to resist power, we have to claim our rights when our rights are denied or overridden, establish strategies that Foucault would qualify sometimes as "counterconducts" and sometimes as "resistances." But the relation between power and freedom, precisely because it presupposes a reciprocal implication of the two terms, would not be able to be reduced to being thought of on the basis of the sole mode of contradiction. Foucault writes,

Consequently, there is not a face-to-face confrontation of power and freedom as mutually exclusive facts (freedom disappearing everywhere power is exercised), but a much more complicated interplay. In this game, freedom may well appear as the condition for the exercise of power the same time its pre-condition, since freedom must exist for power to be exerted, and also its permanent support, since without the possibility of recalcitrance, power would be equivalent to physical determination. (EEW3, 342)

Likewise, if there is no exteriority in the relations of power, we have to recognize paradoxically the enormous extension of practices of freedom right within the power relations:

for, if it is true that at the heart of power relations and as a permanent condition of their existence there is an insubordination and a certain essential obstinacy on the part of the principles of freedom, then there is no relationship of power without the means of escape or possible flight. Every power relation implies, at least virtually, a strategy of struggle, in which the two forces are not superimposed, do not lose their specific nature, or do not finally become confused. (EEW3, 346)

Therefore, power and freedom, subjectification and resistance, are taken into what Foucault identifies as a relation of reciprocal incitation.

The second consequence is then immediately practical. In the 1970s, Foucault added to the trajectory of his theoretical research a series of militant engagements: from the experiment of Le Groupe d'Information sur les Prisons (abbreviated as GIP: "Prison Information Group") to the gay movement. These militant engagements nourish his reflections in a direct manner. On the basis of this "experiment" (or experience) – which is a genuine practical matrix of theoretical problematizations – what is at issue is to think of the political consequences of this "reciprocal incitation." As Foucault says,

I agree ... that liberation is sometimes the political or historical condition for a practice of freedom. Taking sexuality as an example, it is clear that a number of liberations were required vis-à-vis male power, that liberation was necessary from an oppressive morality concerning heterosexuality as well as homosexuality. But this liberation does not give rise to the happy human being imbued with a sexuality to which the subject could achieve a complete and satisfying relation. Liberation paves the way for new power relations that must be controlled by practices of freedom. (EEW3, 283–284)

Freedom is always susceptible of being overtaken and redirected by means of power relations. This is perhaps the whole political problem of the political will to reform, to which Foucault will be strongly opposed while he is involved with the GIP. But, at the same time, there is always freedom, even where the power relations seem the most saturated and the most confining. The coupling – in the oppositional mode – between power and liberation therefore becomes the ternary and open structure of power/strategies of liberation/practices of freedom. This in fact opens Foucault's political reflection to another part of his investigations, which will be ethics.

The third consequence, finally, bears on the very nature of the relation between power relations and phenomena of resistance that Foucault evokes. We have already seen their reciprocal (logical) implication and their reciprocal (political) incitation. The theoretical danger – and Foucault is immediately aware of this danger – is that this reciprocal referential structure opens out onto a purely dialectical conception of the relation between power and resistance. Undoubtedly, this explains why Foucault never uses the term "counter-power." It also explains why the term "counter-conduct" is only used briefly and then is rapidly abandoned. If resistance is limited to being only an *other of power* (that is, in its own way, *another power*), and if, inversely, all power survives only because it is applied to liberties, this "perpetual reversal" is, literally, a dialectical circle (EEW3, 346). This is why it is necessary to insert, within the structure that connects the two terms and that renders them indissociable from one another, an element of radical dissymmetry.

This element, which is going to allow Foucault to assert what he will call "the intransitivity of freedom," is of a qualitative nature. It summons a decisive notion, that of *production*. If we start in fact from Foucault's definition of power understood as "action on the action of humans," the essence of power is of a managerial nature. What is at issue is to inflect, correct, and profitably administer conduct and therefore govern it. Power is applied; it reacts to freedom and governs it. It creates nothing in the strict sense. In contrast, freedom is translated – including when it appears right within the mesh of power – by what Foucault identifies as an irreducible capacity to invent, to inaugurate, and to experiment in relation to itself and in relation to others. In Foucault's thought, freedom is the name of this abundant, permanent production to which the reproductive, secondary, and managerial essence of power is applied. The difference is therefore of an ontological nature. Even if power and freedom cannot be thought of in separation, nothing indicates that they are equivalent – because freedom alone is capable of inventing the world. It is this dissymmetry that even though it cannot entertain the idea of a total exteriority from the relations of power allows paradoxically for its intransitivity.

And, in fact, the word "production" (of subjectivity, of ways of life, etc.), once it is uprooted from the sole register of economic production (which is in reality the register of *re-production* of merchandise), will be placed by Foucault at the center of the ethical analyses that, in the last years of his work, will bear on the historical ways in which these "practices of freedom" appear. The ethical stake par excellence, to produce oneself, is in reality the primary political gesture – insofar as this invention unmasks the incapacity of power to be something other than the secondary, although inevitable, management of the ontological potency of subjectivities. It is in this sense that "ethics is the reflective form that freedom takes" (EEW1, 284). From this viewpoint, the analytic of powers is a propaedeutic to the ethics, and, inversely, the ethics is the inevitable extension of the political interrogation of the reciprocal implication of power and freedom.

Judith Revel

SEE ALSO

Biopolitics
Biopower
Freedom
Governmentality
Knowledge
Sovereignty
State
Friedrich Nietzsche

SUGGESTED READING

Allen, Amy. 2008. *The Politics of Our Selves: Power, Autonomy, and Gender in Contemporary Critical Theory*. New York: Columbia University Press.
Deleuze, Gilles, and Félix Guattari. 1987. *A Thousand Plateaus: Capitalism and Schizophrenia*, trans. Brian Massumi. Minneapolis: University of Minnesota Press.
Revel, Judith. 2010. *Foucault, une pensée du discontinu*. Paris: Fayard.

65

PRACTICE

"**P**RACTICE" IS A key term for Foucauldians. One must be careful not to immediately equate Foucault's focus on practices with some form of pragmatism or action theory. Instead, we must treat "practice" as a metaphysical term, a word that expresses what there is in the world. Thus, "practice" is not to be immediately understood as the opposite of "theory." As Gilles Deleuze says in his conversation with Foucault published as "Intellectuals and Power," "Practice is a set of relays from one theoretical point to another, and theory is a relay from one practice to another" (ELCP, 206). What this means is that "theory" and "practice" are relative terms to each other: theory is a kind of practice (namely, the practice of evaluating practices) and practice is what follows from theory (namely, practices are the effects produced from arrangements of power/knowledge). In other words, we theorize because of practices, and there are practices because knowledge is not an inert, disinterested enterprise.

If one were to perform an ontological assay of Foucault's philosophy, some would argue that everything that is would fall into three categories: statements, forces, and selves. Each of these ontological categories corresponds to a particular method of Foucauldian analysis: archaeology, "a historical ontology of ourselves in relation to truth through which we constitute ourselves as subjects of knowledge"; genealogy, "a historical ontology of ourselves in relation to a field of power through which we constitute ourselves as subjects acting on others"; and ethics, "a historical ontology … through which we constitute ourselves as moral agents" (EEW1, 262). Although the metaphysical categories might be treated as distinct, Foucault's thought development suggests that his methodology became more and more unified over time. At first, in the archaeological period, the focus was on statements. As Foucault started adding nondiscursive forces into this purview, archaeology morphed into genealogy. Finally, toward the end of his life, Foucault moved past the power-knowledge dualism of his previous works and turned to what kinds of subjectivity are possible given one's place in the overall constellation of power and knowledge. Thus, even as the ontological categories increased, the methods for analysis did not. One reason for the continual methodological evolution of Foucault's thought, I argue, is Foucault's constant interest in analyzing practices.

Regardless of whether Foucault is doing archaeology, genealogy, or ethics ("problematization"), the "objects" of research are always practices. What are practices? We ask about practices in the plural because there are always many practices working together at any moment, the pinpointing of one of which is to abstract a practice from its overall constellation of practices. Foucault tells us in "Questions of Method" that practices are "places where what is said and what is done, rules imposed and reasons given, the planned and the taken-for-granted meet and intersect" (EEW3, 225). Thomas Flynn writes that a practice, imagined by itself, is "a preconceptual, anonymous, socially sanctioned body of rules that govern one's manner of perceiving, imagining, judging, and acting" (Flynn 2005, 34). Foucault's theoretical task, then, is to strip otherwise plain historical affairs down to the practices that came to constitute the given scenario. What the practices will look like depends on the practices being analyzed and the Foucauldian method used to analyze them. Regardless of which method is used, however, Foucault seeks to find two particular "effects" of the practice: "prescriptive effects regarding what is to be done (effects of 'jurisdiction') and codifying effects regarding what is to be known (effects of 'veridiction')" (EEW3, 225). In other words, practices determine both the way in which subjects will act and the truth claims those subjects can make. In Foucault's later works, he will focus on how a given subject navigates between jurisdiction and veridiction by means of "games of truth" (cf. EFS and ECF-COT).

Foucault discusses the centrality of practices in his work in the pseudonymous essay "Michel Foucault." There he tells the reader that his project, "a critical history of thought" (EEW2, 459), achieves its goals not by "proceeding upward to the constituent subject which is asked to account for every possible object of knowledge" but by "proceeding back down to the study of the concrete practices by which the subject is constituted in the immanence of a domain of knowledge" (EEW2, 462). By focusing on practices, on "what 'was done'" (ibid.), one is able to break free from what Foucault calls "anthropological universals" such as madness, delinquency, and sexuality. This break from anthropological universals shows that Foucault is not interested in how people, individual and independent, begin to "practice" in particular ways. Instead, Foucault seeks to show how the practices themselves *form* people into the kinds of people who do certain things (jurisdiction) and hold certain things as true (veridiction). This focus on practices is how Foucault offers an alternative to the transcendental phenomenologist and the hermeneutist. Instead of constituting a transcendental, tradition-laden subject who then "looks at" states of affairs and interprets them, Foucault reconstitutes the very practices that made up both the "subject" and the "object" or state of affairs. As such, Foucault's writings are dry and impersonal: facts are presented, correlations made, and local examples given. There is no "spirit of its time" in Foucault's work; his analysis is "grey, meticulous, and patiently documentary ... it must record the singularity of events outside of any monotonous finality; it must seek them in the most unpromising places" (EEW2, 369).

Having spoken of practices in general, we now move to the three main kinds of practices that Foucault analyzes: *discursive practices*, *practices of power* (also called *dividing practices*), and *practices of the self*. The study of discursive practices, although present in all of his works, corresponds to the archaeological method; similarly, and with the same disclaimer, dividing practices correspond to the genealogical method; and practices of the self correspond to the later works on problematization and ethics. I will discuss each kind of practice in turn.

Foucault states in *The Archaeology of Knowledge* that archaeology is a "task that consists of not – of no longer – treating discourse as groups of signs (signifying elements referring to contents or representations) but as practices that systematically form the objects of which they speak" (EAK, 49). To treat discourse as a set of practices is to describe discursive practices. Foucault writes in his summary of the lecture course "The Will to Knowledge" that discursive practices "are characterized by the demarcation of a field of objects, by the definition of a legitimate perspective for a subject of knowledge, by the setting of norms for elaborating concepts and theories" (EEW1, 11). This definition corresponds to Foucault's description of "discursive formations" in *The Archaeology of Knowledge*: discursive objects, enunciative modalities, concepts, and strategies. For example, when Foucault analyzes madness, he is not interested in giving a commentary or to decipher old documents to figure out "what they meant." He instead focuses on "what they said," the very *statements* made. We can define discursive practices as those practices that serve as the conditions for the possibility of statements. Consider a "madman." It is not the case that there were (first) "madmen," therefore bringing about a discourse on "madness." Foucault argues that "madness" (the idea of madness) comes first, thus classifying certain people as "madmen." This is, according to Foucault, the case for every object of scientific discourse: the science (the *connaissance*) comes first. After this discursive practice takes place, another practice, the determination of discursive objects, occurs. Therefore, one cannot speak of "madmen" independently of the discourse of madness. It is the discourse, not the "madmen" per se, that Foucault seeks to study. It is worth noting that one cannot look at discursive objects without also incorporating enunciative modalities (who gets to speak scientifically about madness?), concepts (the notion of "sanity," for example), and strategies (the need to eliminate threats to societal order). All of these "activities" are the "practices" that Foucault studies when doing archaeology.

Genealogy, Foucault's second phase, deals with dividing practices or practices of power. Johanna Oksala states that these "are practices of manipulation and examination that classify, locate and shape bodies in the social field" (Oksala 2005, 3).

One type of dividing practice is "disciplinary practice." Disciplinary practices are described in great detail in *Discipline and Punish*. First, there are the practices that create "docile bodies" by means of the spatial arrangement of individuals (distribution), the control of activity, the organization of genera, and the composition of forces. These disciplinary practices create individuals that can be arranged, trained, and organized into machine-like groups. The arrangement, training, and organization of individuals is brought about by means of correct training. How docile bodies are trained also constitutes disciplinary practices: hierarchical observation, normalizing judgment, and the examination.

There are also dividing practices that affect the entire population and not just individual bodies. These are called "biopolitical practices," which deal with "a multiplicity of men, not to the extent that they are nothing more than their individual bodies, but to the extent that they form, on the contrary, a global mass that is affected by overall processes characteristic of birth, death, production, illness, and so on" (ECF-SMD, 242–243). This kind of practice includes the practices of government (including pastoral power), health codes, statistics, normalizing practices, and economic policies. Sexuality serves as a practice that straddles disciplinary and biopolitical spheres. It is disciplinary insofar as one's sexuality is monitored and "trained"; it is biopolitical insofar as sexuality affects birth rates and infection rates (in the case of sexually transmitted diseases). Race similarly works between both fields, primarily owing to the role of sexuality in Foucault's account of race.

In the genealogical works, practices seem more obvious given the work required to produce docile bodies and optimal populations. Of course, one can see a parallel between the words "practice" and "training." Practices are commonly referred to when describing an apparatus (*dispositif*) of power, so much so that Giorgio Agamben defines an apparatus directly as a "set of practices and mechanisms" (Agamben 2009, 8), although Foucault himself never describes apparatuses in terms of practices, preferring instead to describe them in terms of relations and strategies of power/knowledge (cf. EPK, 196).

The third phase of the Foucauldian project deals with a third kind of practice: practices of the self. These practices involve "the way a human being turns him- or herself into a subject" (EEW3, 327). These practices differ from discursive practices, which objectify human beings as objects of science (archaeology); they also differ from dividing practices, which objectify human beings in terms of power arrangements (genealogy). The practices of the self are *subjectifying*; they "permit individuals to effect by their own means, or with the help of others, a certain number of operations on their own bodies and souls, thoughts, conduct, and way of being, so as to transform themselves" (EEW1, 225). These practices are covered in Foucault's works from the 1980s prior to his death. Drawing primarily from Hellenic schools such as the Stoics and Cynics, Foucault analyzes a variety of ancient practices of the self and wonders what our current possibilities are for self-creation. There are four main kinds of practices of the self that Foucault analyzes in his readings of the Hellenic thinkers: ascetic practices, self-examination (contrasted with disciplinary examination), the interpretation of dreams (oneirocriticism), and self-writing. Foucault also focused on the practices of the self that were revealed by the Enlightenment movement, which for our purposes we will call "practices of freedom" (namely truth-telling and philosophical critique). It is worth noting that the practices of the self seem more like "practice" in the sense of rehearsing and preparing, compared to the other kinds of practices, in which one is *subjected* instead of *subjectifying*.

Thus, regardless of which Foucauldian technique one uses, one is studying practices. One could say that for Foucault everything is the result of practices. *It is practices all the way down.* There are practices and counterpractices; nothing is simply "there" that becomes the "victim" of practices: even these "victims" are themselves a set of practices. To use an example from the first volume of *The History of Sexuality*, there is no such thing as "homosexuals" who became discriminated against because of a heterosexist configuration of power; the very heterosexist configuration produces both "heterosexuals" and "homosexuals." Similarly, the division of people into different races did not become "racist" one day; the very division of people into different races is the racism. This is why Foucault describes power as being everywhere: practices go all the way down. Foucault tells us that power requires resistance (EHS1, 95). This is true because any practice has to maneuver around other practices. Similarly, when one "fights the power," one is simply enacting counterpractices to standing practices. These counterpractices, however, are nonetheless practices.

Unfortunately, other than the definition of "practice" given by Foucault in "Questions of Method," there are no other abstract definitions in the other works. There are lots of practices analyzed in Foucault's works, far too many to list here. However, I think we can conclude with some claims about practices, regardless of whether Foucault explicitly names them in his interviews and writings:

1. *Everything of Foucauldian interest results from practices.* In order to do any Foucauldian analysis on a given state of affairs, practices must be available for analysis. One way to test if someone is being sufficiently Foucauldian would be to explore whether the subject matter analyzed has been investigated as a practice instead of as a priori givens.

2. *Practices connect discourse, power, and subjectivity.* Given that one cannot cleanly separate archaeological, genealogical, and ethical aspects of a practice, there is something in the very practices themselves that crosses all three axes of Foucauldian interest.

3. *Every practice is connected to a problematization.* There is no practice independent of a greater problematization to which it responds. Of course, these problematizations are themselves the result of practices. Another way to say this is that *every practice has a history*, and the goal of genealogy is to produce that history.

4. *For every practice, there could be a counterpractice.* This is why the practices of freedom are so important. Philosophical critique explores which counterpractices might be possible in our ever-continuing quest to resist the domination of particular practices.

5. *Practices themselves are neither "positive" nor "negative," although they are all dangerous.* Practices – even those that we might like – must be scrutinized and analyzed to determine how power operates through them. Foucault states in his interview with Paul Rabinow and Hubert Dreyfus that "everything is dangerous, which is not exactly the same as bad. If everything is dangerous, then we always have something to do" (EEW1, 256).

6. *There are a finite number of practices at any given time.* Our clue comes from *The Archaeology of Knowledge*'s claim that there is a rarity of statements. Given the finite number of discursive practices inside of an *episteme*, I conjecture that there is also a rarity in nondiscursive practices. Since power is always local and from the "ground up," there are only so many ways to move with power, so many ways to transgress in a given scenario, so many ways to make oneself, so many ways to critique, and so on.

Brad Stone

SEE ALSO

Archaeology
Body
Dispositif *(Apparatus)*
Ethics
Genealogy
Race (and Racism)
Truth

SUGGESTED READING

Veyne, Paul. 1997. "Foucault Revolutionizes History," in *Foucault and His Interlocutors*, ed. Arnold Davidson. Chicago: University of Chicago Press, pp. 146–182.

66

PRISON

OUCAULT MAINTAINS A singular relation with the prison, and one that is really different from the relation he had with madness. He does not work within a penitentiary establishment and was never imprisoned. At the beginning of the 1970s, owing to protests, he participated in the organization called Groupe d'Information sur les Prisons (GIP: "Prison Information Group") and in this way experiences struggles (riots and hunger strikes) that develop within the establishments in order to change the standards for the inmates. Foucault collects and distributes information, and encourages, and relates the speeches of, prisoners in revolt. Over two years, he mobilizes his energy "in order to make the prison be known" by publishing the pamphlet called "Intolérable." With this commitment, the battle against the prison became Foucault's notoriety, and the success of his work *Discipline and Punish* (1975) became the symbol of his thought. It is probably not necessary to emphasize this now, but he was the first, on the basis of this experience, to make the prison an object of thought. The prison institutes a new regime of punishment. It brings to an end the tortures of the condemned in favor of their infinite surveillance, for which the figure of Jeremy Bentham's Panopticon is the valuable instrument. Thus Foucault draws up the history of the development of this power and shows how much this model has been a success in capitalist as well as in communist regimes. It is a success because with the prison this kind of power importantly produces a new figure and object of knowledge: the delinquent. Foucault's work on the prison initiates a number of research monographs, in particular in history, from the students and associates of the French historian Michelle Perrot.

But if Foucault is the first philosopher to problematize penal existence and to outline its brief history since its invention at the end of the eighteenth century, to his eyes, the penal prison is contextualized in a network of territory and disciplinary power, although not constituting the network's center. Of course, a certain number of characteristics of the disciplinary concentrated in the prison (characteristics such as the use of time, training of bodies, and individual surveillance) were extended into the schools, asylums, factories, and barracks throughout the nineteenth century. Nevertheless, Foucault shows, notably in his 1973 course at the Collège de France called "Psychiatric Power," that this apparatus is not proper to the prison. But, we find its declension in the asylum. Likewise, he is concerned with historicizing this microphysics of power by emphasizing how much, since its creation and juridical inscription, the prison has become an institution to be reformed. It is this double characteristic that interests Foucault, not that he wishes to become a prison reformer or a critical penal theoretician. Instead, he perceives there a possible weakness, a space of resistance, a leverage point. It is these forms of subjectification that in fact interest him: to understand how a prisoner in this restricted space from which he would not be able to get outside constructs himself as a subject.

Philippe Artières

SEE ALSO

Body
Madness
Normalization
Resistance
Space
The Visible
Gilles Deleuze

SUGGESTED READING

Artières, Philippe, Laurent Quéro, and Michelle Zancarini-Fournel. 2003. *Le groupe d'information sur les prisons: Archive d'une lutte, 1970–1971*. Paris: Editions de L'IMEC.
Macey, David. 1993. *The Lives of Michel Foucault*. New York: Vintage, chap. 11, "'Intolerable.'"

67

PRISON INFORMATION
GROUP (GIP)

THE ACTIVITIES OF Le groupe d'information sur les prisons (GIP: The Prison Information Group) occurred over 1971 and 1972. Its members included Michel Foucault (whose personal address appeared on GIP publications as the GIP's official location) but also Pierre Vidal-Naquet, Jean-Marie Domenach, Casamayor (which was the pseudonym for Serge Fuster), Maurice Clavel, Gilles Deleuze, Robert Badinter, and Jean Genet. The roots of the GIP go back to events of fall 1970. In September 1970 and then again in January 1971, several imprisoned members of a Maoist-inspired movement called Gauche prolétarienne went on a hunger strike in order to be recognized as political prisoners (rather than being treated as common criminals). Daniel Defert, who was a member of the group charged with preparing the lawsuits for the imprisoned (the group was called Organisation des prisonniers politiques [OPP]), proposed to Foucault that he generate a commission of inquest concerning the prisons. It was "at this moment," as Foucault says, that he "concerned himself" with the prisons and established the GIP (FDE1a, 1072). In order to understand the GIP, we must ask what the GIP was, what it did, and what it accomplished.

So, first we must ask for what purpose the GIP was established. It seems that Foucault accepted Defert's proposal because such an inquest looked to be the logical next step following *The History of Madness*. However, whereas Defert seems to have proposed a "commission of inquest" (making use of a judiciary term), Foucault created an "information group," hence the name he gave to the group (see FDE1a, 1042–1043; also Artières, Laurent, and Zancarini-Fournel 2003, 34–36). As Foucault says in the "GIP Manifesto," which he read aloud on February 8, 1971, "Hardly any information has been published on the prisons. The prisons are one of the hidden regions of our social system, one of the black boxes of our life. We have the right to know, we want to know" (FDE1a, 1043). Foucault's transformation of the inquest commission into an information group explains why Deleuze says, much later, in the short interview called "Foucault and Prison," after Foucault had died, that "Foucault had been the only one, not to survive the past [Deleuze mentions the past of May 1968], but to invent something new at all levels" (Deleuze 2007, 272). According to Deleuze, the GIP was an entirely new kind of group. What made the GIP new, according to Deleuze, was its "complete independence." It was completely independent because, being "localized," it concerned itself only with the prisons (Deleuze 2007, 276–277). It was not based on an ideology, or, more precisely, it was not based on something like a morality or a universal truth; it was not a totalizing movement. It had nothing to do with a political party or a political enterprise. What was at issue for the GIP was not a sociological study of prisons. It was not reformist, and it did not want to propose an ideal prison (FDE1a, 1072). What was at issue for the GIP was "to let those who have an experience of the prison speak," "literally to hand over the speaking to the inmates" (FDE1a, 1043, 1072). The former inmates and families of inmates were to speak "on their own account" and "in their own name" (Deleuze 2004, 206, 209). As the "GIP Manifesto" says, "We shall not find the information [we are seeking] in the official reports. We are asking for information from those who, somehow, have an experience of the prison or have a relation to it" (FDE1a, 1043). The GIP sought to avoid, as Deleuze says in "Intellectuals and Power," "the indignity of speaking for others" (Deleuze 2004, 208).

In fact, the GIP tried to avoid the indignity of speaking for others by distributing a questionnaire to the inmates. The GIP was not, however, allowed to distribute the questionnaire inside the prisons. Instead, every Saturday, Foucault tells us in an interview published in March 1971 (FDE1a, 1046), he and other members of the GIP went to the visitor gate of La Santé Prison and distributed the questionnaire to the families of inmates who were waiting in line. The first Saturday, Foucault says, the families of the inmates gave the GIP members a cold welcome. The second time, people were still distrustful. The third time, however, was different. Someone said that "all that is just talk, it should have been done a long time ago." Then suddenly, exploding with anger, a woman starts to tell her entire story: she speaks of the visits, the money she gives to the inmate she is visiting, the wealthy people who are not in prison, she speaks of the filth in the prisons. Thus the woman speaks in her own name, on her own account. And, when she starts to tell her story, it seems that the GIP has succeeded in letting those who have an experience of the prison speak. The GIP had given speech over to the inmates. As Deleuze says, "This was not the case before" (Deleuze 2007, 277).

What was made known by the questionnaire? The questionnaire was composed of eleven sections. The section topics and the questions contained in them are not surprising. They concern the conditions of visitations, conditions of the cells, the food, what sort of exercise, what sort of work, knowledge of rights, and the types of discipline and punishments used in the prisons. However, two questions seem remarkable. On the one hand, under the category of "Visites," the questionnaire asks whether its respondent can describe the conditions of visitations and, in particular, "those conditions which appear to you to be the most intolerable." On the other hand, under the category of "Discipline," and after asking about solitary confinement, the questionnaire asks the respondent what is "most intolerable after being deprived of freedom." The only apparently extant copy of the GIP questionnaire is, in fact, filled in by an unknown former inmate. In response to the question of what constitutes the most intolerable conditions of the visits, the former inmate had written that it is "the 'screws' [that is, the police] behind your back who are trying to see whether you are exchanging family letters. It's shameful." The answer to the second question of what is most intolerable after solitary confinement is: "One is, all the same, on solid ground [after being freed from solitary confinement]. [But] one has suffered." These answers indicate that what the inmates spoke of was shame and suffering. It is the shame and the suffering in the prisons that was the most intolerable. The knowledge of intolerable shame and suffering explains why Deleuze says that Foucault "was very shocked by the results [of the questionnaire]. We found something much worse [than bad food and poor medical treatment], notably, the constant humiliation" (Deleuze 2007, 273). The pamphlet that the GIP published was called "Intolerable." And Foucault says in an interview that "simply, I perceive the intolerable" (FDE1a, 1073).

We come now to the second question: what did the GIP do? This question itself contains two other questions that are inseparably connected. What did the GIP do with the information about intolerable suffering, shame, and humiliation? What did the inmates and families become as a result of what the GIP did? The two questions are inseparable because, as Foucault reports, the GIP wanted to minimize "the difference between those making the inquiry and collecting the information and those who are responding to the inquiry and providing information" (FDE1a, 1046). In a rare occasion, Foucault then speaks of an "ideal": "The ideal would be for us that the families communicate with the prisoners, that the prisoners communicate among themselves, that the prisoners communicate with public opinion. That is, we'd like to break apart the ghetto" (FDE1a, 1046). All that the GIP was doing was providing the "means," the means to express, the means to communicate, the means to make the information circulate "from mouth to ear, from group to group" (FDE1a, 1046–1047). By being simply a "means" to express the intolerable in its "raw state" (FDE1a, 1073), the GIP broke apart the ghetto-like difference but also made the intolerable "echo" (FDE1a, 1045). In "Foucault and Prison," Deleuze also speaks of the "echo" made by the GIP. In fact, he says that the GIP "amplified" the inmates' voices; its means made their voices "resound" (*retentissement*) (Deleuze 2007, 280). In fact, in this late interview, Deleuze says that "the goal of the GIP was less to make [the inmates] speak than to design a place where people would be forced to listen to them, a place that was not reduced to a riot on the prison roof, but would ensure that what they had to say passes through" (Deleuze 2007, 277). The conclusion we must draw is that in the GIP, the ones doing the inquiry became means or, as Deleuze would say, "relays" (Deleuze 2007, 289, 206–207). But then, moving to the side of the ones responding to the inquiry (the second part of our question), we must notice that they, too, were no longer simply inmates or prisoners. In a 1972 text for *Le Nouvel Observateur*, Deleuze says the inmates are judging the forms that their collective actions must take within the framework of the specific prison within which they find themselves (Deleuze 2004, 204). In the same text, Deleuze recounts that a new kind of public gathering is taking place. It has nothing to do with "public confession" or with a "traditional town meeting." Instead, former prisoners are coming forward and saying what was done to them, what they saw: physical abuse, reprisals, lack of medical care (Deleuze 2004, 205). In fact, Deleuze reports that at one such gathering the prison guards tried to shout down the former inmates. The inmates, however, silenced the prison guards by describing the brutality that each one had committed. The inmates used the very sentence that the prison guards had used to intimidate the inmates: "I recognize him" (ibid.). Thus, at the least, we have to say that the inmates became speakers. But they also became writers by simply responding to the questionnaire. The importance of writing is seen in the fourth GIP pamphlet (from late 1972), which published, without correcting punctuation or spelling (that is, in their "raw state"), letters written from prison by a certain "H. M." Deleuze wrote a short commentary to accompany the publication of the letters. Deleuze claims that H. M.'s letters bear witness to complementary or opposed personalities, all of which, however, "are participating in the same 'effort to reflect.'" In fact, Deleuze says that H. M.'s correspondence "is exemplary because its heartfelt reflections express exactly what a prisoner is thinking" (Deleuze 2004, 244). We can then even conclude that the amplification of the inmates' voices was done so that they became thinkers.

We come then to the third question: what happened then? As Deleuze says in "Foucault and Prison," the GIP was a "thought-experiment," but like all experiments it had mixed results (Deleuze 2007, 273). On the side of the ones responding to the questionnaire, there were risks. Accompanying the protests and uprising that continued over the two-year period, there was a rash of suicides in the prisons as a kind of last-ditch protest. In fact, H. M. committed suicide, and the fourth GIP pamphlet was devoted to suicides in the prisons. On the side of the ones collecting the information, the GIP side, there were risks too. In a 1971 interview, Foucault speculated that the authorities might react to the GIP's actions by throwing all of its members in jail. Most importantly, however, soon after the GIP was disbanded in 1972, the prison authorities clamped down on the prisons again. As Deleuze reports in "Foucault and Prison," Foucault came to believe that the GIP had been a failure (Deleuze 2007, 279). Foucault had the impression that the GIP had served no purpose. "It was not repression," Foucault says in Deleuze's words, "but worse: it was as if someone speaks but nothing was said" (Deleuze 2007, 277). Yet, Deleuze insisted that the GIP had been a success in a different way. Although it did not succeed in bringing about long-lasting concrete changes in the French prisons, the GIP did produce "new conditions for statements." It was successful, according to Deleuze, insofar as it made possible "a type of statement about the prison that is regularly made by the inmates and the non-inmates, a type of statement that had been unimaginable before" (Deleuze 2007, 280). In other words, we could say that the GIP's success appeared not in the prisons themselves but in the statements, concepts, and books it made possible. For instance, the former inmate Serge Livrozet wrote a book called *De la prison à la revolte*, for which Foucault wrote a preface (Livrozet 1999; FDE1a, 1262–1267). Although the GIP documents constantly state that they are not trying to raise the inmates' consciousness (FDE1a, 1044), and although Foucault constantly says that the GIP is not providing the inmates with knowledge (FDE1a, 1289), the GIP in fact gave the inmates and their families a new way of relating to themselves. The GIP not only was a relay for the inmates' voices but also a relay for thinking. In this way, the GIP was a success in the unification of theory and practice or philosophy and politics.

Leonard Lawlor

SEE ALSO

> *Philosophy*
> *Politics*
> *Power*
> *Prison*
> *Gilles Deleuze*

SUGGESTED READING

Artières, Philippe. 2013. *Groupe d'information sur les prisons. Intolérable.* Paris: Gallimard. (2013). 2013. *Révolte de la prison de Nancy. 15 janvier 1972.* Paris: Le Point du Jour, 2013.
Artières, Philippe, Laurent Quéro, and Michelle Zancarini-Fournel. 2003. *Le groupe d'information sur les prisons. Archive d'une lutte, 1970–1971.* Paris: Editions de L'IMEC.
Deleuze, Gilles. 2007. "Foucault and Prison," in *Two Regimes of Madness,* trans. Ames Hodges and Mike Taormina. New York: Semiotext(e), pp. 272–281.
Livrozet, Serge. 1999. *De la prison à la révolte.* Paris: L'esprit frappeur.
Spivak, Gayatri Chakravorty. 1994. "Can the Subaltern Speak?" in *Colonial Discourse and Post-Colonial Theory: A Reader,* ed. Patrick Williams and Laura Chrisman. New York: Columbia University Press, pp. 66–111.

68

PROBLEMATIZATION

P ROBLEMATIZATION IS ONE of the centermost ideas in Michel Foucault's methodological repertoire. It has proven quite difficult to understand many crucial aspects of Foucault's methodology without a proper understanding of problematization. Hence it has proven quite difficult to understand how Foucault deployed his methodological tools in the course of his inquiries in order to develop his provocative claims about the objects of these inquiries without a proper understanding of problematization. Hence it has also proven quite difficult to understand how Foucault made use of his methodological equipment and with what modality of critical intent without a proper understanding of problematization.

Foucault himself, in an important 1984 interview with his then-assistant François Ewald, said of his entire career of work: "The notion common to all the work that I have done since *History of Madness* is that of problematization" (EPPC, 257). It is well known that Foucault is famous for sweeping retrospective reflexive redescriptions. Some have accordingly been inclined to dismiss such remarks of Foucault's as this. But in this case, dismissing the remark is symptomatic of a problem at a more general level. At this more general level, it is notable that very few of Foucault's commentators have seriously considered the role played by the analytic of problematization in his methodology. Among those who have addressed the idea of problematization in their interpretations of Foucault, one common view is that problematization has something to do with a third methodological phase in Foucault's work such that the arc of his thought forms a sequence from archaeology to genealogy to problematizations of ethics and the subject. Unfortunately, this interpretation fails to give problematization the more central structural role it plays in Foucault's work. Both archaeology and genealogy, which are not incompatible methodologies, should be seen as embedded in a style of thinking that proceeds as an inquiry into the problems that motivate and facilitate the responsive development of new practices, techniques, and styles.

I shall here show that, with respect to the sweeping self-redescription cited previously, Foucault ably assessed himself. Problematization is a notion that informs the full array of Foucault's inquiries (Koopman 2013). To show this in compact fashion, I shall address the following two questions in turn: What is problematization for Foucault? Where does problematization appear in Foucault?

What is problematization for Foucault? Problematization should be seen as a key piece of analytical equipment in Foucault's methodological repertoire. Regarded as such, the notion plays a dual role. In its first role, problematization is a form of analytic activity, or a modality of philosophic inquiry. In this sense, "problematization" is a verb. It denotes something that the inquirer does. It is often said that Foucault problematized the seemingly stable assumptions of heteronormative sexuality. Indeed, he did. After reading Foucault, and living for a while with that reading, it is difficult not to feel as if our sexuality is terribly problematic. Sex has been a problem for us for a long time. Foucault helps us feel the full force of the problem and the particular locales where that force is most excited. The problem at hand is not the result or product of Foucault's analysis. To think so would be to ascribe more power to a philosopher than any philosopher ever could have. Philosophers do not make problems so much as they clarify and intensify them. It is not that Foucault turned sex into a problem but rather that Foucault gave coherence to a problem we all already implicitly had a sense of. Every teenager knows how problematic sexuality is. But very few teenagers, and not many more adults, understand this set of problems in a way that facilitates ethical responsiveness. What Foucault offers is a way of understanding ourselves through our problems such that we might more usefully respond to who we are. If Foucault problematized, it was because something was already in some way problematic, and yet not coherently or sensibly so. If problematization in the first sense is a mode of the activity of inquiry, then problematization in the second sense is the object of inquiry corollary to such activity. In this sense, "problematization" is a noun, referring to that bundle of problematic material that we find problematic, about which we feel anxious, and over which we tend to obsess, both as individuals and at the more general level of society and culture. One way of summarizing Foucault's notion of problematization in its two senses is to see acts of problematization as giving coherence to the extant problematization that is the object on which the act operates. The activity of problematization renders an object of problematization more coherent – but also more challenging.

Problematization in this dual sense possesses all of the hallmarks of Foucault's work. Problematizations are historical objects, and therefore are to be analyzed as historical phenomena. Problematizations are composed of a bundle of contingently combined practices and therefore are to be analyzed in terms of the way they are both funded by practices and further sponsor the elaboration of new practices. The problematization that is disciplinary power, for example, was both funded by monastic rituals of temporal structure and military rituals of spatial organization and at the same time served to sponsor a wide swath of modern practices such as spatio-temporal techniques of imprisonment. Problematizations that are made possible by practices also make further practices possible. In this sense, problematizations form conditions of possibility for the present and act as limits on who we are and who we might yet become. Whereas for Kant such limits were uncrossable laws of reason as such, for Foucault these limits form deep historical barriers to who we take ourselves to be. As historical but not transcendental limits, problematizations are capable of being crossed over. But this would never be easy, nor would it ever be obvious to us how we might restructure the problematizations in which we find ourselves placed.

One function played by problematization as an act of inquiry is to make clear just how difficult it is, how problematic it feels, to respond to the problematizations in which we find ourselves embedded. There are certain things to which we feel that we must devote some kind of work. Nobody escapes the thrall of sex today (even if for some that thrall takes the form of censuring the sex lives of others). Sex for us is one of those things about which nobody can be agnostic. Nobody has nothing, nothing at all, to say about sex. Yet how difficult it is for any of us to respond usefully to this problematic. There is a vast ensemble of practices, techniques, and rationalities in which our sex is all wrapped up and packaged. Adopting a free and ethical relation to our sexuality proves enormously difficult as a result. We find ourselves the subjects of profound constraints. There remains the nagging motivation that we must somehow find a way to ethically respond to these conditions of who we are and who we could yet become. We, all of us, are just like those teenagers struggling with their sexuality. We, all of us, were at some time, and still remain at some times, those teenagers. Perhaps for biographical reasons Foucault felt these problems more poignantly than many of us do. But we all know some of what he felt. If in his final writings Foucault was devoting himself to elaborating the problematization of sexuality in antiquity, then there is the sense that this problematization somehow still informs who we are today, such that part of what Foucault was doing was elaborating the conditions of his own action, and presumably with an eye toward facilitating a more free and reflective ethical relation to the self.

Two examples, both Foucault's own, can conclude this discussion of how problematization functions in Foucault's work. Elaborating on the retrospective self-interpretive claim cited earlier, Foucault continues in the interview: "In *History of Madness* the question was how and why, at a given moment, madness was problematized through a certain institutional practice and a certain apparatus of knowledge" (ibid.). According to this self-interpretation, the project of that book was to analyze the practical conditions of knowledge and power that contingently coalesced at different moments in modernity so as to institute disruptions and difficulties concerning madness and unreason that motivated the elaboration of those new practices, institutions, and techniques that eventually led to our contemporary practices treating objects of mental illness. Foucault continues in response to his interviewer:

"Similarly, in *Discipline and Punish* I was trying to analyze the changes in the problematization of the relations between crime and punishment through penal practices and penitentiary institutions in the late eighteenth and early nineteenth centuries" (ibid.). The project of this book, likewise, was to analyze the congeries of practices that in the years under consideration began to form a composite problematization that motivated the elaboration of radically different punitive and criminal mechanisms than had been customary until that time.

Where does problematization appear in Foucault? Having specified how problematization functions in Foucault's work, we are now in a good position to assess the accuracy of his self-interpretive claim that this notion informs his work at least as far back as the early 1960s. Most readers are accustomed to the frequent references to this notion in Foucault's late writings of the early 1980s. But few have tracked the notion further back. Yet once one goes looking for it, one finds this idea at key junctures in most of Foucault's major works.

It should be noted in the first place that the notion of problematization was not explicitly thematized as such in Foucault's work until the late seventies. It was in his 1978 Collège de France course lectures, posthumously published under the title of *Security, Territory, and Population*, that the concept first appears to have assumed explicit methodological status. The inaugural lecture of the series, given on January 11, offers a comparative discussion of three episodes of illness (leprosy in the Middle Ages, the plague at the end of the Middle Ages, and smallpox in the context of eighteenth-century practices of inoculation) in terms of the "problem" structuring each episode: "In short, it will no longer be the problem of exclusion, as with leprosy, or of quarantine, as with the plague, but of epidemics and the medical campaigns that try to halt epidemic or endemic phenomena" (ECF-STP, 10). A little later into the course, the February 1 lecture opens with a discussion of "the specific problems of population" and "the problem of government" (ECF-STP, 88). Throughout the remaining lectures, the category of "the problem" assumes increasing methodological gravity in Foucault's analyses of the forms of power, government, and political rationality characteristic of the objects of his inquiry. In work prior to 1978, the concept (as well as the words "problématisation" and "problématique" themselves) appears, though in obviously inchoate usages, as for example in other mid-seventies writings, including the 1975 book *Discipline and Punish* (EDP, 227), the *Abnormal* course lectures from winter 1975 (ECF-AB, 134, 139), and the short 1976 essay "The Politics of Health in the Eighteenth Century" (EFR, 274). In even earlier work, we find the idea itself clearly anticipated in Foucault's archaeological writings. Foucault wrote in *The Order of Things* of "an archaeological analysis of knowledge itself" as explicating "the conditions that make a controversy or problem possible" (EOT, 76). And even as early as *History of Madness* (a work, by the way, that would surely be as genealogical as it is archaeological on any interpretation of these distinct but compatible historical methodologies) there are a handful of key passages in which Foucault seems to be doing what he later said he had done, namely inquiring into the history of madness by deploying analytic procedures treating madness in terms of the problematization that made it possible (EHM, 381, 419, 458). Going back even further, one of the very first appearances of "problématique" in Foucault's work, if indeed not the very first, is located in his very first publication, his 1954 "Introduction" to the phenomenologist Ludwig Binswanger's *Dream and Existence* (FDE1, 79).

A final example will be conclusive. Consider Foucault's 1970 review of two important books by Deleuze published in 1968. Foucault tells his readers that the lesson of Deleuze's books is that, "We must think problematically rather than question and answer dialectically" (EEW2, 359). If Deleuze's books represented a watershed event in contemporary French philosophy because they displaced the until then dominant style of French Hegelianism according to which the motion of thought traverses from position to negation through contradiction, then it is of no small import that Foucault locates the other side of a watershed in terms of a quite different motion of thought as transitioning through problems toward difference and repetition. Years later, Deleuze repaid compliments to Foucault in strikingly similar terms: "One thing haunts Foucault – thought.... To think means to experiment and to problematize" (Deleuze 1988, 116). If this is right, then it will continue to prove enormously difficult to understand Foucault's thought, and that toward which he directed his thought, without an understanding of that thought as enacting a problematization of that which conditions us as our present problematization.

Colin Koopman

SEE ALSO

Critique
Madness
Resistance
Sex
Gilles Deleuze

SUGGESTED READING

Koopman, Colin. 2013. *Genealogy as Critique: Problematization and Transformation in Foucault and Others*. Bloomington: Indiana University Press.

69

PSYCHIATRY

"To become other than what one is," Foucault wrote, "that too, is philosophy" (EEW1, 327). For Foucault, unless utterly dominated (EEW3, 342), and although always within limits, we are free to become other than what we are because there is no innate psychic structure determining our lives. Foucault wrote genealogies, including more than one genealogy of mental illness and psychiatry, because he wanted to show that what we are (psychiatrized subjects) is historically contingent and that what we think is human nature (certain facts about the human psyche) is a set of constructs particular to our own time. Philosophy, for Foucault, should not aim to tell us truths about what it is to be human but should change what this is, or give us the tools to change ourselves. For Foucault, philosophy is political because it is a technology for social and personal change. Foucault would call his early methodology, archaeology, "a line of attack" (EAK, 206), and he would say that his later methodology, genealogy, is "not made for knowing, but for cutting" and for "shattering" (EFR, 88). Foucault does not aim to establish new knowledges but to cut and shatter what we currently consider knowledge. The psychological sciences, and first and foremost psychiatry, were among the things that Foucault cut up, shattered, and attacked. In conversation, he once said that "The art of living is to kill psychology.... If one cannot manage to do that in life, it isn't worth living" (FDE2a, 1075, my translation). Foucault's final "ethical" works on the aesthetics of the self can thus be read as attempts to kill psychology or, more modestly, to find and describe alternatives to the psychologized self. These works show that an aesthetic rather than a medico-scientific or psychological approach to the self is possible since it has existed in the past. Although that particular past is irretrievable (EAIF, 231), remembering that it existed opens up the possibility of "killing" the psychologization of our selves in the present, as well as the possibility of forging new approaches to our lives. But why were the psychological sciences so problematic for Foucault? Why, in his opinion, did they call for assassination?

The human sciences in general are problematic for Foucault because they claim to give us knowledge about ourselves, about human beings, about human nature, thus denying our freedom to be other than what we are, and the psychological sciences are arguably the most pernicious subset of these sciences for a variety of reasons. For one, the psychological sciences – compared to other human sciences such as anthropology or sociology – are pervasive: we do not go to anthropologists or sociologists on a regular basis to learn about who we are, but many people go to psychiatrists and psychotherapists, and even those who do not (or cannot afford to) visit psychiatric experts will engage in a popularized form of psychologizing themselves and others. Whether actively psychiatrized or not, we are saturated by psychologizing discourses. The discourses of the psychological sciences, the most respected (because it is the most "scientific") of which is psychiatry, have become omnipresent, with psychologists and psychiatrists serving as experts on talk shows, writing columns in women's magazines, talking on the news after every crisis or tragedy, writing books for laypeople, informing disciplines such as criminology and pedagogy, and serving as experts in courts of law. This last case particularly concerned Foucault, and he called it "Ubuesque" and "grotesque" (ECF-AB, 35) because it meant that psychiatrists had seized not just disciplinary power but the power of life and death, legal-juridical or sovereign power. Another reason that the psychological sciences are particularly pernicious, compared to other sciences, is that they set up institutions in which people can be incarcerated and dominated for the rest of their lives. Moreover, not only do the psychological sciences have their own institutions but they invade *all other institutions*, infiltrating the school, the hospital, the prison, the court of law, the family, and the workplace. To take just one example, many people now have to pass a personality test designed by psychiatrists in order to compete for a job.

In the late 1940s and early 1950s, Foucault pursued an education both in philosophy and in psychology, and the psychological sciences – psychiatry most prominently – remained a focus of his philosophical attention throughout his life. He received a *licence de philosophie* from the École Normale in 1948, a *licence de psychologie* in 1949, and in 1952 he earned not only the *agrégation de philosophie* but also a *Diplôme de psycho-pathologie* from the Institut de psychologie de Paris. Foucault's first teaching position was in psychology, not philosophy, at the University of Lille. Foucault's critical engagements with psychiatry and the psychological sciences extend throughout his oeuvre, beginning with his earliest work, *Maladie mentale et personnalité*, reedited as *Maladie mentale et psychologie* (1954), and resurfacing as sustained themes in Foucault's course lectures from 1973–1974 and 1974–1975, published as *Psychiatric Power* (2008) and *Abnormal* (2004). For the purpose of this article, I will focus on the *History of Madness* (2006 [1961]), Foucault's most sustained and arguably most significant engagement with psychiatry.

History of Madness is described by Foucault not as a history of psychiatry but as an "archaeology of … silence" (EHM, xxviii). For Foucault, an archaeology is a study of what made a certain discourse – or, in this case, the absence or silencing of a discourse – possible. Thus, in writing an archaeology of silence rather than a history of psychiatry, Foucault is not so much concerned with what made psychiatric discourses possible as what made the silencing of madness possible. As it turns out, psychiatry was a key condition of this possibility. Positing, in this early work, something like an essential experience of madness, Foucault argues that what we hear about in psychiatric discourses and in the words of the mentally ill themselves is no longer madness but what has been allowed to be said once madness was silenced.

Foucault traces the experience of madness through the Renaissance, when madmen and women were perceived in at least three different ways: as tragic, eschatological figures ("Cosmic Madness"), as ironic jousting partners with reason ("Critical Madness"), and as figures of sin (gluttony, avarice, drunkenness, and sloth all being described as *follies* at this time). There is a self-recognition in the mad person during this period: as a figure of death and sin, the madman or woman reminds us that we will all die, that we are all sinners, and that all of our mortal projects are futile and vain. At the same time, madness gives access to fundamental truths of human existence that are not available to reason, and madmen are often figures who tell the (uncomfortable) truth. For instance, the fools in Shakespeare see and say what others cannot. As objects of uneasy identification and reminders and speakers of undesired truths, Foucault claims that the Renaissance response to the mad was to send them into exile or to cast them off to sea. Consequently, the mad were associated with wandering, the amorphousness of water, and a geographical freedom. Drawing on art and literature from the period, Foucault illustrates this thesis with references to Shakespeare, Cervantes, and Bosch.

In contrast to the Renaissance, in the Age of Reason madness was no longer seen as a jousting partner with reason but as the very absence of reason. Far from giving humans access to truths not available to reason, madness was *un*reason, one form of immoral idleness among others (such as poverty, vagabondage, and libertinage). Madness was a chosen, moral failing, deserving of punishment. Since Enlightenment man was defined by his rationality, the mad were dehumanized, and consequently so thoroughly othered that an identification with them – uneasy or otherwise – became impossible. As others, inhuman, the mad were seen as animals, but were also blamed for having chosen animality as other animals were not. The mad had irremediably foresaken their humanity. The Enlightenment response to madness was consequently punitive: confinement and forced labor. A key moment in this archaeology of silence is the creation of the Hôpital Général in 1657, at the beginning of the classical age, which marked the "Great Confinement" not only of the mad but of other unreasonable people – libertines, vagabonds, those who did not work, and criminals. Housed promiscuously together, the mad were nevertheless singled out from their fellow inmates by virtue of their bestialization. Their departure from reason alone was seen as incorrigible, and thus dehumanizing. As such, the mad alone could be put on display and forced to perform tricks for the entertainment of spectators, and could live in the same conditions of material deprivation as domesticated animals, lacking adequate food, clothing, and shelter from the damp and cold.

The next great moment in Foucault's archaeology of silence is Philippe Pinel's "liberation" of the mad at Bicêtre in 1794 – at the beginning of the modern era. With this gesture, and the consequent birth of psychiatry, the understanding of madness changed again. Now madness was viewed by doctors and experienced by the mad themselves as a mental form of illness, in the realm of pathology rather than morality or sin. The relation of madness to truth was reformulated: no longer in dialogue with reason or revelatory of fundamental truths (as in the Renaissance), and no longer an absence of reason or the negation of truth (as in the classical age), modern madness was an *object* of medical reason and truthful scientific discourse. This epistemic shift with respect to madness resulted in some basic material ameliorations in the living conditions of the mad, since their preferred treatment was no longer exile, confinement, or punishment but therapy and cure. Nevertheless, within asylums, all mad men and women continued to be confined (if not in chains then within walls), and continued to be corporally punished if they did not behave according to the dictates of doctors. If they were "liberated," it was in the sense that those who behaved no longer dwelled in dungeons. Foucault contests that this was an even partial "liberation," however, since he suggests that psychiatry could only afford to release the (well behaving) mad from their material chains because it had begun the successful shackling of their souls. The mad whose souls were not yet in chains, moreover – those who still outrageously misbehaved – were returned to material constraints: to straightjackets or mind-numbing regimes of drugs.

Just as Foucault contests that Pinel liberated the insane in 1794, so he rebuts the argument that Freud liberated the mad further a century later. If, after a hundred years, psychoanalysis appeared to "liberate" the mad beyond Pinel's removal of their chains, allowing them to leave the asylum and to speak, it was only because four generations of psychiatry had fettered the souls of the mad so thoroughly that there was now little fear that they would speak anything but the discourses of medicine that the analysts wanted to hear. The "cosmic" truths of madness had by then been so deeply buried that the mad could safely be released not only from chains but from institutional walls and from silence. Broken, and having nothing left to say that did not parrot the psychiatrists – to whom they deferred, whose authority they had accepted, whose discourses they had internalized – the mad (and indeed the rest of us) could now be trusted to present themselves voluntarily for psychotherapy and to say nothing in that clinical space that challenged the medical view of the mind. Although the dominant view and experience of madness and mental experience more generally is thus now the medical one, Foucault argues that echoes of a "cosmic madness" continue to be heard in the works of writers and artists such as Nietzsche, Artaud, Goya, and Van Gogh.

Throughout the *History of Madness*, Foucault argues that the fact that the first psychiatrists were doctors gave them the justification, disguise, or authority to take control of people's bodies, but that the work they did in the asylums was not medical. According to Foucault, psychiatrists simply represent and embody the norms, morality, or values of a particular society, and their job is to assimilate mental patients to these norms. Early psychiatrists such as Tuke and Pinel were aware that they were not using their medical expertise and scientific knowledge in their work with the mad. They were self-consciously assimilating patients into the values of their society, including its sexual norms: the patients whom they considered "cured" were those who would marry and be ideal spouses, who would have children and be ideal parents, or who fulfilled their assigned roles in the heterosexual family. In this early work, Foucault argues that just like the mad had to submit to a bourgeois work ethic within the asylum, they needed to submit to the values of the patriarchal bourgeois family. The mad had long had minority legal status, but they had not actually been treated like children. Now, however, they are theorized and treated as such. The psychiatrist, as the "adult," represents to the mad "both domination and destination," both the power to which one submits and the power that one is destined to become through assimilation. In the asylum, when unreason rebelled against reason, this was seen as a mere failure of a child to submit to the authority of the father. Foucault argues that madness was in this way reduced to a father-child drama, however madness was once about much bigger things. When psychoanalysis "discovers" Oedipal complexes at the root of all neuroses and psychopathologies, it is discovering something that was created recently in asylums: these petty parent-child squabbles are not what madness was about before the asylum reduced it to this. So reduced, however, it was safe to let the mad out of the asylums and to allow them to speak because one knew that they would talk about nothing more threatening than the mommy-daddy-baby discourses that Freud wanted to hear. Even today, psychiatry and psychoanalysis depoliticize and individualize madness, transforming what might have been social critique into family dramas of incest and genes.

Modern science claims to tell us something about madness, or mental illness, but before these sciences could even begin to work, the mad had to already be separated out from the sane. To be an object of scientific knowledge to begin with, this division had to have already occurred. Yet this division was a constitutive act – it changed madness into something that is no longer in dialogue with reason; it subjugated madness so that what was studied was not the pure phenomenon of madness. Psychiatry thus studies an object of its own invention. Foucault wants to show that madness was not always divided from nonmadness, reason was not always divided from nonreason. In the Renaissance, reason and madness were in dialogue, madness threatened with a tragic truth. In contrast, mental illness is a "serene world," and the language of psychiatry is a "monologue," and what is being monologued about is not madness but mental illness, a much safer thing.

When Foucault wrote the *History of Madness*, he had not yet coined many of the terms for which he is now known, and in particular he had not yet theorized disciplinary power. It is nevertheless tempting and possible to read Foucault's *History* through the lens of this later concept as it is contrasted with sovereign power – and indeed, Foucault does something like this in his 1973–1974 course lectures, "Psychiatric Power." In Foucault's later terminology, the classical age was an age of sovereign power. Power entailed the use of brute physical force; it was laborious and inefficient, depending on material weapons and chains and struggles between bodies. With Pinel, that power was supplemented and eventually all but replaced by a newer, cleaner, lighter, more elegant, and efficient form of power: discipline. Disciplinary power does not wield a sword or threaten death but controls people's minds or souls, thereby getting them to control themselves so that physical force is not necessary. Disciplined individuals appear to be free and perceive themselves as free. Having internalized what is expected of them, they regulate themselves. As such, there is no need for physical constraints or physical punishments. The irony, for Foucault, is that the superfluousness of shackles only shows how dominated we are by the disciplinary constitutions of our souls. Pinel's "liberation" of the mad and placement of them in the first psychiatric asylums, and Freud's further "liberation" of these same individuals and placement of them on the analyst's couch, like the shift from torture to prison, illustrates the replacement of sovereign power with disciplinary power. This is a power that functions not through laws but through norms, or is a normalizing form of power.

Foucault's course lectures from 1973–1974, "Psychiatric Power," revisit much of the ground covered by the *History of Madness*, once again providing a history of the emergence of psychiatric discourses and practices. This time, however, Foucault is equipped with the theory of disciplinary power that he was developing at the time in *Discipline and Punish*. The first lectures in this series provide a detailed account of disciplinary power as it may be contrasted point by point with sovereign power, and describe psychiatric power as an example of discipline. In these same lectures, Foucault critiques some of his arguments as well as his methodology in *History of Madness*, claiming that the earlier work, in contrast to the current one, was a history of representations (its examples taken from art), essentialized madness, focused on institutions rather than power relations, and also committed the error of seeing psychiatric power as paternal – or patriarchal – power, reproducing the family within the asylum and assimilating patients into familial subjects. In fact, Foucault now argues, the family is an institution of sovereign power, in contrast to the asylum, which is a site of disciplinary power.

The following year, in his lecture series "Abnormal," Foucault will change his mind again with respect to the psychiatry-family relation, arguing that the family has been thoroughly co-opted by disciplinary power and biopower, and thus the comparison between the family and doctors remains relevant, except that the order of influence is reversed: in *History of Madness*, Foucault argues that doctors act like fathers, but in *Abnormal* Foucault will argue that parents act like doctors. It is thus not so much that the (psychiatric) hospital is a familial space but that the family home has become a clinic. It is not that doctors take on the power of fathers, or function as patriarchs, but that under biopower parents of both sexes defer to doctors: their power is a medicalized one but subjugates parents to doctors rather than allowing them to take on a medical authority of their own. The family, Foucault argues throughout *Psychiatric Power* and *Abnormal*, is thus, like the school, prison, and the court of law, another institution that psychiatry has annexed, and the ever-shifting tensions and allegiances between parents and doctors are ones that Foucault traces throughout both his 1973–1974 and 1974–1975 lecture courses.

Despite changes in methodology and the development of new tools (for instance, his models of power) between the 1960s and the 1970s, and despite a new and important argument associating psychiatry with racism that emerged in Foucault's 1974–1975 and 1975–1976 lectures (ECF-AB, 316–318; ECF-SMD, 60–111), many arguments remain constant between the *History of Madness* and *Psychiatric Power* and *Abnormal*. Most notably, Foucault continues to argue that psychiatry is a form of social or moral hygiene rather than a medicine or science, and that psychiatrists are masquerading as doctors in order to pass off their normalizing task as truth and cure.

Chloë Taylor

SEE ALSO

Abnormal
Archaeology
Biopower
Madness
Power

SUGGESTED READING

Gros, Frédéric. 1997. *Foucault et la folie*. Paris: Presses Universitaires de France.
Huffer, Lynne. 2010. *Mad for Foucault: Rethinking the Foundations of Queer Theory*. New York: Columbia University Press.

70

PSYCHOANALYSIS

PSYCHOANALYSIS RUNS THROUGH Foucault's body of work. From his first publications on mental illness and the existential significance of dreams in the mid-1950s to his last seminars on the history of sexuality and care of the self in the early 1980s, there is for Foucault an abiding concern with Freud and the modern science of psychology.

Depending on the project he is involved with in any given period of his philosophical career, Foucault's critical engagement with psychoanalysis shifts in focus. Within the context of Foucault's early work on the semantics of linguistic expression, psychoanalysis appears as a theory of meaning that comes close to accounting for such expressiveness, while ultimately failing for lack of an appreciation of poetic and mythological language.

In Foucault's work in the early to mid-1960s on the institutionalization of psychiatric discourse and the constitution of the "medicalized" psychological patient, psychoanalysis appears as an exemplary positivist science and is criticized as such on the grounds of its implicit continuation of the early modern moral evaluation of madness. Yet, within this same context, Foucault offers a positive assessment of psychoanalysis. Foucault credits psychoanalysis with reopening the discursive exchange between modern, scientific psychology and madness; it thus gives voice to madness after a long period of silence during the classical period.

It is the *form* of this conclusion that is telling. If the details of Foucault's remarks on psychoanalysis change according to the vantage point from which he views Freud's work, the *tone* of those remarks remains constant: they are always both positive and negative or critical.

Accordingly, "ambivalence" in the Freudian sense may serve as a guiding heuristic in reading Foucault's engagement with psychoanalysis. As Laplanche and Pontalis define "ambivalence" in *The Language of Psycho-analysis*, it is "[t]he simultaneous existence of contradictory tendencies, attitudes or feelings in the relationship

411

to a single object" (Laplanche and Pontalis 1973, 26). Further, as Freud develops the notion of "ambivalence [*Ambivalenz*]" in "Mourning and Melancholia," a subject is ambivalent toward a cathected object insofar as he or she differentiates the object from him- or herself, investing it with love and significance; the subject also reverts to a primary narcissism by which she or he wants to make the object his or her own through incorporation.

These features of Freudian ambivalence might serve as broad contours of an "ambivalent" reading of Foucault's engagement with psychoanalysis; they might also outline a reading of Foucault from a Freudian perspective. The following does not substantiate such a reading of Foucault and Freud. Rather, it merely sketches the possibility of such a reading from the details of Foucault's writings on psychoanalysis.

Foucault's first two publications are critical studies of psychology: *Mental Illness and Personality* (1954), which was revised and retitled as *Mental Illness and Psychology* (1962), and "Introduction: Dream, Imagination, Existence" in the French translation of Ludwig Binswanger's *Dream and Existence* (1954).

The essay *Dream and Existence* that Foucault introduces in the French edition is an example of the *Daseinsanalyse* that Binswanger developed by combining the Heideggerian notion of *Dasein*, which "remove[s] [psychology] from its hoary metaphysical and religious rut," concerning the question of the mind–body relation (EDE, 83) with Freud's treatment of dreams as central to the psychic life of individuals. These two factors combine in the composition of what Binswanger calls a "personal life-history" (EDE, 86).

Foucault highlights Binswanger's insistence that *Daseinsanalyse* draw on "myth, religion, and poetry" (EDE, 84). "The theme of [Binswanger's] 1930 essay," Foucault writes, "[is] existence in that mode of being of the dream in which it announces itself in a meaningful fashion." What interests Foucault is the expressiveness of poetic and mythic language, and Binswanger's attention to such expressiveness in crediting dreams their full, existential significance (EDE, 33).

All discursivity "implies a world of expression which precedes it, sustains it, and allows it to give body to what it means" (EDE, 35). Even with respect to the dream experience, which it purports to treat in its full significance, Freudian psychoanalysis "fail[s] to acknowledge this structure of language" and so "never gets a comprehensive grasp of meaning" (ibid.). Despite the direct link between Binswanger and Freud – and the successes of the former relative to the latter – Foucault concludes in unequivocal fashion: "Psychoanalysis has never succeeded in making images speak" (EDE, 38).

It is possible to read this conclusion as contradictory. As suggested earlier, it might also be possible to read Foucault's conclusion ambivalently. A similar tone appears in Foucault's other early engagement with psychology: *Mental Illness and Personality* (1954)/*Mental Illness and Psychology* (1962). In revising the work, Foucault replaces a Marxist approach to institutional discourse with a historical account of the "constitution" of the modern experience of madness; such "historicization" of mental illness draws the second edition of the work close to psychoanalysis.

Foucault connects the discourse between mental illness and psychology to the "evolved" language in which the mentally ill patient experiences madness. On the discursive encounter between madness and psychology, consider Foucault's rejection of organic explanations of mental illness: "[I]t is only by an *artifice of language* that the same meaning can be attributed to 'illnesses of the body' and 'illnesses of the mind'" (EMIP, 10, emphasis added). Foucault situates madness in a linguistic register, both as experienced by the patient and as analyzed by the therapist. Psychoanalysis, aptly termed "the talking cure" by Freud's patient Anna O., is by Foucault's discursive standards the modern, scientific form of psychology par excellence.

Second, consider Foucault's "evolutionary" model of language. The madman's struggles with the present are manifested in language: "Dialogue … is replaced by a sort of monologue" (EMIP, 23–24). The monological breakdown of the mentally ill patient takes on a historical character once dialogue is seen in an evolutionary light: "A whole social evolution was required before dialogue became a mode of interhuman relation," and the patient who loses his capacity for dialogical exchange "regresses through this whole social evolution" (EMIP, 23). It is at this point that Freud appears in Foucault's discursive history of madness: "A whole side of Freud's work consists of a commentary on the evolutive forms of neurosis" (EMIP, 19); Foucault even credits Freud with a "stroke of genius" in "go[ing] beyond the evolutionist horizon … [and] reach[ing] the historical dimension of the human psyche" (EMIP, 31).

By drawing on mythopoetic "explanatory themes," Freud transcends the "evolutionary horizon" preserved in language. He thus arrives at the discursive history of the mentally ill patient; such mythopoetic themes are "the raw material of evolution," both "individual and social" (EMIP, 24). As vocally as he champions Freudian "regressive analysis" for using the expressive potential of myth and poetry (EMIP, 28), Foucault just as quickly criticizes Freud for "extrapolat[ing]" mythopoetic forms into the "biological reality" of the "death instinct." The "evolutive" potential within language becomes instead a compulsion to repeat the past. Dismissively, Foucault concludes, "[t]his, no doubt, is to give to the facts a name," but such "naming" is at the same time a "reject[ion] [of] any form of explanation" (EMIP, 34).

The *History of Madness* (1961) is a fuller realization of the discursive-historical approach that Foucault adopts in the revised edition of *Mental Illness*. Such methodological overlap with psychoanalysis, and Foucault's interest in the issue of the constitution of madness and modern psychiatry, figure in the intensification of his engagement with psychoanalysis. A Janus-faced figure appears at this theoretical juncture: the mad, modern subject à la Nietzsche and Artaud, and the medical persona as modern practitioner of the new science of psychiatry.

Psychoanalysis appears in the *History of Madness* along with the birth of the asylum and the modern, scientific objectification of madness. If "the psychiatry of the nineteenth century ... converge[s] on Freud" (EHM, 510), it does so along two related pathways.

From one direction, Foucault traces the historical path to Freud from the "York Retreat" introduced by William Tuke. Tuke's "Retreat" anticipates Freud in the "'big family' atmosphere formed by the community of the insane and their keepers at the Retreat" (EHM, 489). This link between the treatment of madness and the family is both classical (ibid.) and modern: "[F]rom this point onwards ... the discourses of unreason became inextricably linked to the half-real, half-imaginary dialectic of the Family" (EHM, 490). From this perspective, psychoanalysis appears as an updating of the family dialectic, which in the interim between Tuke and Freud had become "historical[ly] sediment[ed]" (ibid.).

From the other direction, Foucault traces the line from Phillipe Pinel to Freud. By exorcising religion from the asylum, Pinel was able to legislate a secular morality: treatment is a matter of normalizing the madman in conformity with proper society (EHM, 493). Since the cloistered space of the asylum is not a second Eden in which the madman reclaims his natural (religious) goodness, as in Tuke's bucolic retreat, Pinel had to balance the isolation of the asylum with its inclusion in bourgeois society (EHM, 495).

Foucault presents three "principal means" by which Pinel realizes this difficult task: the imposition of silence, a purely reflexive form of recognition, and the introduction of a process of "perpetual judgment" (EHM, 495–503). Although Freud is anticipated in each of these structures – by reopening a dialogue between reason and madness, practicing a scientific observation of the self-constituting mad subject, and reversing the judgmental condemnation of the mentally ill (EHM, 510) – it is only by way of Pinel's "fourth structure" that we arrive fully at Freudian modernity: "the medical persona [*le personnage médical*]" (EHM, 503).

Although by all appearances the very image of the modern empirical scientist, the medical persona introduced by Pinel is in fact an amalgam of the moral authorities present in early modern society: "Father and Judge, Family and Law" (EHM, 506). Once "every moment of this story" of the medical persona is transposed into a "psychoanalytic narrative," the story of psychoanalysis reveals the Freudian analyst as no more than the modern version of classical moral authority: Dr. Freud as father, judge, and enforcer of the moral law (EHM, 507).

Here the possible ambivalence of Foucault's attitude toward psychoanalysis is harder to discern. Foucault is critical of the concealed moralizing of modern psychiatry, but he identifies Freud with the medical persona, which likens him to the modern subject in company with Nietzsche, Artaud, and Nerval. In what sense, then, does Freud fail where Nietzsche and Artaud succeed; namely, in articulating the expressive excess contained in the position of the modern subject?

A possible answer to this question lies with Jacques Lacan, the other modern "persona" of the psychoanalytic tradition. If Freud acknowledges, reluctantly, his subjective presence in the analytic setting – and his own importance in coalescing around himself the burgeoning science of psychoanalysis – Lacan draws these matters to the very center of his psychoanalytic practice.

During his 1981–1982 lecture course at the Collège de France on the hermeneutics of the subject, Foucault considers this "subjective" difference between Freud and Lacan. Although psychoanalysis in general is a "form of knowledge" that "questions, interrogat[es], and require[s] ... the very old and fundamental questions of the *epimeleia heautou* [care of the self]" (ECF-HOS, 29), the problem with the Freudian version of that "form of kowledge" is that it has forgotten "the question of the relations between truth and the subject" (ECF-HOS, 30).

Foucault then praises Lacanian psychoanalysis on the same grounds as he criticizes Freud. By asking the question of "the price the subject must pay for saying the truth," Lacan surpasses Freud in "reintroduc[ing] into psychoanalysis the oldest tradition ... of the *epimeleia heautou*" (ECF-HOS, 30). Nevertheless, Lacan's positive efforts remain futile because of his psychoanalytic approach, which "pose[s] the question of the relations of the subject to truth ... in terms of knowledge [*conaissance*]" (ibid.).

As with Binswanger, Foucault's engagement with Lacan is characterized by an ambivalence between two different forms of psychoanalysis: Lacan is favored over Freud but criticized for his commitment to a psychoanalytic framework that pairs subjectivity with knowledge. Still, this critical assessment of Freud relative to Lacan casts Foucault's attitude toward psychoanalysis in the *History of Madness* in a new light.

At no particular point in his work does Freud speak from the extra-significant position of the modern subject. Still, in "identif[ying] the irruptive signifier," Freud does more than simply "[rediscover] the lost identity of meaning" (EHM, 546). Freud might succeed *in toto* where he fails *in specie*: as founded on the "irruptive signifier," the *Standard Edition* as a whole might be the mad "absence of an *œuvre*" produced by the modern subject (ibid.).

A "*personal*ized" reading of Freud's oeuvre is possible, though, only if the shortcomings of psychoanalysis are not endemic to the science. To confirm or dismiss this possibility, one would need to consult *The Order of Things* (1966).

Foucault here numbers psychoanalysis as one among the "human sciences." But psychoanalysis is also unique in "advanc[ing] toward the unconscious" directly (EOT, 374). In going straight to what the other sciences approach indirectly, "psychoanalysis moves toward the moment ... at which the contents of consciousness articulate themselves ... upon man's finitude" (ibid.).

Foucault also shows how the distinctiveness of psychoanalysis explains its insufficiency as a "general theory of man" (EOT, 376). The mad subject pronounces in each of their acts the death that figures human finitude; the finitude, that is, "upon the basis of which we are, and think, and know" (EOT, 375). In attending to the mad subject, psychoanalysis thus reveals in "the forms of madness" the very basis of the human sciences (EOT, 376).

Despite its unceasing advance toward the unconscious as the source of what makes the modern subject knowable, psychoanalysis is insufficient to its own task. Psychoanalysis fails in this regard because it does not operate "within the limits of a praxis in which it is not only the knowledge we have of man that is involved, but man himself" (ibid.).

In order to realize its promise as *the* human science, psychoanalysis would have to be combined with ethnology as the other "counter-science" of modern man (EOT, 381). An ethnological psychoanalysis would maintain (ethnologically) the unity of a sign system through its various expressive transformations; it would also identify (psychoanalytically) the "lacuna" from which such transformations arise (EOT, 380). Psychoanalysis would supply "th[e] great caesuras, furrows, and dividing-lines ... [that make man] a possible area of knowledge" (EOT, 378); ethnology would keep man as the object of study from disappearing into those lacunae. In short, the last chapter of *The Order of Things* lays out the realization of Freud's project of an "anthropological psychoanalysis" in *Totem and Taboo* by supplying a workable psychoanalytic praxis (EOT, 379).

Interestingly, Foucault realizes this Freudian project in a distinctly Lacanian fashion. In combining ethnology and psychoanalysis, Foucault envisions the "discovery that the unconscious ... *is* in itself, a certain formal structure" (EOT, 380). Since the character of such a structural unconscious is linguistic, Foucault here echoes Lacan's claim that the unconscious is structured as a language.

If *The Order of Things* is an archaeology of the human sciences in general, Foucault describes the "history of the deployment of sexuality" in the first volume of *The History of Sexuality* (1976) as "an archaeology of psychoanalysis" in particular (EHS1, 130). Foucault here turns his attention to the historical a priori of power and knowledge that constitute modern humans as sexed subjects. Given sex and knowledge as the theoretical coordinates of this late work, the directness of its engagement with psychoanalysis is unsurprising.

In reference to the "repressive hypothesis," according to which nothing need be said about sex because there is nothing that calls for comment or consideration, Foucault sets Freud apart, slightly, from such modern "Victorianism" (EHS1, 5). If the repressive hypothesis is correct in that we moderns pass over sex in silence, then psychoanalysis is an exception: Freud spoke of sex and enabled sex to speak itself. Since Foucault here inaugurates a multivolume work on sex, and in so doing aims to say what has been left unsaid in our collective sexual histories, he would seem to stand beside Freud as an exception to the general rule of repression.

However, Foucault's aim is to give the lie to the repressive hypothesis. The point is not to show that we are sexually liberated but rather to ask how we came to see ourselves as repressed in the first place. With respect to the repressive hypothesis,

Foucault acknowledges that he is not alone in dismissing it as a false lead: "[T]he assertion that sex is not 'repressed' is not altogether new. Psychoanalysts have been saying the same thing for some time" (EHS1, 81). If we are not sexually repressed, as both Foucault and Freud – as well as Marcuse – maintain, if we are instead prolix in and about our sexuality, what role does the "talking cure" play in the "multiplicity of discourses" that define modern sexuality (EHS1, 33)?

Foucault overturns the repressive hypothesis in order to abandon its implicit model of juridico-discursive power. Foucault models power differently: modern disciplinary power corresponds to the institutional imperative on the subject to "tell the truth" about him- or herself (i.e., to speak of his or her sex plurally). Such power is exercised at every point where "excited speech" is oriented toward truth, and the subject is figured as something to be known. Sex is then the matrix through which the force of truth- and knowledge-oriented discourse is directed toward political ends that reinforce the moral and socioeconomic order of bourgeois society (EHS1, 130, 139).

Psychoanalysis openly discusses sex; in its candor, it would seem to be in a position to reveal the complicity of sexual practices – and the discourse about such practices – in the biopolitics of population control and regulation (EHS1, 53). However, psychoanalysis remains complicit in enforcing the dominant trends in modern political life; it does so because it operates by an "injunction to lift psychical repression" (EHS1, 130). Psychoanalysis thus dismisses the repressive hypothesis at the social level in order to recuperate it at the psychic level. Hidden behind an apparent openness, psychoanalysis continues to serve the sociopolitical ends of late (bourgeois) capitalism.

Adrian Switzer

SEE ALSO

> *Care*
> *Finitude*
> *Hermeneutics*
> *Human Sciences*
> *Madness*
> *Sex*
> *Sigmund Freud*

SUGGESTED READING

Binswanger, Ludwig. 1957. *Sigmund Freud: Reminiscences of a Friendship*, trans. Norbert
  Guterman. New York: Grune and Stratton.
Derrida, Jacques. 1998. "'To Do Justice to Freud': The History of Madness in the Age of
  Psychoanalysis," trans. Michael Naas and Pascale-Anne Brault, in Jacques Derrida,
  Resistances of Psychoanalysis. Stanford, CA: Stanford University Press, pp. 70–118.
Moore, Carmella C., and Holly F. Matthews. 2001. *The Psychology of Cultural Experience*.
  Cambridge: Cambridge University Press.
Shepherdson, Charles. 2000. *Vital Signs: Nature, Culture, Psychoanalysis*. New York: Routledge.

71

RACE (AND RACISM)

ALTHOUGH FOUCAULT'S ACCOUNT of race thinking and of the history of racism is somewhat sketchy, it has proved seminal for at least five reasons. First, his idea of biopolitics has proved highly productive for isolating the specific kind of racism that led to the holocaust (e.g., Dickenson 2004, 3–4; Geulen 2004, 30, 271). Second, by understanding race in terms of "the biological existence of a population" (EHS1, 137) and by tracing that concern back to the eighteenth century and the emergence of a discourse of population that monitors birth and death rates and where "sex became a 'police' matter" (EHS1, 24–25), Foucault gave new significance to the growth of *Polizeiwissenschaft* in Prussia in the eighteenth century and in particular to the work of Heinrich Gottlob von Justi (EHS1, 25) and Johann Peter Frank (EEW3, 95, 405). This has born fruit in a number of historical studies (e.g., Figal 2008). Third, Foucault's general approach is well suited to what has been called the "polyvalent mobility" of the concept of race in the sense that it is continually shifting or being reinscribed (Stoler 1995, 89; 1997, 191). For example, Foucault described how the Nazis combined state racism with a revival of the legend of warring races (ECF-SMD, 82). Fourth, Foucault's revival of the idea of a race war has proven illuminating in other contexts such as political theory and geography (Girardin 1998, 194; Mendieta 2004, 53). Finally, and most controversially, Foucault is seen as having offered an account of racism that allows its broadening to the point where it can be applied to describe prejudice against all those considered by society to be "abnormal."

Even though Foucault had at his disposal the resources to write a new account of the history of the concept of race, not least because of the work he had already done in *The Order of Things* where he described the shift from natural history to biology at the beginning of the nineteenth century, he chose not to do so. According to the original plan for the *History of Sexuality*, Foucault intended the sixth, final, volume to be on "Populations and Race," but he abandoned the idea. On another occasion Foucault announced his ambition "to trace the full development of a biological-social racism" (ECF-SMD, 61), but he stepped back from this too. What he did do was show that in the French context the early eighteenth-century historical discourse of races associated most notably with Henri de Boulainvilliers was transformed into "the theory of races in the historico-biological sense" (ECF-SMD, 60) in the second quarter of the nineteenth century and then linked with evolutionism (ECF-SMD, 256) (see Bernasconi 2010). He organized this account around a distinction between "racism in its modern, 'biologizing,' statist form" (EHS1, 149), which he sometimes presented as being organized around the idea of racial purity (ECF-AB, 133; ECF-SMD, 81) and "racism in the traditional sense of the term" (ECF-SMD, 87), or as he called it in the final lecture of the course *Abnormal* "ethnic racism" (ECF-AB, 316). However, the fact that with few exceptions (e.g., ECF-SMD, 103 and 257) he virtually ignored race-based slavery and the specific place of race in colonialism and imperialism has led to the charge that his account is provincial in the sense that it belongs to a historiography "locked in Europe" (Stoler 1995, 60). Nevertheless, this has not stopped a prominent African thinker, Achille Mbembe, from using Foucault's notion of biopower to illuminate colonial occupation (Mbembe 2008).

Foucault was not writing a history of racism in the conventional sense but a "genealogy," which he defined early in the 1976 lecture course as a "coupling together of scholarly erudition and local memories, which allows us to constitute a historical knowledge of struggles and to make use of that knowledge in contemporary tactics" (ECF-SMD, 8). It is in these terms that Foucault's work must finally be judged. He chose to begin his account with Boulainvilliers because of the latter's impact on the development of a specific brand of French racism that flourished at the end of the nineteenth century and that continued to have echoes in the France of his day (ECF-SMD, 262–263). Foucault believed that racism was indispensable to the functioning of the modern state: "death of the inferior race … will make life … healthier and purer" (ECF-SMD, 255). And at the time it was a genuine question for Foucault as to whether biopower could function without racism (ECF-SMD, 263).

At one point in *Society Must Be Defended*, Foucault provocatively reserved the term "racism" for a period that began at the end of the nineteenth century (ECF-SMD, 65). Although he conceded later in the same lecture course that there had indeed been prior racisms, the discrepancy is explained by the fact that Foucault's focus throughout was on state racism (ECF-SMD, 254). Nor was this decision to locate racism so late entirely without precedent. Hannah Arendt drew a distinction between race thinking and racism that had the same effect of dating the advent of racism to the second half of the nineteenth century, although, unlike Foucault, she showed a strong interest in the racism of imperialism (Arendt 1973, 158–184). As with Foucault, Arendt – relying on French scholarship – highlighted Boulainvilliers, but for Arendt the crucial figure was Count Arthur de Gobineau, whereas for Foucault it was Benedict Augustin Morel, the author of *Traité des Dégénerescences Physiques, Intellectuelles et Morales de l'Espéce Humaine* (1857). Foucault argued that

Morel transformed the notion of degeneration in such a way as to prepare for what came to be known as the eugenics movement (ECF-AB, 134). Morel's focus was on the way that the sins of the parents are visited on their children: although the children of alcoholics may not themselves be alcoholics, through inheritance they nevertheless come to suffer deformities or other problems. It was because Morel invited societies to address the potential dangers that Foucault was able to give him such a central place in the history of biopolitics (Morel 1857, 356, 661).

Foucault is said to have understood biologizing racism very broadly insofar as he employed it to cover all forms of degeneration, including alcoholism. The main basis for this claim is the assertion in *Abnormal* where Foucault described a new racism that "is not so much the prejudice of one group against another as the detection of all those within a group who may be carriers of a danger to it. It is a racism that permits the screening of every individual within a given society" (ECF-AB, 317). In that context, he wrote of a racism "against the abnormal, against individuals who, as carriers of a condition, a stigmata, or any defect whatsoever" that is hereditary (ECF-AB, 316). It is quite possible that Foucault meant simply to show the broadening of what were conceived of as hereditary traits, but some commentators have extended Foucault's concept of racism to include, for example, not only mental deficiency and mental illness but also so-called sexual deviance (McWhorter 2009, 31–35, 291–293). To be sure, at one point in *Society Must Be Defended*, albeit without explicit reference to Morel, he refers to "all those biological-racist discourses of degeneracy (*dégenérescence*), but also all those institutions within the social body which make the discourse of race struggle function as a principle of exclusion and segregation and, ultimately, as a way of normalizing society" (ECF-SMD, 61). It is not altogether clear why Foucault was so insistent on calling this a racism, except perhaps to anticipate the way the two technologies, the technology of eugenics and that of psychology, came together in National Socialism (ECF-AB, 317).

Although Foucault's account of the history of the various concepts of race and of the history of racism lacks detail, its importance for the development of his own work, as well as for subsequent scholarship in critical philosophy of race, cannot be doubted. It was at the heart of his claim that, at the beginning of the second half of the nineteenth century, a long-prepared-for shift took place when sovereign power, organized around the sovereign's power to take life or let live, was complemented – and to a certain extent displaced – by what he called "biopower," a term he had used already in the first volume of *The History of Sexuality* to refer to "what brought life into the realm of politics as an object of explicit calculation" where what was at stake was the life not of the individual but of large units of population such as races, nations, or even the species as a whole (EHS1, 143–145). Biopower was manifested in a new right that was attributed to the state, the right to intervene to make live or let die (ECF-SMD, 241–248). Among the ways in which this new right of the state to "let die" manifested itself was through genocide and the discourse of eugenics and racial hygiene, where it is a question of eliminating biological threats to the population (ECF-SMD, 256), particularly those associated with race mixing.

These discourses around racial hierarchization and race mixing were ways of fragmenting the biological continuum of the human species (ECF-SMD, 254–255). The fragmentation was most pronounced in the way the discourse of race struggle became "the discourse of a centered, centralized, and centralizing power" to become "the discourse of a battle that has to be waged not between races, but by a race that is portrayed as the one true race, the race which holds power and is entitled to define the norm, and against those who deviate from that norm, against those who pose a threat to the biological heritage" (ECF-SMD, 61). Racism comes to be defined as "a way of introducing a break into the domain of life … between what must live and what must die" (ECF-SMD, 254). The terms in which this was done help to explain Foucault's broadening of the concept of racism to the extent he does. A whole politics concerned with the family, marriage, education, social hierarchization, and property, accompanied by a long series of permanent interventions at the level of the body, conduct, and health, finds its justification in "the mythical concern with protecting the purity of the blood and ensuring the triumph of the race" (EHS1, 149).

What Foucault himself understood by "race" is not clear, but the best indication is to be found in his review in *Le Monde* in October 1976 of Jacques Ruffié's *De la biologie à la culture*. Only one of the four parts of the book was devoted to race and racism, but Foucault chose to focus on that part. He noted that, according to Ruffié, race is now understood by biologists as a population, which is a statistical concept and must be understood in terms of genetics, not morphology. Furthermore, there have never been human races as such but only a process of "raciation," which is in fact negative insofar as any tendency toward racial purity reduces the possibility of adaptation (FDE3, 96). Here Foucault finds a way to link his account of racism in terms of a discourse of populations going back to the eighteenth century with the current talk about "populations" in biology, but in such a way that biology might liberate us from the concept of race that it gave us. It is only a hint but it seems that one might find here Foucault's own answer to his question of whether we might be liberated from biopolitics (FDE3, 97).

Robert Bernasconi

SEE ALSO

> *Abnormal*
> *Biopolitics*
> *Biopower*
> *Henri de Boulainvilliers*

SUGGESTED READING

Elden, Stuart. 2004. "The War of Races and the Constitution of the State: Foucault's 'Il faut défendre la souété' and the Politics of Calculation," *Boundary* 2, 29, no. 1:125–151.

Holt, Thomas C. 2001. "Pouvoir, savoir et race. A propos du cours de Michel Foucault 'Il faut defendre la societe,'" in *Lectures de Michel Foucault*, volume 1: *A propos de "Il faut défendre la societe,"* ed. Jean-Claude Zancarini. Paris: ENS Editions, pp. 81–96.

Mader, Mary Beth. 2011. "Modern Living and Vital Race: Foucault and the Science of Life," *Foucault Studies* 12:97–112.

Magiros, Angelika. 1995. *Foucaults Beitrag zur Rassismustheorie*. Hamburg: Argument.

72

REASON

MICHEL FOUCAULT'S UNDERSTANDING of reason is a historicist one.
Given the centrality of his historicist understanding to his work, it is surprising that he does not offer an explicit, sustained treatment or analysis of reason. Despite this lack, Foucault's historicist understanding of reason is consistently definitive of his work.

Foucault's early archaeological writings, especially *The Order of Things* and *The Archaeology of Knowledge*, present a historicist treatment of the presuppositions, implementation, and aims of broadly scientific reason. His middle genealogical writings, particularly *Discipline and Punish* and *The History of Sexuality*, present an equally historicist treatment of historical, political, and public reason. His late ethical writings, particularly *The Use of Pleasure* and *The Care of the Self*, follow suit in dealing with the contrast between "classical," modern, and contemporary uses of reason and personal employment of reason in the formation of the self. However, though less so in *The Archaeology of Knowledge* than in the other books, references to reason are usually implicit and often almost incidental and even occasionally ambiguous regarding its historical nature. Nonetheless, these works are exemplary exercises in the application of Foucault's historicist understanding of reason, both in terms of his methodology and in terms of the characterization of their subject matter (see EOT, xxii, 30, 61, 342, 383; EAK, 8, 13, 121, 131, 181, 191, 201; EDP, 97, 103, 112, 140, 183; EHS1, 24, 55, 69, 78, 95; EHS2, 50, 87; and EHS3, 67, 135, 157).

Foucault opposes what he sees as traditional philosophy's idealization of reason; an idealization effected through appeals to and reliance on reason construed as an ahistorical or transhistorical universal. As we might put it, Foucault certainly accepts that there is *reasoning*, but he does not accept that there is *reason* above and beyond delineatable historical modes of reason. His own understanding of reason is of historically contingent, goal-oriented, and justificatory procedures with varying methods and correctness criteria. Regarding his own interests, he focuses on communal or collective modes of reason, primarily historical, political, public, and scientific ones. These modes are, respectively, reckoning and justificatory practices in historical organization and narration; in political end-directed and validating activities; in social problem-solving and norm-setting practices; and in the structuring and doing of science.

The key question regarding Foucault's understanding of reason is whether his historicization of reason means he rejects what I will call "basic" reason as a *capacity*, as essentially different from and as underlying historically or contextually conditioned practical reason. What is at issue is the traditionally fundamental conception of basic reason as the capacity to discern truth/accuracy and to gauge effectiveness and productivity in diverse circumstances, a capacity minimally characterized by disposition to reflectively or unreflectively accept and apply what are considered the unconditional standards of rational thought: the law of noncontradiction, the principle of identity, and the law of excluded middle.

Whether Foucault countenances basic reason, even if he ignores it, or historicizes it, is a matter of major importance because if historicized, basic reason ceases to be universal and can no longer define rational entities or designate a capacity that might be shared by human and nonhuman intelligent beings. More specifically, if basic reason is historicized and does not transcend contextually conditioned reckoning as the capacity exercised in such reckoning, then reason would be no more – though no less – than collections of temporally and contextually developed goal-attainment and validation procedures; procedures wrongly promoted by philosophers to the status of an ahistoric universal that human beings supposedly instantiate. If Foucault does historicize basic reason, as he seems to do, if he understands reason to be exhausted by modes of conditioned reckoning, then what most consider the grounds of rational thought and action ultimately dissolve into so many more consequences of power relations and, as he often insists, power and knowledge are indeed of a piece.

Additionally, if Foucault does historicize basic reason and makes reason entirely contingent on particular contextual and temporal circumstances and activities, reason cannot be universal and historical modes of reason or what we might call reckoning practices can be shared by different groups, and more so by different species, only by sheer coincidence. Historicization of basic reason, therefore, would effectively make the concept of a rational entity vacuous and in effect replace it with the unproductively inclusive concept of a goal-directed entity.

Despite occasional remarks apparently at odds with a historicist view of reason, the textual evidence is all but conclusive that Foucault does historicize basic reason and that he does not acknowledge the philosophical concept of basic reason as having a referent, rejecting the concept as a manufactured one. In *The History of Madness*, Foucault implicitly introduces his historicist understanding by detailing how reason was conceived in the "classical" and modern periods and the isolation of the insane in asylums, and he uses madness to explore how the contemporary language of reason developed partly through efforts to redefine and stigmatize madness or "unreason" as the new leprosy in order to better control it (EHM, 46–47, 102, 109, 138–140, 242–243). But it is later, in "What Is Enlightenment?" where he responds to Kant's view of enlightenment, that Foucault states in a key passage that the investigation of the limits of knowledge (i.e., the critique of reason) "is no longer going to be practiced in the search for formal structures with universal value, but rather as a historical investigation into the events that led us to constitute ourselves and to recognize ourselves as subjects" (EFR, 45–46, 32–50).

This rejection of "formal structures" is historicization of Kant's a priori and thus is, in effect, rethinking the categories of understanding as historically contingent. This rethinking is a firm closing off of conceptual room for reason as a universal and so it is a preclusion of ahistorical or transhistorical basic reason (EFR, 36, 38, 49–50). Foucault's rethinking is also clear in his response to a question about how Kant's distinction between theoretical and practical reason influenced German thought and whether in his own work he offers "another fuller version of reason." Foucault implicitly concurs that he does, answering: "I do not believe in a kind of founding act whereby reason ... was discovered or established." He adds that there was no event that constituted "*the* bifurcation of reason." Instead there was an "abundance of branchings, ramifications, breaks and ruptures" (EPPC, 28–29). Additionally, Foucault asserts that examination of reason's history reveals that rather than being some Platonic form in which we participate, reason "was born ... from chance" and that it was historical compilations of complex practices that "slowly forged the weapons of reason" (EFR, 78). Again, Foucault states "that reason is self-created" (EPPC, 28).

These assertions not only manifest Foucault's historicist understanding of reason but also explain his methodology in the sense of showing why he "tried to analyze forms of rationality: different foundations, different creations, different modifications in which rationalities engender one another, oppose and pursue one another" (EPPC, 28–29). That is, contrary to philosophical tradition, Foucault thinks that instead of seeking to better understand and perfect our application of ahistorically conceived reason, we instead have to work at "isolating the form of rationality presented as dominant, and endowed with the status of the one-and-only reason, in order to show that it is only *one* possible form among others" (EPPC, 27). It is by isolating given rationalities as the dominant ones in particular epochs, and in problematizing those rationalities by exploring marginalized alternatives or proffering new alternatives, that Foucault dismantles perception of them as instantiating universal reason.

Foucault appreciates how his historicization of reason is rejected by many; he responds to such rejection by saying that "every critique of reason or every critical inquiry into the history of rationality" faces a kind of "blackmail." The blackmail is that when the question of critiquing reason arises, "either you accept rationality or you fall prey to the irrational." Foucault holds that many see critiques of what I am calling basic reason as "impossible" because those critiques require application of precisely what is being critiqued (EPPC, 27). It is notable that Foucault also uses the charge of blackmail with respect to consideration of the Enlightenment (EFR, 42–43) and that it was at the core of the dispute he had with Derrida that kept the two apart for a decade (EHM, 550–574).

The trouble here is that critiques of basic reason do seem to be impossible because basic reason is necessarily presupposed and employed in the conduct of any such critique. To see basic reason as open to critique is already to understand reason as historical, but as Hilary Putnam argues, temporally and contextually contingent principles, standards, and practices cannot determine what basic reason is because basic reason is itself operant in the interpretation of those principles, standards, and practices. For Putnam and like-minded philosophers, what I am calling basic reason is regulative and therefore is and must be independent of all historically diverse conventions and practices it regulates. It is precisely because basic reason is independent of our conventions and practices that it enables us to evaluate and critique all of our activities and institutions.

Foucault also is too quick with his charge of blackmail because neither Putnam nor those who share his views automatically reject critiques of particular historical modes of reason; for instance, as employed by alchemists or flat-earthers. Those who reject critiques of basic reason do not thereby charge critics of historical modes of reasoning with falling prey to irrationality. The blackmail charge looks fair to Foucault only because, by including basic reason in his historicization of reason, he is disallowing the distinction Putnam and others assume between basic reason and proper and improper applications of reason.

If there were only historical modes of reason, only temporally and contextually limited reckoning practices, precluding critiques of reason would be in fact privileging one set of reasoning or reckoning standards and casting all critiques of it as irrational, so in Foucault's view Putnam and company are defending a dominant rationality rather than basic reason. Unlike Putnam and most philosophers who conceive of us as rational entities and therefore as *exponents* of reason, Foucault conceives of us as *makers* of reason as we engage in the perpetual process of employing various end-achieving and justificatory practices as well as knowingly and unknowingly – but purposefully – coloring and manipulating facts, intentions, and expectations in the course of achieving our goals. To this extent, and though their conceptions of reason vary importantly, Foucault and Hume agree that reason functions only to serve our "passions," our arational and even irrational interests. For Foucault, then, rather than exercising a capacity in applying basic reason, we muddle through the myriad influences, challenges, and obstructions that power relations and the physical world cascade on us and, in the process, bestow on our productive tactics and procedures the status of being the fruits of a transhistoric universal.

C. G. Prado

SEE ALSO

> *Archaeology*
> *Language*
> *Madness*
> *Practice*
> *Immanuel Kant*

SUGGESTED READING

Braver, Lee. 2007. *A Thing of This World: A History of Continental Anti-Realism*. Evanston, IL: Northwestern University Press.

Dreyfus, Hubert L., and Paul Rabinow. 1983. *Michel Foucault: Beyond Structuralism and Hermeneutics*, 2nd ed. Chicago: University of Chicago Press.

Gutting, Gary, ed. 1994. *The Cambridge Companion to Foucault*. Cambridge: Cambridge University Press.

May, Todd. 1993. *Between Genealogy and Epistemology: Psychology, Politics, and Knowledge in the Thought of Michel Foucault*. University Park: Pennsylvania State University Press.

Miller, James. 1993. *The Passion of Michel Foucault*. New York: Simon and Schuster:.

Prado, C. G. 2000. *Starting with Foucault: An Introduction to Genealogy*, 2nd ed. Boulder, CO: Westview Press.

73

RELIGION

OUCAULT HAD NO systematic philosophy of religion, but his writings did exhibit a multifaceted religious interest. Each of the major areas he investigated engaged religious themes: madness, medicine, language and literature, the prison institution, sexuality, political practice, and the technologies of the self. Jeremy Carrette has brought together in one volume (ERC) the scattered writings in which Foucault touched on religion and has also written an important book-length study of Foucault and religion (Carrette 2000). Among Foucault's claims is that medical knowledge developed not from the replacement of the supernatural by the pathological but rather by the appearance of the "transgressive powers of the body and of the imagination" (ERC, 55). For him, the privileged space of a sexuality that is spoken emerges in the wake of the "death of God" as Nietzsche rather than Hegel and Feuerbach understood it (ERC, 70, 85–86). Of course, sexuality is central to Foucault's understanding of the impact of religious practices. Even in the absence of the never published fourth volume on sexuality and Christianity, the three volumes in the history of sexuality series as well as numerous articles indicate the formation of a privileged place for sexual desire and speaking truthfully of it within Christian culture.

Perhaps the most controversial of Foucault's writings treating religion are contained in his approach to the Iranian Revolution of 1978. These writings, along with many articles critical of Foucault's approach, have been collected by Janet Afary and Kevin Anderson (Afary and Anderson 2005). They do not do complete justice to Foucault's originality in his attentiveness to the religious dynamics of the revolution and in his prescience of the significance of Islamic movements for contemporary political analysis.

Even if Foucault's reflection on religion is dispersed among a variety of topics and formulations, it is not deprived of a center because Foucault's proclamation of the death of man is the other side to Nietzsche's announcement of God's death. Foucault's thought is particularly open to the religious dimension of culture because it problematizes the identity of the secular person. The severe techniques he developed in his archaeological and genealogical practices were ways of breaking the spell humanism had placed on the modern vision. In doing so, Foucault reintroduced into the contemporary landscape of thought that negative theology that had "prowled the confines of Christianity" for a millennium (EEW2, 150). Although Foucault never elaborated on the analogy, he explicitly compared his own thought with negative theology, and his choice of the comparison is illuminating. It points first of all to Foucault's own experience of a fundamental personal conflict in his earlier intellectual interests as a "religious question" (ERC, 98). On the one hand, he was passionately involved in the new literary work of such writers as George Bataille and Maurice Blanchot, which for him at the time displaced interest from a narrative of man to the being of language within which notions of the human are fashioned. On the other hand, Foucault said that he was attracted to the structuralist analysis carried out by the anthropologist Claude Lévi-Strauss and the historian of religion George Dumézil, both of whom dispersed human reality among cultural structures. That Foucault considers the religious problem as the common denominator for both interests indicates that all four thinkers, although in very different ways, unleashed styles of reflection and forms of experience that overturned for him the modern identity of man. Foucault's negative theology is a critique not of the conceptualizations employed for God but of that figure of human finitude scattered in calendars of life, language, and labor. Is this religious sensibility not reflected in his own customary refusal of identities? In his inaugural lecture at the Collège de France, he spoke of his desire for anonymity:

> I would really like to have slipped imperceptibly into this lecture, as into all the others I shall be delivering, perhaps over the years ahead. At the moment of speaking, I would like to have perceived a nameless voice, long preceding me, leaving me merely to enmesh myself in it, taking up its cadence, and to lodge myself, when no one was looking, in its interstices as if it had paused an instant, in suspense, to beckon to me. (EAK, 215)

This earlier search for anonymity found striking expressions. For example, Foucault says: "I am no doubt not the only one who writes in order to have no face" (EAK, 17). And in 1964 he compared the writer to the martyr: "Writing is now linked to sacrifice and to the sacrifice of life itself; it is a voluntary obliteration of the self"(ELCP, 117). The negative theology that characterized the asceticism of Foucault's methods foreshadowed his mature conception of the philosophical life itself with its practices of spirituality. As Carrette has noted, the future of religion after Foucault is to deal with a terrain stripped of an ideal that is transcendent and normative. That emptiness is nevertheless an invitation for an embodied spirituality.

James Bernauer

SEE ALSO

Christianity
Literature
Outside
Practice
Revolution
Georges Bataille
Friedrich Nietzsche

SUGGESTED READING

Afary, Janet, and Kevin B. Anderson. 2005. *Foucault and the Iranian Revolution: Gender and the Seductions of Islamism*. Chicago: University of Chicago Press.

Bernauer, James, and Jeremy Carrette, eds. 2004. *Michel Foucault and Theology: The Politics of Religious Experience*. Burlington, VT: Ashgate.

Carrette, Jeremy. 2000. *Foucault and Religion: Spiritual Corporality and Political Spirituality*. London: Routledge.

74

RESISTANCE

RESISTANCE IS ONE of the most contested and divisive concepts in Foucault's thought. Whereas some commentators strongly argue that it is the debilitating lacuna of his genealogies of power, at the same time, and seemingly paradoxically, others maintain that it is the key to understanding what they are all about – the driving motivation of his critical inquiries of power.

When Foucault introduces his influential conception of power in the form of short propositions over three pages of volume one of *The History of Sexuality*, he explicitly states the inseparability of resistance and power. The fifth proposition contends: "Where there is power, there is resistance" (EHS1, 95). In other words, if Foucault is accepted as being a theorist of power, we also have to read him as a theorist of resistance.

What makes his position contested – and original – is the way he understands the relationship between power and resistance. Immediately after stating their interdependence, he adds, "yet or rather consequently, this resistance is never in a position of exteriority to power" (ibid.). He forbids us to think that resistance is outside of power and also denies that we could ever locate it in a single point: "there is no single locus of great Refusal, no soul of revolt, source of all rebellions, or pure law of the revolutionary" (ibid.). To view the relationship between power and resistance as external would mean misunderstanding the relational character of power. Because power is not something that an individual acquires, holds, or gives away, its existence depends on resistance. Since power exists only in a relation, resistance must be located in these very same power relations. Foucault explains that there are a plurality of resistances that are present everywhere in power relations and "play the role of adversary, target, support, or handle" (ibid.). Points of resistance are the "odd term in relations of power" (EHS1, 96), its blind spot or evading limit. Power is thus not a deterministic machine but a dynamic and complex strategic situation.

This understanding of resistance as an effect of power, or as its self-subversion, has led commentators to conclude that the technologies of power that constitute forms of the subject are never completely successful. Judith Butler (Butler 1997, 93), for example, argues that for Foucault resistance inevitably appears in the course of subjectification that exceeds the normalizing aims by which it is mobilized, or through convergence with other discursive regimes. This inadvertently produced discursive complexity undermines the teleological aims of normalization. Insofar as power always accidentally produces resistance, even the most disciplined subject can be engaged in it.

What still appears as a problem in Foucault's account is how the subject is able to deliberately instigate resistance. For his critics, the main problem is not admitting that some strategies of power are too complex to always succeed and, inevitably, there will be failures. They would insist that these failures do not yet constitute resistance. Our idea of resistance implies an intentional strategy, a deliberate attempt to subvert power. On the basis of Foucault's understanding of both power and the subject, it is not evident how the normalized subject, constituted by power, is capable of engaging in resistance and, furthermore, on what grounds such an attempt could be advocated or justified.

Foucault's late texts on power are important in this context. They should be read as a deliberate attempt to elaborate on his rudimentary account of resistance in volume one of *The History of Sexuality* and to answer the criticism that had been leveled against it.

In an interview given in 1984, shortly before his death, Foucault admitted that when he first became interested in the problem of power, some of the concepts and ideas linked with it were poorly defined and unclear. It was only later that he acquired a clearer sense of the problem (EEW1, 299). He continues by distinguishing between power and domination. Although it is impossible to step out of the social field structured by power relations, it is possible to effect changes in it. We can free subjects from states of domination – situations in which the subject is unable to overturn or reverse the power relation – and put them in a situation in which power relations are interchangeable, variable, and allow strategies for altering them. Foucault goes as far as to set this as an explicit aim:

> I do not think that a society can exist without power relations, if by that one means the strategies by which individuals try to direct and control the conduct of others. The problem, then, is not to try to dissolve them in the utopia of completely transparent communication but to acquire the rules of law, the management techniques, and also the morality, the ethos, the practice of the self, that will allow us to play these games of power with as little domination as possible. (EEW1, 298)

Hence, although there can be no overall liberation from power, there can and should be particular emancipations from different systems of domination: from oppressive relations of power and the effects of the employment of certain normalizing techniques. Foucault lists specific transformations that have proven to be possible in his lifetime: in our ways of being and thinking, relations to authority, relations between the sexes, and the way we perceive insanity or illness (EFR, 46–47).

This view of resistance as aiming at liberation from particular states of domination appeals to a shared commitment to the value that is freedom and involves an understanding of negative freedom. In another late interview, "Subject and Power," Foucault claims that power relations arise when there is action on the actions of others. Power only functions on free action; it is an action on action (EEW3, 341–342). It is thus always exercised on free subjects. Here, however, free means no more than being able to act in a variety of ways. Subjects free of domination are capable of resistance in the sense that they are able to instigate shifts in power relations by acting in different ways to influence each other's behavior. Resistance to domination poses a more difficult challenge, however. Even though power relations are essentially fluid and reversible, what usually characterizes domination is that these relationships have become stabilized through institutions. This stabilization means that the mobility of power relations is limited and that there are strongholds that are difficult to suppress because they have been institutionalized in courts, codes, and so on. Although Foucault recognizes that resistance to states of domination often requires collective political action, the accounts he gives of it are rare.

An important discussion occurs in his Collège de France lecture course "Security, Territory, Population" held in 1978. Foucault explicitly poses the question of resistance against the spread of modern technologies of power – governmentalization – in his lecture on March 1, 1978: "Just as there have been forms of resistance to power as the exercise of political sovereignty, and just as there have been other, equally intentional forms of resistance or refusal that were directed at power in the forms of economic exploitation, have there not been forms of resistance to power as conducting" (ECF-STP, 195)? He replies by arguing that as governmentality refers to a specific form of power that focuses on the conduct of people, the way in which they behave, resistance against it must take the form of *counterconduct*. He discusses various movements – religious and political – that have historically developed in tandem with the growth of governmentality and whose objective was a different form of conduct: to be conducted differently, by other leaders, toward other objectives, and through other procedures and methods.

Foucault's late work on practices of the self provides his fullest account of resistance, but the project was cut short by his untimely death. The last two volumes of *The History of Sexuality* study ancient ethical practices and technologies of the self. Foucault also significantly discusses their relevance for the contemporary art of living in his late interviews and lectures.

The two volumes appeared in a very different form from the one that Foucault had originally planned and proposed. He indicates in the introduction to volume two that there was an analytical axis missing from his previous work. To be able to study the history of "the experience of sexuality," he also needed, besides the methodological tools with which his archaeologies and genealogies had provided him, to "study the modes according to which individuals are given to recognize themselves as sexual subjects" (EHS2, 5). He then turned to studying the historical constitution of the self: the forms of understanding subjects create about themselves and the ways they form themselves as subjects through historically changing technologies of the self. Whereas his earlier genealogical studies investigated the ways that the power/knowledge apparatus constitutes the subject, in his late work the emphasis is on the subject's own role in implementing or refusing forms of subjectivity. His late work thus brings into focus a new component of the constitution of the subject – modes of relation to oneself – and thus presents a more elaborated understanding of the subject than is found in his earlier writings.

This third axis of analysis also makes possible a more sophisticated understanding of resistance: the government of the self by oneself becomes its principal domain. Foucault advocates "a politics of ourselves" that does not attempt to find an authentic or true self but aims at a creative transformation of ourselves. In his rare but important comments in interviews with the gay press, he argued that the gay movement did not need scientific knowledge about sexuality but an art of life: "We don't have to discover that we are homosexuals … we have to create a gay life. To *become*" (EEW1, 163).

In his late thinking, Foucault also returns to the idea, found in his early work, of the subversive role of art. The practices of the self are closely linked, or even fused with aesthetics. He describes them in several contexts in terms of art of life and aesthetics of existence. They are ways of living and thinking that are transgressive in the extent to which, like a work of art, they are not simply the products of normalizing power. The target of these practices is primarily modes of normalization: the forms of power that produce docile forms of subjectivity. Resistance against forms of subjectification cannot be situated outside the networks of power in Foucault's thought since subjectivity is only possible within them. This means that resistance also becomes possible only within them, through the subject's creative practices that help to constitute forms of subjectivity; through refusal and adoption of forms of subjectivity. Resistance comes to mean contesting determinations, of refusing what we are told we are.

For Foucault, the problem with modern power is that it is normalizing power: it is individualizing and yet totalizing. It "separates the individual, breaks his links with others, splits up community life, forces the individual back on himself and ties him to his own identity in a constraining way" (EEW3, 333). The modern state is a sophisticated structure, into which individuals can be integrated, but under the condition that their individuality is shaped in a determinate form, and submitted to a very specific pattern. The way to resist this normalizing power is by shaping oneself and one's lifestyle creatively: by exploring possibilities for new forms of subjectivity, new fields of experiences, pleasures, relationships, modes of living and thinking.

Technologies of the self are not separate from technologies of domination, which had been the focus of Foucault's earlier studies, and he points out necessary links between them (EPT, 181). Hence, technologies of the self do not introduce a totally autonomous subject to Foucault's late thinking. But neither are technologies of the self simply extensions of techniques of domination disguised as voluntary. Foucault theorizes a subject with relative independence in regard to the constitutive power/knowledge apparatus: a subject capable of critical self-reflection and deliberate transformation of the self. As Gilles Deleuze (Deleuze 1988, 101) argued, Foucault's fundamental idea was that of a dimension of subjectivity derived from a power/knowledge apparatus without being dependent on it. The constituted subject is capable of turning back on itself: of critically studying the processes of its own constitution but also deliberately subverting them and effecting changes in them.

In his late texts and interviews, Foucault emphasizes the importance of *critique*. He sees it as an essential form of resistance and links it to the legacy and attitude of the Enlightenment. For Foucault, governmentalization is the process through which individuals are subjugated in modern society, and this subjugation is effected essentially through mechanisms that adhere to truth. Critique is "the movement by which the subject gives himself the right to interrogate truth on its effects of power and question power on its discourses of truth." It is "the art of voluntary insubordination, that of reflected intractability" (EPT, 47).

In Foucault's introduction to *The Use of Pleasure*, as well as in his late interviews, he also introduces the concept of "problematization." It is closely linked to the possibility of critique and refers to the way in which certain forms of behavior, practices, and actions can emerge as possible objects of social critique, politicization, redescription, and ultimately change. He explains that for a practice, a domain of action, or a behavior to enter the field of political problematization it is necessary for a certain number of factors to have first made it uncertain, to have made it lose its familiarity, or to have provoked a number of difficulties around it. This is the result of social, economic, and political processes, but their role is only that of instigation. Effective problematization is accomplished by thought. When thought intervenes, it does not assume a unique form that is the direct result or the necessary expression of the social, economic, or political difficulties. It is an original or specific response, often taking many forms, sometimes contradictory in their aspects. "Thought is freedom in relation to what one does, the motion by which one detaches oneself from it, establishes it as an object, and reflects on it as a problem" (EFR, 388). Foucault thus recognizes that philosophical thought and social critique form an important condition of possibility for political change and as such a significant aspect of resistance to hegemonic forms of power.

In sum, resistance against domination and the normalizing effects of power/ knowledge must advance on multiple fronts. It consists of creative transformations of the self, communal forms of counterconduct, and critical interrogation of our present.

Joanna Oksala

SEE ALSO

Conduct
Contestation
Critique
Power
Problematization
Strategies (and Tactics)
Transgression

SUGGESTED READING

Butler, Judith. 1997. *The Psychic Life of Power, Theories in Subjection.* Stanford, CA: Stanford University Press.
Deleuze, Gilles. 1988. *Foucault*, trans. Seán Hand. Minneapolis: University of Minnesota Press.
Heyes, Cressida. 2007. *Self-Transformations: Foucault, Ethics and Normalized Bodies.* Oxford: Oxford University Press.
McGushin, Edward. 2007. *Foucault's Askesis: An Introduction to the Philosophical Life.* Evanston, IL: Northwestern University Press.
McWhorter, Ladelle. 1999. *Bodies and Pleasures: Foucault and the Politics of Sexual Normalization.* Bloomington: Indiana University Press.
Oksala, Johanna. 2005. *Foucault on Freedom.* Cambridge: Cambridge University Press.
O'Leary, Timothy. 2002. *Foucault and the Art of Ethics.* London: Continuum.

75

REVOLUTION

FOUCAULT RARELY SPEAKS about revolution in his work, and then only in relatively marginal texts. However, where he does speak of it, he accords great importance to the concept, suggesting, in particular, that "all modern thought, like all modern politics, has been dominated by the question of the revolution" (FDE3, 266, my translation; cf. EPPC, 121). Foucault does not exempt himself from this historical horizon of revolutionary thought and politics but rather grasps it deliberately. As with so many concepts, Foucault shows us that revolution, far from being a simple, objective, fundamental category, is of a recent date. For Foucault, the concept of political revolution is the product of a particular episode in the history of thought.

Foucault is a thinker of discontinuity, who sees history as marked by radical cleavages (EEW2, 431). The discontinuities he studied were primarily in the domain of discourses, revolutions in the sense of "scientific revolutions," as Thomas Kuhn famously called them. Foucault himself uses the word "revolution" in this regard but generally shies away from it, preferring to use the word "transformation" (FDE2, 59). This is at least in part deliberately in order to distinguish his approach from that of Kuhn (see FDE2, 239–240). Instead, Foucault mainly reserves the word "revolution" for its political sense.

Foucault's studies tend to deflate the importance of political revolutions as historical events. Although many of the cleavages he finds in his historical inquiries occur around the time of one revolution in particular, the French Revolution of 1789, they do not neatly coincide with it. Foucault talks about the French Revolution in many places, as might be expected, given that he lived in France, a society that honors the event as its founding moment, and that most of his works focus on French history. Still, the position of the French Revolution in the cases he studies is always equivocal: *The Birth of the Clinic* sees medicine already going through major changes before the revolution, though these decisively radicalize after it; in the *History of*

Madness, Foucault sees madness as reappearing immediately prior to the revolution as a result of reforms; and in *Discipline and Punish*, France's new penal code results from the revolution, but in other countries the decisive changes occur before it and without any local revolution spurring it. Foucault is clear that it was not revolution that actually created these changes, even if he also holds that the French Revolution "completely turned upside down" the various institutions his histories had dealt with (FDE3, 411). One can infer then that the revolution is as much the effect as it is the cause of the changes.

Foucault would seem to assign particular importance to the Revolution in his remark that "we still have not cut the head off the king" in political theory in the first volume of his *History of Sexuality* (EHS1, 88–89). However, the point here is precisely that cutting the head off the king in reality failed to achieve a crucial shift in political theory, or indeed in politics itself, insofar as it continued to be dominated by a "sovereign" model of power.

None of Foucault's books thematizes revolution, then; for his explicit views on the subject, one has to look elsewhere. He first explicitly engaged with the theme only in the late 1970s, and then only in interviews, and in his 1976 lecture series "Society Must Be Defended." Foucault locates the first political use of the notion of revolution with French philosopher Henri de Boulainvilliers in the seventeenth century. Boulainvilliers employed the notion literally, as a matter of politics revolving, a turn of the wheel of history by which empires rise and then fall, just as the earth revolves around the sun (ECF-SMD, 193).

More generally, however, Foucault sees revolutionary discourse as founded on the notion of a struggle between opposing forces underlying politics. Revolution is thus understood as a matter of a decisive inversion of the balance of forces, victory for one side or the other (ECF-SMD, 79). Revolutionaries struggle deliberately to produce a final inversion, whereas "antirevolutionary" discourses are opposed to it, defending the state against those who would usurp the existing order. Both sides, however, for Foucault take their cue from the notion of society as struggle; it is only that antirevolutionaries understand themselves as dominant and hence seek to maintain this dominance (ECF-SMD, 81). Racism is thus understood by Foucault as "inverted" revolutionary discourse, which demands the protection of the pure master race (ibid.). Similarly, he notes the possibility that a revolutionary discourse might end up being the discourse of a dominant faction, as in the Soviet Union, on the basis that an oppressed class that has seized power needs to maintain its dominance (ECF-SMD, 83).

In relation to the French Revolution, Foucault discusses a view of revolution as a final reconciliation of historical tendencies, as their logical development (ECF-SMD, 232–233). This position, I think, can be broadly described as Hegelian, though Foucault does not explicitly make that reference. It is not completely at odds with understanding revolution as a victory in a struggle between forces, as evidenced by Marx's dialectical historicism (ECF-SMD, 233–234).

Foucault in *Society Must Be Defended* locates his own thought as lying in the tradition that thinks of politics as the struggle between forces. This gives rise to an apparent antinomy in his position vis-à-vis revolution: on the one hand, he describes it as a limited episode in the history of thought, and on the other locates himself inside this episode. This antinomy is repeated in his remarks regarding revolution in interviews from around the same time. On the one hand, there he bemoans the fact that progress toward revolution has stagnated and urges a return to it. On the other, he criticises the extent to which revolution has been a dominant category of political thought since 1789.

Regarding the claim that revolutionary politics has stagnated, Foucault (FDE3, 398), speaking in 1977, after the collapse of the Chinese Cultural Revolution, argues that we find ourselves for the first time since 1830 in a situation in which no revolution is taking place that we can point to as something to rally toward. Indeed, Foucault notes that the situation in 1830 was less serious because there was an ongoing possibility of harking back to the French Revolution. Whatever the reason, Foucault thinks we find ourselves in a situation where the masses in the West have ceased to desire revolution (FDE3, 85). In the face of this mass opposition to revolution, a minority who continue to advocate revolution have succeeded only in creating an association of revolution with "extreme intellectual elitism" and terrorism. Foucault argues, however, that only mass desire for revolution can bring revolution about, not terror. This leads him to conclude that: "In my opinion, the role of the intellectual today must be to re-establish the same status of desirability for the image of revolution that existed in the 19th century." "To do this," he argues, "it is necessary to invent new modes of human relations, which is to say new modes of knowledge, new modes of pleasure and of sexual life." Foucault's claim is that these new relations can "be transformed into a revolution and render it desirable" (FDE2, 86).

The compatibility of his pro-revolutionary attitude with his critique of revolution can be seen in these remarks: Foucault wants revolution only on condition that it can be a new kind of revolution, different from what has gone before. This indeed may imply that politics as we are used to understanding it will cease to exist (FDE3, 267; cf. EPPC, 122). There is nothing assured about this, however; it might not happen. Hence, for Foucault the task of the intellectual is "to try to know, with the most honesty possible, whether revolution is desirable" (FDE3, 267, my translation; cf. EPPC, 122). Importantly, he adds the caveat here "that only those who accept risking their lives to make it come about can answer this question ultimately" (FDE3, 269, my translation; cf. EPPC, 124).

There is an apparent contradiction here still between the idea that intellectuals are supposed to make revolution desirable and the idea that they should be questioning whether it is desirable. However, the two tasks are compatible: to make us want revolution can combine with the honest posing of the question of whether it is desirable; we try to make it desirable, because it is not yet clearly desirable, through changing reality, not merely engaging in a publicity exercise on behalf of revolution. It is not the intellectual's task to incite revolution regardless of the context. For Foucault (FDE3, 476), no philosophical position is truly in and of itself "revolutionary," or indeed conservative. Thus Hegel or Nietzsche, for example, can be used for either revolutionary or conservative purposes. The point here is that philosophers think about the world in a sophisticated way that does not simply automatically commend the same course of political praxis in all situations.

The problem with revolutionary thought for Foucault (FDE3, 279–280) is that it aims at "*the* revolution," that it presupposes that history is directed toward a singular revolution and bases history and politics around this contextualization of the present. Foucault (FDE3, 530) argues that such ways of thinking are demobilizing in practice by deferring everything away from local, immediate struggles toward a grand struggle. Instead of aiding struggle, then, the notion of revolution becomes a point around which power is constituted (FDE3, 551). For Foucault, this is how the concept of the revolution has operated since its entry into European thought a couple of centuries ago. It

> constituted a gigantic effort to domesticate revolts within a rational and controllable history: it gave them a legitimacy, separated their good forms from their bad, and defined the laws of their unfolding; it set their prior conditions, objectives, and ways of being carried to completion. Even a status of the professional revolutionary was defined: by thus repatriating revolt, people have aspired to make its truth manifest and to bring it to its real end. (EEW3, 450)

Against this tendency to domesticate revolution by seeing it as an absolute and singular rupture, Foucault characterizes it as a "type of codification" of power relations (EPK, 122). It is thus not merely a break but a kind of status quo in itself, even if a revolution is by definition temporary; it will collapse into a nonrevolutionary codification (EPPC, 219). That it is a codification furthermore implies that a revolution has its own specific inherent structure and hence "that there are many different kinds of revolution, roughly speaking as many kinds as there are possible subversive codifications of power relations, and that one can moreover perfectly well conceive of revolutions which leave essentially intact the power relations which allow the state to function" (FDE3, 151, my translation; cf. EPK, 122–123).

Thus, revolution is never absolute, nor does one revolution necessarily particularly resemble another. Foucault argues that revolutionary thought has been universalist in insisting that all revolutions must follow the same model (FDE2, 816). When applied globally, this implies Western revolutionaries are guilty of an "imperialism of the universal discourse," or alternatively of "exoticism" (presumably what Saïd would call "orientalism"). That is, they either see every revolution in the world as according to a Western model or as utterly different, and thus impossible to understand at all.

Foucault made these remarks in 1975, but he would go on to apply them concretely in relation to the Iranian Revolution a few years later. Here, he tries to analyze what he saw firsthand in Iran in its uniqueness as a political event. Predictably, the Left in the West either interpreted Iranian events according to their model or refused to recognize its status as a revolution. For Foucault, its specificity lay, most obviously, in the way Shia Islam operated politically, and also, he suspects, in a status as the first revolt of global modernity, against global systems rather than a merely national situation, representing a new kind of insurrection (FDE3, 716). These comments, however, pertain to the protest movement that forced out the Shah. In 1979, when the Ayatollah Khomeini returned and contested power after the Shah's departure, the Revolution entered a phase that saw it accord with conventional Western notions of revolution, at which point, says Foucault (Afary and Anderson 2005, 239), it was recognized as such for the first time.

Mark Kelly

SEE ALSO

> *History*
> *Politics*
> *Power*
> *Race (and Racism)*
> *Resistance*
> *Henri de Boulainvilliers*

SUGGESTED READING

Afary, Janet, and Kevin B. Anderson. 2005. *Foucault and the Iranian Revolution: Gender and the Seductions of Islamism*. Chicago: University of Chicago Press.

76

SELF

FOUCAULT'S CONCEPTION OF self is antifoundationalist and radically historical. Although the term "self" (*soi*) appears most consistently in Foucault's later writings, courses, and interviews on the Greco-Roman and early Christian worlds, his analysis of self in antiquity must be situated in the context of his lifelong work on subjectification and his metatheoretical challenge to standard conceptions of subjectivity. In Foucault's works, self is a temporally contingent term that emerges within a history of subjectivity as a modern problem to be rethought. As Foucault put it in a 1980 lecture, "I have tried to get out from the philosophy of the subject through a genealogy of the subject, by studying the constitution of the subject across history which has led us up to the modern concept of the self" (EBHS, 202). Foucault's contestation of traditional understandings of subjectivity challenges, in particular, the metaphysical substantival self, the psychological self as personality with interiority or depth, the psychoanalytic self as ego (*le moi*), and the phenomenological self as a subject of consciousness. Foucault's historicizing conception of subjectivity also differs from poststructuralist accounts of a psycholinguistic subject.

Foucault's antifoundationalist interrogation of self as a problem to be rethought can be situated as part of a broader postwar critique of the rationalist Cartesian subject. His uniquely genealogical approach to self historicizes subjectivity not as a history of consciousness but as a genealogy of reflexive practices. The result of a movement of reflection or doubling, self emerges and disappears in particular historical moments without being fixed by a definite article (the or *le*); self is neither the pronominal first-person entity (I or *je*) nor the locus of individual identity designated by what Foucault calls the modern concept of the self (*le soi*). Rather, self in Foucault's work is better conceived as the reflexive effect of subjective problematization: a series of recursive yet singular instances of form-giving that emerge within a historico-philosophical project "whose goal is a history of truth" (EHS2, 11).

This Foucauldian approach to self can be further explored in relation to three specific themes that appear consistently over the course of Foucault's oeuvre: ethics, power, and transformation. First, self is central to Foucauldian ethics, which Foucault defines as the relation of *soi* to *soi*, of self to itself or others. As the site of an ethical problematization, self emerges as a response to the Socratic question "how is one to live?" In his work on the Greco-Roman world, Foucault explores self in its "etho-poetic" (EHS2, 13) function as a style to be given to one's conduct and one's life: self as self-cultivation. This understanding of self reframes subjectivity as a form produced by recursive, ascetic practices of self-care: *epimeleia heautou* in Greek (EHS3, 45), *sui cura* in Latin (EHS3, 45), *souci de soi* in French (FHS3, 61). These arts of self or techniques of existence (*technē tou biou* [EHS3, 43]) turn life, or *bios*, into an aesthetic material to be fashioned through practices of *askesis* (EHS3, 68). Significantly, Foucault contrasts Greek and Roman ascetic exercises with later Christian practices of austerity that focus on self-sacrifice and the renunciation of self. According to Foucault, Christianity inaugurates a new method of self-scrutiny – the hermeneutic principle – and the speaking of that hermeneutic project through a confession of the self. In modernity, confessional self-revelation forms what Foucault calls the "repressive hypothesis" (EHS1) of a subjectivity that is rationally objectified and morally coded through a sexual core buried deep within the psyche. Thus the modern psychological self emerges via a scientistic, rationalist incitement to speak that turns sexuality into "the seismograph of our subjectivity" (EEW1, 179).

Framed as part of a history of reflexive practices, the experience of *askesis* – "testing oneself, examining oneself, monitoring oneself in a series of clearly defined exercises" (EHS3, 68) – is also "a practice of truth" (ECF-HOS, 317) that is "central to the formation of the ethical subject" (EHS3, 68). This perspective on *askesis* underscores Foucault's further elaboration of ethics as a historically shifting relation between subjectivity and truth. "I have always been interested in the problem of the relationship between subject and truth" (EEW1, 289), Foucault says in a 1984 interview. In that context, Foucault distinguishes between the ancient privileging of self-care over self-knowledge and its modern reversal in the "Cartesian moment" (ECF-HOS, 14) when philosophy makes self-knowing "into a fundamental means of access to truth" (ECF-HOS, 14) at the expense of self-care. Unlike the ancient approach to truth through ascetic practices of self-care, the modern rationalist self remains untransformed in its quest for truth. Importantly, Foucault points out that the ancient modes of access to truth reemerge over the course of Western history in other moments of "self-testing," particularly during the Renaissance and the nineteenth century (ECF-HOS, 251). Such descriptions of historically specific moments and practices that reemerge asynchronously, as temporal ruptures within their own ethos, highlight the coexistence of seemingly self-contradictory forms of ethical subjectivity within Foucault's simultaneously diachronic and recursive conceptions of time.

The second theme, subjectivity and power, focuses on self as a function of power-knowledge and what Foucault later calls governmentality. In the summary of his 1980–1981 course at the Collège de France, Foucault describes ethical subjectification as a problem that emerges at the intersection of two themes in his work: a history of subjectivity and an analysis of governmentality. From this perspective, Foucault's earlier work on madness, illness, and delinquency can be seen retrospectively as part of a larger fabric that embeds ethical reflection on self in an analysis of power-knowledge. The concept of governmentality in particular allows Foucault to reconceive the history of subjectivity as bound up not only with repressive and productive forms of subjectification but also as a domain for self-creation and practices of freedom. Governmentality thus has two related objectives that bear on Foucault's conception of self: first, to critique standard understandings of power as centralized, unitary, and emanating from a single source; and second, to analyze power as a domain of strategic relations between individuals and groups. Foucault describes this second aspect of governmentality in terms that resonate with his description of ethics: "the government of self by self (*de soi par soi*) in its articulation with relations to others" (FDE2a, 1033).

Placing the self at the intersection of a history of subjectivity and a history of governmentality has important implications for rethinking subjectivity in political terms. A range of critics, especially Habermasians and feminists, have challenged what they view in Foucault as a politically impoverished conception of self that does not allow for free will, individual agency, or collective social and political action. If, however, one considers Foucault's definition of governmentality as "a strategic field of power relations in their mobility, transformability, and reversibility" (ECF-HOS, 252), possibilities emerge for reconsidering political subjectification at the intersection of subjectivity and governmentality. Differentiating the subject of governmentality from "a juridical conception of the subject of right" (ECF-HOS, 252), Foucault explicitly links power with ethics: "the analysis of governmentality ... must refer to an ethics of the subject defined by the relationship of self to self" (ibid.). Emphasizing this point, Foucault describes "politics as an ethics" (EFR, 375). These and other articulations of the relation between ethical subjectification and governmentality suggest that in Foucault the ethical subject is capable of political acts of resistance, contestation, and even revolt. These acts can be conceived as ethico-political practices of freedom that transform the self in its relation to itself and others. As Foucault puts it in a 1984 interview, ethics as "the conscious [*réfléchie*] practice of freedom" (EEW1, 284) "is thus inherently political" (EEW1, 286).

This theme of transformation constitutes the third and in many ways most important lens through which to understand self in Foucault's thought. Foucault consistently asserts the ethical and political importance of self-transformation: a conception of subjectivity in which self "can eventually change" (EEW1, 177). This theme functions in Foucault's thinking in multiple ways. First, self-transformation names the principle of discontinuity as it relates to the history of subjectivity in Foucault's work. Self, as a concept, is subject to change: self in one period is not self in another. To take the most obvious example, despite its importance for Foucault's conceptual exploration of ethical subjectification, ancient Greek self-reflexivity is radically different from modern instantiations of the self, and any attempt to argue for a continuity between ancient Greek and modern forms of subjectivity would deny the principles of temporal discontinuity and epistemic difference that distinguish Foucauldian genealogies from standard histories. In that sense, the history of self in its transformations is itself nothing more than a self-reflexive movement of return that tracks the epistemic limits of our own attempts to apprehend the alterity of the past.

On a second level, transformation describes a uniquely Foucauldian approach to games of truth that modify the self in its genealogical quest for knowledge. Foucault's genealogies dramatize the play between subject and object in a philosophical pursuit of truth that unfolds in the archive. From this perspective, Foucault's archival work is itself a transformative practice: an art of the self or technique of existence. In his descriptions of his own contact with the materiality of history's traces, Foucault describes a self-transformative erotic practice of thinking and feeling in which he, a knowing subject, is changed by his own repeated encounters with the "poem-lives" (EEW3, 159) he finds in the archive. Ultimately this archival method has the capacity to transform, in a rereversal of the "Cartesian moment" (ECF-HOS, 14), the subject–object relation that structures the modern analytic of finitude Foucault describes in *The Order of Things*. In this archival *ars erotica*, the contact between a knowing subject and an archival object produces a shift, a play in the present-day epistemic and ethical field that Foucault calls freedom. Thus Foucault's self-transformative archival method is inextricably linked to an ethical subjectification whose condition of possibility is freedom: "freedom," Foucault says, "is the ontological condition of ethics" (EEW1, 284); and again, he says, "the freedom of the subject in relation to others ... constitutes the very stuff [*la matière même*] of ethics" (EEW1, 300).

Finally, this notion of a self-undoing ethical subjectification through a practice of freedom links the theme of transformation to desubjectification. Toward the end of his life, Foucault describes his own work as a "philosophical exercise" whose purpose is "to free thought from what it silently thinks, and so enable it to think differently" (EHS2, 9). This freeing of thought from its own thinking is impelled by a curiosity that undoes the subject, enabling "one to get free of oneself" (EHS2,

8). This self-release ("*se déprendre de soi-même*" [FHS2, 15]) is brought about by a self-testing participation in games of truth: an "*askesis*, an exercise of oneself in the activity of thought" (EHS2, 9).

Retrospectively, this self-undoing relation to thinking could be said to describe an ethical approach to a non–self-identical dissolution of the subject that recurs repeatedly over the course of Foucault's work. From the "limit-experiences of the Western world" (EHM, xxx) that Foucault first explored in *History of Madness* (1961), through the troubled mirror of *The Order of Things* (1966) and the self-fracturing irony of *The History of Sexuality* (1976), to the final volumes on the radical alterity of practices of self-care in the ancient world, Foucault's histories describe a subject that is coextensive with a continually transforming "outside." Again and again, Foucault's work stages games of truth as histories of the present in which the modern "I" is freed from the illusion of a self-sameness that traps it: "I discover myself absent at the place where I am, since I see myself over there" (EEW2, 179).

Foucault's repeated invocations of self-undoing construe philosophical *askesis* as an ethical encounter, where the self-reflective symmetry of the "I" is disrupted by the material traces of the past's alterity in ways that put the modern subject into question. As Foucault puts it in "On the Ways of Writing History," the problem "in our time, is to erase one's own name, to come to lodge one's voice in the great anonymous murmur of discourses" (EEW2, 291). That move into the murmur entails what Foucault calls "the knower's straying afield of himself" (EHS2, 8), away from the rationalist Cartesian subject into the anonymity of proliferating forms of existence. In this sense, self in Foucault is an emergence of forces whose modern form – "man" – "is in the process of disappearing" (EOT, 385), "like a face drawn in sand at the edge of the sea" (EOT, 387).

Lynne Huffer

SEE ALSO

Care
Christianity
Governmentality
Life
Man
Outside
Subjectification
Truth
René Descartes

SUGGESTED READING

Allen, Amy. 2008. *The Politics of Ourselves: Power, Autonomy, and Gender in Contemporary Critical Theory*. New York: Columbia University Press.

Davidson, Arnold. 2003. "Ethics as Ascetics: Foucault, the History of Ethics, and Ancient Thought," in *The Cambridge Companion to Foucault*, 2nd ed., ed. Gary Gutting. Cambridge: Cambridge University Press, pp. 123–148.

O'Leary, Timothy. 2002. *Foucault and the Art of Ethics*. London: Continuum.

Veyne, Paul. 1997. "The Final Foucault and His Ethics," trans. Catherine Porter and Arnold I. Davidson, in *Foucault and His Interlocutors*, ed. Arnold I. Davidson. Chicago: University of Chicago Press, pp. 225–233.

77

SEX

"SEX IS BORING" (EFR, 340). This quip, only half tongue in cheek, is a reminder to his interviewer that Foucault is not so much interested in talking about sex as he is in analyzing how it came to be a subject of such interest: sex is boring compared to the question "why do we ask about sex?" Foucault spent the last years of his life justifying, and refining, his answer to that question. He sought to articulate the basic assumptions about sex, which are so familiar that we have difficulty getting a critical perspective on them. Foremost among them is the assumption that sex is a (natural) given. He argued instead that "sex" is not a constant but one of the effects of our experience of a sexuality that itself, like any experience, is "the correlation between fields of knowledge, types of normativity, and forms of subjectivity in a particular culture" (EHS2, 4). What Foucault finds more interesting than sex is the fact of this historically specific experience of sexuality and the ethical possibilities connected to it. Insisting on the recent coinage of the term, his work can be seen as establishing that, although sex in the boring sense might be a historical universal, sexuality in the sense that interests us, that in which we have an interest, is very recent. It is not a historically contingent experience to think, as we do, that each individual has a sexuality and that this sexuality holds the key to the truth about ourselves. In the process of tracing the genealogy of that present experience of sexuality, Foucault's work both confirms and extends his way of conceiving of ethical problems and identifying the stakes of related political struggles.

In a tribute written in 1963, Foucault celebrated the inventiveness of Bataille's transgressive sexuality, seeing in it an appropriate mode of "resistance," which he prophesized might "one day … seem as decisive for our culture … as the experience of contradiction was at an earlier time for dialectical thought" (ELCP, 33). A few years later, Foucault offered this as one definition of humanist thought: "any philosophy which thinks that sexuality is made for loving and proliferating" (FDE2, 65). In some sense, it was thus clear from the start that Foucault's attempt to find an alternative to humanism required an alternate account of sexuality. However, despite these early signs of its importance, sexuality did not become an object of explicit study for him until *The History of Sexuality*, the first volume of which was published in 1976.

That first volume, subtitled *The Will to Knowledge*, presents the justification for, and broad outline of, Foucault's project for the history of sexuality. Rather than reconstituting a history of sexual practices, or even a history of the ideas about sex, Foucault's major work on the subject sought to figure out "how an 'experience' came to be constituted in modern Western societies, an experience that caused individuals to recognize themselves as subjects of a 'sexuality'" (EHS2, 4). When, how, and why did it become "obvious" that each person has a sex and that sexuality is constitutive of identity? In trying to answer these questions, Foucault traced the emergence of the knowledge and power structures that make contemporary experiences of sexual subjectivity possible. He tracked how power came to operate through the current configuration of sexuality to produce and control sexual subjects. For sexuality, as for madness or punishment in earlier works, Foucault began his description of the current power configuration by taking issue with what he identifies as the standard narrative on which that power depends. *History of Madness* used a genealogical study to counter the narrative according to which modern psychiatry, beginning with the emblematic tale of Pinel liberating the insane from their chains in 1793, developed as a progressive rationalization, becoming a science and operating on the side of progressive politics, or increasing liberation. *The History of Sexuality* is likewise structured as a critical response to a dominant narrative, in this case the story of our progressive liberation from the repression of natural sexuality, for which the Victorian age stands as a symbol. Driven by a Nietzschean suspicion that the value of these stories lies in their making possible a certain dominant position, Foucault underlined the effect of "the Repressive Hypothesis" in these terms: "If sex is repressed, that is, condemned to prohibition, nonexistence and silence, then the mere fact that one is speaking about it has the appearance of a deliberate transgression" (EHS1, 6). Thus Foucault's counternarrative is not just a historical corrective to the dominant story about sexuality; it challenges *both* the dominant moralizing order, which excludes "perverse" sexualities, *and* discourses, practices, and institutions that position themselves as the liberating revolutionaries fighting for recognition of sexuality's natural place and importance.

Foucault claimed that historical investigation reveals that there may well have been an increased policing of language and stricter rules on what can be spoken of in polite company in the Victorian era but that this went hand in hand with what he calls a discursive explosion. Beyond the chastening of language, Foucault saw not censorship but instead a complex "apparatus for producing an ever greater quantity of discourse about sex" (EHS1, 23), a proliferation of political, economical, and technical incitements to talk about sex. Managing and controlling sexuality became the concern not just for the law, or for moral authorities, but also for various domains of knowledge (demography, architecture, pedagogy, economics, etc.). Drawing on his work in *Discipline and Punish*, Foucault mobilized a conception of power "that replaces the privilege of the law with the viewpoint of the objective, the privilege of prohibition with the viewpoint of tactical efficacy" (EPK, 102). Discipline "is not ensured by right but by technique, not by law but by normalization, not by punishment but by control" (EHS1, 89), and it is thus to mechanisms of technique, normalization, and control that Foucault looked to track the discipline of bodies in the domain of sexuality. Understanding power's relation to sexuality involves much more than understanding what is forbidden. Foucault's conception of power implies that mechanisms of control are productive even as they exercise restriction. Power is a double relation described by the term "subjectivation," which Foucault used to emphasize that becoming a subject and being subjected are two aspects of a single operation. The work of the historian is thus not simply to chronicle the shifts in prohibitions through time but, more importantly, to attend to the varied ways in which prohibitions and incitements function to create both social experiences and objects of knowledge. Consider the question of infantile sexuality. Foucault found infantile sexuality to have been sustained, as much as restrained, by the worry that developed around it in the Victorian era. By training parents and teachers to detect and fight any manifestations of sexual interest in children or in the redesigning of homes to segregate the nursery so as to limit the exposure of children to a sexuality that was being confined to the marital bedroom, Foucault saw practices that do not reduce the importance of sexuality in childhood so much as constitute it as a multifaceted and ever more prevalent problem. Although the avowed ambition of the Victorian era may have been to restrict sexuality to the monogamous married couple, the effects of the power that enforced this norm included the production of specific forms of sexuality. New perversions came to be fixed as objects of concern and, as these were incorporated into individuals, new figures appeared. With an emerging fear of deviant sexualities came a new specification of dangerous individuals. Whereas sodomy laws had long been on the books, in the nineteenth century the homosexual appears as a "personage," an individual of whom it is thought that "nothing of what he is escapes his sexuality" (EHS1, 43, translation modified). This is, for Foucault, a new sexuality; it is a new experience bound up with a new form of subjectivity for which sexuality is central.

As he sketched the project for a history of sexuality understood as a product of a particular type of power, Foucault insisted that "[w]e must conceptualize the deployment of sexuality on the basis of techniques of power that are contemporaneous with it" (EHS1, 150). He lamented that "the representation of power has remained under the spell of the monarchy" and that "in political thought and analysis we *still have not cut off the head of the king*" (EHS1, 87, emphasis added). This methodological bias has meant excessive, or exclusive, focus on the law, which Foucault countered through extensive analysis of the multiple ways in which norms contribute to the ways discipline operates. He further sought to break the "spell of the monarchy" by arguing that, although political analysis may not yet have recognized it, in the last couple of centuries a new form of power has emerged to challenge the sovereign model. His hypothesis was that the dominant regime of power in the Western world is undergoing a shift from the regime of sovereignty to the regime of biopower. Although both are forms of power over life and death, Foucault identified them as operating according to two different asymmetries. Whereas sovereignty's mission was to make die or let live, biopower's mission is to make live or let die. With this change in mission comes a change in objects – sovereignty governs subjects, biopower manages populations. Managing a population, through norms, with the objective of making live, according to Foucault, is the general picture of the form of power that is "the formative matrix of sexuality" (EPK, 186). Thus the history of sexuality that Foucault argued needed to be written would consider the ways in which norms operate at the level of bodies through anatomodiscipline and at the level of populations through biopower in such a way as to both control and sustain sexuality as it is presently experienced.

When, after a long hiatus and indeed only after Foucault's death, the subsequent volumes of *The History of Sexuality* were published, it appeared that the project had changed. There is some debate as to the importance of the change, but Foucault himself described the shift as one from the perspective of power to the perspective of the subject on which power operates, away from techniques of power toward the analysis of techniques of the self, as he tracked the origin of what he took to be the crucial move to the idea that sexuality provides the key to the truth about the self (ETS, 16–49). Foucault had identified the pastoral tradition and Christian confession as the beginning of practices that encouraged man to look for the truth of himself by examining his desire. However, to understand the emergence of this "man of desire," he found himself having to go further back to a time in which, beneath a thematic similarity, he found a whole different distribution of problems and practices concerning sex. The result of this work is organized in three volumes that involved studying the slow formation during antiquity of a hermeneutic of the self. *The Use of Pleasure* looks at classical Greek discourses on the proper measure for sexual activity; *The Care of the Self* follows these problems through the Greek and Latin texts of the second century; and, finally, *Confessions of the Flesh* outlines the constitution of the doctrine of desire. (The second and third volumes were published in 1984; a fourth volume, almost complete before Foucault's death, remains unpublished.)

The Use of Pleasure investigated ancient Greece to try to understand how, why, and in what form sexual activity became a subject for moral concern. To answer this, Foucault looked at prescriptive texts that propose rules of moral conduct but are also practical in the sense of providing the means for the free man to interrogate his own conduct. Although it was a moral problem, Greek thought did not treat sex as something requiring the imposition or justification of limits, or the codification of acceptable acts. Rather, the task was to establish the principles that should regulate the "use of pleasure." Foucault analyzed three areas (body, marriage, love of boys) to insist on the specificity of the ancient problems. Sexual temperance was thought of in conjunction with temperance in other bodily needs: eating, drinking, sex, and sleep were all questions of diet. Sex within marriage had to be governed by the principles of household economics – the challenge was to maintain throughout time the hierarchical structure proper to a household. Sexual relations between men and boys had to be governed in such a way as to accommodate the principle that passivity is appropriate only for women or slaves. Around these three themes Foucault articulated the logic of prescriptive texts in such a way as to emphasize that what they prescribe is an obligation to style one's conduct in a way befitting a free adult male.

According to the method Foucault develops in this work, describing a moral problem requires determining the ethical substance, the mode of subjectivation, the form of ethical elaboration, and finally the telos of the moral subject. Thus, to take one example, the injunction to marital fidelity marks a whole series of different moral problems depending on the specific cultural context. The ethical substance might be the respect of strict rules of behavior, mastery of desires, or the intensification and permanence of sentiments for one's spouse; the mode of subjectivation might be submission to the condition of belonging to a social group that accepts the injunction to fidelity, but it might also involve practicing fidelity as a way of prolonging a certain spiritual tradition, or responding to a call to give one's personal life a particular form of perfection; the form might be the lengthy assimilation of a series of precepts or regular control of one's behavior, the sudden renunciation of all pleasure, or an ongoing examination of all movements of one's desire. All these variations mean that respecting a prohibition on sexual relations outside of marriage is not always the same act; it can participate in a whole series of different ways of constituting the self as a moral subject. Thus, where other commentators see only familiar injunctions to limit certain sexual activities, Foucault argues that "these themes of sexual austerity should be understood, not as an expression of, or commentary on, deep and essential prohibitions, but as the elaboration and stylization of an activity in the exercise of its power and the practice of its liberty" (EHS2, 23). Emphasizing that apparent continuity of experiences between different eras and contexts is the result of anachronistic reading that fails to take into account epistemological and ontological shifts, Foucault makes the case that sex is neither a natural nor a universal given. At the same time, his analyses of the elaboration of practices of freedom in other contexts clearly point toward the necessity of understanding the analogous practices in the present and the possibilities of resistance.

Commenting in 1978 on what he termed a massive evolution toward a liberal rewriting of the laws (including for instance the decriminalizing of homosexuality), Foucault warned that this movement might be counterbalanced by a shift toward the creation of a generalized fear of sexuality. He detected in this double movement signs of a new method for the management of sexuality. Rather than forbidding certain acts, sexuality might now be managed by responding to, and of course sustaining if not creating, a certain fear that the sexuality of certain parts of the population poses a threat to the others. Indeed, he predicted that sexuality was on the way to being cast as a stalking universal danger, a specter haunting all social relations "between men and women, between children and adults and possibly between adults themselves" (EPPC, 281). As we observe the evolution toward legal accommodation of homosexual marriage, we would do well to remember both that warning and the connections between sex and race that biopower supposes and produces. Understanding sex as Foucault does enables one to discern the ways in which today discourses, practices, and institutions that rest their authority on narratives concerning "dangerous populations" stoke racist fears as a strategy against certain sexualities or brandish the dangers of certain sexualities in order to justify racial exclusion. Resisting those modalities of domination at a collective level is one of the tasks Foucault leaves us with, encouraging us to vindicate his contention that "sex is not a fatality: it is a possibility for creative life" (EEW1, 163).

Foucault's understanding of (our interest in) sex as a characteristically modern Western experience has had an impact on innumerable scholars and activists. Some stayed close to Foucault's work (see, for instance, Arnold I. Davidson's reading of Foucault as an ethical thinker or the connection to psychoanalysis [Davidson 2001]), whereas others drew on its basic suggestions to formulate their own projects. Indeed, the novel understanding of the dynamics of power that the first volume of *The History of Sexuality* provided had a galvanizing effect by suggesting whole new avenues of research in a variety of fields. Biopolitics became a key term for some analyses of contemporary power (see, for instance, Giorgio Agamben's *Homo Sacer: Sovereign Power and Bare Life* [Agamben 1998]). The contention that sexuality should be considered as an effect of power-knowledge provided new perspectives for feminism, then for gender studies, (post)colonial studies, and queer theory. In some of the landmark pieces, Gayle Rubin argued that sexual stratification is as important a consequence of Western industrialization as class inequalities or racial or ethnic discrimination (see Rubin 1984); Ann Stoler showed how Foucault's conceptual framework could reframe the analysis of race and sexuality in colonial and postcolonial studies (see Stoler 1995); and Judith Butler focused attention on the performativity of both sex and gender by exploring the ways in which juridical power produces the subjects it controls (see Butler 1990). These and other voices were important in making sex central to thinking critically about emancipatory projects, focusing on the productive as well as the repressive functions of power. Inspired by Foucault's insistence on the connections between forms of pleasure and forms of community, George Chauncey's *Gay New York* offers an ethnography of sexual subcultures that confirms Foucault's speculative insights while contesting the periodization Foucault put forward (see Chauncey 1995). More personal descriptions of the transformative

effect of *The History of Sexuality* include Ladelle McWhorter's analysis of its importance both for critical thinking and for her life (see McWhorter 1999) and David
Halperin's account of the impact on gay intellectuals and activists of Foucault's ideas
as to the possibilities of strategic self-transformation (see Halperin 1995). Although
many of the specific historical claims he made continue to be contested (by friends as
well as foes), the effects of Foucault's suggestions continue to proliferate in the work
of scholars, activists, and many others. His work made it both possible and necessary
to think in new ways about the interests we have in sex.

Olivia Custer

SEE ALSO

> *Biopower*
> *Homosexuality*
> *Subjectification*
> *Technology (of Discipline, Governmentality, and Ethics)*

SUGGESTED READING

Agamben, Giorgio. 1998. *Homo Sacer: Sovereign Power and Bare Life*, trans. Daniel Heller-
    Roazen. Stanford, CA: Stanford University Press.
Butler, Judith. 1990. *Gender Trouble: Feminism and the Subversion of Identity*. London: Routledge.
Chauncey, George. 1995. *Gay New York: Gender, Urban Culture, and the Making of the Gay Male
    World, 1890–1940*. New York: Basic Books.
Davidson, Arnold. 2001. *The Emergence of Sexuality: Historical Epistemology and the Formation of
    Concepts*. Cambridge, MA: Harvard University Press.
Halperin, David. 1995. *Saint Foucault: Towards a Gay Hagiography*. Oxford: Oxford University
    Press.
McWhorter, Ladelle. 1999. *Bodies and Pleasures: Foucault and the Politics of Sexual Normalization*.
    Bloomington: Indiana University Press.
Rubin, Gayle. 1984. "Thinking Sex: Notes for a Radical Theory of the Politics of Sexuality," in
    Pleasure and Danger, ed. Carole Vance. London: Routledge and Kegan Paul, pp. 267–319.
Stoler, Ann. 1995. *Race and the Education of Desire*. Durham, NC: Duke University Press.

78

SOVEREIGNTY

SOVEREIGNTY HAS BEEN the central concept of the Western political tradition since early modernity. However, it is the counterconcept of Foucault's political theory. First, sovereignty constitutes the negative pole of Foucault's oeuvre in contrast to which Foucault's exploration of power relations unfolds. Second, sovereignty is the theoretical object that defines the political objective of Foucault's work in an antagonistic way.

Sovereignty, according to Foucault, is the "right to take life or let live," a right that ultimately resides in and is exercised as the "right to kill" (ECF-SMD, 240–241; EHS1, 136). One of the interesting features of Foucault's theses on power is that his theoretical innovations are generally introduced as counterpoints to sovereignty. Initially, discipline is juxtaposed with sovereignty (EDP, 208; ECF-SMD, 36). Later, biopower is juxtaposed with sovereignty (EHS1, 138–139; ECF-SMD, 241). Still later, security is juxtaposed with sovereignty. Security is treated in close connection with disciplinary power whose panoptic formation is put forth as "the oldest dream of the oldest sovereign" (ECF-STP, 36–37, 44–45, especially 66). The opposition between sovereignty and other forms of power is also prevalent in the descriptive markers Foucault uses. Foucault depicts discipline as the "non-sovereign power," or "the exact, point-for-point opposite of the mechanics of power that the theory of sovereignty described" (ECF-SMD, 36; EDP, 208). Biopower is the power to "to 'make' live and 'let' die" instead of the sovereign power to "take life" and, as such, it is "precisely the opposite right" of sovereignty (ECF-SMD, 241). Similarly, biopower is defined as the power *over* life in contrast to the power *of* life that designates sovereignty (ECF-SMD, 247). Overall, sovereign power functions as the conceptual counterpoint for new modalities of power whose emergence and workings Foucault so skillfully depicts. However, it is important to keep in mind that in each case the contrast is more of an analytical separation and polarity than a practical one. Although Foucault is insistent on painting the different modalities of power in

distinct colors, often repeating the stark opposition between them in different itera-
tions, he also complicates this picture by showing how these distinct forms articulate
with each other in complex ways, coloring their field of operation into a multiplicity
of hues and shades arising from their different combinations in practice.

The centrality of sovereignty to Foucault's oeuvre is not simply the result of a
rhetorical strategy that augments the originality and difference of his innovations
and thereby greatly enhances the persuasiveness of his arguments. Sovereignty, or
at least the dominant discourse of sovereignty, also functions as the target in opposition to which Foucault directs his inquiries. Foucault's political theory is under-
girded by a conceptual (and political) struggle against sovereignty, an attempt to
invert and think beyond it (EPK, 95). This tendency is not only implicit in his insistence that we must look beyond the state and the law toward social mechanisms of
domination in order to understand the workings of power in modern societies. It is
also part of an explicit demand to "eschew the model of Leviathan in the study of
power" (EPK, 102) and to "cut off the King's head" in political theory (EPK, 121).
Since such a programmatic pronunciation is a rare occurrence in Foucault's volu-
minous discourse, especially in light of his general aversion to overarching normative, political, and theoretical projects, it is not to be taken lightly. This demand
can be understood not simply as a theoretical imperative to move away from the
juridical, prohibitive model of power encapsulated in sovereignty but also to reorient our inquiries toward those multiple and heterogenous sites, local extremities,
in which relations of force are exercised and produce real effects (EPK, 96–103;
ECF-SMD, 45). The demand also contains the political imperative of redirecting
our attention to localized resistances "outside, below, and alongside the State apparatuses" (EPK, 60). Accordingly, the possibility of emancipation resides neither in
conventional politics defined by the election of parliamentary representatives nor
in radical politics directed at the acquisition of state power. Rather, Foucault suggests focusing our struggles on the incessant critique of the relations of power
from the perspective of situated and specific counterforces that use the techniques
of power against it in order to push back on domination without falling back into
sovereignty. "If we are to struggle against disciplines, or rather against disciplinary
power, in our search for a non-disciplinary power," argues Foucault, "we should
not be turning to the old right of sovereignty; we should be looking for a new right
that is both anti-disciplinary and emancipated from the principle of sovereignty"
(ECF-SMD, 39–40).

There are at least two different strategies to map sovereignty in Foucault's
thought, though these tend to move together and overlap at several points. One
strategy is by assuming a diachronic perspective, delineating the various historiciza-
tions of sovereignty in Foucault's work. From such a perspective, we would be in
error to view sovereignty as a static concept; sovereignty is embedded in multiple
political-theoretical discourses, which evolve along with the societies in which these

discourses and their corresponding relations of power operate. In this light, we can identify three different phases in the evolution of sovereignty.

The first phase, beginning in the Middle Ages, is the manifestation of sovereignty as princely power or kingship. In the various forms of monarchical sovereignty, power is intimately personal and vested in the monarch. Its symbol is the sword. It is based on the threat of taking life. Such power is concerned with "deduction," "subtraction," "appropriation," and "seizure"; in short, extraction (EHS1, 136). It extracts bodies, wealth, products, and lives. Its primary preoccupation is with the safety and the maintenance of rule in a given territory (ECF-STP, 11, 65, 96). The laws that rule over the people in that territory are relations of command and obedience. Those who defy or transgress these commands, enemies and criminals, are legitimately punished with a corporeal vengeance (EHS1, 135–136). Sovereign power manifests its might in violent, excessive, spectacular, and intermittent forms of punishment (such as the execution of Damiens the regicide) in which the king's power and the fear of this power are ritualistically affirmed before the spectator public (EDP, 3–6, 33–35, 47). Sovereign power is never completely absolute and total but restricted by divine law, tradition, customary practices, and, later, natural rights. However, as Mbembe (2008) has persuasively shown, the operation of sovereignty over the colonies constitutes an important exception in its absolutism.

The second phase in the evolution of sovereignty roughly corresponds to the seventeenth and eighteenth centuries, in which monarchical sovereignty gives way to popular sovereignty. Power is no longer in the purview of a single person; it is (more or less) democratically distributed and legitimated. Law made by (or in the name of) the people now assumes supreme power. Because of its predominantly juridical nature, sovereign power operates in a repressive, prohibitive fashion. It is the capacity to make and enforce the rules by which society functions. It coincides with the monopoly of legitimate violence. However, this is also the time in which sovereignty loses monopoly over the functioning of power in society. Just as sovereignty augments its participatory and popular nature, it attenuates its centrality. This is because a new form of power has emerged and become pervasive in the social sphere, operating through networks, in capillary form, beyond and under the state. Sovereignty is challenged by disciplinary power, as one of the landmarks of emerging capitalist society.

In contrast to how the individual is represented in social contract theories, as the abstract, juridical subject of sovereign power, the disciplines construct the body as the bearer of power relations, at once its conduits and objects. New fields of knowledge and power emerge and intersect on the body, distinguishing, classifying, controlling, and normalizing the individual, constructing its subjectivity, and functioning ultimately by the internalization of obedience and control by the same individual (EDP, 26–27, 138, 170, 203). The body is ranked, distributed, circulated, enclosed, and differentiated, imposed to conform through detailed measurement, economization, and hierarchization, and subjected to constant supervision. In this subjection, the individual's political as well as economic capacities are reproduced – "the body becomes a useful force only if it is *both a productive body and a subjected body*" (EDP, 26, my italics).

Even though theories of sovereignty continue to emphasize the unitary character of power, its exercise in juridical form, and its workings on preexisting subjects (ECF-SMD, 44), sovereignty now appears to be waning. This transformation is manifest in the shift of techniques of punishment from public and spectacular torture on the scaffold to a strictly regimented daily routine behind bars. Instead of excessive violence, a silent and anonymous gaze operates within an enclosed, concentrated, constructed space (ECF-STP, 11, 44). Instead of the visibility of the sovereign, discipline works through the visibility of its subjects (EDP, 171, 187). Imprisonment as the more efficient, continuous, and regular form of punishment transfers the formerly personal power of the sovereign to the social body and enables the reappropriation of the prisoner's force for the utility of the public, through compulsory work and moral correction as well as a series of "infra-penalities" that subject deviations from the norms to new mechanisms of punishment (EDP, 109, 124, 178). Discipline is not limited to the prison, of course. In fact, the prison, the school, the military barracks, the mental asylum, the hospital, and other institutions increasingly resemble each other in terms of the way in which power operates within and through them, exercised on bodies within their panoptic spatial formations. A disciplinary society is well under way, Foucault contends, even if the prohibitive and egalitarian pretensions of popular sovereignty tend to conceal corporeal domination and normalization from view (EDP, 222; ECF-SMD, 37, 56).

The third phase of sovereign power, identifiable particularly since the nineteenth century, is one in which sovereignty survives largely by incorporating disciplinary tactics. However, its relevance and dominance are challenged, now because discipline is complemented by another modality of power that takes as its object "man-as-species." Biopower, or the administration of life through specific technologies, such as forecasts and statistics, is directed at regulating the health, fertility, and mortality of the social body in aggregate form, at the level of the population as a whole. Hygiene, urbanization, environment, medicine, and sexuality come to constitute novel areas in which governmental apparatuses seek to intervene and regulate, in order to make the population prosper and proliferate. Laws continue to exist, but they are increasingly transformed into tactics that serve the needs of managing the well-being of the population.

In later lectures, Foucault discontinues the use of the term biopower, substituting security in its place and reconceptualizing government on the basis of probability and risk calculations (ECF-STP, 6). Unlike sovereignty, security is not concerned with ruling over people in a territory; unlike discipline, it is not concerned with ruling over bodies in an enclosed space. Rather, security, echoing biopower, has population in a milieu as its object; it is concerned with the regulation of expansive circuits as they follow their own course (ECF-STP, 11, 20, 45) and the administration of the ensemble of relations between men and things: habits, opinions, qualities, and resources, as well as cycles, flows, and natural contingencies (ECF-STP, 96). Underlying this transformation is the general shift in Foucault's definition of the political, moving away from the model of continuous warfare toward that of the "conduct of conduct" (EEW3, 341). The reformulation of the problem of biopower in the form of security, and soon after, as the "art of government" (EC-STP, 79), then leads Foucault to present a genealogy of the modern state that runs through pastoral power and *raison d'État* and that moves toward an analysis of political economy and liberalism as its contemporary frameworks (ECF-BBIO).

An important consequence of the emergence of biopower/security for sovereignty is the change of focus in power relations – from death to life. The growing concern with the administration of life and the improvement of well-being results in the concomitant fading away of death from the political. As a result, death as the stake of politics begins to escape the grasp of power; it becomes depoliticized, individualized, and politically obsolete (ECF-SMD, 241). Foucault argues:

> In the right of sovereignty, death was the moment of the most obvious and most spectacular manifestation of the absolute power of the sovereign; death now becomes, in contrast, the moment when the individual escapes all power, falls back on himself and retreats, so to speak, into his own privacy. Power no longer recognizes death. Power literally ignores death. (ECF-SMD, 248)

However, we also see that the sovereign right over life and death has not completely disappeared, whether in the form of capital punishment, warfare, or policing. In what way can the persistence of sovereignty be explained under contemporary conditions defined by the power over life? In other words, if power's preoccupation has become "making live," how is it possible to account for the continuation of "taking life"? Foucault argues that thanatopolitics is the "reverse of bio-politics" (EEW3, 416). He intimates that this reversal has to do with the persistence of sovereignty within the biopolitical problematic, despite its retreat. However, even though Foucault calls modern states "demonic combinations" of sovereign power and biopower, the nature of their combination remains equivocal (EEW3, 311). This brings us to the second strategy of mapping sovereignty in Foucault's thought, that of looking at how he theorizes the conjunction between different forms of power in a synchronic fashion.

Foucault often remarks how the emergence of new modalities of power have decentered sovereignty and led to a transformation, or at least a transition, a "juridical regression," a reversal in the right to kill (EHS1, 136, 144; EDP, 208). However, he describes this shift in different, almost diametrically opposing, ways. On the one hand, he occasionally takes a strong position, asserting that the sovereign right to kill has been "replaced" or "supplanted" (EHS1, 138, 140). He argues, for example, that because of the symbiosis and mutual enabling between capitalism and disciplinary power, "traditional, ritual, costly, violent forms of power, … soon fell into disuse and were superseded by a subtle, calculated technology of subjection" (EDP, 221). Similarly, summing up the transformation in power relations, Foucault asserts, "the old power of death that symbolized sovereign power was now carefully supplanted by the administration of bodies and the calculated management of life" (EHS1, 138–139).

On the other hand, Foucault also makes the converse point, emphasizing a mutual coexistence and interaction among different modalities of power rather than a replacement or supplementation by their sequential progression. "So, there is not a series of successive elements, the appearance of the new causing the earlier ones to disappear," he posits, "[t]here is not the legal age, the disciplinary age, and then the age of security. Mechanisms of security do not replace disciplinary mechanisms, which would have replaced juridico-legal mechanisms" (ECF-STP, 8). Rather than a strict succession of techniques, he contends, it is the "dominant characteristic" of the power regime that changes and the old techniques are made to work with or in the new ones (ECF-STP, 9–10). Even though there is a move "from a regime dominated by structures of sovereignty to a regime dominated by techniques of government," the new techniques do not replace sovereignty but rather instigate its sharpening (ECF-STP, 106–107).

According to Esposito (Esposito 2008, 43), the problem is that Foucault never decides his position. Esposito maintains that evidence can be found for two opposing theses regarding the relationship of biopower and sovereignty in Foucault's thought. One is the position that views the emergence of biopower as a radical break from sovereignty and emphasizes the differences and the novelty of biopower as well as its opposition to the features of sovereignty (the "discontinuist hypothesis"). The other position views biopower more in continuity with sovereign power and stresses their complementary character and superimposition on one another (the "continuist hypothesis"). Although on the one hand Foucault indicates the withdrawal and disappearance of sovereignty, on the other hand he postulates its continuing relevance and even its resurgence. In sum, Esposito contends, Foucault "continues to run simultaneously in both directions," leaving the connection between life and politics as an open question.

Foucault does not fully problematize the precise nature of the relationship between different modalities of power and the complementarity of their functioning but rather gives different and at times incompatible indications that present us with a real problem, and this lacuna has led to the flourishing of much scholarship addressing this question. Agamben (1998), for example, argues for the always already biopolitical nature of sovereignty. In contrast, Rose (2001) and Rabinow and Rose

(2006) put more emphasis on the increased dominance of biopower in the contemporary period. Dean (2001), for example, differentiates the articulation of biopower and sovereignty according to whether the political regimes in question are liberal, whereas Butler (2004) finds in the "liberal" war against terror, particularly as spatialized in Guantanamo Bay prison, elements indicating the resurgence of sovereignty within the field of governmentality.

These different views, inspired by the productive ambiguities across Foucault's major texts, enable us to isolate different structural articulations of the relationship between the forms of power in his thought more clearly and robustly. These articulations, which I will call (using metaphors from the organic world) *symbiosis*, *invasion*, and *parasitism*, are not necessarily mutually exclusive, nor always consistent, but they point us toward different models of synchronicity. Symbiosis, as one of the ways in which Foucault intimates the nature of the relationship, refers to a situation in which different modalities of power are separate but in a mutual interaction that is either beneficial to both or at least does not harm one while benefiting the other. Indications for this model of articulation can be found in Foucault's references to the relationship between different forms of power in various ways, such as coexistence, conjoining, dovetailing, embedding, complementation, support, and intersection.

For example, despite the fact that they are relegated to different regions, have different techniques, and are embedded in different legitimating discourses and fields of knowledge, Foucault points out that disciplinary power and sovereign power coexist and, in fact, enable and facilitate each other's exercise and development. Foucault's description of this relationship approximates terms suggestive of that between different layers of the base-superstructure model of Marxist theory, in this case substituting disciplinary power for the base and sovereign power for the superstructure. In this spirit, Foucault argues that disciplinary power functions within society through norms on which the laws of juridical power are "superimposed." On the one hand, sovereignty facilitates the development of disciplinary power both by functioning as a discourse of critique against absolutism, paving the way for the proliferation of disciplinary mechanisms, and by concealing the domination inherent in them from view. On the other hand, disciplinary power enables the democratization of sovereignty and increases the domain and effectiveness of state institutions (ECF-SMD, 37; EPK, 73). Foucault suggests that the juridical subject of sovereignty is an ideological representation, whereas the individual as the subject of discipline is a fabricated reality; in other words, both of these characterizations appear as two faces of the same subject, and thus they coexist and depend on each other. Sovereignty enables the functioning of discipline, and discipline ensures submission as the condition and support of juridical rights and liberties (EDP, 194, 222; EHS1, 144). Overall, Foucault contends, the pervasiveness of discipline "constituted the other, dark side" of the democratization of sovereign power (EDP, 222). In a parallel fashion, biopower and disciplinary power also coexist and operate in tandem, both establishing power over life but at different scales and with different techniques (EHS1, 139). Coinciding in concrete areas of operation such as sexuality, city planning, and housing projects, they also "intersect along an orthogonal articulation" (ECF-SMD, 253).

Invasion is the second way in which Foucault describes the relationship between different modalities of power. Foucault's descriptions suggesting invasion include colonization, penetration, infiltration, and permeation. The difference between symbiosis and invasion is that the latter involves a deeper connection, a more significant and thorough entanglement in which different modalities function in a combinatory fashion, mostly beneficially and resulting in reciprocal modification, utilization, accentuation, and containment (ECF-SMD, 241–242, 248–260; ECF-STP, 8, 107). For example, the "humble modalities, minor procedures" of disciplinary power (such as surveillance, normalizing judgment, and examination), Foucault argues, "invade the major forms [including law], altering their mechanisms and imposing their procedures" (EDP, 170). In this light, the generalization of imprisonment as the main form of punishment attests to the colonization of law by disciplinary power (EDP, 232). At the same time, Foucault locates the continuing presence of sovereign power in the recalcitrance of torture in the contemporary penal system, and yet this sovereign power is "enveloped, increasingly, by the non-corporeal nature of the penal system" (EDP, 16). Another example in which Foucault finds the invasion of sovereignty by discipline is the medal commemorating the military parade, where the visibility of the monarch is transferred on the visibility of his subjects (EDP, 189). Napoleon, with his spectacular embodiment of monarchical sovereignty and his simultaneous efforts to organize the state along panoptic lines, is exemplary of the entwined conjunction of sovereignty and discipline (EDP, 217).

Similarly, the institution of the police, as an important manifestation of the link between different forms of power, suggests that disciplinary power has "infiltrated the others, sometimes undermining them, but serving as an intermediary between them, linking them together, extending them and above all making it possible to bring the effects of power to the most minute and distant elements" (EDP, 216). At the same time, biopower also "penetrate[s]" and "permeate[s]" sovereignty (ECF-SMD, 241). The police, Foucault further argues, as one of the "technological assemblage[s]" deployed as part of the "art of government," along with diplomacy and the army, becomes the technique that ensures the regulation of the population, its numbers, necessities, health, activities, and economy, which thereby guarantees the longevity and strength of the state (ECF-STP, 312, 322–327). Foucault ventures, "The governmentalization of the state has nonetheless been what has allowed the state to survive" (ECF-STP, 109). Biopower also interacts with discipline: "[I]t does dovetail into it, integrate it, modify it to some extent, and above all, use it by sort of infiltrating it, embedding itself in existing disciplinary techniques" (SMD, 242). Eventually, Foucault concludes, the result is an interactive triangulation of different yet coexistent modalities of power (ECF-STP, 354).

Parasitism, as a third way of viewing the relationship between different modalities of power, refers to their dependence on the use of a new and external technique in order to coexist, combine, and function in conjunction. For the purpose of solving the problem of the synchronic operation of contradictory modalities of power, particularly the coexistence of the machinery of death and the political concern for life, which Foucault calls "one of the central antinomies of our political reason" (EEW3, 405), he proposes the concept of racism. Accordingly, racism is the method of distinguishing between "what must live and what must die" (ECF-SMD, 254), and it functions as the key mechanism that ties together sovereignty, discipline, and biopower. Racism, Foucault suggests, is the "basic mechanism of power, as it is exercised in modern States" – the mechanism that transforms the ability of states to produce death and destruction at hitherto unprecedented levels without letting go of the hold on life, both individually and at the aggregate level (ECF-SMD, 254).

Once it appears on the scene, racism brings different forms of power together, binds them to each other, and activates their simultaneous functioning while it feeds on and lives off all forms of power. Racism necessitates the preservation of state sovereignty for the protection of the "pure race." Sovereignty, already supported by "medico-normalizing techniques" rather than "magico-juridical rituals," in turn utilizes the discourse on race struggle (which, until then, has been used to challenge sovereignty) for its own ideological purposes (ECF-SMD, 80–83). Through the institutionalization of racism, the otherwise receding sovereign power is able to exercise its power to kill and to demand life. While racism thus legitimates sovereignty, it also legitimates the further government of life. In order to establish the health and purity of life on which racism depends, biopower must further penetrate society and ensure its well-being (however selectively). Sovereignty is now exercised not for the elimination of criminals or enemies but in order to achieve the elimination of the threat to the species and the improvement of one's own race. Similarly, biopower is exercised to strengthen and further cultivate the power of the state (ECF-SMD, 255–258). Hence, Foucault argues, the discourse of racism, present in the Nazi and Soviet states in particular and the workings of modern states in general, enables the uneasy and evolving coexistence of the different modalities of power into a conjunction where they are "absolutely coextensive" (EFC-SMD, 260). Such a parasitic articulation of the preoccupation with the vital processes of the population with the familiar power over life and death through racism creates horrific political consequences, not only for those who become the victims of this conjunction but also (suicidally) for the very population these forms of power are intended to protect.

In sum, sovereignty in Foucault's discourse is a versatile and rich concept, functioning as a negative point of reference for both his theoretical innovations and political aspirations while at the same time serving as an evolving and dynamic modality of power under increasing challenge and pressure by its novel counterparts. Despite the presence of certain internal contradictions and tensions in his oeuvre, in part owing to the evolution of Foucault's thought over time, the general tenor of Foucault's writings points us in the direction of the claim that neither disciplinary power nor biopower completely replaces sovereign power but that the latter survives, at times by incorporating and actively utilizing these new modalities, at times by being conquered by them from within, and at still other occasions being agglomerated with them by the dangerous parasitism of racism. Even when we decapitate the discourse of sovereignty within political theory, as Foucault has inspired us to do, we find that sovereignty itself does not disappear. In spite of having left its comfortable residence in the body of the beheaded king long ago, sovereignty manages to endure, revive, and reinvent itself as the power over life with, in, through, despite, *and* ultimately because of the power of life itself.

Banu Bargu

SEE ALSO

> *Biopower*
> *Body*
> *Governmentality*
> *Power*
> *Race (and Racism)*
> *State*

SUGGESTED READING

Agamben, Giorgio. 1998. *Homo Sacer: Sovereign Power and Bare Life*, trans. Daniel Heller-Roazen. Stanford, CA: Stanford University Press.

Butler, Judith. 2004. "Indefinite Detention," in *Precarious Life: The Power of Mourning and Violence*. London: Verso, pp. 50–100.

Dean, Mitchell. 2001. " 'Demonic Societies': Liberalism, Biopolitics, and Sovereignty," in *States of Imagination: Ethnographic Explorations of the Postcolonial State*, ed. Thomas Blom Hansen and Finn Stepputat. Durham, NC: Duke University Press, pp. 41–64.

Esposito, Roberto. 2008. *Bíos: Biopolitics and Philosophy*, trans. Timothy Campbell. Minneapolis: University of Minnesota Press.

Mbembe, Achille. 2008. "Neuropolitics," in *Foucault in an Age of Terror*, ed. Stephen Morton and Stephen Bygrave. London: Palgrave Macmillan, pp. 152–182.

Rabinow, Paul, and Nikolas Rose. 2006. "Bio-power Today," *BioSocieties* 1, no. 2:195–217.

Rose, Nikolas. 2001. "The Politics of Life Itself," *Theory, Culture and Society* 18, no. 6:1–30.

79

SPACE

FOR FOUCAULT, SPACE is the product of historical transitions and directly affects the ways things are understood, ordered, and transformed in the present. It is shot through with relations of power and shapes and is shaped by knowledge. Discussions of spaces run through Foucault's historical writings, but space only rarely took center stage as an object of analysis in itself. Three key pieces – an unpublished lecture and two interviews: "Of Other Spaces," "Questions on Geography," and "Space, Knowledge, Power" – are often seen as the key places to look for Foucault's ideas on space. Yet his work as a whole is infused with a much more pronounced, and arguably interesting, spatial attunement.

The lecture "Of Other Spaces" or "Different Spaces" discusses the term *heterotopia*, which might be more accurately translated as "another place." It was a lecture given to architects in 1967, but Foucault only permitted its publication shortly before his death (FDE4, 752–762). The piece is widely discussed for its reorientation of contemporary thought to questions of space.

> The great obsession of the nineteenth century was, as we know, history: themes of development and of suspension, themes of crisis and cycle, themes of the ever-accumulating past, with its overload of dead men, the threat of global cooling … the present epoch may be above all the epoch of space. We are in the epoch of simultaneity: we are in the epoch of juxtaposition, the epoch of the near and far, of the side-by-side, of the dispersed. We are at a moment, I believe, when our experience of the world is less that of a long life developing through time than that of a network that connects points and weaves its skein. (FDE4, 752)

What Foucault does in this piece is offer a brief history of space, before using the idea of differently ordered spaces to think about alternative orderings in the present.

He stresses that "space itself, in the Western experience, has a history" not simply in terms of different arrangements but in its very understanding. He appears to be fairly indiscriminate in his use of geographical vocabulary, using terms such as *place*, *lieu*, *espace*, and *emplacement* in what might appear to be a fairly loose way. There is, however, an understanding of how the meanings attached to these terms have changed. Foucault suggests that in the Middle Ages there was a "hierarchized ensemble of places [*lieux*]." These are often in contrasting pairs: sacred and profane; protected and open, exposed places; urban and rural places; supracelestial, celestial, and terrestrial places; and so on. Foucault calls this "medieval space – a space of localization." This was opened up by Galileo, who Foucault gives credit for constituting an infinite and infinitely open space. To think of a thing's place was now only to conceive of it as a point in its movement. The medieval space of localization was replaced by extension. In the contemporary period, the understanding of space on the basis of extension has itself been replaced by the notion of site [*emplacement*]. Foucault is interested in what might be called networks of connections through ideas such as series, trees, and lattices: "The site is defined by relations of proximity [*voisonage*] between points or elements" (FDE4, 753). The most concrete question that arises from this understanding of place [*place*] or site is that of demography: "We are in an epoch where space takes for us the form of relations among sites" (FDE4, 752–754).

Thus the lecture moves beyond the historical to look at the present moment, suggesting a distinction between utopias – nonplaces or happy places – and heterotopias, which are actually existing alternative spatial orderings. Foucault calls utopias "sites with no real place" and heterotopias "counter-sites, kinds of effectively enacted utopias" (FDE4, 755). He gives plenty of examples. He talks of the "crisis heterotopias" that existed in primitive societies for people in states of crisis or transition but that we retain in such sites as the boarding school, military barracks, or the honeymoon hotel. There are heterotopias of deviation such as rest homes, psychiatric hospitals, prisons, and old people's homes. Foucault then moves through a range of different spaces: the cemetery; theatres, cinemas, gardens, and carpets; museums and libraries – accumulations of time and, in contrast, sites of fleeting time – traveling fairgrounds; Polynesian vacation villages; and various others, including Muslim hammans, Scandinavian saunas, American motel rooms, brothels, ships, and Jesuit colonies in South America (FDE4, 756–762). Foucault did not develop these ideas further, but they have been taken up by a range of writers since their publication.

In 1976, in the first issue of the new journal *Hérodote*, Foucault responded to a range of questions from radical French geographers (FDE3, 28–40). *Hérodote* was named after the Greek writer Herodotus, who the founders of the journal wished to honor not simply for his historical writings but for his geographical sensitivity. In the interview, Foucault recognizes his own "spatial obsessions" (FDE3, 33) but continually tries to get the geographers to recognize the power and knowledge aspects to the spatial questions or topics they present him with.

> *Territory* is no doubt a geographical notion, but it's first of all a juridico-political one: the area controlled by a certain kind of power. *Field* is an economico-juridical notion. *Displacement*: what displaces itself is an army, a squadron, a population. *Domain* is a juridico-political notion. *Soil* is a historico-geological notion. *Region* is a fiscal, administrative, military notion. *Horizon* is a pictorial, but also a strategic notion. (FDE3, 32)

Foucault raises a whole range of examples to illustrate and illuminate his answers in a rich piece whose many facets have still not been fully exploited by geographers. His closing comments are, however, widely cited:

> Now I can see that the problems you put to me about geography are crucial ones for me. Geography acted as the support, the condition of possibility for the passage between a series of factors I tried to relate.... Geography must indeed necessarily lie at the heart of my concerns. (FDE3, 39–40)

What is much less well known is that Foucault went back to the journal a couple of issues later and posed some questions back to the geographers (FDE3, 94–95). His questions looked at the relation of strategy; the scientific status of the geographers' attempt at a "knowledge of spaces"; the link between space, production, and power more generally; and the geography of medicine. The editors commissioned a number of responses by Francophone geographers (some translated in Crampton and Elden 2007). Foucault was further pressed on some of these claims in an interview with Paul Rabinow entitled "Space, Knowledge, and Power" that originally appeared in the architecture journal *Skyline* (EFR, 239–256). Foucault highlights a shift during the eighteenth century where discourses on architecture and planning became more explicitly politicized, or perhaps politics became more explicitly spatialized, where "every discussion of politics as the art of the government of men necessarily includes a chapter or a series of chapters on urbanism, on collective facilities, on hygiene, and on private architecture" (EFR, 240).

In terms of questions of knowledge, it is striking how often Foucault uses spatialized vocabulary to describe it. He writes his history of madness as a history of limits, a limit that is always a division (EHM, xxix–xxx), and regularly uses terms such as threshold, transgression, and boundary. Foucault suggests that the spatial metaphors he used were not his own choices but ones that emerged from the subject matter he was examining: spatial techniques, not metaphors (EFR, 254). To read Foucault as simply using spatial metaphors in his histories would be seriously misleading. In *The*

Archaeology of Knowledge and elsewhere, he uses the military term *réparage* to designate mapping, locating (EAK, 116). This political-strategic understanding becomes more prominent in his later writings, although it can be seen in his earlier histories, too. It is in these historical writings, rather than the three shorter pieces noted earlier, that we find more careful examinations of space. Here Foucault uses space in a more active sense, where spatial orderings change how discipline works, how the mad are confined, how sexuality is regulated, and how cities are governed. This can be found in his work looking at madhouses and lazarettos, plans for hospitals, prisons, and idealized cities, the army camp, and the public school.

This spatial analysis is pronounced in *The History of Madness*, where Foucault examines how lepers, the venereally diseased, and the mad are excluded, confined, or otherwise positioned by the operations of power. This operation, Foucault suggests, often works in at least two registers, where the asylum replaced the lazaretto both in the "geography of haunted places and in the landscape of the moral universe" (EHM, 71). Foucault's analyses of the spaces of the Tuke's retreat in York are filled with a sensitivity to the ordering of space, through the architectural design and the landscaping of the grounds. Foucault returns to similar topics a decade later in the *Psychiatric Power* lectures (ECF-PP), yet now with a more explicitly developed conceptual vocabulary of power.

Foucault's work on medicine also demonstrates these interests. The opening line of *The Birth of the Clinic* makes this explicit: "This book is about space, about language, and about death; it is a question of the gaze" (EBC, ix). Foucault suggests that there are three levels of spatialization of medicine, where the disease is defined by its *place* in a family, its situation in an organism, and then "all the gestures by which, in a given society, a disease is circumscribed, medically invested, isolated, divided up into closed, privileged regions, or distributed throughout cure centers, arranged in the most favourable way." There are three registers: classifications of knowledge, the body, and the space of political, economic, and social struggle. It is in the latter that the basis for changes to medical knowledge must be situated (EBC, 16). The last is more fully explored not in *The Birth of the Clinic* but in some remarkable lectures given to the Institute of Social Medicine in Rio de Janeiro in October 1974 (FDE3, 40–58, 207–228, 508–521). Here Foucault looks at the architectural design of hospitals, where they are situated in relation to the towns they serve, and how medicine exceeds the bounds of the institution into the wider community. He states that the "question of the hospital at the end of the eighteenth century was fundamentally a question of space" (FDE3, 518).

The classic spatial form analyzed in *Discipline and Punish* is Jeremy Bentham's design for the Panopticon. Yet the focus on this model is perhaps misjudged: Foucault only discusses it relatively briefly, and notes that he came to it through his earlier work on hospital architecture. In *Discipline and Punish* and a few other places (i.e., FDE3, 517–518), Foucault introduces it as the combination of two different forms of spatial ordering: the exclusion of the leper and the ordering of the plague town. In a town affected by the plague, areas are quarantined, people's movement is controlled, and there is careful surveillance and inspection. Foucault describes it as an operation of "multiple separations, individualizing distributions, an organization in depth of surveillance and control, an intensification and a ramification of power" (EDP, 198). In an idealized prison such as a Panopticon, the space of exclusion is itself divided and controlled: a combination of two previously contrasting models.

This book is arguably more interesting for the broader phenomenon of panopticism, which is a means by which society as a whole is surveyed and ordered. Foucault states that "discipline is above all, analysis of space; it is individualization through space, the placing of bodies in an individualized space which permits classification and combinations" (FDE3, 515). This includes such means as enclosure, partitioning, coding or recoding of spaces, and their classification in a rank. These operate both at the level of physical space – architecture, landscapes, town plans, designs for army camps, and furniture and other objects of control – and in attendant plans, tabulations, organizations, and schemes. Foucault outlines how these work in three pairs that recall some of his concerns in *The Order of Things*: "tactics, the spatial ordering of men; taxonomy, the disciplinary space of natural beings; the economic table, the regulated movement of wealth" (EDP, 141–149; see FCF-FDS, 215, 223–224).

In *The History of Sexuality* and his lectures, Foucault provides plenty of other examples of spatial orderings. In his work on governmentality, for instance, he suggests that territory as an object of government has been displaced, with a new emphasis on population, but still provides considerable attention to the design of towns, the spaces of security, and what he calls the "qualities of territory" (ECF-STP). Many of the collaborative projects he was involved with in the 1970s showed attention to these topics, with projects on green spaces, urban infrastructure, transport systems, and hospital architecture (see Elden 2008). There are other places where Foucault discusses space, in terms of literature, art, or the ordering of libraries (FDE1, 407–412; EDL; ELCP). This widespread interest in space is one of the reasons he has been such an influential thinker within the discipline of geography. Foucault is less interested in providing a definition of space than with outlining different ways in which space has been understood, transformed, and effected, and the effects it has. With Foucault's historical studies predominantly concentrating on the seventeenth to the nineteenth centuries, it is unsurprising that the notion of extended, calculable space is preeminent; spaces that are classified, segmented, ordered, and where exclusions are made and policed. As Foucault declares, "Space is fundamental in any form of communal life; space is fundamental in any exercise of power" (EFR, 252).

Stuart Elden

SEE ALSO

Madness
Outside
Painting (and Photography)
Plague
Strategies

SUGGESTED READING

Crampton, Jeremy, and Stuart Elden, eds. 2007. *Space, Knowledge and Power: Foucault and Geography*. Aldershot: Ashgate.
Driver, Felix. 1985. "Power, Space and the Body: A Critical Assessment of Foucault's Discipline and Punish," *Environment and Planning D: Society and Space* 3:425–446.
Elden, Stuart. 2001. *Mapping the Present: Heidegger, Foucault and the Project of a Spatial History*. London: Continuum.
    2007. "Governmentality, Calculation, Territory," *Environment and Planning D: Society and Space* 25, no. 3:562–580.
Flynn, Thomas R. 1991. "Foucault and the Spaces of History," *The Monist* 74, no. 2 (April): 165–186.
    1997. *Sartre, Foucault, and Historical Reason*, volume 1: *Toward an Existentialist Theory of History*. Chicago: University of Chicago Press.
    2005. *Sartre, Foucault, and Historical Reason*, volume 2: *A Poststructuralist Mapping of History*. Chicago: University of Chicago.
Gregory, Derek. 1994. *Geographical Imaginations*. Cambridge, MA: Blackwell.
Hannah, Matthew. 2000. *Governmentality and the Mastery of Territory in Nineteenth-Century America*. Cambridge: Cambridge University Press.
Hetherington, Kevin. 1997. *The Badlands of Modernity: Heterotopia and Social Ordering*. London: Routledge.
Philo, Chris. 1992. "Foucault's Geographies," *Environment and Planning D: Society and Space* 10, no. 2:137–161.
    2004. *A Geographical History of Institutional Provision for the Insane from Medieval Times to the 1860s in England and Wales: The Space Reserved for Insanity*. Lewiston: Edwin Mellen.
Soja, Edward W. 1989. *Postmodern Geographies: The Reassertion of Space in Critical Social Theory*. London: Verso.
Teyssot, Georges. 2000. "Heterotopias and the History of Spaces," in *Architectural Theory since 1968*, ed. K. Michael Hays. Cambridge, MA: The MIT Press, pp. 296–305.

80

SPIRITUALITY

S PIRITUALITY IS NOT primarily a religious or theological concept for
Foucault. Rather, he defines it as "the set of these researches, practices, and
experiences, which may be purifications, ascetic exercises, renunciations, con-
versions of looking, modifications of existence, etc., which are, not for knowledge
but for the subject, for the subject's very being, the price to be paid for access to the
truth" (ECF-HOS, 15). Spirituality, then, has to do with the way in which the subject
gains access to the truth. In other words, it has to do with the relation between subjectivity and truth (ECF-HOS, 2). This relationship between subjectivity and truth
entails three distinctive "postulates" (ECF-HOS, 15). First, the subject does not have
in its nature or structure any automatic right or inherent access to the truth. In other
words, the very being or structure of the thinking, perceiving, willing subject blocks
its access to the truth. Second, the subject, in order to gain access to the truth, must
undergo a conversion, must transform her very being or structure qua subject. The
subject must, as Foucault frequently puts it, "pay a price in its very being qua subject." This price involves a labor (*askesis*) performed by the subject on itself in order
to transform its way of being in order to bring about a "conversion of the gaze" and
a modification of its manner of existing. The subject must undergo something like
a trial (*épreuve*). This price having been paid, the subject will achieve a new mode of
existing and perceiving in which it will be able to grasp truth. Finally, the truth that
one gains by paying the price of conversion is not simply a matter of correspondence
or coherence but rather has "return effects" on the subject: "[T]he truth gives beat-
itude to the subject; the truth gives the subject tranquility of soul" (ECF-HOS, 16).
Truth, in other words, does not primarily qualify a thought or statement in its relation to a given state of affairs or to other statements in a system but rather it "fulfills
or transfigures his very being" (ibid.).

Foucault argues that "throughout the period we call Antiquity, and in quite
different modalities, the philosophical question of 'how to have access to the truth'

472

and the practice of spirituality (of the necessary transformations in the very being of the subject which will allow access to the truth) ... were never separate" (ECF-HOS, 17). In other words, the primary task for the philosophers of antiquity was the labor through which the subject was able to undergo a conversion and consequently gain access to the truth understood as the fulfillment of one's being.

The modern era of truth begins when philosophy and spirituality become detached from each other and when access to truth no longer requires spirituality: "In European culture up to the sixteenth century, the problem remains: What is the work I must effect upon myself so as to be capable and worthy of acceding to the truth? To put it another way: truth always has a price; no access to truth without ascesis" (EEW1, 279). Descartes, according to Foucault, helped to usher in this modern age "when he said, 'To accede to truth, it suffices that I be any subject that can see what is evident.' Evidence is substituted for ascesis.... This change makes possible the institutionalization of modern science" (EEW1, 279). In the modern era, the subject is related to truth through knowledge understood as a purely mental or cognitive experience of evidence that allows us to verify the relationship between statements and objective states of affairs. In other words, the thinking, perceiving subject is thought to have a natural right and capacity to know the truth and therefore does not need to pay a price in its very being in order to gain access to truth. Furthermore, truth in the modern sense does not have any "return effects" on the subject who knows. Rather it merely has to do with the relationship between propositions and states of affairs and is indifferent to the subject who makes the propositions (EEW1, 279; ECF-HOS, 15–19).

It should be clear that Foucault's interest in spirituality cannot be described as epistemological – rather the fundamental point is that the relationship of subjectivity and truth is not exclusively epistemological but rather is ethical and even political. It is ethical insofar as the subject must transform her relationship to her self and the way she lives in order to gain access to the truth and to live a true life (EEW, 279). It is political, in a broad sense, because spirituality defines not only the subject's relation to herself, her life, and truth but to other subjects and to the political community. Returning to antiquity, Foucault shows that individuals practiced spirituality (i.e., philosophy) in order to gain access to the truth that was necessary for effective political engagement, in particular in order to become capable of speaking the truth before the assembly (see especially ECF-HOS; ECF-GSO; ECF-COT). True discourse was central to the function of the democratic polis; hence truth was political (see ECF-GSO; ECF-COT). Furthermore, spirituality involved relationships of spiritual direction. In order to learn to properly conduct oneself – to properly govern oneself – one needed the assistance of a spiritual director: one allowed oneself to be governed and directed by another in order to bring about the self-transformation necessary to be capable of governing oneself truly. Only once one has become capable of truly governing oneself can one begin to govern others in the political field of the polis. Thus spirituality entailed multiple interconnected relationships of power and government – the government of the self by the spiritual director, the government of the self by her self, and the democratic government of other citizens in the political field.

Foucault's genealogies show that the spirituality of ancient philosophers was incorporated into Christianity and deeply transformed by this appropriation (see, for example, ECF-HOS, 10). Central to the development of Christianity was the formation of intense and permanent relationships of spiritual direction involving very precisely defined practices and forms of subjectivity. It is this effort at spiritual direction – the government of souls – that takes shape as the Christian pastorate, or what Foucault calls "pastoral power" (ECF-STP, 115-190). It is a field of complex relationships of power and knowledge in which pastors govern the souls of the individual members of the flock. Pastoral power governed individuals in a way that was quite different from the simple enforcement of laws. The pastor did not wield power in the manner of a political sovereign who rules over subjects. Rather, pastors governed individuals through practices of spiritual direction geared toward the spiritual growth and salvation of the individual being directed. In other words, whereas sovereign power imposes the law on the anonymous totality of subjects, the pastor comes to know each individual intimately and customizes his efforts toward the specific spiritual needs, temptations, habits, and traits of the individual. Pastoral power produced individualized knowledge of the thoughts, desires, and behaviors of individuals that it used to help guide individuals toward their own salvation. In pastoral power, the production of truth is central to the government of souls.

The growth of pastoral power gave rise to numerous forms of resistance. In other words, as individuals came to feel the increasing power of pastoral government in their lives and even in their own thoughts and desires, they revolted against it. But these revolts are not like the political revolutions that aim to overturn a sovereign or rewrite the law: "They are revolts of conduct" (ECF-STP, 196). They are what Foucault calls "counter-conducts" (ECF-STP, 201). They aim not to escape from government as such but rather to create other ways of governing oneself and others that run counter to the pastoral government of life. In other words, counter-conducts seek out a different way of practicing spirituality and spiritual direction, different forms of *askesis*, and different relationships to spiritual directors.

It is a crisis of conduct, then, that set the stage for Descartes and the rise of a modern era in which philosophy and science are detached from spirituality. "If Descartes' philosophy is taken as the foundation of philosophy, we should also see it as the outcome of this great transformation that brought about the reappearance of philosophy in terms of the question: "How to conduct oneself"" (ECF-STP, 230)? In other words, Descartes' philosophy can be seen as a form of counter-conduct insofar as it attempts to define a form of the government of the self, the conduct of the mind, toward the truth. But Foucault notes that "the extraordinary thing in Descartes' texts is that he succeeded in substituting a subject as founder of practices of knowledge for a subject constituted through practices of the self" (EEW1, 278). This brings us back to the point where we can see the rupture of philosophy and spirituality. In his effort to define a form of self-government, a spiritual practice that will lead one to the truth, Descartes ends up displacing spirituality as the relationship of subjectivity and truth: "With Descartes, direct evidence is enough. After Descartes, we have a non-ascetic subject of knowledge" (EEW1, 279).

The implications of Foucault's genealogy of spirituality for his diagnosis of our present actuality are profound. The most controversial aspect of these is apparent in Foucault's reports from Iran during the period just before the overthrow of the Shah, about which Foucault wrote: "For the people who inhabit this land, what is the point of searching, even at the cost of their own lives, for this thing whose possibility we have forgotten since the Renaissance and the great crisis of Christianity, a *political spirituality*?" (Afary and Anderson 2005, 209; FDE3, 694). This claim must be seen in light of Foucault's analysis of spirituality as the transformative relationship between the subject and truth, and his genealogy of the rise and dispersal of Christian pastoral power. Since the time of Descartes and in the modern era, in which spirituality has been separated from the quest for truth in philosophy and science, the West has "forgotten" its own political spirituality. What fascinated Foucault about the Iranian Revolution was the way in which it was, he thought, a "revolt of conduct." It suggested the possibility of a new configuration of spirituality, a new form of the government of oneself and others. In other words, what made this revolution a *political spirituality* was not its commitment to Islamic doctrines so much as the way it gave expression to "the will to discover a different way of governing oneself through a different way of dividing up the true and the false – this is what I would call 'political spirituality'" (EEW3, 233).

Foucault's thought reminds us of the spiritual potential harbored in our literature, ethics, politics, and forms of knowledge. He sought out revolts of conduct operating in the modern West – modern art and literature, prisoner rights movements, gay rights, women's movements, and the Solidarity movement in Poland, to name a few. His genealogy of the relation between spirituality and philosophy suggested the possibility of a renewal of spirituality, and political spirituality, in our intellectual lives. This does not mean that he sought some sort of theocracy or faith-based politics. Nor does it mean that he was engaged in a retrieval of particular spiritual or political forms from the past. Rather it means that he was decidedly in favor of proliferating experiments in the transformation of subjectivity in order to gain access to the truth and to search for new forms of the connection between government (of self and others) and truth.

Edward McGushin

SEE ALSO

Christianity
Conduct
Ethics
Revolution
Self
Truth
René Descartes

SUGGESTED READING

Afary, Janet, and Kevin B. Anderson. 2005. *Foucault and the Iranian Revolution: Gender and the Seductions of Islamism*. Chicago: University of Chicago Press.

Carrette, Jeremy. 2000. *Foucault and Religion: Spiritual Corporality and Political Spirituality*. London: Routledge.

McGushin, Edward. 2007. *Foucault's Askesis: An Introduction to the Philosophical Life*. Evanston, IL: Northwestern University Press.

81

STATE

FOR MOST OF his career, Foucault said nothing in particular about the state. He did not begin to reflect on it until the mid-1970s. His interest in the concept intensified in the late 1970s before again disappearing from view in the 1980s. In the short period of time that he wrote and spoke about the state, primarily in three courses at the Collège de France between 1976 and 1979, however, his reflections developed significantly around his invention of the new concept of "governmentality"; that is, of variable "governmental rationalities," discourses that shape the state.

The lack of attention to the state before the mid-1970s is surprising inasmuch as much of Foucault's work before that point had already been political, from the *History of Madness* in 1961 to *Discipline and Punish* in 1975. He dealt with political issues without thematizing the state as such, though of course he did not completely exclude the state, which would be all but impossible when discussing questions of public policy, as these works do (ECF-BBIO, 77). He neither ignored nor denied the existence of the state, nor refused to use its name, but he did not focus on it. Still, even this lack of thematization of the state was a relatively radical refusal, given a prevailing expectation that any political work had to address the question of the state. Foucault therefore deliberately chose to bracket the question. When he did come to address it, he did so in a way consonant with the earlier bracketing, by arguing that too much weight was given to the state in political theory and that this needed to be corrected by "cutting the head off the king."

Beginning in 1976 with his lecture series "Society Must Be Defended" and the first volume of his *History of Sexuality*, Foucault put the state in its place, within the framework of his radically novel account of power. Whereas earlier political theory had tended to see the state as the command center of social power relations, Foucault assigned power priority over the state, with the latter as "superstructural" in relation to the former (EPK, 151). For him, "the state is a codification of multiple

477

power relations which permit it to function" (FDE3, 151, my translation; cf. EPK, 122). Although the state may be an enormously important point for the organization of power relations (FDE2, 812), power relations preexisted the state and it is ultimately to them that we must turn to understand politics.

Foucault's distinctive perspective means seeing the state, revolution, politics, and war as essentially the same, inasmuch as they are each different codifications of power relations. The obvious differences we see between war and peace are, for him, the products of the differential operations of power.

Foucault sees his position here as an outgrowth of a certain tendency in the history of the theory of the state. In *Society Must Be Defended*, he traces reflection on the state to a "historico-political discourse" that emerged once the state was established as such toward the end of the sixteenth century. The state had emerged via the expulsion of war to limit the state, ending the medieval situation in which the right of substate actors to use force was ended in favor of a state monopoly of violence (ECF-SMD, 49). A discourse then emerged, first around the English Civil War, that argued that the state was not natural, as it had seemed before, but rather the tool for the domination of a class who had conquered the country as invaders centuries earlier, thus advocating the reopening of the concealed war and overthrow of that class (ECF-SMD, 50). Against this view emerged the view, most prominently exemplified by Thomas Hobbes, that the state mediates or subsumes the war that comes before, urging support for the state. Other accounts of the state followed. Around the French Revolution, a conception of the state as synonymous with the nation arose, identified with Abbé Sieyès in particular, which Foucault (ECF-SMD, 219) sees as making a decisive break with all previous perspectives, including Rousseau's superficially similar position. Thereafter, yet another perspective arises, which viewed conflict over state power as an attempt to produce a universal state (ECF-SMD, 225).

Foucault's own perspective harks back to the oldest view of the state, as the product of a conflict that it does not reconcile, though his position is more complex than any earlier view: he does not see the conflict as between two groups, does not see any group as ever decisively capturing state power, and does not believe in the possibility of a universal state.

The different theories of the state have had powerful recursive effects, within a power-knowledge nexus, on the way politics was actually organized. This recursivity is at the heart of Foucault's 1978 lecture series "Security, Territory, Population." *Society Must Be Defended* effectively ends its account of the history of state in the nineteenth century, with Foucault going on to study the actual constitution of the state after that point. Foucault's next two years of Collège de France lectures (resuming after a hiatus in 1977) fill out this lacuna.

The explicit theme of the lectures of these two years is not so much the state as *government*. For Foucault, government is a very large area of discourse, encompassing questions of personal conduct as well as statecraft, but here Foucault is in fact focused on government in the narrow sense; that is, the intersection of governmentality with the state, what he calls the "government of the state" (ECF-STP, 89). The coincidence of government and state occurs initially through a theory of state that Foucault calls *raison d'État*. This term appears untranslated in the English version of the lectures, though Foucault in his own lectures in English in the United States uses the phrase "reason of state" (EEW3, 406–407). This mode of governmental reason took the state as the sole object of government, privileging it, making it synonymous with government or politics (ECF-STP, 287). *Raison d'État* for Foucault is the first self-conscious theoretization of the state form in history. It is more than a theory, however; it is a governmental rationality, which means it had a direct influence on the way the state was run in practice (see ECF-STP, 276–277). However, this does not mean that the state simply embodied the theory. Although *raison d'État* saw the state as all-powerful, it could not make the state be all-powerful. It could only serve to increase the state's prominence relatively. There were contrary tendencies, in practice and in theory. In particular, *raison d'État* could be said to have generated its opposite, an eschatological revolutionary discourse that posited the complete disappearance of the state as its goal (ECF-STP, 356).

This way of thinking, though diametrically opposed to *raison d'État*, nevertheless for Foucault belongs to the same general conception of the state by according it much more importance than it should have. Here we see an instance of the overvaluation of the state that Foucault elsewhere calls "state-phobia" (ECF-BBIO, 76). He coined this phrase in relation to twentieth-century thought, but it was clearly already present in the nineteenth century. Foucault sees state-phobia as taking two forms. Most obviously, it takes the form of viewing the state as a "cold monster" (a phrase of Nietzsche's that Foucault invokes here), which is anarchist in its implication that the state is generically evil. More subtly, there is a discourse that reduces the state to certain specific functions. As Foucault notes, it is not obvious how such a view overvalues the state, since it sees the power of the state as distinctly limited. However, it does view the state as the crucial point in the power structure, the point both to be attacked and to be won in politics. This position is surely supposed to represent Marxism. Against all forms of overvaluation of the state, Foucault argues that "the state, doubtless no more today than in the past, does not have this unity, individuality, and rigorous functionality, nor, I would go so far as to say, this importance. After all, maybe the state is only a composite reality and a mythicized abstraction whose importance is much less than we think" (ECF-STP, 109).

Is not Foucault himself state-phobic in making such remarks? Not in the sense he means. Throughout his career, he is consistently hostile to the use of the notion of the state as a central concept in political theory, and what he calls state-phobia is part of the overvaluation he opposes. For Foucault, to hate the state is a mistake, if only because it makes the state more important than it is in reality.

Relatedly, Foucault holds that it is not the *étatisation* (literally "state-isation") of society that is the political problem in relation to the state today, "so much as what I would call the 'governmentalization' of the state" (ECF-STP, 109). It is not that Foucault thinks that *étatisation* has never been a problem – at least, he clearly claims in *The Will to Knowledge* that Nazism was an "unlimited *étatisation*" (FHS1, 197; cf. EHS1, 150), albeit one that served as a cover for what was going on in terms of micropowers (cf. ECF-BBIO, 77). Rather, he simply does not think that this is the current problem. Instead, the contemporary situation is marked by an opposite tendency, the hegemony of a state-phobic governmentality, which is the subject of his next series of lectures, 1979's "The Birth of Biopolitics." This governmentality is neoliberalism.

Foucault argues that *raison d'État*'s focus on the state made the state autonomous but that other governmentalities can produce different state forms (ECF-BBIO, 6). In liberalism, the state is justified solely by reference to its function of ensuring the freedoms of subjects outside the state, in civil society. The state is seen as a potential danger to these freedoms, requiring restriction. In neoliberalism, this vision acquires a particularly economic complexion: the state is justified only to the extent that it helps an economy of private enterprise without impinging on it. Liberalism produces no theory of the state, only of government, argues Foucault (ECF-BBIO, 91).

Foucault suggests a three-stage account of historical state forms: first the feudal, sovereign state, followed by the administrative, disciplinary state, and then more recently the governmental state (ECF-STP, 110). *Raison d'État* is associated with the second of these stages, which Foucault also refers to as the "police state." Neoliberalism must be identified with the third. That the state today is for Foucault peculiarly "governmental" does not, however, imply that he thinks that government is unique to this form of state. Rather, he thinks that the state today has been peculiarly "governmentalized," that this governmentalization is essential to the state today, and indeed "has allowed the state to survive" (ECF-STP, 109). The reason government has been crucial to the survival of the state is that it straddles the boundary between the state and its outside, thus providing the means for the adjustment of the state in relation to external pressures. However, this is a matter only of a growth in prominence of government in relation to the state form: government is older than the state; "the state is an episode in Governmentality" (ECF-STP, 248). Indeed, the state is founded on government: the state as a concept is distinctive of "governmental reason" (ECF-STP, 286).

A point of difficulty and possible confusion here is how to link this description of the state back to the diagnosis of contemporary "biopolitics" in *Society Must Be Defended*. Foucault characterizes contemporary states as concerned with the "bioregulation" of populations (ECF-SMD, 250). He names the mechanism by which the life protected by biopolitics is differentiated from that which can be killed or allowed to die "state racism," referring it explicitly to the state (ECF-SMD, 256). The reason that this is "state" racism, one can surmise, is that the state has a decisive role in relation both to the regulation of populations and to the use of force. Biopolitics ultimately, however, is rather indifferent to the division between the state and its outside, though it obviously requires some form of state. It is not a governmentality, and for Foucault it is instantiated in forms as diverse as Nazism and neoliberalism. Governmentality is, however, crucial to it, as the means of coordinating biopolitics across the boundary of the state, whether by focusing on the state or seeking to limit it.

Mark Kelly

SEE ALSO

> *Biopolitics*
> *Governmentality*
> *Power*
> *Resistance*

SUGGESTED READING

Jessop, Robert. 2006. "From Micro-powers to Governmentality: Foucault's Work on Statehood, State Formation, Statecraft and State Power," *Political Geography* 26, no. 1: 34–40.

82

STATEMENT

N *THE ARCHAEOLOGY OF KNOWLEDGE*, the statement initially appears as the basic, irreducible element that constitutes discourses, just as the atom is the basic unit that comprises all molecules: "At first sight, the statement appears as an ultimate, undecomposable element that can be isolated and introduced into a set of relations with other similar elements ... [t]he atom of discourse" (EAK, 80). (Foucault's use of an analogy to physics here is worth noting because he will use similar analogies in his later analyses of power relations.) However, Foucault explains, this atomic analogy is not entirely correct: although groups of statements do constitute discourses, the statement is not so much an element or unit as a function, which he terms the "enunciative function." Foucault observes, in a passage giving his most succinct definition of the statement, that:

> I could not define the statement as a unit of a linguistic type (superior to the phenomenon of the word, inferior to the text); but that I was dealing with an enunciative function that involved various units (these may sometimes be sentences, sometimes propositions; but they are sometimes made up of fragments of sentences, series or tables of signs, a set of propositions or equivalent formulations); and, instead of giving a "meaning" to these units, this function relates them to a field of objects; instead of providing them with a subject, it opens up for them a number of possible subjective positions; instead of fixing their limits, it places them in a domain of coordination and coexistence; instead of determining their identity, it places them in a space in which they are used and repeated. In short, what has been discovered is not the atomic statement ... but the operational field of the enunciative function and the conditions according to which it reveals various units. (EAK, 106)

Foucault arrives at this definition first by distinguishing the statement from a series of similar phenomena (propositions in logic, sentences in language, and speech acts in analytical philosophy). He then identifies a number of the statement's characteristics, each again distinguished from a misunderstanding (which are noted in the series of "instead of" phrases in the preceding quotation). This procedure allows him to define the statement as an "enunciative function" that constitutes discourses and can be analyzed with "archaeological" methods.

Although there are similarities and overlaps between these various concepts, a statement cannot be simply defined as or reduced to a proposition, a sentence, or a speech act. In the first case, there may be multiple different statements – which are situated in different discursive groupings or discourses – which express only one proposition. For example, the statements "No one heard" and "It is true that no one heard" express only one proposition but are not equivalent. In a novel, the former could be "an observation made either by the author, or by a character," but the latter "can only be in a group of statements constituting an interior dialogue" (EAK, 81). These two statements, in other words, have different enunciative characteristics, even if they are logically equivalent. Nor can statements be equated to sentences. Although ungrammatical statements like "Of course!" or "Hey, you!" can legitimately and correctly be called sentences, there are other statements that simply cannot be so described. Conjugation tables (such as, in a Latin textbook, "*amo, amas, amat*"), for example, are not sentences but are most definitely statements (EAK, 82). Finally, statements are not reducible to speech acts either. To give but one example, some speech acts require multiple statements to be effective. The act of becoming engaged to be married requires both a proposal and an acceptance – two quite distinct statements. Foucault explains: "When one wishes to individualize statements, one cannot therefore accept unreservedly any of the models borrowed from grammar, logic, or 'analysis.' ... Although the statement sometimes takes on the forms described and adjusts itself to them exactly, it does not always do so" (EAK, 84).

The next step toward a definition of the statement is to bring out certain characteristics by contrasting them with common misconceptions. Foucault enumerates four such contrasts in the preceding definition. First, "instead of giving a 'meaning' to these units, this function relates them to a field of objects" (EAK, 106). Statements are correlated to a field of objects, but (following the distinctions just made) not as names are correlated with their designees, propositions with referents, or sentences with meanings: "It is linked rather to a 'referential' that is made up not of 'things', 'facts', 'realities', or 'beings', but of laws of possibility, rules of existence for the objects that are named, designated, or described within it, and for the relations that are affirmed or denied in it" (EAK, 91). That is, statements' referentials define "the possibilities of appearance and delimitation of that which gives meaning to the sentence, a value as truth to the proposition" (EAK, 91). Statements demarcate what meanings are possible for sentences. Second, statements do not presuppose a speaking subject as cogito; rather, they create the possibility of assigning one (or more) subject position(s) to a group of signs. A mathematical treatise may encode multiple subject positions: the personal author, whose voice speaks in the acknowledgments and preface; a person-neutral subject position which speaks in the statement of axioms; and other positions (EAK, 94). Third, statements function within a network of other statements – it is this complex web that distinguishes a statement as such: "There is no statement that does not presuppose others; there is no statement that is not surrounded by a field of coexistences, effects of series and succession, a distribution of functions and roles" (EAK, 99). Statements will effectuate distinct enunciative functions by virtue of their position within such a discursive web. Finally, statements have a material existence – they serve to place the units (sentences, propositions, etc.) in a usable space by being voiced, written, published, and so on under certain circumstances. Thus a sentence may be reiterated in different contexts, in which it constitutes different statements, with different effects. But statements, too, are thus limited "by all the other statements among which it figures, by the domain in which it can be used or applied, by the role and functions that it can perform" (EAK, 103).

Each of these four distinctions illustrates that statements serve to demarcate or delimit a field of objects and their possible, permissible, impossible, and impermissible combinations. Thus, what distinguishes and defines a statement is not its form (as proposition, sentence, etc.) but its enunciative function – which is itself reflective of the discursive field in which the statement is realized and which the statement in turn reciprocally serves to constitute. This field includes "all the other formulations with which the statement appears," "all the formulations to which the statement refers," "all the formulations whose subsequent possibility is determined by the statement," and "all the formulations whose status the statement in question shares" (EAK, 98–99). In this sense, the statement is a key element of a discourse, for "discourse can be defined as the group of statements that belong to a single system of formation" (EAK, 107).

The field or set of statements thus described emerges "as the locus of particular events, regularities, relationships, modifications and systematic transformations; in short … as a practical domain that is autonomous" (EAK, 121). Foucault's "archaeological method," then, can be understood as the "analysis of statements" – historical, noninterpretive analysis that "questions them as to their mode of existence, what it means to them to have come into existence, to have left traces, and perhaps to remain there, awaiting the moment when they might be of use once more; what it means to them to have appeared when and where they did – they and no others" (EAK, 109).

Richard A. Lynch

SEE ALSO

> *Archaeology*
> *Language*
> *Literature*
> *Parrēsia*
> *Truth*

SUGGESTED READING

Deleuze, Gilles. 1988. *Foucault*, trans. Seán Hand. Minneapolis: University of Minnesota Press.
Gutting, Gary. 1989. *Michel Foucault's Archaeology of Scientific Reason*. Cambridge: Cambridge University Press.

83

STRATEGIES (AND TACTICS)

"S TRATEGIES" AND "TACTICS" are both concepts that derive from Foucault's general approach to power as a practice rather than an institution or a substance. Insofar as power is understood as a "multiplicity of force relations" (EHS1, 92) whereby one set of actions modifies another, any general treatment of power must be anchored in singular force relations. Only once these specific relations have been accounted for can Foucault go on to investigate how these singular instantiations coordinate with other force relations and thereby form an apparatus. In Foucault's oeuvre, "tactic" will refer to these local force relations, whereas "strategy" will denote the coordination of these particular instances.

In Foucault's examinations of madness, sex, or confinement, his approach consistently identifies the most local applications of force, including the power a doctor exercises over patients, the power a father exercises over his wife and children, or the power a boss exercises over workers (FDE2a, 379). Yet these are only properly called "tactics" to the extent that they are enveloped by a strategy that integrates these local force relations of power and employs them in a global agenda. Foucault's work is perhaps best known for identifying two major strategies operative in modern society: the disciplinary and the biopolitical. Speaking of these forms strictly as strategies, discipline and biopolitics are abstract forms that stand independent of any particular institution. For instance, "discipline" refers to the conduct imposed on a limited group of individuals in a confined space, and it matters little if we examine inmates in a prison, students in a school, or patients in a hospital. Although the panoptic form that organizes all of these relationships is exemplified by Bentham's Panopticon, insofar as it is strategy it is not reducible to any single individual or text: "It is the diagram of a mechanism of power reduced to its ideal form; its functioning, abstracted from any obstacle, resistance or friction, must be represented as a pure architectural and optical system: it is in fact a figure of political technology that may and must be detached from any specific use" (EDP, 205). Yet this is not at all to say that strategies operate as abstract forms imposed from the outside onto concrete tactics. Rather, strategies and tactics are absolutely immanent to each other as well as co-conditioning. That is, discipline could not be effective at the global level if it did not find its support in precise relations between doctors and patients, teachers and students, and so on. Conversely, no single tactic would function were it not conjoined and coordinated with other tactics. Foucault will call this co-dependence between strategies and tactics their "double conditioning" (EHS1, 99–100), but "double" here does not refer to any kind of copying or modeling between tactics and strategies. We would misunderstand this relationship completely if we thought tactics were miniature copies that emanated from a model strategy: "[T]he father in the family is not the 'representative' of the sovereign or state; and the latter are not projections of the father on a different scale. The family does not duplicate society, just as society does not imitate the family" (EHS1, 100). Strategies do not exist before tactics. Rather, the tactical relationship that defines the family is conjoined with other tactics in medicine, statistics, and psychiatry to form a strategy, and the "double conditioning" between strategies and tactics must refer to the way in which strategies enable particular force relations to find their consistency and stability, whereas tactics must anchor a strategy in precise and concrete points of support.

This heterogeneity of tactics and strategies is important when we consider the fact that although tactics are often carried out quite explicitly by individuals at the local level, the way in which they are connected to one another to form a comprehensive system is entirely anonymous in Foucault's account. That is to say, there is no subject who invents or is responsible for carrying out a strategy, and furthermore, the strategy that comes to envelop a tactic may be quite antithetical to the aims of those who "invented" any particular practice. Yet the anonymity of strategies does not result in a kind of physical determinism: even though strategies coordinate tactics to form a general line of force, the particular force relations that are traced out and conjoined are by no means entirely stable. This instability derives from the contingent nature of any tactical relation. Although these local force relations do anchor strategies and function as their points of support, their tenuous nature constantly harbors the possibility of a redistribution or realignment of any broader strategy of power. Thus, because tactics are not only the concrete supports of any strategy but also the site of these strategies, we might say that tactics are situated as a sort of hinge between the potentially totalizing effects of strategies and the resistance to these very strategies.

How does a simple relationship between confessor and pastor, doctor and patient, or inmate and guard transform itself into the restructuring of complex political strategies such as biopower or disciplinary power? An example is instructive. In Foucault's lectures at the Collège de France from 1977–1978, we find several maneuvers at the tactical level that are essential to the struggle against the Christian pastorate, including tactical shifts in eschatology, Scripture, mysticism, the community, and *askesis*. Let us briefly examine *askesis*, which will of course become a major theme in Foucault's late work.

One of the tenets of the Christian pastorate is that the pastor must be concerned with the conduct of each and every individual so as to guarantee their salvation. This functions in part through what Foucault calls a "complete subordination" (ECF-STP, 178) whereby each and every individual completely renounces his will and submits himself to the pastor. This relationship of servitude is manifested in the minute details of monastic life and ultimately comes to take the form of a "test of good obedience" within the monastic institution. Referring to these tests of obedience, Foucault explains, "As soon as an order is given to a monk, he must immediately stop whatever he happens to be doing at the time and carry out the order without wondering why he has been given this order or whether it wouldn't be more worthwhile to continue with what he was doing" (ECF-STP, 176). Accordingly, this form of power relies on a complete renunciation of the will, and the sincerity of the renunciation is guaranteed by a series of tests. However, the Christian pastorate will enter a "crisis" when this test of obedience and the renunciation of the will becomes a test of *askesis*. These ascetic practices, defined by Foucault as "an exercise of self on self" (ECF-STP, 205), involves the self-imposition of a series of tests such as fasting, whipping oneself, or burning oneself that become progressively more difficult and insufferable. But the intent of these exercises is essentially incompatible with pastoral obedience because these self-imposed sufferings ultimately create an individual who "becomes the guide of his own asceticism" (ECF-STP, 205). That is to say, through these tests, the ascetic no longer stands in a position of servitude to a superior but rather achieves mastery over himself and his body – a self-mastery that is antithetical to the pastoral obedience to another. This is merely a single tactical reversal, but when it is coordinated with other practices such as mysticism, eschatology, and so on, a crisis and restructuring at the strategic level is brought about.

Examples of tactical reversals such as this, where a dominated group or individual seizes on a tactic as a means of escape, help us see why Michel de Certeau, following both von Clausewitz and Foucault, will declare, "a tactic is an art of the weak" (Certeau 2002, 37). However, what is essential to note is that although this tactical reversal is opposed to the Christian pastorate's call for obedience, this is not an opposition that operates from outside the pastoral system of power. Rather, asceticism resists pastoral power by reimplementing or reutilizing its own elements, such as the "test," and thereby must be defined as an immanent form of counter-conduct or resistance. Foucault emphasizes the immanence of resistance when he writes, "the struggle [against pastoral power] was not conducted in the form of double exteriority, but rather in the form of the permanent use of tactical elements that are pertinent to the anti-pastoral struggle insofar as they fall *within*, in a marginal way, the general horizon of Christianity" (ECF-STP, 215, my emphasis). Thus, whenever we find an instance of resistance or opposition in Foucault's work, we must be careful that it is not actually based on practices of "reimplementation" or "reutilization," or even repetition, that underpin oppositions to a strategy. In sum, because resistance occurs at the tactical level, and because tactics and strategies are co-conditioning and immanent to each other, any resistance to strategies such as pastoral power, disciplinary power, or biopower must be anchored in tactics constituting these very strategies. That is, the possibility of an escape or flight from any strategic regime is always immanent to every specific application of power, and this aspect of power derives from the "double conditioning" of tactics and strategies, whereby unstable tactical relations constitute potentially totalizing strategies and these strategies are built on unpredictable, tenuous tactical relations.

John Nale

SEE ALSO

Biopolitics
Discipline
Politics
Power

SUGGESTED READING

Certeau, Michel de. 2002. *The Practice of Everyday Life*. Berkeley: University of California Press.
Deleuze, Gilles. 1988. "Strategies or the Non-stratified: The Thought of the Outside (Power)," in *Foucault*, trans. Seán Hand. Minneapolis: University of Minnesota Press, pp. 47–69.
Derrida, Jacques. 1985. "The Ends of Man," in *Margins of Philosophy*, trans. Alan Bass. Chicago: University of Chicago Press, pp. 109–136.
Thompson, Kevin. 2003. "Forms of Resistance: Foucault on Tactical Reversal and Self-Formation," *Continental Philosophy Review* 36, no. 2:113–138.

84

STRUCTURALISM

WHEN FOUCAULT WAS asked in 1969 if he was a structuralist, he answered with a riddle: "What's the difference between Bernard Shaw and Charlie Chaplin? There is none, because they both have a beard, except Chaplin, of course" (FDE1, 788). For two reasons, Foucault's relation to structuralism is particularly difficult to characterize. First and most simply, structuralism has never been defined by a clear set of doctrines or ideas. It is traditionally seen as a movement that has its roots in the early twentieth century, in the linguistics of Ferdinand de Saussure, and that was later developed by French scholars who worked in fields as different as anthropology (Claude Lévi-Strauss), psychoanalysis (Jacques Lacan), Marxism (Louis Althusser), literature (Roland Barthes), and history (Foucault) (for a general historical survey, see Dosse 1998). What all these authors share intellectually is not directly apparent, and it is not without reason that when in 1983 Foucault reflected on the heyday of structuralism, he admitted that "no one really knew what [structuralism] was" (FDE4, 431; see also FDE2, 268).

To further complicate the situation, Foucault himself gave contradictory assessments of his relation to structuralism. From the early 1960s on, especially with the publication of *Birth of the Clinic* in 1963, he clearly and unapologetically embraced structuralism. The apotheosis of this structuralist period is *The Order of Things*, which was originally to be entitled *The Archaeology of Structuralism* (Dreyfus and Rabinow 1983, 17), and in which he analyzed "in terms of structure the birth of structuralism itself" (FDE1, 583). For a short while after the publication of *The Order of Things*, Foucault did not mind being called a structuralist. To an interviewer who claimed that he was "the priest of structuralism," he replied that he was only its "altar boy," because he was part of a movement that had begun long before him (FDE1, 581). Soon thereafter, however, he tried to distance himself from the structuralist movement, to the point of calling those who believed he had ever been a structuralist "idiots, naïves and ignoramuses" (FDE2, 296). In 1972, he significantly altered *Birth of the Clinic* for its second edition, notably by erasing several of the first edition's explicit references to structuralism.

But Foucault's reversal took more the form of a visceral self-defense than that of a fleshed-out argument, and his position ended up being at times incoherent. For instance, at the end of the "Foreword" to the English edition of *The Order of Things*, he claimed that he had "used none of the methods, concepts, or key terms that characterize structural analysis" (EOT, xiv). But in a conference presentation given that same year (1970), he explained that what he had done in his work was "only to have recourse to the structuralist method" (FDE2, 133). One year later, he flipped back and affirmed that he had "never, at any time, used the methods peculiar to the structural analyses" (FDE2, 209–210, 216). Interestingly, in the early 1970s, Georges Dumézil, who strongly influenced Foucault throughout his career, was uttering similar contradictory statements about his own position toward structuralism (see Eribon 1992, 329–334).

Foucault was probably more exasperated by structuralism as a label that was uncritically and automatically stamped on his work than as a method for studying cultural issues. Instead of trying to determine whether Foucault was a structuralist, it is more enlightening to look at the points of intersection between some general aspects of structuralism and Foucault's work. Whether these commonalities are sufficient to win Foucault a membership card in the structuralist club will depend on how exclusive one wants this club to be, but at the very least this analysis will make clear that Foucault rode the wave of structuralism that took over France as he was beginning his work.

Already in his very first interview, given in 1961, Foucault explained that he had been greatly influenced by Dumézil's idea of structure (FDE1, 168). Dumézil had showed in his analyses of myths how the same structure can be found, with some modifications, in the myths of radically different cultures. In good structuralist fashion, a structure was therefore independent from its concrete elements. After the publication of *The Order of Things* in 1966, Foucault presented his book as a type of Dumézilian work, in which he had tried to show how there is "an isomorphism between discourses at a given time period" (EOT, xi). Against historians who believe they can fully explain a discourse by reducing it to its social and economic conditions, Foucault emphasized the importance of the structural level: one must "take into consideration the force and consistency of ... isomorphisms" (FDE1, 591).

Although *The Order of Things* marks the pinnacle of Foucault's focus on discursive isomorphisms, he kept privileging structures and rules over substantial elements in his later works. Most radically, in *The Archaeology of Knowledge*, he explained that what he wished to do was "to dispense with 'things'," which meant to define objects "without reference to the *foundation of things*, but by relating them to the body of rules that enable ... them [to be formed] as objects of a discourse and thus to constitute the conditions of their historical appearance" (EAK, 48). As Foucault later said of sexuality, for instance, its "fundamental characteristics … correspond to the functional exigencies of the discourse that must produce its truth…. It is the 'economy' of discourses, that is to say their intrinsic technology, the necessities of their operation, the tactics that they employ, the effects of power which underlie them and which they transmit – it is this … that determines the fundamental characteristics of what they say" (EHS1, 68–69). "Sexuality" was for Foucault nothing more than the nodal point of a set of "functional exigencies," very much like for Saussure the knight in a chess game is not defined substantially (by its shape, color, size, matter, etc.) but structurally: any object can be a knight as long as it follows the rules that knights must follow (Saussure 1995, 153–154; see Veyne 1978, 423, for the rapprochement between Foucault's method and the Saussurean chess analogy).

Several important methodological consequences follow from the primacy given to structures over their elements. First, the relations governing the elements within or between structures are not causal but "of a logical kind, like implication, exclusion, [and] transformation" (FDE1, 607). Foucault criticized the traditional historians' focus on causal relations: "one must get rid of the prejudice according to which a history without causality would not be a history" (FDE1, 607). Acknowledging the influence of linguistic structuralism, the new type of history that he advocated looked at the problem of "the insertion of logic into the very heart of reality" (FDE1, 824). After the publication of *The Order of Things*, Foucault played down this type of abstract terminology and claimed instead that "language can be analyzed in its formal properties only if we take into account its concrete functioning" (FDE1, 595). Yet even in later works he continued to show very little interest in causal relations, which have always been front and center in traditional historiography, and kept focusing on structural relations of implication or exclusion. For instance, in *Discipline and Punish* he was not primarily interested in the causes of the emergence of modern prisons. What he tried to do was to show that there is a relation of implication between the modern modality of power, which he called "the disciplines," and a series of elements that include not only prisons but also schools, the army, hospitals, psychiatry, and criminology. The disciplines also logically exclude practices that were typical of the power of the Old Régime, such as torture. Torture was thus presented by Foucault as being "irrational" in relation to the disciplines (FDE4, 26).

Second, inasmuch as a structure is not an aggregation of discrete elements but a holistic system, a transformation of one element is necessarily accompanied by the transformation of all the other elements (see FDE1, 839). This implies that the transition from one structure to another can only occur in a block: history is discontinuous. In *The Order of Things*, the three discourses on which Foucault focused (the discourses on natural creatures, on economic exchanges, and on language) are transformed synchronically and abruptly, since these discourses are the three elements of one structure, or *episteme*. Foucault wanted to abandon "the grand and old biological metaphor of life and evolution" that had plagued the traditional, continuous type of history since the nineteenth century (FDE2, 280–281).

Third, Lévi-Strauss had claimed that the fundamental difference between ethnology and history is not a difference in goals, objects, or methods but in the fact that ethnology, unlike history, is primarily concerned with the *unconscious* conditions of social existence (Lévi-Strauss 1958, 24–25). In that regard, Foucault's history is an application of Lévi-Strauss's ethnology to Western civilization. He tried to "find in the history of science, of knowledge [*connaissances*] and of human knowledge [*savoir humain*] something that would be like their unconscious" (FDE1, 665–666; see also EOT, xi). There is, however, a crucial difference between Foucault's and Lévi-Strauss's concepts of the unconscious: Foucault always conceived of the unconscious as something thoroughly historical, whereas Lévi-Strauss claimed that it remains fundamentally the same in every civilization (Lévi-Strauss 1958, 28, 224–225; see Revel 2008, 126).

Last, and most importantly, Foucault found in structuralism an efficient weapon against humanism. His main target was Jean-Paul Sartre, to whom he opposed Lévi-Strauss, Lacan, and Dumézil (see FDE1, 513–516). As Foucault said in a laconic formula, with structuralism "the 'I' has exploded … it is the discovery of the 'there is'" (FDE1, 515; see also FDE1, 591). Hence he makes the following counterintuitive statement in *The Order of Things*: the classical *episteme* "has made possible these individualities that we call Hobbes, or Berkeley, or Hume, or Condillac" (FMC, 77; see also FDE2, 59–61). Methodologically, the structural dissolution of the subject undermined "the great myth of interiority" and therefore the "old exegetic tradition" that required identifying the "true thought of an author" (FDE1, 592). Foucault wanted instead to "determine the conditions of [a statement's] existence, to fix as exactly as possible its limits, to establish its correlations with the other statements with which it might be linked, to show what other forms of enunciation it excludes" (FDE1, 706). Accordingly, Foucault relentlessly attacked the writing of "commentaries," which "by definition admits an excess of the signified over the signifier" (FNC, xii), and gave himself the task of making "visible what is invisible only because it is too much on the surface of things" (FDE1, 772).

Anti-humanism had emerged early in French thought, and independently from structuralism (Geroulanos 2010). Foucault himself identified at least three other breaches made to the Sartrean subject: the philosophy of Nietzsche (FDE1, 775; FDE4, 48), the literary works of Blanchot and Bataille (FDE1, 614–615; FDE4, 48), and a new kind of history, which according to Foucault had its origin in Marx and had been developed by the *Annales* school (FAS, "Introduction"; FDE1, 700; FDE2, 280–281). Despite this overdetermination of anti-humanism, Foucault's repeated mentions of structuralism's ability to "call into question the importance of the human subject, of human consciousness, of human existence" (FDE1, 653; see also FDE3, 590, and FDE4, 52) suggest that his own anti-humanism must have owed a good deal to structuralism.

Superficially, Foucault's relation to structuralism can perhaps best be described as a marriage of convenience that ended in a bitter divorce. Yet even when, after the publication of *The Order of Things*, he decided that he had never been a structuralist, he still stressed that his method belonged to the broad and recent historical transformation that structuralism best exemplifies. Whether his approach to history should be located "next to [structuralism]," as he once claimed, or "within it," as he denied (FDE1, 779), was perhaps not for him to decide, since he lucidly admitted that his own discourse was dependent on "conditions and rules of which [he was] very largely unaware" (EOT, xiv). This concession, which follows a strong repudiation of structuralism, indicates how much he owed to this movement.

Patrick Singy

SEE ALSO

Archaeology
History
Language
Statement
Jean-Paul Sartre

SUGGESTED READING

Canguilhem, Georges. 1967. "Mort de l'homme ou épuisement du cogito?" *Critique* 24: 599–618.

Davidson, Arnold. 1997. "Structures and Strategies of Discourse: Remarks Towards a History of Foucault's Philosophy of Language," in *Foucault and His Interlocutors*, ed. Arnold Davidson. Chicago: University of Chicago Press, pp. 1–17.

Deleuze, Gilles. 2004. "How Do We Recognize Structuralism?" in *Desert Islands and Other Texts 1953–1974*, trans. Michael Taormina. New York: Semiotext(e), pp. 170–192.

Dosse, François. 1998. *History of Structuralism*, trans. Deborah Glassman, 2 vols. Minneapolis: University of Minnesota Press.

Dreyfus, Hubert L., and Paul Rabinow. 1983. *Michel Foucault: Beyond Structuralism and Hermeneutics*, 2nd ed. Chicago: University of Chicago Press.

Eribon, Didier. 1992. *Faut-il brûler Dumézil? Mythologie, Science et Politique*. Paris: Flammarion.

Geroulanos, Stefanos. 2010. *An Atheism That Is Not Humanist Emerges in French Thought*. Stanford, CA: Stanford University Press.

Lévi-Strauss, Claude. 1963. *Structural Anthropology*. New York: Basic Books.

Revel, Judith. 2008. *Dictionnaire Foucault*. Paris: Ellipses.

Saussure, Ferdinand de. 1995. *Cours de linguistique générale*. Paris: Payot and Rivages.

2000. *Course in General Linguistics*, trans. Roy Harris. Chicago: Open Court.

Veyne, Paul. 1984. *Writing History: Essay on Epistemology*, trans. Mina Moore-Rinvolucri. Manchester: Manchester University Press.

2010. *Foucault: His Thought, His Character*, trans. Janet Lloyd. Cambridge: Polity Press.

85

SUBJECTIFICATION

I N A SHORT text published in 1982 as an Afterword to Hubert Dreyfus and Paul Rabinow's book *Michel Foucault: Beyond Structuralism and Hermeneutics*, Foucault offers his most extended discussion of subjectification. However, this is not, in the retrospective view he offers there, his only engagement with the idea. In fact, he writes, "I would like to say, first of all, what has been the goal of my work during the past twenty years. It has not been to analyze the phenomena of power, nor to elaborate the foundations of such an analysis. My objective, instead, has been to create a history of the different modes by which, in our culture, human beings are made subjects" (EAIF, 208).

As with many of Foucault's reflections on his work, one must treat this sweeping retrospective assessment cautiously. Foucault had a tendency to define the entirety of his work from the perspective of the particular theoretical approach he was developing at the moment. Moreover, by 1982, Foucault was developing what has come to be called his ethical period, focused on the modes of self-fashioning particular among the ancient Greeks. Nevertheless, there is a certain interpretive power to be gained by looking at his work through this lens. In order to do so, we need to understand what he means by the term "subjectification" and then see how it appears in the works both before and after this Afterword was published.

The key to understanding the concept is offered by Foucault in a quick summary: "There are two meanings of the word *subject*: subject to someone else by control and dependence, and tied to his own identity by a conscience or self-knowledge. Both meanings suggest a form of power which subjugates and makes subject to" (EAIF, 212). In coining the term "subjectification" (*subjectivation*), Foucault is making a double reference. On the one hand, he refers to the philosophical tradition, and in particular the modern philosophical tradition, in which the concept of the subject as a center of experience plays a central role. On the other hand, he refers to political subjection as a mode of having power exercised over oneself. The histories he develops can be seen as ways of bringing this double reference together, of show-ing how the historical development of the subject of experience is at the same time the formation of someone who is politically subjected or subjugated. In order to see this, we need to understand Foucault's view of the emergence of a particularly mod-ern type of power and its operation in the power-knowledge nexus that is central to Foucault's genealogical works.

Power is usually thought of as repressive, as setting limits to what people can do or as preventing people from doing things. Foucault calls this the "juridico-dis-cursive" view of power (EHS1, 82). However, with the emergence of modern tech-nologies and their intersection with various practices of power and knowledge, a different type of power has emerged, one that might be called creative rather than repressive. Rather than stopping or preventing something or someone from being or doing something, this modern type of power makes something emerge, it puts something in place that was not there before. In the Afterword in which Foucault defines subjectification, he writes of power that, "it incites, it induces, it seduces, it makes easier or more difficult; in the extreme it constrains or forbids, absolutely; it is nevertheless always a way of acting upon a subject or acting subjects by virtue of their acting or being capable of action" (EAIF, 220). By inciting, inducing, and seducing, modern power does not merely repress. That is something it does only, as Foucault says, "in the extreme." More commonly, it makes something emerge in the social field.

Perhaps the most striking example of power's making something emerge is that of the modern soul in *Discipline and Punish*. Foucault insists that:

> It would be wrong to say that the soul is an illusion, or an ideological effect. On the contrary, it exists, it has a reality, it is produced permanently around, on, within the body by the functioning of a power that is exercised on those pun-ished – and, in a more general way, on those one supervises, trains and corrects, over madmen, children at home and at school, the colonized, over those who are stuck at a machine and supervised for the rest of their lives. (EDP, 29)

To say that the soul is an illusion or an ideological effect would be in keeping with the juridico-discursive view of power. Essentially, the idea would be that the modern soul (or what is often called in American psychology *personality*) is simply a smoke screen for the reality that lies beneath or beyond it. For example, for Marxists the real struggle lies at the level of economic relationships. Discussions of psychological makeup only obscure this.

If the modern soul, however, is real – if our personalities are actually produced (and not, for instance, simply obscured) by the mechanisms Foucault describes in *Discipline and Punish* and elsewhere, then power does not operate simply through what it prevents or represses but also by what it creates. And, as a corollary to this, there is no Archimedean point for political struggle. Resistance cannot be anchored in a particular set of relationships, say the state or the economy. Instead, it must arise wherever we are created to be the kinds of beings that (a) on reflection we would not accept being and (b) that reinforce other oppressive social conditions. Politics is both subtler and more widespread than it would be in a Marxist or liberal model.

If modern power is a matter of the way we are created in many of our practices, then it will also have an intimate bond with knowledge. Foucault illustrates this in *Discipline and Punish* in his discussion of the rise of psychology and its relationship with the creation of the modern soul. Whereas in earlier periods the individuals distinguished and marked in a society were its leaders, with the rise of the interventions of modern power it is instead the people on the ground that are individualized: characterized by personality type, assessed with respect to proposed norms, and ultimately manipulated (i.e., created in certain ways) in order to integrate them into the social order. As Foucault comments, "All the sciences, analyses or practices employing the root 'psycho-' have their origin in this historical reversal of the procedures of individualization" (EDP, 193). The emergence of psychological science and knowledge over the course of the nineteenth and twentieth centuries is inseparable from the practices of power by which the modern soul is created.

The point Foucault presses regarding psychology in *Discipline and Punish* is an instance of a more general view. As he comments in the introduction to that book, "[W]e should abandon a whole tradition that allows us to imagine that knowledge can exist only where power relationships are suspended and that knowledge can develop only outside its injunctions, its demands and its interests....We should admit rather that power produces knowledge ... that power and knowledge directly imply one another" (EDP, 27). This is Foucault's description of his famous concept of power-knowledge. If modern power operates at the level of our daily practices, creating us to be certain kinds of beings rather than others, and if those practices involve various kinds of knowledge, then power and knowledge are intimately entwined. Who we are and how we know ourselves (or are known by others) are inseparable both from one another and from the political relationships characteristic of our society.

With these ideas in hand, we can understand the double reference of Foucault's definition of subjectification. In the modern period, to be subject to relations of power and to be a subject, one of self-knowledge, are two aspects of the same process. It is through the operation of our creation in particular ways, and the self-knowledge that accompanies it, that we are made subject to the political orders in which we find ourselves. It is not because we are prevented from being what we otherwise might be (or at least not primarily because of that) but rather because, in our practices and in the knowledge that those practices involve, we are being molded daily as certain kinds of doers and knowers that we become subject to that which governs us. In fact, we can go a step further and say that, in good part, it is precisely those practices and their accompanying knowledge that govern us, or through which we govern and police ourselves. The concept of subjectification captures this operation of modern power and its focus on how we are created through its operation.

Alongside the analyses of *Discipline and Punish*, the first volume of Foucault's *History of Sexuality* also provides stark examples of subjectification. In the chapter entitled "Domain," he offers brief descriptions of "the hysterical woman, the masturbating child, the Malthusian couple, and the perverse adult" (EHS1, 105). The hysterical woman is the female whose sexualized body is filled with nervous energy, ready to break out into various symptoms. The masturbating child is the youngster whose sexuality must be monitored and prevented from expression in order to promote healthy development. The Malthusian couple is the positive figure among these. It is the couple that conforms to social, economic, and procreative norms. Finally, the perverse adult is the character of pathological sexuality, perhaps most prominently represented by the homosexual.

Each of these types of subjectification is, in keeping with the theme of the book, a product of a particular focus on sex. Whereas *Discipline and Punish* is concerned with the rise of psychology and the types of subjectification it creates, the first volume of *The History of Sexuality* is focused more on the changes in religious (and later, psychiatric) practices that make sexuality the key to understanding who we are. These two approaches are not, of course, either exclusive or exhaustive. Because the creative operation of modern power occurs through practices, one would expect that different practices would mold us in different ways. In the case of *Discipline and Punish* and the first volume of *The History of Sexuality*, these different ways of molding, although distinct, also have points of intersection (for example, around psychoanalysis).

The significance of the fact that different practices induce different types of power effects lies in the lesson that we must be careful not to reduce any particular person to a specific type of subjectification. Even though, for instance, there is a "hystericization of women's bodies" (EHS1, 104), there is nobody who is solely a hysterical woman and nothing else. Because of people's exposure to different practices and their power arrangements, we are all at least partially the product of the power relations of those different practices. Subjectification is a complex process. It does not arise solely along one register or in conformity with a single type of power arrangement. Foucault's goal in discussing various types of subjectification is not to describe particular people but rather particular forces that can act in concert or at cross-purposes in the creation of who we are.

Although the concept of subjectification arises later in Foucault's work, one can see it in a nascent way in some of his earlier works. In particular, his first extended work, *The History of Madness*, traces the increasing isolation of madness from reason and the different ways in which the former is categorized and intervened on. It also suggests, through its description of the intersection of medical practice and theory, the way those labeled mad are encouraged to have certain self-understandings that will lead them to behave, and thus become subjects in accordance with those self-understandings. In particular, the discussion of the interventions of Samuel Tuke and Philippe Pinel, who blamed madness on the mad themselves and sought to change them through different types of self-recognition and guilt, intersects with the treatment of the rise of psychology as a subjectifying practice in *Discipline and Punish*.

Not all of Foucault's earlier works lend themselves to interpretation in terms of subjectification. In particular, those works that focus more exclusively on the discursive aspects of practice, for example *The Order of Things* and *The Archaeology of Knowledge*, seem remote from concerns with how we are molded into particular subjects. This is because, by focusing on discourse rather than on the intersection of practices with people (and especially with people's bodies), they do not take up the moments in which people's lives are molded by the practices in which they are engaged. This is not to say that these works are irrelevant for an understanding of how we come to be particular subjects. The changes in economic discourse described in *The Order of Things*, for instance, bear on how we think of ourselves. However, although these works do have bearing on our current self-understanding, they do so indirectly, not through a depiction of processes of subjectification.

Looking forward from *Discipline and Punish* and the first volume of *The History of Sexuality* to Foucault's last works, one can see subjectification in operation, but in a changed form from these two works. One might, at first, describe this change as one of emphasis. Whereas the two works already discussed focus on how power creates certain subjectifications, the last two volumes of *The History of Sexuality* are more concerned with how people subjectify themselves in certain ways. This does not mean that Foucault has abandoned his view of power. Far from it. Rather, under the influence of his reading in ancient philosophy, he shifts his emphasis from the way we are created by our practices to how we go about creating ourselves within and through them.

In his introduction to the second volume of *The History of Sexuality*, Foucault reflects on the difficulties of coming to grips with the sexual subject. He writes:

> It seemed to me that one could not very well analyze the formation and development of the experience of sexuality from the eighteenth century onward, without doing a historical and critical study dealing with desire and the desiring subject.... This does not mean that I proposed to write a history of the successive conceptions of desire, of concupiscence, or of libido, but rather to analyze the practices by which individuals were led to focus their attention on themselves, to decipher, recognize, and acknowledge themselves as subjects of desire. (EHS2, 5)

Foucault marks this shift by introducing the term *problematization*. He wonders why various themes, and sexuality in particular, become problems that societies seek to solve through the norms and practices of people's living. And, as is common with him, he uses that idea retrospectively to interpret his own work. He considers his career to have successively dealt with problematizations of madness, discursive practices, and crime, each corresponding to different rules: normalization, epistemic rules, and disciplinary norms. He states, "And now I would like to show how, in classical antiquity, sexual activity and sexual pleasures were problematized through practices of the self, bringing into play the criteria of an 'aesthetics of existence'" (EHS2, 5).

Subjectification, then, does not leave the field in Foucault's later works. Instead, it is inflected in a different way. Rather than focusing on how people are made to be subjects of one kind or another, the later works seek to concentrate on how people create themselves as subjects through the ways they take up the problematizations presented to them by their society and their culture. This should not be taken to mean that Foucault's work shifts from treating people as passive objects to treating them as active subjects, nor to be understood more broadly as a shift from a determinist position to an embrace of free will. The free will/determinism debate is not a helpful lens through which to view Foucault's work. And as for passivity and activity, *Discipline and Punish* recounts various instances of resistance to disciplinary forms of subjectification, whereas the second and third volumes of *The History of Sexuality* emphasize the constraints within and, more important, *through* which people conduct their "aesthetics of existence." The shift is perhaps better described as one of emphasis. Whereas *Discipline and Punish* and the first volume of *The History of Sexuality* emphasize the social practices through which subjectification occurs, the second and third volumes are more concerned with the ways in which people view and take up themselves within the context of those practices.

Throughout much of Foucault's career, then, and particularly in what are sometimes called the *genealogical* and *ethical* phases of his work, Foucault is concerned with processes of subjectification. This is in keeping with his more general project of a history of the present, of seeking to understand how we came to be who we are today. It should not be surprising that in this larger project subjectification has an important part to play. If one seeks, as Foucault does, to understand who we are at the level of our practices, from the ground up as it were, then a central concern has to be one of how those practices make us into the kinds of subjects we are. By introducing the term *subjectification* as a means of understanding this process, or better this set of distinct but intersecting processes, Foucault isolates a perspective through which we can view some of the most persistent concerns of the trajectory of his work.

Todd May

SEE ALSO

Care
Dispositif *(Apparatus)*
Ethics
Power
Problematization
Resistance

SUGGESTED READING

Allen, Amy. 2008. *The Politics of Our Selves: Power, Autonomy, and Gender in Contemporary Critical Theory*. New York: Columbia University Press.
Deleuze, Gilles, and Félix Guattari. 1987. *A Thousand Plateaus: Capitalism and Schizophrenia*, trans. Brian Massumi. Minneapolis: University of Minnesota Press, pp. 131–164.
May, Todd. 2006. *The Philosophy of Foucault*. Montreal and Kingston: McGill-Queen's University Press.

86

TECHNOLOGY (OF DISCIPLINE, GOVERNMENTALITY, AND ETHICS)

F OUCAULT USED THE word "technology" in conjunction with a family of words related to the Greek *technē*, which is usually taken to mean the art, craft, or skill involved when something is intentionally produced. Thus, he wrote about techniques and technologies of power, techniques, technologies, and arts of government, and, finally, techniques, technologies, and arts of the self in relation to the ancient Greek practice of *technē tou biou*, or the "art of living." The variations on this family of words are not stable across the French and English versions of Foucault's texts. For example, the English version of a lecture delivered at the University of Vermont in 1982 ("Technologies of the Self") has him referring to the four major "technologies" that provide matrices of practical reason: technologies of production, which enable us to produce and transform things; technologies of sign systems, which enable us to use signs, meanings, and symbols; technologies of power, "which determine the conduct of individuals and submit them to certain ends or domination"; and technologies of the self, "which permit individuals to effect by their own means, or with the help of others, a certain number of operations on their own bodies and souls, thoughts, conduct, and way of being, so as to transform themselves in order to attain a certain state of happiness, purity, wisdom, perfection, or immortality" (EEW1, 225). By contrast, the French version of this lecture uses "technique" in all cases where the English has "technology," including the title of this lecture, which appears in the *Dits et écrits* as "*Les techniques de soi*" (FDE4, 785). The nuance between "technology" and "technique" is lost in these translation problems.

However, even where the original and translated texts are consistent, Foucault sometime switches between the terms "art," "technology," and "technique" in close proximity to one another. For example, in the 1983 interview "On the Genealogy of

Ethics: An Overview of Work in Progress," he identifies the specific character of the relation to the self that was involved in the ancient Greek ethics discussed in *The Use of Pleasure*. The ancient Greek self-relation insisted on moderation and self-mastery in the use of the pleasures so that one acted on the self with the purpose of giving one's life certain values: "It was a question of making one's life into an object for a sort of knowledge, for a *technē* – for an art" (EEW3, 271). Later in the same interview, he refers to a broad "technology of the constitution of the self," which in different ways in different periods of European culture makes use of writing. In the next paragraph, he refers to the "techniques of the self," such as writing and other spiritual exercises, that can be found in different forms in all cultures (EEW3, 277). Insofar as there is a rule governing his use of these distinct terms, it is that he uses "art" and "technology" to refer to the overall relation to a particular object in pursuit of a given goal, whereas "technique" is reserved for the particular instruments and means employed to produce the desired result. Thus, in a 1982 interview ("Space, Knowledge and Power"), he distinguished the contemporary narrow sense of "technology," whereby it is limited to certain kinds of material technology such as the technology of wood, fire, or electricity, from the wider sense of the word, in which government is also a form of technology: "the government of individuals, the government of souls, the government of the self by the self, the government of families, the government of children, and so on" (EEW3, 364). In this context, he glosses the meaning of the Greek *technē* in a way that covers all four domains of human endeavor mentioned earlier (technologies of production, signification, power, and the self) as "a practical rationality governed by a conscious goal" (EEW3, 364).

Foucault's characterization of particular technologies of power, government, or the constitution of the self in the broad sense of the term follows the schema of the Aristotelian concept of cause. In each case, the features that distinguish a given technology correspond to each of the four senses in which, according to Aristotle, one thing may be the cause (*aition*) of another. First is the *material* cause, or matter of which the thing is made; in this sense, the stone of which it is carved is the material cause of a statue. Second is the *formal* cause, or what it is that makes this a certain kind of thing; an exercise of power, for example, occurs whenever there is action on the actions of others or on the self. Third, the *efficient* cause is that which produces the thing in question; the activity of the sculptor or the kinds of action on the material produce the desired object. And, finally, we have the telos, or end of the operation in question. This way of defining a given *technē* or technology, enabled the description of continuities and changes in whatever technology is being discussed, in a manner that paralleled the analysis of transformations in discursive formations enabled by the complex concept of discourse outlined in *The Archaeology of Knowledge*.

Consider the example of discipline as a distinct political technology for the exercise of the sovereign power to punish those convicted of breaking the law. In *Discipline and Punish*, Foucault refers to discipline as a "technology of power" (EDP,

23, 131), a "political technology of the body" (EDP 26, 30), and a "subtle, calculated technology of subjection" (EDP, 221). He expands on the idea of discipline as a particular type or technology of power, "a modality for its exercise," in suggesting that it comprises "a whole set of instruments, techniques, procedures, levels of application, targets" (EDP, 215). Perhaps the clearest way to show that disciplinary power is a technology is to contrast it with the other technologies that could have been adopted in the exercise of the power to punish in the latter half of the eighteenth century. The first of these was the power of the sovereign that operated in public ceremonies by inflicting marks of its superior force on the body of the condemned, as described in gruesome detail in the account of the torture and execution of the regicide Damiens that opens *Discipline and Punish*. The second was the democratic power of society that operated by means of signs to the population at large of the inevitability and the inconvenience of the punishment that would follow the perpetration of any criminal act. In contrast to both of these technologies of punishment, penal incarceration involved a series of techniques for the coercion and training of individuals convicted of crimes. These were applied behind prison walls and aimed at the transformation of the behavior of the criminals rather than at affecting the minds of the rest of the population.

This disciplinary technology of power was distinguished first by the *material* to which it was applied: the body of the convicted criminal neither as an enemy of the sovereign nor as a representation of illegality but "the body, time, everyday gestures and activities; the soul too, but insofar as it is the seat of habits" (EDP, 128). Second, the disciplinary technology of power is distinguished by the *modality* of its exercise: rather than a display of superior force or an art of representation, punishment should rest on "a studied manipulation of the individual" (EDP, 128). Third, discipline employed a distinct set of *techniques* that were neither instruments of torture nor complexes of representation but rather "forms of coercion, schemata of constraint, applied and repeated. Exercises not signs: time-tables, compulsory movements, regular activities, solitary meditation, work in common, silence, application, respect, good habits" (EDP, 128). Finally, the *goal* of discipline was neither the demonstration of the sovereign's overwhelming power nor the restoration to the subject of the fundamental rights and duties established by the social contract but "the obedient subject, the individual subjected to habits, rules, orders" (EDP, 128).

Now let us examine governmentality as a technology. Foucault's initial presentation of the concept of governmentality in his lecture of February 1, 1978 referred to the sixteenth-century literature on the art of government rather than to the technology or techniques of state power. However, his subsequent development of the concept made it clear that what was at issue were the different technologies deployed in the exercise of sovereign or state power. His lecture of February 8, 1978 presented his general approach to power as one that sought to go behind the institutions in which power was exercised, such as armies, hospitals, schools, and prisons, in order to discover "what we can broadly call a technology of power" (ECF-STP, 117). The aim of the studies of governmentality that followed was to adopt this same methodological principle in order to resituate the modern state "in a general technology of power that assured its mutations, development and functioning" (ECF-STP, 120).

In fact, as the remaining 1978 lectures make clear, Foucault's studies of governmentality sought to identify the historical series of technologies of state power that have produced the institutions, techniques, and aims of modern political government. Thus, the Tanner lectures ("'*Omnes et Singulatim*': Toward a Critique of Political Reason") delivered in 1979 retrace the origins and some of the mutations of the technology of pastoral power in order to suggest that problems associated with the postwar "welfare state" may be seen as one of many reappearances of "the tricky adjustment between political power wielded over legal subjects and pastoral power wielded over live individuals" (EEW3, 307). In a similar manner, "The Subject and Power" describes contemporary state power as a unique combination of totalizing and individualizing power because of the degree to which it has integrated and transformed the techniques of Christian pastoral power. The contemporary state, Foucault suggests, can be seen as "a modern matrix of individualization, or a new form of pastoral power" (EEW3, 334).

The lecture delivered at the University of Vermont in 1982 gives a different account of the sources of what Foucault here referred to as the "political technology of individuals" (EEW3, 404). In this lecture, as in the Tanner lectures, he refers to the postwar welfare state in suggesting that the coexistence of massive destruction of human lives alongside institutions oriented toward the care of individual life remains one of the "central antinomies" of modern political reason (EEW3, 405). The focus of his inquiry in the Vermont lecture is to identify the particular techniques and technology of government that were taken up within the context of reason of state (*raison d'État*) "in order to make of the individual a significant element for the state" (EEW3, 409–410). His answer is that it was the science of police that was developed in Europe during the seventeenth and eighteenth centuries that provided the rationale for individual lives becoming a focus of concern for the state. It was theorists of police science such as Louis Turquet de Mayerne (1550–1615), N. Delamare (1639–1723), and Johan H. G. von Justi (1720–1771) who "recognized the necessity of defining, describing, and organizing very explicitly this new technology of power, the new techniques by which the individual could be integrated into the social entity" (EEW3, 410).

Although he does not explicitly refer to the Aristotelian schema in connection with the analysis of governmentality, it is clear that this schema continues to provide an intellectual framework for his survey of the different technologies of government that have contributed to the formation of the modern state. The differences between sovereign and pastoral power, between reason of state, police, and liberal government are identified with reference to the material object or substance of government (territories, flocks, populations, societies), the form of relationship to the governed (absolute rule, concern for spiritual or biological well-being, constant monitoring, respect for natural operation), the techniques employed (laws, apparatuses of security), and the aims of government (preservation of sovereign power, strength of the state, well-being of the population, happiness and freedom of individuals, and so on).

Finally, we shall look at ethics as a technology. The same Aristotelian schema informs Foucault's study in the second and third volumes of *The History of Sexuality*. These volumes describe "technologies of the self" that are found first in texts relating to classical Greek sexual ethics and second in texts from around the third century BCE to around the third century CE that discuss Greek and Roman practices of care for the self (*epimelia heautou*). Foucault presents these practices as a contribution to the genealogy of morality but one that focuses on the ethical relationship of the self to the self. As he suggests in the introduction to volume two of *The History of Sexuality*, subtitled *The Use of Pleasure*, "there is a whole rich and complex field of historicity in the way the individual is summoned to recognize himself as an ethical subject of sexual conduct" (EHS2, 32). More generally, he suggests, the different historical forms of this relationship of the self to the self may be defined as distinct technologies of the self, in accordance with the four dimensions of the causal relationship identified by Aristotle. First, there is the part of the self or *ethical substance* that is the object of ethical concern. For the ancient Greek ethics discussed in volume two of *The History of Sexuality*, this was the *aphrodisia* or acts linked to pleasure and desire. In the case of the Christian ethics that came later, it was the flesh. Sexuality in the modern sense, Foucault suggests, "is a third kind of ethical substance" (EEW1, 264). Second, there is the *mode of subjectification or subjectivation* (*mode d'assujettisement*), which refers to the manner in which individuals are supposed to relate to themselves as ethical subjects. For example, they can consider themselves subjects of an art or aesthetics of existence, of divine or natural law, or of universal laws imposed by reason. Third, there are the kinds of activities undertaken, the kinds of ethical work of the self on the self, or the practices or techniques (*technē*) employed that correspond to an asceticism in the broad sense of the term. Finally, there is the goal or type of being the self aspires to become; that is, the telos of the particular form of ethical conduct.

Foucault makes use of this complex concept of technologies of the self in order to show that what might appear to be the same ethical prescription in different cultures or periods, such as the requirement of sexual fidelity between marital partners, is in fact different along one or another of these dimensions (EHS2, 26–28). Further, changes may occur in a given epoch at different rates along some or all of these levels. For example, while ancient Greek and Stoic forms of care of the self retained a similar ethical substance, there were changes in the mode of subjectivation, in the kinds of techniques employed, and in the goal. Christian ethics involved a series of further changes: the ethical substance was no longer *aphrodisia* but concupiscence or flesh; the mode of subjectivation is that of subjection to divine law, the forms of asceticism change and the goal becomes a matter of purity of the soul and the attainment of immortality (EEW1, 267–268). It is perhaps in this area of care of the self that we see best how Foucault's use of the idea of technologies or techniques fits in with his archaeological and genealogical approach to history. As Nietzsche would have said, there is no univocal meaning of a practice; there are only interpretations.

Paul Patton

SEE ALSO

Discipline
Ethics
Governmentality
Power
Self

SUGGESTED READING

Martin, Luther H., Huck Gutman, and Patrick H. Hutton, eds. 1988. *Technologies of the Self: A Seminar with Michel Foucault*. Amherst: University of Massachusetts Press.
Revel, Judith. 2008. *Dictionnaire Foucault*. Paris: Ellipses.

87

TRANSGRESSION

O F ALL THE terms in the Foucauldian lexicon, "transgression" has perhaps
had the greatest impact, both within later "poststructuralist" work and even
outside it (and outside academic discourse as well). As Suzanne Guerlac has
noted, it was taken up, after Foucault's use of it, by *Tel Quel* writers such as Philippe
Sollers and Julia Kristeva; from there it spread outward to the point of general cultural saturation. But at the outset it had a very specific meaning, and a very specific
job to do (see Guerlac 1997).

The starting point for this popularity of the word "transgression" is Foucault's
"Preface to Transgression," an essay written in the 1963 memorial issue of the review
Critique devoted to Georges Bataille, who had died the previous year (ELCP, 29–52).
(*Critique* itself had been founded by Bataille, in 1946, so one can easily grasp the
symbolic importance of this issue.)

First, we should note what transgression meant for Bataille. Writing in and
against the Durkheimian tradition, Bataille from the first had been concerned with
rethinking the role of the sacred in modern societies: How had modern societies
lost touch with the sacred? What was its basic importance? And what would be the
consequences of a return to it? Durkheim's answer was that the sacred was the force
of human society itself coming together (in periodic festivals and celebrations) and
that a modern, rational form of the sacred should serve as the basis of a reinvigorated
French republic (see Stoekl 1989).

Bataille, inverting Durkheim, sees the sacred as not inherently rational or constructive but containing a "left hand" element that founds but also disrupts cultural
coherence and continuity. Indeed the two sides are inseparable: interdiction (accompanied by the "right-hand" sacred of consecration and conservation) assures the bal-
ancing of accounts of cultural and economic practices, the coherence of social and
sexual reproduction. But interdiction is meaningless without the imperative of transgression (the left-hand sacred), the force of negation that precisely does not lead to

positive results: nonreproductive sexuality and the wantonly destructive expenditure of economic rituals like potlatch, as well as laughter, poetry, and so on. Bataille's point is that the relation between interdiction and transgression is precisely *not* dialectical: transgression is not simply subordinated to interdiction in order to facilitate a constructive, progressive historical movement, just as negativity is not always fully recoverable within a coherent historical movement. In *L'Erotisme* (*Death and Sensuality*), Bataille writes:

> [T]ransgression has nothing to do with the primal liberty of animal life: it opens the way beyond the usually observed limits, but it retains these limits. Transgression exceeds without destroying a profane world, of which it is the complement. Human society is not only the world of work. Simultaneously – or successively – the profane and sacred worlds make it up, which are its two complementary forms. The profane world is the world of interdiction. The sacred world opens onto limited transgressions. It's the world of festivals, sovereigns and gods. (Bataille 1987, 67–68, translation modified)

Without interdiction, transgression would be only "natural," sex as mere organic activity, death as something undergone without foresight: the world of animals. The human world is the world of awareness and anguish before death, the world of useless play and dangerous sexual exuberance – but this is only possible so long as interdiction and utility are established *against* transgression. Transgression by itself is nothing; it "needs" interdiction to "function" (not that it is comprehensible as a simple function).

For Bataille, interdiction in the end finds its supreme meaning in intensifying transgression: we conserve, so to speak, only in order to spend, we live and establish barriers to activity that violates rules only to engage in activity that fundamentally transgresses those rules. Thus, nihilistic religions that seem only to provide barriers – that establish a terrifying interdiction as the highest value – ultimately serve to intensify the "experience" of transgression. Again, in the chapter on transgression in *Death and Sensuality*, Bataille writes: "In Christianity and Buddhism ecstasy is founded on the going-beyond of horror. The accord with excess that carries everything before it is even more intense in religions in which fear and nausea have more profoundly eaten at the heart. There is no feeling more forcefully productive of exuberance than that of nothingness" (Bataille 1987, 69, translation modified).

Interdiction and transgression are inseparable, but for Bataille transgression seems in the end logically if not chronologically prior. Just as certain kinds of clothing exist primarily to intensify sexual pleasure, for Bataille interdiction serves to intensify the movement of "exuberance." The horror of the void, the fear of risk, incites one to move in the opposite direction, just as suspension over an abyss invites one to jump. Transgression is the moment of passing over the limit, but, paradoxically, its limitlessness is itself founded on the necessity of the limit. Transgression is contained in, and contains, the limits set by interdiction, and yet the very movement of social life, the very thing that makes life worth living and makes it something other than animal life, lies in the passage over those limits.

With all this said, one should note that Bataille's theory is one of society. It attempts to explain social phenomena: the ultimate workings, and meaning, of religion. It is therefore in a sense also a religious theory: it justifies and affirms the "experience" of the sacred and provides meaning only in the more profound meaninglessness of transgression (unbridled sexuality, play, spending without return, uncontrolled artistic and ludic activity). Bataille is concerned with telling us why we live and what our ultimate motivations are, whether we recognize them (or *can* recognize them, since they operate against limits) or not. He is, in other words, at least in his arguments on the sacred, a social commentator.

Foucault, in "Preface to Transgression," is up to something else. His concerns ultimately turn on textuality and the role of language in it. In his presentation/revision of Bataille, Foucault asserts that sexuality, like God, is no longer capable of setting the outer limits of humanity or the limits of the individual. Sexuality for Foucault appears to be something like what Bataille called eroticism; since God has died, sexuality "points to nothing beyond itself" (ELCP, 30). (Although Foucault uses the term "sexuality," "eroticism" in Bataille's sense would probably be preferable, since Bataille is not discussing the phenomenon of sexuality examined by the contemporary medical or social sciences, which clearly have little concern for transgression or interdiction.)

As conveyed by the writings of the Marquis de Sade, sexuality now is a profanation that "links, for its own ends, an overcoming of limits to the death of God" (ELCP, 33). Through the endless permutations of Sade's novels, written in the mode of blasphemy, directed precisely against a God who does not exist, we come to recognize that sexuality, rather than something outside us (as biological or cultural imperative), setting our personal limits, even authorized by theology (in its reproduction-affirming mode), instead "marks the limit within ourselves and designates us as limit" (ELCP, 30). Endlessly written sexuality is now internal, referring back to no animal ("natural") state; it cannot be incorporated in a benign reproduction under the aegis of an infinite, and infinitely limiting, God. Rather, it turns on itself, always generating new permutations, new senseless variants: "Not that it [sexuality] proffers any new content for our age-old acts; rather, it permits a profanation without object, a profanation that is empty and turned inward upon itself and whose instruments are brought to bear on nothing but each other" (ELCP, 30).

> The interdiction previously provided by God, and by a naturalizing sexuality, is now situated *in* us: it is a constituting line crossed and recrossed by an endless language. Transgression is an empty profanation, the sacred devoid of God, devoid

even of the sacred, an endless movement in us that accomplishes nothing, guarantees nothing; it "is neither violence in a divided world (an ethical world) nor a victory over limits (in a dialectical or revolutionary world); … its role is to measure the excessive distance that it opens at the heart of the limit" (ELCP, 35).

One has the sense, nevertheless, that there is something positive in all this. Perhaps in a Heideggerian mode (filtered through Blanchot), Foucault argues for a transgression that "contains nothing negative, but affirms limited being – affirms the limitlessness into which it leaps as it opens this zone to existence for the first time" (ELCP, 35) (on Foucault on Blanchot, see EFB). What is this affirmation? "Perhaps it is simply an affirmation of division, but only insofar as division is not understood to mean a cutting gesture, or the establishment of a separation or the measuring of a distance, only retaining that in it which may designate the existence of difference" (ELCP, 36).

Transgression is an affirmative movement, opening the possibility of difference, but only in and at the limit, not outside; it does not provide a stabilizing boundary, even in the infinite. It is not scandalous; there is nothing "demonic" about it (ELCP, 37). Transgressive difference is instead the movement not of a productive negativity making possible revolutionary action, but only an "affirmation that affirms nothing, a radical break of transitivity" (ELCP, 36) – what Blanchot calls "contestation."

Division "is" the nonorigin of difference, the "existence of difference" as affirmation not affirming any "thing." Heideggerian Being here morphs into a proto-Derridean *différance*, with the difference being that Foucault can still write of the "existence" of difference. And that difference with Derrida is, I think, significant. The paradox of Foucault's transgression is that, in the end, its difference from Hegelian contradiction is not really transgressive in Foucault's own terms. After all, it *exists*, through the difference it affirms…. What then is the status of this *existence*? How can it be transgressive?

Foucault's larger goal in his essay on transgression is to dispute the primacy of the authorial subject and, from there, the role of a constructive or constitutive negativity. The "experience" is that of the space where experience's language fails, "from precisely the place where words escape it, where the subject who speaks has just vanished" (ELCP, 40). With transgression in and against the internal limit, finitude is lodged in, and transgresses, the space of the absent autonomous subject. Once again, a Heideggerian note, but the result is quite un-Heideggerian, and indeed un-Bataillean: transgression entails the sheer proliferation of language, language repeating and transgressing itself "to infinity," finding its "uninterrupted domain" (ELCP, 48), permuting endlessly in the void of an authorial, and authoritative, subjectivity ("transgressing the one who speaks" [ELCP, 44]). This language doubling and differing from itself, autotransgressing, is a movement that, in Foucault's view, renders obsolete the earlier model of Hegelian (and Kojèvian) negation (for a Derridean critique of this endless mirroring and replication, see Gasché 1986). The dialectic proposed a productive negativity, the uptake of destruction in the creative elaboration of spirit, ending in, literally, *the end*, a steady-state of Spirit at the close of history (this was Kojève's rewriting of Hegel, which had an enormous influence in France between the wars, as well as after World War II; see Kojève 1947). But by 1963 the dialectic, especially as espoused in the version put forward by French Marxist intellectuals (including Sartre), not to mention the French Communist Party, was starting to show its age. The problem was in the question of replacement. Foucault poses the rhetorical question: "[Must we] find a language for the transgressive which would be what dialectics was, in an earlier time, for contradiction?" (ELCP, 40). He seems to want it both ways: no to a simple replacement of dialectical-philosophical discourse, but yes to some other model of philosophy as transgressive discourse. But is "some other model" not merely a version of replacement?

That is the central problem: is contradiction to be *replaced* by another philosophical discourse? Are we really that far from negation, and from the *Aufhebung*? The answer is not at all clear: philosophy only "regains its speech and finds itself again only in the marginal region which borders its limits" (ELCP, 43), coming from the impossible space between "a purified metalanguage" and "the thickness of words enclosed by their darkness" (ibid.). A philosophy will appear, in other words, that transgresses the space between a coherent technical discourse and the madness of proliferating language.

The answer to the question of replacement, then, is both yes and no. Foucault's transgressive duality (the line and its crossing) seems to anticipate much of the later *Tel Quel* project – the paradoxical effort to establish a rigorous theory of a prelogical "chora sémiotique," as Kristeva called it (Kristeva 1984) – and therefore there could be no simple replacement of Hegelian dialectics but only a repetition, with a difference, the endless turning of philosophical discourse around its internal limit, the necessary but unassimilable space of transgression. But the important thing to note here is that Foucault is nevertheless attempting to work out the logic of a philosophical discourse that would *come after*, in one way or another, the coherent philosophical language of dialectics. It seems, then, that he wants it both ways: on the one hand, transgressive discourse is an infinite murmuring, a differential affirmation, reminiscent of Sade's endless permutations or Borges's library of Babel. This avant-garde ideal is doubled by the suggestion (posed as a question) that dialectics (contradiction) will find its successor in a transgressive language that would, we can easily conclude, destroy the legitimacy of dialectical philosophies, not least Marxism, and lead to some sort of (rigorously marginal) philosophical discourse, founded not on contradiction but on transgressive language (which is in fact yet to be found, and perhaps cannot be found: "must we find?"). Discrediting Hegelianism (read, in the 1963 French context: Marxism) and putting forward some conjunction of Bataille/ Nietzsche would thus ultimately have to be seen as a political gesture, as well as a purely postpolitical one. The demise of a theoretical/practical Marxism, after all, is not just a matter of the contestation of language: it would have (and has had) real consequences in the world.

Derrida would later strongly indicate, in his essay on Bataille, the difficulty of scrapping Hegel and moving on (Derrida 1978a). Indeed Derrida's Bataille is situated in and against Hegel, thereby addressing what seems the main problem in Foucault's (and thereby perhaps Derrida is situated in and against Foucault as well): the replacement of Hegelian contradiction with transgression, asserted or implied, is quite simply not a Bataillean strategy. The ringing (albeit qualified) statements about the demise of dialectics are mistaken. Indeed, to replace Hegel, to "liberat[e] ... thought from all forms of dialectical language," as Foucault puts it (ELCP, 51), is itself to carry out a fully dialectical move, as not only Derrida was aware but Bataille (according to Derrida) as well.

As Derrida notes at the outset of his essay, "Contrary to Bataille's experience, this [shrugging off of Hegel] puts one, without seeing it or knowing it, within the very self-evidence of Hegel one thinks oneself unburdened of…. Hegelian self-evidence seems lighter than ever at the moment when it finally bears down with its full weight" (Derrida 1978a, 251; italics Derrida's). Derrida specifically notes the word transgression (in italics) and then notes as well (in a footnote in *Death and Sensuality*) that for Bataille the very use of the term transgression is Hegelian: "It is useless to insist upon the Hegelian character of the operation" (Derrida 1978a, 275). Foucault's version of transgression is clearly at issue in both these passages. One can perhaps answer Derrida, however, by noting that Foucault's main formulation of the "language of transgression" is posed primarily *as a question*. Derrida the famously attentive reader seems to miss this. (In any event, one has the sense that Foucault could have avoided the ambiguities of an antidialectical dialectical position by recalling Deleuze's formulation: "Negation is *opposed* to affirmation but affirmation *differs* from negation…. Affirmation is the enjoyment and play of its own difference" [Deleuze 1983, 188; italics Deleuze's].)

Bataille himself in fact proposes not simply replacing (or sublating) but rather *doubling* Hegel, ironically enough in a way very similar to Foucault's internalization of the limit: in Bataille's Hegel, or Hegel as Bataille, the radical negativity that Hegel must expel in order to constitute the dialectic is (impossibly and always already) incorporated within it, in a final postdialectical dialectical move, resulting in a (transgressive, Foucault would say) doubling of "absolute knowledge" (*le savoir absolu*) by not knowing (*le non-savoir*) (Bataille 1988, 108–111). Thus, interestingly enough, Bataille anticipates Foucault's situation of transgression in the death of God (or of Spirit), the internalization of the limit transgression, all the while affirming not the negation or the going beyond of Hegel but his repetition – with a difference. Bataille thus affirms not sheer "language to infinity," but instead the doubling of a Hegelian end of history with the historically resistant but sociologically grounded movements of eroticism, laughter, and poetry: dialectical negativity not abolished or superseded but "out of a job."

If for Bataille transgression was never restricted to a sheer play of language, the same soon came to be the case for Foucault as well. By the time of "Nietzsche, Genealogy, History" (1971) (ELCP, 139–164), we can see how the movement of a seemingly subjectless language, murmuring infinitely, reflecting its permutations around and across an internal limit, morphs into a subjectless history, consisting of a temporal movement elaborating itself without the intervention of God, spirit, or great men. The micromovements of historical detail are now extralinguistic to the extent that the subjectless *littéraire*/postphilosopher, implied in Foucault's proto–*Tel Quel* version of transgression, is succeeded by the patient and painstaking genealogist-historian, working tirelessly in the *hémicycle* of the Bibliothèque Nationale. The two autobiographical personae of Foucault – textual transgressor and genealogist – are curiously related. Both certainly entail the death of an overarching subjectivity and ceaseless textual elaboration. But by moving away from a Bataille-inspired transgression, Foucault ultimately doubles Bataille even more rigorously, since Bataille himself was, by profession, a patient archivist-librarian – at that ultimate fantasia of the library, the Bibliothèque Nationale.

Allan Stoekl

SEE ALSO

> *Contestation*
> *Difference*
> *Marxism*
> *Space*
> *Georges Bataille*
> *Maurice Blanchot*
> *Jacques Derrida*
> *Georg Wilhelm Friedrich Hegel*
> *Martin Heidegger*

SUGGESTED READING

Bataille, Georges. 1987. *Death and Sensuality*, trans. Mary Dalwood. London: Marion Boyars.
 1988. *Inner Experience*, trans. Leslie Anne Boldt. Albany: The SUNY Press.
Deleuze, Gilles. 1983. *Nietzsche and Philosophy*, trans. Hugh Tomlinson. New York: Columbia University Press.

Derrida, Jacques. 1978a. "From Restricted to General Economy, a Hegelianism without Reserve," in *Writing and Difference*, trans. Alan Bass. Chicago: University of Chicago Press, pp. 251–277.

Gasché, Rodolphe. 1986. *The Tain of the Mirror*. Cambridge, MA: Harvard University Press.

Guerlac, Suzanne. 1997. *Literary Polemics: Sartre, Valéry, Breton*. Stanford, CA: Stanford University Press.

Kojève, Alexandre. 1947. *Introduction à la lecture de Hegel*. Paris: Gallimard.

Kristeva, Julia. 1984. *Revolution in Poetic Language*, trans. Margaret Waller. New York: Columbia University Press.

Stoekl, Allan. 1989. "1937: The Avant-Garde Embraces Science," in *A New History of French Literature*, ed. Denis Hollier. Cambridge, MA: Harvard University Press, pp. 928–935.

Tauchert, Ashley. 2008. *Against Transgression*. Malden, MA: Wiley-Blackwell.

88

TRUTH

I N HIS FINAL works, Foucault explains his overall project as a "history of truth" centered on the relations between subjectivity and truth. Whereas the early archaeology focuses primarily on the formation of new objects and discourses of knowledge, and later, genealogy focuses on techniques of power and self-formation, the problematic of truth is the overriding framework through which Foucault develops these analyses. Throughout all of his work, in fact, Foucault's question is how discourse, institutions, politics, and subjects are established within regimes of truth.

To emerge as a knowable object in reality is also always to enter into a regime of truth, according to Foucault. A regime (or game) should be understood as a set of rules and constraints divided between true and false discourses and practices (EEW1, 297). With this notion, Foucault displaces the traditional correspondence theory of truth, which holds that our knowledge must correspond with or reflect pregiven objects in reality. In order to correspond with these objects, a certain form of subjectivity is required that would be able to access the truth of these objects and hold onto this truth over time. In the history of philosophy, this subject usually takes on a set of universal and ahistorical characteristics that are necessary to have access to such knowledge. When the subject possesses these characteristics naturally and without any necessary history or practice, Foucault calls this kind of subject one that possesses truth through *self-evidence*.

Foucault's philosophy of truth resists the notion that there is either an a priori constituted subject or a pregiven object and instead examines the historical constitution of the subject, the object, and their interrelation. If truth, in Foucault's thought, is involved with correspondence, it can only be one that is historically produced (Gros 2004, 11–12). His entire philosophical career involves a critique of the notion of *self-evidence* and the subject and object that would naturally correspond in such a relation. In his philosophy of truth, it can be seen that each period of his thought involves a critique of self-evidence from a different vantage point, whether it be the history of scientific discourse, the immanence of power and knowledge, or the subject's relation to itself.

Through the critique of self-evidence, Foucault situates the problem of truth at the historical level, excavating the historical conditions of possibility of a given regime of truth. This is the aim in combining key insights of the Kantian analytic with history, in what Foucault calls the *historical a priori*. Instead of asking what it is that makes possible a universal subject capable of knowledge in general, it asks what embeds a subject within a particular regime of truth, what practices are required, what discourses are accepted, and what cost is paid for the subject to enter into that reality. At the same time, the question is one of the conditions behind an object becoming a positive figure of knowledge. What procedures, what order of space, visibility, and time, what institutions, and what relations of power were required for an object such as madness, perversion, delinquency, or the anthropological ideas of the human being to emerge as knowable objects? For Foucault, a regime of truth is the nexus between the historical conditions of possibility of the subject and the historical conditions of possibility of the object. It is the site where truth names the constraints and modalities required of both subject and object to enter the positivity of reality and engage in a set of possible relations (EEW2, 459–460; EEW3, 242–254).

Reflections on truth at the level of history generally tend toward the view that truth is without history entirely, or that its history can only be one of progressive unfolding and clarification. The latter, teleological view claims that through time we are finally able to grasp the great truths of labor, life, language, psychology, sexuality, human rights, liberal government, and so on. These were truths that always existed outside of history, but to discover them it required the test of time and the trial and error of finite human practice: slowly through history, the infinite unshakeable truth reveals itself in the finite.

Instead of a universal theory of truth modified by the modalities of teleological, revealing, or obscuring history, Foucault thinks of a topology of truth in its history and geography. Truth is linked to history in the modality of the event, which requires an examination of its conditions of emergence and its geography of instantiation. Truth is produced within a certain set of circumstances and produces a certain set of behaviors and constraints. The truth-event opposes the notion of self-evident demonstrative truth that can be found in any place or any time regardless of the circumstances. In short, Foucault would like to study a "truth which does not belong to the order of what is, but to the order of what happens, a truth, therefore, which is not given in the form of discovery, but in the form of the event, a truth which is not found but aroused and hunted down: production rather than apophantic" (ECF-PP, 237).

In his archaeological texts from *History of Madness* through *The Archaeology of Knowledge*, Foucault develops a methodological principle: the rejection of the universal from the start in order to examine the *event* of knowledge and its rules of construction. Traditionally, the history of science has taken the "universality" of a scientific discovery and used it as a filter to examine the history of errors and mistakes leading up to this truth. The truth then allows us to separate it from all of the errors and ideologies that led up to its discovery (Gros 2004, 13). In short, the purity of the scientific lineage leading up to this truth is extracted from its accidental and erroneous history.

Foucault's archaeological method is the inverse of this. Instead of starting with the universal, he starts with a particular discourse and excavates the archaeological conditions that made such a discourse possible. As he would later explain in a lecture at the Collège de France:

> [I]nstead of deducing concrete phenomena from universals, or instead of starting with universals as an obligatory grid of intelligibility for certain concrete practices, I would like to start with these concrete practices and, as it were, pass these universals through the grid of these practices.... It was the same question in the case of madness.... If we suppose that it does not exist, then what can history make of these different events and practices which are apparently organized around something that is supposed to be madness? (ECF-BIO, 3; see also EAK, 207)

Madness should be supposed not to exist, in the sense that it does not have any ahistorical or universal reality that we can use to interpret its particular historical variations. Instead, the key to understanding the truth regime of madness is found in the rules and practices by which madness was produced as an object to be known and controlled, along with the forms of subjectivity that it produced and constrained. So, the truth of madness is not to be discovered internal to some true or false definition of "madness in itself" but is instead the very reality produced by a game of truth. Truth does not correspond to some pregiven object, as in the classical correspondence theory of truth, but instead truth is itself productive of and produced by reality.

It should be noted here that Foucault is not interested in any and all games of truth or a critique of science as such. His interest, instead, is in those discourses and games that involve the truth of the human subject, or how "the subject himself becomes an object of possible knowledge" (EEW2, 460). Namely, the task is to see how a possible "science of the human" developed and how a truth game was crystallized around the human. As Frédéric Gros writes, "man is fundamentally thought in [Foucault's] work as *an animal of truth*" (Gros 2004, 11, Gros's italics). All of Foucault's analyses aim to excavate the processes through which man has become both an object and a subject of truth: from the human sciences to the incitement of discourse where the subject seeks to constantly produce and discover an inner truth through confession and self-examination (see EHS1).

The analysis of madness can then be situated as the initiation of Foucault's studies of man's enmeshment within a game of truth. *History of Madness* examines how the Renaissance understanding of madness as a force inhabiting the entire cosmos was transformed into a psychological truth of the human being. How was the seat of the truth of madness shifted from the fabric of the cosmos to an exclusive location within the human being? Furthermore, how did the truth of madness as the irrational exterior to human reason serve to found the truth interior to modern reason?

Foucault shows that the division between madness and reason is not established on some pure rational decision. It is not a positivistic universal that can retrospectively be separated from its accidental history. Instead, the modern truth regime of madness is rooted in a political and economic history of division: the great confinement of the mad and the poor across Europe in the seventeenth century. This position of exclusion was a fundamental condition of possibility for the division between madness and reason and for the emergence of mental illness as a scientific discourse and object of study. In the great confinement, the mad had not been separated from indolence and other forms of social deviance. Yet, it was in this space of confinement where the first doctors of mental illness began to articulate a scientific discourse based on the emergent order of visibility and sayability. However, even the scientific basis on which these doctors could make their statements about mental illness was lacking. This construction was instead based on a complicated subjection of the mad through new structures of recognition and reflexivity. The famous liberation of the mad from their chains in France was coupled with the development of a whole new structure of subjection whereby the mad were led to recognize and internalize their own illness: physical chains substituted for psychical ones. Further, this was a discourse rooted in a figure of authority, the medical person, which did not yet have a scientific basis for understanding madness.

In this sense, the scientific status of the truth of madness as mental illness is shown to have its archaeological roots in a game of division and exclusion that is not evidenced on the surface of its discourse. The *self-evidence* of the mad subject as a natural scientific object to be studied is thrown into question, and the event of madness in its formation of rules and divisions is shown to be the proper site of investigation of its truth regime. The self-evidence of knowledge would set up a direct correspondence wherein the subject is not transformed or constrained in order to come into relation with the truth. Instead Foucault studies the processes through which this relation between subject and object is made possible: at what price and with what history does an object emerge as something that can be known? What effects of constraint, obedience, and subjection must subjects pass through in order to be knowable as objects of truth?

Foucault's aim is not, however, to claim that the scientific discourse of mental illness is in itself *true* or *false* or even ideological. Mental illness possesses its own truth regime and a reality that is not at all illusory. The task is not to propose its falsification by referencing some greater truth but instead to expose its conditions of construction, thus demonstrating that truth never rests purely on its own foundations but is always bound to a relation of otherness in its ties to a long institutional and political history. As Foucault claims in his final unpronounced notes to his final lecture at the Collège de France, "truth is never the same" (ECF-COT, 340).

Foucault's archaeological examination of scientific discourse initiated a number of critiques against the Marxist theory of truth, critiques that were further developed in his genealogy of power. In fact, Foucault claims that the prominent power-knowledge dyad of this period was intended as a displacement of Marxist ideology theory (FCF-GDV, 74–78). Generally speaking, ideology theory supposes that a critique of a given discourse as false or ideological will allow one to attain a deeper underlying truth: smashing the veneer of ideology opens up the path of the real and the true. For Foucault, there is no deeper layer of reality that can be found underneath the surface and there is no deeper truth that he claims to reveal underneath the divisions and constraints of a truth regime.

Ideology theory claims, furthermore, that false appearances are due strictly to the machinations of power and that the brilliance of truth could tear down this facade. This schema is evidenced in the great battling cry of political analysis and activism: "We must speak truth to power." This cry is quite familiar to the history of the West, such that Foucault situates its emergence with the Greeks, all the way back to Sophocles' *Oedipus Rex* and Plato's political philosophy (EEW3, 30–32). This cry supposes that if we were able to penetrate the iron gates of power with all of the brilliant and incriminating truths it has been hiding, then power would simply collapse and lose the legitimate grounds for its justification. In short, it is supposed that truth and power are external to one another and that power can only legitimate itself through an illusory or deceptive relation to the truth. Foucault's intervention into political analysis is to show that we should no longer consider truth and power in relations of externality but instead consider them in a field of immanence. Every form of power is supported by a network of truth relations, and every regime of truth carries with it effects of power (EEW3, 132–133). Just as he refused it in the study of madness, Foucault will refuse the claim that a truth regime is false or ideological because it is produced by and produces relations of power. Instead, he will aim to show that truth is itself immanent to power and produces power relations.

Truth, then, is not a strictly epistemological problem where the purity of knowledge is opposed to the effects of coercion produced on the subject through power. Instead, truth involves relations of force that compel certain conducts and produce forms of subjectivity. As Foucault explained in an interview, "My problem is to see how men govern (themselves and others) by the production of truth (… not the production of true utterances but the establishment of domains in which the practice of true and false can be made at once ordered and pertinent)" (EEW3, 230). This definition of his problem, which could apply to his entire corpus, points to the way in which the direction of human conduct is always compelled by a discourse or ordering of the true and the false. Political power is unintelligible without the deployment of truth as a matrix through which subjects govern themselves and others.

In moving away from epistemological models to a study of political regimes of truth, Foucault will study the role of truth in relation to the history of juridical forms. The relationship between what he will call veridiction (the establishment of veridical domains or truth regimes) and juridical forms or jurisdiction is present in most of his studies during the 1970s. These analyses show the points at which political technologies move between a foundation and legitimation rooted primarily in juridical forms to one rooted primarily in a regime of truth. Generally speaking, this is the framework of analysis for *Discipline and Punish*. In this work, Foucault provides a genealogy of the process through which the juridical question of "what did you do?" is displaced by a question of truth about the subject: "who are you?" (EDP, 17–19). The whole apparatus of disciplinary power is predicated on this new technology of truth that seeks to find the truth of the individual, rather than one that seeks to establish whether a certain infraction was broken, requiring a codified punishment. Modern governmental power is thus primarily supported by veridiction, the division between the true and the false, and only secondarily tied to jurisdiction, the division between the permissible and the nonpermissible.

In a series of lectures from 1973 in Rio de Janeiro, "Truth and Juridical Forms," Foucault traces out an even longer history of this relation between truth and jurisdiction, leading from the Homeric era, through the tragedy of Oedipus and the medieval practices of inquiry, up to the practices of examination and panopticism in the eighteenth and nineteenth centuries (EEW3, 1–89). What these histories show is the increasing instantiation and prioritization of procedures of truth over jurisdiction in the field of politics. Stated otherwise, there were always procedures of truth embedded within jurisdiction, but increasingly truth became a principle of verification, rationalization, and individualization, exerting a much greater force than jurisdiction itself.

Modern veridical forms have increasingly moved away from truth-events and rituals (such as the Homeric trial by test or combat) toward a reign of demonstrative truth where there is a totalizing grid of all possible subjects to be known and controlled. The Panopticon is one such example of a totalizing *tableau vivant* where all subjects can be placed and known at all times. In this case, we see how demonstrative truth is not tied to a purely scientific history but a political history that set up the conditions for subjects to be observable, controllable, and visible at all times and all places.

In Foucault's final works on the technologies of subjectivity, the problematic of the government of human beings (self and others) by truth is developed to focus more extensively on the government of self by truth. If his earlier studies examined the government of others by truth in more depth, his later work will show the network that flows between self and other, and between politics and ethics. These late studies do not come at the expense of the studies on power but instead deepen the analysis of the government of human beings by truth. A theory of power in itself was never his aim, explains Foucault, but rather a study of techniques of subjection and reflexivity: "I am working on the history, at a given moment, of the way reflexivity of self upon self was established, and the discourse of truth linked to it" (EEW2, 452).

The analysis of technologies of subjectivity, furthermore, deepens the critique of self-evidence and the demonstrative reign of truth. Here, Foucault examines the different rituals and procedures through which subjects recognize or speak truths of themselves. With each of these late studies, he accounts for a different set of practices that are required of the subject to encounter or speak a truth, and none of them begin with the idea of a natural subject with immediate access to the true (EEW1, 290). Since Descartes, philosophy has searched for a direct and natural relationship between the subject who knows and the object it knows. In what Foucault cautiously terms the "Cartesian moment," the subject takes on a form of self-evidence where there is a direct interior link between the *I think* and its access to a clear and distinct truth (ECF-HOS, 14). This Cartesian moment founds a relationship between subjectivity and truth that is free from ritual, practice, *askesis*, and self-transformation. It is a form of subjectivity freed from what Foucault calls "spirituality," or the set of necessary transformations required of the subject to access the truth (ECF-HOS, 15–16). Foucault's interest in the practices of self in antiquity addresses a variety of different modes of spirituality; that is, the modes of how the subject is formed in relation to an event of truth.

Foucault assigns a term for this relationship between subjectivity and the event of truth in his 1979–1980 course at the Collège de France, "Du Gouvernement des Vivants": *alethurgy* or *alethurgical forms* (FCF-GDV, 8–9). Alethurgy combines the Greek word for truth, *aletheia*, with the verb for work or production, *ergon*. Thus, etymologically speaking, *alethurgy* refers to the production of the truth. Foucault certainly has a critique of Heidegger in mind here by proposing a reformulation of the Greek term to emphasize the *production* of truth rather than its *unveiling* or *disclosure*. For Foucault, truth has no underlying substratum to be unveiled or disclosed. Instead, alethurgical forms will consider the production of truth through rituals and practices where the subject manifests, recognizes, speaks, or forms an obligation to truth. Whereas archaeology investigated the historical event through which a broader regime of truth came into place at the level of scientific discourse, alethurgy will focus more directly on the event of truth as it occurs through the practices and rituals carried out by and through the subject. What are the rituals and procedures through which a truth gains its force at the level of the subject? What effects of transformation does truth have on the subject, and how have we established such a devotion to truth in the history of the West?

Here it might be asked, and Foucault poses this question himself: why continue using the notion of truth for these practices and rituals? The archaeological studies emphasized the process through which the human became an object of scientific discourses of truth. Yet, Foucault wants to show that truth had a different history and a different set of rules prior to the modern scientific understanding of truth as objective and demonstrative. Truth has not always presented itself as an ahistorical and unconditioned object (see also Detienne 1999). These studies in antiquity aim to restore the modality of the event to the advent of truth. In a late interview, Foucault clarified this emphasis on truth:

> After all, why truth? How did it come about that all of Western culture began to revolve around this obligation of truth which has taken a lot of different forms? Things being as they are, nothing so far has shown that it is possible to define a strategy outside of this concern. It is within the field of the obligation to truth that it is possible to move about in one way or another, sometimes against the effects of domination which may be linked to structures of truth or institutions entrusted with truth.... Thus, one escaped from a domination of truth not by playing a game that was totally different from the game of truth but by playing the same game differently, or playing another game, another, with other trump cards. (EEW1, 295)

There is no pure outside to the truth game but only a different set of rules and a different set of possible cards. Foucault's studies of the ancient world do not then seek to escape games of truth but to examine a different set of rules and cards by which these games were played. In order to do this, they analyze games of truth that are specifically tied to the character of the event: in terms of rituals, practices, forms of speech, and *askesis*.

In this movement to examine a whole different set of truth games free from the demonstrative reign of self-evidence, Foucault will show the different forms in which truth was not primarily predicated on an epistemological but rather an ethical (or political) relation in antiquity. For example, in *The Hermeneutics of the Subject*, he shows that modern philosophy has entirely overlooked the fundamental link between the care of the self (*epimeleia heautou*) and truth in antiquity. The maxim at Delphi, know thyself (*gnōthi seauton*), has almost completely overshadowed this other history. Foucault shows the Hellenistic practices through which self-care was always required of the subject in order to have access to truth, and where self-knowledge only had meaning with respect to a preliminary care of the self. A reexamination of the figure of Socrates in *The Apology* illuminates the centrality of this theme of self-care. Here, Socrates is fundamentally a character who urges others to take care of themselves, and it is only through such care that they might eventually attain the path to wisdom. This theme is clearly present in all of Stoic philosophy as well, and Foucault shows that it was, in fact, a fundamental concern of all of antiquity.

In *The Courage of Truth*, Foucault extends his studies of *parrēsia* (frank speech or fearless truth-telling) from the previous year's course, "The Government of Self and Others," and shows the way in which the true discourse of a subject is bound not to a condition of knowledge but an ethical and political condition. For example, in Plato's *Laches*, Socrates' ability to speak the truth is predicated not on a correspondence with his knowledge but on an ethical relation of mastery he has achieved in his deeds. Thus, it is through the harmony between words and deeds that Socrates has access to the true and frank discourse of *parrēsia*. The Cynics radicalize this harmony and ask the question: what is the form of life such that we can make the brilliance of the truth appear in the very form of our existence? The Cynics arrive at a point where *parrēsia* becomes a confrontational form of life over and above a confrontational form of speech. Thus, we see that the *alethurgical* appearance of truth is already produced in the mode of existence itself, in the *bios*, which does not necessarily await the articulation of the *logos* to become visible: "In short, Cynicism makes life, existence, *bios*, what could be called an alethurgy, a manifestation of truth" (ECF-COT, 172). Arriving at the end of Foucault's philosophical career, we are quite far from the reign of self-evidence. Instead truth is manifested in the scandalous practice of Cynic critique, one that brilliantly appears through *bios* rather than *logos* with the force of an event.

In concluding, it is worth considering two critiques often posed to Foucault's philosophy of truth. The first is the claim that Foucault is nothing more than a radical relativist and so must not be able to tell us very much about truth. This claim fails to grasp the nature of a regime of truth that is precisely not just any set of rules or rituals but ones that have been historically instantiated to have determinate effects on the very being of the subject. The radical relativist would have no interest in games of truth, because the radical relativist thinks that there are no rules of constraint and that any and all acts may pass as true depending on the beliefs or opinions of the individual. This position could not be further from Foucault's view that we must understand the specific constraints that lead us to formulate and carry out truths on ourselves, whether it be in scientific studies that objectify the subject, practices of power that conduct the subject, or in the ethical relations that the subject holds to itself. Truth is always embedded within a network of constraints and possible actions.

The second critique leveled against Foucault asks about the truth content of his own utterances that he produces in his books, essays, and interviews. In response to this question, Foucault claims that his books should be read as experiences and not as factual claims to be verified as true or false (EEW3, 239–246). Foucault's aim in writing philosophy is not to expose us to some deeper truth, for this would return his work to the very ideology theory that his work aims to displace. Instead, these experience books aim at the immanent critique of the intolerable effects of power and subjection that certain discourses of truth hold for the subject. The aim is not

526 / DON T. DEERE

to break free from the regime of truth as such but to locate the points of resistance where the rules of the games might be constructed otherwise. These points of resistance are most often located in those places where Foucault sees the possibility of restoring the status of truth as event over and against a demonstrative truth that appears self-evident.

This philosophy of truth is certainly not one that seeks to provide a theory of truth as such. It is instead a critical history of different truth regimes, with the aim being not to show that any particular regime is true or false but to demonstrate the rules of construction and the effects and constraints that these regimes have on the subject. In our own time, these constraints have increasingly become ossified around the self-evident and necessary notion of truth as demonstration (see also Lorenzini 2010). Foucault's histories aim to shatter the self-evidence of demonstrative truth by showing that truth is itself an event with its own conditions, history, and spatiotemporal foundations.

Demonstrative truth is true regardless of its place or time; dwelling everywhere, it can be known by anyone at any time. It is a truth waiting to be discovered and one that is progressively clarified and grasped through history. The truth-event is by contrast like a lightning bolt that transforms those who come into contact with it. It is a truth belonging to the order of force and not to the order of knowledge. This truth is a

> dispersed, discontinuous, interrupted truth which will only speak or appear from time to time, where it wishes to, in certain places; a truth which does not appear everywhere, at all times, or for everyone; a truth which is not waiting for us, because it is a truth which has its favourable moments, its propitious places, its privileged agents and bearers. It is a truth which has its geography. (ECF-PP, 236)

In this sense, all of Foucault's studies aim at studying truth as an event to show the conditions of space, time, the distribution of bodies, knowledge, and power that enable a particular truth to emerge and gain force at a particular time and place. If Foucault's own discourse is allied to a truth claim, it is to the character of truth as an event. It is a discourse that works to produce this effect of transformation on the level of force and not strictly on the epistemological level of what is to be known. Perhaps, then, a different experience of truth in its force as an event could open the points of contingency where this "animal of truth" might shatter the dominion of demonstration with the brilliance of a lightning bolt.

Don T. Deere

SEE ALSO

> *Historical a Priori*
> *Knowledge*
> *Parrēsia*
> *Power*
> *Self*
> *Spirituality*
> *Martin Heidegger*

SUGGESTED READING

Detienne, Marcel. 1999. *The Masters of Truth in Archaic Greece*. Cambridge, MA: Zone Books.

Flynn, Thomas R. 1985. "Truth and Subjectivation in the Later Foucault," *Journal of Philosophy* 82, no. 10:531–540.

Gros, Frédéric. 2004. "Michel Foucault, Une Philosophie de la Vérité," in *Michel Foucault: Philosophie Anthologie*, ed. Arnold I. Davidson and Frédéric Gros. Paris: Éditions Gallimard, pp. 11–25.

Lorenzini, Daniele. 2008. "'El Cinismo Hace de la Vida Una *Aleturgie*.' Apuntes Para Una Relectura del Recorrido Filosófico del Último Michel Foucault," *Revista Laguna* 23:63–90.

2010. "Para Acabar con la Verdad-Demostración. Bachelard, Canguilhem, Foucault y La Historia de los 'Regímenes de Verdad,'" *Revista Laguna* 26:9–34.

Prado, C. G. 2006. *Foucault and Searle on Truth*. Cambridge: Cambridge University Press, chap. 3.

Revel, Judith. 2009. "Vérité/Jeux de Vérité," in *Le Vocabulaire de Foucault*. Paris: Éditions Ellipses, pp. 64–65.

89

VIOLENCE

FOUCAULT'S MOST EXPLICIT discussion of violence occurs in his late text "Subject and Power," originally an interview conducted by Paul Rabinow in 1982. One of his key objectives in this text is to understand what constitutes the specificity of power relations, and he is therefore forced to inquire into its relationship to violence. He poses essentially the same question as Hannah Arendt did in her definitive study of violence, *On Violence* (1970), namely whether violence is simply the ultimate form of power, "that which in the final analysis appears as its real nature when it is forced to throw aside its mask and to show itself as it really is" (EEW3, 340). He also follows Arendt in his negative reply and puts forward an oppositional view of the relationship between power and violence: they are opposites in the sense that where one rules absolutely the other is absent: "Where the determining factors saturate the whole there is no relationship of power; slavery is not a power relationship when man is in chains" (EEW3, 342).

Foucault defines violence in this text in narrow terms as physical harm to the body: "A relationship of violence acts upon a body or upon things; it forces, it bends, it breaks on the wheel, it destroys, or it closes the door on all possibilities" (EEW3, 340). He distinguishes it from power by arguing that a power relationship is a mode of action that does not act directly and immediately on others' bodies but rather acts on their actions: it is a set of actions on other actions. This means, first, that the one over whom power is exercised is thoroughly recognized as a subject, as a person who acts. Second, he or she must be free, meaning here that when faced with a relationship of power, a whole field of possibilities – responses, reactions, results, and possible inventions – may open up and be realized. Violence, on the other hand, acts directly and immediately on the body. Its opposite pole can only be passivity and its only response to resistance an attempt to break it down. It is not an action on an action of a subject but an action on a body or things.

This neat separation of power from violence restores the possibility of a critique of violence, as some of Foucault's commentators have aptly pointed out. Thomas Flynn (Flynn 2005, 244–245, 250), for example, notes that for Foucault all violence attaches to relations of power, but not all relations of power necessarily entail violence. It is rather the species of power that Foucault calls "domination" and Flynn labels "negative" power with which violence is necessarily associated. It refers to power relations that are nonconsensual and have become institutionalized in a way that the individuals embedded in them are unable to overturn or alter (EEW1, 299).

In light of Foucault's earlier writings on power, the categorical distinction he makes between power and violence in this late text is, however, in many ways perplexing. It seems as if there had been almost a complete reversal in his views. In his original and extensive work on modern forms of power such as disciplinary power, for example, Foucault seemed to have argued for exactly the opposite: any clear distinction between power and violence is untenable. Foucault had also used the model of war for analyzing the functioning of power relations, and had argued for the superiority of this model in comparison to all contractual models of power.

Foucault's characterization of disciplinary power in *Discipline and Punish* is in many ways strikingly similar to his late definition of violence: disciplinary power is power that acts directly on bodies. It oversteps the rules of law and right and is addressed to bodies, to "man-as-body." It is exercised through constant surveillance, observation, and examination but also through more manifestly violent means of manipulating bodies through a closely meshed grid of material coercions. The violence of disciplinary power is markedly different from the violence characterizing earlier forms of punishment, however. It does not subject the body to violence that is spectacular and disproportional but, on the contrary, disciplinary violence is carefully hidden, meticulous, and economical. It focuses on the details of the body, on single movements, on their timing and rapidity. It organizes bodies in space and schedules their every action for maximum effect. Unlike older forms of bodily coercion such as public tortures, slavery, and hangings, disciplinary power does not operate by mutilating the body, but this does not mean that it should be understood as nonviolent.

Foucault sets disciplinary power in opposition to juridical power. Whereas juridical power operates with the binary framework of legal and illegal, disciplinary power is capable of making more nuanced distinctions through the functioning of norms. The contrast to juridical power is illuminating in terms of understanding the fusion of disciplinary power with new forms of violence. Although juridical power is arguably founded on violence, and the threat of violence forms its necessary condition of possibility, the relationship between power and violence at least appears instrumental. The exercise of police violence, for example, is intended to be restrictive and punitive and is reserved for those who break or contest the law. The sharp distinction that Arendt, for example, makes between power as an end in itself and violence as merely the means for securing it seems to hold in the case of juridical power. What characterizes disciplinary power, on the other hand, is that the dividing line between power and violence becomes permeable, at times totally indistinguishable. Disciplinary power/violence is not only punitive but also corrective, rehabilitating and restoring. In short, it produces subjectivity.

Another important instance in Foucault's oeuvre that seems to question the possibility of a categorical distinction between power and violence occurs in his Collège de France lecture course "Society Must Be Defended" (*Il faut défendre la société*) held in 1976. He introduces the course by noting that he would like to begin a series of investigations into whether war can provide a principle for the analysis of power relations. Rather than war being seen as a disruptive principle, he wants to treat it as a principle of intelligibility for understanding history, power, and society. With the model of war, Foucault attempts to offer an alternative to what he calls "the economic models of power": power should not be regarded as a right, which can be possessed in the way that one possesses a commodity. It is not something that the individual can hold, and that he or she can surrender, either as a whole or in part so as to constitute a political sovereignty (ECF-SMD, 13). Rather than understanding political power in terms of contracts, laws, and the establishment of sovereignty, we should understand it in terms of an unending and shifting struggle, a movement that makes some dominant over others. In the first lecture, Foucault famously inverts Clausewitz's (1984, 87) dictum that war is the continuation of politics by other means and chooses as his working hypothesis the claim that politics is the continuation of war. He distinguishes this model from the juridical contract schema represented by Hobbes and his contractarian followers by claiming that the essential opposition is not between the legitimate and the illegitimate but between struggle and submission (ECF-SMD, 17). This war is thus not the abstract, Hobbesian war of every man against every man but a concrete historical struggle in which groups fight groups. Foucault claims that Western political thought has been dominated by social contract theories focusing on the constitution of sovereignty and positing the contract as the matrix of political power. This discourse has covered up the memory of real war that lies at the genesis of sovereignty. As Foucault polemically formulates his aim, it is to show how the birth of states, their organization, and juridical structures are not the result of a contract but arise from and are maintained in the blood and mud of battles. Violence must be understood as fundamentally constitutive of our social and political reality in this sense.

Although it is thus important to take seriously Foucault's late distinction between power and violence and its significance for critiques of violence, this distinction is not the most original contribution that Foucault makes for our understanding of violence. If Foucault's understanding of violence is reduced to a categorical distinction between consensual power and coercive violence, we lose sight of what is most original and important in his approach to it. All definitions of violence, including the ones that Foucault himself provides, must be understood in the light of his understanding of power and knowledge as political acts, and their extension and validity must be open to constant contestation.

When we analyze power on the level of individual acts, it is possible to make fairly clear distinctions between acts of power and acts of violence. When we move to the level of governmentality and attempt to analyze the technologies of power, the distinction becomes more problematic. The practices and institutions of government, in the broad sense of the term, are always enabled, regulated, and justified by a specific form of reasoning or rationality that defines the ends and the appropriate means of achieving them. The analytics of power technologies must concentrate not only on the actual mechanisms of power but also on the rationality that is part of the practices of governing. If we think of a power network as a game, as Foucault has also suggested (e.g., FDE3, 542), then the analysis of the techniques of government would mean an analysis of both the implicit and the explicit rules that this game conforms to. On this level, it is difficult to start with a clear distinction between violence and power because the rules, to a large extent, determine what is understood as acts of power or as acts of violence in the specific game. Moreover, different rules or rationalities are compatible with different forms of violence.

We could take the example of "domestic violence" and argue that it is only in a certain cultural and historical context that it even exists. Forms of behavior that we now conceptualize as domestic violence have only very recently been understood as forms of violence at all. Another example could be "terrorism." Because our descriptions of the world are inevitably the expression of hegemonic power relations, there cannot be any objective or purely descriptive definitions of terrorism and terror. Many of the recent critical analyses of terrorism acknowledge Foucault's claim that we should rather attempt to study the political effects of using such a label. Judith Butler (Butler 2004, 87–88), for example, has emphasized that various forms of violence are called "terror" not because there are valences of violence that can be distinguished from one another on objective grounds but because the label functions as a way of characterizing the violence waged by political entities deemed illegitimate by established states. The use of the terms "terror" and "terrorism" works to delegitimize certain forms of violence committed by political entities that are not state centered, and at the same time they sanction a violent response by established states. In other words, terror does not describe a distinct type of violence but a form of violence that is illegitimate. It is not a descriptive notion but a prescriptive notion, the intelligibility of which depends on the normative claim that it makes.

The always partial, power-laden, and arbitrary nature of all interpretative acts is itself often referred to as violence. Foucault oversteps his narrow definition of violence as bodily harm when he describes the "violence" of the interpretative act itself. Following Nietzsche, he claims that any interpretation of reality is always a form of violence in the sense that knowledge "can only be a violation of the things to be known," not a simple recognition or identification of them (EEW3, 9). The task of his genealogical approach is not to expose and record the hidden and essential meaning of our history. Instead, we have to acknowledge that every interpretation is "the violent or surreptitious appropriation of a system of rules" (EEW2, 378). History as interpretation is itself a series of violent acts, and Foucault's genealogies must be understood as weapons in this silent war.

On the basis of Foucault's analytics of power, it is thus ultimately impossible to secure any categorical, context-free definition of violence. On the contrary, the implication is that we must be wary of all such definitions because of their ignoble histories and inescapable political effects. We must be mindful of Nietszche's assertion that "only that which is without history can be defined" (Nietzsche 1996, 60). Foucault's genealogies should be read as attempts to uncover the underpinning rationality of historically specific practices of power and to study the extent to which this rationality implies and is compatible with specific forms of violence. His most important legacy is not in providing us with a philosophically accurate definition of power and violence but rather in demonstrating how all definitions and social objectivities, including the meaning of violence, are constituted in power/knowledge networks and are therefore matters of political contestation and struggle.

Joanna Oksala

SEE ALSO

> *Contestation*
> *Discipline*
> *Knowledge*
> *Power*
> *War*
> *Friedrich Nietzsche*
> *Carl von Clausewitz*

SUGGESTED READING

Arendt, Hannah. 1970. *On Violence*. San Diego: Harcourt Brace.
Butler, Judith. 2004. *Precarious Life: The Powers of Mourning and Violence*. London: Verso.
Clausewitz, Carl von. 1984. *On War*, ed. Michael Howard and Peter Paret. Princeton, NJ: Princeton University Press.
Flynn, Thomas R. 2005. *Sartre, Foucault, and Historical Reason*, volume 2: *A Post-Structuralist Mapping of History*. Chicago: University of Chicago Press.

Hanssen, Beatrice. 2000. *Critique of Violence: Between Poststructuralism and Critical Theory.*
New York: Routledge.

Nietzsche, Friedrich. 1996. *On the Genealogy of Morals*, trans. Douglas Smith. Oxford: Oxford
University Press.

Oksala, Johanna. 2010. "Violence and the Biopolitics of Modernity," *Foucault Studies* 10:23–43.

2011a. "Lines of Fragility: A Foucauldian Critique of Violence," in *Philosophy and the Return
of Violence: Studies from this Widening Gyre*, ed. Christopher Yates and Nathan Eckstrand.
New York: Continuum, pp. 154–170.

2011b. "Violence and Neoliberal Governmentality," *Constellations: An International Journal of
Critical and Democratic Theory* 18:474–486.

90

THE VISIBLE

T HE VISIBLE IS the part of reality that is given to a gaze or by means of a gaze. The Western philosophical tradition identifies this gaze with a sensation and reduces this sensation to the sense of the view. The visible then would be what is given immediately to a view, and what is knowable would be what is given as a representation of an external reality (Rorty 1979, 38–45). In all senses, the view is most often thought of as the primordial condition of theory's neutrality. Sensible contemplation, knowledge, and truth have in principle been connected together since the time of Aristotle's *Metaphysics* (FDE2, 240–245).

Foucault constructed his own conception of the visible against this identification of the visible in the sense of the view, understood as sensory knowledge and subjective perception of reality. In the first place, the visible is the product of a conceptual structuring whose historical forms must be studied from the semiological, epistemological, and political viewpoint. That is, the forms of the visible depend on a historical *regime*. Even if one presupposes the identity of sensory perception, we do not, at each historical moment, see the same *things* or the *same* thing (Shapiro 2003, 8–11). Thus it is really the case that the visible is given to a gaze, but this gaze does not correspond to a "pure" sensory experience; it is necessarily "armed" (EBC, 51) and structured by a signifying system that implies institutions and concepts. According to Foucault, the historicity of the visible shows that there is no absolute heterogeneity between conceptual organizations and sensory experience. Certain objects become visible, gazable, and problematizable because of the intersection of power, knowledge, and forms of ethical subjectification.

If there is a distinction in modernity between words and things, or yet between what can be stated and the visible, it is that knowledge is an "assemblage" (*agencement*) of statements and visibilities. It is impossible to translate images into words completely and to reduce the visible to what can be stated (Deleuze 1988, 39). Nevertheless, this heterogeneity is not a natural given. It belongs to our historical system of reference. During the Renaissance, there was no difference in nature between words and things: "[L]anguage and the gaze intersect to infinity" (EOT, 39, translation modified). The classical *episteme* established a specific form of the visibilities of things by means of representation, whereas the modern *episteme* will anchor representation in the figure of man, the "gazed upon spectator" whose task is to know himself as well as nature, which stands over and against him. Obviously, Foucault's concept of "regimes of visibility" is situated in opposition to the phenomenological tradition, and in particular to Merleau-Ponty, insofar as Merleau-Ponty wanted to rediscover, by means of a perception freed from the weight of the intelligible, "the conceptless language of things."

This critique of phenomenology is, however, tempered by the third great principle structuring Foucault's conception of the visible: the coimplication between the visible and the invisible. Whereas to Merleau-Ponty incarnate vision assumes the chiasmic interweaving between the visible and the invisible, the reversibility between the one who sees and the one who is seen, in Foucault the invisible is a visible that is so close that we do not see it. The visible and the invisible are "of the same material and of the same indivisible substance. Its invisibility, the visible has it only because it is purely and simply visible" (EDL, 104–105, translation modified). The task of philosophy will consist precisely in showing what is invisible on the basis of the very fact of its extreme visibility, "to render visible what is invisible only because it is too much at the surface of things" (FDE3, 540, my translation). Moreover, despite the fact that Foucault has never valorized an ontology of vision (as Martin Jay has argued), some (such as Stefano Catucci) have called his thought "pictural" not only because of the strategic importance of his thought's visual character but also because the image (as Michel de Certeau has said) seems to "institute" the text and thereby lead the reader to "see" his present differently (as John Rajchman has argued).

Thus, we can say that Foucault has studied the historicity of regimes of visibility by bringing to light, on the one hand, the relation between the visible and what can be stated, and, on the other hand, the relation between the visible and the invisible, and he has done this in three large domains: in the epistemology of psychiatry and medicine; in a reflection on painting and its relation to the forms of knowledge; and in the study of modern strategies of surveillance and control. In the *History of Madness*, madness passes from its status of having an absolute and invisible existence in the night of the world to "a thing to be gazed upon" (EHM, 145, translation modified). In the modern asylum, madness is then continually called forth by the psychiatric gaze to be the object of a spectacle. Thus we could say that the history of madness is that of its becoming progressively more visible for a medical gaze that objectifies it under the forms of a discourse. In *The Birth of the Clinic*, Foucault actually proposes to retrace *an archaeology of the medical gaze*. Foucault shows how the clinic, which is the new form of medical experience, which asserts itself near the beginning of the nineteenth century, does not derive from a return to the "conceptless" perceived that the old forms of medical empiricism had imitated. The clinical gaze is constructed by a practice that is bound up with theory and thereby arises from a new relation of the visible to the invisible and from its articulation in relation to the division of the said and the nonsaid (EBC, Chapters VII–VIII). Foucault describes clinical experience as the "domain of the careful gaze and of an empirical vigilance receptive only to the evidence of visible contents. The eye becomes the [depositary] and source of clarity" (EBC, xiii). The "blink of an eye" of clinical medicine is directed always at what is visible in the illness, but this visible is no longer composed, as it was in the eighteenth century, of signs or symptoms that refer to an invisible essence of the illness. The real has the structure of a language that is nothing other than the "language of the things" themselves (EBC, 109). Since the condition of visibility of the illness is the mastery of a clinical gaze and a clinical language, the perceptual and epistemological structure that orders the clinic is that of an "invisible visibility"; the meaning is the surface of things, but the meaning remains invisible so that it cannot be read (EBC, 165). The givenness that the infinite task of rendering the invisible visible (by means of a language that adheres to the observation of things) confronts is this antinomy between a meaning on the surface and that is yet illegible. Even if this complete reversibility of the visible into what can be stated is destined to remain a utopia, the clinical antinomy excludes from the domain of possible knowledge all of what falls outside the gaze. The possibility of the clinic is located in this radical return of the regime of visibility that, on the one hand, depends on the potential ascent of the medical gaze "supported and justified by an institution" (EBC, 89) and, on the other hand, on the transformation of the discursive structure of medicine.

The relation of language to the visible is also at the center of *Raymond Roussel*. In the poem "La vue," Foucault's Roussel aims to bring to light "the first openness of words and things" by means of the appearance of the everyday world in which the visible is somehow the world of "absolute language": "[H]ere we have the enigmatic visibility of the visible and why language has the same birth certificate as that of which it speaks" (EDL, 146–147, translation modified). However, this pure language of things shows already the overcoming of the viewpoint of the observer who still remains at the center of the gaze described in *The Birth of the Clinic*. By the same centripetal movement that undoes language by means of literary language, Roussel also destroys the centrality of the subject in favor of a "gazeless visibility," to which "the eye can no longer dictate its viewpoint" (EDL, 106). If, for Roussel, language "inclines toward things" and is continually reopened by a "prolixity internal to these things themselves," Magritte's canvases are "unmade calligrams" that show not only the slippage between plastic representations and linguistic representations but also the limits of this very distinction between images and language. The paradoxes of the visibility of Magritte's canvases contest the division instituted by Western painting (the image implies resemblance, and resemblance is equivalent to an assertion) while showing the limits of a mode of thought that revolves around the representation of things by images and the assertion of images by words (ENP, 32–33).

In this sense, painting shows the diagram of an epoch (i.e., the diagram of our epoch), exactly as Velasquez's *Las Meninas* showed, by means of the play of visibility and invisibility, the kernel of the classical age. The characters in the picture gaze on a scene for which they are themselves the scene. The spectator is visible for the painter present in the picture, but his image is nowhere to be found in the picture itself. However, a mirror, in the back of the scene, lets us see the invisible and what is external to the picture. But, this mirror reflects nothing that can be found in the same space as itself. The mirror makes visible what all the characters of the picture are gazing on, what orders the representation, but it is itself invisible to the characters of the picture. If this picture is, according to Foucault, "the representation of classical representation," this is because "the profound invisibility of what one sees is inseparable from the invisibility of the one who sees – despite all the mirrors, reflections, imitations, and portraits" (EOT, 16). Since "the profound invisibility" coincides with extreme visibility, one can assert that the visibility of things in the classical *episteme* is based on the invisibility of the knowing subject (here the spectator) who cannot be represented in the representation.

In *Discipline and Punish*, the relation between visibility and invisibility translates the asymmetry of power relations. The Panopticon, the carceral architectural apparatus (*dispositif*) conceived by Bentham, is structured so that each individual is under permanent surveillance by a centralized gaze: the "actor is alone, perfectly individualized, and constantly visible" (EDP, 200). This permanent visibility must induce in the detainee the consciousness of being able to be under surveillance during every moment by a gaze with the result that the detainee interiorizes the gaze and starts to observe himself. The absolute visibility of each organizes the control of time, proceeds to a centralized individuation, and implies a punitive action being exercised on potential behaviors: the conduct created in this way assures a sort of automatic function of power (EDP, 201). But, the asymmetry between the one doing the surveillance and the one under surveillance is only apparent, since the officials doing the surveillance are themselves under control of the principle of absolute visibility. Insofar as it is a model of disciplinary power, the Panopticon "becomes a transparent building in which the exercise of power may be controlled by society as a whole" (EDP, 207, translation modified). Thus, "visibility is a trap"; it is a trap as much for the ones gazed on as for the ones doing the gazing (Roustang 1976, 187). Bentham has thus set up the principle that power must be visible but not verifiable, since at each moment the one doing the surveillance must be visible, whereas anyone whatsoever will be able to play the role of supervisor. In a regime of absolute visibility, the gaze of the system is, fundamentally, blind. The total visibility guaranteed by the Panopticon is complementary with the dram of a society completely transparent to itself, a society in which each will be able to see, from the point of view he occupies, the whole of the society. Thus the invention of panoptic mechanisms is contemporaneous with the advent of the reign of modern public opinion (EPK, 146–165).

If the Panopticon constitutes something like the reverse of liberalism's freedom of the individual, then the absolute visibility of society is counterbalanced by the invisibility of the economic process as a whole. In his lectures on Adam Smith and on Smith's principle of the "invisible hand," Foucault accentuates not the intelligence that would make use of a holistic view of the totality of the economic processes. Instead, Foucault stresses the necessity of the "hand's" invisibility insofar as it is a principle that remains in the background, unawares, so that it can make possible the actions of economic agents: "Invisibility is not just a fact arising from the imperfect nature of human intelligence which prevents people from realizing that there is a hand behind them which arranges or connects everything that each individual does on their own account. Invisibility is absolutely indispensable. It is an invisibility which means that no economic agent should or can pursue the collective good" (ECF-BBIO, 280). The relation between the absolute visibility of the social process and the invisibility as the central principle of a nontotalizable economic process is truly at the heart of liberalism.

However, in his last course at the Collège de France, "The Courage of Truth," Foucault seems to develop a political concept of the visible that amounts to an alternative to the modern concept of surveillance. Being a tool of the interiorization of control, the complete visibility of existence becomes a principle of the manifestation of the true, which is made visible by means of the body. In fact, for the Cynics, "the very body of the truth is made visible, and laughable, in a certain style of life" (ECF-COT, 173). The Cynics' life must be public in all aspects; it must be put on view for the gaze of others in its most everyday and material reality. One has to live without blushing from what one does, by showing in his own entirely visible conduct the dissolution of the traditional, habitual limits of shame and of the dominant moral system. Thus, the Cynic is "something like the visible statue of the truth" (ECF-COT, 310, translation modified). Here, the absolute visibility of existence seems to be completely overturned into a subversive conduct that turns the manifestation of the "true" into the central principle of a "militant life."

Luca Paltrinieri

SEE ALSO

Knowledge
Language
Normalization

Painting (and Photography)
Phenomenology
Power
Xavier Bichat
Maurice Merleau-Ponty
Raymond Roussel

SUGGESTED READING

Deleuze, Gilles. 1988. *Foucault*, trans. Seán Hand. Minneapolis: University of Minnesota Press.

Jay, Martin. 1993. *Downcast Eyes: The Denigration of Vision in Twentieth-Century French Thought*. Berkeley: University of California Press.

Merleau-Ponty, Maurice. 1968. *The Visible and the Invisible*, trans. Alphonso Lingis. Evanston, IL: Northwestern University Press.

Rorty, Richard. 1979. *Philosophy and the Mirror of Nature*. Princeton, NJ: Princeton University Press.

Roustang, François. 1976. "La visibilité est une piège," *Les Temps Modernes* 33:1567–1579. Collected in Philippe Artières et al. 2010. *Surveiller et punir de Michel Foucault. Regards critiques 1975–1979*. Caen: PUC-IMEC, pp. 183–200.

Shapiro, Gary. 2003. *Archaeologies of Vision: Foucault and Nietzsche on Seeing and Saying*. Chicago: University of Chicago Press.

91

WAR

I N *DISCIPLINE AND PUNISH* (1975), Foucault uses "war" (or at least "battle") as a "model" for understanding social relations. But this epistemological use of "war" did not last. In consulting the Collège de France lecture courses, we see him conduct a genealogy of the war model in "Society Must Be Defended" (1975–1976). As a result of this investigation, the use of "war" in volume one of *The History of Sexuality* (1976) is no longer epistemological but rather practical: "war" is seen as a "strategy" for integrating a differential field of power relations. Then, toward the end of the 1970s, perhaps in dismay at discovering in his genealogical investigation a deep relation between the war model and state racism, in "Security, Territory, Population" (1977–1978) Foucault drops "war" to move to "governmentality" as the "grid of intelligibility" of social relations.

In *Discipline and Punish*, Foucault held to what we can call a Deleuzean concept of "emergence" for analyzing social relations. To understand social power, we have to see macrolevel social relations (for instance, those between "experts and subjects," "men and women," or "bourgeoisie and proletariat") as emerging from a "microphysics of power" by means of a resolution or integration of a multiplicity or differential field of force relations. It is in this emergence scheme, moving from social relations back down to the microphysics from which they emerge, that Foucault uses the war model rather straightforwardly in *Discipline and Punish*:

> Now, the study of this micro-physics presupposes that the power exercised on the body is conceived not as a property, but as a strategy, that its effects of domination are attributed not to "appropriation," but to dispositions, maneuvers, tactics, techniques, functionings; that one should decipher in it a network of relations, constantly in tension, in activity, rather than a privilege that one might possess; that one should take as its model a perpetual battle rather than a contract regulating a transaction or the conquest of a territory. (EDP, 26)

In the 1975–1976 lecture courses, published as *Society Must Be Defended*, Foucault conducts a genealogy of the epistemological use of "war" as a model for social relations. In *Society*, Foucault proceeds by inverting the Clausewitzian saying that "war is politics by other means," or better, by showing that Clausewitz had himself inverted an older discourse whose formula "politics is war by other means" had put war as the model or "grid of intelligibility" for social relations (ECF-SMD, 163). In fact, Foucault finds that war as a grid of intelligibility has been "posited" for our historical discourse (ECF-SMD, 164). In other words, whereas a statement from an earlier discourse about, say, the Trojan origins of the Franks, would be neither true nor false for us, statements in the discourse in which the grid of intelligibility for social power is war would have a truth value for us: they could be demonstrated to be either true or false (ibid.).

The content of the war model has three aspects: (1) social power relations are anchored in a given historical war so that politics "sanctions and reproduces" the result of that war; (2) political struggles are continuations of that same war; and (3) a final decision that ends politics can only come in a final battle (ECF-SMD, 15–16). These three aspects produce three novelties of the war model: (1) it is the first historical-political discourse in postmedieval Europe; (2) it enshrines an explicit perspectivalism, in that the speaking subject must be on one side or the other of the social binary; and (3) as a result of the anchoring of politics in specific historical sequences, there are singular rather than universal rights (ECF-SMD, 52).

What Foucault finds as the results of his genealogy of the war schema was most likely dismaying to him, for he finds one of its main origins in the "race war" theory of Boulainvilliers and the seventeenth- and eighteenth-century French reactionary petty nobility, as well as the final imbrications of it in contemporary state racism and biopower (ECF-SMD, 258–261). We must remember here that "race" for Boulainvilliers was not a modern biological racism but indicates a "people" like the Franks, Gauls, Romans, or Celts in struggle with another "people" (ECF-SMD, 77). Although the analysis of these peoples might certainly involve "physico-biological facts" (ECF-SMD, 54), "race" was not so much a biological object in itself as a discursive strategy in a social struggle (ECF-SMD, 61).

Foucault begins his genealogy of the war model by dismissing the "false paternity" of the social war discourse in Machiavelli and Hobbes. Rather than a political tactic as it was for Machiavelli (ECF-SMD, 164, 169) or a philosophical principle as it was for Hobbes (ECF-SMD, 89–99), "war" in the social war discourse is real historical war. There is thus a dual birth of the social war model, in the English revolutionaries in the 1630s, who point back to the Norman Conquest (ECF-SMD, 99–109), and in the French petty nobility in the 1690s, who point back to the victory of Clovis and the Franks over the Gallo-Romans (ECF-SMD, 144–155). In reading the English revolutionaries and the French petty noble Boulainvilliers, Foucault notes a paradox: it is with the defeat of the noble right to war, when war becomes the monopoly of the state, that the social war model arises (ECF-SMD, 49). For Boulainvilliers, history, or the clash of unequal forces, is always stronger than nature and its theoretical equality (ECF-SMD, 157). Thus we must focus on how the military institutions are integrated into the general political economy of each society, for this holds the key to the clash of unequal forces in war. Boulainvilliers can thus point out the difference between heavily armed warriors who support themselves via feudal land ownership and the king, who can afford an army of foot soldiers through his powers of central taxation (ECF-SMD, 159).

Moving out of the French Revolution and through the nineteenth century, Foucault traces first how the notion of war as a grid of intelligibility of the social was overcome by the theme of "national universality" (ECF-SMD, 239). With characteristic panache, Foucault ties this overcoming to the birth of dialectical philosophy (ECF-SMD, 236–237). He then moves on to consider the relation of modern biological racism to the birth of modern "biopolitics" (ECF-SMD, 243). (It is beyond the scope of this entry to do more than note the strange absence of the Atlantic slave trade from Foucault's account of modern biological racism, though it should be noted that he does appeal to "colonization" [ECF-SMD, 257].) First, Foucault notes how nineteenth-century revolutionaries transformed the race struggle (of "peoples" in conflict) into class struggle at the same time as "race" in the biomedical sense was born (ECF-SMD, 60–62, 254–255). Thus, as society came to be seen in the evolutionary sense of being engaged in a struggle for existence, it became seen as biologically monist, as a substance into which foreigners have invaded or infiltrated and in which deviants are produced within society as degeneration (ECF-SMD, 80–81). Racism thus introduces a "break" in the domain of life that biopolitics places under the control of the state (ECF-SMD, 255), and it thus allows a justification of the "murderous function of the State" as the violence that is deployed to combat the biological threat to the race under its protection (ECF-SMD, 256). Thus the state plays a new role when biological racism is introduced; it is no longer an instrument of one race against another, as it was in the struggle of "peoples," but in the birth of modern racism, the state becomes the protector of the integrity, superiority, and purity of the national race (ECF-SMD, 81) as well as being charged with regenerating the purity of the race under the crucible of war (ECF-SMD, 257). Thus we see racism as an inversion of revolutionary discourse; race discourse for Boulainvilliers had been a weapon against state (royal) sovereignty, but it is now used by the state to protect its sovereignty via medical normalization and eugenics (ECF-SMD, 81).

From there, Foucault traces twentieth-century transformations of racism, revealing why the most murderous states are those most immersed in biopolitics and hence racism (ECF-SMD, 258). First is Nazi state racism, which is reinscribed in the prophetic discourse from which race struggle once emerged, as we see in the Nazi myths of popular struggle: the Germans victimized by the Versailles treaty and awaiting a new Reich, which will usher in the apocalypse, the end of days (ECF-

SMD, 82). The specificity of the Nazis, however, comes not in their recycling of old myths but in their simultaneous unleashing of sovereign murderous power and life-administering biopower throughout the entire biological reality of the people under the control of the state, a combination that ultimately makes the state suicidal in its desire to expose the people to the purifying violence of constant and intense exposure to death (ECF-SMD, 259–260). Finally, Foucault treats Soviet scientific racism, in which the class enemy becomes biological threat, and medical police eliminate class enemies as if they were a biological threat (ECF-SMD, 83, 261–262).

As a result of conducting his genealogy of the war model in *Society*, Foucault comes to nuance his use of "war" in volume one of *The History of Sexuality*, published in 1976, the year in which the "Society" lectures were delivered. In this volume, war is no longer seen as a grid of intelligibility that reveals a regime of truth governing a particular historical discourse. Rather, it is seen as a practical option for "coding" the multiplicity of force relations; that is, an optional and precarious "strategy" for integrating them:

> Should we turn the expression around, then, and say that politics is war pursued by other means? If we still wish to maintain a separation between war and politics, perhaps we should postulate that this multiplicity of force relations can be coded – in part but never totally – either in the form of "war," or in the form of "politics"; this would imply two different strategies (but the one always liable to switch into the other) for integrating these unbalanced, heterogeneous, unstable, and tense force relations. (EHS1, 93)

The context for this remark, we should recall, is subtle and ambiguous. It comes in the "Method" section of Part IV of the work, "The dispositif of sexuality." The ambiguity of Foucault's position is set up by his remark a moment earlier when he discusses power as decentered: "[P]ower's condition of possibility, or in any case the viewpoint which permits one to understand its exercise … and which also makes it possible to use its mechanisms as a grid of intelligibility of the social order, must not be sought in the primary existence of a central point" (ibid.). Here we see Foucault's famous ambivalence toward Kant: no sooner does he say "condition of possibility" then he has to nuance it.

Thus, at this point, Foucault has "power" as the grid of intelligibility for social relations and "war" as an active strategy of political practice; looking at the social field in terms of power lets us see war as a possible strategy for integrating a multiplicity of force relations, whereas power "itself" can only be seen if we look at it *as* such a multiplicity: "It seems to me that power must be understood in the first instance as the multiplicity of force relations immanent in the sphere in which they operate and which constitute their own organization" (EHS1, 92). So, in volume one of *The History of Sexuality* the "multiplicity of force relations" is the grid of intelligibility for power, which is in turn the grid of intelligibility of the social field. These successive grids of intelligibility reveal a dynamic social ontology, an interactive realism, in which war is a strategy for action in the social field, a way of integrating the multiplicity of force relations that constitute that field and thereby constituting the protagonists of political history as engaged in a "war by other means." The looping effect or self-fulfilling prophecy here should be clear: it's almost a cliché to say that naming yourself and others as warriors tends to create the reality in which others treat you as such and you respond in kind since they have just proved your point!

At the end of volume one of *The History of Sexuality*, we find Foucault's first published theses on state racism and biopower. After the publication of the lecture courses, we can now see this analysis as having been developed in the last lecture of *Society Must Be Defended* (ECF-SMD, 239–263). The outlines of Foucault's treatment of sovereign power as the right to decide life and death in this volume are well known. The sovereign power to decide life and death has a formal derivation from absolute Roman *patria potestas*, but survives in diminished form in classical legal theory, so that only when a threat to the sovereign is present can the right be exercised. The sovereign has only an indirect hold on the life of the subject in regard to external enemies; here the sovereign can indirectly expose the subject to death by compelling him to defend the sovereign in war. But in response to an internal threat, the sovereign can exercise a direct power and put the subject to death (EHS1, 135). So the sovereign has a "dissymmetrical" right with regard to the life of subjects, being able to reach life only via death, by killing or refraining from killing. The symbol of such sovereign power is the sword, and the major form of power is by means of deduction (*prélèvement*) (EHS1, 136). The power over life is transformed in the modern West, however. There are many forms of power, not just deduction, for the aim is no longer simple enrichment of the sovereign but an intensification of forces. Thus life becomes the positive object of administration, and death is just the reverse side of life. Two symptoms reveal this transformation: first, the increased bloodiness of war, for modern states must defend everyone, not just the sovereign; and second, the death penalty became the scandal of a power that administers life (EHS1, 136–138).

Perhaps dismayed at the results of his genealogy of the war schema, Foucault moves in the fourth lecture of "Security, Territory, Population" to "governmentality" as the model for social relations, as its grid of intelligibility. Rather than social relations being seen as war, we are asked to see social relations as the "conduct of conduct," as the leading of men's lives in quotidian detail. There is still the Deleuzean concept of integration of a multiplicity of differential elements and relations as embedded in the interplay of power and resistance in practices, but the grid of intelligibility is no longer war but governmentality. Along with the change in the grid of intelligibility comes a change in the nature of the relations. It is no longer "force" relations but relations of "actions" that are to be integrated. Foucault's formula is now that "to govern ... is to structure the possible field of action of others" (EAIF, 221). Now we must avoid reading Foucault as if a concern with subjectivity comes to replace a concern with power. Rather, subjectivity is the mode in which power operates in governmentality; the conducting of the conduct of our lives is done by inducing us to subjectify ourselves in various ways, as sexual subjects, or indeed as self-entrepreneurs.

John Protevi

SEE ALSO

Life
Multiplicity
Power
Race (and Racism)
State
Violence
Henri de Boulainvilliers
Carl von Clausewitz

SUGGESTED READING

Deleuze, Gilles. 1994. *Difference and Repetition*, trans. Paul Patton. New York: Columbia University Press.
Han, Béatrice. 2002. *Foucualt's Critical Project: Between the Transcendental and the Historical*, trans. Edward Pile. Stanford, CA: Stanford University Press.
Nealon, Jeffrey. 2007. *Foucault Beyond Foucault: Power and Its Intensifications since 1984*. Stanford, CA: Stanford University Press.

II

PROPER NAMES

92

LOUIS ALTHUSSER (1918–1990)

I T IS STRANGELY difficult to describe the precise philosophical, theoretical, and even political relations between Foucault and Althusser. To refer this difficulty to Althusser's Marxism (or rather his continued use of a certain terminology derived from the texts of Marx, Lenin, and Mao) and Foucault's studied avoidance of this terminology does little to clarify matters. That Althusser thought within Marxism, a field that was anything but homogeneous and free of conflict, and that he expressed himself in a Marxist idiom, in no way prevented his work from coinciding with Foucault's, just as the fact that Foucault went to great lengths to speak in any other idiom than the Marxist did not prevent them from speaking about the same thing, often as the same time, as if both felt that their historical moment, by all accounts a dramatic and fecund one, imposed specific problems on them. Indeed, it seems that it is precisely the degree of convergence between Althusser and Foucault, a convergence that is not the same thing as agreement between them but rather the proximity of exploring many of the same theoretical regions, that makes it difficult to grasp their connections. This difficulty is all the more acute in that the conversations and debates between them, and between their works, were usually indirect, addressed without naming each other or in most cases without referring to specific texts.

It is not difficult to identify the common notions that caused their theoretical trajectories to intersect at certain precise points. Foucault, as Althusser announced in *For Marx*, had been his student (Althusser 1969, 257), not simply in the formal sense but with, if not through, Althusser developed a passionate attachment to French "épistémologie," the line of thought represented by such figures as Cavaillès, Koyre, Bachelard, and, above all, Canguilhem, and a hostility to the particularly French variant of phenomenology that could best be described as Cartesian. Both Althusser and Foucault endorsed Cavaillès' call for a philosophy of the concept to replace the philosophies of consciousness (Cavaillès 1970), and this commitment marked their work from beginning to end. In their respective realms, whether the history of madness or the history of Marxism, their common rejection of a certain notion of the subject as origin allowed or compelled them to see discontinuities, breaks, and ruptures where others had seen linear progress, and to argue, much to the shock of their readers, that there was no single object of Marxist theory or of the discourse on madness but rather a series of absolutely disparate objects. The fact that their shared "theoretical anti-humanism," the idea that something called man was not the transcendental essence of history but rather a theoretical (and political) construct internal to history, provoked their critics – sometimes the same critics (as in the case of Sartre), sometimes different – to similar expressions of outrage is surely significant. As Althusser liked to say, the meaning of a philosophy lies in its effects, especially the attacks it provokes.

Another fairly obvious point of convergence between the two men was the refusal to consider theories independently of the material and institutional forms in which they were incarnate. Thus, for Foucault the history of the concept of madness could not be understood separately from the forms of coercion and confinement to which those deemed mad were subject. Even the history of medicine, or more specifically the histories of pathology and epidemiology, could not be disentangled from the institutional forms of segregation, constraint, and observation that formed its material conditions of possibility. Similarly, for Althusser, ideology, the system of ideas that justified and contributed to the reproduction of class exploitation, did not exist in the form of a false consciousness that might be dispelled by true ideas but was consubstantial with the material apparatuses and practices that governed a given society at a given historical moment. For both men, the very notion of the individual as subject as the origin of thought, speech, and action, was a historical phenomenon produced by very specific apparatuses, a form of subjection that imprisoned the individual and compelled him to speak and to act. Again, their critics accused them of remarkably similar errors: a denial of human freedom, the freedom to think and criticize freely, a political pessimism masquerading as a left-wing functionalism, and a vision of a domination so total that every act of resistance could only secure its reproduction.

Finally, both Althusser and Foucault understood themselves as working within the specificity of a historical moment that was not governed by "Zeitgeist" or worldview but was the site of conflict and multiplicity in which they had to take a position. Althusser called this the theoretical conjuncture, Foucault simply "the present." Althusser extended the Leninist concept of a political conjuncture marked by a relationship or rather series of relationships of disparate forces within which any political action took place to the philosophical realm, which he understood as a field of conflicting forces in which he was caught and in which he had no choice but to intervene. Foucault, from a very different starting point and set of references, arrived at a similar position. In his commentary on Kant's "What Is Enlightenment?" (EEW1, 303–320), he notes that Kant accounts for the conditions of possibility of philosophical speculation in two radically different ways. The first concerns the transcendental conditions of thought that confer on its content a universality. This is of course the standard image of Kant as the author of the three Critiques. Foucault, however, points to another Kant, the philosopher of the present and the contemporary, who feels compelled to produce "a particular analysis of the specific moment at which he is writing and because of which he is writing" (EEW1, 309). This is perhaps the most decisive connection between Althusser and Foucault, which, more than the others, makes intelligible the points of both convergence and divergence that constitute the precise character of their relationship.

It was in fact these common notions, the conditions of possibility of their proximity, that brought the two men into conflict at certain precise points. The first of these conflicts occurred around the appearance of the *History of Madness* in 1961. Althusser's reaction to the book, as reported in his correspondence, was one of enormous excitement and enthusiasm ("as crepusculary as Nietzsche, but as clear as an equation") (Althusser 1998, 215). He saw the *History of Madness* as a history full of discontinuities and reversals, of a concept that despite its status in the psychiatry of the mid-twentieth century was determined as much by political, legal, and philosophical concerns as by anything understood as scientific, a history as it was, not as it was supposed to be. It is all the more striking then that the only written trace of his reading, lecture notes from a course on structuralism in 1962–1963, contained a critique above all of Foucault's own theorization of his work in the original preface (removed from subsequent editions). Foucault's project of an archaeology of a silence, the gradual silencing of madness by means of its transformation into "mental illness," seemed to Althusser to suggest an inversion of the notion of reason as origin and grounds of the history not simply of thought but of civilization itself: it is madness that becomes the transcendental origin, that which civilization must exclude and repress in order to be itself, as if reason were the negation of the madness and nonsense that preceded it. Whether or not Foucault learned of this critique, the work that followed *The Birth of the Clinic* focused on modes of discourse, quite independently of the subject understood as its origin or the real object that discourse was supposed to represent.

At the same time, Althusser and his colleagues in 1966 initiated a discussion (of which Althusser's contribution was published posthumously as "Three Notes on a Theory of Discourse" [Althusser 2003, 33–84]) investigating the ways in which an object of knowledge did not precede discourse but was only constituted in it, as well as what Althusser had begun to call the "interpellation" of the subject of discourse, the way in which the role of the subject and origin of discourse was attributed retroactively to individuals as one of its effects. As in the case of Foucault in *The*

Archaeology of Knowledge (1969), Althusser realized that even that gesture by which discourse was granted a materiality, its irreducibility to an expression or representation, led to a kind of dualism of discursive and nondiscursive practices. It was only too clear that the individual's constitution as a subject free and therefore legally responsible (and punishable) for his actions could not be understood as a discursive effect alone but involved the social "apparatuses" ("appareils," a word common to both Althusser and Foucault) in which discourses were inextricably embedded. This discovery coincided with the general radicalization around May 1968, the challenges to which impelled both men to write two of their most influential texts, Althusser's "Ideology and the Ideological State Apparatuses" (1970) and Foucault's *Discipline and Punish* (1975).

It was in the latter work that Foucault criticized Althusser most openly (although not by name), referring to the "Ideology and the Ideological State Apparatuses" essay published five years earlier. Althusser had preserved the language of Marxism, including above all the notion of ideology, which had come to mean the system of ideas that inclined individuals to accept and submit to the established order but had done so to transform its meaning. For Althusser, ideology could not be understood as having the form of ideas, of consciousness or even of discourse. Instead, as he announced in his essay, "ideology has a material existence": ideology exists only in apparatuses in which the body, above all, is at stake. But his exposition, as evidenced by the countless interpretations that followed the publication of the essay, unfolded in an uneven and contradictory manner. In particular, the notion that ideology interpellated individuals as subjects could be understood as the production of a fictitious subjectivity or a drama of recognition. In the opening chapter of *Discipline and Punish*, Foucault, who had earlier denounced the very notion of ideology as "idealist" (as concerned with minds rather than bodies and with consciousness rather than material forces [EPK, 58]), reformulated Althusser's theory by rejecting the very notion of ideology, especially insofar as it was used to explain the constitution of subjects. Ironically referring to the religious concept of the soul, instead of the preferred terminology of personality, consciousness, or subjectivity, as if to confront the latter terms with their theological origins, Foucault argues that we can only begin to understand "the genealogy of the modern 'soul'" if we reject any notion that it is an illusory "ideological effect" (EDP, 29). In keeping with his project of a microphysics of power, Foucault focuses much more closely than Althusser on the way in which this "soul" is not only real and material, rather than a false representation, but is "produced permanently around, on, within the body" (EDP, 29) by a disciplinary power. Not only has discipline, the set of strategies and tactics whose objective is to secure the utility and docility of the body, replaced ideology in his analysis, but the material production of the soul around the body has replaced the notion of the interpellation of the subject.

But this was not the only focal point of Foucault's critique of the "Ideological State Apparatuses" essay. The other was its apparent insistence on the state as the locus of power, the site from which class domination emanated and therefore, despite Althusser's explicit denial, tended to reproduce the distinction between the state and civil society. Foucault repeatedly stressed that the disciplines were not localized in the state and that the "privately owned" factory, for example, made use of the same disciplinary techniques as the prison or the army (moreover citing Marx in support of his demonstration). The model of political struggle that privileged the state and the seizure of state power, as well as the juridical struggle over legal rights, had to be replaced by the model of politics as a perpetual battle, never a zero-sum game in which one does or does not have rights or privileges but a constantly shifting relation of forces. As such, there could be no single confrontation between the oppressed and the oppressor but only an effect of domination that results from innumerable particular struggles. Interestingly, this brought Foucault into greater proximity to Althusser, who was in the early and mid-1970s working on Machiavelli. In volume one of *The History of Sexuality*, Foucault would praise Machiavelli as one of the few "to think [of] the power of the Prince in terms of relations of force." He added, however, that the time had come to move beyond the person of the Prince to understand "the strategy immanent in force relations" (EHS1, 101).

This implicit debate, a final reflection on the difficulties encountered by the radical movements to which both Althusser and Foucault had been committed, was suspended after 1976. Foucault's subsequent work on governmentality was not intended to supplant the earlier work but neither was it a continuation of it. The final years of the decade, difficult for both men for reasons not entirely unrelated, sent them along very different paths. Fittingly, it was only the final act of Althusser's madness, the murder of his wife, that reunited them. Foucault was, until his death, one of the most frequent visitors to the psychiatric hospitals where Althusser spent most of the remainder of his life, the never-forgetful witness of his former teacher's own history of madness.

Warren Montag

SEE ALSO

> Dispositif *(Apparatus)*
> *Marxism*
> *Power*
> *State*

SUGGESTED READING

Althusser, Louis. 1969. *For Marx*, trans. Ben Brewster. London: New Left Books.
    1998. *Lettres à Franca (1961–1973)*. Paris: Stock/IMEC.
    2003. *The Humanist Controversy and Other Writings (1966–1967)*, trans. G. M. Goshgarian. London: Verso.
Cavaillès, Jean. 1970. "On Logic and the Theory of Science," trans. Theodore J. Kisiel, in *Phenomenology and the Natural Sciences*, ed. Joseph J. Kockelman and Theodore J. Kisiel. Evanston, IL: Northwestern University Press, pp. 353–412.
Montag, Warren. 2002. *Louis Althusser*. London: Palgrave.

93

THE ANCIENTS
(STOICS AND CYNICS)

A VERY LARGE PART of Foucault's investigations concern, in Western modernity (the sixteenth to the twentieth centuries), the organization of kinds of knowledge and the mechanisms of power. However, Foucault has over the course of his life studied, at three different times, ancient history and ancient philosophy. The first time was in 1971, in his first course at the Collège de France (*La volonté de savoir*, FCF-LSV). This course interrogated the appearance, in the West, of a discourse (philosophy) that claimed to be universal, true, just, disinterested, neutral, objective, and pure. Foucault shows how this discourse presupposes the great sociopolitical revolutions of ancient Greece. These ancient Greek revolutions include the determination of a justice as the establishment of human measure and human order, and no longer as the manifestation of the wild force of the gods; the invention of a currency that is able to circulate throughout the polis and to symbolize the social bond; the institution of a law (*nomos*) that is anonymous and impartial; and the characterization of crime as "pollution" (*miasma*). All of these characteristics (objectivity, universality, neutrality, and purity) are found again as criteria for philosophical discourse both in classical Greece and later in the West. In 1971, Foucault showed that the invention of this true discourse was based at the same time on a certain number of exclusions: rejection of tragic speech that insists on the unbearable dimension of the true; the elimination of revolutionary speech when it denounces the hypocrisy of the consensus and the scandal of injustices; and separation among those who claim to have the right to speak, between the pure and the impure. This first large study of Greek thought is presented therefore as the realization of Nietzsche's program of the description of the will of Western truth (at once the practical root of philosophical discourse and the denunciation of the obscurities produced by this discourse). Next, at the end of the 1970s, Foucault studied, on the basis of Plato's political texts in particular, the way in which governmentality in the Greek polis involves nothing like a pastoral style. The modern state introduces, with the idea of *raison d'État*, the care of the individual as a principle of government. But, in the 1980s, Foucault devoted, exclusively this time, his investigations to ancient culture and thought: the collection of courses at the Collège de France (from 1981 to 1984) and his published books (the second and third volumes of *The History of Sexuality*, respectively subtitled *The Use of Pleasure* and *The Care of the Self*, EHS2 and EHS3). One can reorganize this collection of investigations around three major notions: Greco-Latin antiquity: *epimeleia heautau* or *cura sui* (the care of the self), *parrēsia* or *libertas* (frank speaking), and *aphrodia* or *voluptas* (the pleasures of love).

The concept of care of the self is studied by Foucault essentially in the version that the great Hellenistic and Roman philosophers have given to it (even if Foucault recognizes the importance, in Plato, of this concept through which he characterizes the character of Socrates as a master of the care of the self). In a very general way, what is at issue for Foucault is to rethink the problem of the relation between subjectivity and truth. In the modern West, there are two general ways in which this relation has been structured. The first is philosophical (the Cartesian moment). One has to interrogate the nature of the subject as the foundation of knowledge and of the recognition of truth, the very condition of science. The second is religious (the Christian moment, reactivated later by psychology). Here one has to pose the question of a true knowledge of the subject itself. And to gain this true knowledge, one has to propose methods of introspection, analysis, and self-decipherment (hermeneutics), through which a subject would be able to become conscious of his authentic identity and his secret nature, and by means of the verbalization addressed to another (a confessor, a psychoanalyst), he would become aware of his hidden desires. When Foucault undertakes the study of the ancients on the basis of the concept of the care of the self, he attempts specifically to show that these two great ways of posing the problem of the relation between subjectivity and truth (transcendental interrogation or confessional techniques) do not hold for antiquity. On the one hand in fact, Foucault shows that the care of the self poses the question of the relation between the self and truth not at the level of transcendental conditions but of ascetic ones. The subject is capable of truth on the condition of performing on himself a certain kind of work, a certain number of transformations and purifications that are indispensable if he wants to gain access to the truth. The possibility for a subject to know the truth does not depend on a rational demonstration but on a spiritual transformation. On the other hand, the care of the self structures a relation between the self and truth that is irreducible to the Christian modality of interior decipherment. The care of the self is constituted by a sect of techniques that Foucault calls "techniques of subjectification," in the sense that the subject is called by these techniques to construct himself, to fashion for himself an internal consistency, to obligate himself to certain regularities of behavior. One really has to understand primarily that the care of the self for the ancients constituted in no way an invitation to narcissism (the idea that one would turn oneself into an object of adoration), or an elicitation to egoism (the idea that one would be concerned with prioritizing one's own affairs over those of others). The care of the self is a long, difficult enterprise of self-construction that demands the advice of a master of virtue and an arduous discipline. The primary objective of these exercises lies in obtaining a certain kind of concentration, an intensification of self-presence, and thereby it avoids the dispersion and the scattering of the subject. We know about some of these exercises: an examination each morning through which one prepares for the events of the day by anticipating the things that might be rather unpleasant so that one does not lose one's temper when they happen; an examination each evening in which I go over my day once more in order to take stock of the progress accomplished toward my ideal of mastery and wisdom; then the analysis of representations by which I differentiate within what happens to me between what does not depend on me (the content of events) and what depends on me (the meaning that I am going to give to them); a meditation on death through which I obligate myself to consider lucidly my future disappearance so that I will not let myself be carried away by ephemeral passions and fleeting desires; the patient study of nature, which teaches me to understand that a causal chain runs through all phenomena and that everything that happens must therefore have its reason; and finally the exercises of endurance (fasting, depriving oneself) through which I manufacture for myself a patience that will help me bear the unpredictable things of existence. Through these exercises, each of us must learn to turn back toward oneself. But this turning back cannot be assimilated to introspection. The problem is not to know oneself better or to throw oneself into the investigation of one's hidden intimacy or one's secret nature. Through these exercises, one learns rather to interiorize schemas of appropriate action (to react courageously to catastrophes, etc.) and to provide for oneself rules of behavior (not to lose one's temper, etc.). But this interiorization of principles holds only because it allows me to make visible, in the exteriority of my social relations and of my attitudes, qualities of order and harmony (this is an aesthetics of existence). The care of the self does not lead one to detach himself from the world and from others. It leads one to act, with others and in the world, in a rational way. It is especially in the Stoics (Seneca, Epictetus, and Marcus Aurelius) that Foucault finds the evocation of these techniques of the self, but the care of the self can also be Epicurean. The care of the self then takes on a more communitarian form. Friendship gives to each a confidence and a consistency that helps him flee from false pleasures. Nevertheless, one has to notice that the skeptics are never mentioned by Foucault. Skepticism in fact presents, within Hellenistic and Roman wisdom, a peculiar aspect that is particularly difficult to integrate within the general framework of the care of the self: the theme of an empty subject and an effort of desubjectification.

The second important concept is that of *parrēsia*. *Parrēsia* designates a kind of speech that is courageous and open to risk. For example, Socrates refuses to flatter or sweet-talk his judges. Out loud, he proclaims his convictions, even though he puts himself in danger of death by expressing them. In the same way, when Plato confronts Dionysus of Syracuse, he does not hesitate to criticize the tyrant and instead praises justice, thereby provoking Dionysus's anger. Foucault shows the interest in *parrēsia* especially within the democratic framework. Democracy can remain authentic and not decline into demagoguery, only because there are courageous men who do not hesitate to stand up to the passions of the people in order to try to make their ideal of the public good triumph. In a democracy corrupted and manipulated by rhetoricians, *parrēsia* becomes negative. It becomes the license given to everyone to say whatever comes to mind. There is, however, a second face to *parrēsia*, its ethical face. Foucault studies it on the basis of a description of Cynic philosophy. In the Cynics, *parrēsia* is connected to a way of life. The Cynics make use of rough language and are deliberately provocative. They go from city to city and harangue the crowds by violently denouncing the vile compromises, the atrocious hypocrisies, the ridiculous customs that one finds everywhere in human societies. But this freedom of speech is total in the Cynic because he makes for himself no concessions. He lives like a dog, sleeps outside, and possesses nothing but a stick, a bag, and an old coat. For Foucault, the Cynic allows us to ask philosophy the question of the "true life." The true life, however, is not a harmonious, ideal, resplendent life. It is a life constructed like a permanent test: how is one to free oneself from social hypocrisies, depend really on no one, and imitate nature? In philosophy, the Cynic represents the way of dissonance and scandal.

The last concept constructed by Foucault is *aphrodisia*. In a very general way, Foucault investigated in the ancients a problematization of sexuality that is irreducible to modern readings. Western modernity constructs sexuality on the basis of three major notions: moral interdiction, the man/woman difference, and concupiscence. For Foucault, sexuality in the ancients is structured on the basis of different landmarks. The first is the obsession with mastery. Sexual pleasures are not considered to be bad in themselves. Instead, they are seen as involving a certain kind of risk because of their internal energy. They risk carrying us away, leading us astray. Therefore we have to define strict rules of use so that we do not let ourselves be overrun by them. Then there is the exultation of activity. The true line of division does not pass between man and woman but between an active position and a passive position in the sexual relation. Finally, sexuality does not give rise, in the ancients, to techniques of self-decipherment. Instead, sexuality leads to regulation. One would then find here again the general framework already mentioned in relation to the care of the self. Sexuality does not allow us to know ourselves better. It refers instead to a tumultuous sequence of existence that we have to give a regular, harmonious form.

Overall, Foucault's summoning up of the ancients has an essentially disturbing function. Traditionally, ancient philosophy has been for us a reference point for what is obvious in philosophy. In ancient philosophy, we investigate the foundation, the confirmation by origin, of the eternity of our certainties. In contrast, Foucault investigates, in the culture and thought of the ancients, an element of destabilization, a factor of historicization: the historicity of truth and of the subject, the historicity of philosophy and of sexuality. The ancients for Foucault disturb our modern certainties. And they are able to do this, to disturb us in this way, not because their truths would be *truer* but because they are *other*.

Frédéric Gros

SEE ALSO

Christianity
Ethics
Friendship
Hermeneutics
Parrēsia
Psychoanalysis
Plato
Sex

SUGGESTED READING

Gros, Frédéric, and Carlos Lévy, eds. 2003. *Foucault et la philosophie antique*. Paris: Kimé.
Hadot, Pierre. 1995. *Philosophy as a Way of Life: Spiritual Exercises from Socrates to Foucault*, ed. Arnold Davidson. Oxford: Wiley-Blackwell.

94

GEORGES BATAILLE (1897–1962)

IKE MANY FRENCH theorists of his generation, Foucault's thinking was deeply influenced by the work of Georges Bataille. Historically, Foucault's assistance in the posthumous publication of Bataille's *Œuvres completes* (1973) as well as his frequent contributions and editorial consultation to *Critique*, a journal founded by Bataille, clearly indicate the esteem with which he held Bataille and his work. (See "A Preface to Transgression," ELCP, note 1.) Philosophically, however, the influence of Bataille's work is almost always unmarked in Foucault's texts and thus more difficult to trace.

Foucault only wrote one essay explicitly on the work of Georges Bataille, "A Preface to Transgression" (ELCP). Written in 1963, this essay begins to work out some of the insights about the self-enclosed character of prohibition and transgression that then comes to full-blown articulation in Foucault's 1976 reorientation of the "Repressive Hypothesis" in volume one of *The History of Sexuality* (EHS1). It is the restricted and thus illusory character of liberation that transgression promises that Foucault traces in Bataille's work in this early essay – an insight that becomes central to his reconfiguration of not only sexuality but also power in the later volume one of *The History of Sexuality*. Because of the singular essay's focus on transgression as well as a long-standing reading of Bataille as a literary bad boy of eroticism and the sacred, most scholarship on the connections between Foucault and Bataille tends to emphasize their shared focus on sexuality and this limited, if vexing, character of transgression as a complex register of modern Western subjectivity. This emphasis is certainly warranted, given Bataille's early writings (1930s) – both fictional and theoretical – on the politically, epistemologically, and psychologically disruptive force of eroticism and sexuality, especially in early twentieth-century European resistances to fascism. (See especially his fictional works *Blue of Noon* and *Story of the Eye* as well as the collected writings in *Visions of Excess* and *Erotism: Death and Sensuality*.) But if we are to grasp how Foucault's infamous call in volume one of *The History of Sexuality* to reconceive Western subjectivity through "bodies and pleasures" (EHS1, 157) may be situated in Bataille's work, we need a broader understanding of Bataille's epistemological intervention in the various projects of modernity. From that perspective, we can begin to see how Foucault's ongoing effort, across his early and later work to grasp and thereby transform our historical present through the excavation of subjugated knowledges can be traced back to the radical shift in perspective that Bataille articulated in the language of general economy.

As the Second World War ended and the cold war emerged, Bataille entered what Michel Surya describes as a period of intense production and seriousness, in which the Dada and surrealist scandals from the 1930s became "a distant and disparate echo" (Surya 2002, 372) and the question of political economy in its broadest sense took hold of his writing. The result is *The Accursed Share*, volumes I–III, as well as *Theory of Religion*, wherein Bataille enacts his self-avowed "Copernican transformation: a reversal of thinking – of ethics" (Bataille 1991, 25), which he calls "general economy." Radically reorienting us from the epistemological and political projects of modernity, where clarity and precision are the hallmarks of insight, argumentation, and principles of evaluation, "general economy" is best approached obtusely, through characterization rather than definition. Bataille frames it in the early pages of volume one of *The Accursed Share* as the study of "the movement of energy on the earth" (Bataille 1991, 10), especially the persistent exclusion of excess energy, which Bataille called "nonproductive expenditure" as early as 1933 ("The Notion of Expenditure," 1985, 117), from all modern epistemologies, politics, ethics, and religions. To grasp such a large, amorphous and yet pervasive omission leads Bataille to a methodology of "general economy," wherein "a human sacrifice, the construction of a church or the gift of a jewel were no less interesting than the sale of wheat" (Bataille 1991, 9). Not simply a methodology that sets the intellectual free from the rigor of disciplinary training, Bataille's analyses are grounded in the ongoing effort to grasp nonproductive expenditure – that is, to grasp excess – without recourse to the restricted economy of transgression/prohibition. For his various analyses in *The Accursed Share* (these three volumes include topics such as the sacrificial practices of the Aztecs, military formations of early Islam and Lamaism, a fascinating advocacy of The Marshall Plan, extended readings of Lévi-Strauss and Nietzsche, prolonged meditations on eroticism and sovereignty beyond the logic of transgression, and the political and ethical questions of communism and capitalism, among others) as well as later works on religion and eroticism, this involves a thorough critique of the insidious logic of utilitarianism and all its various guises – a critique that arguably also animates a great deal of Foucault's thinking, especially in his genealogies.

Foucault's wide array of objects of study has constantly been a source of bewilderment and admiration. From his early work in *The Order of Things* and *The Archaeology of Knowledge* to demarcate the boundaries of disciplines and, to use his later language of biopolitics, decipher the productive and normalizing effects of those boundaries through omission, Foucault is consistently attuned to the silences of those phenomena that remain unfocused, unexamined – undisciplined. He is constantly concerned with how "Mendel spoke the truth, but was not *dans le vrai*" (EAK, 224). While this attunement can be traced to many sources, perhaps most of all to Husserl, the kind of move we find in Bataille's general economy helps us to understand some of Foucault's most continuous obsessions: the spatialization of reason, the attention to shifting scales of investigation (micro, macro, local, distant), the critical capacity of subjugated knowledges and the tricky methodology of excavating them, and the demarcation of the abnormal (delinquents, criminals, madness, sexual deviants, and so on) in the ever-narrowing confines of modern "normal" life. These are also Bataille's obsessions, albeit taken up in different terms and emphases. To follow these trajectories is to give a completely different orientation to moments in Foucault's texts such as the early one in volume one of *The History of Sexuality* when he tells us that he is not aiming to disprove the Repressive Hypothesis but rather to put "it back within a *general economy* of discourses on sex in modern societies since the seventeenth century" (EHS1, 11, my emphasis). Such moments begin to proliferate in Foucault's texts once one is sensitive to them, leading us to see how some of Bataille's most challenging and groundbreaking work animates Foucault's very thinking, in ways so profound that they are difficult – but crucial – to decipher.

Shannon Winnubst

SEE ALSO

> *Sovereignty*
> *Transgression*
> *Maurice Blanchot*

SUGGESTED READING

Bataille, Georges. 1991. *The Accursed Share*, volume 1. New York: Zone Books.
Hollywood, Amy. 2002. *Sensible Ecstasy: Mysticism, Sexual Difference, and the Demands of History.* Chicago: University of Chicago Press.
Mitchel, Andrew J., and Jason Kemp Winfree, eds. 2009. *The Obsessions of Georges Bataille: Community and Communication.* Albany: The SUNY Press.
Surya, Michel. 2002. *Georges Bataille: An Intellectual Biography.* London: Verso.
Winnubst, Shannon. 2006a. *Queering Freedom.* Bloomington: Indiana University Press.
  ed. 2006b. *Reading Bataille Now.* Bloomington: Indiana University Press.

95

XAVIER BICHAT (1771–1802)

N *THE BIRTH OF THE CLINIC*, Foucault presented the anatomist and physiologist Xavier Bichat (1771–1802) as the defining figure of modern medicine: since the nineteenth century, medicine has been living in "the age of Bichat" (EBC, 122). In order to understand how Bichat's work transformed medicine, it is first necessary to get a sense of how *Birth of the Clinic* transformed the history of medicine. This book, which Foucault once complained had been greeted by "total silence" when it was published (FDE3, 88), offers a new interpretation of the emergence of modern medicine in the early nineteenth century. For two centuries, doctors and historians have for the most part stuck to a positivist interpretation: modern medicine emerged when physicians began to observe more and theorize less. Up until the end of the eighteenth century, moral and religious taboos supposedly prevented physicians from dissecting corpses, and it is only when these cultural obstacles were lifted that a new, truly scientific kind of medical knowledge became possible.

Foucault argued that "this reconstruction is historically false" (EBC, 125). Mentioning the examples of well-known eighteenth-century physicians and surgeons like Morgagni, Hunter, Tissot, and Desault, he pointed to the fact that dissecting corpses was relatively common before Bichat. The historiographical implications of this minor historical rectification are important: Foucault agreed with other historians that the early nineteenth century marked a rupture in the history of medicine, but this rupture was now in need of a new, nonpositivist explanation.

What Bichat accomplished was therefore not to improve medical knowledge gradually by dissecting more corpses than physicians before him (although he certainly dissected many). More fundamentally, what he and other physicians after him accomplished was "a recasting at the level of knowledge [*savoir*] itself.... It is not the same game, somewhat improved, but another game" (EBC, 137). This game, in which death has become the source of disease as well as a technical instrument of knowledge, is centered on the new notion of "pathological life" (EBC, 153).

Before Bichat, a disease had been conceptualized as an essence, a pathological species, "inserting itself in the body, where it is possible" (EBC, 136). For instance, in the eighteenth century, "the same spasmodic disease can move from the lower abdomen …, toward the chest …, and finally toward the head…. The organs are the concrete supports of the disease, they never constitute its indispensible conditions" (EBC, 10). Even an eighteenth-century pathological anatomist like Morgagni, who is traditionally considered to be a precursor of modern medicine, belonged to this early modern configuration of medicine. Morgagni opened up corpses of people who had been sick and found lesions in their bodies. For him those lesions were the seats or causes of diseases – *De Sedibus et Causis Morborum* (1761) was the title of his most influential work – but, unlike what they were to become in the nineteenth century, they were not the diseases themselves (EBC, 140).

What were the epistemological transformations that made possible Bichat's new form of medical knowledge? Instead of focusing on organs, like most earlier pathological anatomists, Bichat focused on tissues, of which he described twenty-one. According to this system, each organ can be divided into its constitutive tissues. Most importantly, the divisions between tissues are revealed by the ways morbid processes are occurring. For instance, a morbid process often takes place in only one of the tissues of an organ, and in this way effectuates a "real division" between the different tissues of this organ (EBC, 131, 150). Additionally, the morbid process affecting the tissue of an organ might spread to other organs, if the latter are constituted of the same tissue, because "a pathological phenomenon follows in the organism the privileged path prescribed by tissue identity" (EBC, 149). If Bichat created modern pathological anatomy, it is therefore "only insofar as the pathological spontaneously anatomizes" (EBC, 131).

Foucault described other Bichatian principles governing tissues and their relations (EBC, 149, 152). What is crucial is that "these principles define the rules of the pathological cursus and describe in advance the possible paths that it must follow" (EBC, 152). A disease is no longer something that comes from the outside and attacks the body; it is now a modification of life itself. As Bichat declared, a pathological phenomenon is the augmentation, diminution, or alteration of a physiological phenomenon (ibid.). More profoundly, disease is the "silent work" of death, which is present in the unavoidable wear of organs as soon as they are being used (EBC, 158). Hence we see the following historical reversal that marks the modern period: "It is not because he falls sick that man dies; it is fundamentally because he is mortal that he may fall sick" (EBC, 155).

But death is not only something that is present within the living body. With Bichat, it became a "technical instrument" (EBC, 144). For the first time in the history of medicine, there is a "conceptual mastery of death" (EBC, 141). Before Bichat, a common criticism made against pathological anatomy was that death has effects on the body that cannot be distinguished from the pathological phenomena themselves.

For instance, it was difficult to separate in a corpse morbid decomposition from the gangrene that had afflicted the person when she was living (EBC, 134). Thanks to the new organization of clinics that followed the French Revolution, it became possible to open up corpses very soon after death and thus lessen this difficulty (EBC, 141). In a most important conceptual innovation, Bichat also showed that death is a process: not all the organs die at once. For instance, he demonstrated by means of experiments on animals that the death of the brain causes the death of the heart only indirectly, through the intermediary death of the lungs. In living beings, the relations between these organs were invisible; it is only by using death instrumentally that Bichat managed "to illuminate organic phenomena and their disturbances" (EBC, 143). Death became "the great analyst, which shows the connections by unfolding them, and which bursts open the wonders of genesis in the rigor of decomposition: and one should let the word *decomposition* stumble under the weight of its meaning" (EBC, 144, Foucault's italics).

Bichat's revolution is as radical as it is simple: it is now "the body itself that has become ill" (EBC, 136). Today we take for granted the rules of the game that Bichat and his contemporaries established only in the early nineteenth century: "For us, the human defines, by natural right, the space of origin and of distribution of disease: a space whose lines, volumes, surfaces and routes are laid down, in accordance with a now familiar geometry, by the anatomical atlas" (EBC, 3). This is not to say that Foucault had any illusion as to the scientific validity of most of Bichat's ideas. What mattered to him was that Bichat had triggered an epistemological transformation, which "can take place even in a system of affirmations that would be scientifically false" (FDE2, 29). Doctors today might not find in Bichat's work much that is scientifically true, yet at the epistemological level they still follow the rules of his game.

In Foucault's work, Bichat is explicitly mentioned only in the narrow context of the history of clinical medicine. Yet there are indications that point to the larger role he played in Foucault's overall interpretation of the history of modernity. Because of the intimate connection between death and life – death working its way through life, death as an instrument for understanding life – Foucault drew a parallel between Bichat and the nineteenth-century obsession with death in the works of many artists and writers, such as Goya, Géricault, or Baudelaire (EBC, 171). For the same reason, he also noted the significance of the chronological overlap between Bichat and the Marquis de Sade (1740–1814): "Is not Bichat, after all, the contemporary of the man who introduced suddenly, in the most discursive of languages, eroticism and its inevitable point, death?" (EBC, 171; see also 195). Although Foucault did not make the following rapprochement as explicitly as one would have expected, Bichat is even more directly linked to the comparative anatomist Georges Cuvier (1769–1832), who plays in *The Order of Things* a role very similar to Bichat's in *Birth of the Clinic*. Cuvier transformed animal taxonomies whereas Bichat revolutionized pathological anatomy, but both have been crucial actors in the emergence of the modern concept of *life*, which is one of the key concepts of the modern *episteme*. Foucault in fact described Cuvier's and Bichat's accomplishments in somewhat similar terms: "From Cuvier onward, it is life in its non-perceptible, purely functional aspect that provides the basis for the exterior possibility of a classification" (EOT, 268); and "From Bichat onward, the pathological phenomenon was perceived against the background of *life*" (EBC, 153, Foucault's italics). From an archaeological point of view, Cuvier and Bichat had an equivalent historical function: they brought about the same epistemological transformation, the magnitude of which we are still feeling today. However, since according to Foucault modern medicine has been more deeply ingrained within the modern *episteme* than any other discipline (EBC, 197), and since Bichat personifies this type of medicine, it is perhaps he, more than Sade, Cuvier, or anyone else, who best represents our historical moment.

Patrick Singy

SEE ALSO

> *Body*
> *Death*
> *Life*
> *Georges Canguilhem*

SUGGESTED READING

Huneman, Philippe. 1998. *Bichat, la vie et la mort*. Paris: Presses Universitaires de France.

96

LUDWIG BINSWANGER
(1881–1966)

F OUCAULT DISCUSSED THE work of the Swiss psychiatrist Ludwig Binswanger only in a small group of texts of the 1950s, and above all in a long introduction to a French translation of the physician's 1930 article "Traum und Existenz." Moreover, Foucault did so with a purpose and a language that are very different from his subsequent work, which led many scholars to ignore these early writings. They seem in fact to stand on their own, isolated within the Foucauldian corpus. After having sketched the core of Foucault's discussion of the work of Binswanger, we will try to place it in the context of some biographical facts, his interest in the problem of anthropology, and some later methodological self-reflections on his early work of the 1950s.

Ludwig Binswanger, the director of the famous Bellevue clinic in Kreuzlingen, was one of the founders of so-called existential or phenomenological psychiatry, and the initiator of *Daseinsanalyse*, a combination of Husserlian and, above all, Heideggerian themes and psychopathology. His work is spread across a very large period of time, but Foucault seemed particularly interested, in addition to the work he introduced, by his works of the 1940s and 1950s, the "Heideggerian period" of Binswanger's speculation.

Generally speaking, the young Foucault's interest in existential psychiatry and *Daseinsanalyse* comes from the fact that this medico-philosophical way of thinking allowed him to avoid the alternative between, on the one hand, a psychology based on the mechanistic causality of the sciences of nature, and, on the other hand, an explanation of pathology that reduced it to historical external factors. Moreover, as he wrote in 1954, "phenomenological analysis no doubt rejects any *a priori* distinction between normal and pathological" (EMIP, 56) – an emerging preoccupation in Foucault's thought. Given his intellectual orientation both toward psychology and the three Hs (Hegel, Husserl, Heidegger) that dominated his – and his generation's – philosophical formation, it is not a surprise to see him engaged in an enterprise of explanation, divulgation, and development of Binswanger's work.

In Foucault's 1954 little book on mental illness and psychology (EMIP, 1954, 1961), reedited in 1961 with huge changes after the publication of *History of Madness*, the chapter dedicated to existential psychology is the place where he mentions, with clear but not unconditioned sympathy, Binswanger, alongside Jaspers, Minkowski, and Roland Kuhn. The context is a discussion of the particular existential structures of the pathological world, as individuated by phenomenological analysis (spatiality, temporality, the dimension of one's own body, etc.). Foucault remarked here that Binswanger brilliantly studied mental pathologies as disturbances of the existential dimension of temporality. In his *Über Ideenflucht* (Binswanger 1933), he showed how the temporal experience of the maniac is fragmented, and how that of the schizophrenic is constituted by an alternation of a fragmented time and a suspension of temporality in a sort of eternity (EMIP, 51). A few pages later, Foucault mentions probably the most famous of the clinical cases reported by Binswanger, that of Ellen West (Binswanger 1957a), as a case of a disorder of sense of her own body and its place in space, according to the existential dimension of the rise and the fall. But if the contexts of these cursory remarks remained those of a historical and theoretical introduction to contemporary psychology, the essay on Binswanger's article on dream is where Foucault actively, and uniquely, endorsed the method of *Daseinsanalyse*.

The introduction to *Dream and Existence* is a text that largely goes beyond the task of explaining and commenting on another text, and it is a very complex work in which a lot of threads are intertwined. The effect of estrangement is increased by the fact that Foucault speaks in a phenomenological and Heideggerian jargon about themes like fundamental human freedom, the dialectic between images and imagination, and the authenticity of existence. We can individuate at least four main topics in this text that are impossible to summarize: a criticism of Freud's naturalism about dreams and the unconscious; the individuation of the phenomenological problem of understanding the act of expression; the importance of the existential dimension of spatiality; and the relation between imagination and images.

In order to focus on the specific fascination the young Foucault felt for Binswanger, we have to look at the first paragraph of the introduction, where the problem is that of the possibility of building an anthropology in its relations to a Heideggerian ontology. Binswanger's particular form of analysis is interesting because it doesn't aim to build a new form of psychology or a new kind of autonomous philosophical speculation but at the same time conceives itself as fundamental to objective and experimental knowledge of man. This is because its method is fully determined by its object, namely man, or better, the being of man, *Menschsein* (FDE1a, 94). *Anthropology* – that is the proper name of this effort – is opposed to every form of positivism, to every naturalistic form of psychology that takes man as *homo natura*; on the contrary, it is placed from the beginning in the domain of an ontological reflection on the *Dasein*. This anthropology focuses on the concrete content of what in Heideggerian terms can be described as the transcendental structure of the *Dasein*. But if anthropology is opposed to positivism, it is not, on the other hand, a form of a priori philosophical speculation. Neither science nor philosophical abstraction, it is the study of the real and concrete content of human existence as it experiences itself. Binswanger's work blurs the boundary – which Heidegger himself seems to have drawn too neatly – between anthropology and ontology, and places itself in a zone of exchange between these two domains (FDE1a, 95). That is precisely the function of Binswanger's insistence on the dimension of spatiality in dreams, and particularly on the direction that goes from the rise to the fall and vice versa (perfectly illustrated by the case of Ellen West). To this vertical dimension of spatiality both the temporality and the authenticity of existence are linked. This means that with a spatial analysis of dreams we are able to leave the domain of anthropology and enter that of ontology, namely the domain that concerns the mode of being of existence as being-in-the-world. This passage from anthropology to ontology, Foucault argues, is not abstract, not a priori, but rather comes from a concrete reflection on man: it is existence itself that shows its ontological basis (FDE1a, 137).

Foucault tells us that the theme of Binswanger's article is not so much dream *and* existence, but dream as a modality of existence, as one of the ways in which existence shows itself. Dream is a mode of expression of existence considered as a global structure. This is one of the sources of Foucault's comparison between Freud's *Traumdeutung* and Binswanger's work on dreams. Freud – Foucault says – brilliantly individuated the semantics of dreams, but he stopped there: "The Language of the dream is analyzed only in its semantic function. Freudian analysis leaves its morphological and syntactic structure in the dark…. The peculiarly imaginative dimension of the meaningful expression is completely omitted…. Psychoanalysis has never succeeded in making images speak" (EDE, 35, 38). For the young Foucault, this is precisely the problem that the existential and phenomenological method of Binswanger is able to resolve. The logic of dream is not given by censorship, Foucault argues, but it is a compromise between the authentic movement of imagination and its adulteration in the crystallized form of the image. In fact, it is not correct to say that dreams are made of images, because oneiric images are nothing but a single frozen moment in the original flux of the imagination of the dreamer: "to have an image is to leave off imagining" (EDE, 71). Discussing Sartre and Bachelard, among others, Foucault is here interested in theorizing about the perennial movement of imagination, which reflects a fundamental freedom, in opposition to the fixity and instantaneousness of images. Dreams are the original place of the movement of imagination, and this is also why, from a more practical point of view, the physician has to keep in mind that his patient's illness is not an entity, a state, but a cut in the flux of temporal and spatial existence (EDE, 66).

How can we make sense of this theoretical interest in phenomenological psychiatry, and how can we place it in the context of Foucault's works that followed? An answer to the first question might be found in his intellectual biography. Between the end of the 1940s and the beginning of the 1950s – to put the facts in line – Foucault met Daniel Lagache, followed Georges Gusdorf's lectures on psychopathology at the École Normale Supérieure, followed Merleau-Ponty's courses on psychology at the Sorbonne (where he encountered an important reference shared by Merleau-Ponty, his *maître* Canguilhem, and Binswanger: Kurt Goldstein and *Gestalttheorie*), as well as Henry Ey's lectures at the Saint-Anne hospital. In 1952, he took a *diplôme* in psychopathology and worked in the laboratory where H. Labory experimented on the first neuroleptic, and he started to teach thought psychology at the École Normale Supérieure and the University of Lille, which he continued to do until 1955. During 1952 and 1954, he and Jaqueline Verdeaux, with whom he worked in a laboratory of experimental psychology at the Saint-Anne hospital, traveled a few times to Switzerland. There he met Roland Kuhn and Binswanger himself, and discussed with Binswanger his introduction, Heidegger, and phenomenology.

To answer the second question is more complicated. In addition to his work on Binswanger's anthropology, in the late 1950s Foucault translated and introduced Kant's *Anthropology*; we might say that what was at first a philosophical interest in anthropology became later a historical theme, in the last part of *The Order of Things*. All of his work on anthropology surely was very useful when he attempted to historicize all this knowledge about man. But on a methodological level, and even if he spent his career constantly criticizing the transcendental subject of phenomenology, Foucault gave, at least on two occasions, some interesting genetic self-explanations that are worth reporting. In 1980, Foucault answered an explicit question about his early work on Binswanger in this way:

> My reading of what was called "existential analysis"… was important for me during the time I was working in psychiatric hospitals and while I was looking for something different from the traditional schemas of psychiatric observation, a counterweight to them.… And I believe that Roland Laing was impressed by all that as well.… But we moved on to other things.… [E]xistential analysis helped us delimit and get a better grasp on what was heavy and oppressive in the gaze and the knowledge apparatus of academic psychiatry. (EEW3, 257–258)

And in a 1984 text, he added:

> To study forms of experience … in their history is an idea that originated with an earlier project, in which I made use of the methods of existential analysis in the field of psychiatry and in the domain of "mental illness." For two reasons … this project left me unsatisfied: its theoretical weakness in elaborating the notion of

experience, and its ambiguous link with a psychiatric practice which it simultaneously ignored and took for granted. One could deal with the first problem by
referring to a general theory of the human being, and treat the second altogether
differently by turning, as is so often done, to the "economic and social context";
one could choose, by doing so, to accept the resulting dilemma of a philosophical
anthropology and a social history. But I wondered whether, rather than playing
on this alternative, it would not be possible to consider the very historicity of
forms of experience (EFR, 334).

Paolo Savoia

SEE ALSO

Phenomenology
Psychiatry
Martin Heidegger

SUGGESTED READING

Basso, Elisabetta. 2007. *Michel Foucault e la Daseinsanalyse. Un'indagine metodologica*. Milan:
    Mimesis.
Binswanger, Ludwig. 1933. *Über Ideenflucht*. Zurich: Art. Institut Orell Füssli.
    1957. "Ellen West," in *Schizophrenie*. Pfullingen: G. Neske.
Herzog, Max. 1994. *Weltentwürfe: Ludwig Binswangers phänomenologische Psychologie*. Berlin:
    Walter de Gruyter.
Kuhn, Roland, and Henri Maldiney. 1971. "Préface," in Ludwig Binswanger, *Introduction à
    l'analyse existentielle*. Paris: Les Éditions de Minuit.
Lanzoni, Susan. 2003. "An Epistemology of the Clinic: Ludwig Binswanger's Phenomenology
    of the Other," *Critical Inquiry* 30:160–186.
    2005. "The Enigma of Subjectivity: Ludwig Binswanger's Existential Anthropology of
    Mania," *History of the Human Sciences* 18:23–41
Spiegelberg, Herbert. 1972. *Phenomenology in Psychology and Psychiatry: A Historical Introduction*.
    Evanston, IL: Northwestern University Press.

97

MAURICE BLANCHOT (1907–2003)

WE NOW KNOW that Foucault displayed an intense interest in literature in the early 1960s, that between 1961 and 1965 he wrote a number of articles and a book (*Raymond Roussel*) devoted to literature, that in private conversations he had told Paul Veyne that he wanted to write like Blanchot, whom he had been reading since the late 1940s or early 1950s, that his last major piece of writing on literature from this period was entitled *Maurice Blanchot: The Thought of the Outside*, that with Roger Laporte he edited the special issue of *Critique* devoted to Blanchot (dated June 1966), and that in an interview he declared Blanchot to be at the summit of any thinking of literature, calling him "the Hegel of literature" (FDE2, 124).

In an interview with Raymond Bellour, Foucault had extremely high praise for Blanchot, going as far as to say that Blanchot "made all discourse on literature possible" (FDE1, 593). According to Foucault, literature is "what constitutes the outside of every work [*œuvre*]" (ibid.). Literature is "not a mode of language, but a hollow that traverses, like a great movement, all literary languages"; it is "the empty void where all works reside" (ibid.). It is also Blanchot that he credits with thinking through the relation between "the author" and "the work." The work is not "a project of its author" or that of his existence, Foucault proclaims, it is "'the streaming of the eternal outside'" (ibid.).

Frédéric Gros in *Michel Foucault*, his volume for the popular series "Que sais-je?," isolates a number of themes in Foucault's writings on literature – the mirror, the infinite, murmur, space, distance, the outside, the void, simulacra, doubling, multiplication of surfaces, transgression, disappearance of the subject, nothingness, the absence of work, and madness – some of which Foucault owes to a reading of Blanchot, who starting in 1953 was regularly contributing essays to *Nouvelle Revue Française*. With essays such as "Madness *par excellence*" (1951) and writings on Sade, Hölderlin, and Artaud, Blanchot had already displayed an interest in madness and the extremes of unreason. So when in the "Preface" to the original edition of *Folie et déraison* (written in 1960 and published in 1961) Foucault writes that madness is nothing else than "absence of work [*l'absence d'œuvre*]," he may have been drawing inspiration from the notion of work [*l'œuvre*] in Blanchot (EPHM, xxxi). (After 1972, this preface did not appear in the later editions of the text.) Between the publication of *Folie et déraison* and its expansion as *Histoire de la folie à l'âge classique* (1972), Foucault published an article entitled "La folie, l'absence d'œuvre" (appearing as an appendix to *Histoire de la folie* until 1972) in which the influence of Blanchot's work on his thinking of madness is readily apparent.

In this 1964 article, Foucault writes about the relationship of Western culture to its limits, to what is excluded from it and is considered to be the forbidden, the intolerable, and the transgressive. Madness, the quintessential limit-experience, can only be welcomed by literature and art. Noting the "strange proximity" between madness and literature (EAW, 548), Foucault defines madness as "a *reserve* of meaning," this reserve to be understood as "a figure that retains and suspends meaning" (EAW, 547). Madness as such a "reserve" does not manifest or narrate the birth of a "work [*œuvre*]" but rather it "refers to the empty form [*la forme vide*] from where the work comes," the site where the work never ceases to be absent, even though "it will never be found" there (EAW, 548). The work, turned toward the elemental depth, is said to be and not be there and by definition escapes comprehension. There, in this "pale region," the "twin incompatibility" of the work and madness becomes apparent (ibid.). This is also "the place that the language of literature approaches" (ibid.). This language, Foucault writes, should not be defined by what it says or by its structures but by its "being." This being, which needs to be interrogated, is related to "the double" and "the void" that hollows it out. It thus belongs to the region where "the experience of madness has been enacted" (ibid.). Madness would then be this absence of work (*l'absence d'œuvre*), this unworking or worklessness. (Blanchot seems to have adopted Foucault's notion of "the absence of work" in his own writings [Blanchot 1992, 424].)

Foucault's major essay devoted to Blanchot, *Maurice Blanchot: The Thought of the Outside*, begins by invoking the saying attributed to Epimenides, the sixth-century BCE Cretan philosopher-poet. Foucault distinguishes the Epimenidean "I lie," which he claims shakes the foundations of Greek truth, from "I speak," which inaugurates any discussion of modern literature. Contrary to widely held belief, modern literature is not characterized by self-reference or a doubling back (EEW2, 148). The event that we understand as "literature" is only, on the surface, of the order of an interiorization; rather it is a matter of "a passage to the 'outside'" (ibid.). Literature, Foucault writes, is language distancing itself from itself, not a folding back [*repli*] but a gap [*écart*], a dispersion rather than a return of signs to themselves (EEW2, 149). The "subject" of literature – what speaks – is thus "less language than the void" (ibid.). For Foucault, "I speak" functions counter to "I think," the indubitable certainty of the "I" and its existence. Whereas thought leads to deepest interiority, "I speak" distances, disperses, and effaces that existence.

There is an incompatibility between the appearance of language in its being, Foucault writes, and the consciousness of the self in its identity. The being of language only appears for itself in the disappearance of the subject. Access to this relation can be gained only through a form of thought that he dubs "the thought of the outside [*la pensée du dehors*]" (EEW2, 150). Foucault remarks that it would be necessary, at some point, to define the fundamental forms and categories of this thought and its sources. It may have had its source in Pseudo-Dionysus and the mystical thinking subsequent to Christianity, but its first "rending" in modern times is to be found in the writings of Sade. According to Kevin Hart, Foucault perhaps attributes the thought of the outside to Pseudo-Dionysus because the latter has "a vision of the deity as above or beyond what is unified." For Pseudo-Dionysus, God is thought of as abiding "beyond the reach of the distinction between unity and multiplicity" (Hart 2004, 140). Foucault adds that the "experience" of the outside was also given voice by Hölderlin, Nietzsche, Mallarmé, Artaud, and Bataille (EEW2, 151). But above all others, it is the work of Maurice Blanchot that is the thought itself.

Neither reflection nor the vocabulary of fiction is adequate to expressing the thought of the outside. For Foucault, this thought is "not reflection, but forgetting; not contradiction, but a contestation that effaces; not reconciliation but reiteration [*ressassement*]" (EEW2, 152). Reflexive language, which always leads thought to a dimension of interiority, needs to be directed toward the outside, cast toward the void that undoes it. The space of fiction is limited to the experiences of the body, the limits of the will, and the ineffaceable presence of others (EEW2, 153). If the fictitious resides in the impossible verisimilitude of what lies between things and people (ibid.), then the language of fiction requires a conversion.

Rather, the "movement of attraction," what Foucault names "the pure, most naked, experience of the outside" (EEW2, 154), and the withdrawal of the companion in Blanchot's *récits* lay bare what precedes all speech, what underlies all silence: the continuous streaming or flowing [*ruissellement*] of language (EEW2, 166). What language is in its being is a formless murmur or rumbling [*rumeur informe*] (EEW2, 167). According to Foucault, Blanchot narrates the experience of the anonymity and boundlessness of language – a "site without geography" (EFB, 54). The being of language, language that is spoken by no one, is the effacement of the one who speaks (EEW2, 166). In language, which places "the origin" in contact with death, "every existence [in their shared transparency] receives through the assertion 'I speak' the threatening promise of its own disappearance, its future appearance" (EEW2, 168).

After 1965, Foucault's interest shifts to what he called the "sacralization" and "institutional valorization" of literature (FMFE, 81). His concern, he explains to Roger-Pol Droit, is in how a certain number of discourses have been given a particular function and a sacralization and how in Western society literature has operated as a substitute for all other discourses (FMFE, 78). Opposed to "a kind of exaltation of literature as a structure of language that can only be analyzed in itself, starting from itself" (FMFE, 82), an exaltation that estimates writing to be in itself subversive and revolutionary, Foucault's concern is now about "how a culture had decided to give such a singular and strange position to the writer," as its voice and spokesperson (FMFE, 83). Nonetheless, he still portrays Blanchot's general approach as "a desacralization of literature," crediting Blanchot alongside Klossowski, Bataille, and Nietzsche (FMFE, 83) with allowing him to "break free [*se débarasser*]" from philosophy (FMFE, 88). Perhaps it is Foucault's reading of Blanchot that may have contributed to his desire to address "the outside" of social practices and the mechanisms of power in society.

Blanchot himself wrote two assessments of Foucault's work: an early article in 1961, "L'oubli, la déraison [Forgetting, Unreason]," an appreciation of Foucault's *Histoire de la folie*, which was published in *Nouvelle revue française* and later appeared in revised form as a chapter in *The Infinite Conversation*. Also, a slim volume, *Michel Foucault as I Imagine Him*, containing brief but penetrating analyses of Foucault's works, which could also serve as a corrective to misreadings of Foucault's work, was published in 1986 after his untimely passing away.

One of the correctives Blanchot issues is of the prevalent interpretations of the notion of the subject in Foucault's work: "The subject does not disappear; rather its excessively determined unity is put in question" (EFB, 76). What is of significance is "its disappearance (that is, the new manner of being which disappearance is), or rather its dispersal, which does not annihilate it but offers us, out of it, no more than a plurality of positions and a discontinuity of functions (and here we reencounter the *system of discontinuities* …)" (EFB, 76–77). Another corrective concerns the interpretation of madness. What particularly catches Foucault's attention in his writings on madness, Blanchot explains, is "the act of exclusion" and not what is excluded (EFB, 65). In examining the power of exclusion that divides society into the reasonable and the unreasonable (EFB, 65), Foucault tackles problems that have always belonged to philosophy (reason and unreason), but he treats them from the angle of history and sociology (EFB, 66). According to Blanchot, Foucault is not calling into question reason itself but rather "the danger of certain rationalities or rationalizations," in the same way that he is not interested in the concept of power in general but rather in relations of power, their formation, specificity, and activation (EFB, 90).

Blanchot's brief essay on Foucault not only alludes to the perceptive manner in which each thinker interpreted the other's writings but also demonstrates how much their readers could learn from reading them together.

Kas Saghafi

SEE ALSO

Literature
Outside
Georges Bataille

SUGGESTED READING

Blanchot, Maurice. 1987. "Michel Foucault, as I Imagine Him," in *Foucault/Blanchot. Maurice Blanchot: The Thought from Outside, by Michel Foucault, and Michel Foucault as I Imagine Him, by Maurice Blanchot*, trans. Jeffrey Mehlman and Brian Massumi. New York: Zone Books, pp. 61–109.
    1992. *The Infinite Conversation*, trans. Susan Hanson. Minneapolis: University of Minnesota Press.
Foucault, Michel. 1998. "The Thought of the Outside," in *Aesthetics, Method, and Epistemology: Essential Works of Foucault, 1954–1984*, ed. James D. Faubion. New York: The New Press, pp. 147–169.
Hart, Kevin. 2004. *The Dark Gaze: Maurice Blanchot and the Sacred*. Chicago: University of Chicago Press.

98

HENRI DE BOULAINVILLIERS (1658–1722)

HENRI DE BOULAINVILLIERS (1658–1722), who preferred to be known as Boulainvilliers, is perhaps best remembered today as an early opponent of Spinoza's philosophy. In the period immediately after his death (many of his works were published posthumously), he was best known for advocating the interests of the French nobility against absolute monarchy, and it is for that reason that Foucault devoted three lectures of the course "Society Must Be Defended" (SMD) to him in February and March 1976. Current interest in Foucault's discussion of Boulainvilliers tends to focus on the fact that Boulainvilliers used terms like *race* and *blood* in his account, thereby suggesting that he could be considered an early theorist of racial differences.

Some of Foucault's readers, particularly in the English-speaking world, seem to have been unaware that Boulainvilliers had long played a role in French discussions of the history of race thinking. Augustin Thierry, to whom Foucault also refers extensively in SMD, had already argued in 1820 as a young man of twenty-five that Boulainvilliers had shown that the nobility were the representatives of the conquerors of Gaul and that it was on that basis that they could call the land of Gaul their own (Thierry 1845, 89). This was suggested to him by such passages as the following: "It is certain that since the conquest the original French have been the true nobles and are the only ones who could be, whereas the prospects (*fortune*) of the Gauls were restricted by the will of the conqueror" (Boulainvilliers 1727, I:39). The widespread, but largely unsubstantiated, view that Boulainvilliers was "one of the real ancestors of racism" (Poliakov 1975, 126) received support from a monograph by André Devyer (Devyer 1973, 353–390) just a few years before Foucault delivered his lectures. The recognition that a large portion of Foucault's discussion of Boulainvilliers is not original to him but was a report of the genealogy constructed by the young Augustin Thierry, although later revised by him, accounts for the shift in the reception of Foucault (Venturino 2003 contrasts with his less critical discussion in Venturino 1993). Boulainvilliers was a spokesperson of the nobility, but Thierry reinterpreted him so that he could be understood as a historian of racial conflict, and this is how Foucault presented him: as a theorist of race war (which as an explanatory device held sway until it was replaced by the class war in the middle of the nineteenth century) (ECF-SMD, 60, 80).

In contrast to Foucault, the weight of current scholarly opinion has returned to the earlier view that because Boulainvilliers did not have an idea of biological inheritance and because he was primarily a defender of the aristocracy, he is better understood as a theorist of class than of race (Simar 1922, 24). That this is the better reading is confirmed by the fact that Boulainvilliers was following earlier usage in understanding *race* as a synonym for *rang* or rank (Boulainvilliers 1727, III:204). On that basis, he argued that a noble birth is the most common means to attain virtue (Boulainvilliers 1732, 7–8). He associated noble birth with "a tradition of virtue, glory, honor, sentiments for dignity and goods, which is perpetuated in a lengthy continuation of races" (Boulainvilliers quoted in Devyer 1973, 548). But, in spite of the advantages that accrued to the nobility, race was not destiny. Virtues were rendered hereditary by education (Boulainvilliers 1975, 135).

Nevertheless, the fact that Foucault's account is at very least problematic in strictly historical terms does not mean that it does not succeed in all respects. It was also Foucault's intention to write the genealogy of a certain discourse that appealed to history rather than to first principles. By the end of the nineteenth century this in France was largely a right-wing discourse (ECF-SMD, 135). When at the very end of "Society Must Be Defended" Foucault referred to the racism among socialists of the Dreyfus era, many in his audience would have known that the dominant right-wing racists of the period, Gaston Méry and Edouard Drumont, drew on the rivalry between the Gauls and the Latins and in so doing belonged to the tradition of Boulainvilliers.

Foucault's account of Boulainvilliers still has another level. Notwithstanding the association Foucault sketches between Boulainvilliers and the French rightwing, some commentators have recognized that Foucault presented Boulainvilliers as to some degree a forerunner not only of his own genealogical method and of the theme of power as relational (Marks 2008, 88 and 92), but also of his own view that politics is the continuation of war by other means.

Robert Bernasconi

SEE ALSO

Abnormal
Body
Race (and Racism)

SUGGESTED READING

Boulainvilliers, Henri de. 1727. *Histoire de l'ancien gouvernement de la France*. 3 volumes. The Hague: Aux depens de la Compagnie.
　1732. *Essais sur la noblesse de France*. Amsterdam: N.p.
　1975. *Œuvres Philosophiques*, volume 2, ed. Renee Simon. The Hague: Martinus Nijhoff.
Devyer, André. 1973. *Le sang épuré*. Brussels: Editions de Université de Bruxelles.
Ellis, Harold A. 1988. *Boulainvilliers and the French Monarchy*. Ithaca, NY: Cornell University Press.
Furet, François. 1984. "Two Historical Legitimations of Eighteenth-Century French Society: Mably and Boulainvilliers," in *The Workshop of History*, trans. J. Mandelbaum. Chicago: University of Chicago Press, pp. 125–139.
Marks, John. 2008. "Michel Foucault: Bio-politics and Biology," in *Foucault in an Age of Terror: Essays on Biopolitics and the Defence of Society*, ed. Stephen Morton and Stephen Bygrave. London: Palgrave Macmillan, pp. 88–105.
Poliakov, Leon. 1975. *The History of Anti-Semitism*, volume 3, trans. Miriam Kochan. New York: The Vanguard Press.
Simar, Theophile. 1922. *Études critique sur la formation de la doctrine des races*. Brussels: Maurice Lamertin.
Thierry, Augustin. 1845. "On the Antipathy of Race which Divides the French Nation," in *Historical Essays*. Philadelphia: Carey and Hart, pp. 89–91.
Venturino, Diego. 1993. "A la politique comme à la guerre? A propos des cours de Michel Foucault au Collège de France," *Storia della Storiografia* 23:135–152.
　2003. "Race et historie. Le paradigme nobiliaire de la distinction social au debut du XVIIIe siecle, in L'idée de 'race' dans les sciences humaines et la litterature (XVIIIe–XIXe siecles)," ed. Sarga Moussa. Paris: L'Harmattan, pp. 19–38.

99

GEORGES CANGUILHEM
(1904–1995)

THE NAME GEORGES Canguilhem evokes a philosophical dignity for Foucault because of his intellectual importance in postwar France and the continuing relevance of his methods and subject matter. It is Canguilhem who, in elaborating on the French tradition in the history of science, best posed the question of Enlightenment to the generations coming of age after the war. Raised the son of a tailor in a family with peasant roots, Canguilhem's early success at school led him to Paris for *lycée* and on to the École Normale Supérieure. After studies in philosophy, Canguilhem taught at a number of *lycées* before being posted to Toulouse, where he undertook medical studies in order to continue his philosophical education by studying concrete human problems (Canguilhem 1991, 34). With the German occupation and rise of the Vichy regime, Canguilhem quit his post, objecting to the use of philosophy as an instrument for furthering state morality. Continuing his medical studies, he was appointed to replace Jean Cavaillès at the University of Strasbourg and also became active in the Resistance around this time. Although a pacifist associated with "Alain" (the pseudonym for Émile-Auguste Chartier) well into the 1930s, Canguilhem came to believe that armed resistance was necessary. He finished his studies in medicine during this period with the thesis that would establish his reputation after the war, *A Sketch of Some Problems Concerning the Normal and the Pathological* (Canguilhem 1991). After the war, Canguilhem gained a reputation for his severity as general inspector of philosophy and jury member for the *agrégation*, eventually defending his thesis in philosophy, *La formation du concept de réflexe*, under Gaston Bachelard, whom he would replace as director of the *Institut d'histoire des sciences et des techniques* at the University of Paris in 1955 (Lecourt 2008, 56). Canguilhem became well known for his 1955–1956 inaugural course on "Science and Error," which inquired into the status of error in the sciences in order to better understand its place in human life. In 1956, he also famously criticized the scientific pretensions of psychology, arguing that as long as psychology remained ungrounded in philosophy, in a concrete account of the human being, it is an instrument without an end, open to use by industry and the state for the control of employees and citizens. This is the Canguilhem that Foucault would elect as his *bon maître*.

Canguilhem was director of Foucault's thesis, publisher of *The Birth of the Clinic*, and a staunch supporter in the face of existentialist critics (Macey 1993). But consider also Foucault's personal profession of his debt to Canguilhem in 1965:

> When I began to work ten years ago, I did not know you – not your books. But what I have done since, I certainly would not have done it if I had not read you. [My work] carries the imprint of your mark. I can't tell you very well how, neither in which precise places, nor in which points of "method"; but you should know that even, that above all my "counter-positions" … are only possible beginning from what you have done, from this layer of analysis that you introduced, from this "eidetic epistemology" that you have invented. (Eribon 1991, 103)

Instead of Canguilhem's emphasis on the role of vitalism in the history of the life sciences, for example, Foucault argued that a mortalism made the life sciences possible (EBC, 145). Yet, despite this and other "counter-positions," Canguilhem's manner of doing the history of sciences was the starting point for Foucault's own archaeological works. In 1978, Foucault repeated this claim in his introduction to the English-language translation of the expanded edition of Canguilhem's medical thesis, *Le Normal et le pathologique* (1966), while also extending it to other postwar French intellectuals as well as his own genealogical works (Canguilhem 1991). Canguilhem became the essential philosopher for those who would rethink the subject (Canguilhem 1991). Foucault updated this "Introduction" in 1984 – it is the last text he would sign – though it appeared in early 1985, now entitled "Life: Experience and Science" (EEW2, 465–478). Although Foucault was not able to prepare a new essay as he had wanted, he did make a number of changes, suggesting a reevaluation of both his own and Canguilhem's work, for the last version of the essay highlights the "philosophical dignity" of Canguilhem's work in the history of the sciences. And although there is less discussion of vitalism, more emphasis is placed on the philosophical endeavor to root scientific concepts in the activity of the living through the problem of error. As Canguilhem himself later says, his work had attempted to correct a long tradition in the history of medicine that viewed truth as the successive denunciation of previous error by reminding it that error is proper to living things themselves before being the object of the scientist. He states, "[t]o fight against illness is to attempt to help life recover from some error" (my translation from Canguilhem's 1987 acceptance speech for the gold medal from the Centre National de Recherche Scientifique, text from Fonds Georges Canguilhem,

Paris). As Foucault finds, Canguilhem's philosophical value comes from his attempt to rethink the relation between the subject, life, and knowledge on the basis of the problem of error (EEW2, 477). And this relation is one of the major problems for modern thought.

Emerging in the late eighteenth century, the question of Enlightenment sought to know the moment when the West had first asserted the autonomy of its own rationality and the status of the present in relation to this moment (EEW2, 467). The traditional focus on reason's universality opened onto other inquiries, ones in which philosophers would study reason's history and geography in order grasp it in its vitality – its historical birth and life, its present crises and maladies. These concerns became especially relevant after 1945, since the history of European colonialism, the new powers of science and technology, and the violent legacy of modern revolutions had brought forth so many questions about the extent to which rationality is an instrument of liberation or domination, enlightenment or despotism (EEW2, 470). Today the question of Enlightenment seeks to examine "a reason whose structural autonomy carries the history of dogmatisms and despotisms along with it – a reason, therefore, that has a liberating effect only provided it manages to liberate itself" (EEW2, 469). By studying the history of scientific rationalities as aspects of culture, Canguilhem gives the historian the task of posing their meaning for the subject. And the examination of their critical rectifications in the search for truth suggests that the search for truth is a power by which the subject is itself called into question (Canguilhem 2002, 20–23). And this provokes Foucault to ask: "How is it that the human subject took itself as a possible object of knowledge? Through what forms of rationality and historical conditions? And, finally, at what price? That is my question: At what price can subjects speak the truth about themselves?" (EEW2, 444). Canguilhem's work is essential because it formulates the question of Enlightenment for postwar France.

Whereas Foucault identifies different national traditions according to which this question was taken up, Canguilhem's version is the culmination of a French tradition in the history of science (EEW2, 470–471). Here the question was taken up in the nineteenth century by positivists, beginning with Saint-Simon and Comte, who considered himself Kant's successor (Gutting 2005, 90). For Comte, the emergence of positive sciences out of religious and metaphysical consciousness marks the beginning of man's maturity, his break with previous consciousness and emergence as a rational, self-aware being. The development of a positive social science would be useful for identifying areas of life in which immaturity lingered and excluding its errors once and for all (Comte 1853). Moreover, a positivist history of science would be a means of excluding error from future possible scientific endeavors. Historical epistemology (Lecourt 2008, 51–52) grows out of this by means of a critical reflection on positivist theses by the likes of Bachelard or Koyré, yet for Foucault it is only Canguilhem's work that brings the subject into question. Although the appearance of Husserlian phenomenology on the Parisian scene in 1929 may have played an important role in shaping French philosophy in the decades to come, by connecting Canguilhem to historical epistemology, Foucault suggests that his work is a response to problems that had been developing in France since the nineteenth century. Moreover, Canguilhem breaks with the traditional focus on mathematics or physics, visible in Bachelard, Koyré, or Cavaillès, since this allows the history of science to be done without real concern for the subject who knows. Doing the history of such disciplines allows the historian to sidestep the question of the relation between history and philosophy under the assumption that the universal develops according to its own logic once it has broken with experience. And such work thereby occludes concern about the geography and history of diverse scientific rationalities and their meaning for the subject. By focusing on intermediate sciences, like physiology, anatomy, and biology, Canguilhem begins to transform what it means to philosophize on the basis of a critique of French history of science, but with implications that go far beyond its domain.

Canguilhem reworks the French history of science regarding its methods and its objects (EEW2, 470–473). The discontinuity of a scientific rationality over time, a theme as old as the history of science, is no longer asserted as a static fact of history as in Koyré, nor is a radical break with the experiential world supposed as a condition of a science's appearance as in Bachelard. Instead, discontinuity is a part of Canguilhem's analyses because science produces discontinuities within itself. Sciences are truthful discourses, "that rectify and correct themselves, and that carry out a whole labor of self-development governed by the task of 'truth-telling' [*dire vrai*]" (EEW2, 471). The history of a science is the account of normative ruptures instituted in the search for norms giving better access to truth. The sciences are not instructive insofar as they break with experience but insofar as they have been able to rectify their own procedures and correct their own errors. Therefore, writing the history of science becomes a recurring task, since successive transformations in the norms for speaking true [*dire vrai*] entail the reshaping of this very history (EEW2, 472). But scientists as such are not the legitimate historians of their disciplines, since they are oriented by the object of science, an unchanging being, rather than science as it exists, a becoming oriented by the value of truth. Furthermore, since the historian investigates the process by which truth is sought, a recounting of diverse theories or paradigms of knowledge is excluded as a proper object for the historian, since these give a picture of what was known but not the process by which the true is distinguished from the false. This is an "indispensable theoretical reflection" formed from within the history of science since it frees this work from the obligation of repeating what contemporary science regards as true or false, proposing instead to study the extent to which a particular scientific rationality has been and is able to free itself from its own norms, its own truths (EEW2, 473). The historian of science studies the normativity of veridical discourses.

Canguilhem proposes that the life sciences, especially in their connection to medical discourse, are the best places to study the history of veridical discourses, since they prohibit the sort of formalization found in mathematics and physics. The sciences of life exhibit an uncertain but undeniable connection between veridical discourses and human life insofar as they bear the mark of the distinction between health and illness within themselves thanks to concrete, nonscientific human experience (Canguilhem 1991, 222). These discourses have therefore found themselves constantly confronted with the specificity of living things, thereby giving vitalism a special role in their history, since it appears as a perpetual counterbalance to attempts to reduce living beings to physical and chemical constants. So even though vitalism may be regarded as false by a reductionist science, it constitutes part of the normativity of the life sciences, since contemporary biological concepts, like that of reflex motion, are historically dependent on them (Canguilhem 1955). Thus, rather than attending to theories, Canguilhem focuses on concepts, since these cut out particular phenomena for scientific study while respecting the peculiarity of the living beings that are studied. Essential to the normativity of the life sciences, the concept becomes the object of their historian. As Foucault puts it, Canguilhem studies the concept of life as both a property of life and as an attempt to explain life (EEW2, 475). This makes the endeavor to know a way of living, not a way of denying life, and the history of science a philosophical discipline, since it reveals the vitality of this rationality.

According to Foucault, Canguilhem's most important work is *The Normal and the Pathological*, first published in 1943 and then again in 1966 with important additions. In these two parts of the book, the reader finds "how the problem of the specific nature of life has recently been inflected in a direction where one meets with some of the problems that were thought to belong strictly to the most developed forms of evolution" (EEW2, 476). Foucault alludes here to the problem of error, which is central to Canguilhem's thought but not explicitly addressed in his major publications in the history of science before 1966. Recalling that between 1943 and 1966 work on the mechanisms of heredity had enabled an understanding of the living in terms of genetic error, Foucault can be read as suggesting that the error Canguilhem originally studied in the concept of life was later discovered by the life sciences and medicine in life itself, giving a significant scientific confirmation of Canguilhem's historical and philosophical work.

To better grasp Foucault's claim, consider the problem of error in Canguilhem's earlier work. Error is clearly a problem for those who would know, since the scientist wants to avoid making an error in judgment by taking the false for the true, or the true for the false, even though it is a condition of possibility for scientific work (Canguilhem 2011, 644–646). Although error in its usual sense pertains to the human pursuit of knowledge, it has its origins in the experience of failure provoked by the costly trials and errors of living (Canguilhem 1991, 130). Acting without knowledge, without even consciousness at first, the living attempt to attain their ends however possible, with any techniques at their disposal. Consciousness arises only in the face of failure, when a risk taken leads to suffering or illness, making subjectivity dissatisfaction with one's condition (Canguilhem 1991, 222; Canguilhem 2002, 364). The project of seeking knowledge is therefore undertaken in the face of error or failure; that is, in the face of conscious impotence. Medicine and the life sciences are key fields of study, since medicine in all its cultural forms is an attempt to relieve suffering that produces a will to know through its own failures to heal (Canguilhem 1991, 229). As early as 1938, Canguilhem argues that the birth of science from the failures of technique, which happen because of its error in assuming an agreement between needs and things, shows that this error is creative as such in man (Canguilhem 2001, 504). The pursuit of knowledge, though, is an erroneous one, since it is not oriented by the aim of solving any particular problem but solely by the will to know; that is, to grasp the true and avoid the false. Respecting the mutual exclusivity of these values, the search for knowledge seeks to expel all errors from itself, even though it is only error that renders the will to know possible. The continual pursuit of knowledge may be the purest risk possible, since it is guided by no value other than that of truth. But a problem known, and thus resolved to a certain extent, becomes the basis for a new technique, a new way in which the living can attempt to dominate its environment. Such risking, such trial and error, in the attempt to prosper is normativity itself, whereas obedience to established values and norms is normality (Canguilhem 1991, 228). Moreover, the being that can risk itself, experience failure, and recover is healthy, whereas the being that is unable to risk itself and incapable of tolerating changes to its milieu is ill, and as this holds for the living, it also holds for the pursuit of knowledge as a way of living. This notion of error as a permanent contingency for the living "allows [Canguilhem] to bring out the relationship between life and knowledge and to follow, like a red thread, the presence of value and norm" (EEW2, 477). It is not that Canguilhem deduces knowledge from life but rather that knowledge is one of many ways of living, each with its own way of becoming. The problem of error therefore also teaches that where there is knowledge there are orienting values and enabling norms; that is, power.

The risk scientific rationalities pose in addressing human problems – whether these be physical, psychological, social, or political – can be seen, for Canguilhem, in their judging according to standards of truth and falsity alone. In this manner, positivism seeks to reduce the distinction between normal and pathological states to merely quantitative variations of basic physiological functions. But to do this is to deny the basis of the distinction between health and illness in living, and this haunts the entire history of positivist attempts to undo the distinction (Canguilhem 1991). It also denies the value of error, the value of erring for living beings, and demands that humans conform to the rigid contours of the true. Although medicine and medical theorists have suffered from this problem, Canguilhem also worries about the human sciences, in particular psychology. In the endeavor to study the human as a scientific object, such sciences seek the laws that will give an exhaustive account of the object's behavior, thereby enabling its strict control. In such a situation, though, the erratic being that is man is an inevitable affront to the scientific project. It is at this point that the human sciences are revealed as pseudosciences in service to social and political projects of control, and, where this fails, extermination. The true horror here is that these projects operate in the name of health and security from disease, thereby denying the human liberty that is rooted in the errancy of the living. In response, philosophy must counter the humanization of the sciences by dehumanizing them. Canguilhem therefore studies the life sciences and medicine to counter the human sciences, since their history so clearly reveals the value of life's errors. This also helps explain his proposal to study psychologists in the way they study others, as insects (Canguilhem 2002, 379–380).

By 1966, the new science of heredity, grounded in molecular biology, promised a scientific power to diagnose certain genetic forms as errors. Science had gained the ability to define living individuals according to their particular genetic errors and risk, thereby making possible endeavors to correct certain forms of life through genetic manipulation (Canguilhem 1991, 280–281). This causes Canguilhem great anxiety, since it sets the stage for a new humanization of science and a gene police that judges and eliminates the errors of life according to paradigms of normality. Although the appearance of genetic knowledge confirms the primacy of error for the living and allows Canguilhem to develop the problem of error in terms of information theory (Canguilhem 2002, 360–364), it also risks the thought that the errors of life are strictly scientific concerns. As Foucault portrays him, the philosophical dignity of Canguilhem's work is confirmed by the extent to which it remains at the center of problems that contemporary biological knowledge raises for us: that status of error in living beings when this is established scientifically rather than in the events of life. Whereas Foucault embraces the extension of scientific error to the living in his attempt to think the true (FDE2, 967–972), Canguilhem remains anxious.

Samuel Talcott

SEE ALSO

Knowledge
Life
Friedrich Nietzsche

SUGGESTED READING

Canguilhem, Georges. 1991. *The Normal and the Pathological*, with an introduction by Michel Foucault, trans. C. Fawcett. New York: Zone Books originally published in 1943 and 1966.

——— 1994. *A Vital Rationalist: Selected Writings from Georges Canguilhem*, ed. F. Delaporte, trans. A. Goldhammer. New York: Zone Books.

——— 2001. *Œuvres complètes*, tome I: *Écrits philosophiques et politiques (1926–1939)*. Paris: Vrin.

——— 2002. *Études d'histoire et de philosophie des sciences concernant les vivants et la vie*. Paris: Vrin.

——— 2005. "The Object of the History of Science," in *Continental Philosophy of Science*, ed. Gary Gutting. London: Blackwell.

——— 2008. *Knowledge of Life*, trans. Stefanos Geroulanos and Daniela Ginsburg. New York: Fordham University Press.

——— 2011. *Oeuvres complètes*, Volume 1, Braunstein and Schwartz, eds., Vrin: Paris.

Comte, Auguste. 1853. *The Positive Philosophy of Auguste Comte*, trans. Harriet Martineau. London: J. Chapman.

Eribon, Didier. 1991. *Michel Foucault*, trans. Betsy Wing. Cambridge, MA: Harvard University Press.

Gutting, Gary. 2005. *Continental Philosophy of Science*. London: Blackwell.

Leblanc, Guillaume. 2010. *Canguilhem et la vie humaine*. Paris: Presses Universitaires de France.

Lecourt, Dominque. 2008. *Georges Canguilhem*. Paris: Presses Universitaires de France.

Macey, David. 1993. *The Lives of Michel Foucault*. New York: Vintage.

100

GILLES DELEUZE (1925–1995)

FOUCAULT AND DELEUZE first met in 1952 at the house of Deleuze's friend Jean-Pierre Bamberger, after Deleuze and Bamberger had attended a talk by Foucault, the junior lecturer in *psychologie* at Lille University. However, it was not until 1962 that they became friends, following a failed attempt by Foucault to have Deleuze appointed at the University of Clermont-Ferrand, where Foucault was then professor of philosophy (Dosse 2010, 365). Deleuze reviewed Foucault's *Raymond Roussel* in 1963 (Deleuze 2004, 72–73) and *Les Mots et les choses* in 1966, describing the latter as "a great book, brimming with new thoughts" (Deleuze 2004, 90–93). His equally celebratory reviews of *The Archaeology of Knowledge* and *Discipline and Punish* reappeared in revised form in the book published after Foucault's death (Deleuze 1988).

Their collaboration during the 1960s revolved around shared interests in Nietzsche and in the work of Pierre Klossowski, on whom Foucault published an essay in 1964 (EEW2, 123–135). Deleuze's essay on Klossowski appeared in *Critique* the following year before reappearing as an appendix to his 1969 *Logic of Sense* (Deleuze 1990). In 1966, Foucault and Deleuze became editors of the French edition of Colli-Montinari's *Complete Works of F. Nietzsche*. Their coauthored "General Introduction," published in 1967 as part of volume 5, which included Klossowki's translation of *The Gay Science*, expressed the hope that this edition would bring about a "return to Nietzsche" (FDE1, 564). Deleuze's 1962 *Nietzsche and Philosophy* left a strong impression on Foucault (Macey 1993, 109). He referred to Deleuze's analysis of the play of reactive forces in his presentation at the conference organized by Deleuze at Royaumont Abbey in 1964 (EEW2, 277). In their 1972 "Intellectuals and Power" interview, Foucault credited *Nietzsche and Philosophy* with advancing the understanding of power (ELCP, 213). Late in his life, Foucault referred once again to Deleuze's "superb book about Nietzsche" and to his role in the French rediscovery of Nietzsche during the 1960s (EEW2, 438, 445).

Over and above these honorific acknowledgments, the effects of Deleuze's reconstruction of Nietzsche's concept of will to power in terms of force relations are apparent in Foucault's writing about the nature of power during the 1970s. Deleuze's concept of a transcendental field of force relations, encompassing all of the means by which bodies of different kinds may act on each other, forms the basis of Foucault's analysis of power in volume one of *The History of Sexuality*. Foucault suggests that power must be understood "in the first instance as a multiplicity of force relations immanent in the sphere in which they operate," and as the processes by which these force relations are transformed and support or contradict one another, and as the strategies in which they take effect (EHS1, 92–93). As such, power's condition of possibility "is the moving substrate of force relations which, by virtue of their inequality, constantly engender states of power" (EHS1, 93). It follows from this understanding of power as the effect of relations between different forces that the power of a body resides not "in a certain strength we are endowed with" but in the fluctuating field of relations to other bodies. The power even of a single body is dispersed in such a manner that "power is everywhere, not because it embraces everything, but because it comes from everywhere" (ibid.).

In 1969, Foucault published a short review of *Difference and Repetition*, followed by a much longer article in 1970 on this book and its companion *The Logic of Sense* (FDE1, 767–771; EEW2, 343–368). This article begins with the much-quoted remark that "perhaps one day, this century will be known as Deleuzian" (EEW2, 343). Less frequently noted is the first part of this sentence, in which Foucault places Deleuze's work in "enigmatic resonance" with that of Klossowski. Indeed, Foucault's reading of Deleuze's books is framed by themes shared with Klossowski's work, such as the overturning of Platonism and the revaluation of simulacra. In Deleuze's case, he argued, this overturning took the form of a perversion of Platonism, the gesture of which is "to displace oneself insidiously within it, to descend a notch, to descend to its smallest gestures – discreet but moral – which serve to exclude the simulacrum" (EEW2, 345). Foucault presents *The Logic of Sense* as "the boldest and most insolent of metaphysical treatises," where metaphysics is understood as a discourse dealing with extra-being and "the materiality of incorporeal things – phantasms, idols, and simulacra" (EEW2, 347).

At the same time, following Deleuze's reworking of the Stoic concept of events as incorporeal effects produced by bodies and states of affairs and expressed in propositions, this metaphysics of phantasms is also a metaphysics of events, the essential elements of which Deleuze had formulated in his major thesis for the Doctorat d'État, *Difference and Repetition* (1968). Foucault recounts Deleuze's diagnosis of the subjection (*assujettissement*) of difference to forms of identity in the history of philosophy and endorses the project of "liberating" difference through the invention of an "acategorical" thought. He points to the overriding concern of both these books with the nature of thought. Deleuze's search for a new image and a new practice of thought requires abandoning the constraints of the common sense and good will that have dominated the philosophical tradition. It requires abandoning the subordination of both difference and repetition to figures of the same in favor of a thought without contradiction, without dialectics and without negation, one that embraces divergence and multiplicity: "the nomadic and dispersed multiplicity that is not limited or confined by the constraints of the same" (EEW2, 358). It requires an acategorical thought and a conception of being as univocal that revolves around the different rather than the same. Being here is understood as the recurrence of difference in the sense that Deleuze gives to Nietzsche's eternal recurrence. Whereas for Nietzsche's Zarathustra this remained an intolerable thought, Foucault finds the thought of eternal recurrence as difference enacted in Deleuze's texts. As a consequence of the lightning storm that bears the name of Deleuze, "new thought is possible; thought is again possible" (EEW2, 367).

Neither Deleuze nor Foucault were directly involved in the upheavals of May 1968, although both were deeply affected by them. In 1969, Foucault was responsible for Deleuze's appointment to the philosophy department at the newly established University of Paris VIII at Vincennes. They collaborated on a number of political activities throughout the early 1970s, including the Prisoner's Information Group established by Foucault, Daniel Defert, and others at the beginning of 1971 with the aim of bringing to the public at large the voices of those with direct experience of prisons (FDE2, 174–182; Defert and Donzelot 1976). Both took part in a number of other campaigns, such as the antiracism movement inspired by the shooting of a young Algerian in the Paris neighborhood known as the Goutte d'Or (Dosse 2010, 309–313). Deleuze participated in Foucault's seminar at the Collège de France in 1971–1972 devoted to the case of Pierre Rivière. Both men contributed to several issues of the journal *Recherches*, published by Guattari's Centre d'études, de recherches et de formation institutionelles (CERFI), including the infamous issue on homosexuality entitled *Trois milliards de pervers* (Guattari 1973).

The high point of their common political and theoretical engagement was undoubtedly the "Intellectuals and Power" interview, conducted in March 1972 and published later that year in the issue of *L'Arc* devoted to Deleuze (ELCP, 205–217). They reject the idea that there is a single "totalizing" relation between theory and practice in favor of the idea of a plurality of more fragmentary relations. In their view, theory is neither the expression nor the translation of a practice, whereas practice is neither the application of theory nor the inspiration of theory to come. Rather, theory is itself a local and regional practice that operates as a series of relays from one practice to another, whereas practices are relays from one theoretical point to the next. Deleuze advances the much-quoted formula that epitomizes the pragmatism of their approach: theory should be considered a toolbox, or a pair of spectacles that may or may not provide a useful view of the world. If a theory does not help in a given situation, the theorist-practitioner should make another (ELCP,

208). In turn, Foucault suggests that it was one of the lessons of the upsurge of direct political action at the end of the 1960s in France that the masses have no need of enlightened consciousnesses in order to have knowledge of their situation. The problem is rather that their own forms of knowledge are blocked or invalidated. The role of the intellectual therefore does not consist of bringing knowledge to or from the people but of working within and against the order of discourse within which the forms of knowledge appear or fail to appear. More generally, it consists of struggling against the forms of power of which he or she is both the object and the instrument.

Foucault connected the problem of finding adequate forms of struggle to the prevailing ignorance of the nature of power. He considered existing theories of the state and state apparatuses, along with the theory of class power associated with Marxism, to be inadequate for understanding the nature of power and the forms of its exercise. He credited Deleuze's *Nietzsche and Philosophy* as well as his work with Guattari with advancing the manner in which this problem is posed (*Anti-Oedipus* was published in March 1972). He implicitly referred to his earlier comments about working within the order of discourse and knowledge in suggesting that identifying and speaking publicly about the centers of power within society is already a first step in turning power back on itself: "If the discourse of inmates or prison doctors constitutes a form of struggle, it is because they confiscate at least temporarily the power to speak on prison conditions – at present, the exclusive property of prison administrators and their cronies in reform groups" (ELCP, 214).

Many of the points made in this landmark interview continued to reverberate through the publications of Deleuze and Foucault in the years that followed. Much of Foucault's work during the 1970s sought to develop new conceptual tools for understanding power and its relation to knowledge or theory. The first lecture of his 1976 course at the Collège de France takes up the question implicitly posed by his 1972 remarks about the relative lack of understanding of the nature of power and sets out a series of heuristic principles designed to reorient the study of power away from the juridical, political, and ideological apparatuses of the state and toward the material operations of domination and subjectification throughout society, along with the formations of knowledge that accompany them. At the outset of this lecture, Foucault returns to the inhibiting effects of global theories in relation to "subjugated knowledges," defining his genealogical approach as one that targets "a combination of erudite knowledge and what people know" – the technical knowledge of the practitioners of particular forms of power and the disqualified knowledge of those subject to them – and suggesting that this would not have been possible were it not for "the removal of the tyranny of overall discourses, with their hierarchies and all the privileges enjoyed by theoretical vanguards" (ECF-SMD, 8).

His 1982 text "The Subject and Power" offers much the same analysis of the totalization of micropowers by a dominant or ruling power that he gave a decade earlier (EEW3, 326–348). But Foucault's understanding of power had by this time taken a new turn following his discovery of governmentality and his renewed focus on the freedom of those over whom power is exercised. He no longer conceived of power in terms of the interplay of bodies and forces but in terms of "action upon the actions of others" (EEW3, 341). His analyses of the means by which power is exercised included techniques for the government of whole populations by institutions exercising sovereign power. His 1978–1979 lectures on liberal and neo-liberal governmentality included a polemic against forms of "state-phobia" that relied upon an essentialist conception of state power exemplified by Deleuze and Guattari's concept of the state as an apparatus of capture (Patton 2010).

Deleuze and Foucault's 1972 interview already showed signs of their divergent theoretical trajectories. At one point, for example, Deleuze endorses and attributes to Foucault the idea that theory is "by nature opposed to power," even though Foucault has just suggested that theory always takes place within an order of discourse and knowledge that is governed by forms of power (ELCP, 208). Deleuze appears to understand "theory" to mean something like the conception of philosophy as the creation of concepts that he later described as "in itself" calling for "a new earth and a people that do not yet exist" (Deleuze and Guattari 1994, 108). However, this conception of theory continues to rely on the repressive conception of power that Foucault soon came to challenge. Deleuze refers here to the radical fragility of the system of power and its "global force of repression" (ELCP, 209, translation modified). They drifted apart following the publication in 1976 of volume one of Foucault's *History of Sexuality* and his criticism of the represssive conception of power. A letter that Deleuze wrote to him in 1977, subsequently published as "Desire and Pleasure," set out a series of questions that reflected differences between Foucault's account of the formation of the Western apparatus of sexuality and Deleuze and Guattari's conception of assemblages of desire and power (Davidson 1997, 183–192; Deleuze 2007, 122–134). Some of these points bearing on the relation of desire to power and the primacy of movements of deterritorialization or lines of flight in any given assemblage were restated several years later in a footnote in *A Thousand Plateaus* (Deleuze and Guattari 1987, 530–531). More generally, Deleuze's questions point to more profound differences in their relations to psychoanalysis and the kind of critique each was prepared to undertake (Grace 2009).

In response to questions from James Miller some years later, Deleuze insisted that there was no single cause of their estrangement but a number of contributing factors: "The only important thing is that for a long time I had followed [Foucault] politically; and at a certain moment, I no longer totally shared his evaluation of many issues" (Miller 1993, 298). The issues on which their evaluations around this time diverged sharply included Israel-Palestine, the so-called new philosophers, and the Croissant Affair (Dosse 2010, 314). Works by "new philosophers" such as André Glucksmann's *La Cuisinière et le mangeur d'hommes* and Bernard-Henry Levy's *La barbarie à visage humaine* combined Foucauldian theses about the "Great Confinement" with claims derived from Solzhenitsyn and other dissidents about Soviet totalitarianism (Glucksmann 1975; Lévy 1977). In 1977, Foucault published a three-page review of Glucksmann's *Les Maîtres penseurs* in *Le Novel Observateur* that praised the book for tracing the origins of the Soviet Gulag to the manner in which nineteenth-century German philosophy linked the state and the revolution (FDE3, 277–281). One month later, Deleuze published a denunciation of the "new philosophers" in which he expressed his disgust at their martyrology of the victims of the Gulag and accused them of trafficking in large, empty concepts such as The Law, The Power, The Master, and so on (Deleuze 2007, 139–147).

Klaus Croissant had been one of the defense lawyers for members of the Red Army Faction (RAF) in 1975. After having been charged with supporting a criminal organization and jailed on more than one occasion, he fled to France in summer 1977 and applied for political asylum. After his arrest by French authorities in September 1977, Foucault, Deleuze, and Guattari were among those who joined a committee established to oppose his extradition and agitate for his release from prison. Their activities were to no avail, as Croissant was finally extradited on November 16. Foucault and Deleuze were among the small crowd of protesters outside La Santé prison when he was removed. Foucault published several pieces against the extradition of Croissant, but he refused to sign a petition circulated by Guattari and signed by Deleuze, among others. Macey claims that what was unacceptable to Foucault in the petition was a characterization of the West German state as "fascist" (Macey 1993, 394). Eribon offers a slightly milder version of the unacceptable petition, suggesting that it presented West Germany as drifting toward "police dictatorship" (Eribon 1991, 260). Deleuze and Guattari's opinion piece in *Le Monde* on November 2 contains no characterization of the West German state as fascist, nor any suggestion that it was becoming a police dictatorship, although it does reflect a more critical stance toward "the German governmental and judicial model," which they describe as in "a state of exception" (Deleuze 2007, 149). Whatever may have been the text of the petition, Foucault preferred to restrict his support to the lawyer and to the right of accused parties to legal representation.

From this point on, Foucault and Deleuze rarely saw one another. Some years later, Deleuze wrote: "We worked separately, on our own. I am sure he read what I wrote. I read what he wrote with a passion. But we did not talk very often. I had the feeling, with no sadness, that in the end I needed him and he did not need me. Foucault was a very, very mysterious man" (Deleuze 2007, 286).

Paul Patton

SEE ALSO

Difference
Governmentality
Power
Friedrich Nietzsche

SUGGESTED READING

Davidson, Arnold, ed. 1997. *Foucault and His Interlocutors*. Chicago: University of Chicago Press.
Defert, Daniel, and Jacques Donzelot. 1976. "La charnière des prisons," *Magazine littéraire* 112/113:33–35.
Deleuze, Gilles. 1988. *Foucault*, trans. Seán Hand. Minneapolis: University of Minnesota Press.
   2004. *Desert Islands and Other Texts 1953–1974*, ed. David Lapoujade, trans. Michael Taormina. New York: Semiotext(e).
   2007. *Two Regimes of Madness: Texts and Interviews 1975–1995*, rev. ed., trans. Ames Hodges and Mike Taormina. New York: Semiotext(e).
Deleuze, Gilles, and Félix Guattari. 1987. *A Thousand Plateaus: Capitalism and Schizophrenia*, trans. Brian Massumi. Minneapolis: University of Minnesota Press.
   1994. *What Is Philosophy?* trans. Hugh Tomlinson and Graham Burchell. New York: Columbia University Press.
Dosse, François. 2010. *Gilles Deleuze and Félix Guattari: Intersecting Lives*, trans. Deborah Glassman. New York: Columbia University Press.
Eribon, Didier. 1991. *Michel Foucault*, trans. Betsy Wing. Cambridge, MA: Harvard University Press.
Glucksmann, André. 1975. *La Cuisinière et le mangeur d'hommes*. Paris: Seuil.
Grace, Wendy. 2009. *"Faux Amis*: Foucault and Deleuze on Sexuality and Desire," *Critical Inquiry* 36, no.1: 52–75.
Guattari, Félix, ed. 1973. *Trois Milliards de Pervers: Grand Encyclopédie des Homosexualités*. Paris: Recherches, Mars.
Lévy, Bernard-Henri. 1977. *La barbarie à visage humaine*. Paris: Grasset.
Macey, David. 1993. *The Lives of Michel Foucault*. New York: Vintage.
Miller, James. 1993. *The Passion of Michel Foucault*. New York: Simon and Schuster.
Nail, Thomas, Nicolae Morar, and Daniel Smith, eds. 2013. *Between Deleuze and Foucault*. London: Continuum.
Patton, Paul. 2010. "Foucault and Normative Political Philosophy," in *Foucault and Philosophy*, ed. Timothy O'Leary and Christopher Falzon. London: Wiley-Blackwell, pp. 204–221.

101

JACQUES DERRIDA (1930–2004)

N THE ENGLISH-SPEAKING academy, the proper names Derrida and Foucault are often uttered together, emblematic of a kind of thinking that passes under the various names of postmodernism, poststructuralism, continental philosophy, French theory, and simply Theory. But despite this reception, in each thinker's oeuvre the work of the other is minimally present, both in specific invocation and in a more generalized engagement. Foucault and Derrida were not major influences on or interlocutors for one another, at least not as is avowed in their writings and certainly not when compared to their relations with others. However, their one explicit debate reveals certain important features of their thinking, particularly concerning their attitudes toward the institution of philosophy.

Some basic facts of their relationship are well known. They first met at the École Normale Supérieure, where Foucault was teaching psychology when Derrida enrolled as a student in 1952. Derrida would later remark on his teacher's eloquence, authority, and brilliance in speaking. Foucault published his first major work, *Madness and Unreason: History of Madness in the Classical Age*, in 1961, and in 1963 Derrida presented a complex and to a large degree critical reading of this work in "Cogito and the History of Madness." By all accounts Foucault, who was in the audience when Derrida first delivered the paper, reacted well and supported its publication in *Revue de métaphysique et de morale*. He also gave high praise to Derrida's other publications of the 1960s, including *Writing and Difference*, in which the "Cogito" essay reappeared, and in 1967 Derrida joined him on the editorial board of *Critique*. The next public event in their relationship was the publication of Foucault's "Reply to Derrida" in February 1972 in the Japanese journal *Paideia* (as part of an issue devoted to Foucault and literature, in which Derrida's essay also appeared). But more significant was Foucault's reworking of this text into "My Body, This Paper, This Fire," published later in 1972 as an appendix to the second edition of *Madness and Unreason* (now titled simply *History of Madness in the Classical Age*, and without the original

Preface on which Derrida in part relied to advance his argument). Particularly in its second iteration, this response was extremely critical both of Derrida's essay and of his work in general. The most damning lines from this response also appeared in *Le Monde* on June 14, 1973 under the title "Selon Michel Foucault 'Une petite pédagogie'," in a double-page dossier devoted to Derrida's writings (Naas 2003, 198). It is not known exactly why Foucault's attitude changed so dramatically. Derrida himself traced it to a disagreement in late 1967 over the publication in *Critique* of an essay by Gérard Granel, which gave Derrida high praise and claimed that the Cogito essay exposed a fatal flaw not only in *Madness and Unreason* but in Foucault's archaeological method as a whole (Granel 1967, 897). Whatever the reason, after "My Body" was published the two did not speak for another ten years, until 1982, when Foucault protested Derrida's arrest in Prague. They maintained friendly relations until Foucault's death in 1984, and in 1991 Derrida gave the paper "'To Do Justice to Freud': The History of Madness in the Age of Psychoanalysis" at a conference marking the thirtieth anniversary of the publication of *Madness and Unreason*. Finally, in his late seminars Derrida briefly discussed some of Foucault's work, focusing on *Discipline and Punish* and volume one of *The History of Sexuality*. In *The Beast and the Sovereign, volume I (2001–2002)*, Derrida discusses Foucault's understanding of biopolitics while critiquing Giorgio Agamben's *Homo Sacer* (Derrida 2009, 324–333). In his 1999–2000 seminar on the death penalty, Derrida questions Foucault's opposition between the visible and the invisible in *Discipline and Punish* (Derrida 2012). This second point is raised briefly in *For What Tomorrow*, amid Derrida's reflections on his relation to Foucault and other thinkers he engaged critically in his early work (Derrida and Roudinesco 2004, 12). It may well be that Derrida discusses Foucault's work in other seminars still to be published.

The debate thus begins with Foucault's *History of Madness*. Even though Derrida will make claims about its whole, two sections of this book are particularly relevant to the exchange to come. The first is the Preface, where Foucault outlines his aims and articulates the difficulties he faces in achieving them. The book follows a basic historical sequence: from the Middle Ages and the Renaissance, where madness plays a role in society as a link to supernatural truth, to the classical age, inaugurated through madness's exclusion and ending with madness emerging as mental illness confined in psychological discourse. Foucault maintains that we remain in this last stage, where reason has silenced the dialogue it once had with madness, and he describes his work not as a strict history but as "the archaeology of that silence" (EHM, xxviii). The paradoxical nature of this project is immediately apparent. How can one speak of an excluded silence produced by reason without participating in the very process of exclusion? And how does one access a thing such as madness if it truly has been silenced? Foucault acknowledges these tensions, without claiming to resolve them. He also oscillates between intimating that madness has no reality outside the discourse of reason and speaking of it as if it does, however inaccessible it remains today.

The second relevant section of the *History of Madness* is the opening of Chapter 2, "The Great Confinement." Here Foucault gives a brief reading of Descartes' First Meditation and argues that madness receives special treatment in the method of doubt (EHM, 44–47). Foucault claims that Descartes entertains the possibility of sense errors and dreaming, including them in his method of doubt and so in the experience of thinking. By contrast, Descartes excludes madness as relevant to his method, rigorously separating it from thought as such. "One cannot suppose that one is mad, even in thought, for madness is precisely a condition of impossibility for thought … madness is simply excluded by the doubting subject, in the same manner that it will soon be excluded that he is not thinking or that he does not exist." Descartes' treatment of madness is thus of a piece with the great confinement, in which the mad were locked up en masse along with other undesirables, excluded from all commerce with society at large. "Madness has been banished. While *man* can still go mad, *thought*, as the sovereign exercise carried out by a subject seeking the truth, can no longer be devoid of reason." With Descartes, madness falls silent in the face of reason.

The next text in the debate is Derrida's "Cogito and the History of Madness." This essay begins with a short introduction, in which Derrida reflects on having been a student of Foucault, finding himself "already challenged by the master's voice within him" before he even speaks. But this relation of power is simultaneously contested, since Derrida claims that the master within "is also challenged by the disciple that he himself is" (Derrida 1978, 31–32). Although brief – one paragraph – these remarks raise the themes of mastery and pedagogy, destabilizing an understanding of the active schoolmaster as sovereign over the passive student. Cast as a site of contestation and struggle, the teacher–student relation will remain in play in the remainder of the debate.

Derrida then proceeds by outlining as well as questioning Foucault's project in general terms. Derrida's understanding of the *History of Madness* is here guided by its Preface, from which he quotes extensively, and focuses on two main themes. The first concerns Foucault's thesis that reason has silenced madness and the description of his project as an archaeology of this silence. Derrida questions Foucault's ability to speak from a position outside the order of a generalized reason, since language itself is located in this order. He thus suggests that Foucault cannot avoid complicity with reason's silencing of madness. Although noting that Foucault himself raises such questions, Derrida nonetheless claims that he does so "in too lateral and implicit a fashion" and does not "acknowledge their quality of being prerequisite methodological or philosophical considerations" (Derrida 1978, 35, 38). The second theme analyzed is that of the search for the common root that precedes the division between reason and madness, a project that Derrida claims is opened but "left in the shadows" by Foucault (Derrida 1978, 39). Here Derrida questions Foucault's view that this division takes place in the classical age and involves an external differentiation between reason and its other. Instead, Derrida proposes that the classical event is a secondary phenomenon, derivative of divisions internal to reason more generally understood that can be traced back to the Greeks. Similarly, Derrida pursues the implications of Foucault's association of the division between reason and madness with the origin of history. Taking this seriously, Derrida argues, also undermines the privilege of the classical age. Derrida thus proposes that the relations between reason, madness, and history must be different from what Foucault suggests. The possibilities of both madness and history do not arise only in the classical age but are explained by a broader understanding of reason and its relation to its others.

This sets the stage for the most famous section of Derrida's essay, his contestation of Foucault's reading of Descartes. This proceeds in two phases. First, Derrida argues that Descartes does not treat madness differently from sense errors and dreaming. Rather, he claims that all three are equally excluded from truth, since all leave untouched the realm of the intelligible. The possibility of madness is one step among others in the method of doubt, and Derrida maintains that the only reason it is passed over in favor of dreaming is because it is not common or universal enough. It is thus not convincing to the "nonphilosopher," who Derrida claims Descartes gives voice to at this moment in the text, and so "is not a useful or happy example pedagogically" (Derrida 1978, 51). Further, Derrida argues that madness returns to thought in the hypothesis of the evil genius, for the global doubt this introduces, of both sensory and intelligible truth, is a hyperbolization of insanity. This places the possibility of madness firmly inside the realm of thought.

Second, Derrida raises the stakes further by arguing that the cogito itself is not the paradigm of reason defined in the absence of madness, as Foucault would have it, but "it is valid *even if I am mad*.... Whether I am mad or not, *Cogito, sum*. Madness is therefore, in every sense of the word, only one *case* of thought (*within* thought)" (Derrida 1978, 55–56, Derrida's italics). This, for Derrida, is the cogito's "mad audacity," a madness that goes beyond even that of the evil genius. And Derrida labels it the philosophical moment par excellence, linking it to Plato's "Good beyond being." The cogito thus answers to the project of uncovering the common root of the division between madness and reason, one not located solely in the classical age. However, in a further twist, Derrida suggests that this moment of madness is not found in the cogito as it is written in Descartes' text. To reflect on it or retain it, to communicate it in language, is already to reduce this moment to a kind of rational order. It is thus not a root that lies in historical time. But neither is it located outside of time altogether, as eternal or timeless, a "*philosophia perennis*." Rather, Derrida argues that "the historicity proper to philosophy is located and constituted in the transition, the dialogue between hyperbole and the finite structure, between that which exceeds the totality and the closed totality, in the difference between history and historicity" (Derrida 1978, 60). Between the finite and beyond, the cogito thus provides the basis for an understanding of the relations between reason, madness, and history different from that offered by Foucault.

The nature of Derrida's critique is thus complex in its structure. In its broadest expression, Derrida agrees with Foucault's claim that Descartes has interned madness. But he has displaced both the madness in question and the site of its internment. At issue is not the ordinary madness that Foucault claims is confined in the First Meditation. Rather, it is the hyperbolic madness of philosophy as such, and it is in the Second Meditation that it is cast outside, an exclusion reinforced in Descartes' later appeal to the natural light and to God. It is for this reason that Derrida claims that Foucault risks "a violence of a totalitarian and historicist style" (Derrida 1978, 57), for he follows Descartes in denying the madness inherent in philosophical reason. Not that this risk could be avoided, for Derrida also asserts that the excessive moment of hyperbole is compromised as soon as one speaks. Derrida suggests that the value of Foucault's work is to help us appreciate this point, praise that is of course not without a sting.

It is a sting that Foucault's "My Body, This Paper, This Fire" returns to its sender with a redoubled force. This essay contains two main lines of argument. First, Foucault provides a detailed critique of Derrida's alternative interpretation of Descartes' First Meditation. Opposing him on several key points, Foucault argues that Derrida misses important differences at work in Descartes' text, neglecting "literal differences between words ... thematic differences of images ... textual differences in the arrangement and the opposition of the paragraphs" (EHM, 562). Further, Foucault charges that underlying Derrida's misreading is a fundamental failure to understand the nature of the meditation as a genre. A meditation operates, Foucault argues, in two registers at once, as the deduction of systematic truths and as an exercise to be performed. While Derrida has focused on the first, he appears oblivious to the second and so fails to appreciate those moments of the text aiming more to achieve a change in the meditating subject – to bring about a series of extra-textual events – than to communicate any truth. Foucault then offers a reading of the First Meditation informed by this distinction, one only slightly longer than that offered in the *History of Madness*, confirming his original hypothesis that madness is excluded by Descartes.

Second, Foucault argues that this misreading of Descartes is indicative of Derrida's tendency to reify the sovereign position of philosophy as master of all domains, something Foucault himself rejects. Foucault does not advance this point by analyzing Derrida's praise of philosophy in his interpretation of the cogito in the Second Meditation – this aspect of Derrida's reading he barely mentions. Instead, he focuses on Derrida's claim that the rejection of madness in the First Meditation is made by the hypothetical nonphilosopher supposedly invoked by Descartes.

According to Foucault, Derrida claims this because to acknowledge philosophy's exclusion of madness would be to accept philosophy's limits. Better to relegate the rejection to a prephilosophical naivete and maintain philosophy's power to dominate its others. But more broadly, and more cutting, Foucault extends this diagnosis to Derrida's writings as a whole. He asserts that such a move involves "a reduction of discursive practices to textual traces; the elision of events that are produced there, leaving only marks for a reading," and that behind this strategy is "a historically well-determined little pedagogy, which manifests itself here in a very visible manner. A pedagogy which teaches the student there is nothing outside the text ... a pedagogy that inversely gives to the voice of the masters that unlimited sovereignty that allows it indefinitely to re-say the text" (EHM, 573). With these words, Foucault grants Derrida the status of a master while mercilessly attacking the value of this position.

Reflecting on the significance of this debate, one is struck by the sharp difference that emerges in these two thinkers' attitudes toward philosophy. Although Derrida argues that the affirmative madness of the cogito is lost as soon as Descartes writes, he nonetheless emphasizes this moment's necessity as philosophy's driving force, and the necessity that we pursue this in our own thought in turn. Foucault, by contrast, belittles Derrida's praise of philosophy, confining both disciple and discipline to a past better left behind. (This difference is brought out more clearly in the first version of Foucault's response, "Reply to Derrida." There Foucault opens with general remarks concerning Derrida's relation to philosophy as it is taught in France, remarks still critical but less biting than those closing "My Body," and is also explicit about his own attempt to break free of this institutional framework [EHM, 575–578]). This difference reflects their institutional positions at the time of writing. "Cogito and the History of Madness" was Derrida's first public presentation in Paris and his third publication. No longer a student but not yet a master, the young assistant at the Sorbonne seems to be knocking on philosophy's door, asking for admittance. It is thus no surprise that Derrida affirms philosophy so strongly in supporting Descartes against Foucault's reading, even as he asserts himself as an independent force with which to reckon. The author of "My Body, This Paper, This Fire" was in a markedly difference space. Recently elected to the Collège de France, Foucault had turned his back on the traditional academy and seems to relish the opportunity to slam the door on philosophy one more time. Of course, for neither thinker are these texts the last word on the matter – this particular praise of philosophy quickly disappears from Derrida's writings, and Foucault could be said to return to the discipline in much of his late work. Nonetheless, the texts of this exchange remain significant events in the trajectories of philosophical engagement followed by both Derrida and Foucault.

As mentioned earlier, although "My Body" was the last text in the exchange to be read by both thinkers, it is not the last text relevant to the debate as a whole. In "'To Do Justice to Freud'" Derrida examines the position of Freud in the *History of*

Madness (Derrida 1998). He argues that in this work Freud occupies an ambivalent position, and he extends his analysis briefly to other works of Foucault, primarily *The Order of Things* and volume one of *The History of Sexuality*. Relevant to the earlier debate, Derrida also underlines certain other passages of the *History of Madness* where the evil genius makes an appearance, and claims that these support his original critique. Any comprehensive engagement with Derrida and Foucault would thus need to incorporate this essay's claims. Equally if not more significant is the posthumous publication of the two thinkers' seminars, and not just because, as I have already indicated, Derrida discusses other texts of Foucault's in this venue. Containing a wealth of material, these works make possible further exploration of their debate (immediately calling for further investigation is the theme of sovereignty) as well as opening up many new topics of research.

Samir Haddad

SEE ALSO

Madness
René Descartes

SUGGESTED READING

Boyne, Roy. 1990. *Foucault and Derrida: The Other Side of Reason*. London: Unwin Hyman.
Derrida, Jacques. 1978. "Cogito and the History of Madness," in *Writing and Difference*, trans. Alan Bass. Chicago: University of Chicago Press, pp. 31–63.
———. 1998. "'To Do Justice to Freud': The History of Madness in the Age of Psychoanalysis," trans. Michael Naas and Pascale-Anne Brault, in Jacques Derrida, *Resistances of Psychoanalysis*. Stanford, CA: Stanford University Press, pp. 70–118.
———. 2009. *The Beast and the Sovereign*, volume 1, trans. G. Bennington. Chicago: University of Chicago Press.
———. 2012. *Séminare: La peine de mort, volume 1 (1999–2000)*. Paris: Galilée.
Derrida, Jacques, and Elizabeth Roudinesco. 2004. *For What Tomorrow … A Dialogue*, trans. J. Fort. Stanford, CA: Stanford University Press.
Granel, Gerard. 1967. "Jacques Derrida et la rature de l'origine," *Critique* 246:887–905.
Naas, Michael. 2003. "Derrida's Watch/Foucault's Pendulum: A Final Impetus to the Cogito Debate," in *Taking on the Tradition: Jacques Derrida and the Legacies of Deconstruction*. Stanford, CA: Stanford University Press, pp. 57–75.

102

RENÉ DESCARTES (1596–1650)

FOUCAULT'S ENGAGEMENT WITH Descartes is articulated in multiple statements and interpretations, most of which are brief but evocative, scattered
across many different projects spanning the course of many years. Given this, it
should not be surprising that the interpretation of Descartes' thought that emerges
in Foucault's writings appears fragmentary and ambivalent. Yet, despite this, there is
a remarkable continuity in Foucault's relation to Descartes. On more than one occasion, Foucault insisted that "we must not forget that Descartes wrote 'meditations' –
and that meditations are a practice of the self" (EEW1, 278; see also EHM, 562,
and ECF-HOS, 358, for example). This injunction ties together the central themes
that define Foucault's encounter with the work of Descartes. First, this line makes
obvious reference to Descartes' *Meditations on First Philosophy*. Foucault returned
to this text, and in particular to the First Meditation, time and again in his writing,
research, and lectures. Although this is not the only work of Descartes that Foucault
thought or wrote about, it is clearly the one that held the most interest for his own
project. Second, this injunction draws our attention to the meditational character
of Descartes' text. What interests Foucault is not primarily the logical structure of
Descartes' arguments but rather the style and function of the discursive practices of
which the *Meditations* are composed. In other words, Foucault's aim is to examine
what the text *does*, how it functions or *happens* as a series of events, not to evaluate its
logical validity or truth value. Third, Foucault identifies the function of this text as
a "practice of the self." The *Meditations* employ a set of procedures and techniques
aimed at the transformation of the self or subject who is meditating. In other words,
the *Meditations* have what Foucault calls an "ascetic" dimension. They are part of
an *askesis* – a labor or exercise that one performs in order to change oneself. Finally,
Foucault suggests here and elsewhere that the meditational or functional character of
the *Meditations* is something that *we* tend to forget. This forgetting, as Foucault sees
it, is constitutive of the contemporary academic discipline of philosophy. Foucault's

work reminds us of this aspect of the *Meditations* and in so doing makes us aware of our historical situation in relation to Descartes' text. Foucault's study of Descartes attempts to explain how and why it is that we tend not to focus on the meditational quality of the text, to reanimate the text's meditative dimension, and to show how Descartes' work is in fact part of a historical process that has constituted the kinds of practices that define us today.

In *History of Madness* and *The Order of Things*, Foucault sees Descartes' work primarily as a sign or example of a larger, and largely unconscious, historical event taking place. While each text presents us with an original insight into the historicity of Descartes' thought, it was the brief but controversial passage from *History of Madness* that garnered the special critical attention that eventually led Foucault to develop his understanding of Descartes' thought. For this reason, we will set aside the import of his remarks in *The Order of Things* and focus on his comments in *History of Madness*.

In *History of Madness*, Foucault charts a dramatic shift in the experience or perception of unreason, madness, and the mad that takes place around the time of Descartes (see EHM, part I, chaps. 1, 2). In the sixteenth and early seventeenth centuries, Foucault argues, there was no absolute distinction between unreason and reason, between madness and sanity. For example, skeptical philosophers such as Montaigne insisted that the most seemingly rational, sane, lucid-thinking person could in fact be mad at the very moment of their greatest lucidity. No clear borders marked out a space of rational thought over and against a space of derangement. But a new experience of madness comes to replace this one. Foucault points to Descartes' First Meditation as a "sign" of this new experience. Descartes takes up the skeptical method of doubt – he seeks to set aside all opinions for which he can find a reason to doubt. As part of the method, Descartes wonders whether it is possible to doubt his immediate actuality. But he hesitates because only a madman would doubt this, and Descartes can be sure that he is not mad. According to Foucault, this passage demonstrates a new perception of madness. Descartes seems to presuppose and to safely assume that if one is thinking rationally – that is, methodically, logically – then one is not and cannot be mad. Madness and reason are cleanly distinguished from one another and there is no overlap. The skepticism of Montaigne, in which reason is always potentially madness, is not thinkable for Descartes.

Shortly after the publication of *History of Madness*, Jacques Derrida offered a deconstructive reading of the book. Derrida singled out Foucault's interpretation of Descartes and claimed that "the sense of Foucault's entire project can be pinpointed in these few allusive and somewhat enigmatic pages" (Derrida 1978, 32). Derrida argued that Foucault had fundamentally misunderstood the meaning of Descartes' text, which far from excluding madness from reason in fact radicalizes it as part of his project of methodical and hyperbolic doubt. Furthermore, according to Derrida, this misreading is symptomatic of Foucault's flawed historicism. Foucault posits a historical point of rupture where reason separates itself from madness. This implies – and

Foucault attempts to describe – a prior time where reason and madness participated in an undivided experience, where the two communicated with one another. But, communication is only possible where there is meaning, sense, or reason, and madness or unreason is precisely the absence of these qualities. Thus Foucault is wrong both in his reading of Descartes and in his historicist account of the relation between history and madness. There could never be in history any time when madness and reason are either undifferentiated or absolutely differentiated.

Derrida's challenge served as an opportunity for Foucault to revisit the *Meditations* and expand on his reading of them. In his response to Derrida, Foucault writes that we "must keep in mind the title itself of 'Meditations'" (EHM, 562). Keeping this in mind means paying attention to the nature of the "discursive events" from which the text is composed. In a "pure demonstration," in a text composed exclusively or primarily of arguments, statements are linked by formal rules and ought to be understood and evaluated according to their logical validity. Consequently, "the subject of the discourse is in no sense implied in the demonstration" (ibid.). In other words, in a text devoted to logical demonstration, each statement takes place, or happens, as the result of the application of the formal rules of logic, and the aim of the demonstration is to arrive at the proper conclusion, which follows necessarily from the sequence. The essence of an argument is in the relation of each statement to the others. The existence and status of the subject who writes or reads is absolutely not essential to the meaning or structure of the text. In a logical analysis, we are not interested in the relation of the statements to the subject who thinks them or the effects they might bring about in or on that subject. But a meditation, on the other hand, "produces, as so many discursive events, new enunciations that bring in their wake a series of modifications in the enunciating subject" (EHM, 563). This is the ascetic or meditative dimension of the text. Insofar as the meditation aims at bringing about modifications in the subject, it is a practice of the self – a practice that aims at the transformation of the subject.

In *The Hermeneutics of the Subject*, Foucault returns to this very point. In this text, he defines meditation "not as the game the subject plays with his thought but as the game thought plays on the subject" (ECF-HOS, 358). In the case of the First Meditation, Foucault writes that "Descartes is not thinking about everything in the world that could be doubtful.... Descartes puts himself in the position of the subject who doubts everything.... This, then, is not at all an exercise carried out on thought and its content. It is an exercise by which, through thought, the subject puts himself in a certain situation" (ibid.).

The *Meditations*, according to Foucault's reading, include both demonstrative reason and meditative, ascetic thinking. In his reply to Derrida, Foucault traces the two kinds of discursive practices as Descartes employs them in the development of doubt in the First Meditation. Foucault follows and paraphrases the sequence of demonstrative statements up to the point where the doubt requires ascetic thinking.

Descartes states a principle of practical reason: do not trust someone who has deceived you. He notes that the senses have deceived him on numerous occasions. Therefore, the senses should not be trusted. This is merely sound reasoning. The concluding statement follows logically from the previously established statements. But, though Descartes now has arrived at the valid logical conclusion of his argument, he finds himself unable actually to doubt his senses. Even though the senses have deceived him, he cannot make himself question the certainty that he is here in this room, in these clothes, even though it is nothing other than his supposedly unreliable senses that convince him of these facts. In other words, the immediate actuality of the subject, the givenness of the existing subject who is trying to doubt here and now, resists logical doubt. It is at this point, according to Foucault, that the discursive procedure of the text shifts from the demonstrative order to the ascetic. When Descartes raises the specter of madness and then summarily dismisses it, he does so in the context of an ascetic practice. He is looking for a device that will modify his subjective state, and madness is not effective because Descartes knows that he is not mad. How does he know this? According to Foucault, this is the sign that Descartes is already caught up in a form of knowledge that excludes madness. This is why Descartes dismisses madness and instead reaches for the device of the dream. Dreaming is a condition experienced by rational subjects in which they are deceived about their immediate surroundings. According to Foucault, the sequence of statements in which Descartes considers the possibility that he might be dreaming does not have a demonstrative function – it is not organized according to principles of inference. Rather, this discursive sequence is ascetic in function. Its purpose is to take effect in the subject who thinks it. The key to this sequence is not the logical relation of one statement to another but rather the modification of the subject who is meditating. This modification is possible when one meditates on the nature of dreaming, because in this meditation one is reminded that in an actual dream one is often sure of being awake. Consequently, Descartes no longer knows if he is asleep or awake – consequently his relation to his own immediate actuality, his very presence in the room, has been modified. This modification opens up the possibility of continuing doubt just at the point where demonstrative reasoning had reached its limit.

Why is it that this function of the *Meditations* tends to be overlooked? Why do we tend to focus on the statements solely in terms of their demonstrative order? To answer these questions, we must turn to Foucault's genealogies of governmentality and care of the self. In this research, Foucault traced the formation, transformation, and circulation of relations of power, knowledge, and practices of the self at the heart of Western civilization. Although our civilization has developed many different technologies of control, one central trend is the focus on self-government, or "care of the self." In order to better understand these technologies, Foucault developed a genealogy that traced them to their roots in Western philosophy, which, he discovered, was originally a practice of care of the self. Care of the self was both an attitude (concern, vigilance) and a labor that one carried out with the aim of self-realization in a true, beautiful, noble existence, self-mastery, or a status of peace within oneself (see ECF-HOS). Foucault's studies show that ancient Greek, Hellenistic, and Roman philosophy was primarily devoted to care of the self. In other words, it was not first and foremost a disinterested, theoretical pursuit that aimed at producing objectively true propositions. Rather, philosophy was a kind of training for life that involved a labor self-formation and self-transformation: the truth sought by philosophers was a true life. This truth was the result of self-transformation and was the reward for that transformation. Furthermore, this practice of care required forming relationships of government, spiritual direction, between individuals. The philosopher acted as a spiritual director to the student so that the student could arrive at the point where he could take care of himself, govern himself, and live properly.

This practice of self-transformation and spiritual direction was taken up by early Christian thinkers, monastics, and ascetics and later became the provenance of what Foucault named "pastoral power." The Church developed its distinctive mechanism of spiritual direction – pastoral power – by taking over the framework of care of the self from ancient philosophy (see ECF-STP lectures of February 8, 15, and 22). Pastoral power entailed establishing permanent and intense relationships between individuals, in which some – pastors – govern others not by dominating them or repressing them but rather by taking care of the salvation of their souls. The pastor guides, or governs, the conduct of the individual through a variety of practices of spiritual direction, confession, and penance that come to invest the whole life, including the inner life, of the governed.

As pastoral power intensified and gained ground in Western civilization, it became the object of resistance and generated numerous revolts and reform movements. Foucault argues that "the general problem of 'government' suddenly breaks out in the sixteenth century" (ECF-STP, 88). Foucault sets Descartes' text within this field of contestation. Descartes' thought is motivated by the desire to govern his own thoughts, to outline and follow a method for arriving at truth. He develops his rules for conducting – in other words for governing – the mind in the pursuit of truth (*Rules for the Direction of the Mind*). Furthermore, the truth Descartes seeks is not a speculative truth. As he writes in Part 6 of the *Discourse on Method*, his aim is to find and employ a method for arriving at useful knowledge, knowledge that could more generally help improve the government of life. Descartes' text therefore presents us with what Foucault calls technologies of government – arts of conducting oneself and others based on a method of discerning practical, governmental, truth: "If Descartes' philosophy is taken as the foundation of philosophy, we should also see it as the outcome of this great transformation that brought about the reappearance of the question: 'How to conduct oneself?'" (ECF-STP, 230). Descartes' thought is an effort to develop and practice a science of self-government.

Descartes' thought represents an attempt to resist the pastoral government of life by positing an alternative form of government founded on philosophical truth. But Foucault notes that "the extraordinary thing in Descartes' texts is that he suc-ceeded in substituting a subject as founder of practices of knowledge for a subject constituted through practices of the self" (EEW1, 278). Descartes stands at a turning point in Western civilization:

> In European culture up to the sixteenth century, the problem remains: What is the work I must effect upon myself so as to be capable and worthy of acceding to the truth? To put it another way: truth always has a price; no access to truth without ascesis.... Descartes, I think, broke with this when he said, "To accede to truth, it suffices that I be any subject that can see what is evident." (EEW1, 279)

In other words, as a result of the turn toward evidence as the grounds of knowledge, the ascetic grounds of knowledge come to be obscured, neglected. Foucault, some-what ironically, names this change the "Cartesian Moment" (ECF-HOS, 14). He writes that, "This change makes possible the institutionalization of modern science" (EEW1, 279). It also obscures the ascetic, meditative dimension of thought.

Foucault seemed almost compelled to invoke Descartes' name and work at key points in so many of his different studies over the years. When he did so, he con-sistently returned to the ascetic dimension of Descartes' work. Despite this consis-tency, Foucault's reading of Descartes leaves us with some unresolved tensions. For example, Descartes' thought seems, in Foucault's works, to be both determined by the historical structures or processes taking place around and beyond it and yet an agent of transformation in history. Similarly, Foucault sometimes emphasizes the fact that in Descartes we have the beginning of modern scientific thought and the disqualification of *askesis*. At other times, Foucault places the accent on the idea that Descartes wrote meditations, that he was engaged in a spiritual exercise in order to gain access to truth. Ultimately, Foucault's encounter with Descartes provides a window on the movement of Foucault's thought as well as unique insight into the historical and philosophical meanings of Descartes' work.

Edward McGushin

SEE ALSO

Madness
Philosophy
Jacques Derrida

SUGGESTED READING

Derrida, Jacques. 1978. "Cogito and the History of Madness," in *Writing and Difference*, trans. Alan Bass. Chicago: University of Chicago Press, pp. 31–63.

McGushin, Edward. 2005. "Foucault's Cartesian Meditations," *International Philosophical Quarterly* 45:41–59.

103

SIGMUND FREUD (1856–1939)

FREUD AND FOUCAULT: How are we to understand the "and" that stands between "Foucault" and "Freud"? Its placement suggests a point of contact between the two thinkers who are named on each side of it. But is this connection specific? Is it that Foucault and Freud both think some one thing but in other regards differ? Or is the "and" a generic sign, naming in general an affinity or alliance between the two thinkers? If it is the latter, then what is the nature of their community? Further, how are we to conceive of a society that spans such a long time period – one that reaches from the beginning to nearly the end of the twentieth century?

For two thinkers concerned with unearthing the conditions of the present, whether those conditions are conceived, as in Freud, as "phases of development" of the psychosexual organization of an individual psychology (Freud 1949, 197ff), or, with Foucault, as the historical periodization of different modes of knowledge, every community – every present connection between persons (or institutions or social phenomena) – stands in relation to the past circumstances that determine it.

This is not to say that Foucauldian archaeology and genealogy or Freudian psychoanalysis are explicable simply in terms of their pasts, as if psychoanalysis is already prefigured in the work on hypnotism by Jean-Martin Charcot or that Georges Canguilhem's *The Normal and the Pathological* (1943/1966) already contains Foucault's critique of modern scientific positivism. In a 1983 interview with Gérard Raulet, Foucault puts this point succinctly: "There is nothing necessary in [the] order of ideas" (EEW2, 434).

Foucault draws from the phenomenological tradition; he was trained in the philosophy of the history of science; his work shows signs of Marxism and structuralism; and his idea of genealogy is borrowed from Nietzsche. Yet the character of Foucault's thought stands out against the backdrop of these influences; as he explains in the same interview with Raulet, "[many of Canguilheim's students] were neither Marxists nor Freudians nor structuralists. And here I am speaking of myself"

(EEW2, 437). By denying allegiance to the three dominant trends of thought in France in the 1950s and 1960s, Foucault positions his work outside the main currents of mid–twentieth-century French thought.

The same is true of Freud: psychoanalysis is clearly indebted to the study of hysteria in the late nineteenth century. However, Freud's discovery of the unconscious, his notion of a part-psychic, part-physical "drive [*Trieb*]," and the advancements in technique accomplished in analysis make the new science of psychoanalysis distinctly modern (cf. EEW2, 251ff). Foucault signals as much by including Freud with Nietzsche and Marx in his 1967 article for the *Cahiers de Royaumont: Nietzsche*. Together, this group of thinkers defines the discursive character of modern life: "[T]he nineteenth century – and particularly Marx, Nietzsche, and Freud – have put us back into the presence of a new possibility of interpretation; they have founded once again the possibility of a hermeneutic" (EEW2, 271–272).

Here as previously, Freud is not considered in isolation. Whether it is Freud in company with French Marxism à la Herbert Marcuse and Louis Althusser, or Freud together with Nietzsche and Marx, Foucault's tendency is to think of Freud in community with others. What this suggests is that to engage Freud is to face questions of inheritance, intellectual genealogy, and traditions of thought: Freud, the great thinker of the family in modern times, cannot be critically interrogated without raising issues of filiation and association.

Just as issues of association and lineage shape Foucault's and Freud's respective projects from the outside through the influence of the past and present, those same issues and their "present historical" temporality are prominent *within* their respective thoughts. In the *Three Essays on the Theory of Sexuality* (1905), for example, Freud posits three stages of infantile sexual development; he does so, however, only on the evidence of the "fragmentary manifestation[s] of [infantile] sexuality" that appear in a person's mature psychology (Freud 1949, 179). Similarly, the psychological factors that contribute to Dora's fingering of her reticule during therapy, and the connection in her mind between this small purse and past events in her sexual development, are significant only insofar as they are manifest in the present (Freud 1949, 76ff).

Foucault, too, is a historian of the present. As he explains in his 1984 piece on Kant's essay "What Is Enlightenment?" a critical genealogy is a "historical investigation into the events that have led us to constitute ourselves and to recognize ourselves as subjects of what we are doing, thinking, saying" (EEW1, 315). To think, interpret, and criticize is always a present undertaking, but it is inflected by the past. So, the community named in "Foucault and Freud" is at once historical, conditioned by all that has shaped and determined their respective projects and defined their common ground and their points of difference while being also a contemporary gathering of persons and ideas.

What this means is that we are party to the society of Foucault and Freud: we who think in the present continue to work in their company. The "and" between them, which involves both thinkers, implicates us as well. The "and" that bonds Freud to Foucault poses to us questions of association, of filiation; it raises issues of the responsibilities and ethics of living and thinking with others, especially when the others with whom we think can no longer answer for themselves; and it draws out the historical conditions of our own thinking, our lives, and our intellectual efforts to communalize.

The history of the twentieth century *as* the history of the present is another name for the community named by "Freud and Foucault." If Foucault opens his review of Gilles Deleuze with the idea that "perhaps one day, this century will be known as Deleuzian" (EEW2, 343), we might take his hesitation to indicate something other than uncertainty about the future. Foucault's "perhaps" suggests that "this century" has already been designated. One day this may change and we will see ourselves as Deleuzians; in the meantime, we are all already members of the intellectual community named in "Foucault and Freud."

These reflections on community, intellectual filiation, and our present Freudian-Foucauldian circumstances are borrowed, in part, from the lecture Jacques Derrida gave in 1991 to commemorate Foucault. As Derrida asks, "Would Foucault's project have been possible without psychoanalysis, with which it is contemporary and of which it speaks little? ...Does the project owe psychoanalysis anything? What? ... In a word, what is the situation of psychoanalysis at the moment of, and with respect to, Foucault's book?" (Derrida 1998, 76).

The questions Derrida pose here are specific, as is fitting in interrogating the work of Foucault; the book project in question in this regard is Foucault's *History of Madness*. Yet, by generalizing Derrida's point, and doing so in order to implicate ourselves, we raise a number of related questions: Would our project be possible, that of thinking ourselves under our present conditions, were it not for Foucault and Freud? What debt do we owe these thinkers? Further, what is the situation of the community named by "Foucault and Freud" at this moment? What does membership in such a society require and entail?

As we have already noted, these issues of community and social belonging (and their obverse, issues of abnormality and dysfunctional nonbelonging) are familiar to the work of both thinkers. Freud maintained the importance of social and filial relations in analysis in determining individual psychology; he also conceived of the group of practicing psychoanalysts as an extended family, or as members of a common tribe. Early in his career, Freud invited other therapists and doctors into his home each week as part of the "Wednesday Psychological Society"; throughout his career, Freud continued to exercise strict paternal control over the clan, and would expel members, as he did to Alfred Adler and Carl Jung, for their divergence from psychoanalytic doctrine.

There is no corresponding archaeological or genealogical society that Foucault oversaw in his lifetime. Indeed, and despite the community of intellectuals that

Eleanor Kaufmann imagines between Foucault and others based on their writing laudatory essays to one another (see Kaufmann 2001), to the extent that Foucault considered issues of membership and belonging, it was to distance himself from given intellectual traditions. In a 1980 interview with *Le Monde* – conducted under conditions of anonymity and published as "The Masked Philosopher" – Foucault rejects the need for a contemporary "society of scholars": "People sometimes complain that there is no dominant philosophy in France. So much the better for that!" What is better than belonging to a community of thinkers, Foucault continues, is a willingness to "think otherwise [and] to do something else" (EEW1, 327).

Of course, a desire for anonymity and a preoccupation with nonmembership is a kind of fixation on the opposite; and Foucault was constantly concerned in his work with group dynamics, from the mentally ill gathered within institutional walls to prisoners living together under the threat of disciplinary power. Biographically, Foucault identified with the protest groups in Tehran during the Iranian Revolution in 1978; and the history of sexuality project can be read as a theoretical exercising of personal issues of gay identity and the social significance of being a homosexual.

Foucault, then, like Freud, is a preeminently social thinker. The question, which can only be addressed through a study of their particular textual encounters on the topics of community, society, and affiliation, is what the nature of their shared social thought is and how this past community influences our own present ways of thinking about ourselves in society.

In the context of Foucault's early psychological writings – "Introduction" to the French translation of Ludwig Binswanger's *Dream and Existence* (1952), *Mental Illness and Personality/Psychology* (1954/1962), and *History of Madness* (1961) – the "and" of "Foucault and Freud" names "madness [*folie*]" or "unreason [*déraison*]." By listening to unreason, which in the nineteenth century lost its means of addressing reason because of the turn in psychology toward scientific positivism, Freud implicitly critiques the same psychological tradition as Foucault. In turn, Foucault, in company with Binswanger, who was himself part of Freud's inner circle, charges modern psychiatry with objectifying unreason as madness and thereby silencing it. In place of the categorical and etiological diminishment of unreason, under the title of madness or mental illness, Binswanger treated the mentally ill patient existentially by considering his or her self-constitution as a biography and life's narrative.

In *History of Madness*, Foucault places Freud at the end of a historical lineage that begins in the classical period with Pinel and Tuke. Yet, in coming *after* the history of early modern psychology, Freud also comes *before* it in returning to madness and allowing unreason to speak. In this way, Freud encompasses the whole history of modern psychology – a historical feat that his own psychoanalytic approach to time and history makes explicable; here is Foucault commenting on this aspect of Freud's thought in his 1968 "response" to the Paris Epistemology Circle: "The desire to make historical analysis the discourse of continuity, and make human consciousness the originating subject of all knowledge and all practice, are the two faces of one and the same system of thought." Foucault continues this line of thought by citing the corrective effect that "psychoanalytical, linguistic and then ethnological research" has had on this premodern notion of continuous, conscious history (EEW2, 301). An implication of Foucault's response is that he, too, is modern, which is to say psychoanalytic, in his archaeological study of the history of madness.

Beyond the idea that Foucault keeps company with Freud and psychoanalysis in practicing history in a similarly discontinuous fashion, the issue of community and societal belonging appears explicitly in the pages of *History of Madness* as "the Great Confinement" of criminals, the poor, the morally debauched, and the mentally ill during the classical period of European history (EHM, 158ff). Freud is implicated in this history in participating in the modern equivalent of classical internment: by identifying the pathologies from which the mad suffer and classifying cases according to observable symptomologies, Freud collectivizes the mentally ill just as decisively as did the wardens of the eighteenth-century asylum. As Foucault puts this last point in his "summary" for his 1973–1974 lecture course at the Collège de France: "[Psychoanalysis is] a reconstitution of medical power as truth-producer, in a space arranged so that the production would always remain perfectly adapted to that power" (EEW1, 47).

Is there a sense in which Foucault does the same? The society of the mad named by "Nietzsche and Artaud" – and, on a few occasions, Freud is included in this society – recurs throughout *History of Madness* (EHM, 351–352, 510–511). The problematic of "unreason" is made to identify a select society: Nietzsche and Artaud (and Freud). Each in his own way participates in unreason, and this bonds each of them to the others in the history of modern thought. Foucault's suggestion is that all we must do is join this Nietzschean-Artaudian-Freudian society in order to reverse the scientistic turn that reason generally and psychology specifically took in the late nineteenth and early twentieth centuries.

Issues of communalization and society are central as well to Foucault's remarks on Freud in *The Order of Things* (1966). Toward the end of the volume, Foucault considers psychoanalysis together with ethnology as premiere instances of the human sciences: "[P]sychoanalysis and ethnology are not so much two human sciences among others, but ... they span the entire domain of those sciences" (EOT, 379). An "ethnological psychoanalysis" similar to what Freud envisions in *Totem and Taboo* (1912–1913) would apply the Freudian insight into the unconscious to the inexplicit determinants of a society. It would in turn make the unconscious a social structure whose significance was guaranteed by the various practices of a given culture: "By this means, ethnology and psychoanalysis would succeed, not in superimposing themselves on one another ... but in intersecting like two lines differently oriented" (EOT, 380).

Finally, the issues of community and affiliation that run through all of the textual exchanges between Foucault and Freud become fully articulated in Foucault's late history of sexuality project. Freud and psychoanalysis are near constant points of reference for Foucault in the first volume of *The History of Sexuality* (1976). At the beginning of the book, in considering the "repressive hypothesis" that defines modern sexuality, Foucault turns to Freud: "Perhaps some progress was made by Freud" in overturning the idea of our own sexual repression. Yet, owing to his clinical "circumspection" and "medical prudence," Freud did not go far enough (EHS1, 5), hence the need for Foucault to continue Freud's work.

Subsequently, Foucault presents psychoanalysis as a "*scientia sexualis*" characterized by the "clinical codification" of discourse on sex and sexuality and the hermeneutic role played by the listener to such discourse (EHS1, 65ff). Finally, Foucault ends the book as he began it: with Freud. In envisioning a people to come who will wonder in retrospect at our modern preoccupation with the truth of sex – and notice the complex historical temporality of this vision – Foucault imagines future generations who will laugh at the charge of "pansexualism" once brought against Freud. From this future vantage point, the error of this judgment against Freud will lie with those who dismissed it in order to overcome a perceived modern prudishness, for they will be the ones who proved blind to Freud's genius: "[Freud placed sexuality] at one of the critical points marked out for it since the eighteenth century by the strategies of knowledge and power" and thereby impelled the proliferation of sex in modern discourse (EHS1, 158–159).

But it is in the middle section of the book that issues of community and filiation appear most explicitly. Here, under the heading of "The Deployment of Sexuality," Foucault identifies two interrelated forms of societal power: a "deployment of alliance" and a "deployment of sexuality" (EHS1, 106–107). Foucault discusses the past ways in which these "deployments" have intersected and interacted; it is a history that culminates with psychoanalysis, according to which the disparate bonds of alliance are reorganized around the basic family unit and sexual, disciplinary power is exercised over these extended social connections through the prohibition against incest (EHS1, 112–113).

In that Foucault's discussion recalls Freud's discussion of (much) the same in *Totem and Taboo* – with alliances being figured there in totemic clan affiliations and sexuality being deployed through the taboo against incest (cf. Freud 1955, 8ff) – we might read this section of *The History of Sexuality* as working out in some detail the promised ethnological psychoanalysis that Foucault imagines at the end of *The Order of Things*.

If this last suggestion presents a viable reading of the middle sections of Foucault's first volume of *The History of Sexuality*, then it outlines a Freudian framework through which we might read the second and third volumes of the same history. While Foucault focuses in these last works on what might seem like personal or private issues, on such things as techniques of care of the self and practices of self-writing, these are all set against the wider backdrop of a sexual ethics. Further, Foucault draws his examples for such an ethics from the ancients, specifically from different schools or groups of ancient philosophers – the Stoics are of particular importance in the third volume of the project, subtitled *The Care of the Self* (1984).

What this suggests is that the "and" between himself and Freud continues to influence Foucault to the end of his intellectual career. In trying to reverse the order of a Freudian sexualization of social alliances, and thereby model a productive social norm based on the practices of the ancient Greeks and Romans, Foucault continues to work with basically Freudian themes of social alliance and sexuality.

Adrian Switzer

SEE ALSO

Psychoanalysis
Sex
Georges Canguilhem

SUGGESTED READING

Davidson, Arnold I. 2001. *The Emergence of Sexuality: Historical Epistemology and the Formation of Concepts*. Cambridge, MA: Harvard University Press.

Derrida, Jacques. 1998. "'To Do Justice to Freud': The History of Madness in the Age of Psychoanalysis," trans. Michael Naas and Pascale-Anne Brault, in Jacques Derrida, *Resistances of Psychoanalysis*. Stanford, CA: Stanford University Press, pp. 70–118.

2001. "Cogito and the History of Madness," trans. Alan Bass, in *Writing and Difference*. New York: Routledge, pp. 36–76.

Freud, Sigmund. 1949. *A Case of Hysteria, Three Essays on the Theory of Sexuality, and Other Works (1901–1905)*. The Standard Edition of the Complete Psychological Works of Sigmund Freud 7. London: The Hogarth Press.

Ginsburg, Nancy, and Roy Ginsburg. 1999. *Psychoanalysis and Culture at the Millennium*. New Haven, CT: Yale University Press.

Kaufmann, Eleanor. 2001. *The Delirium of Praise: Blanchot, Deleuze, Foucault, Klossowski*. Baltimore: The Johns Hopkins University Press.

104

JÜRGEN HABERMAS (1929–)

J ÜRGEN HABERMAS IS a German philosopher and social theorist, and the leading representative of the second generation of the Frankfurt school approach to critical theory. Born in 1929, Habermas was roughly a contemporary of Foucault's; unfortunately, the vicissitudes of academic specialization and Foucault's untimely death precluded any in-depth exchange of ideas between the two men. Habermas has had a long, prolific, and varied career, in which he has made significant contributions to a wide range of fields, including the philosophy of language, social theory, moral philosophy, legal and political theory, and, most recently, philosophy of religion. As wide-ranging as it is, his work centers on a common core: the theory of communicative rationality. Habermas's central insight is to recast both theoretical and practical reason in communicative terms, construing rationality as an intersubjective process of giving and asking for reasons (as Habermas would say, redeeming claims to truth or normative validity) in a discourse that is structured by certain counterfactual ideals (the most important of which are maximal participation and inclusion and a willingness to be guided by what Habermas calls the unforced force of the better argument). With the theory of communicative rationality, Habermas strives to break out of the aporias generated by the philosophy of consciousness. Having come of age as an intellectual in West Germany in the wake of the Holocaust and in the shadow of his more pessimistic Frankfurt school predecessor Theodor Adorno, Habermas also aims to deploy the normative resources found in the concept of communicative rationality to provide a solid normative grounding for the project of critical theory.

Foucault once acknowledged, with regret, that "the Frankfurt school was practically unheard of in France" when he was a student (EPPC, 26). He lamented this situation, claiming, with only a hint of self-deprecating irony, that if he had been familiar with the Frankfurt school earlier on he might have avoided some missteps and blind alleys in his earlier work (ibid.). The lack of rapprochement between the

French philosophy of science in which Foucault was trained and the Frankfurt school is, Foucault notes, "a strange case of non-penetration between two very similar types of thinking which is explained, perhaps, by that very similarity. Nothing hides the fact of a problem in common better than two similar ways of approaching it" (ibid.). Although he does not specify which works of the Frankfurt school he has in mind here, he suggests that the thread that connects his work to the Frankfurt school is the attempt to offer a "rational critique of rationality," which Foucault explains is "a question of isolating the form of rationality presented as dominant, and endowed with the status of the one-and-only reason, in order to show that it is only *one* possible form among others" (EPPC, 27). To be sure, the attempt to offer a rational critique of rationality draws Foucault's work into proximity with one of the most important works of the first generation of the Frankfurt school, Horkheimer and Adorno's dark masterpiece, the *Dialectic of Enlightenment* (Horkheimer and Adorno 2002; for discussion, see McCarthy 1991 and Hoy 1986). However, in light of Habermas's own trenchant critique of that text (Habermas 1987b, 106–130), this proximity does not necessarily bring Foucault any closer to Habermas himself.

To complicate matters even further, although Foucault professed some familiarity with and even interest in Habermas's work, and expressed some hesitation about Habermas's notion of the ideal speech situation (on both points, see EEW1, 298), he never offered a sustained discussion or critique of Habermas's work. Habermas, for his part, did develop a sustained critique of Foucault, devoting two lectures in his *Philosophical Discourse of Modernity* to Foucault's work (Habermas 1987b, 238–293). However, this critique is based on an incomplete reading of Foucault's work, since Habermas appears to have composed it prior to the publication of volumes 2 and 3 of *The History of Sexuality* (EHS2 and EHS3) and without having read Foucault's important late essays on Kant, critique, and the Enlightenment project. Near the time of Foucault's death, a formal exchange of ideas between Foucault and Habermas was in the planning stages, but even that was apparently the source of misunderstanding (for Foucault's version of events, see EPPC, 34; for Habermas's, see Habermas 1994). In any event, it was slated for November 1984 (Habermas 1994, 150), so it never took place.

As a result of these misunderstandings and missed opportunities, the Foucault-Habermas debate remains largely a second-order affair – the product of the secondary literature on these two thinkers – and a contentious one at that. In the remainder of this entry, I will first enumerate Habermas's major criticisms of Foucault, indicating how commentators have responded to these charges on Foucault's behalf. I shall then turn the tables and sketch out some Foucault-inspired criticisms of Habermas.

In his lectures on Foucault in *The Philosophical Discourse of Modernity* (Habermas 1987b, 238–293), Habermas presents three major criticisms, the second of which is further subdivided into three parts. First, he criticizes Foucault's ambiguous use of the concept of power, which is employed simultaneously as an empirical and a transcendental concept, resulting in paradoxical critical positivism – paradoxical because positivism at least aspires to be value-free, and hence it cannot, in Habermas's view, also be critical. Second, Habermas charges Foucauldian genealogy with reductionism of three types: it reduces meaning, truth and validity, and normativity to power relations. The first form of reductionism mires genealogy in presentism; the second, in relativism; the third, in cryptonormativism. Third, because genealogy "deals with an object domain from which the theory of power has erased all traces of communicative actions entangled in lifeworld contexts" (Habermas 1987b, 286), Foucault's analysis of power is unsociological in two senses. First, the assumption that power relations are coextensive with the social body and cannot be eliminated leaves Foucault unable to explain how social order is possible, since the possibility of social order depends on some non–power-laden (in the sense of nonstrategic; hence, Habermas would also say communicative) forms of interaction. Second, Foucault cannot adequately explain the relationship between individual and society, since he presents individuals as copies mechanically punched out by disciplinary power relations rather than as autonomous individuals.

In the background of each of these criticisms is Habermas's more general charge that Foucault, like Nietzsche, Heidegger, and Horkheimer and Adorno before him, is an anti- or counter-Enlightenment thinker. Foucault's late essays on Kant and the Enlightenment project, not discussed in Habermas's lectures in *Philosophical Discourse of Modernity*, no doubt complicate this picture considerably. However, in a subsequent essay (Habermas 1994), in which Habermas does address Foucault's later work on Kant, Habermas declines to reconsider his interpretation of Foucault's earlier work in light of these later texts. On the contrary, he interprets Foucault's embrace of a certain – admittedly somewhat idiosyncratic – understanding of the Kantian Enlightenment project as standing in stark contradiction to his earlier work. Moreover, he suggests that it is the productive yet ultimately unsustainable contradiction in Foucault's work between his critical analysis of power and his unmasking of the will to truth that leads him "in this last of his texts, back into a sphere of influence he had tried to blast open, that of the philosophical discourse of modernity" (Habermas 1994, 154).

Contra Habermas, however, Foucault's defenders have argued that one can read even Foucault's work from his early and middle periods as aiming to transform the Kantian Enlightenment project from within by exploring the historically and socially specific, and hence contingent, conditions of possibility for subjectivity and agency in late Western modernity (see Allen 2008). This is in fact how Foucault presents his own philosophical oeuvre in essays such as "What Is Enlightenment?" (EEW1, 303–319). Such a reading considerably complicates Habermas's interpretation of Foucault as an antimodern young conservative who sets out to abstractly negate the Enlightenment project only to find himself unwittingly drawn back into its orbit. Recent scholarship also calls into question Habermas's claim that Foucault's genealogies present the subject as a mechanically punched out copy. Indeed, challenging this reading is particularly important in light of Foucault's late work on practices of the self, which presupposes a capacity for deliberate self-transformation that would seem impossible if Habermas's reading of Foucault's middle-period work is correct. The fuller picture of Foucault's account of subjection that emerges from thinking through the transition from his middle-period genealogies to his late work on practices of the self is that of a self who engages in practices of self-formation and self-discipline, though these practices take place within rather than outside power relations (see McWhorter 1999). Commentators have also rethought the normative stance of Foucault's critique by uncovering, for example, an implicit norm of freedom at work in Foucault's texts (see Oksala 2005). Such a reading challenges Habermas's assertion that Foucault reduces normativity to power relations.

Whereas the bulk of the literature that makes up the Foucault-Habermas debate consists either of extensions or further articulations of Habermas's central charges (see Honneth 1991; McCarthy 1991) or of attempts to defend Foucault against Habermas's criticisms, a small portion of it turns the tables around and offers Foucauldian criticisms of Habermas's work. For example, James Tully (Tully 1999) argues that Habermas's principal objections to Foucault – the charges of presentism, relativism, and cryptonormativism – can be successfully turned around against Habermas. With respect to the first objection, Tully argues that Habermas's reconstructive defense of the decentered, postconventional, autonomous subject and the social institutions and forms of life that make such subjects possible (see Habermas 1990) is insufficiently critical of its own present. As Tully puts it, "the arguments for the universality of the decentred subject are structured in a way that insulates it from criticism." Hence, "at the center of Habermas' form of reflection is a form of the subject which is taken for granted at the outset and protected from, rather than opened to criticism by the forms of analyses characteristic of his philosophy (Tully 1999, 111–112). Turning Habermas's charge of relativism around, Tully casts doubt on Habermas's strong claims to universalism and the context transcendence of validity claims. Tackling the charge of cryptonormativism, Tully maintains that the price Habermas pays for his normative grounding of critical theory is utopianism. In so doing, Tully echoes – and also complicates – one of Foucault's own passing critical remarks about Habermas (EEW1, 298). Habermas's assumption that communicative action and discourse can be *even in principle* (if not, as Habermas fully admits, in practice) isolated from relations of power is utopian, as Tully argues, in two senses: first, "in the strict sense that there is 'no place' where humans communicate and dispute norms without putting into play relations of power"; and, second, even if one interprets, as one should, Habermas's notion of communication free from domination as a regulative idea, "to approach communicative games [in this way] is to abstract oneself from what is really going on and the possibilities of concrete freedom *within them*, the only kind of freedom available to humans" (Tully 1999, 131).

Tully's fourth and final point turns on the very idea of a rational critique of rationality. Whereas Foucault claims that this idea is both the central impetus of his work and the thread that connects him to the Frankfurt school (EPPC, 27), Habermas famously maintains that such a project is self-undermining, since it ends in performative contradiction (see Habermas 1990, 76–109). As Tully sees it, all that Foucault needs to do here to avoid the dreaded performative contradiction is simply "to refuse to enter into the form in which Habermas structures the debate" (Tully 1999, 121), by refusing to identify the rationality that he is critiquing with reason per se. As Foucault himself puts this point, in response to a question about Habermas's defense of the modern, Enlightenment conception of reason (reformulated as communicative reason): "that is not my problem, insofar as I am not prepared to identify reason entirely with the totality of rational forms which have come to dominate.... For me, no given form of rationality is actually reason" (EPPC, 35). The point of Foucault's rational critique of rationality, then, is not to indict reason per se but rather, as discussed earlier, to isolate "the form of rationality presented as dominant, and endowed with the status of the one-and-only reason, in order to show that it is only *one* possible form among others" (EPPC, 27). The point, in other words, is to reveal the contingency of those forms of rationality that we take to be universal and necessary and hence open up the possibility of moving beyond them.

Another Foucault-inspired line of criticism of Habermas's work focuses on his conception of power. The criticism focuses on Habermas's tendency in his two-volume magnum opus *The Theory of Communicative Action* (Habermas 1984; Habermas 1987a) to use the term "power" to refer only to the functionally integrated administrative political system (i.e., the state). The result of this terminological choice is that Habermas tends to refrain from analyzing the core functions of the lifeworld – the reproduction of society, culture, and personality – in terms of power relations. As a result, Axel Honneth criticizes Habermas's distinction between system and lifeworld on the grounds that it generates two inversely related and equally problematic fictions: the fiction of a norm-free economic and administrative political system and that of a power-free lifeworld (Honneth, 1991, 298ff). Similarly, Nancy Fraser maintains that it is "a grave mistake to restrict the use of the term 'power' to bureaucratic contexts," for this renders Habermas's theory of communicative action incapable of fully illuminating gender dominance and subordination, which is secured largely through the lifeworld domain of the traditional nuclear family (Fraser 1989, 121). The upshot of this criticism is that Habermas's conception of the lifeworld presents an object domain from which all traces of power have been erased.

Although Habermas insists in response that the lifeworld "by no means offers an innocent image of 'power-free spheres of communication'" (Habermas 1991, 254), critics doubt whether his attempts to theorize the role that power plays in the lifeworld are satisfactory (see Allen 2008; Allen 2010). For instance, Habermas's colonization of the lifeworld thesis, explored in detail in the second volume of *The Theory of Communicative Action* (Habermas 1987a), highlights the ways in which increasingly complex systems of power and theoretical forms of power intrude on lifeworld contexts, producing pathological effects. However, this response does not meet the force of the objection, which concerns precisely Habermas's lack of an account of power relations that are *internal* to the lifeworld itself. Habermas's second way of theorizing power in the lifeworld, his notion of systematically distorted communication, is initially more promising. In instances of systematically distorted communication, power relations, in the form of a strategic orientation toward success (as opposed to a communicative orientation toward mutual understanding), penetrate the structures of communicative action themselves (Habermas 2001). The analysis of systematically distorted communication hence comes much closer to addressing Honneth's and Fraser's worry. However, this comes at a high cost for Habermas. Because systematically distorted communications are both prima facie communicative and *latently* strategic, they are neither fully strategic nor fully communicative. In order to maintain the normative basis for his theory, Habermas needs to be able to distinguish between interactions that are *genuinely* communicative and those that are merely *apparently* so; and yet, the only way he can make this distinction is by appealing to the notion of communicative action, which may, for all we know, be subject to systematic distortions. Although this circle is not necessarily a vicious one, it does raise the vexing question of how confident we can ever hope to be in making the distinction between communicative and strategic actions. In the background here is the Foucauldian worry that it is not possible to disentangle power from validity once and for all.

A final Foucauldian criticism of Habermas concerns his account of autonomy, a concept central to Habermas's normative project. The worry here is that Habermas's robust account of autonomy is plausible only insofar as we are overly sanguine about the depth and complexity of the relationship between normalizing, disciplinary, and biopolitical power relations and the modern autonomous subject. If, as Foucault has shown, the subject is constituted by power relations, then this means, as Judith Butler points out, that "power pervades the very conceptual apparatus that seeks to negotiate its terms, including the subject position of the critic" (Butler 1995, 39). This suggests that if we accept Foucault's (and Butler's) analysis of subjection, we must confront the possibility that what looks like autonomy may in fact be something else entirely.

Foucault makes a similar point when he admits that, if we accept his archaeological and genealogical recasting of Kant's notion of critique, "we have to give up hope of ever acceding to a point of view that could give us access to any complete and definitive knowledge of what may constitute our historical limits" (EEW1, 316). Accepting this means accepting something more demanding than the mere fallibilism that Habermas recommends (see Habermas 2003). It means accepting that "the theoretical and practical experience we have of our limits, and of the possibility of moving beyond them, is always limited and determined; thus, we are always in the position of beginning again" (EEW1, 316–317). This is tantamount to acknowledging the ultimate contingency of our historically determined epistemological and normative starting points. In light of Habermas's staunch defense of the project of modernity – however flawed and incomplete the project of modernity may be, it nonetheless represents for Habermas the result of a historical learning process – this may be the most serious and fundamental disagreement between the two thinkers.

Amy Allen

SEE ALSO

Critique
Power
Immanuel Kant

SUGGESTED READING

Allen, Amy. 2008. *The Politics of Our Selves: Power, Autonomy, and Gender in Contemporary Critical Theory*. New York: Columbia University Press.
2009. "Discourse, Power, and Subjectification: The Foucault/Habermas Debate Reconsidered," *The Philosophical Forum* 40, no. 1 (Spring): 1–28.
2010. "The Entanglement of Power and Validity: Foucault and Critical Theory," in *Foucault and Philosophy*, ed. Timothy O'Leary and Christopher Falzon. Oxford: Wiley-Blackwell.
Ashenden, Samantha, and David Owen, eds. 1999. *Foucault contra Habermas: Recasting the Dialogue between Genealogy and Critical Theory*. London: Sage.
Biebricher, Thomas. 2005. *Selbstkritik der Moderne: Foucault und Habermas im Vergleich*. Frankfurt: Campus Verlag.
Butler, Judith. 1995. "Contingent Foundations: Feminism and the Question of 'Postmodernism,'" in *Feminist Contentions: A Philosophical Exchange*, ed. Linda Nicholson. New York: Routledge, pp. 629–647.
Fraser, Nancy. 1989. "Foucault on Modern Power: Empirical Insights and Normative Confusions," in *Unruly Practices: Power, Discourse and Gender in Contemporary Social Theory*. Minneapolis: University of Minnesota Press.
Habermas, Jürgen. 1987a. *The Theory of Communicative Action*, volume 2: *Lifeworld and System: A Critique of Functionalist Reason*, trans. Thomas McCarthy. Boston: Beacon Press.
1987b. *The Philosophical Discourse of Modernity: Twelve Lectures*, trans. Frederick G. Lawrence. Cambridge, MA: The MIT Press.
1990. *Moral Consciousness and Communicative Action*, trans. Christian Lenhardt and Shierry Weber Nicholsen. Cambridge, MA: The MIT Press.
1991. "A Reply," in *Communicative Action: Essays on Habermas's Theory of Communicative Action*, ed. Axel Honneth and Hans Joas. Cambridge, MA: The MIT Press.
2001. "Reflections on Communicative Pathology," in *On the Pragmatics of Social Interaction*, trans. Barbara Fultner. Cambridge, MA: The MIT Press.

2003. "Introduction: Realism after the Linguistic Turn," in *Truth and Justification*, ed. Barbara Fultner. Cambridge, MA: The MIT Press.

Honneth, Axel. 1991. *The Critique of Power: Reflective Stages in a Critical Social Theory*, trans. Kenneth Baynes. Cambridge, MA: The MIT Press.

Horkheimer, Max, and Theodor Adorno. 2002. *Dialectic of Enlightenment: Philosophical Fragments*, trans. Edmund Jephcott. Stanford, CA: Stanford University Press.

Hoy, David Couzens. 1986. "Power, Repression, Progress: Foucault, Lukes, and the Frankfurt School," in *Foucault: A Critical Reader*, ed. David Couzens Hoy. Oxford: Blackwell, pp. 123–148.

Hoy, David Couzens, and Thomas McCarthy. 1994. *Critical Theory*. Oxford: Blackwell.

Kelly, Michael, ed. 1994. *Critique and Power: Recasting the Foucault/Habermas Debate*. Cambridge, MA: The MIT Press.

McCarthy, Thomas. 1991. "The Critique of Impure Reason: Foucault and the Frankfurt School," in *Ideals and Illusions: On Reconstruction and Deconstruction in Contemporary Critical Theory*, ed. Thomas McCarthy. Cambridge, MA: The MIT Press, pp. 43–75.

McWhorter, Ladelle. 1999. *Bodies and Pleasures: Foucault and the Politics of Sexual Normalization*. Bloomington: Indiana University Press.

Oksala, Johanna. 2005. *Foucault on Freedom*. Cambridge: Cambridge University Press.

Saar, Martin. 2007. *Genealogie als Kritik: Geschichte und Theorie des Subjekts nach Nietzsche und Foucault*. Frankfurt am Main: Campus Verlag.

Tully, James. 1999. "To Think and Act Differently: Foucault's Four Reciprocal Objections to Habermas's Theory," in *Foucault contra Habermas*, ed. Samantha Ashenden and David Owen. London: Sage Publications, pp. 90–142.

105

GEORG WILHELM FRIEDRICH HEGEL (1770–1831)

T IS OFTEN said that Foucault belonged to a generation of French intellectuals whose defining mark was a "generalized anti-Hegelianism," to invoke Deleuze's famous expression for any form of thought that aspired to think of difference or alterity beyond the confines of identity and representation. And certainly, both the methodology and insights of Foucault's historical studies bear testament to a vigilant questioning of the unity and integrity of reason and the order and finalism of history. In this sense, it is right to place Foucault alongside others, such as Louis Althusser, Gilles Deleuze, and Jean-François Lyotard, who, above all, sought to escape the strictures of what they saw as the highest expression of the philosophical commitment to truth, identity, and being: the Hegelian system's teleology and totalization.

But Foucault himself was more circumspect. Acknowledging that he indeed lived in an age that was attempting precisely to flee Hegel, he once wrote, paying tribute to his teacher and mentor, the towering scholar of Hegelian thought, Jean Hyppolite, that:

> really to escape Hegel involves an exact appreciation of the price we have to pay to detach ourselves from him. It assumes that we are aware of the extent to which Hegel, insidiously perhaps, is close to us; it implies a knowledge, in that which permits us to think against Hegel, of that which remains Hegelian. (EAK, 235)

The proximity to Hegel was, for Foucault, biographical and conceptual.

Foucault first encountered Hegel at his elementary school, Henri-IV, in Poitiers. There Jean Hyppolite patiently, though only briefly (he departed for an appointment at the University of Strasbourg only two months after Foucault's arrival), led the students through the *Phenomenology of Spirit* [1807]; it was an experience that Foucault was later to recall as hearing not just the voice of a teacher but that of Hegel, even perhaps the voice of philosophy itself. This early encounter, along with the publication of Hyppolite's French translation of the *Phenomenology* (the first volume appearing in 1939 and the second in 1941) as well as his monumental commentary, *Genesis and Structure of Hegel's Phenomenology of Spirit* (1946), was to mark Foucault throughout his subsequent career as it was this work of Hegel's, above all others, that he was continually to employ as a kind of touchstone both against which and with which to think.

Foucault again came under the tutelage of Hyppolite at the École Normale Supérieure, where in 1947, in fulfillment of the requirements for the second year Diplôme d'Études Supérieures, he is reported to have submitted a thesis entitled "The Constitution of a Transcendental in Hegel's *Phenomenology of Spirit.*" The manuscript has not apparently survived, but the title alone indicates not only that Foucault's engagement with the *Phenomenology* had continued and deepened but that what was to be one of the defining concerns of his own work – the status of the transcendental – began to take shape precisely in the conceptual space defined by Hegel's thought.

Foucault pursued this concern with the genesis and structure of the transcendental to its roots in Kant's thought in the translation, introduction, and notes for the latter's *Anthropology from a Pragmatic Point of View* (1798; French trans. 1964) that he prepared between 1959 and 1960 in Hamburg, under Hyppolite's titular supervision at the Sorbonne (Foucault had actually worked alone on the project), as the complementary thesis to his principal thesis, "Madness and Unreason: The History of Madness in the Classical Age." Hyppolite, recognizing that he was not competent to assess the principal thesis itself – as it was an exploration of the historical constitution and transformation of madness into mental illness – invited his colleague, the esteemed historian of medicine and science Georges Canguilhem, to serve as its *rapporteur*. In his report, Canguilhem found that the work brilliantly displayed what he called a "dialectical vigor" in its distinctive historical methodology, a vigor that he judged to have come, at least in part, from Foucault's "sympathy with the Hegelian vision of history and from his familiarity with the *Phenomenology of Spirit*" (Canguilhem 1997, 26).

Now, if we turn from biography to the works themselves and the conceptual frameworks with which they operate, we can see that Hegel's thought, and the *Phenomenology* in particular, continued to define the very task of philosophy itself for Foucault throughout his career. This is especially evident if we consider three central problematics that Foucault sought to study – madness, knowledge, and subjectivity – and what is arguably the underlying methodological issue of his entire oeuvre: history.

The History of Madness (1961) contains sparse but decisive evidence of its author's deep familiarity with the *Phenomenology*: the entirety of the study is framed in terms of the trajectory leading from the initial confinement of madness, by way of its delineation, in the classical age, from unreason (*déraison*) to its reemergence, in modernity, in the form of an alienation or contradiction at the very heart of reason itself. This last moment is embodied, Foucault argues, in Diderot's figure of Rameau's nephew, and the status of this character serves as a kind of grid through which Foucault constructs his historical account. Rameau's nephew is also a pivotal character in the *Phenomenology*, as Hegel takes him as the exemplar of the extreme form of alienation that he named "derangement (*Zerissenheit*)," a nihilistic condition that, he contends, arose throughout European society at the juncture between the collapse of the medieval world of culture and the advent of the conflict between otherworldly faith and pure insight that was to define the Enlightenment and its ultimate descent into the Terror. In this sense, *History of Madness* marks its proximity to Hegel precisely at that point at which it seeks to think against him by thinking that which exceeds the parameters of Hegel's own analysis of madness, namely the ways in which the practices of division and classification themselves not only created the condition of alienation to which they were purported to respond but ultimately confined alienation itself within the interiority of the subject, placed it at the very core of reason, and thereby gave birth to the supposedly liberating, more humane, configuration of power-knowledge that became the science and practice of psychiatry. *History of Madness* thus proposes nothing less than to isolate the historical conditions under which Hegel's own account of the history of modernity operates.

In *The Order of Things* (1966), Foucault shows that Hegelian phenomenology first becomes possible as a distinctive form of knowledge by virtue of the mutation that he tracks between the historical a prioris (the grids of intelligibility) of the classical and the modern epochs. Foucault's central thesis here is that, in the classical age, the period from the mid-seventeenth through the end of the eighteenth century, the rules under which genuine truth claims can be asserted and assessed permit the complete unification of all knowledge, a universal *mathesis*. The mutation into modernity, Foucault demonstrates, is marked by the fracturing of this unifiability. One of the lines on which it breaks is that which separates the empirical and the transcendental. Modern philosophy still strives after the unification of all knowledge, but it must do so in a way that addresses this breach. Accordingly, Foucault says, the need for the project of Hegelian phenomenology arises precisely at this juncture: it seeks to integrate the domain of the empirical within the interiority of consciousness in its process of revealing itself to itself, what Hegel called experience or spirit and what Foucault terms a "field, at once, empirical and transcendental" (EOT, 248). In this sense, then, Foucault circumscribes the project of the *Phenomenology* by demonstrating it to be but one more manifestation of the dogmatic anthropological slumber from which we have only recently begun to awaken, a project at once still our own and yet no longer who we are.

Foucault returns to the question of the historical a priori under which the project of the *Phenomenology* becomes possible late in his career in the lecture course entitled *The Hermeneutics of the Subject*, which he delivered at the Collège de France in 1982. The lectures that year were devoted to an exploration of the relationship between subjectivity and truth. Specifically, they sought to identify the historical lines from which the distinctly modern subordination of subjectivity to truth descended: the requirement that one must first prepare oneself in order to attain insight into the essence of reality or into the nature of knowledge. Foucault argues, through a subtle and extensive reading of ancient texts from Plato to Seneca, that the modern arrangement is a profound reconfiguration of the relation as it was understood in the thought of classical and late antiquity, where truth is continually placed in service to self-transformation. The historical trajectory of the investigation is thus set, as it was in *History of Madness*, by the *Phenomenology*. But here it is not a specific analysis or figure from this work that proves decisive; rather, as it was in *The Order of Things*, it is the very aim and methodology of the *Phenomenology* itself that is at issue, for the genealogy that Foucault traces shows this to be the ultimate culmination of the epistemological project of modernity and thus of gaining access to truth through the transformation of the subject of knowledge itself: the *Phenomenology* demands of its readers that they give themselves over to the logical and historical process of immanent self-examination that the work unfolds and, by so doing, they are able to establish that knowledge of truth (absolute knowing) is possible and what the content of such knowledge is. As such, Foucault situates the very project of the *Phenomenology* itself as the philosophical exemplar of the modern hermeneutical form of the care of the self (see ECF-HOS, 25–30, 486–487).

Underlying all of these problematics, however, is of course the issue of history: how is the past to be depicted? Canguilhem, as we saw, found in *History of Madness* a thinker that he took to be in full sympathy with the Hegelian vision of history. But it is perhaps here, more than anywhere else, that Foucault sought to think against Hegel and, in doing so, to take the full measure of what remained of Hegel in his own thought.

Hegel, beginning with the *Phenomenology*, famously insisted that the justification of absolute knowing required a historical demonstration. The set of orientations and norms that silently define and mold a social order, what Hegel called a "shape of a world," together embody a conception of the very nature of reality itself, a truth claim that, as it is tested out by those leaving under its aegis and found lacking in some definite respect, is historically transformed into a subsequent shape that incorporates what was found valid in the previous shape and alters what had failed. History is thus, for Hegel, the movement of determinate negation and, as such, it is essentially continuous and progressive. Furthermore, insofar as it culminates in the full accord of the shape of a world with the nature of reality itself, the very possibility of absolute knowing is established and, in this sense, the history at issue is fundamentally teleological as well.

For Foucault, the question of history was a matter of accounting for the historical shifts and breaks that archaeological excavation uncovers. Foucault consistently recognized that the rules governing the various discursive formations that he studied were nothing more than series of events possessing a variable, though tenuously stable, regularity; that they were a bare coherence of positions and sequences and nothing more. From his earliest mature writings, he sought to work out a theory of historical transformation that would account for the various levels at which a break or shift between historical a prioris occurs. He knew that to do so, to remain faithful to their fragile cohesiveness, required rejecting the conventional explanatory models – of creation (theological), of sense-giving acts (psychological), and of evolution (biological) – as these all sought to tether such a movement, in different ways, back to a set of ultimately determinative forces and processes that possess a unitary origin, which they continually unfold, and that proceed according to the inevitability of necessity (see EAK, Part IV, Chapter 5). But because the archaeological method only unearths the transcendental conditions that govern the formation of a discursive body, it is beyond its purview to account for what exactly produced such a rupture, what Foucault called the problem of "epistemological causality" (EOT, xiii).

Foucault held that, as assemblages of events, discursive formations are inherently material. Events, though themselves incorporeal, necessarily take effect in and through materiality. They are thus materially dispersed. Foucault therefore came to see that the problem of epistemological causality is a problem of how these dispersed constitutive elements are forged into interrelated networks and sequences. That is to say, how do events become regularized series and how does one discursive formation, one arrangement of regularized series, give way to another?

Foucault's answer is that the materiality and contingent relationality of history, what he called its positivity, demands of historical investigation that it disavow both continuity and teleology as unwarranted presuppositions. Fidelity to the positivity of history requires instead a method that affirms events as random accidents, reversals, both small and large, and deviations of all kinds that history is populated by, sometimes discrete, sometimes intertwining, lines of descent, and that these lines sometimes forge determinate series that coalesce and erupt in specific, fragile constellations. Such a view of history is necessarily concerned with historical materiality and, specifically, with the way in which this is shaped and molded in and through practices of regulation, control, discipline, and governance. To depict the past in all its positivity thus demands genealogy, for only such a methodology as this is capable of attending to the utter contingencies, discontinuities, and materialities that define the historical field.

Foucault's proximity to and distance from Hegel is thus ultimately marked at the point of historical method, for in detaching genealogy from phenomenological history, Foucault sought nothing less than to think of discontinuity in relation to continuity without sacrificing the former to the latter. The question of how much of Hegel remains in the method of genealogy is the question, then, of to what extent the project of identifying historical shifts and breaks is predicated on a capacity to compare our present epoch with those that have preceded it. Insofar as prior ages remain in some sense our own, insofar as they have shaped us as we are and thereby remain intelligible to us, is not genealogy an examination that presupposes the very kind of continuities that it explicitly appears to reject?

Anti-Hegelianism, Foucault reminds us, may prove in the end to be nothing more than "one of his [Hegel's] tricks directed against us, at the end of which he stands, motionless, waiting for us" (EAK, 235).

Kevin Thompson

SEE ALSO

Experience
Finitude
History
Jean Hyppolite

SUGGESTED READING

Allen, Amy. 1998. "Foucault's Debt to Hegel," *Philosophy Today* 42:71–79.
Baugh, Bruce. 2003. *French Hegel: From Surrealism to Postmodernism.* New York: Routledge, chap. 8.
Butler, Judith. 1987. *Subjects of Desire: Hegelian Reflections in Twentieth-Century France.* New York: Columbia University Press, chap. 4.
    1997. *The Psychic Life of Power: Theories in Subjection.* Stanford, CA: Stanford University Press.
Canguilhem, Georges. 1997. "Report from Mr. Canguilhem on the Manuscript Filed by Mr. Michel Foucault, Director of the Institut Français of Hamburg, in Order to Obtain Permission to Print His Principal Thesis for the Doctor of Letters," in *Foucault and His Interlocutors*, ed. Arnold Davidson. Chicago: University of Chicago Press, pp. 23–27.
Cutrofello, Andrew. 1993. "A History of Reason in the Age of Insanity: The Deconstruction of Foucault in Hegel's Phenomenology," *Owl of Minerva* 25, no. 1:15–21.
D'Hondt, Jacques. 1986. "On Rupture and Destruction in History," *Clio* 15, no. 4:345–358.
Fillion, Réal. 2005. "Foucault after Hyppolite: Toward an A-Theistic Theodicy," *Southern Journal of Philosophy* 43, no. 1:79–93.
Lawlor, Leonard. 2003. *Thinking Through French Philosophy: The Being of the Question.* Bloomington: Indiana University Press.
Roth, Michael S. 1988. *Knowing and History: Appropriations of Hegel in Twentieth-Century France.* Ithaca, NY: Cornell University Press, Afterword.

106

MARTIN HEIDEGGER (1889–1976)

FOUCAULT'S WORK CAN be linked to that of Heidegger via a series of themes, such as nihilism, technology, truth, a critique of humanism, and their respective relations to Nietzsche. Wherever one begins, however, complex stories emerge in which proximities and differences compete and often overlap to the point where forging it all into one perspective is impossible. Both thinkers confront a history through which thought has arrived at an impasse. They both think it necessary to restructure and redirect philosophical thought in order to resolve this impasse, and they both treat the practice of thinking as inseparable from close attention to the structure and history of thinking itself. Within this broad area of agreement, ontology, subjectivity, and finitude feature prominently, but these themes are in turn developed in divergent ways, leading to quite different outcomes. A perspective on this complex relation can be opened up by considering the role of time in their respective critiques of the relation between philosophy and anthropology.

In *The Order of Things*, Foucault considers the transition from the classical to the modern period, which he regards as having drawn thought into an impasse from which it has struggled to escape. If knowledge is a representation of the world and representation an activity of the subject, then knowledge can only be grounded in an account of the subject as one who represents. The attempt to know the subject in this way is reflected in Kant's account of space and time as forms of sense, and his deduction of the transcendental conditions for the possibility of our experience of the world. But Kant's procedure committed thought to treating the human as at once an empirical being and the bearer of a set of transcendental conditions; that is, as what Foucault calls "an empirico-transcendental doublet" (EOT, 318), a being that appears on both sides of the divide and is therefore bound to elude itself. In complementary fashion, the human sciences emerging in the nineteenth century set out to understand the human in a quite different way, but the organization of "objective" knowledge of the human in scientific form demanded a rigorous foundation, and this demand in turn called for an inquiry into the human as the finite subject who represents. The analysis of representation led back to Kant and to a transcendental inquiry into the conditions of knowledge, but insofar as a human being is conditioned by biology, social and economic reality, and language, knowledge of the subject was found to depend in turn on knowledge of these further objective conditions. As Foucault describes it, this led to a fluctuating movement between branches of inquiry while a fixed point on which the body of thought as a whole might rest remained out of reach.

The difficulty is centered on the finitude of the human and led, as Foucault describes, to a call for an "analytic of finitude," a discourse addressing "a fundamental finitude which rests on nothing but its own existence as a fact, and opens upon the positivity of all concrete limitation" (EOT, 315). In addition, this same discourse should deal directly with the concrete instances of finitude in human existence, without referring them to some deeper underlying condition. But as long as what counted as knowledge was restricted to representations of objective reality, this would remain an impossible task. The account of knowledge would therefore have to change in order that acquiring knowledge of the conditions of representation not reopen the same question over again while at the same time also permitting it to address the positivity of concrete human existence. Phenomenology promised answers to these issues. Husserl had sought an adequate basis for the sciences in a more fundamental knowledge of the subject and had devised a methodology and a new conception of objectivity in order to achieve this. Moreover, it is easy to make the link from the analytic of finitude as Foucault describes it here to the existential analytic that Heidegger carries out in *Being and Time*. This is directed precisely toward a determination of the essential finitude of Dasein, which it finds in a temporal finitude defined by Dasein's relation to its own mortality and formalized in the account of the original temporality of Dasein in Division Two of *Being and Time*. What is clear for both Heidegger and Foucault is that the question of human finitude, its relation to concrete human existence and to knowledge, cannot be addressed at an epistemological level alone and that an ontological reflection is also required.

For Heidegger, the history of philosophy can be read as a forgetting of the question of Being as such, which he regarded as having been so concealed by the metaphysical tradition that philosophy had ceased to take it seriously as a question at all. Underpinning his call to remedy this neglect is the ontological difference between beings and Being. Whereas the question of what a thing is leads to an account of its essence, a consideration of essence itself leads to a quite different account of the conditions under which disclosure occurs at all. In this way, the most basic sense of what it means to be – to be anything at all – is disentangled from notions of objectivity and rethought as the question of Being as such. Since we are the beings engaged by this question, the disclosure of Being occurs in and through our existence. However, in Heidegger's view, the philosophical tradition failed to inquire into this existence appropriately; for example, Descartes identified the "I" simply as a thinking thing, and thereby placed it alongside things in the world, its being merely modified by the addition of thinking. When Kant identified the question "What is man?" as fundamental to philosophy, it seemed that this error may have been corrected and the way opened to a philosophical anthropology that could set thinking on a secure footing. However, Heidegger remained critical, arguing in *Kant and the Problem of Metaphysics* that Kant did not deliver on this promise. In his analysis of transcendental imagination, Kant brought to light the importance of time in the formation of experience but did not pursue the inquiry far enough to uncover the temporal character of its foundation in the transcendental subject, which as a result remained obscure, leaving the inquiry into the Being of the subject incomplete. Moreover, Kant's anthropological inquiries remained, for Heidegger, incomplete and poorly conceived: as they are concerned with the faculties of the soul, they cannot be simply empirical, yet as they do not engage what is for Heidegger the fundamental theme of transcendence, they cannot carry through their analyses sufficiently to reveal the grounds of their own possibility, and the grounds of the possibility of metaphysics itself. Heidegger argues that an ontology of the subject as a subject and not as an empirical object requires an account of the temporal structure of the transcendental imagination (Heidegger 1990, 92); that is, the temporal structure of the synthetic activity by which intuitions are subsumed beneath concepts and our experience given structure and coherence.

Heidegger's attention to the ontological structure of Dasein is a direct response to this problem. Recognizing the ontological difference, it treats the existence of Dasein as a form of disclosure through which Being is presented, and does so in such a way that neither Dasein nor Being is treated as an object of knowledge. Rather than limiting this clarification of the disclosure of Being to the way that we understand, reason, and perceive the world, Heidegger extended his analysis to include the practical aspect of our existence, the way our actions take shape around concerns and aims, the way we share our world with others, settle into familiar routines, and sometimes act with a freedom born out of a readiness to confront our basic existential condition. However, while Heidegger presents the existential analytic in Division One of *Being and Time*, it is in Division Two that the properly ontological aspect of the account comes to the fore, as it is here that Heidegger sets out his conception of original temporality that underpins the account of Dasein's finite existence in Division One. The Being of Dasein is temporal in the sense that each of the fundamental modes by which it exists, and by which it discloses Being, has a temporal structure. Together, these constitute the original unity that is the ecstatic temporality of Dasein. Fundamental to Heidegger's account is that Dasein's temporality is more fundamental than our everyday sense of time and cannot be derived from it. While Heidegger provides a radical analytic of human finitude (without any appeal to infinity or eternity), he accords a fundamental priority to the ontological dimension of Dasein's concrete existence as that which is responsible for Dasein's existence occurring as it does, and as that from which thinking must take its lead. Dasein is the site of the disclosure of Being, and the further thinking presses in its attempt to grasp the condition of Dasein as disclosive, rather than simply as disclosed, the further it is drawn toward the event of disclosure itself and to Being. From this perspective, making up for what was missing in Kant entails insisting that anthropology can never adequately become a grounds for philosophical thought, because the more fully such thinking engages with its true grounds, the further it moves from the terrain of anthropology.

Foucault rarely referred to Heidegger directly in his published work, but there are a number of passages where he appears to have Heidegger very much in mind. For the most part, these are critical in tone (though not too much need be read into this), but there is one more positive reference. In 1954, Foucault published an introduction to Ludwig Binswanger's *Dream and Existence*, a study in existential psychiatry influenced by Heidegger. The practice of Daseinanalysis it proposes and develops is indebted to the existential analytic of Dasein set out in *Being and Time*, and Foucault's enthusiasm for Binswanger implies at least a degree of enthusiasm for Heidegger as well. There are passages in which Foucault praises an inquiry closely aligned to the existential analytic that Heidegger undertook in *Being and Time*, and in terms similar to those in which he appears to describe that analytic elsewhere. However, it is also clear that even at this early stage Foucault had serious reservations over the form of Heidegger's inquiry. Explaining his interest in Binswanger, Foucault refers to the way Binswanger's analysis of existence avoids any a priori distinction between ontology and anthropology (EDE, 32). This is in sharp contrast to Heidegger, for whom this distinction was fundamental, and anthropology remained compromised by its lack of a properly ontological basis, carrying over a conception of the human from the metaphysical tradition without submitting that conception to revision in the light of a renewed engagement with the question of Being as such. In this way, anthropology was, for Heidegger, to be ranked alongside biology, history, and political science as a science of the human based on a misconceived confidence in the ideal of objectivity. Foucault's comments in the Introduction to *Dream and Existence* therefore seem to be explicitly antiphenomenological, in spite of the alignment with Heidegger implied elsewhere in the same text. Moreover, the true villain of the piece, standing in the wings, is Kant, who installed the distinction between positive science and transcendental philosophy at the heart of thinking, and who saw that the thinking subject cannot be disclosed as a subject through an empirical reflection. Having refused the phenomenological approach, Foucault then also rules out both a "pre-critical" indifference to the distinction between the positive sciences and transcendental philosophy and a simple return to the anthropology that Kant proposed. He seems therefore to have left himself with little room to maneuver. A different solution is required, and he finds it in an interpretation of Kant's anthropology that diverges sharply from that of Heidegger, yet does so through a strategy of reading that recalls Heidegger's "destruction" of the history of ontology, an approach aimed precisely at retrieving possibilities that had been closed off by the metaphysical tradition (Heidegger 1962, §6; Heidegger 1982, §5).

Foucault draws attention to the different roles played by time in the *Critique of Pure Reason* and the *Anthropology*, a difference that arises from the nature of the *Anthropology*'s inquiry into what the human individual "as a free-acting being makes of himself, or can and should make of himself" (Kant 2006, 3), not only by shaping our conduct but also by cultivating our sensibility, understanding, and taste. Kant first explores this through a rehearsal of structures familiar from the *Critique of Pure Reason* (sensibility, understanding, reason) and then through a consideration of pleasure, displeasure, and desire that takes in discussions of topics such as distraction, mental illness, dreams, wit, boredom, and eating alone or in company, before going on to deal with character, physiognomy, and the character of races and the sexes, and more besides. Whereas in the *Critique of Pure Reason* the subject is divided between a transcendental unit that anchors the syntheses of the multiple and the empirical self that appears as an object of intuition, in the *Anthropology* the subject experiments with provisional variations on the human, each of which may be modified or undone in turn. Here, writes Foucault, time is not the transparent condition of synthetic activity but rather that by which it is left obscure and incomplete. Simple determination gives way to a gradual and uncertain activity that Kant names *Kunst*. Time in the *Anthropology* is described by Foucault as the guarantee of a "dispersion that cannot be contained (*qui n'est pas surmontable*)" (EIKA, 89). It is "the dispersion of the synthetic activity with regard to itself" (ibid.), the noncoincidence of synthesis with itself as it works through time. By virtue of this structural incompleteness, Foucault writes, the time of the *Anthropology* eats away at the coherence of synthesis from within, making room for error, correction, repetition, and thereby also a certain freedom (EIKA, 91). The message that Foucault draws from this is that one must avoid a "false" anthropology that seeks to return to a beginning point, whether this be in an empirical sense or by recourse to a transcendental a priori. Instead, he proposes that the a priori of the *Critique of Pure Reason* be repeated "in a truly temporal dimension" (EIKA, 93). Like Heidegger, then, Foucault sees time as the key to Kant's anthropology, and, like Heidegger, Foucault tries to identify the temporal structure of synthesis itself. However, whereas Heidegger directs his attention to the temporal dimension of the synthetic activity of the transcendental imagination, Foucault sees the locus of the problem shift to the anthropology, where the purity of this synthesis is adulterated by the time of concrete life. From the point of view of Foucault's depiction of the way thought in modernity has been caught in an impasse, this disruption of dichotomy between the empirical and the transcendental, between the actual existence and the conditions that make it possible, seems to promise thinking a new future.

However, there are two obstacles that make it impossible simply to take Kant's formulation in the *Anthropology* as a solution to the problem. First, the presentation of time as a linear series of events has to be constituted by an antecedent activity that cannot itself be represented in the series. The transcendental role of time as the condition of the order of experience is thereby kept out of view, but for this reason the disruptive potentiality of temporal dispersion is also blocked; that is, the account sits firmly within the very structure from which Foucault wishes to escape. Also playing a vital role here is language, which is seen as a regulated articulation of the freedoms by which individuals form a community and thereby accomplish a "concrete universal" (EIKA, 102). If time itself is the dimension of the "originary" (*l'originaire*), Foucault endorses the view that it "is not to be found in an already given, secret meaning, but in what is the most manifest path of the exchange" (EIKA, 102–103). This becomes problematic, in Foucault's view, because Kant adopts a "popular" idiom for the *Anthropology*. By appealing to a common language, shared between author and public, it fosters a certainty that, in spite of the dispersion of time, something clear and whole is nonetheless given, or at least almost within our grasp. Taking up a language that is already familiar from our understanding of the world, the *Anthropology* deploys it to grasp the human, time is confirmed as an order of empirical events, and the radical potential of temporal dispersion is lost. So when Foucault writes that the reader of the *Anthropology* is placed in a milieu of "total evidence" where any number of new examples can be found, but that "'popular knowledge' is not the first, the earliest, nor the most naïve form of truth" (EIKA, 94), he is on a path parallel to Heidegger's contrast of authenticity with the common currency of the impersonal "they" (Heidegger 2010, §27). Moreover, like Heidegger, his solution is to recover a temporal form that has been concealed by this semblance of self-evidence. The difference is that for Heidegger an account of the Being of the subject is only possible once a clear distinction is made between everyday time and the original time of the ontological, whereas Foucault welcomes the way the two are folded together in Kant's anthropology (a view that matches the one he sketched ten years earlier in his Introduction to Binswanger's text). But in order that the transformative repercussions of this shift be felt, the screen of self-evidence placed around it when Kant cast anthropology as a "popular" discourse has to be drawn away.

Foucault's work, as it unfolds later in the 1960s and beyond, retrieves the temporal dispersion he found in Kant from the restrictions of the "popular" idiom, allowing dispersion to shape a different understanding of the subject in its relation to ontology and to knowledge. Archaeological method suspends readymade unities (actors, discourses, works, traditions, artifacts) in the analysis of discourse, exposing history as the gradual, piecemeal, and provisional formation of such unities, their temporary stability, and their ultimate deformation. In this way, it turns a forensic eye on the genesis of forms that the analysis of discourse generally either takes for granted or defines as the conditions of possibility for a given class of events. Foucault sees the dispersion of events in their multiplicity challenge the synthetic activity by which such formal characteristics emerge and by which things, ideas, and even thought itself become intelligible. The archaeological analogue of synthesis produces discourse from discourse, according to rules formed within discourse that are transformed along with the shifting patterns they describe and yet for which they nonetheless establish local conditions of existence. As a response to Kant, and to Heidegger's response to Kant, archaeology opens synthesis up to what Foucault again identifies as "temporal dispersion" (EAK, 25). The difference is that now the dispersion is caused not by an underlying linear time that eventually undoes the work of the subject but by plural times that are the formation and deformation of unities and regularities. The division between the transcendental and the empirical is erased, and, in the terms Foucault used in his Introduction to Binswanger, there is no a priori distinction between ontology and anthropology.

Foucault's subsequent introduction of power into his analyses is already well prepared here; the Nietzschean conception of the will to power maps easily onto the transformation in the conditions of existence that comes with the ongoing production of discourse. Similarly, the Nietzschean refusal to see an agent behind the act, or an ideal behind things as they appear, can already be found in archaeology. That said, there is certainly a shift in emphasis in Foucault's work to treat the rules shaping what can be said and done in terms of power and not just in view of the various functions and positions of discourse. With the emergene of power as a theme in Foucault's work also comes a further point of comparison with Heidegger, in that Foucault's insistence that power is not a thing and should not be treated as if it were a substance echoes Heidegger's approach to Being and the ontological difference. The comparison is a valid one, but only up to a certain point, and the point at which it breaks down reveals an important difference between Heidegger and Foucault over the possibility of ethics and its relation to ontology. In *Being and Time*, Heidegger describes how we are thrown into a historical situation we did not choose and cannot master. Even so, it is possible for us to confront our own finitude and thereby modify our relation to our own ontological condition. In this way, we can transcend the immediate conditions of our factical life. What we cannot do is change the fundamental conditions by which Being is disclosed, which make up the temporal structure of our existence. As Heidegger moved beyond *Being and Time*, the attempt to determine the temporal horizons of the meaning of Being gave way to a recognition that Being is historical, or rather that the truth of Being is historical, its disclosure taking different forms in different epochs. Since the prevailing form of the disclosure of Being varies from epoch to epoch, at any one time we stand within an opening that sets the conditions of interpretation without itself being open to such interpretation. It is therefore impossible to draw the different epochs of the history of Being into a single account. Similarly for Foucault, how things appear as objects of discourse, and thus also the way that subjects are situated in relation to them, varies in ways that the discourses themselves cannot describe. In *The Order of Things*, this took the form of a division of history into different *epistemes*, with the working definition of knowledge being internal to each. Even as this large-scale structure gave way to more finely differentiated analyses, it remained the case for Foucault that we become subjects in relation to what can be established as true or false at any given time, and that this is contingent on the prevailing regularities in the relations of power and knowledge. The difference between Heidegger and Foucault here turns on the question of the priority attributed to the ontological order. The history of the truth of Being as described by Heidegger sees the way Being is disclosed change from one epoch to another, but what does not change is that thinking cannot alter the form of the disclosive event of Being. By contrast, Foucault can be said to preserve the ontological difference while dispensing with the priority of the rules of givenness at any time. In this respect, Heidegger's move from a unified temporal horizon of the understanding of Being to a discontinuous history of the truth of Being changes very little from Foucault's perspective. Like Heidegger, Foucault thinks we can address our own finitude (albeit differently), transcend the immediate conditions of our factical life, and modify our relation to the conditions that make us what we are. But this is where the similarity ends, as the relations of power linking us to others, to institutions, and to forms of knowledge that feature in Foucault's account are in a process of continual change to which our own discourses and critical activities can contribute. For Foucault, we can intervene not just in our relation to our own ontological condition, as Heidegger proposes, but in that very condition itself. This is evident in his later writing, where there is greater emphasis on small degrees of change, rather than epochal shifts, and also on the capacity of the subject to modify them, aided by critical discourses directed at very specific local conditions: in "What Is Enlightenment?" Foucault describes this as the "undefined work of freedom" (EEW1, 316). For Foucault, we are contemporaries with power in a way that, for Heidegger, we are never contemporaries with Being.

Time therefore is central to Foucault's philosophy, especially to his divergence from Heidegger. Resituating the "original" temporality by virtue of which things take on actual existence, Foucault places time within the discourse whose unities time forms. Not only does the time of discourse occur only within and as discourse, there is no formal determination of time that can be found repeatedly over a variety of circumstances. Ultimately, it is by virtue of this break with the legacy of formalism that the ontological dimension of Foucault's analyses can be linked to a certain positivity, and this break marks the divergence between his thought and that of Heidegger.

David Webb

SEE ALSO

Finitude
Phenomenology
Ludwig Binswanger
Immanuel Kant

SUGGESTED READING

Han-Pile, Béatrice. 2003. "Foucault and Heidegger on Kant and Finitude," in *Foucault and Heidegger: Critical Encounters*, ed. Alan Milchman and Alan Rosenberg. Minneapolis: University of Minnesota Press, pp. 127–162.

Heidegger, Martin. 1962. *Being and Time*, trans. John Macquarrie and Edward Robinson. New York: Harper and Row.

1982. *The Basic Problems of Phenomenology*, trans. Albert Hofstader. Bloomington: Indiana University Press.

1990. *Kant and the Problem of Metaphysics*, trans. Richard Taft. Bloomington: Indiana University Press.

2010. *Being and Time*, trans. Joan Stambaugh, revised with a Foreword by Dennis J. Schmidt. Albany: The SUNY Press.

Kant, Immanuel. 2006. *Anthropology from a Pragmatic Point of View*, trans. Robert B. Louden and Manfred Kuehn. Cambridge: Cambridge University Press.

107

JEAN HYPPOLITE (1907–1968)

EAN HYPPOLITE WAS the French translator of Hegel's *Phenomenology of Spirit*, for which he also wrote in 1946 a long commentary (*Genesis and Structure of Hegel's Phenomenology of Spirit*); he followed this book with a study in 1952 of Hegel's logic (*Logic and Existence*). In 1954, he was appointed director of the École Normale Supérieure in Paris; he was elected to the Collège de France in 1963. The academic connection between Jean Hyppolite and Foucault is clear. At the École Normale Supérieure in the late 1940s and early 1950s, Hyppolite was Foucault's teacher, and Foucault replaced Hyppolite at the Collège de France in 1969 after Hyppolite died suddenly. The philosophical connection between them, however, is more difficult to determine.

Hyppolite's interpretation of Hegel seemed to have a twofold effect on the evolution of French thought as it entered the 1960s, as the moment of French existentialism, the moment of Sartre and Merleau-Ponty, was starting to fade. On the one hand, Hyppolite stressed that Hegel's thought was not a humanism. If one focuses on the *Phenomenology of Spirit*, and especially if one focuses on the master–slave dialectic (as Kojève did in his famous lectures), humanity plays a key role in that dialectic. However, even the *Phenomenology* ends in "absolute knowledge," a position that transcends humanity. If one focuses on Hegel's *Logic*, as Hypppolite did in *Logic and Existence*, this movement beyond humanity is even clearer. On the other hand, Hyppolite clarified the movement of Hegelian transcendence. Hyppolite recognized that Hegel, before Nietzsche, had aimed at a reversal of Platonism, meaning that the movement beyond did not aim at a second ideal world. Hegel's dialectic, for Hyppolite, is still immanent to experience. Remaining, however, immanent to experience, the dialectic is a singular movement of differentiation, a movement that hollows out a position, placing it in opposition to another position but not in opposition to another position that is *external* to the original position. Therefore, and here we have Hyppolite's strongest influence on the generation of French philosophers that includes Foucault, Derrida, and Deleuze, the central issue in Hegel's thought is difference, the difference between nature and spirit, the difference between experience and logic, the difference between finitude and infinity, and probably most importantly for Foucault, the difference between philosophy and history.

In his inaugural address at the Collège, Foucault acknowledged that he owed a lot to Hyppolite. Foucault added, however, that Hyppolite showed all of us that the task of philosophy lies not in generalization but in reestablishing contact with what precedes it, in drawing as close as possible to "the singularity of history" (EAK, 236). Undoubtedly, the task of all of Foucault's archaeological studies can be summarized in this "task of philosophy." At the same moment as his inaugural address, Foucault also wrote a eulogy for Hyppolite. There he makes this task clearer, saying that, "The problem that Hyppolite never stopped working on is perhaps this one: what is this limitation that is proper to philosophical discourse, the limitation that allows it or makes it appear as the speech of philosophy itself, in a word: *what is philosophical finitude?*" (FDE1, 781, Foucault's emphasis, my translation). The chair that Foucault occupied at the Collège de France was the Chair of the History of Systems of Thought. We can see now that what Foucault called "systems of thought," especially at the end of his career (see EEW1, 201), really concerned this very limitation that connects philosophy back to history. It concerned the difference that makes philosophy finite but that also allows philosophical thought to go beyond that limitation. Repeatedly, Foucault speaks of his histories having the purpose of transformation (see, for example, EAK, 130). It is this difference that allows thought to transform the very conditions in which it finds itself.

Leonard Lawlor

SEE ALSO

Archaeology
Finitude
History

SUGGESTED READING

Hyppolite, Jean. 1974. *Genesis and Structure of Hegel's Phenomenology of Spirit*, trans. Samuel Cherniak and John Heckman. Evanston, IL: Northwestern University Press.
    1991. *Figures de la pensée philosophique*. Paris: Quadrige Presses Universitaires de France.
    1997. *Logic and Existence*, trans. Leonard Lawlor and Amit Sen. Albany: The SUNY Press.
Lawlor, Leonard. 2003. *Thinking Through French Philosophy*. Bloomington: Indiana University Press.

108

IMMANUEL KANT (1724–1804)

SHREDDED BY THE reverberations of a triply polarized conceptual field, the experience of Kant in Foucault's thought can hardly be univocally described. A system of echoes resonates in three chords. Foucault's reading of Kant is split between critique as a *discourse* with lofty transcendental pretensions and critique as the *spiritual attitude* that animates it, in view of the self-transformation required for having experience in which freedom and truth are not mutually exclusive (ECF-HOS, 14–19, 25–30). Foucault's philosophical position with respect to Kant is ambivalent, divided between the need to redress its misguided epistemological ideals and the will to project its useful ontological attitude. The methodological implications for his own thought, in which there are recurrent points of intersection between method and material, are also divided, between points of resistance to the transcendental and moments of interpretive transference. And so the echoes of Kant in Foucault are caught in three layers of distortion: between a discourse described from the outside and its exercise experienced from within; between what is left and what is taken; and between the description and the use of method. This exposition plays out the first to the point of its reprise in the second, with a gesture in the direction of the third.

Aside perhaps from Nietzsche, Kant figures more prominently than any other philosopher in Foucault's otherwise contentious histories. But nothing about the way Kant is portrayed in them is orthodox. Kant is a major reference in Foucault's early analysis of discursive practices and in his late work on practices of the self, but is barely mentioned in the twelve years in between *The Order of Things* and "What Is Critique?" (found in EPT and FQC). Scattered in several texts at the extremities of his work, the scope of Foucault's accounts of Kant varies from terse historical characterizations to full-scale textual analysis. In both the early and the late characterizations, Foucault's Kant is bipolar: the familiar speculative, transcendental thought of the *Critiques* is cast into a field of interpenetration and contestation with the kind of reflection found in popular works such as the *Anthropology* and the Enlightenment essay. The problem of the relation between the two is the leitmotif of the experience of Kant in Foucault.

Kant's importance for Foucault stems in part from Hyppolite, with whom he studied briefly at Lycée Henri-IV in 1945 and who supervised both his Diplôme d'Études Supérieures (a French degree roughly equivalent to an advanced Master's, degree) on Hegel's *Phenomenology of Spirit* in 1949 and his 1961 PhD *thèse complémentaire* at the Sorbonne. The thesis, a translation of Kant's *Anthropology* accompanied by an extensive introduction (published in 2008 as FKF), is Foucault's first and most sustained study of Kant. Hyppolite had reservations about it, notably that Foucault's reading was "inspired by Nietzsche more than by Kant" (Eribon 1991, 114). The fact that Foucault was known to refer to it as his "book on Nietzsche" goes to show that he took the criticism well, to say the least (Potte-Bonneville and Defert 2010). Indeed, if Foucault's Kant is post-Nietzschean, it is surely not a matter of exegetical weakness. One also hears echoes of Heidegger – through whom Foucault came to the study of Nietzsche – in the recurrence to "repetition" and the "originary." But despite its unavowed inspirations, the thesis is by no means merely a student work. Clearly the culmination of years of study and teaching (the *Anthropology* figured in Foucault's teaching at least as early as 1953), its penetrating analysis of the genesis and structure of Kant's text and of its historical significance is of great value for an understanding of his subsequent work. Its interrogation is genetic, systematic, and historical.

The problem of the relation between transcendental and popular standpoints in Kant surfaces at the intersection of the genetic and the systematic register. Foucault addresses Kant's thought as a discursive practice, a form of experience that can be either described from the outside as a closed discursive system on the basis of its materialization in a text or verbal expression or exercised, by lateral insertion, as an opening onto a reality. Critical discourse circularly does the former by means of the latter: it describes forms of experience – ways to sensibly interrogate reality – by using what it describes as its method. The experience of Kant in Foucault is polarized not only between the *Critiques* and *Anthropology* or the Enlightenment essay but also with respect to the priority of the discourse of critique and of the exercise of a critical attitude. We will see that these are not theoretical options like prongs of a fork but directions of a reversible polarity; the one is just the other turned inside out.

Foucault shows that the *Critiques* record an epistemologically oriented version of the practice by describing the form of experience in terms of the conditions under which universal and necessary knowledge is possible. This transcendental critique reaches a level of abstraction apt for its radically general external description by moving inferentially from qualities of reality such as it is given from the inside to an external description of the rules according to which we systematically determine and regulate it as such by way of chains of indispensability relations. Absolutely general regularities are thereby sifted from our experience. The idea underlying Foucault's reading is that this transcendental critique betrays itself as a practice. By foreclosing the objective of self-transformation as a condition of access to truth in a conception of the subject that is also the condition of impossibility of knowledge, it screens itself from the indeterminacy of its experience and denies its self-participation in what it describes, leaving only the description. The practice of transcendental critique functions as though it were not a practice at all but the material record of its exercise in a circuit of distinctions, its image in the mirror. It is as though the conceptual matter of the *Critique* exhausted its practice.

In *The Order of Things*, the historical significance of transcendental critique is tied to its simultaneity with ideology (Destutt de Tracy and Gerando), with which it shares a field of application, representational relations. Their overlap is the hinge in the passage of classical representational to modern anthropological thought. Whereas the Ideologues attempted to capture the nonrepresentative in the very form of representation, critique suspends the analysis of representations by asking how representation itself is possible. Kant's transcendental critique pulls thought out of the infinite space of representations the Ideologues had attempted to exhaustively render scientifically. At the level of nonrepresentative conditions of representation, he unmasks the attempt, and the project of representational thought in general, as dogmatic metaphysics. Paradoxically, for Foucault regrettably, this moment – the simultaneity of Ideology and Kant's critique that denounces it – also paves the way for a new anthropological metaphysics (EOT, 241–242).

The priority in transcendental critique of discursive over practical criteria, of a closed system over its exercise as opening, is reversed in the ontological practices of critique such as recorded in the *Anthropology* and the Enlightenment piece. This explains Foucault's resistance to the objectives of transcendental critique and his antipathy for post-Kantian anthropology, which replays transcendental betrayal and begs the question of the extent to which his own histories of experience do not succumb. With an ontological orientation, anthropological critique reverses this critical practice, taking the results of transcendental critique as given – the capacities and categories through which experience is conditioned – and showing that, transposed from the a priori to the originary temporal flux, they lend their figure to concrete existence.

When they were published toward the end of his life in 1798, Kant had given the *Anthropology* lectures for a quarter of a century, in the midst of which transcendental critique was developed and published in the first Critique. Foucault shows that the relation between the two implies that transcendental critique is a moment in the elaboration of anthropological critique, which reaches a point of stabilization in transcendental philosophy (EIKA, 23). Foucault explains how the anthropocritical repetition brings about a shift in Kant's thought from the cosmological standpoint of the 1760s and 1770s, which takes the world as already given, to a cosmopolitical standpoint, for which the world remains to be made (EIKA, 33). This external standpoint on human beings in the world is adopted mostly in the shorter second part of the *Anthropology* (the Characteristic). The lion's share of the lectures are devoted to the Didactic, in which the figure of human existence is presented as spirit's principle (*Gemüt*). Neither the soul (*Seele*), dispelled as illusory by the Paralogisms of the first Critique, nor the closely related spirit (*Geist*), which animates it with ideas, spirit's principle gives it the living figure it has in experience, the orientation that opens it onto "a virtual totality," a duration that removes it from "indifferent dispersion" (EIKA, 57–62). Freed of the illusions generated by their transcendental use by being restrained to possible experience in its temporal intensity, ideas vivify existence by giving birth to "the multiple structures of totality in becoming that make and undo themselves as so many partial lives that live and die in spirit" (EIKA, 63). Thus Foucault concludes that the very movement that gives birth to "the transcendental mirage" in the *Critique* "prolongs the empirical and concrete life of spirit's principle" in the *Anthropology*, freeing spirit from its determinations and consecrating it for the possibilities of a future of its own making (EIKA, 63). Whereas from a transcendental standpoint spirit implies that "the infinite is never there, but always in essential retreat," from which it "animates the movement towards the truth and the inexhaustible succession of its forms" (EIKA, 65). In its anthropological form, spirit for Foucault is a "secretly indispensable" aspect of the structure of Kant's thought, the reversible basic root of pure reason: both the source of its transcendental illusions and the principle of its movement in experience (ibid.). As discourse, the structure of the *Anthropology* inverts that of the *Critique*: the one repeats the other negatively, like a print repeats a photonegative (EIKA, 66–73). As practice, anthropology makes the passage to transcendental philosophy possible by formulating existence in terms of a play of source, domain, and limit. These specify the relation between man and world, transposing the three capacities of the *Critique*, sensibility, understanding, and imagination, by posing the three basic questions of Kant's thought – what can I know? what must I do? what can I hope for? – backwards. This is why the *Anthropology*, a textbook of empirical lessons and popular exercises, is the record of the practice of critique that gives the capacities of reason described in the *Critique* their "fundamental cohesion" (EIKA, 86). As Kant practiced it in his lectures (and presumably in his life), anthropology is prior to transcendental critique, even though as discourse it was published after it. However, the exercise of critique in the *Anthropology* is also "systematically projected," making it possible for it to grasp truth recast in the element of freedom as transcendental philosophy. Foucault reconstructs Kant's thought in terms of a passage from transcendental critique, which investigates a priori knowledge, to anthropology, which explores the originary relation between temporality and language, to transcendental philosophy, which establishes the fundamental relation between truth and freedom (EIKA, 106). Thus there is a circular relation between anthropological and transcendental practices of critique, reflected by the fact that the *Anthropology* is both popular and systematic: it gives a priori description its true meaning by repeating it in the originary, "the *truly* temporal" medium of concrete existence beyond subjectivity, in which the universal emerges: the always already, never yet there flux of temporality in which truth and freedom are one (EIKA, 92). As discourse, the *Anthropology* repeats the results of the *Critique* backwards, but as practice it is transcendental critique that reverses anthropology.

Transcendental and anthropological critiques share the objective of learning to live with unavoidable illusion. Thus Foucault describes the "anthropological illusion" as "the reverse, the mirror-image of the transcendental illusion": the one is produced by the "spontaneous transgression" by reason's will to know the infinite, the other accounts for the transgression in a "reflexive regression" (EIKA, 122). This inversion generates "false anthropology" in Kant's wake (EIKA, 92). Reflection on the limits and transgression of thought and the possibility of nonpositive affirmation becomes the pretension to be the source of man's self-knowledge, when anthropology serves as the positive foundation of the human sciences. Although Kant's *Anthropology* may well be the birthplace of the illusion, as Foucault maintains in "A Preface to Transgression," noncritical anthropology is inadmissible from a Kantian standpoint, given that anthropology, the reversal of transcendental critique, cannot lay claim to positive knowledge (EEW2, 74). Consequently, Foucault's assessment of post-Kantian anthropological thought is severe. He claims that it exploits its intermediary position between the a priori and the fundamental, entitling itself to the privileges of both (to be preliminary like critique and complete like transcendental philosophy), and that it confuses both necessity and existence, and knowledge and finitude (EIKA, 106). As Foucault has it, the muddle comes from an illusory objective, positive knowledge of "man," or "finitude in itself" (EIKA, 118). For Foucault, the importance of this anthropological illusion is such that the history of post-Kantian philosophy needs to be retold from the perspective of its denunciation, a project that he undertakes as *The Order of Things*.

In that text, Foucault detaches the birthplace of anthropological thought as an epistemological configuration from Kant specifically, to cast it as the result of the general recession of the theory of representation as the universal foundation of discourse in Western culture. He presents it as the organizing principle of a partly philosophical, partly positivistic form of reflection on *man* that is formed as the basis for the series of "quasi-transcendentals" – life, work, and language – the post-Kantian precritical metaphysical categories that emerge at the beginning of the nineteenth century in symmetry with transcendental philosophy. These objective fields of empirical knowledge describe the conditions of possibility of experience from within the being of the object represented, rather than the representing subject, and concern a posteriori truth, rather than the synthetic a priori of all possible experience (EOT, 243–248). Anthropology is discourse on the natural finitude of human beings, an analytics of man as an empirico-transcendental doublet, for which the concrete forms of existence are reductively equated with the limits of knowledge. Kant's distinction between the empirical and the transcendental results in a mixed discourse, in which empirical observation-based knowledge and critical thought overlap, confusing experience from the outside and experience from the inside. In this fold, Foucault proposes, its pathos relieved at the return of "the reign of the humanity," modern philosophy falls asleep "in a new slumber; not of dogmatism, but of anthropology" (EOT, 341). But he also explains how Nietzsche stirs this sleep by showing that the discovery of the finitude of man already implies his decline, thus providing the tools for the destruction of post-Kantian anthropology, the doubly dogmatic historical a priori that served as the universal unreflective grounds of the human sciences. This for Foucault would be required to make the emergence of a new philosophy possible after the death of man. Thus, echoing the alarm with which Hume sprang Kant from dogmatism, it was Nietzsche who woke Foucault up from anthropological slumber, by showing him that the flip side of the finitude of human experience (the "death of God") is its own disintegration (the "death of man"). This calls for a renewal of critique, not of reason, but of the finite form of being from which it is abstracted, of what in post-Kantian thought is called "man." The epistemological interests of Kant's transcendental critique – about how a subject can know something universally and necessarily – can be displaced by interrogation of its ontological presuppositions, about how such a subject can be such a subject. Foucault finds the ill-fated kernel of such a critique not in Nietzsche paradoxically but in Kant's *Anthropology*. There he finds the aim to demystify the anthropological illusion, finitude caught in a "reflexive regression that must account for that regression" that leaves it subjected to absolute subjectivity, to the dialectic of the finite and the infinite (EIKA, 123). Properly practiced as "*true* critique," an ontological attitude of contestation and self-transformation, anthropology aims to free individuals from both finitude and the infinite by initiation into the game of life through a mode of existence in which finitude is "the knot and curb of time where the end is also the beginning" (EIKA, 124).

Foucault insists on the ascetic dimension of this anthropological practice: the *Anthropology* is a "book of daily exercise" that is not "theoretical" or dogmatically "scholastic"; it is neither "the history of culture" nor "the successive analysis of its forms," but "the immediate and imperative practice" through which individuals learn how to "recognize their culture in the school of the world" by being initiated into the game of life, which is its own school, such that they teach themselves how to use the world, its rules, and its prescriptions (EIKA, 53). In this respect, the practice of anthropology aims not to establish a body of empirical knowledge of man through external observation but to transform individuals' relation in a given culture to themselves and to their concrete forms of existence. Indeed, for Foucault, in this pragmatic dimension, the *Anthropology* itself is a user's guide of sorts to the world. Foucault leaves aside this focus on temporal experience after the *Introduction to Kant's Anthropology*, but an underlying concern remains for the critical ascetic practices through which individuals can change their relation to themselves and to their culture in the interest of existence in a mode in which truth and freedom are not mutually exclusive. It surfaces again much later, in the context of reflection on practices of governing in Western culture through which individuals were subjected to a politics of truth, a form of power incompatible with freedom.

In a 1978 lecture, Foucault addresses Kant's critique at the intersection of power relations and spiritual relations in terms of its historical conditioning as a sociopolitical practice. In Kant's essay on Enlightenment, he finds a formulation of critique not as a discourse but as an attitude toward oneself and one's actuality. Foucault's genealogy identifies this form of activity in the social practices in which a form of religious power previously exercised within the Church is transferred to the political sphere, in the context of the Reformation in the sixteenth century, as a means of resisting the effects of governing in which the imperative to obey direction is validated by an appeal to the truth. This governmentalization politicizes the pastoral power exercised in a religious context between God or his representative as a shepherd and his faithful as sheep needing care, protection, and salvation. Indeed, practices of resistance to the biblical pastorate can be seen as precursors to these critical practices, such as second- to fourth-century Gnostic sects, which exercised social and religious transgression motivated by principles internal to the practices that governed them (suicide or destructive sinfulness on the basis of the identification of matter as evil, or systematic infraction of the law on the basis of the entreaty to overturn the world of legality).

Foucault's suggestion is that the attitude of being critical surfaces as a form of counterconduct to these arts of governing, as internal points of resistance that contest the effects of its conflation of power and truth. In a biblical register, one finds a vindication of the direct appeal to Scripture as attenuation of the authority of the magister in order to rectify the individual's relation to the truth. In a juridical register, an appeal to universal natural right supports the recusal of unjust laws based on sovereign fiat. In an epistemic register, the rejection of dogmatic claims to knowledge and truth is habilitated by the application of a criterion of available justification, accepting them only if one has reason to do so. These attitudes of being critical dispose individuals "to interrogate the truth about its effects of power, and power about its discourse on truth" (FQC, 39). They exercise principled refusal of subjection to mechanisms of power based on the will to truth.

In Foucault's reading, what Kant formulates as Enlightenment is precisely this spiritual attitude of being critical. In Kantian terms, it is culture's movement out of its state of minority in which, incapacitated by their lack of courage and decisiveness, individuals are authoritatively denied the use of their own understanding. In a state of minority, they voluntarily submit to external authority, not because they have to but because they lack the courage to use their own reason. In the movement out of this state, individuals come to differentiate the private and the public uses of reason and obey only in the case of the latter, as a citizen and in other social functions, in which it would be incoherent not to obey (in this register, power relations are constitutive of the experience, such that transgression is synonymous with dysfunction). In its public use, enlightened reason does not submit to externally prescribed regulation and direction but holds discourse as a subject in the universal medium in which rules are formulated in the interrogation of the conditions of possibility of experience. Thus Foucault considers that Kant's *Critique* is the theoretical "logbook" of this autonomous public use of reason that is the distinctive mark of the attitude of being critical (EEW1, 309). He finds it exercised in Kant's very formulation of it in the Enlightenment essay as a form of philosophical and historical interrogation that aims to formulate the specificity of the present in its distinctiveness from the past. It poses the problem of its relation to this present and to itself by assessing the possibilities of philosophical reflection, the practices in which they are exercised, and the modalities of participation in them as philosophers. This kind of critical attitude in which philosophical discourse becomes reflective about its position in its own actuality, its belonging to a "we" to which it attributes a philosophical significance, is characteristic of what it means, for Foucault, to be modern. Modernity is a way of being critical.

Besides its philosophical and historical disposition to the present, Foucault characterizes critical modernity as a practice, an ethos, a voluntarily chosen and permanently reactivated way of being that aims to elaborate and transform its relation to actuality and to itself. In this register, freedom is a matter of being critical, the curious exercise of testing the limits of the possibilities of experience by recognizing the contingency in what is presented as universal and necessary, and formulating the regularity of that contingency as another possible way. For Foucault, this philosophical version of the attitude of being critical animates the critical tradition he calls the "ontology of ourselves," which he opposes to the "analytics of truth," a tradition of critique that stems from Kant's transcendental critique (ECF-GSO, 20–21). Whereas the latter can be recognized in the form of analytic philosophy, the former shapes the outlooks of thinkers in the vein of Schelling, Hegel, Schopenhauer, Nietzsche, Weber, Heidegger, the Frankfurt school, and Foucault himself.

Mirroring the effects of the anthropological illusion, critique as analytics of truth is in Foucault's reading incapacitated by a lack of self-awareness about its conception of subjectivity, which leads it to forego the practical and ascetic dimension of philosophy, its function as an exercise of self-transformation. Transcendental critique is disabled by the fact that its access to truth and experience of freedom do not require a transformation of the subject. Since the structure of the knowing subject specifies what it is impossible to know, the idea that access to truth requires a transformation of the subject can get no purchase; it is impossible even to conceive.

Thus it would seem that in his discovery of the attitude of being critique in his later readings of Kant, Foucault distances himself from the relation of circular reversibility between the transcendental standpoint of the *Critiques* and its mirror repetition as ontological exercise in the *Anthropology*. As historical traditions of critique, he presents them as disjunctive options and associates himself exclusively with the latter. The positive assessment of transcendental critique in his earlier work – he credits it with the invention of the form of reflection on limitation and transgression around the possibility of nonpositive affirmation that he considered to be the mark of viable postanthropological philosophy, such as one finds in Nietzsche and Blanchot, for example – has disappeared in his frequent methodological formulations, in which resistance to the transcendental practice of Kantian critique is a recurrent theme. For example, in a debate with Preti, Foucault flatly rejects the notion that the *epistemes* his archaeology describes are historical versions of Kantian categories (FDE3, 372). In *The Archaeology of Knowledge*, he emphasizes the need "to free the history of thought from its transcendental subjection," to strip it of its "transcendental narcissism," in order to define the conditions and historical transformations of knowledge with a regressive analysis that functions outside the transcendental aim of making philosophy as metaphysics possible by functioning at a level of abstraction at which universal and necessary knowledge of the conditions of experience is possible (EAK, 202–203). This, for Foucault, is an incoherent objective that belongs to the anthropological sleep characteristic of modern philosophy. With the epistemological orientation under the spell of the anthropological illusion, bedeviled by a naive conception of the subject, transcendental critique can only bring philosophy further from experience. In Foucault's philosophical assessments and in his methodological reflections, transcendental critique is no longer considered to be an indispensible detour in the exercise of being critical as it was in his reading of Kant's critical anthropology. This gives the impression that Foucault's ontological critique no longer requires transcendental reflection on the conditions of possibility of thought, and that Foucault's debt to Kant is entirely at the level of the attitude of being critical.

It would be hasty to draw such a conclusion. It is important not to lose sight of the side of Foucault's work that echoes transcendental critique, despite his reservations about it. This methodological debt is most visible in the archaeology of discursive practices, but it is present in more or less concentrated form throughout his work. The primary objective of Kant's transcendental critique is, of course, to establish the conditions of possibility of real experience in view of guaranteeing universal and necessary knowledge of it. His overarching concern is the state of the metaphysics of his day, moribund, victim to its lack of self-awareness about the kind of knowledge philosophy can obtain scientifically, given the experience it is possible for the knowing subject to have. The preparatory work of critique aims to make metaphysics possible as a science, dispelling transcendental illusion by curtailing its dogmatic tendency to make claims to knowledge of what it is impossible for us to experience as objectively real, such as God, freedom, and the soul. The guiding thought is that spatiotemporal experience is regulated by the subject's capacities, which impose constraints on what it is possible and impossible to experience as objectively real. Thus, the limitations of the subject's capacities trace the contours of reality as possible, rather than as actual, in reverse. His transcendental method infers the conditions of possible experience from undeniable features of actual experience by setting up chains of indispensability relations that appeal to what is conceivable and inconceivable. The result is the description of a set of subjective capacities, forms of sensibility, and categories that express what is and what is not possible as a form of experience.

Now, in pursuit of the objective to denounce anthropological illusion, Foucault's work exercises a form of this transcendental reasoning that is disconnected from its epistemological objectives. Suspending the ideal of universality and necessity in order to recall the need for self-transformation as a condition of possibility of a modality of existence in which freedom and truth are not incompatible, Foucault replaces the knowing subject with historically and culturally determined anonymous practices as the unit of analysis that fixes the level of abstraction of transcendental description. His procedure echoes Kant's transcendental reasoning nonetheless, reversing it, beginning with practices such as they can be externally found in historical archives, and elaborating them as forms of experience. He describes such ontological capacities – *epistemes*, apparatuses of power, and techniques of self-transformation – as tests of what can actually be experienced otherwise. Transcendental critique functions here as a kind of spiritual exercise embedded in the practice of the attitude of being critical. Despite Foucault's insistence that his method is not transcendental – a betrayal not of the practice but of the discourse of critique – as his own reading of Kant shows, the attitude of being critical and the ontology of ourselves that it orients can only protect itself from reenacting the unavowed positivism of anthropological slumber by the exercise of a transcendental detour, ontologically rather than epistemologically oriented. Although it is less elementary in Foucault's work, this betrayed aspect of his method echoes Kant perhaps even more distinctively than the ones he calls attention to in the Enlightenment essay.

Marc Djaballah

SEE ALSO

Man
Phenomenology
Resistance
Friedrich Nietzsche

SUGGESTED READING

Davidson, Arnold. 2001. *The Emergence of Sexuality: Historical Epistemology and the Formation of Concepts*. Cambridge, MA: Harvard University Press.

Deleuze, Gilles. 1988. *Foucault*, trans. Seán Hand. Minneapolis: University of Minnesota Press.

Djaballah, Marc. 2008. *Kant, Foucault, and Forms of Experience*. London: Routledge.

    2013. "Foucault on Kant, Enlightenment, and Being Critical," in *A Companion to Foucault*, eds. Christopher Falzon, Timothy O'Leary, and Jana Sawicki. Oxford: Blackwell, pp. 264–281

Eribon, Didier. 1991. *Michel Foucault*, trans. Betsy Wing. Cambridge, MA: Harvard University Press.

Gutting, Gary. 1989. *Michel Foucault's Archaeology of Scientific Reason*. Cambridge: Cambridge University Press.

Hacking, Ian. 2002. *Historical Ontology*. Cambridge, MA: Harvard University Press.

Potte-Bonneville, Mathieu, and Daniel Defert. 2010. "Filigranes philosophiques," in *Foucault*. Paris: Les Cahiers de l'Herne, pp. 39–46.

109

NICCOLÒ MACHIAVELLI
(1469–1527)

I N THE OPENING lectures of his 1977–1978 lecture course, "Security, Territory, Population," Foucault distinguishes what he calls the apparatus of security from those of sovereignty and discipline, in the process turning to a discussion of the role of the population in the operation of biopower. In his fourth lecture, given on February 1, 1978, Foucault proposes that underneath the notions of security and population ultimately lies the "problem of government." Indeed, beginning in the sixteenth century, he claims, the problem of government, whether of the self, of the soul, of children, or of states, "breaks out" (ECF-STP, 88). According to Foucault, the question of government arises out of the intersection of two processes – a concentration of state power owing to the demise of the feudal system and a dispersion of religious power attributable to the Reformation and Counter-Reformation – and it is characterized by a concern for the problem of "how to be governed, by whom, to what extent, to what ends, and by what methods" (ECF-STP, 89).

In response to this novel problematic of government, the sixteenth, seventeenth, and eighteenth centuries would see the publication of a number of treatises intended to outline an "art" of political government. What unifies this "immense," "monotonous" literature is not only a shared concern for the problem of government, but also a common "point of repulsion": Niccolo Machiavelli's *The Prince* (ECF-STP, 89).

Published in 1513, *The Prince* would quickly be opposed, Foucault proposes, by a literature of government that is notable less for its negativity than for the fact that it represents "a positive genre, with its specific object, concepts, and strategy" (ECF-STP, 91). For Foucault, one of the most notable of these anti-Machiavellian treatises on the art of government is Guillaume de La Perrière's *Le miroir politique, contenant diverses manières de gouverner* (1555), in which the birth of a novel conception of government can be discerned. But prior to addressing La Perrière's text directly, Foucault provides a discussion of the readings of *The Prince* that can be found in this novel literature of government.

For Machiavelli's opponents, there is one fundamental principle at work in *The Prince*: that the prince exists in a position "of singularity and externality," of transcendence, with respect to his principality. In other words, there exists no natural, fundamental, juridical relation between the prince and his territory or subjects; theirs is a synthetic connection maintained through violence, tradition, or treaty. A corollary of this fundamental principle is that the connection that exists between the prince and his territory is a fragile one, constantly threatened from within and from without by the prince's many enemies. In turn, this principle and its corollary imply a certain imperative: the objective of political power is not to protect a territory and its inhabitants, but rather to maintain, strengthen, and protect the connection that binds them to the prince (ECF-STP, 91–92). Thus, this anti-Machiavellian literature of government argues, the mode of analysis present in *The Prince* is going to have two aspects, the first concerning the dangers posed to the prince's principality (What are the dangers? Where do they come from? Which are the most pressing?); the second concerning the art of manipulating relations of force in such a way as to protect the prince's principality; that is, the prince's connection to his territory and to his subjects. As Foucault explains, then, Machiavelli's *The Prince* is portrayed in the mid-sixteenth-century literature of government as "a treatise on the Prince's ability to hold on to his principality" (ECF-STP, 92).

The importance of this critical portrayal of *The Prince* lies in the fact that in response to Machiavelli's treatise, writers like Guillaume de La Perrière would outline an entirely new conception of government, one that substituted for the prince's "know-how," his ability to maintain power over his territory and subjects, a novel "art of government" that would propose not only a new definition for what it means to govern but also a new object for the intervention of government and a new end for the practice of government. And it is this conception of the "art of government," along with the emergence of the discourse of statistics and the constitution of the population as an object of state intervention, that would ultimately make possible the deployment of the myriad mechanisms of security during the eighteenth and nineteenth centuries. In that respect, the anti-Machiavellian literature of government discussed in his "Security, Territory, Population" lectures is central to an understanding of the security-population-government series that for Foucault lies at the heart of modern society's biopolitical operation.

David-Olivier Gougelet

SEE ALSO

Biopower
Discipline
Population
Sovereignty

SUGGESTED READING

Machiavelli, Niccolò. 2008 [1513]. *The Prince*, trans. Peter Bondanella. New York: Oxford University Press.

110

MAURICE MERLEAU-PONTY (1907–1961)

T IS FAIR – though perhaps much too obvious – to present Foucault as an opponent of phenomenology. As a matter of fact, from *The History of Madness* onward, everything he writes seems to dispute every form of humanism. This criticism would have to include what at the time, thanks to Sartre's identification of phenomenology with existentialism and existentialism with humanism, might have appeared as a kind of necessary phenomenological humanism. There is no subject according to Foucault. There is no primeval experience to which we might return, no experience to which one could trace back the abstractions of theory. There is no plenitude of sense capable of enlightening the constitution of the objects with which we deal. What Husserl thought possible in his last work, *The Crisis of European Sciences*, is for Foucault not possible: there is no possible way of reactivating faded evidence by leading the tradition of the sciences back to the primitive intentionality that would first have nurtured and then deserted them. More deeply, there are no self-evident intuitions, no immediacy. There is such a thing as knowledge just because there is no intuition. There are social practices just because we are not placed within the light of any originary givenness. Seen from this angle, the phenomenological project is grounded on the sand of ancient metaphysical illusions.

Still, it is not so easy to determine Foucault's grounding in relation to that of Husserl and Merleau-Ponty, and this is even more difficult to do in relation to phenomenology. Even if Foucault says that there is no subject, no full and radiating sense, no experience as a primeval belonging to the world, what he puts in their place is something that Husserl's and Merleau-Ponty's phenomenology seem to have already pointed out and developed. We can see this especially if we ignore the vulgarization of phenomenology by a certain type of existentialism, and more so if we ignore the vulgarization to which existentialism itself has often been reduced. In this respect, as Foucault will say in an interview in the mid-1970s, reading Husserl's work was crucial for his intellectual itinerary. The relationship between knowledge and power was not at all "a discovery of mine," as Foucault provocatively claims in that interview. That relationship "lies in a trajectory which gets outlined between Nietzsche's *Genealogy of Morals* and Husserl's *Crisis of the European Sciences*" (FMFE, 126). That is the kind of phenomenology to which we must turn if we want to truly understand Foucault's relationship to Husserl's phenomenology, its French reception, and especially its relation to the way Merleau-Ponty takes up phenomenology.

Nietzsche's *Genealogy of Morals* and the later Husserl father not only *The Crisis of European Sciences*, but also a text like *Experience and Judgment*, whose subtitle is *A Genealogy of Logic*. Husserl conceives his "last" phenomenology as an investigation of the constraints and the coercive mechanisms that function at the basis of knowledge. To know, for Husserl, means first of all to write. That there is no experience without retention has always been the touchstone of Husserl's phenomenology. Similarly, there is no knowledge without writing, without a work of inscription, and without the permanence of a trace. This is the immense expansion that the later Husserl imposes on his thought of the irreducibility of retention. As Husserl shows in *The Crisis*, mathematical idealities come from geometry, and geometry from the practice of land measurement. At this late stage in the development of Husserl's thought, phenomenology wants to reanimate, behind disembodied ideas, the living body of social practices, the multilayered and phantasmatical movement of the *grammata*, the thick plot of "pragmatic anthropology." (Kant's *Anthropology from a Pragmatic Point of View* is what forced Foucault, early in his career, to come to terms with the transcendentalism of the *Critique of Pure Reason*.) In this sense, phenomenology is a genuine genealogy, as Husserl maintained, or an archaeology, as Merleau-Ponty will claim. Indeed, in his late "The Philosopher and His Shadow," Merleau-Ponty states that phenomenology is "a descent in the domain of our archaeology" (Merleau-Ponty 1964a, 165).

If we want to see the traces of a continuity between phenomenology and archaeology (which proves to be stronger than the often recognized discontinuities), we must look at Merleau-Ponty, who held one of the most authoritative positions in the intellectual landscape in which Foucault was trained during the 1940s and 1950s. Foucault follows Merleau-Ponty's lecture courses – at just the moment when a whole generation of French philosophers will be struck with ideas, sparks of inspiration, splinters of thought that will proliferate immediately after Merleau-Ponty's premature death in 1961: psychoanalysis, structuralism, deconstruction, all the directions French thought will take throughout the 1960s. Merleau-Ponty's phenomenology is an archaeology insofar as it is a phenomenology of the primordial, an inquiry into the underlying structures of human experience, a mapping of the practico-corporeal underpinnings of every human expression, experience and knowledge, history and politics. At the basis of all this there is a bodily "I can" (*Ich kann*), as both Husserl and Merleau-Ponty maintain; that is, they maintain that there is a "power" in each and every sense of the word, a bond concerned with the ability to do, with an openness that unfolds into a web of possibilities that encroach on, disentangle from, and oppose each other. This claim also means a bond that has to do with a corresponding number of impossibilities that get outlined within each possibility. In other words, in order that the opening onto possibilities be an opening onto just those possibilities (and not others), there must be some sort of closure.

Naturally, Foucault does not think that there is a primordial structure or foundation; similarly, the later Merleau-Ponty, that of the working notes to *The Visible and the Invisible* is non-foundationalist. But Foucault unquestionably retrieves the idea that there are structures or, more precisely, local organizations, articulations of elements that affect a certain discursive field. For Foucault, there are practical ties, material concatenations on whose shapes the contents of a certain area of knowledge depend; there are the spaces within which a given epistemic sector is able to be formulated or not; there are also postures available or unavailable to the bodies of humans within a certain age and a certain location. Archaeology is the systematic investigation of such a body of submerged statements, human practices, and apparatuses (*dispositifs*). This is a submerged body that blindly and deafly exerts a pressure; it produces effects of sense in accordance with rules and regularities that archaeology will bring back to light; it is a body that shapes the souls of humans, forges and disposes their habits and their bodies, trains them to a certain style of social, political, military, religious, scholastic, and bureaucratic functioning.

Blindly and deafly, we have said. If Foucault argues that there is no constitutive subject, no transcendental entity that weaves the threads of experience, no *plenum* that organizes and radiates the field of experience by infusing into it that quality which we call "sense," he does this not because he is arguing against phenomenology. He is simply developing an idea that is easy to find at the very core of the later Merleau-Ponty's thought. Besides being an affect, sense is an effect. It is a beam that shines through by virtue of the friction sparked between the elements of a mechanical device or at least between those of a disposition and those of an articulated joint. Sense is not something that is but something that makes itself, and it is something that makes itself within an interstitial space. It is a phenomenon of divergence (*écart*). It is not the elements themselves that organize our experience; it is the empty space between the elements. Sense exists as, has the way of being of, the event. But this is precisely the status of what Merleau-Ponty names "flesh," one of the most fertile and problematic concepts among those presented in *The Visible and the Invisible*, his final work. The flesh is a divergence effect (an effect of *écart*), more an interstice than a substance. Merleau-Ponty also describes the flesh as a mirror phenomenon, a play of differences in whose folds one can outline transient, elusive identities. One hand touches the other, according to the pivotal example in *The Visible and the Invisible*, an example that Husserl had already used (in the second book of *Ideas for a Pure Phenomenology and for a Phenomenological Philosophy*). Through its own sensing, the human body then is, within itself, split in two. The body comes to itself through that distance which is the only "self" it possesses. The touching hand becomes the touched hand, the unity of the subject is nothing but the "spatializing" (*espacement*) of this divergence that reproduces itself each time it seems to cancel itself in pure coincidence. As Merleau-Ponty says in *The Visible and the Invisible*, the divergence produces "a reversibility that is always imminent and never realized in fact" (Merleau-Ponty 1968, 147).

Thus, in the opening pages of *The Order of Things*, Foucault interprets Diego Velázquez's *Las Meninas* as an image of the image itself, a sort of infinite reflection of the image (a *mise-en-abyme*). For Foucault, Velázquez had undertaken in this painting a quasi-metaphysical investigation into the laws of representation. That is why *The Order of Things* – this masterful study of the tiny shifts in the most profound roots of modern scientific representation through the disciplines of economy, natural sciences, and linguistics – begins with a splendid baroque reading of this well-known painting. A painter is at work: we see him gazing out from behind the big canvas he is working on. He stares at the subject in front of himself, who is located in our direction. Among other paintings, in the background of the scene, there is a mirror. In the background, the spectator sees other paintings, in the middle of which is a mirror. We should see ourselves reflected in that mirror. But what we see is the subject whose portrait the painter is painting. That subject of course is the King and Queen of Spain. The whole construction wavers around this paradox. The painter is staring at a point outside of the painting, where the Spanish royalty is situated. It is the same point in which we are placed, as spectators of the painting. We are the scene he is reproducing. But he is the scene that our gaze captures. He is the object of the Spanish royalty's gaze, and of ours as well, insofar as we occupy the same place. The key word to which Foucault resorts at this level of his analysis is "reciprocity." In this famous analysis, he says, "The picture in its entirety looks upon a scene for which it is, in its turn, a scene. As something looking and as something looked at, the mirror manifests a *pure reciprocity*" (EOT, 14, my emphasis, translation modified; also EOT, 4).

We might say that "reciprocity" is a word – and a phenomenon – that is eminently Merleau-Pontean. There is no observing subject in the painting. Any hypothetical "subject who looks," were he in the painting, would be an observed subject. "A subject that casts a gaze" might be in the painting only in a sidelong way, as a gaze evoked and, simultaneously, discarded, suggested and cancelled through one and the same gesture. The whole visible area on the surface appears to be surrounded by a deeper and invisible place, which is the very place in which the visibility of the visible is produced. Nevertheless, this invisible is not elsewhere with respect to the visible, it is not something other than the visible. It is not something that we could relocate in the space of the painting if we changed the direction of our gaze. The invisible is the heart of the visible and it is in the visible. But it is there as a trace, so to speak. The invisible is neither a presence nor an absence, neither an "element" among the others in the painting nor something simply outside the painting. The invisible does not embrace but rather pierces the visible. We look from the inner core of the painting, according to Foucault's analysis. The visibility of the painting is produced in the luminous, and yet marginal core of the painting, that is, within the mirror. The archaeologist aims at this visible-invisible core of any "visualization," of any epistemic arrangement (any *mise-en-scène*), of any painting or representation, or scientific paradigm.

If we accept the analysis of *The Visible and the Invisible* (which Merleau-Ponty also developed in his final essay, the 1961 "Eye and Mind"), then we look at the world only insofar as we look from the invisible heart of the world that looks at us. Alluding to something Paul Klee said, Merleau-Ponty observes, "As many painters have said, I feel myself looked at by the things … ; what would be at issue is not seeing into the outside … , but especially to be seen by the outside, to exist in it, to emigrate into it" (Merleau-Ponty 1968, 139). This blind and anonymous gaze from the outside (the outside of which Foucault also speaks in his essay "The Thought of the Outside" [collected in EEW2]) is precisely the element in which the subjective vision, "our" vision, the vision of "our" knowledge and of "our" experience, makes itself. The archaeologist (but also, as Merleau-Ponty would say, perhaps rightly, the phenomenologist) is someone who retrieves the traces of this anonymous gaze, in which not only our gaze has been forged but also and especially the power that such a gaze will have over the world and over the things it will evoke, draw, make visible and measurable, perceptible and manageable. We are a fold of that anonymous "stuff," precisely like the things we talk about, as the things discussed by our sciences (which is naively objectivistic) and captured by our knowledge (which is superficially realistic). We are played by that network of divergences, this system of slidings and shiftings, all the noncoincidences in which what we call experience is constituted. And somehow we even think of this experience as our "own" experience.

Furthermore, as Deleuze has shown us and he was the first (Deleuze 1988, 99–100), one must read the notorious "reappearance" of the subject in the final Foucault through the idea of "the fold." The reappearance of the subject is enigmatic because Foucault had implacably shown that the subject was an object outlined by something and, that man was merely a figure drawn in the sand by an unintentional hand. The Foucault of the "return" to the subject is the Foucault of the Ancients, the tireless decipherer of Greek and successively Roman wisdom, the theoretician of an aesthetics of existence with a Stoic flavor. The wise person is the one who chisels himself just like a marble block, who makes a statue of himself from himself, who molds his shape just like an artist who gives a shape to matter. It is this figure of the wise person, as is well known, that Foucault places before our eyes through the many figures of the self, of the use of pleasures, of *parrēsia* (frank-speaking). Once again, we see that a certain practice or pragmatics of the bodies is at work, but in this case it is the occasion or the event of such a figure in progress, of such a form of life in which ancient wisdom consists. The wise person's body, the flesh carved out as a work of art, the words this person speaks, polished and put into play in the political arena, the soul made "public" and thoroughly political, are the stuff, the wax, the clay, the blank slate on which the traces of that practice get inscribed. The issue of the body, which is the phenomenological theme par excellence and, long before phenomenology, was a Nietzschean theme (as we see clearly in the *Genealogy of Morals*), eventually comes back. But, more precisely, we must say that this theme had never really disappeared. Put simply, the body seen and sifted through by the clinical gaze (*The Birth of the Clinic*), the body torn apart and watched over (*Discipline and Punish*), has now become the body rummaged through and manipulated by the tiny, unceasing, tenacious, ruthless maneuvers of the care of the self.

There is no longer a body-thing on which the trajectories of power get inscribed like incandescent darts; there is no longer the sovereign power that tortures to the point of death; there is no longer the docile body, the body turned into a bundle of fibers, a "plexus" of functions to promote, a filigree of possibilities that biopolitics will bend to its own purposes (*Society Must Be Defended*). There is this body that the wise person takes away from the political space, not with a view to placing it in a more primeval and authentic space, but simply to make the body the space of a different politics. There is this body, this word, this voice, which the wise person makes unavailable for certain practices and powers, so as to make it the place and the occasion of different practices and new powers. The wise person, after all, is not so much the statue produced at the end of a life of ascetical practices (*askesis*); he (or she) is rather the process of the making, the movement that will have produced the statue across time. From both sides, there is the wise person at work, the molding and the molded hand. The doubleness of the wise man can be elaborated further. On the one hand, there is the wise man conceived as a "work" (*œuvre*), as completed artifact, as crystal; that is, as a subject. On the other side, we see the wise man as "activity" and, so to speak, as "unworked" (*désœuvrement*), as movement and escape from the touching hand that never wholly precipitates into the touched hand, as Merleau-Ponty would say. What we are now speaking of is no longer a subject. The wise person is nothing more and nothing less than this escape from oneself, this taking of oneself away from oneself. "Se méprendre de soi" – Foucault once said – is the aim of archaeology. The aim is not truth but a certain exercise, an *askesis*, as it were. This asceticism is something that needs to be fostered, made to happen, let proceed.

If Foucault's itinerary culminates in the theorization of an aesthetics of existence, we might understand this aesthetics as an aesthetics of the event. "I am a pyrotechnician," Foucault claimed, not without some slyness, in the interview where he spoke of Husserl and Nietzsche (cited above). Yet, what did phenomenology really aim at, really "want"? It wanted to produce an "Umstellung," an *overturning* in the subject, as Husserl says in the *Crisis of the European Sciences* (Husserl 1976, 472). Phenomenology wants to bring the constituted object back to the place of its constitution, to show the unobjectifiable source of objective knowledge, and to detach the subject from the illusion of science's objectivism and naturalism. It wants to discover in the transcendental subject *"a new will of life [ein neues Lebenswille]"* (Husserl 1976, 472, Husserl's emphasis). What did Merleau-Ponty's phenomenology want? Not to build up another, more trustworthy form of knowledge, but to place knowledge back within a certain element, within a dimension that Merleau-Ponty described as an origin that always explodes here and yet also over there, precisely at the place where we are, each time forever (Merleau-Ponty 1968, 264). What we have been describing is Merleau-Ponty's idea of "hyperdialectics," the bringing of oneself back to the thread of the becoming of oppositions, the placing of oneself back into the plot of divergences (*écarts*) in perpetual motion, divergences that perpetually bring about effects that assail us.

Although Foucault does not think there is such a constitutive source, he still thinks that there is an element lingering at the margins of the objectivations of each form of power and knowledge. That elusive element is not a source, but it is certainly an unobjective "element." It is nothing full, and just for this reason it belongs to the order of the invisible that lies at the core of the visible. It is this unobjective, invisible aspect that archaeology wants to reactivate, a potency pulsating in power and "out of step" (*contretemps*) with knowledge. After claiming that he is a pyrotechnician (*un artificier*), Foucault says, "I fabricate something that, at the end of the day, must be used in view of an attack, a war, a destruction. I am not in favor of destruction, but I am in favor of the fact that it is possible to go ahead, that some walls can be demolished" (FMFE, 92).

Federico Leoni

SEE ALSO

Outside
Phenomenology
Maurice Blanchot

SUGGESTED READING

Deleuze, Gilles. 1988. *Foucault*, trans. Seán Hand. Minneapolis: University of Minnesota Press.
Husserl, Edmund. 1976. *Die Krisis der Europaeischen Wissenschaften und die transzendentale Phaenomenologie*, Husserliana, Band VI. The Hague: Martinus Nijhoff.
Merleau-Ponty, Maurice. 1964. *Signs*, trans. Richard C. McCleary. Evanston, IL: Northwestern University Press.
    1968. *The Visible and the Invisible*, trans. Alphonso Lingis. Evanston, IL: Northwestern University Press.
    2011. *Phenomenology of Perception*, trans. Donald Landes. London: Routledge.

111

FRIEDRICH NIETZSCHE (1844–1901)

"THE FOLLOWING STUDY will only be the first, and probably the easiest, in this long line of enquiry which, beneath the sun of the great Nietzschean quest, would confront the dialectics of history with the immobile structures of the tragic" (EHM, xxx). These words, which appear in the Preface to the original, 1961 publication of Foucault's doctoral thesis *Folie et déraison: Histoire de la folie à l'âge classique*, could, I would argue, be adapted to stand as an epigram to the entire Foucauldian oeuvre insofar as that oeuvre never loses sight of how that "great Nietzschean quest" framed the ways in which to think of the complex relations of language, truth, power, and the subject. Foucault is, moreover, well aware of this, and he appeals to Nietzsche explicitly at crucial points in his major texts and invokes him often in interviews as he tries to clarify and contextualize his projects. For example, in an interview shortly after the publication of *Discipline and Punish* (1975), Foucault remarked that

> If I wanted to be pretentious, I would use "the genealogy of morals" as the general title of what I am doing. It was Nietzsche who specified the power relation as the general focus, shall we say, of philosophical discourse – whereas for Marx it was the productive relation. Nietzsche is the philosopher of power, a philosopher who managed to think of power without having to confine himself within a political theory in order to do so. (EPK, 53)

And in his final interview, given just a month before his death, he went even further in his identification with Nietzsche:

> I can only respond by saying that I am simply Nietzschean, and I try to see, on a number of points, and to the extent that it is possible, with the aid of Nietzsche's text – but also with anti-Nietzschean theses (which are nevertheless

662

Nietzschean!) – what can be done in this or that domain. I'm not looking for anything else but I'm really searching for that. (EPPC, 251)

Like many of the young philosophers of his generation, Foucault was first drawn to Nietzsche insofar as he felt constrained by the discursive practices of the philosophical discipline. Having "been trained in the great, time-honored university traditions – Descartes, Kant, Hegel, Husserl," when Foucault first came upon Nietzsche's "rather strange, witty, graceful texts," his reaction was to say: "Well I won't do what my contemporaries, colleagues or professors are doing; I won't just dismiss this" (EPPC, 33). In fact, Foucault came to read Nietzsche first in 1953, having been led to him by reading Bataille. From Foucault's friend Maurice Pinguet, we learn that while the two were vacationing that August in Italy, Foucault took with him everywhere his bilingual French-German edition of Nietzsche's *Untimely Meditations*. While enjoying the sights, and soaking up the sun on the beach at Civitavecchia, whenever he had a few moments, "on the beach, on the terrace of a café," Pinguet recalled that Foucault would open up the book and resume his reading (Pinguet 1986, 130).

Foucault's interest in Nietzsche in these early years was not just personal. In 1953, Foucault was teaching at Lille, and in addition to a course on "Connaissance de l'homme et réflexion transcendentale" in which he discussed Nietzsche, he also offered "some lectures on Nietzsche" (FDE1, 19). In 1964, at the first major conference in France to treat Nietzsche seriously as a philosopher – organized by Gilles Deleuze and held at the Abbey at Royaumont – Foucault presented an important paper titled "Nietzsche, Freud, Marx" (EEW2, 269–278), in which he offered an early indication of how those who later would be called the "masters of suspicion" would dominate critical theory in France for the next several decades. And later, in February 1966, he accepted with Deleuze the responsibility for organizing and editing the French edition of the German critical edition of Nietzsche's complete works – the *Kritische Gesamtausgabe* – edited by Giorgio Colli and Mazzino Montinari, coauthoring with Deleuze in 1967 the "General Introduction" (FDE1, 561–563) that appeared at the beginning of the first volume of the French *Œuvres Philosophiques Complètes*, Pierre Klossowski's translation of *Le Gai Savoir*.

While the importance of Nietzsche's analysis of power relations for the works of Foucault's so-called genealogical period is widely acknowledged, it is important to recognize that Nietzsche's influence on and appearance in Foucault's work began well before *Discipline and Punish*. In a 1983 interview, Foucault remarks that he first read Nietzsche "from the perspective of an inquiry into the history of knowledge – the history of reason." It was, in other words, his effort to "elaborate a history of rationality," and not his interrogation of power, that first led him to read Nietzsche (EEW2, 438). Reading Nietzsche made possible one of the decisive events in Foucault's development insofar as Nietzsche showed the way beyond the phenomenological, transhistorical subject. Nietzsche showed, in other words, that "There is a history of the subject just as there is a history of reason." At the same time, Nietzsche also demonstrated to Foucault that "we can never demand that the history of reason unfold as a first and founding act of the rationalist subject" (EEW2, 438).

It is Nietzsche's disclosure of the history of the subject, the history of reason, and the interrelations of these two histories that dominate Foucault's early, archaeological works, works that Foucault himself acknowledged owe "more to Nietzschean genealogy than to structuralism properly so called" (EEW2, 294). To understand what these works owe to Nietzsche, we need only look at the way Foucault deploys Nietzsche first in his *thèse complémentaire*, "Introduction à l'*Anthropologie* de Kant," and again when he returns to many of the same themes in *The Order of Things*. In his *thèse*, which accompanied his translation of Kant's *Anthropology*, Foucault provides an account of the place of Kant's *Anthropology* in relation to the three *Critiques* as well as the *Opus Postumum*. The key to this relation is located in Kant's *Logic*, where the three questions that guide the Critical Philosophy – "What can I know?" "What should I do?" "What may I hope for?" – now appear along with a fourth: "*Was ist der Mensch?*" ("What is man?"). This fourth question, Foucault tells us, "gathers [the first three] together in a single frame of reference" (EIKA, 74), which is to say that the answer to the questions of metaphysics, morality, and religion are, for Kant, ultimately to be found in anthropology.

Foucault further discusses the place of "man" in the *Opus Postumum* as the synthesis of God and world (see EIKA, 105ff). And it is this further point that allows Foucault to come to his conclusion. First, Foucault comments that, "These three terms, God, the world, and man, in their fundamental relationship to one another, get these notions of *source, domain, and limit* going again – the organizational persistence and force of which we have already seen at work in Kant's thought" (EIKA, 105). And it is "in the recurrence of these three notions, their fundamental rootedness, that the movement according to which the conceptual destiny, that is, the problematic, of contemporary philosophy can be seen to take shape" (EIKA, 106). This is to say that for Foucault the entire problematic of post-Kantian philosophy has been located in the interrogation of human finitude, which Foucault understands in terms of Kant positioning man (limit) as the synthesis of God (source) and world (domain). Such an understanding explains Nietzsche's surprising appearance in an "Introduction" to Kant's *Anthropology* insofar as Nietzsche also positions a being – but a being other than "man" – as the synthesis of source (values) and domain (Earth). Foucault thus closes his "Introduction à l'*Anthropologie* de Kant" with the following sentence: "The trajectory of the question *Was ist der Mensch?* in the field of philosophy reaches its end in the response which both challenges and disarms it: *der Übermensch*" (EIKA, 124).

Readers of *The Order of Things* are familiar with the role Nietzsche plays in that text, and this is anticipated in other provocative ways in Foucault's *thèse complémentaire*.

To cite just one example, although Foucault notes that in Kant's *Anthropology* "language is not yet presented as a system to be interrogated" (EIKA, 100), in *The Order of Things* he highlights Nietzsche's role in filling this lacuna insofar as Nietzsche was the first to connect "the philosophical task with a radical reflection upon language" (EOT, 305). It was Nietzsche, in other words, who, long before Heidegger, suggested that one could learn about the genealogy of morality by examining the etymology and evolution of moral terminology (e.g., in the First Essay of *On the Genealogy of Morals*). And it was Nietzsche who recognized that a culture's metaphysics could be traced back to the rules of its grammar, and who recognized that, for example, Descartes' proof of the cogito rested on the linguistic rule that a verb – thinking – requires a subject – a thinker – and that this very same linguistic prejudice leads to the metaphysical error of adding a doer to the deed (see, e.g., Nietzsche 1966, 17; Nietzsche 1967b, I:13). Insofar as all the structuralists based their theories on the view of language as a system of differences, we can therefore understand why Foucault could regard the question of language as the single most important question confronting the contemporary *episteme*, which erupted with the question of language as "an enigmatic multiplicity that must be mastered" (EOT, 305). And insofar as Nietzsche viewed our metaphysical assumptions to be a function of our linguistic rules (grammar as "the metaphysics of the people" [Nietzsche 1974, 354]), and he understood both our metaphysics and our language in terms of the difference between forces, one can understand why Foucault traces the roots of the contemporary *episteme*, which no longer views man as the privileged center of representational thinking and discourse, back to Nietzsche as its precursor.

Turning from Foucault's early work to his genealogical period, we again see the Nietzschean inspiration at the heart of Foucault's thinking about truth, power, and the subject. For Foucault, Nietzsche was the first to address a certain kind of question to "truth," a question that no longer restricted truth to the domain of epistemic inquiry or took the value of "truth" as a given. By posing ethical and political questions to "truth," Nietzsche saw "truth" as an ensemble of discursive rules "linked in a circular relation with systems of power that produce and sustain it, and to effects of power which it induces and which extend it" (EEW3, 132). When Nietzsche claimed, in *On the Genealogy of Morals*, that philosophy must for the first time confront the question of the value of truth (Nietzsche 1967b, III:24), he recognized that "Truth" was not something given in the order of things, and in so doing Foucault credits him with being the first to recognize "truth" as something produced within a complex sociopolitical institutional regime. "The problem," Foucault writes, "is not changing people's consciousness – or what's in their heads – but the political, economic, institutional regime of the production of truth. ... The political question, to sum up, is not error, illusion, alienated consciousness, or ideology; it is truth itself. Hence the importance of Nietzsche" (EEW3, 133).

Throughout his career, Foucault drew inspiration both from Nietzsche's insights linking power, truth, and knowledge and from his rhetoric of will to power, which drew attention away from substances, subjects, and things and focused that attention instead on the *relations* of forces *between* these substantives. Following Nietzsche, for Foucault, "power means relations": "Power in the substantive sense, '*le' pouvoir*, doesn't exist. [...] The idea that there is either located at – or emanating from – a given point something which is a 'power' seems to me to be based on a misguided analysis, one which at all events fails to account for a considerable number of phenomena" (EPK, 198). Where Nietzsche saw a continuum of will to power and sought to incite a becoming-stronger of will to power to rival the progressive becoming-weaker he associated with a degenerating modernity, Foucault saw power relations operating along a continuum of repression and production, and he drew attention to the multiple ways that power operates through the social order while never losing sight of the becoming-productive of power that accompanies the increasingly repressive power of that normalizing, disciplinary, prison society we call "modern." Contrary to the "repressive hypothesis" that functions as one of the privileged myths of modernity, Foucault shows that resistance is internal to power as a permanent possibility. Foucault argues that power relations are not preeminently repressive, nor do they manifest themselves only in laws that say "no." They are also productive, traversing and producing things, inducing pleasures, constructing knowledge, forming discourses, and creating truths (cf. EEW3, 119–120). This fundamental ambivalence between repression and production mirrors Nietzsche's recognition that will to power stands always facing the choice of going under or overcoming.

The final dimension of Foucault's Nietzscheanism we will examine is his thinking on the subject, which as we saw was what first led him to read Nietzsche. Foucault's early desire, as exemplified in his critique of "man," to challenge the epistemic and discursive privileging of the subject was directed very explicitly toward the "subject-function" of "man" as the foundation of the modern, a "subject-function" that he sees alive and well in phenomenology and existentialism. But this was not to be Foucault's final position on this matter, as is made clear when Foucault returns explicitly to reflect on the subject in his late works, for while Foucault has no sympathy for the phenomenological-existential and, in particular, the Sartrean subject (see, e.g., EEW1, 290), he does retrieve a more ambivalent subject whose constitution takes place within the constraints of institutional forces that exceed both its grasp and its recognition.

This is the subject whose genealogy Nietzsche traced in *On the Genealogy of Morals* (Nietzsche 1967b, I:13). In an analysis that Foucault discusses in his important early essay "Nietzsche, Genealogy, History" (EEW2, 369–391), Nietzsche focuses not on the valorization of origins (*Ursprung*) but on a critical analysis of the conditions of the subject's emergence (*Entstehung*) and descent (*Herkunft*). Pursuing this genealogy, Nietzsche locates the subject not as a metaphysical given but as a historical construct whose conditions of emergence are far from innocent. The "subject" is not only a superfluous postulation of a "'being' behind doing," a "doer" fictionally added to the deed. In addition, the belief in this postulate is exploited by slave morality both to convince the strong that they are free to be weak – and therefore are accountable for their failure to be weak – and to convince the weak that they are, in reality, strong and should therefore take pride in having freely chosen – by refraining from action – to be weak. For Nietzsche, "the subject (or, to use a more popular expression, the soul) … makes possible to the majority of mortals, the weak and oppressed of every kind, the sublime self-deception that interprets weakness as freedom, and their being thus-and-thus as a merit" (Nietzsche 1967b, I:13). For this reason, Nietzsche directs his genealogical gaze to the life-negating uses made of the principle of subjectivity in the service of a "hangman's metaphysics" that invented the concept of the responsible subject in order to hold it accountable and judge it guilty (Nietzsche 1968, VI:7).

In *Discipline and Punish*, his most Nietzschean text, Foucault for all practical purposes reproduces Nietzsche's analysis when he argues that the history of the microphysics of punitive power would be an element in the genealogy of the modern "soul" (EDP, 29). Foucault addresses this soul most explicitly in the discussion of the construction of the delinquent as a responsible subject, arguing in Nietzschean fashion that there is a subtle transformation in the exercise of power when punishment is no longer directed at the delinquent's actions (his "doing") but at his very person, his "being" as (a) delinquent. And Foucault returns to this argument at a crucial moment in the first volume of *The History of Sexuality*, when he notes the point at which the homosexual is no longer simply the performer of certain "forbidden acts" but instead has emerged as a subject with a "singular nature," a new "species" (EHS1, 43).

By the end of his career, as his attention turned, in the second and third volumes of *The History of Sexuality*, specifically to sexuality, his thinking moved from the constitution of the subject as an *object* of knowledge and discipline to the ethical practices of subjectification (*assujetissement*) and "the kind of relationship you ought to have with yourself, *rapport à soi*, which [he calls] ethics, and which determines how the individual is supposed to constitute himself as an ethical subject of his own actions" (EEW1, 263, translation altered). In thinking about the construction of the ethical subject, Foucault himself came to see that the question of the subject, or more accurately the question of subjectification – the transformation of human beings into subjects of knowledge, subjects of power, and subjects to themselves – had been "the general theme of [his] research" (EEW3, 327). Even here, however, as his thinking turned to the Greeks and his overt references to Nietzsche diminished, Foucault continued to see his own trajectory framed by the Nietzschean project of creatively constructing oneself through giving style to one's life (cf. EEW1, 261–262).

Alan D. Schrift

SEE ALSO

Genealogy
Power
Gilles Deleuze
Immanuel Kant

SUGGESTED READING

Ansell-Pearson, Keith. 1995. "The Significance of Michel Foucault's Reading of Nietzsche: Power, the Subject, and Political Theory," in *Nietzsche: A Critical Reader*, ed. Peter R. Sedgwick. Oxford: Blackwell, pp. 13–30.

Mahon, Michael. 1992. *Foucault's Nietzschean Genealogy: Truth, Power, and the Subject*. Albany: The SUNY Press.

Nietzsche, Friedrich. 1966. *Beyond Good and Evil*, trans. Walter Kaufmann. New York: Random House.

　　1967. *On the Genealogy of Morals*, trans. Walter Kaufmann. New York: Random House.

　　1968. *Twilight of the Idols*, trans. Reginald J. Hollingdale. Middlesex: Penguin Books.

　　1974. *The Gay Science*, trans. Walter Kaufman. New York: Random House.

Pinguet, Maurice. 1986. "Les Années d'apprentissage," *Le Debat* 41 (September–November): 122–131.

Schrift, Alan D. 1995. *Nietzsche's French Legacy: A Genealogy of Poststructuralism*. New York: Routledge.

Sluga, Hans. 2005. "Foucault's Encounter with Heidegger and Nietzsche," in *The Cambridge Companion to Foucault*, 2nd ed., ed. Gary Gutting. Cambridge: Cambridge University Press.

112

PLATO (428–347 BCE)

FOUCAULT WORKED ON Plato's texts during the final years of his productive life (1981–1984) across three large problematic dimensions: the erotic, the ethical, and the political. The problem of the Platonic erotic was posed on the basis of an interrogation of the relation between boys in ancient culture. In a general way, Foucault shows how sexuality in the Greeks is not considered, as in the Christian epoch, through the filter of a code of interdictions and the requirement of a suspicious decipherment of one's own desire. Instead, sexuality is considered on the basis of the problem of a relation of the self to the self in terms of commandment and government. The *aphodisias* (the things of love) appear, for example, to the Greeks as dangerous, not because they would be a figure of Evil but because their proper energy (the impulse of love, the search for satisfaction of carnal pleasure) risks, each time, to make us lose the rigorous control over ourselves. Just as a master of the home must learn to manage his expenses correctly in order to guarantee his family's prosperity, the sexual subject must manage his pleasures correctly and develop in himself the qualities of moderation. If not, he will only suffer events, he will be carried away by his desires, and he will find himself in a condemnable position of passivity. Within this very general framework that valorizes the principle of activity, homosexual love affairs do not constitute an absolute specificity, because the problem posed is not that of the object of sexual desire (a man or a woman) but that of the internal dynamic of sexuality (a force that is at times difficult to control). For Foucault (in *The Use of Pleasure*), Plato's *Symposium* (Diotima's speech) and his *Phaedrus* (the final myth) represent, within this Greek problematic of pleasures and amorous relations with boys, a certain shift in direction. In effect, Plato no longer poses to the aphrodisist the question of their use (what strategy should be adopted in order to subdue their energy?) but that of their essential nature (what is the truth of love?). Plato represents the passage from the deontology to the ontology of amorous desire. Now, through a moment of reduction and of spiritualization, amorous desire is analyzed as an impulse toward the truth that starts out by directing itself toward the wrong object; the tension that pushes us to look for pleasure with beautiful people is recodified as a restless search for eternal Ideas. For Foucault, Plato is the one who poses the problem of the truth of love and understands the genuine love as the love of the truth. To truly love a young man is to struggle with him against the deceptive illusion of carnal pleasures and to reorient the set of desires toward what unites them in an authentic way: the pure truth of the *logos*. This transformation is central because it poses, within sexual ethics, new principles: the necessity of a difficult struggle and of a permanent purification; the formulation of a rigorous austerity that can go as far as renouncing every relation to the flesh. Platonic erotics proposes ethical demands that will be rediscovered in Christianity.

Foucault's reading of Plato is also very important in the elaboration of a central concept, which is "the care of the self." As the 1982 course at the Collège de France ("The Hermeneutics of the Subject," ECF-HOS) shows, Foucault constructs, on the basis of Plato's *Alcibiades*, the theme of "the care of the self," which for him characterizes ancient ethics – outside of the specific problem of sexual pleasure. In a general way, Foucault is going to oppose an ancient care of the self, whose first formulation is found in Plato, to a modern introspection. This opposition allows him to think that there is something like a history of subjectivity. The ancient subject must take care of himself; that is, the ancient must regularly turn back to himself and examine himself carefully. But this turning back is not introspective. What is not at issue, within the framework of the care of the self, is a psychological self-decipherment, through which the subject would discover his secret nature or his hidden identity. For example, in the *Alcibiades*, Socrates simply asks Alcibiades (who has flaunted his intention to enter politics and concern himself with the affairs of the *polis*) the following question: before you concern yourself with the affairs of others, have you thought of concerning yourself with yourself? However, this is not to say that you would do better to concern yourself with yourself instead of concerning yourself with the *polis*. This question means that you will take better care of others insofar as you take care of yourself correctly. The care of the self does not appear as a narcissistic invitation to be self-centered and be concerned solely with one's own person. It is an invitation to work on oneself, a regulation of one's behavior so that one will be able to act on and with others in a just, coherent, and effective way. For example, how would one be able to claim to dominate the anger of the people or to be able to denounce public corruption, if one has not already done a work on oneself to quiet one's own fits of rage or one's own lust? The order that must reign in the *polis* must also reign in the individual. In the Platonic dialogues, Socrates appears precisely as the master of the care of the self. Foucault's second reference point is the great dialogue of the *Apology*. Here, Socrates is described as the one whose mission is precisely to care in such a way that each takes care of himself. In his final course at the Collège de France

("The Courage of Truth," ECF-COT), Foucault returns to the Platonic form of the care of the self, but by dividing it. This division of the care of the self allows him to establish a fundamental alternative to Western philosophy on the basis of Plato. Plato laid out two ways: that of wisdom and that of metaphysics (ECF-COT, 127). The way of wisdom (presented, according to Foucault, in the *Laches*) demands of the subject that he pose the problem of the form that he must give to his existence, the rules of conduct that he must adopt, the problem of the coherence of his discourse and his actions, of the techniques by which he will be able to obtain ethical results. This first Platonic way is also what Foucault calls an "aesthetics of existence." Taking care of oneself amounts to imposing qualities of order and harmony on one's existence. The second way is that of metaphysics, which Foucault lays out on the basis of the final sentences of the *Alcibiades*. The subject is called not to transform his way of life but to concentrate himself on the nature of his soul, to come to know the soul in its ontological principle, to recognize in the soul the mirror of a divine essence, to use one's soul as a support in order to go behind the curtain of sensible appearances and to merge with with the world of eternal essences. To care for oneself is to rediscover the divine portion of one's soul. This alternative within Platonism is, for Foucault, fundamental, for it outlines two distinct kinds of questioning: How to live? Or what is the soul in its truth? This originary division of philosophy is reconfigured at the end of the 1984 course when Foucault takes into account ancient Cynicism. Cynicism is a philosophy of ethical provocation. The Cynic breaks the set of social codes, transgresses all the social conventions, by leading a scandalous existence. But this different existence constitutes at the same time a call to the transformation of the world by means of the denunciation of its hypocrisies and injustices. In contrast, Platonism, for Foucault, invites a purification of the soul by means of the *logos*. This *askesis* constitutes at the same time a preparation for a higher life in another world, that of the intelligible essences (ECF-COT, 319). Plato then appears as the thinker of the identity between the soul and the *logos*, which founds a philosophy of transcendent truth. Diogenes, in contrast, commits philosophy to the path of the immanent transformation of self and of the world.

In 1983, Foucault proposed a series of lectures on *parrēsia*, a Greek term that means frankness and that Foucault translates by "truth-telling" or even by "the courage of truth." *Parrēsia* designates a speaking that is direct and frank, the kind of speech that clearly states its convictions and takes the risk of making people unhappy. The one who speaks frankly puts himself in danger by stating unbearable truths to those who are listening. Foucault considers that *parrēsia* is a forgotten foundation of Greek democracy. In fact, thanks to *parrēsia*, democracy can remain authentic and does not decline into demagogy. For example, the way in which Socrates addresses himself to his judges during his trial derives from the idea of *parrēsia*. He does not try to seduce them; rather, he provokes them. Plato himself, over the duration of his life, would have undergone this *parrēsia*, at the moment of his confrontation with the tyrant of Syracuse. Foucault studies this story of Plato and Dionysus both in the narrative that Plutarch provides and in Plato's own version in the "Seventh Letter." Two remarks are in order in relation to Foucault's reading of this narrative. First, Foucault observes that Platonic *parrēsia* functions in a framework different from democracy. Plato proves his courage not before a people who are unreliable and who can be influenced; Plato is courageous before an omnipotent tyrant. But, second, what is most important lies in the fact that Plato, by deciding to go to Syracuse, determines philosophy to be a test of oneself and of others rather than as a system of eternal truths made available to future readers. Foucault's interpretation of the "Seventh Letter" is entirely remarkable and original. He finds in this text the statement of a conception of philosophy that is removed from the fascination with a *logos* that is abstract and separated from contingencies. Plato went to Syracuse, as he himself explains, because he considered that philosophy must test its own reality. Philosophy must not simply be *logos* (discourse); it must also be *ergon* (work). In 1983, Foucault strove to establish that Plato, in the "Seventh Letter," defined philosophy as practice, at once as a self-practice and as a political practice (ECF-GSO, 209–219). Philosophy is not a simple system of knowledge that must keep watch over its internal logical validity. Philosophy is a practice: a practice of truth that must test its own reality by accepting its task of standing up to the political world. It is a self-practice that presupposes a whole ascetical work and an internal discipline. Nevertheless, the philosopher is not the one who must constitute political programs that the rulers must carry out. Foucault's analysis of the "Seventh Letter" provides a new presentation of the philosopher-king. This figure does not mean that the philosopher must govern because his knowledge is more extensive and his science is superior. Philosophy does not have to bring to political humans the knowledge that they lack. Philosophy has to bring the demand of an ethical structuration made of patience, courage, and firmness.

Foucault's readings of Plato therefore have been variable and at times contradictory. One can map out four great interpretative strategies. Plato is first presented as the one who simply brings forward a general apparatus of classical Greek thought (this is the example of his erotics in relation to the classical position of sexual relations with boys). But Plato can also be thought of as the one who introduced a forgotten foundation of the ethics of the ancients (this is the example of the care of the self as the Socratic interrogation par excellence). Third, Plato can be thought of as the initiator of a way or of several ways that would outline crucial divisions throughout the whole of Western philosophy (this is the example of the alternative between an aesthetic of existence and a metaphysics of the soul). Finally, in Foucault, through a final, substantial strategy, on the basis of a very precise reading, we see a different Plato appear (this is the example of the "Seventh Letter," which presents philosophy as a practice of the self rather than as a doctrine of knowledge). This complex array of interpretative strategies could be found as well in Foucault's treatment of other great figures of philosophy; for example, Descartes or Kant.

Frédéric Gros

SEE ALSO

Care
Parrēsia
Philosophy
Truth
The Ancients (Stoics and Cynics)

SUGGESTED READING

Davidson, Arnold. 1994. "Ethics as Ascetics: Foucault, the History of Ethics, and Ancient Thought," in *The Cambridge Companion to Foucault*, ed. Gary Gutting. Cambridge: Cambridge University Press, pp. 115–140.

Gros, Frédéric, and Carlos Lévy, eds. 2003. *Foucault et la philosophie antique*. Paris: Kimé.

113

PIERRE RIVIÈRE (1815–1840)

FOR FOUCAULT AND his team (Jean-Pierre Peter, Jeanne Favret Saada, Patricia Moulin, Blandine Barret-Kriegel, Philippe Riot, Alessandro Fontana, and Robert Castel), the Pierre Rivière affair (Rivière being a young Normand who in 1835 violently killed his whole family except for his father and who recounted his act in a memoir) reveals kinds of knowledge and prejudices but also the strategies used by psychiatry in the middle of the nineteenth century in order to have penal justice recognize its importance. Rivière is the very image of the "infamous man," an individual who is taken for a short time into the administrative machinery and is forced to explain his actions. This crime, Foucault emphasizes, does not make a big stir in the judiciary of this time. Rivière remains an insignificant and anonymous character. However, his narrative, a poetical work that possesses a profoundly disturbing power, manages, after 150 years, to throw the 1970s psychiatric institution into crisis. *I, Pierre Rivière, Having Slaughtered My Mother, My Sister, and My Brother* proposes as well an important renovation in the way of writing history. The subjective dimension of the historical work is largely accepted by Foucault, who seeks not to reduce this crime into a sociological, anthropological, or historical logic. What is at issue is to make Rivière's act unassimilable by making it "stick in our throat like anxiety."

Jean-François Bert

SEE ALSO

Abnormal
Madness
Psychiatry

SUGGESTED READING

Foucault, Michel. 1982. *I, Pierre Rivière, Having Slaughtered My Mother, My Sister, and My Brother: A Case of Parricide in the 19th Century*, ed. Michel Foucault, trans. Frank Jellinek. Lincoln: University of Nebraska Press.

114

RAYMOND ROUSSEL (1877–1933)

RAYMOND ROUSSEL WAS a French writer who was influential in Surrealist circles during his lifetime and was an important inspiration for the *nouveau roman* movement in the 1950s and 1960s. He wrote plays, poetry, and novels. His most well-known works are the novels *Impressions of Africa* (1910) and *Locus Solus* (1914) and the autobiographical essay *How I Wrote Certain of My Books* (1935) (Roussel 2001; Roussel 1983; Roussel 1995). Foucault recounts in an interview (EDL) that he first came across Roussel's work, completely by accident, in a secondhand bookshop in 1957. As his fascination with Roussel grew, he decided to write an article for the journal *Critique*, but this quickly grew into a book-length study. The book, published in French with the title *Raymond Roussel* (1963), was not translated into English until 1983, when it was given the more evocative title *Death and the Labyrinth: The World of Raymond Roussel* (EDL).

We can guess that Foucault's fascination with Roussel's work was fed by his own work of the late 1950s and early 1960s. At this time, he was working toward completion of the *History of Madness* (1961) and was already working on the material that would become *The Order of Things* (1966). Roussel's work raises questions both about the positioning of madness in society and about the troubled relation between words and things. Roussel was, famously, a patient of the psychiatrist Pierre Janet, and his work was often interpreted in the light of his mental illness (for example, his death by apparent suicide). And, in the works themselves, the theme of the relation between language and the world of things is constantly explored. Above these concerns, and appealing to another of Foucault's interests, was the theme of death and, in particular, its relation to language.

Foucault presents Roussel as a writer who is anxiously obsessed with language and who is constantly exploring the intimate connection between language and death. In the last line of his book, Foucault generalizes this experience by saying that what we share with Roussel is this "anguish of the signified" (EDL, 169). A shared anxiety in the face of language is both what allows us to understand Roussel's works and what allows us (Foucault) to speak of them. And, it is also what contributes to giving Foucault's own book its labyrinthine opacity, its relentless turning around the question of what Foucault sees as the void that opens up at the heart of language and connects it inexorably with death.

Convolution, repetition, and mirroring were key features of Roussel's work. A significant part of the pleasure of those works comes from the fact that, at one level, they can be approached as a kind of mystery that both resists and invites explanation; in fact, as a mystery that is constantly being explained but in ways that we cannot quite accept as reliable. In *Locus Solus* ("solitary place"), for example, we are introduced to the extraordinary garden of Martial Canterel. A group of visitors is led by Canterel through a series of marvels that he has assembled (literally) using his incomparable powers of engineering and chemistry. These include a series of vignettes, inside large, glass-fronted refrigerators, in which cadavers that have been temporarily reanimated using two substances invented by Canterel ("resurrectine" and "vitalium") reenact the most highly charged moments of their lives, before collapsing again into a state of death. Before any explanation is given, the visitors (and the reader) are taken from window to window to observe the curious actions of the inmates of each refrigerated cell. The scenes are described in meticulous but baffling detail; neither we nor the visitors to the garden have any idea of the significance of the actions we are witnessing. After the eight scenes, Canterel explains both his discovery of the chemical compounds resurrectine and vitalium and, once again in great detail, describes the context of the moments that we had seen being recreated inside the refrigerated cells. This second description is, then, an explanation of the original description, but it is one that is almost as mysterious and inexplicable as the first.

One thread to finding our way through this labyrinth is given to us by Roussel himself in the posthumous text in which he explained how he had written certain of his books. For Foucault, this text demonstrates that Roussel's work should be read not as a series of flights of the imagination but as a technical experiment that is carried out on language in order to expose both the labyrinth that it constructs for us and the abyss on which it rests. In *How I Wrote Certain of My Books*, Roussel explains some of the basic techniques on which he built "certain" of his books (principally *Locus Solus* and *Impressions of Africa*). One technique, for example, consisted of choosing two almost identical words – for example *billard* (billiard table) and *pillard* (plunderer). To these he would add identical words capable of two meanings in order to produce two almost identical sentences with radically different meanings. Hence: "*les lettres du blanc sur les bandes du vieux billard*" [the white letters on the cushions of the old billiard table] becomes "*les lettres du blanc sur les bandes du vieux pillard*" [the white man's letters on the hordes of the old plunderer]. His task was then to construct a narrative that would begin with the first sentence and end with the second sentence. It was this story, Roussel tells us, that was the basis for his novel *Impressions of Africa*.

Hence, for Foucault, these inventions are not primarily the product of a rich, surreal imagination. Rather, they are the products of a process that extracts wonders (in a Jules Verne sense) from the limitless fecundity of language itself: "the reader thinks he recognizes the wayward wanderings of the imagination where in fact there is only random language, methodically treated" (EDL, 40). For Foucault, this is the key to the locked doors of Roussel's work: not so much the mechanics of the process itself, and certainly not the psychopathology of the author, but the sense in which the equal poverty and richness of language is capable of generating a world of crystal clarity and impossible mystery. Underlying all of these experiments is an anxiety about words and their relation to things. Roussel's work both conveys and instills this anxiety: a "formless anxiety" relating to "the stifling hollowness, the inexorable absence of being … [the] expanse that Roussel's narratives cross as if on a tightrope above the void" (EDL, 13, 21). In Roussel, therefore, the effect of the incredibly precise descriptions of the world of things is, paradoxically, to undermine our faith in a direct and faithful relation between words and things.

In 1983, Foucault remarked that, "No one has paid much attention to this book, and I'm glad; it's my secret affair. You know, he was my love for several summers … no one knew it" (EDL, 187). He even goes so far as to say that the Roussel book "doesn't have a place in the sequence of my books" (ibid.). There is indeed no doubt that the book is very different in tone and content from his more widely read works. However, despite Foucault's own wish for it to remain secret, today it serves as an important testament to the crucial role that avant-garde literature played in the early formation of his intellectual project.

Timothy O'Leary

SEE ALSO

Language
Literature
Gilles Deleuze

SUGGESTED READING

Deleuze, Gilles. 1988. *Foucault*, trans. Seán Hand. Minneapolis: University of Minnesota Press. 1994. *Difference and Repetition*, trans. Paul Patton. New York: Columbia University Press.

Roussel, Raymond. 1983. *Locus Solus*, trans. Rupert Copeland Cuningham. London: John Calder.

1995. *How I Wrote Certain of My Books*, ed. and trans. Trevor Winkfield. Cambridge: Exact Change.

2001. *Impressions of Africa*, trans. Lindy Foord and Rayner Heppenstall. London: John Calder.

115

JEAN-PAUL SARTRE (1905–1980)

S ARTRE AND FOUCAULT were arguably the leading intellectuals of their respective generations in France during the second half of the twentieth century. Although their names were frequently associated, often in an adversarial way, their politics and political activism made them colleagues in demonstrations and petitions for causes of the Left in the 1960s and 1970s. Each was sometimes suspected by his critics of harboring anarchist tendencies. On one of the very few occasions when Sartre addressed Foucault's thought explicitly, he argued apropos the latter's "archaeological" structures (*epistemes*) that, whereas history is best conceived as cinema, Foucault offers us a slide show (Sartre 1966, 87). Philosopher of the imaginary, Sartre aptly drew the contrast between their respective philosophies of history with an image, whereas Foucault, master of specialized reason, effectively appealed to the diagram; the Foucauldian diagonal replaced the Sartrean dialectic.

Their differences were famously, if hyperbolically, summarized by Foucault in terms of Sartre's having "closed the parenthesis on the episode in our culture that began with Hegel." Despite his efforts to integrate contemporary culture in the dialectic, Foucault explains, Sartre typically was unable to abandon everything that comes from analytical reason and that plays a profound role in contemporary culture: "logic, information theory, linguistics, formalism. The *Critique of Dialectical Reason*," Foucault continues," is the magnificent and pathetic effort of a man of the nineteenth century to think the twentieth century. In this sense, Sartre is the last Hegelian and, I would even say, the last Marxist" (FDE1, 541–542). In what follows, I shall parse these remarks, discussing what is plausible or excessive and indicating what is simply erroneous.

Although the comparison is complex and multifaceted, I shall focus chiefly on the model of Foucault's Anthropological Quadrilateral. In his ambitious yet masterly *The Order of Things*, Foucault gathers the elements and relations that constitute the grid of intelligibility (the *episteme*) that sets the conditions and charts the limits for what will count as knowledge in what he designates the "modern" period – extending roughly from the late 1700s to the emergence of structuralism in the 1950s. As usual, the argument is spatial in that the relations are mapped both vertically and horizontally, but especially diagonally, through a juncture labeled "Man." This is not the "homo" of *Homo sapiens* or the object of Renaissance *studia humaniora* but the "Man" of the human sciences (*les sciences humaines*), an invention of the nineteenth century likely destined for disappearance in the latter half of the twentieth. It is within this epistemic box and centered on this humanistic node that Foucault would enclose Sartre – a man of the nineteenth century trying to think the twentieth century.

The plausibility of Foucault's charge rests heavily on Sartre's early individualist philosophy of consciousness epitomized in his masterwork, *Being and Nothingness*, but Foucault's charge depends even more on his commitment to dialectical, as distinct from analytical, reason. Long before Sartre's *Critique of Dialectical Reason*, Sartre had distinguished synthetic from analytic reason and associated the latter with bourgeois thought. Characteristically, this epistemic distinction also bore a political and an ethical significance. In Sartre's view, it was such thinking, for example, that brought us the abstraction that would generously confer on the black, the Jew, the Arab, and the woman the "Rights of Man and of the Citizen" while ignoring what was distinctive about the needs and concerns of each group. Sartre could easily subscribe to Foucault's claim that "the 'Enlightenment', which discovered the liberties, also invented the disciplines" (EDP, 222). Both (negative) liberties and (social scientific) disciplines were born of unbridled analytical reason.

If Sartre's alleged discovery of the power of phenomenology to philosophize about a cocktail glass, in Beauvoir's story, led him to study Husserl, it was the title of Jean Wahl's book *Toward the Concrete* (1932) that sparked Sartre's enthusiasm as he moved to and beyond phenomenological description toward dialectical comprehension, and from consciousness to lived experience (*le vécu*). In *The Birth of the Clinic*, Foucault had noted that the emerging case-study method served as a counterexample to the still prevalent Aristotelian dogma that there was no science of the singular (see EBC, xiv, a remark echoed in EDP, 191). But Sartre expanded this thesis by insisting that synthetic, dialectical thinking could overcome the inability of analytical reason to understand the singular by locating it in its sociohistorical context. This was the "singular universal" of the *Critique* and especially of his multivolume existential biography of Gustave Flaubert, *The Family Idiot* (Sartre 1981–1993).

How then did Sartre escape from the rectangular nineteenth-century prison in which Foucault confined him? I suggest that he slipped past the guards incognito – appearing to be a model prisoner while in fact concealing the recalcitrant Other in his very self. Consider a few examples.

The Dialectic. Amid his growing preference for dialectical reasoning, Sartre reserved an ontological space for analytical reason with its structures, functions, and causal analyses, the very intellectual practices Foucault insisted Sartre could not suffer.

It is located in the realm of what he calls the "practico-inert." This term denotes the sedimentation of previous praxes (human actions in their sociohistorical context) and so is ontologically dependent on "free organic praxis." The latter is the fulcrum of Sartre's dialectical thinking as it had been the basis of his individualist philosophy of consciousness in *Being and Nothingness*. In this respect, it might seem that Sartre fits well into the modern *episteme*. But this would misread him as a methodological (and ontological) individualist in his social philosophy, neglecting the crucial role played by "real relations" in his social ontology as elaborated in the *Critique*.

Does that then make him a holist? Even a "structuralist? Not at all. A simple either/or that divides social ontology into holism and individualism overlooks Sartre's explicit appeal to a *dialectical nominalism*, which argues for a "synthetic enrichment" of organic praxes as "mediated" by properly social (interpersonal) relations such as group membership and by practices and processes such as racism or colonialism. So important is the concept of mediation to Sartre's social ontology that Althusser could call him "[t]he philosopher of mediation par excellence." Sartre occasionally called his version a dialectic "with holes." These holes (*trous*) denote organic praxes that are ontologically free ("other-than themselves, nonself-coincidental"). This counters Foucault's claim that the covert telos of Hegelian dialectic is identity, not difference. Whether applicable to the Hegelian dialectic or not, identity is definitely not the goal of the Sartrean. This very "inner distance" marks the Sartrean "self" as ontologically free precisely because man is "not a self but a presence-to-self" (Sartre 1956, 440). Though Sartrean praxis totalizes, it resolutely withstands complete totalization by an Other. The otherness that Hegel's phenomenology is commonly seen striving to overcome in its pursuit of identity is disvalued as a "futile passion" by Sartre in contrast with the anguish of good faith efforts to resist this temptation toward conscious identity. Even the group-in-fusion of the *Critique* is ontologically a revolving set of relations in which each member is both mediated and mediating in the practical "sameness" of common concern but never in the ontological identity of a collective subject. The inner distance, the gap that conditions individual freedom, tames group unity as well, making betrayal a constant threat to the group just as bad faith stalks the individual.

Indeed, it seems that Foucault had already eyed fissures in the walls of this anthropological prison when he designated the two opposing angles of his spatial model "formalization" and "interpretation" (roughly, structuralism and hermeneutics), insisting that they "have become the two great forms of analysis of our time. In fact, we know no others" (EOT, 299). Toward the end of the book, he describes three "counter-sciences" that might presage the path that the future *may* hold for us, namely a kind of "structuralist" linguistics, psychoanalysis, and ethnology that was beginning to marginalize existential humanism even as he wrote. The "structuralist" character of these sciences that counter the human sciences consists in their search for "the totality of formal structures" (EOT, 380) that unconsciously condition those respective pursuits called psychoanalysis and ethnology. Foucault does not foresee the end of the social sciences as such, merely the likely erasure of their manlike face. It is at their "right angle" where the chain of signification crosses the plane of the social that they come into play, for "just as the linear structure of language always produces a possible choice between several words or several phonemes at any given moment," so "the *unique experience of the individual* finds a certain number of possible choices (and of excluded possibilities) in the system of the society" at the point at which the social structures encounter a certain number of possible individuals (and others who are not)" (EOT, 380, emphasis added). This calls for and receives a kind of master counterscience, namely linguistics as a "pure" theory of language; that is, one that *makes no mention of man*. It seems that the nodal point in this alternative model is a function, not an agent. And its "choices" are limited, if not reduced to one – a situation that Sartre rejected in *Being and Nothingness* as freedom-obliterating determinism. Yet the later Foucault seemed to echo Sartre's view when he commented that "where the determining factors are exhaustive, there is no relation of power: slavery is not a power relationship when a man is in chains" (EEW3, 342), a remark Sartre anticipated.

The Free Agent. The ambiguity of "free agency" challenges both Sartre and Foucault at this point. Foucault will face it, though not face it down, with his concept of power as "action on the action of others" that presumes freedom of resistance on the part of the other lest it harden into brute force (see EEW3, 221; EPPC, 83). Sartre, for his part, will gradually acknowledge the historical dimension of "situation" when he admits: "it is history which shows some the exits and makes others cool their heels before closed doors" (Sartre 1968, 80). Perhaps what Foucault disparages as "the neurosis of dialectics" is just the kind of necessary antidote that either cures or destroys freedom according to the amount administered. As Merleau-Ponty posed the problem in 1945, the question is to know what part freedom plays in this new existentialist philosophy and whether we can allow it something without giving it everything (Merleau-Ponty 1964, 77).

Whether these antisciences are the glimmer on the horizon that promises the dawning of a new age or rather the twilight of a fading era, Foucault is careful not to judge. As with so many such crossroads in his thought, he leaves us with the possibility that opens for us the freedom to "think" contrary to our received certitudes. The kaleidoscope has been turned ever so slightly, the mechanism is found to be one cog out of alignment, and the rest is up to us.

Or is it? That is Sartre's abiding conviction, from his early writings through his vintage existentialist mantra that you can always make something out of what you've been made into. The "always make something" denotes his existentialist freedom; the "what you've been made into" designates the "objective possibility" (or impossibility) that dawned on him as his concept of abstract freedom thickened with the aid of historical materialism. Toward the end of his life, Sartre reaffirmed the humanist conviction that "hope is part of man. Human action is transcendent" (Sartre and Lévy 1996, 53).

Late in life, Foucault seemed to approximate Sartre's mantra when he explained:

> I'm very careful to get a grip on the actual mechanisms of the exercises of power; I do this because those who are enmeshed, involved, in these power relations, in their actions, in their resistance, their rebellion, escape them, transform them, in a word, cease being submissive. And if I don't say what needs to be done, it isn't because I believe there is nothing to be done. On the contrary, I think there are a thousand things that can be done, invented, contrived by those who, recognizing the relations of power in which they are involved, have decided to resist them or escape them. From that viewpoint, all my research rests on a postulate of absolute optimism. (EEW3, 294)

We have just seen that the *Critique* does respect the formalization of analytic reason. Sartre even describes his projected study of Gustave Flaubert's life and times as the response to the question whether "today we have the means to constitute a structural, historical anthropology" (Sartre 1968, xxxiv). Yet Sartre accords a three-fold primacy to free organic praxis – epistemic, ontological, and moral. Indeed, he calls comprehension (hermeneutical understanding) "the translucidity of praxis to itself" (Sartre 2004, 74), though allowing in his Flaubert study almost offhand that ideology could cloud the clear vision of consciousness (Sartre 1981–1993, volume 1, 141). Again, he seems held fast in the anthropological quadrilateral by its two meth-odological corners. But, to continue my analogy, each of these confining corners is adapted by Sartre in such a way that they enable him to break free of the neat limita-tions that Foucault would impose on him. We have just seen how Sartre's adoption of the dialectic is not a commitment to identity over difference, except in the admit-tedly "futile passion" to be self-identical. The "othering" character of consciousness (articulated in intentionality) constitutes and sustains the gap in which creativity (the imaginary), the ethical, and the political can function freely, though always "in situation."

In *Search for a Method*, Sartre "repeats with Marxism: there are only men and real relations between men" (Sartre 1968, 74). The ontology of these all-important relations is not addressed explicitly except to call them "real" as presumably opposed to merely "nominal." But one factor enabling Sartre to escape this quadrilateral is his robust ontological realism – precisely what led him to move away from Husserl of the *Ideas*. That rage for nonlinguistic reality liberated him from the confines of Foucault's alleged dalliance with linguistic idealism in *The Order of Things* even as it turned Foucault toward nonlinguistic power relations in his genealogical pursuits. In other words, Foucault, too, seemed aware of that threat toward the end of the book, when he raised the question of "what language must be in order to structure in this way what is nevertheless not in itself either word or discourse, and in order to articulate itself on the pure forms of knowledge" (EOT, 382), for insofar as the sides of the quadrilateral map over the four modalities of the linguistic sign that yield archaeologically the *episteme* of the classical age, even if they are inverted in Nietzschean fashion with "Man" displacing "Name" in the modern model, Sartrean existentialism resists surrender to the empire of the sign or the emerging realm of structuralist "signification." Sartre once quipped, "*le signifiant* [signifier] *c'est moi*." But even this is an exaggeration because the ontological locus of language for Sartre is the *practico*-inert, and the individual is both signifier and signified (*signifiant et signifié*). Ontologically, language does not "speak" the speaker even if it is a basic ingredient of the human situation, as Sartre pointed out in *Being and Nothingness*. For him, too much is at stake in ignoring this constitutive relation, namely the existentialist values of freedom and moral responsibility, to name the two most important. These have remained defining features of existentialist thought. And it is not pushing the envelope too far to note that in several respects the "final Foucault" seemed to gesture in this direction with his talk of experience, as we shall see.

Humanism. Broadly speaking, one can say that humanism, anthropology, and dialectical thought for Foucault are intertwined. While analytical reason, in Foucault's mind, is incompatible with humanism, "dialectic appeals to humanism secondarily" for several reasons: because it is a philosophy of history, because it is a philosophy of human practice, and because it is a philosophy of alienation and reconciliation. For these reasons and because fundamentally it is always a philosophy of return to the self (*soi-même*), dialectic in a sense promises the human being that he will become an authentic and true man. It promises man to man and to this extent is inseparable from a humanist ethic (*morale*). In this sense, the parties most responsible for contemporary humanism are evidently Hegel and Marx (FDE1, 541). And one could add, "Sartre is the last Hegelian and even the last Marxist" (FDE1, 542). The link between humanism and dialectic is perplexing because, among other things, Sartre would have encased "bourgeois" humanism precisely in the bad faith of the bourgeoisie and its analytical rationality: it is confidence in its "right" to govern. In effect, what Sartre despised is the racism, the anti-Semitism and the nascent fascism of the French middle class, as captured in his novel *Nausea* and short story "The Childhood of a Leader." His is a humanism of labor, a "socialist" humanism minus the Socialist Party.

But the humanist ethic? That is another story. A naturalist ethic? Yes. And an ethic of persons and not abstract principles, to be sure, as well as an ethic that is creative and willing to respect and foster the freedom of others. Foucault, who distinguished ethics (action of the self on itself) from morals (a set of principles and codes) (Flynn 2005, 347n7) in *The Uses of Pleasure*, does seem to approximate the Sartrean (actually Nietzschean) notion of moral creativity, but at the risk of slipping into aestheticism. Again, he runs this risk with Sartre, who, noting the resemblance between moral choice and aesthetic creativity in *Existentialism Is a Humanism*, warned his critics not to confuse this with aestheticism, though he predicted they would.

Authenticity. In notes from conversations that Hubert Dreyfus and Paul Rabinow held with Foucault at Berkeley in 1983, we catch glimpses of an ethic for our time that he is in the process of sketching. Following an earlier remark, they ask him: "But if one is to create oneself without recourse to knowledge or universal rules, how does your view differ from Sartrean existentialism?" In reply, Foucault insists that Sartre misses the mark by linking the practice of creativity to the moral notion of authenticity, which Foucault (mis)interprets as faithfulness to a "true self": "The theme of authenticity whether explicitly or not, refers to a mode of being of a subject defined by its adequation to itself (*lui-même*)." On the contrary, Foucault believes that the relation to the self ought to be described in terms of multiple possible modalities, only one of which is authenticity. This requires the practice of certain "techniques of the self" and not merely a shift in discourse (FDE4, 617ff, revised in French edition). One could question whether authenticity is merely one value among equals or, as Sartre seems to imply, enjoys at least a primacy among equals, if not a certain power to trump other considerations, all things being equal. Given the admitted impossibility of reaching a level playing field in a persistent capitalist and racist society – in Sartre's account – perhaps a certain amount of "amoral realism" seemed called for during his four years of fellow traveling with the French Communist Party (1952–1956). But it was their call for justice in addition to a penchant for "direct action" that attracted Sartre to the Maoists in the later 1960s – a politico-ethical stance he seemed to share with Foucault in those years (Sartre, Gavi, and Victor 1974, 79).

A parallel moral matter arises when we consider Foucault's last lectures on *The Courage of Truth* (*parrēsia*) at the Collège de France and at Berkeley the previous term. Briefly stated, his survey of *parrēsia* as a political virtue the first semester (you told the prince the truth even if it cost you your head) and a moral virtue the second (you admitted the truth about yourself even if it cost you your self-image) – raised a mixture of political and ethical issues that transformed and displaced *parrēsia* from the institutional horizon to the horizon of individual practice of *ethos* formation (see FCF-CV, 62). But in fact this "parrēsiastic" account in the broad sense of considering all three poles of truth-telling – the scientific, the political, and the ethical – in their irreducible yet essential interrelationship, Foucault insists, "has characterized philosophical discourse from the Greeks to our day" (ibid.). I leave it to the reader to consider how Foucauldian "*parrēsia*" might map over Sartrean "authenticity" if the cognitive and political dimensions of the latter were elaborated as Sartre proposes (Flynn 2005, 280–282).

Experience. Foucault distinguished two paths taken by French philosophers in the wake of Husserl's famous *Cartesian Meditations* lecture delivered in Paris in 1929. Sartre and Merleau-Ponty pursued the "philosophy of experience, of meaning and of the subject," whereas the philosophy of knowledge, of rationality, and of the concept was followed by Cavaillès, Canguilhem, and presumably himself (EEW2, 466). Still, it is significant that the concept of experience figures importantly throughout his works. Foucault called the *History of Madness* his "experience book" and spoke openly about experience in an interview with Duccio Trombadori late in his career. The last two volumes of his *History of Sexuality* analyze the "experience of sexuality" in the ancient world. Above all, when charting his lifelong inquiries along the three axes or "poles" of his thought (truth, power, and subjectification) with his characteristic appeal to spatial metaphors, he describes the space they enclose and their "matrix" as experience. One should not marvel, then, that Pierre Macherey would call "experience" a concept that lies at the center of Foucault's thought (Macherey 1986, 753–754).

Has Foucault changed his mind? Or was his use of "experience" so polyvalent that it could travel comfortably along the path of the concept? Briefly, I would suggest that what troubles him about the use employed by Sartre and initially by Merleau-Ponty as well was their linkage of experience with consciousness as if the expression "unconscious experience" was an oxymoron – and so it seemed to be for Sartre. But with Merleau-Ponty's notion of "operational intentionality" and the Lacanian understanding of the unconscious structured like a language, the link between consciousness, intentionality, and experience seemed weakened, if not broken entirely. Thus Foucault could raise the question: "Can't there be experiences in the course of which the subject is no longer posited, in its constitutive relations, as what makes it identical with itself? Might there not be experiences in which the subject might be able to dissociate from itself, sever the relation with itself, lose its identity? Isn't that the essence of Nietzsche's experience of eternal recurrence?" (EEW3, 248).

What is the upshot of the foregoing comparison and contrast? To adopt Foucauldian spatial metaphors, one can say that his thought is prismatic (three poles of truth, power, and subjectification rising indefinitely from their experiential matrix), whereas Sartre's thought is pyramidal (all sides converging in a responsible agent whose inner life is free; that is, "othering"). If we choose the model of searchlights or Venn diagrams, one can recognize a certain overlap and intensification of positions from differing perspectives. Each model is suggestive by its very limitations. The challenge, to paraphrase Merleau-Ponty once more, is to award each a voice in the conversation without letting it devolve into a dialogue of the deaf.

Thomas R. Flynn

SEE ALSO

Experience
Parrēsia
Phenomenology
Maurice Merleau-Ponty

SUGGESTED READING

Flynn, Thomas R. 1997. *Sartre, Foucault, and Historical Reason: Toward an Existentialist Theory of History*. Chicago: University of Chicago Press.

———. 2005. *Sartre, Foucault, and Historical Reason*, volume 2: *A Poststructuralist Mapping of History*. Chicago: University of Chicago Press.

Macherey, Pierre. 1986. "Aux Sources de 'Histoire de la folie,'" *Critique* 442 (August–September): 753–774.

Merleau-Ponty, Maurice. 1964. *Sense and Non-Sense*, trans. Hubert L. Dreyfus and Patricia Allen Dreyfus. Evanston, IL: Northwestern University Press.

Sartre, Jean-Paul. 1956. *Being and Nothingness*, trans. Hazel E. Barnes. New York: Philosophical Library.

———. 1966. "Jean-Paul Sartre répond," *L'arc* 30:87–96.

———. 1968. *Search for a Method*, trans. Hazel E. Barnes. New York: Vintage Books.

———. 1981–1993. *The Family Idiot: Gustave Flaubert 1821–1857*, trans. Carol Cosman, 5 vols. Chicago: University of Chicago Press.

———. 2004. *Critique of Dialectical Reason*, volume 1: *Theory of Practical Ensembles*, trans. Alan Sheridan-Smith. London: Verso.

Sartre, Jean-Paul, Philippe Gavi, and Pierre Victor (a.k.a. Benny Lévy). 1974. *On a raison de se révolter*. Paris: Gallimard.

Sartre, Jean-Paul, and Benny Lévy. 1996. *Hope Now: The 1980 Interviews*, trans. Adrian Ven Den Hoven. Chicago: University of Chicago Press.

116

WILLIAM SHAKESPEARE
(1564–1616)

OUCAULT'S REFERENCES TO Shakespeare are infrequent but revealing. Apart from a passing allusion to the sonnets, he refers exclusively to the tragedies and histories. In each case, he calls attention to aspects of Shakespeare's representations of death: first the relationship between death and dreaming, then the relationship between death and madness, and finally the relationship between death and sovereignty.

(1) *Death and dreaming*. In "Dream, Imagination, and Existence," Foucault argues that dreaming interrupts sleep by representing the dreaming subject's own death. This idea prompts him to recall the voice that cries "Macbeth doth murder sleep!" Building on the existential analyses of Heidegger and Binswanger, Foucault contrasts authentic death (the "proper" end of an existing being) with inauthentic death (the "accidental" death that threatens existence from outside). From this distinction, it would be a short step to Freud's opposition between the aims of the death drive and Eros; authentic death would be the aim of the death drive, whereas inauthentic death would be the unintended death that happens to cut flourishing life short. Foucault, however, resists this Freudian interpretation. If to be mortal is to move with sovereign freedom toward a death that is both authentic and adventitious, the two seemingly opposing tendencies must ultimately coincide. Foucault finds this view admirably expressed in the coincidence of the two interpretations of Calpurnia's dream in *Julius Caesar*. Caesar reports, "She dreamt tonight she saw my statue, / Which, like a fountain with an hundred spouts, / Did run pure blood." Calpurnia is right to take her dream to be the ominous sign that it is of the danger that might befall Caesar if he goes to the Capitol. At the same time, Decius Brutus, despite his insincerity, is no less justified in interpreting the dream as an expression of Caesar's sovereign destiny to be Rome's great benefactor. The two interpretations

coincide, for Caesar will fulfill his destiny precisely by unexpectedly falling at the hands of the conspirators. For Foucault, death, in general, resolves an apparent antinomy "between freedom and the world." He concludes that "in every case death is the absolute meaning of the dream." Reiterating the opposition between sleep and death, he returns once more to *Macbeth*: "Shake off this downy sleep, death's counterfeit, / And look on death itself!" (EDE, 54–55).

(2) *Death and madness.* In his other major text from the 1950s, Foucault characterizes both Shakespeare and Cervantes as writers who "attest to the great prestige of madness" during the Renaissance (EMIP, 67). In *History of Madness*, he goes one step further, suggesting that Shakespeare and Cervantes depict a "tragic experience of madness born in the fifteenth century more than they reflect the critical or moral experience of unreason that is nonetheless a product of their era" (EHM, 37). Shakespeare, then, is located on the cusp of a historical divide. From the earlier, tragic point of view, madness is essentially linked to death: to succumb to madness is to cross a threshold from which no traveler returns alive. In support of this idea, Foucault mentions the examples of Ophelia, Lady Macbeth, and King Lear. In later seventeenth-century drama, madness no longer represents a point of no return but becomes instead a stage on a journey, a temporary condition from which it is possible to be redeemed. We may wonder if Lear's madness, cured by sleep, is closer to this later model than Foucault suggests, but the suicides of Ophelia and Lady Macbeth underscore his point. Ophelia's drowning reflects an association of madness and water that runs across the two periods, a continuity that Foucault highlights in the context of wondering why the motif of the ship of fools suddenly came to the fore in fifteenth-century painting and literature (EHM, 12). He does not locate this motif in Shakespeare, but he does suggest that the wanderings of Lear and the Fool attest to the same sort of liberty that was granted to the mad during the Renaissance (EHM, 77). In "Madness and Society" (1970), he mentions Lear's Fool as an exemplary representative of the early modern figure of the "licensed" fool who knows more than everyone else (EEW2, 340).

(3) *Death and sovereignty.* The madness of Lear is referred to again in Foucault's 1973–1974 lectures on psychiatric power, but the emphasis has now shifted to questions concerning political sovereignty. After Lear abdicates and finds himself subject to the tyranny of his ungrateful daughters, his ensuing madness symbolically expresses his transformation from sovereign to subject. Richard III (whose foreboding dream anticipates his own death) is subject to a similar threat. Such crises of sovereignty attest to the fragility of the medieval legal fiction of the "King's Two Bodies." Ernst Kantorowicz, whom Foucault cites in *Discipline and Punish*, argues that this fragility is most perspicuous in Shakespeare's *Richard II*. Foucault observes that by the end of the eighteenth century, the relationship between sovereignty, madness, and death had come to be represented in an entirely new way.

Pinel's description of Willis's cure of George III's madness depicts "a completely different type of power … an anonymous, nameless and faceless power that is distributed between different persons" (ECF-PP, 21). In his lectures on "the abnormal" the following year, Foucault identified "the infamy of sovereignty" or "the discredited sovereign" as "Shakespeare's problem" (ECF-AB, 13). The next year, in *Society Must Be Defended*, Shakespeare's "'historical' tragedies" are said to reflect "the problems of public right," specifically "the problem of the usurper and dethronement, of the murder of kings and the birth of the new being who is constituted by the coronation of a king" (ECF-SMD, 174–175). Shakespeare's "sad stories of the death of kings" are typical of tragedy in general. In modernity, the rise of the novel is correlated with a shift from the juridical problem of right to the statistical problem of the norm. This idea recalls Foucault's earlier discussions of the loss of tragic experience and the differences between Lear's and George III's loss of sanity and sovereignty. In his 1977–1978 lectures, Foucault briefly mentions the theme of the coup d'état in Shakespeare, Corneille, and Racine.

Besides these three major thanatological topoi, Foucault refers in passing to Roussel's "imitation of Shakespeare" (EDL, 98) and to French classical indifference to Shakespeare (in connection with Nietzsche's conception of "great epochs") (EEW2, 384). More suggestive is his allusion in "What Is an Author?" to the notorious authorship controversy: "If I discover that Shakespeare was not born in the house we visit today, this is a modification that, obviously, will not alter the functioning of the author's name. But if we proved that Shakespeare did not write those sonnets which pass for his, that would constitute a significant change and affect the manner in which the author's name functions" (EEW2, 210).

Despite the relative brevity of his remarks about Shakespeare, Foucault has had a major impact on Shakespeare studies, notably through his influence on New Historicist criticism. Richard Wilson recounts some of the Foucauldian themes (such as panopticism and disciplinary power) that critics have found in Shakespeare's plays.

Andrew Cutrofello

SEE ALSO

Death
Madness
Sovereignty
Raymond Roussel

SUGGESTED READING

Howard, Jean E. 2004. "The New Historicism in Renaissance Studies," in *Shakespeare: An Anthology of Criticism and Theory 1945–2000*, ed. Russ McDonald. Malden, MA: Blackwell, pp. 458–480.

Kantorowicz, Ernst H. 1997. *The King's Two Bodies: A Study in Mediaeval Political Thought*. Princeton, NJ: Princeton University Press.

Wilson, Richard. 2007. *Shakespeare in French Theory: King of Shadows*. New York: Routledge, esp. chap. 2: "Prince of Darkness: Foucault's Renaissance," pp. 75–122.

117

CARL VON CLAUSEWITZ
(1780–1831)

CARL VON CLAUSEWITZ was a German general and military theorist. Foucault's engagement with Clausewitz is primarily around the latter's most famous saying, that "war is the continuation of politics by other means." The idea here is that war is an extension, a certain form, of the political process that goes on between nations.

Foucault's best-known mention of this dictum is probably that in volume one of his *History of Sexuality* (EHS1, 93), but he examines it in more detail and names Clausewitz as its originator in the lecture series *Society Must Be Defended* (ECF-SMD, 15). Foucault's move here is to *invert* Clausewitz's dictum, to say that it is not so much that war is a continuation of politics as that politics is a continuation of war. Foucault thus puts himself explicitly at odds with Clausewitz, inasmuch as he seems to be saying the opposite thing to Clausewitz. For Foucault, war shows us the nature of power relations in a way that is concealed in "peaceful" politics but still continues to operate beneath the surface. War and politics are for him different ways of "encoding" power relations. Foucault contrasts this understanding of power with a "juridical" model of power that sees power as essentially a matter of rules and hierarchy. For Foucault, rules and hierarchy are manoeuvres within a social war. From this perspective, he sees himself as following a tradition of European political thought with antecedents including Friedrich Nietzsche, and much of left-wing thought, with its emphasis on class struggle underlying our apparently peaceful institutions. By contrast, Clausewitz would seem to belong to the mainstream of thinking about war and politics, which sees the former as an adjunct to a stable, established politics. Indeed, Foucault thinks his "inversion" of Clausewitz is in fact older than Clausewitz's position, which itself inverted an older position, and which did not in fact originate with Clausewitz (ECF-SMD, 48).

However, it is not clear how much inverting the statement in either direction actually changes its meaning. Whether war is held to be another form of politics or vice versa, a continuity between politics and war is posited. Indeed, Roger Deacon (Deacon 2003) has argued that Foucault's position is much closer to Clausewitz's than the antinomy Foucault stages between himself and Clausewitz indicates. This is not to say that Foucault does not intend to differentiate his position strongly from Clausewitz's – it seems clear that Foucault thinks that the priority he gives to war makes his position the polar opposite of one that gives priority to politics – but rather that Clausewitz's position is more complicated than Foucault's treatment indicates. Along with Julien Reid (Reid 2003), Deacon furthermore suggests that Foucault's position might have been affected by reading Clausewitz. In particular, we perhaps see Clauzewitz' influence in Foucault's frequent use of military vocabulary, most notably his use of the word "strategy."

Mark Kelly

SEE ALSO

Politics
Power
State
Strategies
War

SUGGESTED READING

Deacon, Roger. 2003. "Clausewitz and Foucault: War and Power," *Scientia Militaria: South African Journal of Military Studies* 31, no. 1:37–48.
Reid, Julian. 2003. "Foucault on Clausewitz: Conceptualizing the Relationship between War and Power," *Alternatives: Global, Local, Political* 28 (January–February): 1–28.

Chronology of Michel Foucault's Life
(1926–1984)

The chronology is based on those found at www.michel-foucault.com, especially the chronology composed by Daniel Defert. The chronology is also based on David Macey, *The Lives of Michel Foucault* (New York: Vintage, 1995); Didier Eribon, *Michel Foucault*, trans. Betsy Wing (Cambridge, MA: Harvard University Press, 1991); and James Miller, *The Passion of Michel Foucault* (New York: Anchor Doubleday, 1993).

1926　Born in Poitiers, to Paul-Michel Foucault (surgeon) and Anne Malapert.

1945　In October enters preparatory class (*khâgne*) for the École Normale Supérieure, at Lycée Henri-IV.

1946　In September enters the École Normale Supérieure, rue d'Ulm.

1950　Joins French Communist Party.

1951　Passes the state licensing exam for philosophy (the *agrégation*) on the second attempt.

1952　Successfully completes the diploma course in psychopathology taught by the Institut de Psychologie, Paris. Teaches psychology at the Université de Lille. Quits the French Communist Party.

1954　Publication of Introduction to Binswanger's *Dream and Existence* (Desclée de Brouwer); also publication of *Maladie mentale et personnalité* (*Mental Illness and Personality*) (Presses Universitaires de France).

1955　Director of the Institut Français at Uppsala, Sweden. Meets Roland Barthes.

1956　Begins writing *The History of Madness*.

1958　Director of Centre de Civilisation Française in Warsaw, Poland.

1959　Director of Institut Français in Hamburg, Germany.

1960　Joins the faculty of Université Clermont-Ferrand. Meets Daniel Defert, with whom Foucault is going to share his life.

1961　Presents *The History of Madness* as his principal thesis (directed by Georges Canguilhem) and *Introduction to Kant's Anthropology* as secondary thesis (directed by Jean Hyppolite). Publishes *The History of Madness* under the title *Folie et déraison. Histoire de la folie à l'âge classique* (Plon).

1962　*Maladie mentale et personnalité* is reissued (revised) as Maladie mentale et psychologie (Mental Illness and Psychology) (Presses Universitaires de France). Meets Gilles Deleuze, who has just published *Nietzsche and Philosophy*.

1963　Publishes *The Birth of the Clinic* (Presses Universitaires de France) and *Death and the Labyrinth* (on Raymond Roussel) (Gallimard). Starts the project that will become *Les mots et les choses* (*The Order of Things*).

1965　In October, presents portions of *The Order of Things* in Sao Paolo, Brazil. Participates in the Fouchet commission to reform the university system.

1966　In April, publication of *The Order of Things* (Gallimard). The Paris reaction to the book is generally hostile. Occupies a philosophy teaching position at the Université de Tunis and resides in Sidi Bou Saïd.

1967　At Tunis and Milan gives lectures on Manet, one of which will be posthumously published as *Manet and the Object of Painting* (2004 for the French publication).

1968　In March, Marxist student movement in Tunisia, which is anti-imperialist, is harshly repressed. Foucault tries to help the students who are arrested and imprisoned. Forced to leave Tunis at the end of May, consequently Foucault does not participate in "the events of May '68." In Paris, during the month of May, there are massive student protests and occupation of the universities. The police forcibly retake the universities. In September (after the events of "May '68"), Hélène Cixous invites Foucault to participate in the foundation of a new experimental university in the Paris suburb of Vincennes. At Vincennes, Foucault teaches his first courses on "Sexuality and Individuality" and on Nietzsche.

1969　Publication of *The Archaeology of Knowledge* (Gallimard). In April–May, Foucault makes his first trip to the United States, to the State University of New York at Buffalo. In November, Foucault is elected to the Collège de France (replacing Jean Hyppolite who had died on October 26, 1968).

1970　December 2, inaugural address at the Collège de France, called *L'ordre du discours* (*The Order of Discourse*, translated in EAK, 215–237, as "The Discourse on Language"). Foucault organizes the first meetings of a commission investigating the French prison system; this commission will become the Groupe d'information sur les prisons (GIP: Prison Information Group).

1971　In February, Foucault publishes GIP's manifesto (with historian Pierre Vidal-Naquet, and Jean-Marie Domenach, the director of the Catholic spiritualist journal *Esprit*). GIP engages in several investigations. Foucault becomes increasingly engaged in the struggle against the severe police repression of social struggles in France. Through Jean Genet, Foucault becomes a supporter of the American Black Panthers. In November, Foucault, Sartre, Genet, Claude Mauriac, and Jean-Claude Passeron (in association with other extreme leftist groups) set up, in the Maghrebin district of the Goutte d'or in Paris, a commission investigating racism. Foucault's course at the Collège de France is devoted to "Penal Theories and Institutions." On Dutch television, Foucault debates Noam Chomsky on the existence of human nature.

1972　Foucault returns to Buffalo and presents a lecture called "The Will to Truth and Ancient Greece." On this trip, he visits Attica prison in New York State. Hélène Cixous and Jean Gattegno publish *Cahiers de revendications sortis des prisons*, claims that were assembled by the GIP militants. In December, GIP decides to dissolve in order to allow it to be directed by ex-convicts; it becomes CAP (Comité d'action des prisonniers).

1973　Foucault's course at the Collège de France is "The Punitive Society," which is the preparation for *Discipline and Punish*. In September, *Pierre Rivière* and *This Is Not a Pipe* are published.

1974　Collège de France course is "Psychiatric Power." Lectures widely on antipsychiatry.

1975　Collège de France course is "Abnormal." *Discipline and Punish* is published (Gallimard). In September, Foucault, along with Yves Montand, Claude Mauriac, Régis Debray, Costas Gravis, and Jean Lacouture, intervene in Madrid, Spain, against the Franco death sentences given to several Basque militants. In November, Foucault makes a presentation at Columbia University, New York, on the role that doctors and psychiatrists are playing in the torture of political militants in Brazil. Gilles Deleuze, Félix Guattari, and William Burroughs participate in this conference.

1976　Collège de France course is "Society Must Be Defended." In May, Foucault presents lectures at Berkeley and Stanford. In December, volume one of *The History of Sexuality* is published by Gallimard.

1977   Has a sabbatical leave from the Collège de France. Cornell University Press publishes *Language, Counter-Memory, Practice: Selected Essays and Interviews* (ELCP).

1978   Collège de France course is "Security, Territory, Population." In September, Foucault goes to Tehran, Iran, and publishes article on the Iranian Revolution in the Italian daily *Corriere della Sera*.

1979   Collège de France course is "The Birth of Biopolitics." In the first issue of a new gay journal (*Gaipied*), Foucault gives an interview called "Un plaisir si simple" ("A So Simple Pleasure"). In October, Foucault gives the Tanner Lectures at Stanford University on governmentality called "Omnes et singulatum."

1980   Collège de France course is "The Government of the Living." March 21, Barthes dies; April 15, Sartre dies. In October, Foucault gives the "Howian Lectures" at Berkeley. More than 800 people arrive to hear the lecture "Truth and Subjectivity."

1981   Collège de France course is "Subjectivity and Truth." Foucault protests in favor of the Polish Solidarity movement.

1982   Collège de France course is "Hermeneutics of the Subject." In July, Foucault starts to suffer from a "chronic sinus infection." In October–November, he presents seminars at the University of Vermont on "The Technology of the Self."

1983   Collège de France course is "The Government of Self and Others." In March, Foucault meets with Habermas. In April–May, he lectures at Berkeley on the technologies of the self and has discussions with Hubert Dreyfus, Paul Rabinow, Charles Taylor, Richard Rorty, Martin Jay, and Les Lowenthal. He lectures several times on *parrēsia*. Foucault begins medical treatment for AIDS at the Paris Tarnier-Cochin Hospital under the care of Professor Jean-Paul Escande.

1984   Collège de France course is "Courage of Truth." Publication of volumes two and three of *The History of Sexuality*, subtitled *The Use of Pleasure* and *The Care of the Self*, respectively, both with Gallimard. Foucault is hospitalized in urgent care on June 3. He dies of AIDS on June 25, in the Salpêtrière Hospital in Paris (a hospital about which he had written in *History of Madness*) at the age of 58.

Secondary Works Cited

Afary, Janet, and Kevin B. Anderson. 2005. *Foucault and the Iranian Revolution: Gender and the Seductions of Islamism*. Chicago: University of Chicago Press.

Agamben, Giorgio. 1998. *Homo Sacer: Sovereign Power and Bare Life*, trans. Daniel Heller-Roazen. Stanford, CA: Stanford University Press.

    2009. *What Is an Apparatus? and Other Essays*, trans. David Kishik and Stefan Pedatella. Stanford, CA: Stanford University Press.

Allen, Amy. 1998. "Foucault's Debt to Hegel," *Philosophy Today* 42:71–79.

    2008. *The Politics of Our Selves: Power, Autonomy, and Gender in Contemporary Critical Theory*. New York: Columbia University Press.

    2009. "Discourse, Power, and Subjectivation: The Foucault/Habermas Debate Reconsidered," *The Philosophical Forum* 40, no. 1 (Spring): 1–28.

    2010. "The Entanglement of Power and Validity: Foucault and Critical Theory," in *Foucault and Philosophy*, ed. Timothy O'Leary and Christopher Falzon. Oxford: Wiley-Blackwell.

Althusser, Louis. 1969. *For Marx*, trans. Ben Brewster. London: New Left Books.

    1998. *Lettres à Franca (1961–1973)*. Paris: Stock/Imec.

    2003. *The Humanist Controversy and Other Writings (1966–1967)*, trans. G. M. Goshgarian. London: Verso.

Ansell-Pearson, Keith. 1995. "The Significance of Michel Foucault's Reading of Nietzsche: Power, the Subject, and Political Theory," in *Nietzsche: A Critical Reader*, ed. Peter R. Sedgwick. Oxford: Blackwell, pp. 13–30.

Arendt, Hannah. 1970. *On Violence*. San Diego: Harcourt Brace.

    1973. *The Origins of Totalitarianism*. New York: Harcourt Bruce Jovanovich.

Artières, Philippe. 2013. *Groupe d'information sur les prisons. Intolérable*. Paris: Gallimard.

    2013. *Révolte de la prison de Nancy. 15 janvier 1972*. Paris: Le Point du Jour.

Artières, Philippe, and Jean-François Bert. 2011. *Un succès philosophique: L'histoire de la folie à l'âge classique de Michel Foucault*. Marquette: Presses Universitaires de Caen.

Artières, Philippe, Jean-François Bert, and Luca Paltrinieri, eds. 2011. *Histoire de la folie de Michel Foucault, Regards critiques – 50 ans*. Caen: PUC-IMEC.

Artières, Philippe, and Emmanuel da Silva, eds. 2001. *Michel Foucault et la médecine: lectures et usages*. Paris: Éditions Kimé.

Artières, Philippe, Laurent Quéro, and Michelle Zancarini-Fournel. 2003. *Le groupe d'information sur les prisons: Archive d'une lutte, 1970–1971*. Paris: Editions de L'IMEC.

Ashenden, Samantha, and David Owen, eds. 1999. *Foucault contra Habermas: Recasting the Dialogue between Genealogy and Critical Theory*. London: Sage.

Badiou, Alain. 2009. *Pocket Pantheon*, trans. David Macey. London: Verso.

Barry, Andrew, Thomas Osborne, and Nikolas Rose, eds. 1996. *Foucault and Political Reason: Liberalism, Neo-liberalism, and Rationalities of Government*. Chicago: University of Chicago Press.

Barthes, Roland. 1967. *Writing Degree Zero*, trans. Annette Lavers and Colin Smith. New York: Hill and Wang.

1977. "The Death of the Author," in *Image-Music-Text*, trans. Stephen Heath. London: Fontana Press.

Basso, Elisabetta. 2007. *Michel Foucault e la Daseinsanalyse. Un'indagine metodologica*. Milan: Mimesis.

Bataille, Georges. 1985. *Visions of Excess: Selected Writings 1927–1939*, ed. Allan Stoekl. Minneapolis: University of Minnesota Press.

1987. *Death and Sensuality*, trans. Mary Dalwood. London: Marion Boyars.

1988. *Inner Experience*, trans. Leslie Anne Boldt. Albany: The SUNY Press.

1991. *The Accursed Share*, volume 1. New York: Zone Books.

Baugh, Bruce. 2003. *French Hegel: From Surrealism to Postmodernism*. New York: Routledge.

Baxter, Hugh. 1996. "Bringing Foucault into Law and Law into Foucault," *Stanford Law Review* 48, no. 2:449–479.

Bernasconi, Robert. 2010. "The Policing of Race Mixing: The Place of Bio-power within the History of Racisms," *Bioethical Inquiry* 7:205–216.

Bernauer, James. 1990. *Michel Foucault's Force of Flight*. London: Humanities Press.

2004. "Michel Foucault's Philosophy of Religion: An Introduction to the Non-Fascist Life," in *Michel Foucault and Theology: The Politics of Religious Experience*, ed. James Bernauer and Jeremy Carette. New York: Ashgate, pp. 77–97.

2006. "An Uncritical Foucault? Foucault and the Iranian Revolution," *Philosophy and Social Criticism* 32, no. 6:781–786.

Bernauer, James, and Jeremy Carrette, eds. 2004. *Michel Foucault and Theology: The Politics of Religious Experience*. Burlington, VT: Ashgate.

Bernauer, James, and Jeremy Carrette, and Michael Mahon, 2005. "Foucault's Ethical Imagination," in *The Cambridge Companion to Foucault*, 2nd ed., ed. Gary Gutting. Cambridge: Cambridge University Press, pp. 149–175.

Biebricher, Thomas. 2005. *Selbstkritik der Moderne: Foucault und Habermas im Vergleich*. Frankfurt am Main: Campus Verlag.

Binkley, Sam, and Jorge Capetillo, eds. 2010. *A Foucault for the 21st Century: Governmentality, Biopolitics and Discipline in the New Millennium* (new edition). Newcastle upon Tyne: Cambridge Scholars Publishing.

Binswanger, Ludwig. 1933. *Über Ideenflucht*. Zurich: Art. Institut Orell Füssli.

1957a. "Ellen West," in *Schizophrenie*. Pfullingen: G. Neske.

1957b. *Sigmund Freud: Reminiscences of a Friendship*, trans. Norbert Guterman. New York: Grune and Statton.

Blanchot, Maurice. 1955. "A tout extremité," *Nouvelle Revue Française* 26:285–293.

1961. "L'oubli, la déraison," *Nouvelle Revue Française* 106 (October): 676–686. Reprinted in *L'Entretien infini*. Paris: Gallimard, 1969, pp. 189–199.

1986. *Michel Foucault tel que je l'imagine*. Montpellier: Fata Morgana.

1987. "Michel Foucault as I Imagine Him," in *Foucault/Blanchot*, trans. Jeffrey Mehlman and Brian Massumis. New York: Zone Books, pp. 61–109.

1992. *The Infinite Conversation*, trans. Susan Hanson. Minneapolis: University of Minnesota Press.

1995. *The One Who Was Standing Apart From Me*, trans. Lydia Davis. Barrytown, NY: Station Hill Press.

Borgés, Jorge Luis. 2000. *Borgés: Selected Non-Fictions*, trans. Eliot Weinberger. New York: Penguin.

Boulainvilliers, Henri de. 1727. *Histoire de l'ancien gouvernement de la France*, 3 vols. The Hague: Aux depens de la Compagnie.

1732. *Essais sur la noblesse de France*. Amsterdam: N.p.

1975. *Œuvres Philosophiques*, volume 2, ed. Renee Simon. The Hague: Martinus Nijhoff.

Boyne, Roy. 1990. *Foucault and Derrida: The Other Side of Reason*. London: Unwin Hyman.

Braver, Lee. 2007. *A Thing of This World: A History of Continental Anti-Realism*. Evanston, IL: Northwestern University Press.

Bruns, Gerald L. 2011. *On Ceasing to Be Human*. Stanford, CA: Stanford University Press.

Burchell, Graham, Colin Gordon, and Peter Miller, eds. 1991. *The Foucault Effect: Studies in Governmentality*. Chicago: University of Chicago Press.

Butler, Judith. 1987. *Subjects of Desire: Hegelian Reflections in Twentieth-Century France*. New York: Columbia University Press.

1990. *Gender Trouble: Feminism and the Subversion of Identity*. London: Routledge.

1995. "Contingent Foundations: Feminism and the Question of 'Postmodernism,'" in *Feminist Contentions: A Philosophical Exchange*, ed. Linda Nicholson. New York: Routledge.

1997. *The Psychic Life of Power, Theories in Subjection*. Stanford, CA: Stanford University Press.

2002. "What Is Critique? An Essay on Foucault's Virtue," in *The Political: Readings in Continental Philosophy*, ed. David Ingram. London: Blackwell, pp. 212–226

2004. *Precarious Life: The Powers of Mourning and Violence*. London: Verso.

Canguilhem, Georges. 1955. *La Formation du Concept de Réflexe aux XVIIe et XVIIIe siècles*. Paris: Presses Universitaires de France.

1962. "Monstrosity and the Monstrous," *Diogenes* 40:27–42.

1967. "Mort de l'homme ou épuisement du cogito?" *Critique* 24:599–618.

1975. *Études d'histoire et philosophie des sciences*. Paris: Vrin.

1991. *The Normal and the Pathological*, with an introduction by Michel Foucault, trans. C. Fawcett. New York: Zone Books.

1994. *A Vital Rationalist: Selected Writings from Georges Canguilhem*, ed. F. Delaporte, trans. A. Goldhammer. New York: Zone Books.

1995. "On *Histoire de la folie* as an Event," in *Foucault and His Interlocutors*, ed. Arnold Davidson. Chicago: University of Chicago Press, pp. 28–32.

1997. "Report from Mr. Canguilhem on the Manuscript Filed by Mr. Michel Foucault, Director of the Institut Français of Hamburg, in Order to Obtain Permission to Print His Principal Thesis for the Doctor of Letters," in *Foucault and His Interlocutors*, ed. Arnold Davidson. Chicago: University of Chicago Press, pp. 23–27.

2001. *Œuvres complètes*, tome I: *Écrits philosophiques et politiques (1926–1939)*. Paris: Vrin.

2002. *Études d'histoire et de philosophie des sciences concernant les vivants et la vie*. Paris: Vrin.

2005a [1967]. "The Death of Man, or the Exhaustion of the Cogito?" trans. Catherine Porter, in *The Cambridge Companion to Foucault*, 2nd ed., ed. Gary Gutting. Cambridge: Cambridge University Press, pp. 74–94.

2005b. "The Object of the History of Science," in *Continental Philosophy of Science*, ed. Gary Gutting. London: Blackwell.

2008. *Knowledge of Life*, trans. Stefanos Geroulanos and Daniela Ginsburg. New York: Fordham University Press.

2011 *Oeuvres complètes*, Volume 1, Braunstein and Schwartz, eds., Vrin: Paris.

Carrette, Jeremy, ed. 1999. *Religion and Culture: Michel Foucault*. London: Routledge.

2000. *Foucault and Religion: Spiritual Corporality and Political Spirituality*. London: Routledge.

Catucci, Stefano. 2003. "La pensée picturale," in *Foucault, la littérature et les arts*, ed. Philippe Artières. Paris: Kimé, pp. 127–144.

Cavaillès, Jean. 1970. "On Logic and the Theory of Science," trans. Theodore J. Kisiel, in *Phenomenology and the Natural Sciences*, ed. Joseph J. Kockelman and Theodore J. Kisiel. Evanston, IL: Northwestern University Press, pp. 353–412.

Certeau, Michel de. 2002. *The Practice of Everyday Life*. Berkeley: University of California Press.

Chauncey, George. 1995. *Gay New York: Gender, Urban Culture, and the Making of the Gay Male World, 1890–1940*. New York: Basic Books.

Clastres, Pierre. 1989. *Society against the State: Essays in Political Anthropology*, trans. Robert Hurley and Abe Stein. New York: Zone Books.

Clausewitz, Carl von. 1984. *On War*, ed. Michael Howard and Peter Paret. Princeton, NJ: Princeton University Press.

Cohen, Edward. 1988. "Foucauldian Necrologies: 'Gay' 'Politics'? Politically Gay?" *Textual Practice* 2, no. 1:87–101.

Colwell, Chauncey. 1997. "Deleuze and Foucault: Series, Event, Genealogy," *Theory and Event* 1, no. 2. Accessed November 11, 2010. DOI: 10.1353/tae.1997.0004.

Comte, Auguste. 1853. *The Positive Philosophy of Auguste Comte*, trans. Harriet Martineau. London: J. Chapman.

Crampton, Jeremy. 2007. "Key Term: Conduct of Conduct." http://foucaultblog.wordpress. com/2007/05/15/key-term-conduct-of-conduct/. Accessed December 22, 2010.

Crampton, Jeremy, and Stuart Elden, eds. 2007. *Space, Knowledge and Power: Foucault and Geography*. Aldershot: Ashgate.

Cutrofello, Andrew. 1993. "A History of Reason in the Age of Insanity: The Deconstruction of Foucault in Hegel's Phenomenology," *Owl of Minerva* 25, no. 1:15–21.

Daston, Lorraine, and Francisco Vidal, eds. 2004. *The Moral Authority of Nature*. Chicago: University of Chicago Press.

Davidson, Arnold. 1986. "Archaeology, Genealogy, Ethics," in *Foucault: A Critical Reader*, ed. David Couzens Hoy. Oxford: Blackwell, pp. 221–234.

    1991. "The Horror of Monsters," in *The Boundaries of Humanity*, ed. James Sheehan and Morton Sosna. Berkeley: University of California Press, pp. 36–68.

    1994. "Ethics as Ascetics: Foucault, the History of Ethics, and Ancient Thought," in *The Cambridge Companion to Foucault*, ed. Gary Gutting. Cambridge: Cambridge University Press, pp. 115–140 (2nd ed. 2005, pp. 123–148).

    ed. 1997. *Foucault and His Interlocutors*. Chicago: University of Chicago Press.

    2001. *The Emergence of Sexuality: Historical Epistemology and the Formation of Concepts*. Cambridge, MA: Harvard University Press.

    2003. "Introduction," in Michel Foucault, *"Society Must Be Defended," Lectures at the Collège de France, 1975–76*, trans. David Macey. New York: Picador.

    2008. "In Praise of Counter-Conduct." http://humweb.ucsc.edu/foucaultacrossthedisci-plines/9_Davidson.mp3. Accessed December 22, 2010.

Deacon, Roger. 2003. "Clausewitz and Foucault: War and Power," *Scientia Militaria: South African Journal of Military Studies* 31, no. 1:37–48.

Dean, Mitchell. 2001. "'Demonic Societies': Liberalism, Biopolitics, and Sovereignty," in *States of Imagination: Ethnographic Explorations of the Postcolonial State*, ed. Thomas Blom Hansen and Finn Stepputat. Durham, NC: Duke University Press, pp. 41–64.

Dean, Tim, and Christopher Lane, eds. 2001. *Homosexuality and Psychoanalysis*. Chicago: University of Chicago Press.

Defert, Daniel, and Jacques Donzelot. 1976. "La charnière des prisons," in *Magazine littéraire* nos. 112/113:33–35.

Deleuze, Gilles. 1983. *Nietzsche and Philosophy*, trans. Hugh Tomlinson. New York: Columbia University Press.

    1988. *Foucault*, trans. Seán Hand. Minneapolis: University of Minnesota Press.

    1990. *The Logic of Sense*, trans. Mark Lester. New York: Columbia University Press.

    1994. *Difference and Repetition*, trans. Paul Patton. New York: Columbia University Press.

    1995. *Negotiations: 1972–1990*, trans. Martin Joughin. New York: Columbia University Press.

    1997. "Desire and Pleasure," in *Foucault and His Interlocuters*, ed. Arnold Davidson. Chicago: University of Chicago Press, pp. 183–192. Originally published as "Désir et Plaisir," *Magazine litteraire* no. 325 (October 1994): 57–65.

2004. *Desert Islands and Other Texts 1953–1974*, ed. David Lapoujade, trans. Michael Taormina. New York: Semiotext(e).

2007. *Two Regimes of Madness: Texts and Interviews 1975–1995*, trans. Ames Hodges and Mike Taormina. New York: Semiotext(e) [revised edition].

Deleuze, Gilles, and Félix Guattari. 1987. *A Thousand Plateaus: Capitalism and Schizophrenia*, trans. Brian Massumi. Minneapolis: University of Minnesota Press.

1994. *What Is Philosophy?*, trans. Hugh Tomlinson and Graham Burchell. New York: Columbia University Press.

Deleuze, Gilles, and Claire Parnet. 2007. *Dialogues II*, rev. ed., trans. Hugh Tomlinson and Barbara Habberjam. New York: Columbia University Press.

Derrida, Jacques. 1978. *Writing and Difference*, trans. Alan Bass. Chicago: University of Chicago Press, pp. 31–63 (repr. New York: Routledge, 2001).

1985. "The Ends of Man," in *Margins of Philosophy*, trans. Alan Bass. Chicago: University of Chicago Press, pp. 109–136.

1998. "'To Do Justice to Freud': The History of Madness in the Age of Psychoanalysis," trans. Michael Naas and Pascale-Anne Brault, in Jacques Derrida, *Resistances of Psychoanalysis*. Stanford, CA: Stanford University Press, pp. 70–118.

2009. *The Beast and the Sovereign*, volume 1, trans. G. Bennington. Chicago: University of Chicago Press.

2011. *Voice and Phenomenon*, trans. Leonard Lawlor. Evanston, IL: Northwestern University Press.

2012. *Séminare: La peine de mort, volume 1 (1999–2000)*. Paris: Galilée.

Derrida, Jacques, and Elizabeth Roudinesco. 2004. *For What Tomorrow… A Dialogue*, trans. J. Fort. Stanford, CA: Stanford University Press.

Detel, Wolfgang. 2005. *Foucault and Classical Antiquity: Power, Ethics and Knowledge*, trans. David Wigg-Wolf. Cambridge: Cambridge University Press.

Detienne, Marcel. 1999. *The Masters of Truth in Archaic Greece*. Cambridge, MA: Zone Books.

Devyer, André. 1973. *Le sang épuré*. Brussels: Editions de Université de Bruxelles.

D'Hondt, Jacques. 1986. "On Rupture and Destruction in History," *Clio* 15, no. 4:345–358.

Dickinson, Edward Ross. 2004. "Biopolitics, Fascism, Democracy: Some Reflections in Our Disclosure about Modernity," *Central European History* 37, no. 1:1–48.

Dillon, Michael, and Andrew Neal, eds. 2008. *Foucault on Politics, Security, and War*. London: Palgrave.

Djaballah, Marc. 2008. *Kant, Foucault, and Forms of Experience*. London: Routledge.

2013. "Foucault on Kant, Enlightenment, and Being Critical," in *A Companion to Foucault*, ed. Christopher Falzon, Timothy O'Leary, and Jana Sawicki. Oxford: Blackwell, pp. 264–281.

Dosse, François. 1998. *History of Structuralism*, trans. Deborah Glassman, 2 vols. Minneapolis: University of Minnesota Press.

2010. *Gilles Deleuze and Félix Guattari: Intersecting Lives*, trans. Deborah Glassman. New York: Columbia University Press.

Dreyfus, Hubert L., and Paul Rabinow. 1983. *Michel Foucault: Beyond Structuralism and Hermeneutics*, 2nd ed. Chicago: University of Chicago Press.

Driver, Felix. 1985. "Power, Space and the Body: A Critical Assessment of *Foucault's Discipline and Punish*," *Environment and Planning D: Society and Space* 3:425–446.

Droit, Roger-Pol. 2004. *Michel Foucault: Entretiens*. Paris: Odile Jacob.

Elden, Stuart. 2001a. "The Constitution of the Normal: Monsters and Masturbation at the Collège de France," *Boundary 2*, 28, no.1:91–105.

2001b. *Mapping the Present: Heidegger, Foucault and the Project of a Spatial History*. London: Continuum.

2004. "The War of Races and the Constitution of the State: Foucault's '*Il faut défendre la souété*' and the Politics of Calculation," *Boundary 2*, 29, no. 1:125–151.

2007. "Governmentality, Calculation, Territory," *Environment and Planning D: Society and Space* 25:562–580.

2008. "Strategies for Waging Peace: Foucault as *collaborateur*," in *Foucault on Politics, Security, and War*, ed. Michael Dillon and Andrew Neal. London: Palgrave, pp. 21–39.

Ellis, Harold A. 1988. *Boulainvilliers and the French Monarchy*. Ithaca, NY: Cornell University Press.

Eribon, Didier. 1991. *Michel Foucault*, trans. Betsy Wing. Cambridge, MA: Harvard University Press.

1992. *Faut-il brûler Dumézil? Mythologie, Science et Politique*. Paris: Flammarion.

2001. "Michel Foucault's Histories of Sexuality," *GLQ: A Journal of Lesbian and Gay Studies* 7, no. 1:31–86.

Esposito, Roberto. 2008. *Bíos: Biopolitics and Philosophy*, trans. Timothy Campbell. Minneapolis and London: University of Minnesota Press.

Ewald, François. 1990. "Norms, Discipline, and the Law," trans. Marjorie Beale, *Representations* 30:138–161.

1999. "Foucault and the Contemporary Scene," *Philosophy and Social Criticism* 25, no. 3: 81–91.

Ferguson, Adam. 1966 [1767]. *An Essay on the History of Civil Society*, ed. Duncan Forbes. Edinburgh: Edinburgh University Press.

Figal, Sara Eigen. 2008. *Heredity, Race, and the Birth of the Modern*. New York: Routledge.

Fillion, Réal. 2005. "Foucault after Hyppolite: Toward an A-Theistic Theodicy," *Southern Journal of Philosophy* 43, no. 1:79–93.

Flynn, Thomas R. 1985. "Truth and Subjectivation in the Later Foucault," *The Journal of Philosophy* 82, no. 10:531–540.

1988. "Michel Foucault as *Parrhesiast*: His Last Course at the Collège de France," in *The Final Foucault*, ed. James Bernauer and David Rasmussen. Cambridge, MA: The MIT Press, pp. 102–117.

1991. "Foucault and the Spaces of History," *The Monist* 74, no. 2 (April): 165–186.

1994. "Foucault's Mapping of History," in *The Cambridge Companion to Foucault*, ed. Gary Gutting. Cambridge: Cambridge University Press, pp. 28–46.

1997. *Sartre, Foucault, and Historical Reason: Toward an Existentialist Theory of History*. Chicago: University of Chicago Press.

2005. *Sartre, Foucault, and Historical Reason*, volume 2: *A Poststructuralist Mapping of History*. Chicago: University of Chicago Press.

Foucault, Michel. 1980. "Prison Talk," in *Power/Knowledge: Selected Interviews and other Writings, 1972–1977*, ed. Colin Gordon. New York: Pantheon Books, pp. 37–54.

1983. "The Subject and Power," in *Beyond Structuralism and Hermeneutics*, ed. Hubert L. Dreyfus and Paul Rabinow. Chicago: University of Chicago Press, pp. 208–228.

1988. "Iran: The Spirit of a World without Spirit," in *Michel Foucault. Politics, Philosophy, Culture: Interview and other Writings, 1977–1984*, ed. Lawrence D. Kritzman. New York: Routledge, pp. 211–224.

1998. "The Thought of the Outside," in *Aesthetics, Method, and Epistemology: Essential Works of Foucault, 1954–1984*, ed. James D. Faubion. New York: The New Press, pp. 147–169.

Foucault, Michel, Blandine Kriegel, Anne Thalamy, Francois Beguin, and Bruno Fortier. 1976. *Généalogie des équipements de normalisation*. Fontenay sous-Bois: CERFI.

Fraser, Nancy. 1989. "Foucault on Modern Power: Empirical Insights and Normative Confusions," in Nancy Fraser, *Unruly Practices: Power, Discourse and Gender in Contemporary Social Theory*. Minneapolis: University of Minnesota Press.

Freud, Sigmund. 1949. *A Case of Hysteria: Three Essays on the Theory of Sexuality, and Other Works (1901–1905)*. The Standard Edition of the Complete Psychological Works of Sigmund Freud, volume 7. London: The Hogarth Press.

1955. *Totem and Taboo, and other Works (1913–1914)*. The Standard Edition of the Complete Psychological Works of Sigmund Freud, volume 12. London: The Hogarth Press.

Furet, Francois. 1984. "Two Historical Legitimations of Eighteenth-Century French Society: Mably and Boulainvilliers," in *The Workshop of History*, trans. J. Mandelbaum. Chicago: University of Chicago Press, pp. 125–139.

Gadamer, Hans-Georg. 1990. *Truth and Method*, trans. Joel Weinsheimer and Donald G. Marshall, 2nd rev. ed. New York: Crossroads.

Garlick, Steve. 2002. "The Beauty of Friendship: Foucault, Masculinity and the Work of Art," *Philosophy and Social Criticism* 28:558–577.

Gasché, Rodolphe. 1986. *The Tain of the Mirror*. Cambridge, MA: Harvard University Press.

Gauchet, Marcel, and Gladis Swain. 1980. *La pratique de l'esprit humain*. Paris: Gallimard.

Geroulanos, Stefanos. 2010. *An Atheism That Is Not Humanist Emerges in French Thought*. Stanford, CA: Stanford University Press.

Geulen, Christian. 2004. *Wahlverwandte. Rassendiskurs und Nationalismus im späten 19. Jahrhundert*. Hamburg: Hamburger.

Ginsburg, Nancy, and Roy Ginsburg. 1999. *Psychoanalysis and Culture at the Millennium*. New Haven, CT: Yale University Press.

Girardin, Jean-Claude. 1998. "Avec Michel Foucault, Histoire, théorie politique et racism," *Les Temps Modernes* 601:178–196.

Glucksmann, André. 1975. *La Cuisinière et le mangeur d'hommes*. Paris: Seuil.

Golder, Ben, and Peter Fitzpatrick. 2009. *Foucault's Law*. London: Routledge.

——— eds. 2010. *Foucault and Law*. Surrey: Ashgate.

Grace, Wendy. 2009. "*Faux Amis*: Foucault and Deleuze on Sexuality and Desire," *Critical Inquiry* 36, no. 1: 52–75.

Granel, Gerard. 1967. "Jacques Derrida et la rature de l'origine," *Critique* 246:887–905.

Gregory, Derek. 1994. *Geographical Imaginations*. Oxford: Blackwell.

Gros, Frédéric. 1996. *Michel Foucault*. Paris: Presses Universitaire de France.

——— 1997. *Foucault et la folie*. Paris: Presses Universitaires de France.

——— 2004. "Michel Foucault, Une Philosophie de la Vérité," in *Michel Foucault: Philosophie Anthologie*, ed. Arnold I. Davidson and Frédéric Gros. Paris: Éditions Gallimard, pp. 11–25.

——— 2005. "Le Souci de Soi chez Michel Foucault," *Philosophy and Social Criticism* 31, nos. 5–6:697–708.

Gros, Frédéric, and Carlos Lévy, eds. 2003. *Foucault et la philosophie antique*. Paris: Kimé.

Guattari, Félix, ed. 1973. *Trois Milliards de Pervers: Grand Encyclopédie des Homosexualités*. Paris: Recherches, Mars.

Guerlac, Suzanne. 1997. *Literary Polemics: Sartre, Valéry, Breton*. Stanford, CA: Stanford University Press.

Gutting, Gary. 1989. *Michel Foucault's Archaeology of Scientific Reason*. Cambridge: Cambridge University Press.

——— 1994. *The Cambridge Companion to Foucault*. Cambridge: Cambridge University Press.

——— 2002. "Foucault's Philosophy of Experience," *Boundary 2*, 29, no. 2:69–85.

——— 2005. *Continental Philosophy of Science*. London: Blackwell.

Haber, Stéphane. 2006. *Critique de l'antinaturalisme: Études sur Foucault, Butler, Habermas*. Paris: Presses Universitaires de France.

Habermas, Jürgen. 1984. *The Theory of Communicative Action*, volume 1: *Reason and the Rationalization of Society*, trans. Thomas McCarthy. Boston: Beacon Press.

——— 1987a. *The Theory of Communicative Action*, volume 2: *Lifeworld and System: A Critique of Functionalist Reason*, trans. Thomas McCarthy. Boston: Beacon Press.

——— 1987b. *The Philosophical Discourse of Modernity: Twelve Lectures*, trans. Frederick G. Lawrence. Cambridge, MA: The MIT Press.

——— 1990. *Moral Consciousness and Communicative Action*, trans. Christian Lenhardt and Shierry Weber Nicholsen. Cambridge, MA: The MIT Press.

1991. "A Reply," in *Communicative Action: Essays on Habermas's Theory of Communicative Action*, ed. Axel Honneth and Hans Joas. Cambridge, MA: The MIT Press.

1994. "Taking Aim at the Heart of the Present: On Foucault's Lecture on Kant's *What Is Enlightenment?*" in *Critique and Power: Recasting the Foucault/Habermas Debate*, ed. Michael Kelly. Cambridge, MA: The MIT Press.

2001. "Reflections on Communicative Pathology," in *On the Pragmatics of Social Interaction*, trans. Barbara Fultner. Cambridge, MA: The MIT Press.

2003. "Introduction: Realism after the Linguistic Turn," in *Truth and Justification*, ed. Barbara Fultner. Cambridge, MA: The MIT Press.

Hacking, Ian. 2002. *Historical Ontology*. Cambridge, MA: Harvard University Press.

2006. "Foreword," in Michel Foucault, *History of Madness*. London: Routledge.

Hadot, Pierre. 1995. *Philosophy as a Way of Life: Spiritual Exercises from Socrates to Foucault*, ed. Arnold Davidson. Oxford: Wiley-Blackwell.

2004. *Le voile d'Isis: Essai sur l'histoire de l'idée de nature*. Paris: Gallimard.

Halfin, Igal. 2003. *Terror in My Soul: Communist Autobiographies on Trial*. Cambridge, MA: Harvard University Press.

Halperin, David. 1995. *Saint Foucault: Towards a Gay Hagiography*. Oxford: Oxford University Press.

1996. "Homosexuality," in *The Oxford Classical Dictionary*, ed. Simon Hornblower and Antony Spawforth. Oxford: Oxford University Press, pp. 720–723.

1998. "Forgetting Foucault: Acts, Identities, and the History of Sexuality," *Representations* 63 (Summer): 93–120.

2002a. "The First Homosexuality?" in *The Sleep of Reason: Erotic Experience and Sexual Ethics in Ancient Greece and Rome*, ed. Martha Nussbaum and Julia Sihlova. Chicago: University of Chicago Press, pp. 229–268.

2002b. *How to Do the History of Homosexuality*. Chicago: University of Chicago Press.

Han, Béatrice. 2002. *Foucault's Critical Project: Between the Transcendental and the Historical*, trans. Edward Pile. Stanford, CA: Stanford University Press.

Han-Pile, Béatrice. 2003. "Foucault and Heidegger on Kant and Finitude," in *Foucault and Heidegger: Critical Encounters*, ed. Alan Milchman and Alan Rosenberg. Minneapolis: University of Minnesota Press, pp. 127–162.

2005. "Is Early Foucault a historian? History, history and the Analytic of Finitude," in *Philosophy and Social Criticism* 3 (September): 585–608.

Hannah, Matthew. 2000. *Governmentality and the Mastery of Territory in Nineteenth-Century America*. Cambridge: Cambridge University Press.

Hanssen, Beatrice. 2000. *Critique of Violence: Between Poststructuralism and Critical Theory*. London: Routledge.

Hart, Kevin. 2004. *The Dark Gaze: Maurice Blanchot and the Sacred*. Chicago: University of Chicago Press.

Heidegger, Martin. 1962. *Being and Time*, trans. John Macquarrie and Edward Robinson. New York: Harper and Row.

1982. *The Basic Problems of Phenomenology*, trans. Albert Hofstader. Bloomington: Indiana University Press.

1990. *Kant and the Problem of Metaphysics*, trans. Richard Taft. Bloomington: Indiana University Press.

2010. *Being and Time*, trans. Joan Stambaugh, revised with a Foreword by Dennis J. Schmidt. Albany: The SUNY Press.

Herzog, Max. 1994. *Weltentwürfe: Ludwig Binswangers phänomenologische Psychologie*. Berlin: Walter de Gruyter.

Hetherington, Kevin. 1997. *The Badlands of Modernity: Heterotopia and Social Ordering*. London: Routledge.

Heyes, Cressida. 2007. *Self-Transformations: Foucault, Ethics, and Normalized Bodies*. New York: Oxford University Press.

Hindess, Barry. 1996. "Liberal Government and Techniques of the Self," in *Foucault and Political Reason*, ed. Andrew Barry, Thomas Osborne, and Nikolas Rose. Chicago: University of Chicago Press, pp. 19–36.

Hollywood, Amy. 2002. *Sensible Ecstasy: Mysticicsm, Sexual Difference, and the Demands of History*. Chicago: University of Chicago Press.

Holt, Thomas C. 2001. "Pouvoir, savoir et race. A propos du cours de Michel Foucault 'Il faut defendre la societe,'" in *Lectures de Michel Foucault*, volume 1: *A propos de "Il faut defendre la societe*," ed. Jean-Claude Zancarini. Paris: ENS Editions, pp. 81–96.

Honneth, Axel. 1991. *The Critique of Power: Reflective Stages in a Critical Social Theory*, trans. Kenneth Baynes. Cambridge, MA: The MIT Press.

Horkheimer, Max, and Theodor Adorno. 2002. *Dialectic of Enlightenment: Philosophical Fragments*, trans. Edmund Jephcott. Stanford, CA: Stanford University Press.

Howard, Jean E. 2004. "The New Historicism in Renaissance Studies," in *Shakespeare: An Anthology of Criticism and Theory 1945–2000*, ed. Russ McDonald. Malden, MA: Blackwell, pp. 458–480.

Hoy, David Couzens. 1986. "Power, Repression, Progress: Foucault, Lukács, and the Frankfurt School," in *Foucault: A Critical Reader*, ed. David Couzens Hoy. Oxford: Blackwell.

Hoy, David Couzens, and Thomas McCarthy. 1994. *Critical Theory*. Oxford: Blackwell.

Huffer, Lynne. 2010. *Mad for Foucault: Rethinking the Foundations of Queer Theory*. New York: Columbia University Press.

Huneman, Philippe. 1998. *Bichat, la vie et la mort*. Paris: Presses Universitaires de France.

Hunt, Alan, and Gary Wickham. 1994. *Foucault and Law: Towards a Sociology of Law as Governance*. London: Pluto Press.

Husserl, Edmund. 1965. *Phenomenology and the Crisis of Philosophy*, trans. Quentin Lauer. New York: Harper Torchbooks.

　1970. *The Crisis of European Sciences and Transcendental Phenomenology*, trans. David Carr. Evanston, IL: Northwestern University Press.

　1976. *Die Krisis der Europaeischen Wissenschaften und die transzendentale Phaenomenologie*, Husserliana, Band VI. The Hague: Nijhoff.

　1977. *Cartesian Meditation*, trans. Dorian Cairns. The Hague: Martinus Nijhoff.

　1997. *Psychological and Transcendental Phenomenology and the Confrontation with Heidegger (1927–1931)*, trans. and ed. Thomas Sheehan and Richard E. Palmer. Dordrecht: Kluwer Academic Publishers.

Hyppolite, Jean. 1974. *Genesis and Structure of Hegel's Phenomenology of Spirit*, trans. Samuel Cherniak and John Heckman. Evanston, IL: Northwestern University Press.

　1991. *Figures de la pensée philosophique*. Paris: Quadrige Presses Universitaires de France.

　1997. *Logic and Existence*, trans. Leonard Lawlor and Amit Sen. Albany: The SUNY Press.

Illich, Ivan. 1976. *Medical Nemesis: The Expropriation of Health*. New York: Pantheon.

Ingram, David. 2005. "Foucault and Habermas," in *The Cambridge Companion to Foucault*, 2nd ed., ed. Gary Gutting. Cambridge: Cambridge University Press.

James, William. 1981 [1907]. *Pragmatism*. Indianapolis: Hackett Publishing Company.

Jameson, Fredric. 2009. *Valences of the Dialectic*. London: Verso.

Jay, Martin. 1993. *Downcast Eyes: The Denigration of Vision in Twentieth-Century French Thought*. Berkeley: University of California Press.

　2006. *Songs of Experience: Variations on a Universal Theme*. Berkeley: University of California Press.

Jessop, Robert. 2006. "From Micro-powers to Governmentality: Foucault's Work on Statehood, State Formation, Statecraft and State Power," *Political Geography* 26, no. 1:34–40.

Kant, Immanuel. 2003. "Attempt to Introduce the Concept of Negative Magnitudes into Philosophy (1763)," in *The Cambridge Edition of the Works of Immanuel Kant, Theoretical Philosophy 1755–1770*, trans. and ed. David Walford, with Ralf Meerbote. Cambridge: Cambridge University Press, pp. 203–241.

     2006. *Anthropology from a Pragmatic Point of View*, trans. Robert B. Louden and Manfred Kuehn. Cambridge: Cambridge University Press.

Kantorowicz, Ernst H. 1997. *The King's Two Bodies: A Study in Mediaeval Political Thought*. Princeton, NJ: Princeton University Press.

Kaufmann, Eleanor. 2001. *The Delirium of Praise: Blanchot, Deleuze, Foucault, Klossowski*. Baltimore: The Johns Hopkins University Press.

Kelly, Mark G. E. 2009. *The Political Philosophy of Michel Foucault*. New York: Routledge.

Kelly, Michael, ed. 1994. *Critique and Power: Recasting the Foucault/Habermas Debate*. Cambridge, MA: The MIT Press.

Kharkhordin, Oleg. 1999. *The Collective and the Individual in Russia: A Study of Practices*. Berkeley: University of California Press.

Kojève, Alexandre. 1947. *Introduction à la lecture de Hegel*. Paris: Gallimard.

Koopman, Colin. 2013. *Genealogy as Critique: Problematization and Transformation in Foucault and Others*. Bloomington: Indiana University Press.

     2010. "Historical Critique or Transcendental Critique in Foucault: Two Kantian Lineages," *Foucault Studies* 8:100–121.

Kreager, Philip. 1993. "Histories of Demography: A Review Article," *Population Studies* 47, no. 3 (November): 519–539.

Kristeva, Julia. 1984. *Revolution in Poetic Language*, trans. Margaret Waller. New York: Columbia University Press.

Kuhn, Roland, and Henry Maldiney. 1971. "Préface," in Ludwig Binswanger, *Introduction à l'analyse existentielle*. Paris: Les Éditions de Minuit.

Kvanvig, Jonathan. 2008. "Coherentist Theories of Epistemic Justification," in *The Stanford Encyclopedia of Philosophy (Fall 2008 Edition)*, ed. Edward N. Zalta. http://plato.stanford.edu/archives/fall2008/entries/justep-coherence/.

Lanzoni, Susan. 2003. "An Epistemology of the Clinic: Ludwig Binswanger's Phenomenology of the Other," *Critical Inquiry* 30:160–186.

     2005. "The Enigma of Subjectivity: Ludwig Binswanger's Existential Anthropology of Mania," *History of the Human Sciences* 18:23–41.

Laplanche, Jean, and Jean-Bertrand Pontalis. 1973. *The Language of Psycho-analysis*. New York: Norton and Company.

Lawlor, Leonard. 2003. *Thinking through French Philosophy: The Being of the Question*. Bloomington: Indiana University Press.

     2006. *The Implication of Immanence: Towards a New Concept of Life*. New York: Fordham University Press.

LeBlanc, Guillaume. 2005. *L'Esprit des sciences humaines*. Paris: Vrin.

     2010. *Canguilhem et la vie humaine*. Paris: Presses Universitaires de France.

Lecourt, Dominique. 2008. *Georges Canguilhem*. Paris: Presses Universitaires de France.

Lemke, Thomas. 1997. *Eine Kritik der politischen Vernunft – Foucaults Analyse der modernen Gouvernementalität*. Berlin/Hamburg: Argument.

Levi-Strauss, Claude. 1963. *Structural Anthropology*, trans. Claire Jacobson and Brooke Grundfest Schoepf. New York: Basic Books.

Lévy, Bernard-Henri. 1977. *La barbarie à visage humaine*. Paris: Grasset.

Livrozet, Serge. 1999. *De la prison à la révolte*. Paris: L'esprit frappeur.

Locke, John. 1960 [1690]. *The Second Treatise of Government*, ed. Peter Laslett. Cambridge: Cambridge University Press.

Lorenzini, Daniele. 2008. "'El Cinismo Hace de la Vida Una *Aleturgie*.' Apuntes Para Una Relectura del Recorrido Filosófico del Último Michel Foucault," *Revista Laguna* 23:63–90.

2010. "Para Acabar con la Verdad-Demostración. Bachelard, Canguilhem, Foucault y La Historia de los 'Regímenes de Verdad,'" *Revista Laguna* 26:9–34.

Lynch, Richard A. 1998. "Is Power All There Is? Michel Foucault and the 'Omnipresence' of Power Relations," *Philosophy Today* 42:65–70.

Macey, David. 1993. *The Lives of Michel Foucault.* New York: Vintage.

Macherey, Pierre. 1986. "Aux Sources de 'Histoire de la folie,'" *Critique* 442 (August–September): 753–774.

Machiavelli, Niccolò. 2008 [1513]. *The Prince*, trans. Peter Bondanella. New York: Oxford University Press.

Mader, Mary Beth. 2011. "Modern Living and Vital Race: Foucault and the Science of Life," *Foucault Studies* 12:97–112.

Magiros, Angelika. 1995. *Foucaults Beitrag zur Rassismustheorie.* Hamburg: Argument.

Mahon, Michael. 1992. *Foucault's Nietzschean Genealogy: Truth, Power, and the Subject.* Albany: The SUNY Press.

Marcuse, Herbert. 2007. "Repressive Tolerance," in *The Essential Marcuse: Selected Writings of the Philosopher and Social Critic Herbert Marcuse*, ed. Andrew Feenberg and William Leiss. Boston: Beacon Press.

Marks, John. 2008. "Michel Foucault: Bio-politics and Biology," in *Foucault in an Age of Terror: Essays on Biopolitics and the Defence of Society*, ed. Stephen Morton and Stephen Bygrave. London: Palgrave Macmillan, pp. 88–105.

Martin, Luther H., Huck Gutman, and Patrick H. Hutton, eds. 1988. *Technologies of the Self: A Seminar with Michel Foucault.* Amherst: University of Massachusetts Press.

May, Todd. 1993. *Between Genealogy and Epistemology: Psychology, Politics, and Knowledge in the Thought of Michel Foucault.* University Park: Pennsylvania State University Press.

1994. *The Political Theory of Poststructuralist Anarchism.* University Park: Pennsylvania State University Press.

2006. *The Philosophy of Foucault.* Montreal and Kingston: McGill-Queen's University Press.

2011. "Foucault's Conception of Freedom," in *Michel Foucault: Key Concepts*, ed. Dianna Taylor. Durham, NC: Acumen Publishing, pp. 73–81.

Mbembe, Achille. 2008. "Neuropolitics," in *Foucault in an Age of Terror*, ed. Stephen Morton and Stephen Bygrave. London: Palgrave Macmillan, pp. 152–182.

McCarthy, Thomas. 1991. "The Critique of Impure Reason: Foucault and the Frankfurt School," in *Ideals and Illusions: On Reconstruction and Deconstruction in Contemporary Critical Theory*, ed. Thomas McCarthy. Cambridge, MA: The MIT Press, pp. 43–75.

McGushin, Edward. 2005. "Foucault's Cartesian Meditations," *International Philosophical Quarterly* 45:41–59.

2007. *Foucault's Askesis: An Introduction to Philosophical Life.* Evanston, IL: Northwestern University Press.

McLaren, Margaret A. 2006. "From Practices of the Self to Politics: Foucault and Friendship," *Philosophy Today* 50:195–201.

McSweeney, John. 2005. "Foucault and Theology," *Foucault Studies* 2:117–144.

McWhorter, Ladelle. 1994. "The Event of Truth: Foucault's Response to Structuralism," *Philosophy Today* 38, no. 2:159–166.

1999. *Bodies and Pleasures: Foucault and the Politics of Sexual Normalization.* Bloomington: Indiana University Press.

2009. *Racism and Sexual Oppression in Anglo-America.* Bloomington: Indiana University Press.

Mendieta, Eduardo. 2004. "Plantations, Ghettos, Prisons: U.S. Racial Geographics," *Philosophy and Geography* 7, no. 1:43–59.

Merleau-Ponty, Maurice. 1964a. *Signs*, trans. Richard C. McCleary. Evanston, IL: Northwestern University Press.

1964b. *Sense and Non-Sense*, trans. Hubert L. Dreyfus and Patricia Allen Dreyfus. Evanston, IL: Northwestern University Press.

1968. *The Visible and the Invisible*, trans. Alphonso Lingis. Evanston, IL: Northwestern University Press.

1970. *Themes from the Lectures*, trans. John O'Neill. Evanston, IL: Northwestern University Press.

1973. *Prose of the World*, trans. John O'Neill. Evanston, IL: Northwestern University Press.

2010. *Institution and Passivity*, trans. Leonard Lawlor and Heath Massey. Evanston, IL: Northwestern University Press.

2011. *Phenomenology of Perception*, trans. Donald Landes. London: Routledge.

Milchman, Alan, and Alan Rosenberg, eds. 2003. *Foucault and Heidegger: Critical Encounters*. Minneapolis: University of Minnesota Press.

Miller, James. 1993. *The Passion of Michel Foucault*. New York: Simon and Schuster.

Mitchell, Andrew J., and Jason Kemp Winfree, eds. 2009. *The Obsessions of Georges Bataille: Community and Communication*. Albany: The SUNY Press.

Mol, Annemarie. 2008. *The Logic of Care*. New York: Routledge.

Montag, Warren. 2002. *Louis Althusser*. London: Palgrave.

Moore, Carmella C., and Holly F. Matthews. 2001. *The Psychology of Cultural Experience*. Cambridge: Cambridge University Press.

Morel, Benedict Augustin. 1857. *Traité des dégenerescences physiques, intellectuelles et morales*. Paris: Jean-Baptiste Baillière.

Morton, Stephen, and Stephen Bygrave, eds. 2008. *Foucault in an Age of Terror*. London: Palgrave Macmillan.

Moss, Jeremy, ed. 1998. *The Later Foucault: Politics and Philosophy*. London: Sage.

Naas, Michael. 2003. "Derrida's Watch/Foucault's Pendulum: A Final Impetus to the Cogito Debate," in Michael Naas, *Taking on the Tradition: Jacques Derrida and the Legacies of Deconstruction*. Stanford, CA: Stanford University Press, pp. 57–75.

Nail, Thomas, Nicolae Morar, and Daniel Smith, eds. 2013. *Between Deleuze and Foucault*. London: Continuum.

Nealon, Jeffrey T. 2007. *Foucault beyond Foucault: Power and Its Intensifications since 1984*. Stanford, CA: Stanford University Press.

Neurath, Otto. 1983 [1935]. "The Unity of Science as a Task," in *Philosophical Papers 1913–1946*, ed. Robert S. Cohen and Marie Neurath. Dordrecht: D. Reidel, pp. 115–120.

Nietzsche, Friedrich. 1966. *Beyond Good and Evil*, trans. Walter Kaufmann. New York: Random House.

1967a. *Kritische Gesamtausgabe*, ed. Giorgio Colli and Mazzino Montinari. Berlin: Walter de Gruyter.

1967b. *On the Genealogy of Morals*, trans. Walter Kaufmann. New York: Random House.

1967c. *Le Gai Savoir. Œuvres Philosophiques Complètes*, trans. Pierre Klossowski. Paris: Éditions Gallimard.

1968. *Twilight of the Idols*, trans. Reginald J. Hollingdale. Middlesex: Penguin Books.

1974. *The Gay Science*, trans. Walter Kaufman. New York: Random House.

1982. *Daybreak*, trans. Reginald. J. Hollingdale. Cambridge: Cambridge University Press.

1989. *On the Genealogy of Morals*, trans. Walter Kaufmann. New York: Vintage Books.

1996. *On the Genealogy of Morals*, trans. Douglas Smith. Oxford: Oxford University Press.

Oksala, Johanna. 2005. *Foucault on Freedom*. Cambridge: Cambridge University Press.

2010. "Violence and the Biopolitics of Modernity," *Foucault Studies* 10:23–43.

2011a. "Lines of Fragility: A Foucauldian Critique of Violence," in *Philosophy and the Return of Violence: Studies from this Widening Gyre*, ed. Christopher Yates and Nathan Eckstrand. New York: Continuum, pp. 154–170.

2011b. "Violence and Neoliberal Governmentality," *Constellations: An International Journal of Critical and Democratic Theory* 18:474–486.

2011c. "Sexual Experience: Foucault, Phenomenology, and Feminist Theory," *Hypatia* 26, no. 1:207–223.

O'Leary, Timothy. 2002. *Foucault and the Art of Ethics*. London: Continuum.

2008. "Foucault, Experience, Literature," *Foucault Studies* 5:5–25.

Oyama, Susan, Paul Griffiths, and Russell Gray, eds. 2001. *Cycles of Contingency: Developmental Systems and Evolution*. Cambridge, MA: The MIT Press.

Patton, Paul. 2010a. *Deleuzian Concepts: Philosophy, Colonization, Politics*. Stanford, CA: Stanford University Press.

2010b. "Foucault and Normative Political Philosophy," in *Foucault and Philosophy*, ed. Timothy O'Leary and Christopher Falzon. London: Wiley-Blackwell, pp. 204–221.

2010c. "Activism, Philosophy and Actuality in Deleuze and Foucault," *Deleuze Studies* 4 (Supplement). Accessed December 6, 2010. DOI: 10.3366/dls.2010.0207.

Peeters, Benoît. 2010. *Derrida*. Paris: Flammarion.

Perrot, Michelle. 1980. *L'impossible prison: Recherches sur le système pénitentiaire au XIXe siècle*. Paris: Seuil.

Philo, Chris. 1992. "Foucault's Geographies," *Environment and Planning D: Society and Space* 10, no. 2:137–161.

2004. *A Geographical History of Institutional Provision for the Insane from Medieval Times to the 1860s in England and Wales: The Space Reserved for Insanity*. Lewiston: Edwin Mellen.

Pinguet, Maurice. 1986. "Les Années d'apprentissage," *Le Debat* 41 (September–November): 122–131.

Poliakov, Leon. 1975. *The History of Anti-Semitism*, volume 3, trans. Miriam Kochan. New York: The Vanguard Press.

Poster, Mark. 1984. *Foucault, Marxism, and History: Mode of Production versus Mode of Information*. Stanford, CA: Stanford University Press.

Potte-Bonneville, Mathieu, and Daniel Defert. 2010. "Filigranes philosophiques," in Mathieu Potte-Bonneville and Daniel Defert, *Foucault*. Paris: Les Cahiers de l'Herne, pp. 39–46.

Prado, C. G. 2000. *Starting with Foucault: An Introduction to Genealogy*, 2nd ed. Boulder, CO: Westview Press.

2006. *Foucault and Searle on Truth*. Cambridge: Cambridge University Press.

Protevi, John. 2009. *Political Affect: Connecting the Social and the Somatic*. Minneapolis: University of Minnesota.

Rabinow, Paul, and Nikolas Rose. 2006. "Biopower Today," *BioSocieties* 1, no. 2:195–217.

Rai, Amit S. 2004. "Of Monsters – Biopower, Terrorism, and Excess in Genealogies of Monstrosity," *Cultural Studies* 18, no. 4:538–570.

Rajchman, John. 1985. *Michel Foucault: The Freedom of Philosophy*. New York: Columbia University Press.

1988. "Foucault's Art of Seeing," *October* 44:88–117.

1991. *Truth and Eros: Foucault, Lacan and the Question of Ethics*. London: Routledge.

Rayner, Timothy. 2009. *Foucault and Fiction: The Experience Book*. London: Continuum.

Read, Jason. 2009. "A Genealogy of Homo-Economicus: Neoliberalism and the Production of Subjectivity," *Foucault Studies* 6:25–36.

Reid, Julian. 2003. "Foucault on Clausewitz: Conceptualizing the Relationship between War and Power," *Alternatives: Global, Local, Political* 28 (January–February): 1–28.

2006. "War, Discipline, and Bio-politics in the Thought of Michel Foucault," *Social Text* 86:127–152.

Revel, Jacques. 1992. "Le moment historiographique," in *Michel Foucault: lire l'œuvre*, ed. Luce Girard. Grenoble: Jérôme Millon, pp. 83–96.

Revel, Judith. 1996. "Foucault lecteur de Deleuze: De l'écart à la différence," *Critique* 591–592 (August–September): 723–735.

2008. *Dictionnaire Foucault*. Paris: Ellipses.

2009. "Vérité/Jeux de Vérité," in Judith Revel, *Le Vocabulaire de Foucault*. Paris: Éditions Ellipses, pp. 64–65.

2010. *Foucault, une pensée du discontinu*. Paris: Fayard.

Rorty, Richard. 1979. *Philosophy and the Mirror of Nature*. Princeton, NJ: Princeton University Press.

Rose, Nikolas. 1999. *Powers of Freedom*. Cambridge: Cambridge University Press.
  2001. "The Politics of Life Itself," *Theory, Culture and Society* 18, no. 6:1–30.

Rose, Nikolas, and Mariana Valverde. 1998. "Governed by Law?" *Social and Legal Studies* 7:541–551.

Roth, Michael S. 1988. *Knowing and History: Appropriations of Hegel in Twentieth-Century France*. Ithaca, NY: Cornell University Press.

Roudinesco, Elizabeth, ed. 1992. *Penser la folie: Essais sur Michel Foucault*. Paris: Galilée.

Roussel, Raymond. 1983. *Locus Solus*, trans. Rupert Copeland Cunningham. London: John Calder.
  1995. *How I Wrote Certain of My Books*, ed. and trans. Trevor Winkfield. Cambridge: Exact Change.
  2001. *Impressions of Africa*, trans. Lindy Foord and Rayner Heppenstall. London: John Calder.

Roustang, François. 1976. "La visibilité est une piège," *Les Temps Modernes* 33:1567–1579, collected in Philippe Artières et al. 2010, *Surveiller et punir de Michel Foucault: Regards critiques 1975–1979*. Caens: Presses Universitaires de Caen-IMEC, pp. 183–200.

Rubin, Gayle. 1984. "Thinking Sex: Notes for a Radical Theory of the Politics of Sexuality," in *Pleasure and Danger*, ed. Carole Vance. London: Routledge and Kegan Paul, pp. 267–319.

Ruffié, Jacques. 1976. *De la biologie à la culture*. Paris: Flammarion.

Saar, Martin. 2007. *Genealogie als Kritik: Geschichte und Theorie des Subjekts nach Nietzsche und Foucault*. Frankfurt am Main: Campus Verlag.

Sárkány, Mikhály, Chris M. Hann, and Peter Skalník, eds. 2005. *Studying Peoples in the People's Democracies: Socialist Era Anthropology in East-Central Europe*. Münster: Lit Verlag.

Sartre, Jean-Paul. 1956. *Being and Nothingness*, trans. Hazel E. Barnes. New York: Philosophical Library.
  1966. "Jean-Paul Sartre répond," *L'arc* 30:87–96.
  1968a. *Communists and Peace with A Reply to Claude Lefort*, trans. Martha H. Fletcher et al. New York: George Braziller.
  1968b. *Search for a Method*, trans. Hazel E. Barnes. New York: Vintage Books.
  1981–1993. *The Family Idiot: Gustave Flaubert 1821–1857*, trans. Carol Cosman, 5 vols. Chicago: University of Chicago Press.
  1988. *What Is Literature?* trans. Bernard Frechtman et al., intro. Steven Ungar. Cambridge, MA: Harvard University Press.
  2004. *Critique of Dialectical Reason*, volume 1: *Theory of Practical Ensembles*, trans. Alan Sheridan-Smith. London: Verso.

Sartre, Jean-Paul, and Benny Lévy 1996. *Hope Now: The 1980 Interviews*, trans. Adrian Ven Den Hoven. Chicago: University of Chicago Press.

Sartre, Jean-Paul, Philippe Gavi, and Pierre Victor (a.k.a. Benny Lévy). 1974. *On a raison de se révolter*. Paris: Gallimard.

Saussure, Ferdinand de. 1995. *Cours de linguistique générale*. Paris: Payot and Rivages.
  2000. *Course in General Linguistics*, trans. Roy Harris. Chicago: Open Court.

Sawicki, Jana. 1991. *Disciplining Foucault: Feminism, Power, and the Body*. New York: Routledge.
  2010. "Foucault, Queer Theory, and the Discourse of Desire: Why Embrace an Ethics of Pleasure?" in *Foucault and Philosophy*, ed. Timothy O'Leary and Christopher Falzon. London: Blackwell, pp. 185–203.

Schmidt, James, ed. 1996. *What Is Enlightenment?: Eighteenth Century Answers and Twentieth Century Questions*. Berkeley: University of California Press.

Schrift, Alan D. 1995. *Nietzsche's French Legacy: A Genealogy of Poststructuralism*. New York: Routledge.

Scott, Charles E. 1990. *The Question of Ethics*. Bloomington: Indiana University Press.

Shapiro, Gary. 2003. *Archaeologies of Vision: Foucault and Nietzsche on Seeing and Saying*. Chicago: University of Chicago Press.

Sharpe, Andrew. 2007. "Foucault's Monsters, the Abnormal Individual and the Challenge of English Law," *Journal of Historical Sociology* 20, no. 3:384–403.

— 2010. *Foucault's Monsters and the Challenge of Law*. New York: Routledge.

Shepherdson, Charles. 2000. *Vital Signs: Nature, Culture, Psychoanalysis*. New York: Routledge.

Silverman, Hugh J. 1997. *Inscriptions: After Phenomenology and Structuralism*, 2nd ed. Evanston, IL: Northwestern University Press.

Simar, Theophile. 1922. *Études critique sur la formation de la doctrine des races*. Brussels: Maurice Lamertin.

Simons, Jon. 1995. *Foucault and the Political*. New York: Routledge.

Sluga, Hans. 2005. "Foucault's Encounter with Heidegger and Nietzsche," in *The Cambridge Companion to Foucault*, 2nd ed., ed. Gary Gutting. Cambridge: Cambridge University Press.

Smart, Barry. 1983. *Foucault, Marxism, and Critique*. London: Routledge.

Soja, Edward W. 1989. *Postmodern Geographies: The Reassertion of Space in Critical Social Theory*. London: Verso.

Sournia, Jean-Charles. 1961. *Logique et morale du diagnostic*. Paris: Gallimard.

Spiegelberg, Herbert. 1972. *Phenomenology in Psychology and Psychiatry: A Historical Introduction*. Evanston, IL: Northwestern University Press.

Spivak, Gayatri Chakravorty. 1994. "Can the Subaltern Speak?" in *Colonial Discourse and Post-Colonial Theory: A Reader*, ed. Patrick Williams and Laura Chrisman. New York: Columbia University Press, pp. 66–111.

Still, Arthur, and Irving Velody, eds. 1992. *Rewriting the History of Madness: Studies in Foucault's Histoire de la folie*. London: Routledge.

Stoekl, Allan. 1989. "1937: The Avant-Garde Embraces Science," in *A New History of French Literature*, ed. Denis Hollier. Cambridge, MA: Harvard University Press, pp. 928–935.

Stoler, Ann Laura. 1995. *Race and the Education of Desire*. Durham, NC: Duke University Press.

— 1997. "Racial Histories and Their Regimes of Truth," *Political Power and Social Theory* 13:183–206.

Strauser, Joëlle. 2004. "Loi(s)" in *Abécédaire de Michel Foucault*. Paris: Les Editions Sils Maria et Les Editions Vrin.

Surya, Michel. 2002. *Georges Bataille: An Intellectual Biography*. London: Verso.

Tadros, Victor. 1998. "Between Governance and Discipline: The Law and Michel Foucault," *Oxford Journal of Legal Studies* 18, no. 1:75–103.

Tanke, Joseph. 2010. *Foucault's Philosophy of Art: A Genealogy of Modernity*. New York: Continuum.

Tauchert, Ashley. 2008. *Against Transgression*. Malden, MA: Wiley-Blackwell.

Taylor, Chloë. 2009. *The Culture of Confession from Augustine to Foucault: A Genealogy of the "Confessing Animal."* London: Routledge.

Taylor, Dianna. 2009. "Normativity and Normalization," *Foucault Studies* 7:45–63.

Teyssot, Georges. 2000. "Heterotopias and the History of Spaces," in *Architectural Theory since 1968*, ed. K. Michael Hays. Cambridge, MA: The MIT Press, pp. 296–305.

Thierry, Augustin. 1845. "On the Antipathy of Race which Divides the French Nation," in Augustin Thierry, *Historical Essays*. Philadelphia: Carey and Hart, pp. 89–91.

Thompson, Kevin. 2003. "Forms of Resistance: Foucault on Tactical Reversal and Self-Formation," *Continental Philosophy Review* 36, no. 2:113–138.

— 2008. "Historicity and Transcendentality: Foucault, Cavaillès, and the Phenomenology of the Concept," *History and Theory* 47:1–18.

Tully, James. 1999. "To Think and Act Differently: Foucault's Four Reciprocal Objections to Habermas's Theory," in *Foucault contra Habermas*, ed. Samantha Ashenden and David Owen. London: Sage Publications.

Vallier, Robert. 2005. "Institution: The Significance of Merleau-Ponty's 1954 Course at the Collège de France," *Chiasmi International 7: Life and Individuation*:263–280.

Venturino, Diego. 1993. "A la politique comme à la guerre? A propos des cours de Michel Foucault au Collège de France," *Storia della Storiografia* 23:135–152.

———. 2003. "Race et historie. Le paradigme nobiliaire de la distinction sociel au debut du XVIIIe siecle," in *L'idée de 'race' dans les sciences humaines et la litterature (XVIIIe–XIXe siecles)*, ed. Sarga Moussa. Paris: L'Harmattan, pp. 19–38.

Veyne, Paul. 1984. *Writing History: Essay on Epistemology*, trans. Mina Moore-Rinvolucri. Manchester: Manchester University Press.

———. 1985. "Homosexuality in Ancient Rome," in *Western Sexuality: Practices and Precept in Past and Present Times*, ed. Philippe Artières and André Béjin. Oxford: Oxford University Press.

———. 1997a. "The Final Foucault and His Ethics," trans. Catherine Porter and Arnold Davidson, in *Foucault and His Interlocutors*, ed. Arnold Davidson. Chicago: University of Chicago Press, pp. 225–233.

———. 1997b. "Foucault Revolutionizes History," in *Foucault and His Interlocutors*, ed. Arnold Davidson. Chicago: University of Chicago Press, pp. 146–182.

———. 2010. *Foucault: His Thought, His Character*, trans. Janet Lloyd. Cambridge: Polity Press.

Visker, Rudi. 1995. *Michel Foucault: Genealogy as Critique*, trans. Chris Turner. London: Verso.

Webb, David. 2003. "On Friendship: Derrida, Foucault and the Practice of Becoming," *Research in Phenomenology* 33:119–140.

———. 2013. *Foucault's Archaeology: Science and Transformation*. Edinburgh: Edinburgh University Press.

Wickham, Gary. 2006. "Foucault, Law, and Power: A Reassessment," *Journal of Law and Society* 33, no. 4:596–614.

Wilson, Richard. 2007. *Shakespeare in French Theory: King of Shadows*. New York: Routledge.

Winnubst, Shannon. 2006a. *Queering Freedom*. Bloomington: Indiana University Press.

———. ed. 2006b. *Reading Bataille Now*. Bloomington: Indiana University Press.

Authors' Biographical Statements

Amy Allen is the Parents Distinguished Research Professor in the Humanities and professor of philosophy and women's and gender studies at Dartmouth College. In 2010 and 2012, she was a Humboldt Fellow at the University of Frankfurt.

Philippe Artières is a French historian and head of research at the Centre national de la recherche scientifique in Paris. He is the author of a number of titles, including *1968, années politiques* (éditions Thierry Magnier, collection Troisième Culture, 2008) and *Le groupe d'information sur les prisons: Archives d'une lutte, 1970–1972* (with Michelle Zancarini-Fournel, IMEC, 2001).

Banu Bargu is an assistant professor of politics at The New School. She recently authored the book *Starve and Immolate: From Biopolitics to the Weaponization of Life* (Columbia University Press, forthcoming).

Miguel de Beistegui is professor of philosophy at the University of Warwick. He recently delivered the Lev Chestov Lectures at the Institute of Philosophy of the Academy of Science in Moscow. He is also the principal investigator for the Leverhulme Research Project in Bioethics and Biopolitics. His most recent books include *Proust as Philosopher: The Art of Metaphor* (Routledge, 2012) and *Aesthetics After Metaphysics: From Mimesis to Metaphor* (Routledge, 2012).

Robert Bernasconi is Edwin Erle Sparks Professor of Philosophy at the Pennsylvania State University. He is the author of *How to Read Sartre* (Norton, 2006).

James Bernauer is the Kraft Family Professor in the Philosophy Department at Boston College, where he is also the director of its Center for Christian-Jewish Learning.

Jean-François Bert is a historian of the social sciences. Recent publications include *Introduction à Michel Foucault* (Editions La Découverte, 2011) and *Des Gestes aux techniques. Les techniques dans les sociétés pré-machinistes de André Georges Haudricourt*, édition établie, corrigée et annotée (Maison des Sciences de l'Homme, 2010).

Olivia Custer is a visiting assistant professor of philosophy at Bard College. She has written and lectured extensively on Derrida, Immanuel Kant, and Michel Foucault. She is the co-editor of *L'ex-Yougoslavie en Europe: de la faillite des démocraties au processus de paix* (L'Harmattan, 1997).

ANDREW CUTROFELLO is professor of philosophy at Loyola University, Chicago. He is the author of *Continental Philosophy: A Contemporary Introduction* (Routledge, 2005) and is currently writing a book about philosophical representations of Hamlet.

DON T. DEERE received his BA in philosophy and government from Cornell University and currently is a PhD candidate in philosophy at DePaul University. His areas of research include twentieth-century French philosophy, Latin American philosophy, and the history and philosophy of space.

ANDREW DILTS is assistant professor of political science at Loyola Marymount University. His recent publications include "From 'Entrepreneur of the Self' to 'Care of the Self': Neoliberal Governmentality and Foucault's Ethics," in *Foucault Studies*, 12 (Octobert 2011): 130–146 and "To Kill a Thief: Punishment, Proportionality, and Criminal Subjectivity in Locke's Second Treatise," in *Political Theory*, volume 40, number 1 (February 2012): 58-83. His *Punishment and Inclusion* is forthcoming with Fordham University Press, 2014.

MARC DJABALLAH is associate professor of philosophy at Université du Québec à Montréal. He has published *Kant, Foucault and Forms of Experience* (Routledge, 2008, 2011).

STUART ELDEN is professor of political geography at Durham University. His book *The Birth of Territory* will appear in 2013 with University of Chicago Press.

FRED EVANS is professor of philosophy and director of the Center for Interpretive and Qualitative Research at Duquesne University. His most recent book is *The Multivoiced Body: Society and Communication in the Age of Diversity* (Columbia University Press, 2008, 2011).

THOMAS R. FLYNN is the Sandler Candor Dobbs Professor of Philosophy at Emory University. He is the author of *Sartre and Marxist Existentialism: The Test Case of Collective Responsibility* (Chicago, 1986) and *Sartre, Foucault, and Historical Reason* (vol. 1): *Toward an Existentialist Theory of History* (Chicago, 1997), (vol. 2): *A Post-structuralist Mapping of History* (Chicago, 2005).

ERINN GILSON is assistant professor of philosophy at the University of North Florida. She recently published the article "Vulnerability, Ignorance, and Oppression" in *Hypatia: A Journal of Feminist Philosophy* and is completing a book on the ethics of vulnerability, which will be published by Routledge in fall 2013.

DAVID-OLIVIER GOUGELET is a professor of philosophy at Simpson College. He focuses mainly on contemporary European philosophy (nineteenth- and twentieth-century continental philosophy), and particularly on the role of the concept of biopower in the work of Michel Foucault. He has published on the concepts of race and medicalization in Foucault.

FRÉDÉRIC GROS is visiting assistant professor of philosophy at University Paris East Creteil and the editor of Foucault's final lectures at the Collège de France.

GARY GUTTING holds the Notre Dame Endowed Chair in Philosophy at the University of Notre Dame. His most recent book is *Thinking the Impossible: French Philosophy since 1960* (Oxford University Press, 2011).

SAMIR HADDAD is assistant professor of philosophy at Fordham University. He is the author of *Derrida and the Inheritance of Democracy* (Indiana University Press, 2013).

DEVONYA N. HAVIS is assistant professor of philosophy at Canisius College. She specializes in ethics, twentieth-century continental philosophy, and African American philosophy. Prior to Canisius, Havis was an associate professor of philosophy at Virginia Union University. She holds a PhD in philosophy from Boston College and a BA in religion from Williams College.

JARED HIBBARD-SWANSON is a PhD candidate at Pennsylvania State University. He is currently working on a dissertation that critically analyzes how biopolitics shapes education in democratic states.

LYNNE HUFFER is professor of women's, gender, and sexuality studies at Emory University. She recently received the Florence Howe Award for best feminist scholarship in English from the Modern Language Association (2011).

ARUN IYER teaches philosophy at Seattle University. He has a book under contract with Continuum Press titled *Towards an Epistemology of Ruptures: The Case of Heidegger and Foucault*.

STEPHANIE JENKINS is an assistant professor in the School of History, Philosophy, and Religion at Oregon State University. She recently received her dual PhD in philosophy and women's studies from the Pennsylvania State University.

MARK KELLY is lecturer in philosophy at Monash University. He is the author of *The Political Philosophy of Michel Foucault* (Routledge, 2009).

COLIN KOOPMAN is assistant professor of philosophy at the University of Oregon. He is the author of *Genealogy as Critique: The Problems of Modernity in Foucault* (Indiana University Press, 2012) and *Pragmatism as Transition: Historicity and Hope in James, Dewey, and Rorty* (Columbia University Press, 2009).

JOSHUA KURDYS is a lecturer at the Pennsylvania State University World Campus. He successfully defended his dissertation, "Genealogical Critique in the Later Work of Michel Foucault," in 2011.

LEONARD LAWLOR is Edwin Erle Sparks Professor of Philosophy at Pennsylvania State University. His most recent book is *Early Twentieth Century Continental Philosophy* (Indiana University Press, 2011).

FEDERICO LEONI is a philosopher at the University of Milan. He is co-editor of *Chiasmi International*. He was the invited professor at the Summer School, Université de Toulouse/ Université de Bonn, in September 2012.

RICHARD A. LYNCH teaches philosophy at DePauw University. His recent publications include chapters in *Michel Foucault: Key Concepts* and *A Companion to Foucault*.

MARY BETH MADER is a professor of philosophy and director of graduate admissions at the University of Memphis. She is the author of *Sleights of Reason: Norm, Bisexuality, Development* (The SUNY Press, 2011; Gender Theory Series, ed. Tina Chanter).

BILL MARTIN is professor of philosophy at DePaul University in Chicago. He is the author of nine books, most recently *Ethical Marxism: The Categorical Imperative of Liberation*.

TODD MAY is Class of 1941 Memorial Professor of the Humanities at Clemson University. He is the author of eleven books of philosophy, most recently *Friendship in an Age of Economics* (Lexington Books, 2012).

COREY McCALL is assistant professor of philosophy and religion at Elmira College. His recent articles on Foucault's work include "The Art of Life: Foucault's Reading of Baudelaire's 'The Painter of Modern Life'" and "Foucault, Iran, and the Question of Religious Revolt."

MARGARET A. McLAREN holds the Harriet W. and George D. Cornell Chair in Philosophy at Rollins College. She is the author of *Feminism, Foucault and Embodied*

Subjectivity (The SUNY Press, 2002), which was nominated for an SPEP book award, and has written a number of articles on Foucault.

EDWARD McGUSHIN is an associate professor of philosophy at Stonehill College. In 2007, he published his book titled *Foucault's Askesis: An Introduction to the Philosophical Life* (published by Northeastern University Press in its Topics in Historical Philosophy series).

LADELLE McWHORTER is the James Thomas Professor in Philosophy at the University of Richmond. Her latest book is *Racism and Sexual Oppression in Anglo-America: A Genealogy* (Indiana University Press, 2009).

EDUARDO MENDIETA is professor of philosophy at Stony Brook University. In 2011, he received the Dean's Award for Excellence in Graduate Teaching.

WARREN MONTAG is professor of English and comparative literary studies at Occidental College, Los Angeles, CA. His most recent book is *Philosophy's Perpetual War: Althusser and His Contemporaries* (Duke University Press, 2013).

NICOLAE MORAR is a postdoctoral fellow in bioethics at the Rock Ethics Institute at the Pennsylvania State University. He is also coauthoring a paper with Dan Kelly analyzing the roles disgust should be given in our society, and is co-editing two books: *Biopower: Ethics and Politics in the Twenty-first Century* with V. Cisney and *Intersections in Bioethics: Animals, Environment, and Biotechnologies* with J. Beever (under contract with Purdue University Press).

ANN V. MURPHY is assistant professor of philosophy at the University of New Mexico in Albuquerque. She is the author of *Violence and the Philosophical Imaginary* (The SUNY Press, 2012).

JOHN NALE is visiting assistant professor of philosophy at the University of North Florida. His doctoral thesis on Descartes and the mind-body problem was completed in 2011.

JEFFREY T. NEALON is Liberal Arts Research Professor of English and philosophy at the Pennsylvania State University. His latest book is *Post-Postmodernism; or, the Cultural Logic of Just-in-Time Capitalism*.

HARRY A. NETHERY IV is an advanced PhD student in philosophy at Duquesne University. He recently received the Charles J. Dougherty Graduate Student Teaching Award.

JOANNA OKSALA is a senior research fellow in the Department of Philosophy, History, Culture and Art Studies at the University of Helsinki. She is the author of *Foucault on Freedom* (Cambridge: Cambridge University Press, 2005), *How to Read Foucault* (London: Granta Books, 2007), and *Foucault, Politics, and Violence* (Northwestern University Press, 2012).

TIMOTHY O'LEARY is associate professor of philosophy at the University of Hong Kong. He has published *Foucault and the Art of Ethics* (Continuum, 2002) and *Foucault and Fiction* (Continuum, 2009). He has edited several collections, including *Foucault and Philosophy* (Blackwell, 2010).

LUCA PALTRINIERI is a PhD candidate in philosophy (École Normale Supérieure de Lyon and University of Pisa). He is an associate researcher at the Centre International d'Etude de la Philosophie Française (Ecole Normale Supérieure-Ulm, Paris).

PAUL PATTON is professor of philosophy at the University of New South Wales, Sydney, Australia. He is the author of *Deleuzian Concepts: Philosophy, Colonization, Politics* (Stanford

University Press, 2010), and was elected a Fellow of the Australian Academy of the Humanities in 2011.

CHRISTOPHER PENFIELD is a PhD candidate in philosophy at Purdue University. His entry, "Foucault, Michel," appears in *Encyclopedia of Global Justice* (Springer, 2011).

C. G. PRADO is professor emeritus of philosophy at Queen's University, Kingston, Ontario, and Fellow, Royal Society of Canada. His most recent publications are *Coping with Choices to Die* (2011), *Starting with Descartes* (Bloomsbury Academic, 2009), *Foucault's Legacy* (Bloomsbury, 2009), *Choosing to Die: Elective Death and Multiculturalism* (Cambridge University Press, 2008), and *Searle and Foucault on Truth* (Cambridge University Press, 2006).

JOHN PROTEVI is the Phyllis M. Taylor Professor of French Studies and professor of philosophy at Louisiana State University. He is the 2012 Scots Philosophical Association Centenary Fellow.

JUDITH REVEL is on the faculty at Paris I Panthéon-Sorbonne. She is a board member of the *Centre Michel Foucault*, overseeing the Foucault archives. Her recent publications include *Michel Foucault: Une pensée du discontinu* (Mille et une nuits/Fayard, 2010), *Cahier de l'Herne Foucault* with Ph. Artières, F. Gros, and J.-F. Bert (L'Herne, 2011), and *Dictionnaire politique à l'usage des gouvernés* with F. Brugère, G. le Blanc, M. Gaille, M. Foessel, and P. Zaoui (Bayard, 2012).

KAS SAGHAFI is associate professor in philosophy at the University of Memphis. He researches and teaches in contemporary continental philosophy, philosophy and literature, and aesthetics. He is the author of *Apparitions – Of Derrida's Other* (Fordham University Press, 2010).

PAOLO SAVOIA earned his PhD in philosophy from the University of Pisa. He has published papers on Michel Foucault, the history of sexuality, the history of psychiatry, and the Franco-American tradition of historical epistemology. He is currently enrolled in the PhD program at the Department of the History of Science, Harvard University, where he works on the history of Renaissance medicine.

JANA SAWICKI is Carl Vogt '59 Professor of Philosophy at Williams College. She is currently co-editing *A Companion to Foucault* (Oxford: Blackwell) with Timothy O'Leary and Chris Falzon, as well as the queer theory issue of *Foucault Studies* with Shannon Winnubst. She has recently published a series of essays on Foucault and queer theory.

ALAN D. SCHRIFT is F. Wendell Miller Professor of Philosophy at Grinnell College. He recently edited the eight-volume *History of Continental Philosophy* (Acumen Publishing, 2011) and is currently editing *The Complete Works of Friedrich Nietzsche* for Stanford University Press.

CHARLES E. SCOTT is Distinguished Professor of Philosophy Emeritus and research professor of philosophy at Vanderbilt University. His most recent book is *Living with Indifference* (Indiana University Press).

GARY SHAPIRO is Tucker-Boatwright Professor of Humanities-Philosophy Emeritus at the University of Richmond; his article "Then and Now, Here and There: On the Grounds of Aesthetics, 1961–2011" appeared in *The Journal of Speculative Philosophy* in 2012.

HUGH J. SILVERMAN was professor of philosophy and comparative literary and cultural studies at Stony Brook University. He was executive director of the International Association for Philosophy and Literature and was Fulbright Distinguished Chair of Art

Theory and Cultural Studies at the Vienna Academy of Fine Arts (Vienna, Austria). He passed away in 2013.

PATRICK SINGY is an independent scholar studying the philosophy and history of sexuality and medicine. He is the author of numerous publications, including "A Tergo: Taking History from Behind" (*Pli – The Warwick Journal of Philosophy*, forthcoming) and "The Popularization of Medicine in the Eighteenth Century: Writing, Reading and Rewriting Samuel Auguste Tissot's Avis au peuple sur sa santé" (*Journal of Modern History* 82 (2010): 769–800).

ALLAN STOEKL is professor of French and comparative literature at Pennsylvania State University. He has translated a number of works by Georges Bataille, Maurice Blanchot, and Paul Fournel. His most recent book is *Bataille's Peak: Energy, Religion, Postsustainability* (University of Minnesota Press, 2007). His current project is a study of avant-garde theories of the city from the perspective of questions of sustainability and gleaning.

BRAD STONE is associate professor of philosophy and African American studies at Loyola Marymount University, where he also serves as director of the University Honors Program. Named one of *Princeton Review*'s top 300 professors in the United States, his work on Foucault has been published in *Foucault Studies*, *The Other Journal*, and *Michel Foucault: Key Concepts* (ed. Dianna Taylor).

ADRIAN SWITZER, PHD, is an assistant professor of philosophy at Western Kentucky University. The author of many articles on such figures as Guy Debord, Gilles Deleuze, Michel Foucault, Luce Irigaray, Immanuel Kant, Jean-Luc Nancy, and Friedrich Nietzsche, he is presently completing a manuscript on *Nietzsche and the Politics of May '68*.

SAMUEL TALCOTT is an assistant professor of philosophy at the University of the Sciences. He is the author of "Foucault and Historical Epistemology: Critique and Development of the Philosophy of the Norm," in *Studies in the Philosophy of Michel Foucault: A French Alternative to Anglo-Americanism*, ed. Brian Lightbody (Edwin Mellen Press, 2010).

CHLOË TAYLOR is assistant professor of philosophy at the University of Alberta. She is the author of *The Culture of Confession from Augustine to Foucault* (Routledge 2008, 2010).

DIANNA TAYLOR is associate professor of philosophy and currently holds the Shula Chair in Philosophy at John Carroll University in Cleveland, Ohio. She is editor of *Michel Foucault: Key Concepts* (Acumen, 2011).

KEVIN THOMPSON is an associate professor of philosophy at DePaul University. He has published numerous articles on phenomenology, Foucault, Kant, and Hegel.

ROBERT VALLIER is the academic program director for graduate studies at Columbia University's Paris campus. He is the translator of several French philosophy books, in particular Merleau-Ponty's *Nature*.

POL VAN DE VELDE is professor of philosophy at Marquette University. He recently published *Heidegger and the Romantics: The Literary Invention of Meaning* (Routledge, 2012).

DAVID WEBB is on the faculty at Staffordshire University. He is the author of *Foucault's Archaeology: Science and Transformation* (Edinburgh University Press, 2012).

SHANNON WINNUBST is associate professor in the Department of Women's, Gender and Sexuality Studies at Ohio State University. Her next book is entitled *A Biopolitics of Cool: Neoliberalism, Difference and Ethics*.

Index

abnormal, 3–10, 38, 75
    confession, 319
    diagnosis, 201
    discipline, 320
    disease, 95
    forms of life, 296
    juridicality, 296
    legality, 247
    monster, 302
    pleasure, 210
    population, 298, 319
    power, 300, 317
    racism, 419, 421
    sexuality, 75, 301
abnormality. *See* abnormal
actuality, 10–13, 130
    apparatus, 130
    control, 130
    critique, 648
    history, 198
    intellectual, 225
    knowledge, 299
    philosophy, 188, 196, 648
Althusser, Louis, 203, 266, 267, 288, 490, 610,
    624, 682
analytic philosophy, 17, 87, 648
anatomo-politics, 39, 40, 41, 44, 96, 374
ancient philosophy, 57, 500, 558
ancients, the, 137, 138, 139, 555–560, 615,
    659, 672
apparatus. See *dispositif* (apparatus)
archaeology, 10–13, 183, 184, 201, 405
    archive, 22
    body, 51, 657
    critique, 649

death, 94
difference, 106
discursive formation, 183
ethics, 123
exercise, 660
genealogy, 185, 386, 399
hermeneutics, 183, 184
human sciences, 237, 284
Kantian categories, 649
methodology, 404
phenomenology, 656
practice, 387, 388
psychiatry, 406
sexuality, 435
of silence, 551
time, 636
truth, 386, 523
archive, 20–24, 131, 194–195
    actuality, 349
    archaeology, 348
    contested language, 81
    historical a priori, 203, 204
    history, 130
    statement, 121, 205
    transformative practice, 446
art history, 327
Aufklärung. *See* Enlightenment, the
author, 24–31, 267, 691
    archaeology, 183
    discourse, 201
    event, 143
    historical a priori, 204
    history, 201
    statement, 484
    work, 572

Bataille, Georges, 80, 107, 149, 188, 237, 239,
    289, 322, 430, 449, 493, 560–563
  Nietzsche, 663
  outside, the, 574
  transgression, 509–511, 513–515
Bichat, Xavier, 257–258, 563–567
  death, 94
  illness, 309
  life, 95
  vitalism, 254
Binswanger, Ludwig, 567–572
  anthropology, 635, 636
  death, 689
  Freud, 612
  Heidegger, 633
  imagination, 236
  philosophy, 345
  problematization, 403
  psychology, 412
biohistory, 638
  biopolitics, 42, 43
  medicine, 297
biopolitics, 37–44
  biopower, 46
  body, 311, 660
  control, 84
  governmentality, 45, 48
  human, the, 260
  liberation from, 422
  life, 44
  Morel, Benedict Augustin, 421
  power, 96, 374
  psychoanalysis, 417
  racism, 375, 542
  security, 375
  state, 481
  strategy, 486
  thanato-politics, 460
biopower, 3, 44–51
  discipline, 117, 463
  population, 459
  racism, 421
  sovereignty, 456
Blanchot, Maurice, 188, 289, 326, 430, 493,
    572–577
  anthropology, 649
  contestation, 512
  law, 243
  outside, the, 239
  transgression, 512
body, 38–39, 51–57, 113, 114
  Ancient, 361

  archaeology, 657
  care of the self, 59, 659–660
  Christian, 61
  counternature, 311
  death, 564–565
  deformities, 6
  discipline, 40–41, 96, 111, 112, 113–114, 116,
    316, 458–459, 505, 552
  disease, 95, 564
  economy, 298
  fiction, 574
  finitude, 283, 340
  genealogy, 310–311
  ideology, 552
  institutions, 222
  living, 258, 260
  mastery, 488
  medicine, 201, 298
  mind and, 276, 412
  nature, 313
  norm, 5, 117
  phenomenology, 656, 657
  population, 320
  power, 540, 589
  social body, 217, 220, 286, 292, 305, 365, 381,
    421, 618
  sovereignty, 3, 111, 505
  subjectivity, 97
  transformation, 210
  truth, 353, 538
  violence, 528–529
Boulainvilliers, Henri de, 577–580
  race, 420
  race war, 541–542
  revolution, 439

Canguilhem, Georges, 580–588
  archaeology, 14
  discontinuity, 191, 289
  epistemology, 129
  error, 261
  Hegel, 625
  historical a priori, 204
  history, 187, 189–191
  knowledge, 233–234
  life, 34, 254–257, 262
  limit-experience, 149
  medicine, 296
  monster, the, 300
  reason, 275
  truth, 228
care, 57–61, 507

institutions, 506
  pastoral power, 606
care of the self, 163, 185, 268, 334, 353,
    411, 415
  Ancient, 164, 352, 556–558
  body, 660
  freedom, 362
  Hegel, 627
  homosexuality, 210
  pastoral power, 606
  Plato, 670–671
  self-knowledge, 444, 605–606
  truth, 524, 556
Christianity, 58, 61–64
  communism, 78
  confession, 77, 444
  counterconduct, 72
  desire, 100, 361
  negative theology, 430
  obedience, 70
  pastoral power, 76, 474
  sexuality, 271, 429
  truth, 76
civil society, 64–68
  Althusser, 553
  government, 251
  liberalism, 251
  state, the, 480
Clausewitz, Carl von, 693–695
  politics, 365, 530, 541
  tactics, 488
conduct, 71–74, 311, 545
  abnormality, 6
  Christianity, 488
  counterconduct, 49, 382, 384, 434, 437, 474,
    488, 647
  discipline, 319, 486
  discourse, 521
  ethical, 363
  ethics, 507
  government, 478
  governmental power, 156
  governmentality, 45
  Kant, 634
  monstrosity, 301
  moral, 452
  natural, 311
  pastoral power, 606
  politics, 460
  population, 88
  possibilities, 382
  power, 382, 384, 433, 434, 503, 525, 537

revolt, 474, 475
  self, 389, 444, 452
  sexual, 362
  social relations, 544
  subversive, 538
  surveillance, 316
  wisdom, 671
confession, 75–80
  Ancient, 556
  Christianization, 62
  discipline, 319
  identity, 319
  individualization, 100
  parrēsia, 353
  pastoral power, 606
  pleasure, 360
  power, 100, 359
  secular, 319
  self, 444
  truth, 452, 519
contestation, 80–83
  Blanchot, 512
  critique, 646
  ethics, 445
  outside, the, 574
  phenomenology, 342
  power, 531
  revolution, 71
  social objectivities, 532
  teacher-student, 597
  unreason, 91
control, 40, 83–87
  biopolitics, 38, 39, 40–41
  biopower, 46, 47, 49
  Canguilhem, 586
  capitalism, 39
  crime, 302
  desire, 359, 453
  discipline, 112, 113, 114, 130, 159, 232,
    316, 409
  discourse, 105, 237
  docile bodies, 389
  education, 115
  force-relations, 96
  freedom, 160
  governmentalization, 89
  history, 441, 628
  homosexuality, 208, 209
  liberalism, 179, 251
  life, 258, 542
  norm, the, 117
  object, 233

control (*cont.*)
  population, 417
  power, 46, 156, 379, 433
  psychiatry, 408
  quarantine, 356–357
  racism, 45
  self, 139, 605, 669
  sexuality, 101, 124, 208, 320, 352, 450–451, 452, 454
  subject, 169, 496
  time, 54
  truth, 170
  visibility, 537
critique, 87–94, 159, 197, 642–650
  actuality, 10, 11
  Althusser, 553
  archaeology, 200
  autonomy, 243
  counterpractices, 391
  creation, 352
  Cynicism, 525
  discourse, 121, 641
  finitude, 430
  freedom, 141, 390
  genealogy, 349
  governmentality, 445
  Habermas, 617
  historical limits, 621
  history, 189
  ideology critique, 203, 205, 252
  of modernity, 230
  Nietzsche, 284
  parrēsia, 336
  philosophy, 349
  power, 391, 525
  present, the, 103
  psychoanalysis, 408
  of rationality, 617, 620
  of reason, 347, 426–428
  resistance, 436–437
  self-, 124
  self-evidence, 517
  sovereignty, 462
  spiritual attitude, 641
  struggle, 457
  subject, the, 191, 519
  tragedy and, 277
  truth, 436
  violence, 529
Cynics, the, 188, 268
  history, 198
  nature, 312–313

parrēsia, 558
philosophy, 353–354
Plato, 671
self, 389
truth, 525, 538

death, 94–99, 116, 143, 322, 469, 557
  Ancients, the, 343
  of the author, 24, 25, 26
  becoming other, 343
  Bichat, Xavier, 257
  biohistory, 43
  biopolitics, 460–461
  biopower, 47, 452, 543
  Christian pastorate, 62
  discipline, 409
  disease, 564
  finitude, 33, 230, 341
  freedom, 689
  Freud, 413
  of God, 91, 230, 238, 284, 429, 430, 511, 514, 646
  illness, 309
  interdiction, 510
  knowledge of, 227
  language, 239, 240, 574, 676
  life, 47, 256, 260, 262, 375, 563, 565
  literature, 240, 324–325
  madness, 406, 415
  of man, 91, 133, 284, 430, 646
  medicine, 201
  outside, the, 240
  parrēsia, 558
  pleasure, 362
  population, 320, 372, 389
  psychiatry, 405
  race, 419
  racism, 420, 460–461
  self, 77
  Shakespeare, 689–691
  sovereignty, 40, 45, 83, 544
Deleuze, Gilles, 588
  actual, the, 11
  Clastres, Pierre, 380
  control, 83–84
  desire, 100
  difference, 103, 105–108
  event, the, 144
  finitude, 90
  Hegel, 624
  multiplicity, 305
  negation, 514

Nietzsche, 663
phenomenology, 340
philosophy, 141
practice, 386
Prison Information Group (GIP), 224,
    394–398
problematization, 403
subjectivity, 436, 659
Derrida, Jacques, 595–602
    author, the, 25
    Descartes, 603–604
    différance, 105
    discourse, 205
    Enlightenment, the, 427
    Freud, 611
    madness, 273
    transgression, 512, 514
Descartes, René, 474–475, 602–609
    cogito, 283
    knowledge, 54
    Nietzsche, 665
    phenomenology, 338
    reason, 282
    self, 185
    subject, the, 190
    truth, 473
desire, 99–102, 340
    Christianity, 77, 669
    Deleuze and Guattari, 592
    discipline, 110
    ethical substance, 139, 271, 507
    ethics, 173
    finitude, 341
    homosexuality, 209
    knowledge, 232, 556
    literature, 264
    love, 270, 272
    medicine, 210
    pastoral power, 474
    pleasure, 55, 210, 359–363
    population, 372
    reason, 139
    self-knowledge, 79
    sex, 452–453
    sexual ethics, 138
    sexual freedom, 160
    subject, the, 210, 500
    to know, 351
    truth, 57, 237, 669
    virtue, 271
difference, 102–110, 684
    affirmation, 514

archive, 131
Deleuze, 589
dialectic, 513, 514, 682
discontinuity, 195
epistemic, 446
genealogy, 195
history, 196, 198, 229
Hyppolite, 640
Merleau-Ponty, 657
modernity, 196
multiplicity, 304, 306
ontological, 631, 636, 637
outside, the, 323
representation, 282
systems of difference, 85, 181, 237,
    378, 665
thought, 403
trangression, 512
discipline, 53–55, 110–120, 232–233, 245, 285,
    409, 451, 456, 462–464
    abnormality, 317
    anatomo-politics, 96
    biopolitics, 260
    biopower, 40–41, 47, 375, 459
    body, 53
    capitalism, 39
    care of the self, 353, 557, 619
    control, 83, 130
    freedom, 159
    governmentality, 176, 179, 181
    history, 628
    human sciences, 215
    ideology, 552
    law, 245–246, 248
    military, 316
    neoliberalism, 85
    normalizing, 320
    normation, 321
    population, 320
    prison, 330, 395
    quarantine, 357
    security, 460
    sexuality, 41, 452
    sovereignty, 452, 459,
        504–505
    space, 469, 470
    strategies, 486, 487
    subject, the, 84, 177
    technology, 504–505
    training, 85
disciplines, 37
    medical, 31

discourse, 104–106, 120–126, 206, 388
  Althusser, 551–552
  anthropology, 645
  archaeology, 17–18, 229, 519, 635–637
  archive, the, 20–22, 194
  author, the, 26–30
  Canguilhem, 255
  care of the self, 686
  critique, 641
  death, 98
  Derrida, 205
  desire, 100
  episteme, 492
  event, 145
  government, 478
  historical a priori, 203
  history, 447
  human sciences, 285
  ideology, 521
  institutions, 218
  intellectuals, 591
  language, 213, 236–237, 324
  literature, 574
  madness, 277, 406, 407, 520, 535
  man, 134, 153, 665
  norm, 311
  order, 323
  parrēsia, 260, 335, 525
  philosophy, 513, 640
  power, 351, 666
  race, 422
  reason, 131
  revolution, 439
  rupture, 220
  scientific, 191, 232, 233, 234, 274, 286, 290,
    340, 524
  sexuality, 100, 360, 450, 454
  statements, 82, 205, 482–483, 484
  structure, 491–492
  subject, the, 285, 519
  time, 637
  truth, 290, 473, 518, 521, 523, 526, 555, 584
  war, 541
dispositif (apparatus), 126–133, 389, 486
  archaeology, 657
  biopolitics, 37
  biopower, 46, 48
  discipline, 522
  governmentality, 48
  history, 379
  ideology, 552

madness, 242
  sexuality, 55
  sovereignty, 53
  subjectivity, 347, 435, 436, 550
  truth, 351
divine law, 458, 508
double, 133–136, 341, 487
  doublet, empirico-transcendental, 33, 148,
    153, 214, 231, 630, 645
  doublet, transcendental-empirico, 264, 265,
    283, 310, 329, 341
  identity, 342
  language, 238, 241, 573
  living, the, 258

education, 115, 157, 169, 405, 422, 578, 580
Enlightenment, the, 62, 87, 88, 89, 158, 188,
  196, 197, 291, 349, 390, 427, 436, 617, 618,
  626, 641, 642, 643, 648, 650
ethics, 45, 57, 136–143, 384–385, 453
  ancient, 60, 100, 271, 670–671, 672
  archaeology, 123
  biopolitics, 85
  care of the self, and, 57
  critique, 89
  ethical subjectivity, 56, 57, 60, 173
  freedom, 158
  friendship, 162–163, 271
  Heidegger, 636
  law, 243
  life, 45, 261
  nature, 312
  phenomenology, 134
  politics, 364, 365, 368
  psychology, 404
  Sartre, 685–686
  self, 444–447
  subjectivity, 362–363, 400–401,
    449, 473
  technology, 507–508
  theoretical ethic, 74
  truth, 525
event, 106, 143–147, 219–221, 628, 634–636
  archaeology, 183
  Aufklärung (enlightenment), 197, 349, 426
  of Being, 637
  death, 95, 257
  discursive, 604
  extratextual, 599
  genealogy, 166, 167
  history, 189, 195, 339, 388

literature, 573
multiplicity, 304
philosophy, 196
sense, 219, 657
statement, 194, 203
truth, 518–519, 523–526
experience, 147–153, 168, 278, 571, 687
-books, 525
Christian, 75, 77, 100
conditions of possible, 87, 283, 348, 630, 645, 649
constitution of, 659
of disease, 200
forms of, 642–643, 650
Hegel's concept of, 639
knowledge, 227
of language, 325
limit-, 91–92, 149, 238–239, 621
lived-, 337–339, 341–343
of madness, 15, 406, 407, 413, 603, 604
phenomenology, 295
philosophy of, 345, 347
power, 169
primeval, 655
real conditions of, 350
reflexive, 97–98
science, 583
self, 185–186
sense, 219
sexual, 207
of sexuality, 449–450
subject of, 497
of transgression, 512

finite, the, 340–341, 343
human sciences, 212
truth, 518
finitude, 153–156, 230–231, 283, 340–341, 631
analytic of, 90, 92, 148, 283
death, 33, 95, 96
experience of, 90
human sciences, 214
Hyppolite, 640
Kant, 645–646
literature, 325
madness, 415
medicine, 258
transgression, 322
freedom, 156–162
actuality, 11–12
Ancient, 139

biopolitics, 49
Christian, 139
critique, 648
death, 689
Habermas, 619
history, 198
liberalism, 179–180, 253
negative, 434
power, 222, 382–385, 637
Sartre, 683–684
self, 445, 446–447
stylistics of, 362
thought, 436
transcendental critique, 648
transcendentalism, 141
truth, 644
French Revolution, 87, 130, 276, 438, 439, 440, 478, 542, 565
Freud, Sigmund, 609–616
author, the, 27–28
death, 689
Derrida, 600
desire, 100
dreams, 328, 569
madness, 277, 279, 407, 408, 409
psychoanalysis, 411–417
friendship, 162–163
love, 271, 272
pleasure, 363, 557

genealogy, 170, 173, 195–196, 220, 420
archaeology, 185, 348, 386, 399, 404
biopower, 45
body, 310
desire, 99–100
event, 144
Habermas, 618
Hegel, 628–629
knowledge, 169–173
Nietzsche, 220
ontology, 386
phenomenology, 656
politics, 365, 366
power, 388
power relations, 352
practice, 387, 390
self, 605
sexuality, 435
subject, 57, 443
GIP, 115

governmentality, 42, 47–48, 175–182, 366–368
  Ancient, 555
  biohistory, 32
  biopolitics, 45, 481
  biopower, 37, 49
  civil society, 66
  conduct, 68, 434
  emancipatory politics, 293
  friendship, 163
  liberalism, 251, 253
  neoliberalism, 480
  pastoral power, 70
  politics, 365
  population, 376, 470
  power, 69
  state, the, 479
  subjectivity, 445, 545
  technology, 505–507
  violence, 531
  war, 540

Habermas, Jürgen, 616–624
  self, the, 445
Hegel, Georg Wilhelm Friedrich, 624–630
  archaeology, 14–16
  contestation, 81
  critique, 87, 648
  death of God, 429
  difference, 106
  history, 187
  Hyppolite, Jean, 639–640
  Nietzsche, 663
  phenomenology, 339
  Phenomenology of Spirit, 642
  philosophy, 141, 188
  Sartre, 680, 682
  transgression, 512–515
Heidegger, Martin, 634–636
  Binswanger, Ludwig, 567–569
  contestation, 81
  death, 689
  language, 228
  man, 148
  phenomenology, 339
  psychoanalysis, 412
  transgression, 512
  truth, 523
Henri de Boulainvilliers (1658–1722), 577–580
hermeneutics, 57, 182–187, 682
  confession, 444
  desire, 99
  Freud, 610

Hegel, 627
  language, 238
  psychoanalysis, 614
hermeneutics of the self, 48, 76–78
  biohistory, 32
historical a priori, 17, 21, 22, 103, 149,
    200–207, 229, 349
  archaeology, 348
  Hegel, 626
  human sciences, 350, 646
  man, 284
  sexuality, 416
  shift, 628
  truth, 518
history, 29, 187–200, 219–221, 290, 310,
    518–519
  actual, the, 130–131
  Ancient, 139
  archaeology, 14–16, 309, 596, 635
  archive, 20
  Bataille, 515
  Being, 636–637
  civil society, 66
  counterconduct, 73
  Derrida, 598
  dialectic, 513
  difference, 230, 275
  discontinuity, 104, 255, 267,
    438, 551
  discourse, 122
  event, the, 143–144
  finalism, 624
  genealogy, 166
  Hegel, 625, 626, 627–629
  intellectual, the, 225
  knowledge, 341
  life, 32, 42, 44, 215, 260, 374
  of limits, 91, 468
  of madness, 273, 277, 535
  meaning, 218
  of medicine, 299
  nature, 313, 542
  Nietzsche, 663–664
  phenomenology, 205, 339–340
  philosophy, 346, 354, 583, 640
  politics, 365, 522
  power, 244, 279, 379
  practice, 390
  present, the, 348
  prison, the, 331
  of punishment, 286
  revolution, 439, 441

Same, the, 323
Sartre, 680
of science, 255, 289, 582, 583–584
of sexuality, 450, 452
state, the, 88
structures, 492–493
subject, the, 278, 285, 550
subjectivity, 134, 377, 443,
    445–446
time, 167
of truth, 350, 526
history of the present, 60, 62
homosexuality, 207–212
   freedom, 160
   friendship, 162, 163–164
   liberation, 383
   life, 435
   love, 272
   perversion, 499
   practice, 390
   sexuality, 451, 669
   soul, the, 52
   species, 362, 667
human nature, 7, 65, 144, 158, 159, 165, 177,
   349, 350, 382, 404, 405
human sciences, 212–217, 405
   anthropology, 645
   Canguilhem, 586
   countersciences, 682
   critique, 90
   gaze, the, 201
   historical a priori, 202, 350, 646
   human nature, 308, 313
   humanism, 157
   knowledge, 91, 103, 237, 630
   language, 183
   literature, 266
   madness, 416
   man, 33, 34, 231, 235, 238, 259, 284,
    285–286, 681
   norm, the, 311
   normalization, 92
   postmodernity, 264
   power, 351
   psychoanalysis, 613
   self-knowledge, 14
   soul, the, 52
   truth, 519
Hyppolite, Jean, 641–652
   Collège de France, 346
   Hegel, 188, 624–625
   Kant, 642

institution, 217–224, 279
   abnormality, 5, 6
   archaeology, 18
   biopolitics, 486
   biopower, 47
   care of the self, 185
   control, 84
   discipline, 3, 96, 112, 115, 117, 286, 462
   experience, 150
   freedom, 158, 159
   governmentality, 175
   ideology, 203
   judicial, 246
   knowledge, 170, 348
   language, 237, 238
   madness, 110
   medicine, 469
   normalization, 317
   parrēsia, 686
   pleasure, 164
   politics, 260
   power, 46, 169, 292, 379, 459, 529
   psychology, 405
   racism, 464
   science, 607
   truth, 417, 473
intellectual, the, 167, 224–226, 440–441, 591
Iranian Revolution, 70, 73, 429, 431, 442, 475,
   476, 612

Kant, Immanuel, 641–652
knowledge, 226–236, 341, 518, 534, 631
   abnormality, 7, 319
   Ancient, 312
   archaeology, 13–14, 183, 194, 202, 237, 348,
    386, 402
   Bataille, 514
   Binswanger, 568
   body, 51, 54
   Canguilhem, 584–585
   care, 59
   categories, 107
   Christianity, 76–77
   correspondance, 517, 520
   critique, 87
   Cynicism, 353
   death, 257
   Descartes, 475, 605, 606
   discipline, 111
   discontinuity, 104, 125, 190, 220
   discourse, 121, 551
   dispositif (apparatus), 347

knowledge (*cont.*)
  embodied, 149
  episteme, 192, 681
  ethics, 124, 141
  experience, 148
  finitude, 154–155
  friendship, 163
  gaze, the, 536
  genealogy, 45, 165–166, 167–168, 404, 446
  governmentality, 42
  Hegel, 624, 627
  history, 426, 570, 583
  human sciences, 103, 214–216, 405, 630
  Husserl, 656
  intellectual, the, 440, 591
  interpretation, 531
  Kant, 631, 642–643, 644, 645–646, 649
  language, 237–238, 685
  law, 247–248, 311
  liberalism, 251, 252
  life, 34, 96, 256, 261
  limit-experience, 149
  lived experience, 337
  madness, 274–275, 339, 401, 408
  man, 33, 91, 133–134, 148, 212–213, 214,
    259, 282, 283, 340–341
  medicine, 258, 276, 278, 295, 297, 299, 302,
    309, 429, 563–564
  Merleau-Ponty, 659, 661
  monster, 300
  nature, 309–310
  Nietzsche, 663
  norm, 300
  normalization, 318
  outside, the, 108
  pastoral power, 474
  phenomenology, 631
  philosophy, 255, 626, 672
  population, 286, 373
  positivism, 92
  possibility of, 92, 342
  power, 88, 157, 286, 291, 351, 365, 392, 498
  Prison Information Group (GIP), 398
  psychoanalysis, 415
  rationality, 129
  representation, 148, 282, 630
  scientific, 88, 89, 221
  self, the, 128, 312
  sexuality, 56, 208–209, 360, 451
  space, 468
  subject, the, 387, 473, 475, 519, 556, 613, 667
  subjugated, 561, 591
  transcendental subject, 90
  truth, 526

language, 16–17, 25, 236–243, 492, 677–678
  archaeology, 13
  archive, the, 21
  Blanchot, 573–575
  contestation, 81–82
  death, 676–677
  Derrida, 597, 598
  discourse, 120
  dream, the, 569
  event, the, 183
  finitude, 340
  hermeneutics, 182–183
  Kant, 635
  knowledge, 310
  life, 261
  linguistics, 202
  literature, 572
  madness, 275, 277–278
  man, 430, 683
  Merleau-Ponty, 218
  modern, 213, 285
  Nietzsche, 665
  outside, the, 322–326
  painting, 329
  policing, 450
  population, 373
  propositional, 228
  psychoanalysis, 412–413
  Renaissance, the, 535
  Sartre, 685
  schizophrenia, 108
  scientific, 96
  sovereignty, 112
  subjectivity, 14
  transgression, 511, 512–515
  unconscious, 416
  visible, the, 536–537

law, 243–251
  application of, 302
  desire, 100
  discipline, 463, 529
  freedom, 158
  juridico-discursive power, 44
  liberalism, 252
  madness, 275
  medicine, 208
  monster, 300–301
  norm, the, 451
  pastoral power, 474

pleasure, 353
politics, 366
revolution, 474
sexuality, 451
sovereignty, 113
liberalism, 251–254
biopolitics, 41–42
civil society, 65
freedom, 157–158
governmentality, 178–180
human nature, 311–312
ordoliberalism, 180
politics, 367
population, 370
security, 376
state, the, 460, 480
visibility, 538
life, 40, 254–263, 374–375, 565–566
animal, 341, 511
art of, 444
beautiful, 140
biohistory, 31–35
biology, 52, 202
biopolitics, 42–43
biopower, 44–45, 459
Canguilhem, 584–586
capital punishment, 53
counterconduct, 49
death, 47, 94–98
error, 581
ethical, 140
experience, 343
finitude, 646
forms of, 159, 160, 199, 271, 296, 363, 382, 525, 538
good, 140
government of, 607
history, 215
human nature, 310–311
limit, 149
medicine, 297–298
militant forms of, 198
pathological, 563
politics, 421
population, 48, 373
racism, 420, 422, 464, 480, 542–543
sovereignty, 3, 456–457, 460–461, 544
truth, 558, 606
ways of, 209–211, 368
limit-experience. *See* experience, limit-
literature, 263–270
Blanchot, 572–575

language, 240–241
linguistics, 238
madness, 277–278
outside, the, 322, 324–325
philology, 214
lived-experience. *See* experience, lived-
love, 270–273
Ancient, 100, 360, 556
Cynicism, 354
fraternal, 79
genealogy, 166
Plato, 669–670
pleasure, 210

Machiavelli, Niccolò, 652–655
Althusser, 553
governmentality, 177
war, 541
madness, 51, 227, 278–279, 302, 309, 573
Althusser, 551
Blanchot, 575
coercion, 550
contemporary, 173
Derrida, 596–600
Descartes, 603–604, 605
discourse, 388
experience, 150
Freud, 612–613
Hegel, 626
knowledge, 339
painting, 327
problematization, 401
psychiatry, 405–408
psychoanalysis, 411, 413–414
reason, 15, 110, 426, 499
Roussel, 676
Shakespeare, 690–691
silence, 551
truth, 519–520
visibility, 535
man, 16, 33, 40–41, 90–91, 238, 281–288
Althusser, 550
Aristotle, 260
Binswanger, 568
body, 529
death of. *See* death, of man
desire, 452
double, the, 133–134
error, 585
experience, 148
finitude, 153–155, 230–231, 646
hermeneutics of the subject, 185

man (*cont.*)
    human sciences, 34, 212–216, 681
    humanism, 685
    Kant, 632
    knowledge, 340–341, 645
    language, 430
    liberalism, 252
    life, 34
    madness, 597
    medicine, 295
    modernity, 234, 259
    nature, 308–310
    Nietzsche, 664–665
    outside, the, 324–325, 343
    painting, 329–330
    production, 159
    psychoanalysis, 415
    rationality, 406
    science, 586
    self, 447
    species, 342, 459
    truth, 519
    visibility, 535
Marxism, 288–295
    Althusser, 552
    freedom, 158
    ideology, 203
    phenomenology and, 345
    power, 591
    representation, 202
    state, the, 479
    structuralism, 266
    transgression, 513
medicine, 295–300
    Bichat, 563–564
    biohistory, 42
    biopolitics, 37–38
    criminal psychiatry, 6
    death, 564
    desire, 210
    error, 584, 586
    family, 8
    historical a priori, 200–201
    hospital, 31, 39
    individuality, 257
    law, 208
    madness, 275, 407
    mental medicine, 276
    modernity, 566
    sexuality, 7
    space, 469

    truth, 581
    visibility, 536
    will to know, 585
Merleau-Ponty, Maurice, 655–662
    experience, 687
    freedom, 683
    institution, 218–219
    literature, 265
    man, 148
    painting, 328
    philosophy of the subject, 190
    psychology, 570
    transcendence, 339
    visible, the, 535
monster, 300–301, 311
    abnormality, 5–6
    knowledge, 7
    law, 247
multiplicity, 304–308
    Althusser, 550
    Deleuze, 590
    difference, 107
    discipline, 41
    dispositif (apparatus), 128
    experience, 149
    force relations, 366, 486, 540, 543–544, 589
    Kant, 635
    language, 285, 665
    outside, the, 343, 574
    population, 389
    recurrence, 332
    science, 122

natural history, 34, 52, 104, 184, 213
natural law, 111, 311, 312, 507
nature, 34, 258–259, 308–315
    anthropology, 230
    body, 54
    history, 542
    legality, 249
    monster, the, 5, 247, 300–301
    power, 373
    science, 660
    singular nature, 667
    state of, 65
neoliberalism, 42
    biopolitics, 37
    control, 85
    governmentality, 176, 180–181
    law, 248–249
    multiplicity, 306

state, the, 480–481
Nietzsche, Friedrich, 662–669
  actuality, 131
  communism, 289
  critique, 87, 91–92, 230
  death of God, 429
  Deleuze, 588–589, 590
  finitude, 646
  Freud, 610
  genealogy, 165, 166, 167, 168, 195, 220, 349
  Habermas, 618
  historical a priori, 204
  history, 187, 188–189, 231
  Kant, 642
  knowledge, 232, 531
  literature, 265
  madness, 613
  man, 284–285
  multiplicity, 332
  power, 365, 656
  practice, 508
  psychoanalysis, 414
  reason, 129
  Shakespeare, 691
  state, the, 479
  subject, the, 493, 687
  subjectification, 128
  truth, 35, 237, 290, 348, 350–351, 555
  unreason, 277
  war, 693
normalization, 4–7, 111, 315–322
  abnormality, 3
  control, 85
  desire, 100–101, 359
  discipline, 113, 114, 248, 305, 374, 409, 451, 459
  emancipation, 434
  ethics, 140
  freedom, 160
  human sciences, 215
  law, 245, 246
  man, 215
  medicine, 38, 110, 295–297, 298
  monster, the, 302
  pleasure, 360, 363
  population, 47, 375
  problematization, 137
  resistance, 433, 435–436
  science, 92
  secular morality, 414
  sexuality, 124, 210, 279, 352

  sovereignty, 464
  surveillance, 232

outside, 322–327
  Blanchot, 573–575
  contestation, 80
  difference, 108
  ethics, 447
  experience, 149
  force relations, 236
  language, 81, 131, 238, 239–240
  literature, 572
  madness, 278
  Merleau-Ponty, 659
  phenomenology, 343
  power relations, 619
  truth, 524

painting, 327–334
  dispositif (apparatus), 127
  language, 241
  madness, 274, 275
  Merleau-Ponty, 658–659
  visibility, 537
parrēsia, 268–269, 334–337, 525, 557–558, 686
  confession, 353
  friendship, 163
  hermeneutics of the subject, 185
  Plato, 671–672
phenomenology, 133–135, 337–345, 655–656
  body, 660
  experience, 147–148
  history, 188, 205, 218
  knowledge, 631, 661
  man, 153, 666
  Marxism and, 345
  medicine, 295
  Merleau-Ponty, 219
  painting, 328
  phenomenological psychiatry, 567, 570
  practice, 387
  Sartre, 681
  science, 290
  subjectivity, 285
  visibility, 535
philosophy, 90, 108, 188, 197, 322–327, 404, 640
  academic, 602
  actuality, 196
  ancient, 606
  anthropology, 309, 649

philosophy (*cont.*)
  care of the self, 524
  Cartesian, 192
  of the concept, 255, 549
  Cynicism, 558
  Deleuze, 592
  Derrida, 598, 600
  of difference, 103
  empirical science, 213
  of experience, 255
  finitude, 664
  Heidegger, 631–632
  history, 583
  history and, 193
  human sciences, 187, 212, 586
  Kant, 89
  love, 271
  madness, 600
  man, 281
  modern, 59, 87, 148, 261, 310, 523
  Nietzsche, 646
  Plato, 671–672
  present, the, 102
  professional, 167
  spirituality, 474–475
  of the subject, 121, 141, 443, 687
  transgression, 513
  visibility, 535
photography, 327, 332, 333
plague, 356–359, 402
  space, 470
Plato, 669–674
  care of the self, 556
  love, 270–271
  parrēsia, 335, 558
  simulacrum, 332
  truth, 228, 521, 525, 627
Platonism, 58, 589, 639, 671
pleasure, 362–363
  Ancient ethics, 507
  biopolitics, 37
  body, 55–56
  care of the self, 59
  desire, 99–101, 271
  ethics, 139
  friendship, 163–164, 557
  homosexuality, 209–210
  love, 271–272
  Plato, 669–670
  problematization, 501
  self, 504
  sex, 453

  truth, 352–353
politics, 368
  biopolitics, 42
  body, 660
  Clausewitz, 693–694
  death, 460
  ethics, 49, 445
  intellectual, the, 225
  life, 47, 49, 260, 461
  man, 32, 260
  religion, 73
  resistance, 498
  revolution, 439
  sovereignty, 439
  spirituality, 475
  state, the, 479
  of truth, 89
  war, 541, 553
population, 31, 286, 370–377
  abnormality, 8
  biopolitics, 39–42, 46, 47–48, 389
  biopower, 3, 47, 116–117, 162, 459
  capitalism, 39
  control, 84, 379
  governmentality, 175–176, 470, 652
  human science, 215
  humanism, 157
  liberalism, 251
  medicine, 296, 298
  nature, 311–312
  normalization, 4, 5, 319, 320–321
  police, 178, 463
  race, 419, 421–422
  racism, 464
  sexuality, 55, 417, 452
  state, the, 480, 653
power, 3, 37, 45–46, 68–69, 113, 117–118,
    156–157, 351, 377–386, 486, 497
  abnormality, 3, 7
  analytics of, 44
  biopower, 38, 44
  body, 41, 51, 52, 53, 112, 113
  Canguilhem, 585
  capitalism, 39
  centralized, 176
  Christianity, 75–76
  civil society, 66
  configuration, 450
  control, 84, 85
  death, 45, 96
  Deleuze, 589, 591–592
  desire, 100–101, 359

diagram, 486
discipline, 110, 111, 117, 537
discourse, 123, 285
Enlightenment, the, 88
event, 144
expenditure of, 39
freedom, 49, 157, 160, 222, 291
friendship, 162
genealogy, 165, 169
government, 292
governmentality, 68, 175
Habermas, 618
Heidegger, 636
history, 393
homosexuality, 390
human sciences, 215
ideology, 521–522
individual, the, 114, 115, 117, 169, 285
institutions, 169, 217, 221
judicial model, 181
knowledge, 169, 232, 233, 286, 498, 656
language, 215
law, 243–246
life, 40, 45, 49, 260, 374, 460
lifeworld, 620–621
madness, 268, 278–279, 409, 691
maximizing, 40
medicine, 295
micro-physics of, 52, 540, 552
monster, the, 302
multiplicity, 305–306
nature, 373
Nazism, 41
neoliberalism, 42
Nietzsche, 165, 231, 662, 663, 665–666
normalization, 4–5, 8, 300, 311
normalizing, 316
pleasure, 360
political economy, 65
politics, 365–366
population, 42
practice, 388, 390, 391, 499
prison, 392
psychiatry, 405
psychoanalysis, 613
race, 422
racism, 464–465
relations, 575, 578
resistance, 172, 236, 432–434, 435, 457, 684
revolution, 441
security, 373
self, 127

sex, 417
sexuality, 55, 124, 451–452
slavery, 683
sovereignty, 111, 249, 456–457, 458
spirituality, 647
state, the, 180, 477, 478, 652
subject, the, 48, 89, 172, 186, 221, 496, 523
subjectification, 496, 500
subjectivity, 45, 445
tactics, 486
technologies of, 503, 504–506
territory, 468
truth, 18, 163, 336, 647
violence, 528–532
war, 540, 541, 543–544, 693
power/knowledge, 39, 128, 136, 137, 139, 141,
    176, 208, 232, 243, 245, 249, 274, 278, 279,
    305, 313, 317, 320, 386, 389, 425, 435, 436,
    445, 454, 497, 498, 532, 626, 655
biopower, 32
discourse, 124, 125
governmentality, 89
life, 32, 43
madness, 401
medicine, 38, 45
politics, 531
resistance, 437
sexuality, 416, 450
subject, the, 130
subjectivity, 386
practice, 386–392
actuality, 11
anthropological critique, 643
anthropology, 644, 646
archaeology, 194, 305, 519, 657
archive, the, 21
ascetic, 72, 444–445, 660
body, 54, 112, 360
care, 59
care of the self, 57
Christian, 75
counterpractice, 49, 143
critique, 650
cultural, 613
discontinuity, 195
discourse, 20, 120
discursive, 20, 51, 121, 123, 131,
    203, 229, 266, 269, 279, 304, 552,
    600, 604, 642
economic, 179
ethical, 667
ethics, 136

practice (*cont.*)
  freedom, 93, 141, 156, 157, 159–160,
    383–384, 445, 453
  genealogy, 231–232
  government, 531
  governmentality, 175
  historical a priori, 201
  human sciences, 201
  institution, 221–222
  interpretation, 508
  law, 247
  liberalism, 178
  madness, 339
  medical, 295–296
  minority, 85, 181
  normal, 166, 171
  normalization, 435
  normative, 150
  parrēsia, 335
  philosophy, 197, 352, 648, 672
  pleasure, 363
  power, 176, 366, 486
  power/knowledge, 249
  problematization, 400–401
  psychiatric, 571
  reason, 427
  reckoning, 425
  regime, 517
  resistance, 89, 544
  revolution, 197
  scientific, 228
  of the self, 185–186, 261, 270, 359, 362, 434,
    475, 507, 602, 604, 605, 606–607, 615, 619
  sexual, 210, 417
  sexuality, 84
  social, 60, 296, 575
  spirituality, 473
  statements, 105
  strategy, 487
  subject, the, 518, 613
  subjectification, 377, 498–501
  theory and, 172, 178, 224, 398, 536, 590
  transcendental critique, 643
  truth, 256, 290, 452, 523–524
prison, 115–116, 170, 392–394
  discipline, 459, 505
  Guantanamo Bay, 462
  institution, 221
  painting, 331
  Panopticon, 318
  Prison Information Group (GIP), 395,
    397–398

  school, 113
  space, 470
  struggle, 591
  torture, 409
  visibility, 330
Prison Information Group (GIP), 224, 293,
  392, 394–399
problematization, 137–138, 399–404, 501
  practice, 387, 390
  resistance, 436
  self, 443
psychiatry, 301–302, 404–411
  abnormality, 8–9
  confession, 319
  criminal, 3, 6
  existential, 633
  genealogy, 450
  Hegel, 626
  homosexuality, 208–209
  human nature, 309
  madness, 274
  mental illness, 276
  modern, 612
  morality, 414
  penal justice, 674
  phenomenological, 570–571
  psychoanalysis, 413
  reform, 150
  visibility, 535
psychoanalysis, 411–419
  Canguilhem, 255
  counterscience, 238, 683
  Deleuze, 592
  desire, 100, 556
  Freud, 27–28, 609–610, 611–614
  madness, 279, 407, 408
  Merleau-Ponty, 656
  self, 443
  structuralism, 266

race, 419–424
  biopower, 46, 454
  Boulainvilliers, 577–578
  human, 374
  master race, 439
  population, 31
  postcolonial studies, 454
  sexuality, 389
  sovereignty, 464
  war, 541–543
racism, 419–424
  abnormality, 3, 9

biopolitics, 375, 481
Boulainvilliers, 577
death, 45
immigrant rights, 150
power, 464–465
practice, 390
psychiatry, 410
revolution, 439
war, 541–543
reason, 129, 424–429, 620
analytical, 680–682, 685
Aufklärung (enlightenment), 197
Blanchot, 575
Canguilhem, 582
Derrida, 596–599
Descartes, 282, 603–605
desire, 139
discourse, 131
Enlightenment, 349, 648
Freud, 279, 612
Kant, 105, 644, 645
love, 270
madness, 15, 110, 274, 275, 277, 499,
520, 551
man, 309
Modernity, 626
Nietzsche, 663–664
phenomenology, 218
psychiatry, 406–407, 408
science, 347
space, 562
state, the, 88
unreason, 91, 275
religion, 429–432
Bataille, 511
confession, 77
counterconduct, 73
Kant, 664
madness, 276, 414
subjectivity, 130
resistance, 432–438, 488–489, 498
Bataille, 449
critique, 92
discipline, 305, 501
ethics, 445
event, the, 143
freedom, 683
genealogy, 45
law, 245
multiplicity, 304, 306
pastoral power, 474, 606
power, 117, 172, 236, 384, 390, 647, 666

punishment, 53
sexuality, 124, 359
subjectification, 383
truth, 526
violence, 528
ways of life, 209
revolution, 117, 197, 438–443
Ancient, 555
conduct, 474
human nature, 313
modern, 582
power, 478
race, 542
spirituality, 475
state, the, 479
transgression, 512
Rivière, Pierre, 108, 194, 674–676
Deleuze, 590
Roussel, Raymond, 676–680
dispositif (apparatus), 126
literature, 266
outside, the, 326
visible, the, 536–537
Russian Revolution, 73, 130, 189

Sartre, Jean-Paul, 680–689
Althusser, 550
archaeology, 193
humanism, 655
literature, 265
man, 148
Marxism, 288–289
structuralism, 493
subject, the, 190
transcendence, 339
self, 127, 185–186, 443–449, 503–504
aesthetics of the, 149, 404, 503
Ancients, the, 137
asceticism, 72
ascetism, 488
body, 51, 56, 657
care of the. *See* care of the self
Christianity, 75, 76–78, 139
Descartes, 602, 605–606
distance, 155
ethics, 136, 368
-formation, 140–141
genealogy, 169
governmentality, 68, 368
Habermas, 619
knowledge, 312
language, 574

self (*cont.*)
  love, 270
  pleasure, 210, 361, 362
  power, 172
  -practice, 389–390, 672
  practice of the, 475, 604
  -relations, 159
  resistance, 434–436
  Sartre, 682
  sex, 452, 453
  Soviet culture, 79
  spirituality, 474, 523
  subjectification, 127
  technologies of the, 48–49, 507–508
  -transformation, 643, 646, 648
  truth, 18, 100, 261, 522, 556
  writing, 430
self-knowledge, 134, 157, 352, 496, 498, 524
  self-care, 444
sex, 449–456
  Ancients, the, 18
  biopolitics, 41
  body, 55
  Christianity, 62, 139
  desire, 99, 101
  discourse, 123–124
  friendship, 162
  heterosexuality, 208
  interdiction, 510
  love, 272
  pleasure, 210, 359–362
  police, 419
  problematization, 401
  psychoanalysis, 416–417, 614
  truth, 351
sexuality, 449–455, 492
  abnormality, 7–8, 75, 301
  Ancients, the, 18, 558–559
  archaeology, 123
  Bataille, 560
  biopolitics, 164
  body, 41, 55–56
  Christianity, 139, 271
  confession, 75
  control, 84
  death of God, 429
  Deleueze and Guattari, 592
  desire, 99–100, 101, 362
  discourse, 124, 492
  dispositif (apparatus), 46
  ethics, 136–137, 141, 667
  freedom, 160
  Freud, 614

homosexuality, 207–209
law, 244
liberalism, 179
liberation, 383
nature, 313
normalization, 279, 320
pathological, 499
Plato, 669
pleasure, 210, 359–360, 362
problematization, 138, 400,
  401, 501
race, 374, 389
religion, 499
science, 352, 435, 444
transgression, 510, 511–512
truth, 351
Shakespeare, William, 689–693
  literature, 264, 275
  madness, 406
sovereignty, 3–4, 456–466
  biopolitics, 37, 40–41
  biopower, 44–45, 47, 452
  body, 52, 53, 111–112
  civil society, 64–65
  counterconduct, 73
  death, 96, 544, 690–691
  Derrida, 601
  discipline, 83, 113, 116, 130, 246,
    249, 356
  freedom, 157
  governmentality, 176, 367
  law, 244–245
  life, 260
  madness, 268
  monster, the, 301
  normalization, 315–316, 318
  pastoral power, 474
  plague, 357
  political economy, 381
  politics, 366
  population, 372–373
  power, 530
  psychiatry, 170, 409
  race, 421, 542
space, 466–472
  body, 51
  Canguilhem, 190
  care of the self, 59
  contestation, 81
  death, 240
  discipline, 39, 83, 114, 459, 529
  discursive, 26
  education, 115

ethics, 140
historical a priori, 204
institution, 221
Kant, 630
knowledge, 121, 192, 518
language, 225, 239, 240
life, 258
lived experience, 148
madness, 276
organism, 257
outside, the, 322–325
plague, the, 356–357
politics, 660
power, 127
pre-discursive, 149
psychoanalysis, 613
reason, 562, 603
security, 460
sense, 657
sovereignty, 329
transgression, 512–513
truth, 526
West, the, 378
writing, 266
spirituality, 472–477, 523
critique, 641, 647, 650
Enlightenment, 647
history of the present, 61
homosexuality, 210
negative theology, 430
philosophy, 352
Stoics, the, 313
truth, 556
state, 477–482
abnormality, 5, 296
Althusser, 553
biopolitics, 41
biopower, 4, 117, 464
counterconduct, 73
discipline, 112, 114
family, 8
freedom, 157
governmentality, 175, 176–178, 181, 463,
505–507
governmentalization, 42, 47–48
liberalism, 252
medicine, 41
normalization, 436
ordoliberalism, 180
philosophy, 89
-phobia, 592
politics, 366–368, 381
population, 370, 653

power, 245, 292, 380, 457,
458, 591
racism, 419, 420, 421, 464,
540, 541, 542–543, 544
resistance, 498
revolution, 439, 441, 457
science, 88
society, 49
sovereignty, 460
tactics, 487
war, 542
statement, 17, 127, 482–486
archaeology, 657
archive, the, 20–22, 194
Canguilhem, 233
contestation, 82
Descartes, 604–605
difference, 104–105
discourse, 120–123, 237, 388
dispositif (apparatus), 129–130
event, 145, 183
historical a priori, 204–205
knowledge, 228–229
Prison Information Group (GIP), 398
structuralism, 493
war, 541
Stoics, the, 58, 97, 185, 268, 271, 312, 353, 389,
524, 557, 615
Deleuze, 589
strategy, 486–490
antistrategic, 74, 225
biopower, 44
Clausewitz, 694
counterconduct, 382
discourse, 16, 388
freedom, 160
genealogy, 220
governmentality, 445
Habermas, 621
history, 218
homosexuality, 209
institution, 221–222
law, 245
medicine, 38
power, 68, 118, 123, 172
punishment, 18
resistance, 432–433
sexuality, 99
space, 469
war, 540, 543–544
structuralism, 102, 122, 218, 490–496
archaeology, 664
counterscience, 682

structuralism (*cont.*)
  discourse, 194
  event, the, 219
  human sciences, 347
  language, 665
  literature, 266
  philosophy, 345
  religion, 430
  Sartre, 685
subject, the
  anthroplogy, 91
  Blanchot, 575
  Canguilhem, 582–583
  care, 59
  death, 97
  Descartes, 604–605
  discourse, 285
  experience, 148
  Heidegger, 635
  history, 29
  Kant, 634
  knowledge, 227, 556–557
  language, 239, 325
  liberation, 383
  love, 270
  Merleau-Ponty, 657–658
  Nietzsche, 666–668, 687
  outside, the, 322–323
  parrēsia, 261, 268
  phenomenology, 338, 341
  philosophy, 496
  political economy, 64
  power, 48, 285
  representation, 630
  resistance, 433, 435
  sexuality, 210
  spirituality, 473
  thought, 343
  truth, 57, 76, 417, 436, 517, 523,
    525–526
subjectification, 48, 138, 496–503
  care of the self, 58, 556
  conduct, 69
  desubjectification, 89, 92, 557
  discourse, 351
  dispositif (apparatus), 127–128, 130
  ethics, 173, 445–447, 507, 667
  genealogy, 377
  resistance, 383, 433, 435

tactics, 470, 486–490
  discipline, 54, 215

genealogy, 352
governmentality, 42
history, 218
normalization, 316
power, 118, 451
technology
  body, 52–53
  discipline, 111, 115–117, 233
  discourse, 492
  governmentality, 244, 311
  life, 260, 311
  Panopticon, 486
  philosophy, 404
  power, 373
  psychiatry, 8
  of the self, 76, 79
technology (of discipline, governmentality, and
    ethics), 503–509
transcendental philosophy, 33, 141, 202, 228,
    633, 643, 644
transgression, 509–517
  Bataille, 108, 560–561
  force relations, 236
  language, 238–239
  limit-experience, 149
  monster, the, 301
  outside, the, 322
  reason, 645
truth, 228–229, 517–528
  analytic of, 92, 648
  Ancients, the, 198, 556, 573
  anthropology, 635
  archaeology, 18
  ascesticism, 660
  author, the, 27–28
  Canguilhem, 583–584
  Christianity, 77, 429
  Classical, 626
  confession, 76
  contestation, 81
  critique, 87, 88–89, 436
  Cynics, the, 538
  death, 257
  Derrida, 598, 599
  Descartes, 475, 606–607
  desire, 100, 160, 359, 363, 452
  discourse, 100, 106, 290, 492
  ethics, 444
  freedom, 650
  games of, 149, 218, 336
  genealogy, 45, 446
  governmentality, 196

Habermas, 616, 618
Hegel, 624
Heidegger, 637
historical a priori, 205
history, 191–192
history of the present, 349
ideology, 203
Kant, 644, 645, 646–647
knowledge, 169
language, 240
liberalism, 251
life, 35, 260–261, 606
literature, 267–268
lived-experience, 342
love, 270–271
madness, 309, 339, 407, 408, 596
man, 91, 212, 213, 258, 313, 343
medicine, 295, 581
Nietzsche, 348, 665–666
otherness, 199
parrēsia, 60, 163, 334, 671, 686
pastoral power, 474
philosophy, 142, 347, 351–354,
    672
Plato, 669–670, 671
politics of, 365, 368
power, 237, 291
practice, 387
psychoanalysis, 613
revolution, 441
science, 232, 234, 256, 347, 585
self, the, 185
sex, 417
sexuality, 55, 449
spirituality, 472–473, 475
statements, 484
subject, the, 57, 59, 415, 582, 627
subjectivity, 97
thought, 597
transcendental critique, 643
visible, the, 534
war, 541, 543
will to, 232, 618

violence, 167, 528–534
    Derrida, 599
    madness, 279
    Nazis, the, 543
    power, 110
    racism, 542
    sovereignty, 116, 459
    state, the, 478
    thought, 324
    transgression, 322, 512
visible, the, 534–540
    abnormality, 5
    biopolitics, 311
    death, 257
    Derrida, 596
    discipline, 111, 113, 232, 459, 463
    discourse, 327
    dispositif (apparatus), 126–127
    knowledge, 51
    language, 241, 329
    madness, 275, 327
    mental illness, 520
    Merleau-Ponty, 328, 658–659
    multiplicity, 305
    natural history, 34
    nature, 312
    Panopticon, 79, 116, 318, 330
    sexuality, 7, 209
    sovereignty, 111
    truth, 525

war, 540–547
    biopolitics, 97
    Boulainvilliers, 578
    class, 578
    Clausewitz, 693–694
    genocidal, 62
    law, 245
    politics, 365–366, 367
    power, 365, 529, 530
    race, 419, 578
    sovereignty, 96
    state, the, 478

Lightning Source UK Ltd.
Milton Keynes UK
UKHW031837200520
363560UK00014B/309